Essentials of Pattern Recognition

This textbook introduces fundamental concepts, major models, and popular applications of pattern recognition for a one-semester undergraduate course. To ensure student understanding, the text focuses on a relatively small number of core concepts with an abundance of illustrations and examples. Concepts are reinforced with hands-on exercises to nurture the student's skill in problem solving. New concepts and algorithms are framed by real-world context, and established as part of the big picture introduced in an early chapter. A problem-solving strategy is employed in several chapters to equip students with an approach for new problems in pattern recognition. This text also points out common errors that a new player in pattern recognition may encounter, and fosters the ability of readers to find useful resources and independently solve a new pattern-recognition task through various working examples. Students with an undergraduate understanding of mathematical analysis, linear algebra, and probability will be well prepared to master the concepts and mathematical analysis presented here.

Jianxin Wu is a professor in the Department of Computer Science and Technology and the School of Artificial Intelligence at Nanjing University, China. He received his BS and MS degrees in computer science from Nanjing University and his PhD degree in computer science from the Georgia Institute of Technology. Professor Wu has served as an area chair for the conference on Computer Vision and Pattern Recognition (CVPR), the International Conference on Computer Vision (ICCV), and the AAAI Conference on Artificial Intelligence. He is also an associate editor for the *Pattern Recognition* journal. His research interests are computer vision and machine learning.

Essentials of Pattern Recognition

An Accessible Approach

JIANXIN WU
Nanjing University, China

CAMBRIDGE
UNIVERSITY PRESS

CAMBRIDGE
UNIVERSITY PRESS

University Printing House, Cambridge CB2 8BS, United Kingdom

One Liberty Plaza, 20th Floor, New York, NY 10006, USA

477 Williamstown Road, Port Melbourne, VIC 3207, Australia

314–321, 3rd Floor, Plot 3, Splendor Forum, Jasola District Centre, New Delhi – 110025, India

79 Anson Road, #06–04/06, Singapore 079906

Cambridge University Press is part of the University of Cambridge.

It furthers the University's mission by disseminating knowledge in the pursuit of education, learning and research at the highest international levels of excellence.

www.cambridge.org
Information on this title: www.cambridge.org/9781108483469
DOI: 10.1017/9781108650212

First published 2021

Printed in the United Kingdom by TJ Books Ltd, Padstow Cornwall, 2021

A catalogue record for this publication is available from the British Library.

ISBN 978-1-108-48346-9 Hardback

Additional resources for this publication are at www.cambridge.org/patternrecognition

Contents

The plate section can be found between pages 208 and 209

Figures

Tables

Preface

Pattern recognition, a research area that extracts useful patterns (or regularities) from data and applies these patterns to subsequent decision processes, has always been an important topic in computer science and related subject areas. Applications of deep learning, the current focus of attention in artificial intelligence, are mainly pattern recognition tasks. Although pattern recognition has direct applications in our society, the shortage of well-trained pattern recognition researchers and practitioners is also obvious.

As an introductory textbook, the purpose of this book is to introduce background and fundamental concepts, major models, and popular applications of pattern recognition. By learning the theories and techniques, followed by hands-on exercises, I hope a beginner will nurture the ability for independent problem solving in the pattern recognition field.

Several classic textbooks have been published in this field. Do we need yet another new one (such as this book)? My answer to this question is yes. These widely adopted pattern recognition textbooks were mostly published a decade ago, but nowadays quite a number of characteristics differ significantly from where the pattern recognition area was ten years ago. Deep learning is a typical example of such novel characteristics. The final chapter of this book introduces convolutional neural networks, the most important deep learning model. Recent achievements and views from the pattern recognition research frontier are also reflected throughout this book.

The major goal, and hopefully the most important feature of this book, however, is *to ensure that all readers understand its contents—even a reader who is not strong (or is even slightly weak) in mathematical and other background knowledge related to pattern recognition*. To achieve this goal, I have used many illustrations and examples, emphasized the cause and effect of various methods (e.g., their motivations, applications, and applicable conditions), and have not omitted any steps in the mathematical derivations. I also provide all necessary background knowledge and encourage the reader to obtain hands-on experience when appropriate. I also wish this book will *serve as an excellent reference book for practitioners* in pattern recognition and machine learning (including deep learning).

Chapter 14 is a good example to illustrate these features. Expectation-maximization (EM) is an algorithm that is important in both pattern recognition and machine learning. However, in the classic textbook (Bishop 1995a), EM occupies only seven pages and the core mathematical derivation only two pages! This succinct treatment may be suitable for experienced or talented readers, but not necessarily for the general audience who are interested in learning pattern recognition.

In Chapter 14 of this book, I introduce the EM algorithm's necessity and main idea through an example (the Gaussian mixture model, GMM), which paves the way for a formal description of EM. The EM algorithm, although very short in its mathematical form, is not easy to follow for beginners. I continue to use GMM as a worked example and prepare the derivation and meaning of every step in full detail. Finally, the EM updating equations for the GMM become obvious and neat. In the exercise problems, I ask the reader to derive the EM algorithm independently without resorting to the chapter. In another exercise problem, I ask the reader to independently derive Baum–Welch, another classic EM derivation—with the help of well-designed hints and steps. For this same EM algorithm, I use 17 pages, and I believe this chapter will help readers not only to learn the EM algorithm smoothly, but also to understand its key ideas and its merits and drawbacks.

Obviously, this book can elaborate on only a carefully selected small subset of core contents. However, other important topics are also briefly mentioned in chapters and exercise problems (e.g., locally linear embedding and the exponential family), and I provide pointers to resources at the end of most chapters if a reader wants to dive deeper into pattern recognition. The core contents of this book may also help a reader to form a foundation for understanding deep learning.

This book also emphasizes hands-on experience. Some details, although not relevant to mathematical derivations, are vital in practical systems. These details are emphasized when appropriate in the book. The design of the exercise problems took me one year. In order to fully understand this book, it is essential that a reader completes these problems. Some problems ask a reader to install software packages, read manuals, and solve problems by writing code.

Finally, beyond teaching knowledge, I want to nurture two kinds of ability in this book. First, when presented with a new task, I want to encourage readers to independently solve it by following these steps: analyzing the problem, obtaining an idea to solve it, formalizing the idea, simplifying the formulation, and then solving it. Second, when encountering a problem that may be easily solved with the help of existing resources, I hope readers can actively search and find such resources (e.g., software packages, manuals, products) such that the problem can be solved promptly rather than reinventing the wheel.

It is always a difficult mission to write a textbook. The conception of this book began in July 2013, when I had just returned to my *alma mater*, Nanjing University, and planned to start a new course, Pattern Recognition. Throughout the six-and-a-half-year writing process, I have been grateful to many people for their kind support. A partial list of persons I wish to acknowledge is shown here in an approximate chronological order.

- Professor James M. Rehg at the Georgia Institute of Technology, my PhD supervisor. Jim's suggestions improved some critical parts of this book too.

- My colleagues at the LAMDA (Learning And Mining from DatA) institute, the Department of Computer Science and Technology (and School of Artificial Intelligence) at Nanjing University. The LAMDA institute provides an excellent research environment. Discussions and collaborations with LAMDA director Professor Zhi-Hua Zhou, my fellow teachers, and LAMDA postgraduate students have been very helpful. LAMDA secretaries also saved me a lot of time by taking care of many administrative procedures.
- Students enrolled in my Pattern Recognition courses. After I used a draft of a few chapters as course notes, the enthusiastic and positive feedback I received from them encouraged me to continue the writing process. Interactions in and after the lectures also greatly shaped the presentation of this book. In addition, numerous typos and errors have been pointed out by them. Although a full list of names is not provided here due to limitations on space , they will be acknowledged in this book's accompanying home page.
- Graduate students under my supervision. The collaborative efforts between myself and my supervisees ensured that research efforts in my small group carried on productively. Thus, I had more time to write this book. They were often also the first batch of readers of this book.
- The managers and editors at Cambridge University Press (CUP). Mr. David Liu from CUP visited my office and discussed a potential publication proposal with me when this book's draft was almost finished. His friendly reminders pushed me to devote more time and to finish the book writing and publication process as early as possible. Ms. Lisa Pinto, lead of the higher education branch's development team at CUP, supervised and greatly helped the editing process.
- My dear family members. Before the birth of my son, this book was mostly written at home, either before I went to the office or after I returned. However, since his birth, especially once he learned to walk, I could use only my time in the office, on an airplane, or on a train trip for this book. I wish to thank my wife, son, parents, and parents-in-law for their love and support!

Any feedback or comments are most welcome. Please send them to the following email address: pr.book.wujx@gmail.com.

Notation

$\mathbb{R}$	set of real values
$\mathbb{R}_+$	set of nonnegative real values
$\mathbb{Z}$	set of integers
$\triangleq$	defined as
$(\cdot)^T$	transpose of a matrix
$\mathbf{1}, \mathbf{0}$	vector of all 1s or all 0s, respectively
$\\|\cdot\\|$	norm of a matrix or a vector
$\boldsymbol{x} \perp \boldsymbol{y}$	two vectors $\boldsymbol{x}$ and $\boldsymbol{y}$ are orthogonal
I_n (I)	identity matrix of size $n \times n$
$\det(X)$ or $\lvert X \rvert$	determinant of X when X is a square matrix
$\lvert D \rvert$	size (cardinality) of D when D is a set
X^{-1}	inverse of a square matrix X
X^{+}	Moore–Penrose pseudoinverse of matrix X
$\operatorname{tr}(X)$	trace of a square matrix X
$\operatorname{rank}(X)$	rank of a matrix X
$\operatorname{diag}(a_1, a_2, \ldots, a_n)$	diagonal matrix with diagonal entries being a_i
$\operatorname{diag}(X)$	vector formed from diagonal entries in square matrix X
$X \succ 0$ $(X \succcurlyeq 0)$	square matrix X is positive (semi)definite
$\Pr(\cdot)$	probability of an event
$\mathbb{E}_X[f(X)]$	expectation of $f(X)$ with respect to X
$\operatorname{Var}(X)$ $(\operatorname{Cov}(X))$	variance (covariance matrix) of X
$\rho_{X,Y}$	Pearson's correlation coefficient
$N(\mu, \sigma^2)$	normal distribution with mean μ and variance σ^2
$[\![\cdot]\!]$	indicator function
$\lceil \cdot \rceil$ and $\lfloor \cdot \rfloor$	ceiling and floor functions, respectively
$\operatorname{sign}(x)$	the sign of $x \in \mathbb{R}$, can be 0, 1 or -1
$\propto$	proportional to
x_+	hinge loss, $x_+ = \max(0, x)$
$\mathcal{O}(\cdot)$	big-O notation
$x_{1:t}$	abbreviation for the sequence $x_1, x_2, \ldots, x_t$

Part I

Introduction and Overview

1 Introduction

This book will introduce several algorithms, methods, and practices in *pattern recognition*, with a sizable portion of its contents being the introduction to various *machine learning* algorithms.

Technical details (such as algorithms and practices) are important. However, we encourage the readers to focus on more fundamental issues rather than dwelling on technical details. For example, keeping the following questions in mind will be useful:

- What is pattern recognition? What is machine learning? And what is the relationship between them?
- Given a specific pattern recognition task, what are the input and output of this task? What aspects of the task make it difficult to solve?
- Among the many existing algorithms and methods, which one(s) should be used (or must not be used) for our task at hand? Is there any good reason to support your decision?
- There is no silver bullet that can solve all problems. For example, deep learning has emerged as the best solution technique for many applications, but there are many tasks that cannot be effectively attacked by deep learning. If we have to develop a new method for one task, is there a procedure that can help us?

Although we have not defined these terms—such as pattern recognition and machine learning—it is worthwhile to quickly scan these questions. In fact, there is no crystal clear answer to these questions. For some (e.g., the last two), researchers and practitioners mostly resort to their experiences in choosing a particular plan of attack for their task at hand. An experienced researcher may pick an appropriate algorithm for their task in the first trial. A novice, however, may try all the methods from a handbook in a random order, which means a lot of time, energy, and cost is often wasted before the first working method emerges for this task. Hence, rather than remembering every technical detail of the methods we introduce, it is probably more important to build your own rule of thumb for the following question through our introduction and analyses of these methods: *What is this method good for (or bad for)?*

To answer some other questions, we require knowledge beyond the materials we will introduce in this book. For example, in order to understand what are the input, output, and difficulties in OCR (optical character recognition, a typical pattern recognition task), we need to carefully study at least the specific environment the OCR task will happen in and the level of recognition accuracy that is required. All these factors are beyond the scope of a brief introduction to pattern recognition and machine learning. Although it is impossible to dive into such application-specific details, we will remind the readers about the importance of these factors when appropriate.

There remain questions that have very different answers from different communities or individuals. For example, the questions mentioned above, what is pattern recognition?, what is machine learning?, what is the relationship between them?, can be given quite different answers.

Let us take the widely utilized Wikipedia project as an example.[1] The entry "Pattern recognition" was introduced in Wikipedia as follows, and also involves machine learning, and reflects at least one type of understanding of this subject:

> Pattern recognition is a branch of machine learning that focuses on the recognition of patterns and regularities in data, although it is in some cases considered to be nearly synonymous with machine learning. (Wikipedia, "Pattern recognition," retrieved on October 8, 2016)

Along with our introduction to both subjects, however, we want to emphasize that although machine learning (ML) and pattern recognition (PR) are closely related subjects, *PR is* not *a branch of ML, and neither is ML a branch of PR.*

In this book, we adopt another definition of pattern recognition:

> The field of pattern recognition is concerned with the automatic discovery of regularities in data through the use of computer algorithms and with the use of these regularities to take actions such as classifying the data into different categories. (Bishop 2006)

Pattern recognition is closely related to machine learning, which is defined as follows:

> The field of machine learning is concerned with the question of how to construct computer programs that automatically improve with experience. (Mitchell 1997)

These definitions may seem difficult to grasp at first sight. Let us start with an example that is related to both of them.

1.1 An Example: Autonomous Driving

We will use autonomous driving as an example to illustrate machine learning, pattern recognition, and other subjects.

Ideally, a fully autonomous car (which is not yet commercially available as of today) may operate as follows:

- `T.1.` The car identifies that its owner is approaching and automatically unlocks its doors.
- `T.2.` The car will communicate with the user to learn about the destination of a trip.
- `T.3.` The car will find its way and drive to the destination on its own (i.e., autonomously), while the user may take a nap or enjoy a movie during the trip.

[1] `https://en.wikipedia.org/wiki/Main_Page`

`T.4.` The car will properly notify the user upon its arrival and will park itself after the user leaves the car.

For task `T.1`, a viable approach is to install several cameras on different sides of the car, which can operate even when the engine is switched off. These cameras will watch out vigilantly, and automatically find out that a person is approaching the car. Then the next step is to identify whether the person is the owner of this car. If the answer is yes, and when the owner is close enough to any one of the car's doors, the car will unlock that door.

Because these steps are based on cameras, task `T.1` can be viewed as a *computer vision* (CV) task.

Computer vision methods and systems take as inputs the images or videos captured by various imaging sensors (such as optic, ultrasound, or infrared cameras). The goal of computer vision is to design hardware and software that can work together and mimic or even surpass the functionality of the human vision system—e.g., the detection and recognition of objects (such as identifying a person) and the identification of anomalies in the environment (such as finding that a person is approaching). In short, the input of computer vision methods or systems are different types of images or videos, and the outputs are results of image or video understanding, which also appear in different forms according to the task at hand.

Many subtasks have been decomposed from `T.1`, which correspond to widely researched topics in computer vision, e.g., pedestrian detection and human identity recognition (such as face recognition based on human faces, or gait recognition based on a person's walking style and habits).

Task `T.2` involves different sensors and data acquisition methods. Although we can ask the user to key in the destination from a keyboard, the better way is to carry out this communication through natural languages. Hence, microphones and speakers should be installed around the car's interior. The user may just say "Intercontinental Hotel" (in English) or "Zhou Ji Jiu Dian" (in Chinese). It is the car's job to find out that a command has been issued and to acknowledge (probably also to confirm) the user's command before it starts driving. The acknowledgment or confirmation, of course, is given in natural languages too.

Techniques from various areas are required to carry out these natural verbal communications, such as *speech recognition*, *natural language processing*, and *speech synthesis*. The car will capture the words, phrases, or sentences spoken by the user through speech recognition, will understand their meanings, and must be able to choose appropriate answers through natural language processing; finally it can speak its reply through speech synthesis.

`T.2` involves two closely related subjects: speech processing and natural language processing. The input of `T.2` is speech signals obtained via one or several microphones, which will undergo several layers of processing: the microphones' electronic signal is first converted into meaningful words, phrases, or sentences by speech recognition; the natural language processing module will convert these words into representations that a computer can understand; natural language processing is also responsible for choosing an appropriate answer (e.g., a confirmation or a request for further clarification) in the form of one or several sentences in text; finally, the speech synthesis module must convert the text sentences into audio signals, which will be spoken to the user via a loudspeaker and are the final output of `T.2`. However, the modules used in `T.2` have different intermediate inputs and outputs, often with one module's output being the input of the next processing module.

Items `T.3` and `T.4` can be analyzed in a similar fashion. However, we will leave these analyses to the reader.

In this example, we have witnessed many sensors (e.g., camera, infrared camera, microphone) and outputs of various modules (e.g., existence of a person, human identity, human voice signal). Many more sensory inputs and outputs are required for this application. For example, in `T.3`, highly accurate global positioning sensors (such as the Global Positioning System (GPS) or BeiDou receiving sensors) are necessary in order to know the car's precise location. Radar, which could be millimeter-wave radar or laser based (lidar), are also critical to sense the environment for driving safety. New parking lots may be equipped with RFID (radio-frequency identification) tags and other auxiliary sensors to help the automatic parking task.

Similarly, more modules are required to process these new sensory data and produce good outputs. For example, one module may take both the camera and radar inputs to determine whether it is safe to drive forward. It will detect any obstacle that stands in front of the car, in order to avoid collision if obstacles do exist.

1.2 Pattern Recognition and Machine Learning

The above tasks are all examples of *pattern recognition*, which automatically extracts useful patterns from input data (e.g., pedestrians from images, or text from speech signals), and the extracted patterns are often used in decision making (e.g., whether to unlock the car or to find an appropriate response to a user's speech command).

The word *pattern* can refer to a wide range of useful and organized information in diverse applications. Some researchers use the word *regularity* as a synonym for pattern, both referring to information or knowledge that is useful for future decision making. The word *automatic* refers to the fact that a pattern recognition method or system acts on its own (i.e., without a human in the loop).

1.2.1 A Typical PR Pipeline

There are many options to deal with a pattern recognition task. However, the steps in Figure 1.1 form a typical pattern recognition (PR) pipeline.

A PR pipeline often starts from its input data, which most probably come from various sensors. Sensors (such as cameras and microphones) collect input signals from the environment in which the PR system operates. This step, also termed *data acquisition*, is extremely important for pattern recognition performance.

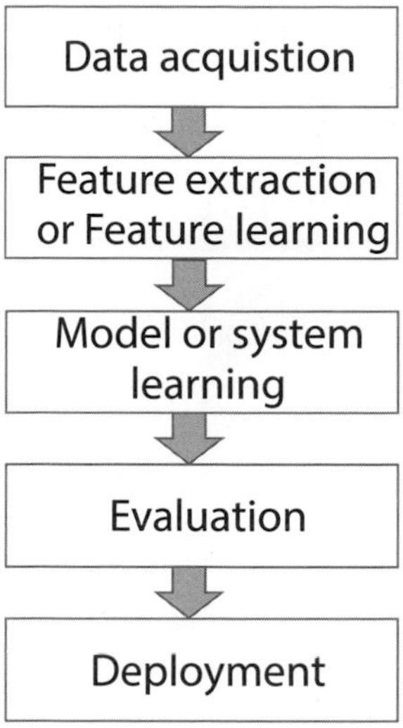

Figure 1.1 A typical pattern recognition pipeline.

The properties of input data can be more important than other steps or components in the PR pipeline. Face recognition from surveillance videos is an example to illustrate this statement. Surveillance videos are useful tools in the investigation of accidents or crimes. However, it is rare that surveillance cameras happen to be within a small distance of where the accident or crime has occurred. When the cameras are far away from the site (e.g., more than 30 meters away), a face will occupy fewer than 20×20 pixels in the video frames. This resolution is too small to provide useful identity information for a suspect, either for a human expert or an automatic computer vision or pattern recognition system. Hence, acquiring high-quality input data is the top priority in achieving a successful pattern recognition system. If a high-resolution facial image (e.g., with more than 300×300 pixels) is available, the face recognition task will become much easier.

Acquiring high-quality sensory input involves experts from many fields, for example, physicists, acoustic engineers, electrical and electronics engineers, and optical engineers. Sensory input data often need to be digitized, and may appear in many different forms such as text, images, videos, audio signals, or three-dimensional point clouds. Beyond input data directly captured by various sensors, a PR method or system can also use the output of other methods or systems in the PR pipeline as its input.

The next step is feature extraction or feature learning. The raw sensory input, even after digitization, is often far from being meaningful or interpretable. For example, a color picture with resolution 1024×768 and three channels (RGB) is digitized as

$$3 \times 1024 \times 768 = 2\,359\,296$$

integers between 0 and 255. This large quantity of integers is not very helpful for finding useful patterns or regularities in the image.

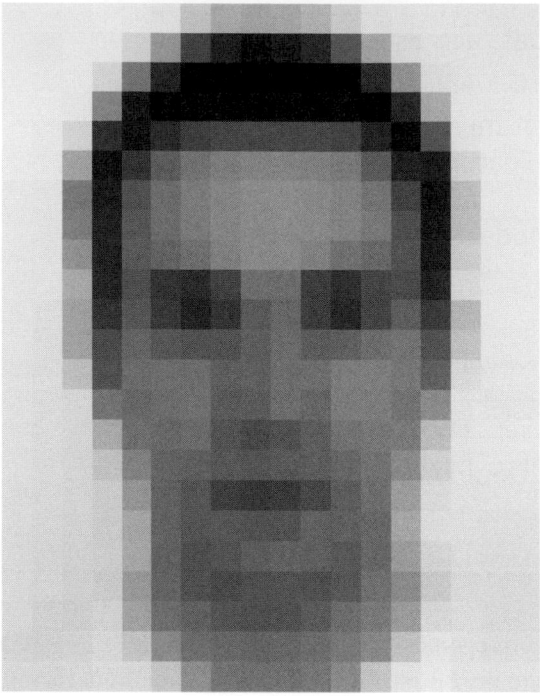

(a) A small grayscale face image

242	242	243	244	243	241	216	192	186	191	203	225	240	241	241	240	239	239
241	240	242	242	228	168	80	34	23	28	50	105	188	237	240	239	239	239
242	241	242	229	134	41	12	9	10	11	12	17	60	170	237	240	240	240
243	242	240	149	28	18	20	20	20	21	20	21	19	57	193	241	241	241
243	241	228	53	26	55	79	88	88	90	91	85	52	26	107	240	242	242
242	241	180	25	67	116	138	149	155	156	154	146	118	54	43	230	242	242
240	239	137	33	99	131	147	157	164	166	162	156	142	89	32	210	242	242
239	238	143	40	108	131	146	157	163	165	164	157	146	104	36	212	242	242
238	238	163	43	113	124	137	153	161	163	155	139	131	110	41	225	242	242
237	237	188	47	97	71	61	85	133	133	83	67	91	100	53	235	241	241
236	234	179	66	108	75	50	72	113	126	82	59	89	120	79	205	241	241
235	232	179	91	123	110	103	106	118	131	118	120	133	140	106	213	240	240
234	231	208	96	129	132	131	118	119	132	134	147	150	143	119	232	238	238
233	230	228	132	124	130	133	113	115	131	126	146	147	137	160	238	237	237
232	229	226	188	128	125	128	105	91	104	117	137	142	144	208	238	238	238
231	228	225	211	146	121	117	109	105	111	117	126	137	158	224	237	237	237
230	227	225	219	167	119	106	80	73	79	91	117	133	178	233	236	236	236
230	227	224	220	185	120	106	109	102	104	122	121	127	189	235	235	234	234
229	226	223	221	187	118	96	104	115	121	120	111	126	177	228	233	232	232
229	226	222	218	169	120	98	90	98	102	101	110	133	158	218	229	229	229
227	222	220	224	178	128	117	103	96	100	112	131	143	175	229	232	229	229
224	222	224	228	212	153	128	123	119	123	129	140	155	212	238	235	232	232
227	226	227	230	229	214	158	132	129	131	137	155	215	238	241	237	235	235

(b) The image seen by a computer

Figure 1.2 (a) A small grayscale image, 23 × 18 in resolution, and enlarged by scale factor 15. (b) It is seen by the computer as a 23 × 18 matrix of integers.

Figure 1.2 shows a small grayscale (single channel) face image (Figure 1.2a) and its raw input format (Figure 1.2b) as a matrix of integers. As shown by Figure 1.2a, although the resolution is small (23 × 18, which is typical for faces in surveillance videos), our brain can still interpret it as a candidate for a human face, but it is almost hopeless to guess the identity of this face. The computer, however, sees a small 23 × 18 matrix of integers, as shown in Figure 1.2b. These 414 numbers are far away from our concept of a human face.

Hence, we need to extract or learn *features*—i.e., to turn these 414 numbers into other numerical values that are useful for finding faces. For example, because most eyes are darker than other facial regions, we can compute the sum of pixel intensity values in the top half of the image (12×18 pixels, denoting the sum as v_1) and the sum of pixel intensity values in the bottom half (12×18 pixels, denoting the sum as v_2). Then the value $v_1 - v_2$ can be treated as a feature value: if $v_1 - v_2 < 0$, the upper half is darker and this small image is possibly a face. In other words, the feature $v_1 - v_2$ is useful in determining whether this image is a face or not.

Of course, this single feature is very weak, but we may extract many feature values from an input image, and they form a *feature vector*.

In the above example, the features are manually designed. Such features often follow advice from domain experts. Suppose the PR task is to judge whether a patient has a certain type of bone injury, based on a computed tomography (CT) image. A domain expert (e.g., a doctor specialized in bone injuries) will explain how to reach a conclusion; a pattern recognition specialist will try to capture the essence of the expert's decision-making process and turn this knowledge into feature extraction guidelines.

Recently, especially after the popularization of *deep learning* methods, feature extraction has been replaced by feature learning in many applications. Given *enough* raw input data (e.g., images as matrices) and their associated labels (e.g., face or nonface), a learning algorithm can use the raw input data and their associated labels to automatically learn good features using sophisticated techniques.

After the feature extraction or feature learning step, we need to produce a model, which takes the feature vectors as its input, and produces our application's desired output. The model is mostly obtained by applying *machine learning* methods on the provided training feature vectors and labels.

For example, if an image is represented as a d-dimensional feature vector $\boldsymbol{x} \in \mathbb{R}^d$ (i.e., with d feature values), a linear model

$$\boldsymbol{w}^T\boldsymbol{x} + b$$

can be used to produce the output or prediction, in which

$$\boldsymbol{w} \in \mathbb{R}^d \quad \text{and} \quad b \in \mathbb{R}$$

are $d + 1$ *parameters* of the linear machine learning model. Given any image with a feature vector $\boldsymbol{x}$, the model will predict the image as being a face image if $\boldsymbol{w}^T\boldsymbol{x} + b \geq 0$, or nonface if $\boldsymbol{w}^T\boldsymbol{x} + b < 0$.

In this particular form of machine learning model (which is a parametric model), to learn a model is to find its optimal parameter values. Given a set of training examples with feature vectors and labels, machine learning techniques learn the model based on these training examples—i.e., using past experience (training instances and their labels) to learn a model that can predict for future examples even if they are not observed during the learning process.

1.2.2 PR vs. ML

Now we will have a short detour to discuss the relationship between PR and ML before we proceed to the next step in the PR pipeline.

It is quite easy to figure out that pattern recognition and machine learning are two closely related subjects. An important step (i.e., model learning) in PR is typically considered an ML task, and feature learning (also called representation learning) has attracted increasing attention in the ML community.

However, PR includes more than those components that are ML related. As discussed above, data acquisition, which is traditionally not related to machine learning, is ultraimportant for the success of a PR system. If a PR system accepts input data that is low quality, it is very difficult, if not impossible, for the machine learning related PR components to recover from the loss of information incurred by the low-quality input data. As the example in Figure 1.2 illustrates, a low resolution face image makes face recognition almost impossible, regardless of what advanced machine learning methods are employed to handle these images.

Traditional machine learning algorithms often focus on the abstract model learning part. A traditional machine learning algorithm usually uses preextracted feature vectors as its input, which rarely pays attention to data acquisition. Instead, ML algorithms assume the feature vectors satisfy some mathematical or statistical properties and constraints, and learn machine learning models based on the feature vectors and their assumptions.

An important portion of machine learning research is focused on the theoretical guarantees of machine learning algorithms. For example, under certain assumptions on the feature vectors, what is the upper or lower bound of the accuracy that *any* machine learning algorithm can attain? Such theoretical studies are sometimes not considered as a topic of PR research. Pattern recognition research and practice often has a stronger system flavor than that in machine learning.

We can find other differences between PR and ML. But, although we do not agree with expressions like "PR is a branch of ML" or "ML is a branch of PR," we do not want to emphasize the differences either.

PR and ML are two closely related subjects, and the differences may gradually disappear. For example, the recent deep learning trend in machine learning emphasizes *end-to-end* learning: the input of a deep learning method is the raw input data (rather than feature vectors), and its output is the desired prediction.

Hence, instead of emphasizing the differences between PR and ML, it is better to focus on the important task: let us just solve the problem or task that is presented to us!

One more note: the patterns or regularities recognized by PR research and practice involve various types of sensory input data, which means that PR is also closely related to subjects such as computer vision, acoustics, and speech processing.

1.2.3 Evaluation, Deployment, and Refinement

The next step after obtaining a model is to apply and evaluate the model. Evaluation of a PR or ML method or model is a complex issue. Depending on the project goals, various performance measures such as accuracy (or error) rate, speed, resource consumption, and even Research and Development (R&D) costs must be taken into account in the evaluation process.

We will leave the discussion of evaluation to Chapter 4. Suppose a PR model or system has passed the evaluation process (i.e., all the design targets have been met by the system); the next step is to deploy the system into its real-world application environments. However, passing evaluations and tests in a laboratory setting does not necessarily mean the PR system works well in practice. In fact, in many if not most cases, the reverse is true. The deployment may encounter environments that are far more complex than expected or assumed during the research, development, and evaluation phases. The real-world raw input data may, not surprisingly, have different characteristics from the data collected for training purposes.

Hence, deployment is rarely the last step in a PR system's life cycle. As shown in Figure 1.3, all the issues that appear in the system deployment phase have to be carefully collected, studied, and corrected (as reflected by the arrow pointing from "Deployment" to "Data acquisition"). The pipeline in Figure 1.3 now supersedes that in Figure 1.1 in order to reflect the importance of feedback.

Depending on the issues, some or even all the steps (data acquisition, feature extraction or learning, model learning, and evaluation) may have to be refined or completely revamped. This refinement process may require many cycles of effort. Of course, if issues are identified earlier in the evaluation step, the system has to be revised before its deployment.

Both data acquisition and manual feature extraction based on knowledge from domain experts are application or domain specific, which will involve background from various subject areas. In this book, we will not be able to go into the detail of these two steps.

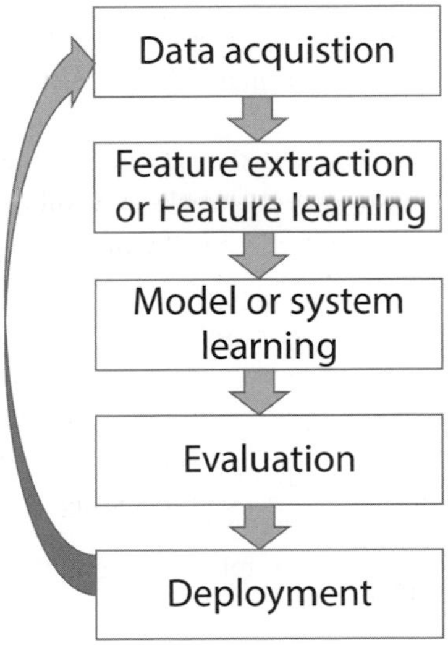

Figure 1.3 A typical pattern recognition pipeline with feedback loop.

The other steps are introduced in this book. For a detailed description of the structure and contents of the rest of this book, please refer to Chapter 3.

Exercises

1.1 Below is an interesting equation I saw in a short online entertainment video clip:

$$\sqrt[3]{a + \frac{a+1}{3}\sqrt{\frac{8a-1}{3}}} + \sqrt[3]{a - \frac{a+1}{3}\sqrt{\frac{8a-1}{3}}}. \tag{1.1}$$

What do you think this equation will evaluate to? Note that we consider only real numbers (i.e., complex numbers will not appear in this problem).

One does not often see this kind of complex equation in an online entertainment video, and this equation almost surely has nothing to do with pattern recognition or machine learning. However, as will be illustrated in this problem, we can observe many useful thinking patterns in the solution of this equation that are also critical in the study of machine learning and pattern recognition. So, let us take a closer look at this equation.

(a) **Requirements on the input.** In a pattern recognition or machine learning problem, we must enforce some constraints on the input data. These constraints might be implemented by *preprocessing* techniques, by requirements in the *data acquisition* process, or by other means.

The requirement for the above equation is specified in terms of a. What will we enforce on the variable a?

(b) **Observing the data and the problem.** The first step in solving a PR or ML problem is often to *observing* or *visualizing* your data—in other words, gaining some intuition about the problem at hand. While trying to observe or visualize the data, two kinds of data are often popular choices: those that are *representative* (to observe some common properties) and those that have *peculiar* properties (to observe some corner cases).

One example of peculiar data for Eq. (1.1) is $a = \frac{1}{8}$. This value for a is peculiar because it greatly *simplifies* the equation. What is the value of Eq. (1.1) under this assignment of a?

(c) **Coming up with your idea.** After observing the data, you may come up with some intuition or ideas on how to solve the problem. If an idea is *reasonable*, it is worth pursuing.

Can you find another peculiar value for a? What is the value of Eq. (1.1) in that case? Given these observations, what is your idea about Eq. (1.1)?

(d) **Sanity check of your idea.** How do you make sure your idea is reasonable? One commonly used method is to test it on some simple cases, or to write a simple prototype system to verify it.

For Eq. (1.1), we can write a single-line MATLAB®/GNU Octave command to evaluate its value. For example, let `a=3/4` assign a value to a; we can evaluate Eq. (1.1) as

```
f = ( a + (a+1)/3*sqrt((8*a-1)/3) )^(1/3) + ...
    ( a - (a+1)/3*sqrt((8*a-1)/3) )^(1/3)
```

What is the value this command returns?

(e) **Avoiding caveats in coding.** The value returned by this command is obviously wrong—we know the result must be a real number. What is the cause of this issue? It is caused by a small caveat in the programming. We should pay special attention to programming details in our prototype system, in order to make sure it correctly implements our idea.

Read the online MATLAB manual and try to fix the problem. What is the correct value? If you use the correct code to evaluate Eq. (1.1) for many different a values ($a \geq 0.125$), can it support your idea?

You might have come up with a good idea that is supported by your code from the very beginning. In this case, you can move to the next part. If not, please observe the data, come up with an idea that is better than your original one, and test it until it is supported by your sanity check experiments.

(f) **Formal and rigorous proof.** Inevitably you will have to formally prove your statements in some tasks. A proof needs to be correct and rigorous. The first step in a valid proof is probably to define your *symbols and notation* such that you can *express your problem and idea precisely* in mathematical language.

Define your notation and write down your idea as a precise mathematical statement. Then prove it rigorously.

(g) **Making good use of existing results when they are available.** In both research and development, we have to make good use of existing resources—e.g., mathematical theorems, optimization methods, software libraries, and development frameworks. That said, to use existing results, resources, and tools means that you have to be aware of them. Thus, it is good to *know major results and tools in subject domains that are close to one's own domain*, even if you are not familiar with their details.

Of course, these resources and tools include those that are developed by yourself. Use the theorem you just proved in this problem to calculate the following expression:

$$\sqrt[3]{2+\sqrt{5}}+\sqrt[3]{2-\sqrt{5}}.$$

(h) **Possibly extending your results to a more general theory.** Some of your results may have the potential to become a theory that is more general and more useful. And it is worthwhile to take this step when there is an indication of such a possibility.

The above equation in fact comes from a more general result: Cardano's method to solve a cubic equation. Gerolamo Cardano was an Italian mathematician, and he showed that the roots of the equation

$$z^3 + pz + q = 0$$

can be solved using expressions related to Eq. (1.1). Read the information at `https://en.wikipedia.org/wiki/Cubic_equation` (especially the part that is related to Cardano's method), and try to understand this connection.

2 Mathematical Background

This chapter provides a brief review of the basic mathematical background that is required for understanding this book. Most of the contents in this chapter can be found in standard undergraduate math textbooks, hence details such as proofs will be omitted.

This book also requires some mathematics that is a little bit more advanced. We will provide the statements in this chapter, but detailed proofs are again omitted.

2.1 Linear Algebra

We will not consider complex numbers in this book. Hence, what we will deal with are all real numbers.

Scalar. We use $\mathbb{R}$ to denote the set of real numbers. A real number $x \in \mathbb{R}$ is also called a scalar.

Vector. A sequence of real numbers form a vector. We use boldface letters to denote vectors, e.g., $\boldsymbol{x} \in \mathbb{R}^d$ is a vector formed by a sequence of d real numbers. We use

$$\boldsymbol{x} = (x_1, x_2, \ldots, x_d)^T$$

to indicate that $\boldsymbol{x}$ is formed by d numbers in a *column* shape, and the ith number in the sequence is a scalar x_i, i.e.,[1]

$$\boldsymbol{x} = \begin{bmatrix} x_1 \\ x_2 \\ \vdots \\ x_d \end{bmatrix}, \tag{2.1}$$

where d is called the length (or dimensionality, or size) of the vector, and the vector is called a d-dimensional one. We use $\mathbf{1}_d$ and $\mathbf{0}_d$ to denote d-dimensional vectors whose elements are all 1 and all 0, respectively. When the vector size is obvious from its context, we simply write $\mathbf{1}$ or $\mathbf{0}$.

[1] The ^{T} superscript means the transpose of a matrix, which will be defined soon.

2.1.1 Inner Product, Norm, Distance, and Orthogonality

The inner product of two vectors $\boldsymbol{x}$ and $\boldsymbol{y}$ is denoted by $\boldsymbol{x}^T\boldsymbol{y}$ (or $\boldsymbol{x}\cdot\boldsymbol{y}$, or $\langle\boldsymbol{x},\boldsymbol{y}\rangle$, or $\boldsymbol{x}'\boldsymbol{y}$, or $\boldsymbol{x}^t\boldsymbol{y}$; in this book, we will use the notation $\boldsymbol{x}^T\boldsymbol{y}$). It is also called the dot product. The dot product of two d-dimensional vectors $\boldsymbol{x} = (x_1, x_2, \ldots, x_d)^T$ and $\boldsymbol{y} = (y_1, y_2, \ldots, y_d)^T$ is defined as

$$\boldsymbol{x}^T\boldsymbol{y} = \sum_{i=1}^{d} x_i y_i. \tag{2.2}$$

Hence, the inner product is a scalar, and we obviously have

$$\boldsymbol{x}^T\boldsymbol{y} = \boldsymbol{y}^T\boldsymbol{x}. \tag{2.3}$$

The above fact will sometimes help us in this book—e.g., making transformations:

$$(\boldsymbol{x}^T\boldsymbol{y})z = z(\boldsymbol{x}^T\boldsymbol{y}) = z\boldsymbol{x}^T\boldsymbol{y} = z\boldsymbol{y}^T\boldsymbol{x} = (z\boldsymbol{y}^T)\boldsymbol{x}, \tag{2.4}$$

and so on.

The norm of a vector $\boldsymbol{x}$ is denoted by $\|\boldsymbol{x}\|$, and defined by

$$\|\boldsymbol{x}\| = \sqrt{\boldsymbol{x}^T\boldsymbol{x}}. \tag{2.5}$$

Other types of vector norms are available. The specific form in Eq. (2.5) is called the ℓ_2 norm. It is also called the *length* of $\boldsymbol{x}$ in some cases. Note that the norm $\|\boldsymbol{x}\|$ and the squared norm $\boldsymbol{x}^T\boldsymbol{x}$ are always nonnegative for any $\boldsymbol{x} \in \mathbb{R}^d$.

A vector whose length is 1 is called a unit vector. We usually say that a unit vector determines a *direction*. Endpoints of unit vectors reside on the surface of the unit hypersphere in the d-dimensional space whose center is the zero vector $\boldsymbol{0}$ and radius is 1. A ray from the center to any unit vector uniquely determines a direction in that space, and vice versa. When $\boldsymbol{x} = c\boldsymbol{y}$ and $c > 0$, we say that the two vectors $\boldsymbol{x}$ and $\boldsymbol{y}$ are in the same direction.

The distance between $\boldsymbol{x}$ and $\boldsymbol{y}$ is denoted by $\|\boldsymbol{x} - \boldsymbol{y}\|$. A frequently used fact is about the squared distance:

$$\|\boldsymbol{x} - \boldsymbol{y}\|^2 = (\boldsymbol{x} - \boldsymbol{y})^T(\boldsymbol{x} - \boldsymbol{y}) = \|\boldsymbol{x}\|^2 + \|\boldsymbol{y}\|^2 - 2\boldsymbol{x}^T\boldsymbol{y}. \tag{2.6}$$

The above equality utilizes the facts that $\|\boldsymbol{x}\|^2 = \boldsymbol{x}^T\boldsymbol{x}$ and $\boldsymbol{x}^T\boldsymbol{y} = \boldsymbol{y}^T\boldsymbol{x}$.

2.1.2 Angle and Inequality

If $\boldsymbol{x}^T\boldsymbol{y} = 0$, we say that the two vectors are orthogonal, or perpendicular, also denoted by $\boldsymbol{x} \perp \boldsymbol{y}$. From the geometry, we know that the angle between these two vectors is 90° or $\frac{\pi}{2}$.

Let the angle between vectors $\boldsymbol{x}$ and $\boldsymbol{y}$ be denoted by θ ($0 \le \theta \le 180^\circ$); then

$$\boldsymbol{x}^T\boldsymbol{y} = \|\boldsymbol{x}\|\,\|\boldsymbol{y}\|\cos\theta. \tag{2.7}$$

The above equation in fact defines the angle as

$$\theta = \arccos\left(\frac{\boldsymbol{x}^T\boldsymbol{y}}{\|\boldsymbol{x}\|\,\|\boldsymbol{y}\|}\right). \tag{2.8}$$

Because $-1 \le \cos\theta \le 1$ for any θ, these equations also tell us that

$$\boldsymbol{x}^T\boldsymbol{y} \le |\boldsymbol{x}^T\boldsymbol{y}| \le \|\boldsymbol{x}\|\,\|\boldsymbol{y}\|. \tag{2.9}$$

If we expand the vector form of this inequality and take the square of both sides, it appears as

$$\left(\sum_{i=1}^{d} x_i y_i\right)^2 \le \left(\sum_{i=1}^{d} x_i^2\right)\left(\sum_{i=1}^{d} y_i^2\right), \tag{2.10}$$

which is the Cauchy–Schwarz inequality.[2] The equality holds if and only if there is a constant $c \in \mathbb{R}$ such that $x_i = cy_i$ for all $1 \le i \le d$. In the vector form, the equality condition is equivalent to $\boldsymbol{x} = c\boldsymbol{y}$ for some constant c.

This inequality (and the equality condition) can be extended to integrals:

$$\left(\int f(x)g(x)\,\mathrm{d}x\right)^2 \le \left(\int f^2(x)\,\mathrm{d}x\right)\left(\int g^2(x)\,\mathrm{d}x\right), \tag{2.11}$$

(in which $f^2(x)$ means $f(x)f(x)$), assuming all integrals exist.

2.1.3 Vector Projection

Sometimes we need to compute the projection of one vector onto another. As illustrated in Figure 2.1, $\boldsymbol{x}$ is projected onto $\boldsymbol{y}$ (which must be nonzero). Hence, $\boldsymbol{x}$ is decomposed as

$$\boldsymbol{x} = \boldsymbol{x}_\perp + \boldsymbol{z},$$

where $\boldsymbol{x}_\perp$ is the projected vector, and $\boldsymbol{z}$ can be considered as the residue (or error) of the projection. Note that $\boldsymbol{x}_\perp \perp \boldsymbol{z}$.

In order to determine $\boldsymbol{x}_\perp$, we take two steps: to *find its direction and norm separately*, and this trick will also be useful in some other scenarios in this book.

For any nonzero vector $\boldsymbol{x}$, its norm is $\|\boldsymbol{x}\|$. Since $\boldsymbol{x} = \frac{\boldsymbol{x}}{\|\boldsymbol{x}\|}\|\boldsymbol{x}\|$, the vector $\frac{\boldsymbol{x}}{\|\boldsymbol{x}\|}$ is in the same direction as $\boldsymbol{x}$ and it is also a unit vector. Hence, $\frac{\boldsymbol{x}}{\|\boldsymbol{x}\|}$ is the direction of $\boldsymbol{x}$. The combination of norm and direction uniquely determines any vector. The norm alone determines the zero vector.

[2] The two names in this inequality are Augustin-Louis Cauchy, the famous French mathematician who first published this inequality, and Karl Hermann Amandus Schwarz, a German mathematician. The integral form generalization of this inequality was by Viktor Yakovlevich Bunyakovsky, a Ukrainian/Russian mathematician.

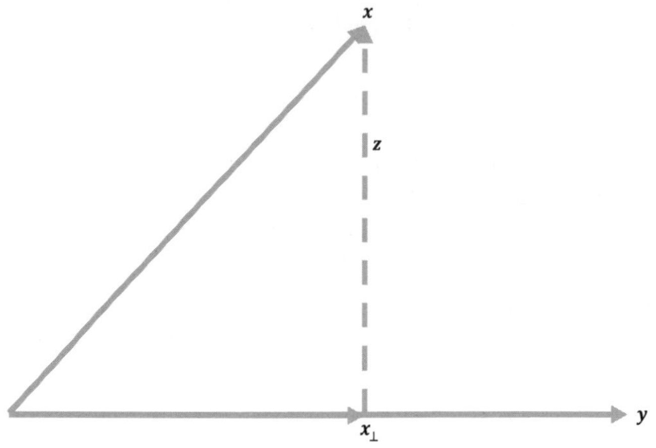

Figure 2.1 Illustration of vector projection.

The direction of $\boldsymbol{y}$ is $\frac{\boldsymbol{y}}{\|\boldsymbol{y}\|}$. It is obvious that the direction of $\boldsymbol{x}_\perp$ is $\frac{\boldsymbol{y}}{\|\boldsymbol{y}\|}$ if the angle θ between $\boldsymbol{x}$ and $\boldsymbol{y}$ is acute ($< 90°$), as illustrated in Figure 2.1. The norm of $\boldsymbol{x}_\perp$ is also simple:

$$\|\boldsymbol{x}_\perp\| = \|\boldsymbol{x}\| \cos\theta = \|\boldsymbol{x}\| \frac{\boldsymbol{x}^T \boldsymbol{y}}{\|\boldsymbol{x}\| \, \|\boldsymbol{y}\|} = \frac{\boldsymbol{x}^T \boldsymbol{y}}{\|\boldsymbol{y}\|}. \tag{2.12}$$

Hence, the projection $\boldsymbol{x}_\perp$ is

$$\boldsymbol{x}_\perp = \frac{\boldsymbol{x}^T \boldsymbol{y}}{\|\boldsymbol{y}\|} \frac{\boldsymbol{y}}{\|\boldsymbol{y}\|} = \frac{\boldsymbol{x}^T \boldsymbol{y}}{\boldsymbol{y}^T \boldsymbol{y}} \boldsymbol{y}. \tag{2.13}$$

Equation (2.13) is derived assuming θ is acute. However, it is easy to verify that this equation is correct too when the angle is right ($= 90°$), obtuse ($> 90°$), or straight ($= 180°$). The term $\frac{\boldsymbol{x}^T \boldsymbol{y}}{\boldsymbol{y}^T \boldsymbol{y}}$ (which is a scalar) is called the projected value, and $\frac{\boldsymbol{x}^T \boldsymbol{y}}{\boldsymbol{y}^T \boldsymbol{y}} \boldsymbol{y}$ is the projected vector, which is also denoted by $\text{proj}_{\boldsymbol{y}} \boldsymbol{x}$.

Vector projection is very useful in this book. For example, let $\boldsymbol{y} = (2, 1)$ and $\boldsymbol{x} = (1, 1)$. The direction of $\boldsymbol{y}$ specifies all the points that possess the property that the first dimension is twice the second dimension. Using Eq. (2.13), we obtain $\text{proj}_{\boldsymbol{y}} \boldsymbol{x} = (1.2, 0.6)$, which also exhibits the same property. We may treat $\text{proj}_{\boldsymbol{y}} \boldsymbol{x}$ as the best approximation of $\boldsymbol{x}$ that satisfies the property specified in $\boldsymbol{y}$. The residue of this approximation $\boldsymbol{z} = \boldsymbol{x} - \text{proj}_{\boldsymbol{y}} \boldsymbol{x} = (-0.2, 0.4)$ does not satisfy this property and can be considered as noise or error in certain applications.

2.1.4 Basics of Matrices

An $m \times n$ matrix contains mn numbers organized in m rows and n columns, and we use x_{ij} (or $x_{i,j}$) to denote the element at the ith row and jth column in a matrix X, that is,

$$X = \begin{bmatrix} x_{11} & \cdots & x_{1n} \\ \vdots & \cdots & \vdots \\ x_{m1} & \cdots & x_{mn} \end{bmatrix}. \tag{2.14}$$

We also use $[X]_{ij}$ to refer to the element at the ith row and jth column in a matrix X.

There are a few special cases. When $m = n$, we call the matrix a square matrix. When $n = 1$, the matrix contains only one column, and we call it a column matrix, or a column vector, or simply a vector. When $m = 1$, we call it a row matrix, or a row vector. Note that when we say that $\boldsymbol{x}$ is a vector, we mean a column vector if not otherwise specified. That is, when we write $\boldsymbol{x} = (1, 2, 3)^T$, we are referring to a column matrix $\begin{bmatrix} 1 \\ 2 \\ 3 \end{bmatrix}$.

There are also a few special cases within square matrices that are worth noting. In a square matrix X of size $n \times n$, the diagonal entries refer to those elements x_{ij} in X satisfying $i = j$. If $x_{ij} = 0$ whenever $i \neq j$ (i.e., when nondiagonal entries are all 0), we say that X is a diagonal matrix. The unit matrix is a special diagonal matrix, whose diagonal entries are all 1. A unit matrix is usually denoted by I (when the size of it can be inferred from the context) or I_n (indicating the size is $n \times n$).

Following the MATLAB convention, we use

$$X = \operatorname{diag}(x_{11}, x_{22}, \ldots, x_{nn})$$

to denote an $n \times n$ diagonal matrix whose diagonal entries are $x_{11}, x_{22}, \ldots, x_{nn}$, sequentially. Similarly, for an $n \times n$ square matrix X, $\operatorname{diag}(X)$ is a vector $(x_{11}, x_{22}, \ldots, x_{nn})^T$.

The transpose of a matrix X is denoted by X^T, and is defined by

$$[X^T]_{ji} = x_{ij}.$$

If X has size $m \times n$ then X^T is $n \times m$. When X is square, X^T and X have the same size. If in addition $X^T = X$, then we say that X is a symmetric matrix.

2.1.5 Matrix Multiplication

Addition and subtraction can be applied to matrices with the same size. Let X and Y be two matrices with size $m \times n$, then

$$[X + Y]_{ij} = x_{ij} + y_{ij}, \tag{2.15}$$

$$[X - Y]_{ij} = x_{ij} - y_{ij}, \tag{2.16}$$

for any $1 \leq i \leq m$, $1 \leq j \leq n$. For any matrix X and a scalar c, the scalar multiplication cX is defined by

$$[cX]_{ij} = cx_{ij}.$$

Not just any two matrices can be multiplied. The multiplication XY exists (i.e., is well defined) if and only if the number of columns in X equals the number of rows in

Y—i.e., when there are positive integers m, n, and p such that the size of X is $m \times n$ and the size of Y is $n \times p$. The product XY is a matrix of size $m \times p$, and is defined by

$$[XY]_{ij} = \sum_{k=1}^{n} x_{ik} y_{kj}. \tag{2.17}$$

When XY is well defined, we always have

$$(XY)^T = Y^T X^T.$$

Note that YX does not necessarily exist when XY exists. Even if both XY and YX are well defined, $XY \neq YX$ except in a few special cases. However, for any matrix X, both XX^T and $X^T X$ exist and both are symmetric matrices.

Let $\boldsymbol{x} = (x_1, x_2, \ldots, x_m)^T$ and $\boldsymbol{y} = (y_1, y_2, \ldots, y_p)^T$ be two vectors. Treating vectors as special matrices, the dimensions of $\boldsymbol{x}$ and $\boldsymbol{y}^T$ satisfy the multiplication constraint, such that $\boldsymbol{x}\boldsymbol{y}^T$ always exists for any $\boldsymbol{x}$ and $\boldsymbol{y}$. We call $\boldsymbol{x}\boldsymbol{y}^T$ the outer product between $\boldsymbol{x}$ and $\boldsymbol{y}$. This outer product is an $m \times p$ matrix, and $[\boldsymbol{x}\boldsymbol{y}^T]_{ij} = x_i y_j$. Note that in general $\boldsymbol{x}\boldsymbol{y}^T \neq \boldsymbol{y}\boldsymbol{x}^T$.

Block matrix representation is sometimes useful. Let $\boldsymbol{x}_{i:}$ denote the ith row of X (of size $1 \times n$), and $\boldsymbol{x}_{:i}$ the ith column (of size $m \times 1$); we can write X in either column format

$$X = \begin{bmatrix} \boldsymbol{x}_{1:} \\ \hline \boldsymbol{x}_{2:} \\ \hline \vdots \\ \hline \boldsymbol{x}_{m:} \end{bmatrix}, \tag{2.18}$$

or row format

$$X = [\boldsymbol{x}_{:1} | \boldsymbol{x}_{:2} | \ldots | \boldsymbol{x}_{:n}]. \tag{2.19}$$

Using block matrix representation, we have

$$XY = [\boldsymbol{x}_{:1} | \boldsymbol{x}_{:2} | \ldots | \boldsymbol{x}_{:n}] \begin{bmatrix} \boldsymbol{y}_{1:} \\ \hline \boldsymbol{y}_{2:} \\ \hline \vdots \\ \hline \boldsymbol{y}_{n:} \end{bmatrix} = \sum_{i=1}^{n} \boldsymbol{x}_{:i} \boldsymbol{y}_{i:}. \tag{2.20}$$

That is, the product XY is the summation of n outer products (between $\boldsymbol{x}_{:i}$ and $\boldsymbol{y}_{i:}^T$, which are both column vectors), X and Y^T have the same number of columns. If we compute the outer product of their corresponding columns, we get n matrices, each of which is $m \times p$. The summation of these matrices equals XY.

Similarly, we also have

$$XY = \begin{bmatrix} \boldsymbol{x}_{1:} \\ \hline \boldsymbol{x}_{2:} \\ \hline \vdots \\ \hline \boldsymbol{x}_{m:} \end{bmatrix} \left[\boldsymbol{y}_{:1} | \boldsymbol{y}_{:2} | \dots | \boldsymbol{y}_{:p} \right]. \tag{2.21}$$

This (block) outer product tells us $[XY]_{ij} = \boldsymbol{x}_{i:}\boldsymbol{y}_{:j}$, which is exactly Eq. (2.17).

For a square matrix X and a natural number k, the kth power of X is well defined, as

$$X^k = \underbrace{XX \dots X}_{k \text{ times}}.$$

2.1.6 Determinant and Inverse of a Square Matrix

There are many ways to define the determinant of a square matrix, and we adopt Laplace's formula to define it recursively. The determinant of X is usually denoted by $\det(X)$ or simply $|X|$, and is a scalar. Note that although the $|\cdot|$ symbol looks like the absolute value operator, its meaning is different. The determinant could be positive, zero, or negative, while absolute values are always nonnegative.

Given an $n \times n$ square matrix X, by removing its ith row and jth column we obtain an $(n-1) \times (n-1)$ matrix, and the determinant of this matrix is called the (i,j)th minor of X, denoted by M_{ij}. Then Laplace's formula states that

$$|X| = \sum_{j=1}^{n} (-1)^{i+j} a_{ij} M_{ij} \tag{2.22}$$

for *any* $1 \le i \le n$. Similarly,

$$|X| = \sum_{i=1}^{n} (-1)^{i+j} a_{ij} M_{ij}$$

for any $1 \le j \le n$. For a scalar (i.e., a 1×1 matrix), the determinant is itself. Hence, this recursive formula can be used to define the determinant of any square matrix.

It is easy to prove that

$$|X| = |X^T|$$

for any square matrix X, and

$$|XY| = |X|\,|Y|$$

when the product is well defined. For a scalar c and an $n \times n$ matrix X,

$$|cX| = c^n |X|.$$

For a square matrix X, if there exists another matrix Y such that $XY = YX = I$, then we say that Y is the inverse of X, denoted by X^{-1}. When the inverse of X exists, we say that X is invertible; clearly X^{-1} is of the same size as X. If X^{-1} exists, then its transpose $(X^{-1})^T$ is abbreviated as X^{-T}.

The following statement is useful for determining whether X is invertible or not:

$$X \text{ is invertible} \iff |X| \neq 0. \tag{2.23}$$

In other words, a square matrix is invertible if and only if its determinant is nonzero.

Assuming that both X and Y are invertible, XY exists, and c is a nonzero scalar, we have the following properties:

- X^{-1} is also invertible and $\left(X^{-1}\right)^{-1} = X$;
- $(cX)^{-1} = \frac{1}{c}X^{-1}$;
- $(XY)^{-1} = Y^{-1}X^{-1}$;
- $X^{-T} = \left(X^{-1}\right)^T = \left(X^T\right)^{-1}$.

2.1.7 Eigenvalue, Eigenvector, Rank, and Trace of a Square Matrix

For a square matrix A, if there exist a *nonzero* vector $\boldsymbol{x}$ and a scalar λ such that

$$A\boldsymbol{x} = \lambda\boldsymbol{x},$$

we say that λ is an eigenvalue of A and $\boldsymbol{x}$ is an eigenvector of A (which is associated with this eigenvalue λ). An $n \times n$ real square matrix has n eigenvalues, although some of them may be equal to each other. The eigenvalues and eigenvectors of a real square matrix, however, may contain complex numbers.

Eigenvalues have connections with the diagonal entries and the determinant of A. Denoting the n eigenvalues by $\lambda_1, \lambda_2, \ldots, \lambda_n$, the following equations hold (even if the eigenvalues are complex numbers):

$$\sum_{i=1}^{n} \lambda_i = \sum_{i=1}^{n} a_{ii}, \tag{2.24}$$

$$\prod_{i=1}^{n} \lambda_i = |A|. \tag{2.25}$$

The latter equation shows that a square matrix is invertible if and only if all of its eigenvalues are nonzero. The summation of all eigenvalues ($\sum_{i=1}^{n} \lambda_i$) has a special name: the trace. The trace of a square matrix X is denoted by $\operatorname{tr}(X)$. Now we know

$$\operatorname{tr}(X) = \sum_{i=1}^{n} x_{ii}. \tag{2.26}$$

If we assume all matrix multiplications are well defined, we have

$$\operatorname{tr}(XY) = \operatorname{tr}(YX). \tag{2.27}$$

Applying this rule, we can easily derive

$$\operatorname{tr}(XYZ) = \operatorname{tr}(ZXY) = \operatorname{tr}(YZX)$$

and many other similar results.

The rank of a square matrix X equals its number of nonzero eigenvalues, and is denoted by $\operatorname{rank}(X)$.

If X is also symmetric, then the properties of its eigenvalues and eigenvectors are a lot nicer. Given any $n \times n$ *real symmetric matrix* X, the following statements are true:

- All the eigenvalues of X are real numbers, hence can be sorted. We will denote the eigenvalues of an $n \times n$ real symmetric matrix as $\lambda_1, \lambda_2, \ldots, \lambda_n$, and assume $\lambda_1 \geq \lambda_2 \geq \cdots \geq \lambda_n$— i.e., they are sorted in descending order.
- All the eigenvectors of X contain only real values. We will denote the eigenvectors as $\xi_1, \xi_2, \ldots, \xi_n$, and ξ_i is associated with λ_i—i.e., the eigenvectors are also sorted according to their associated eigenvalues. The eigenvectors are normalized—i.e., $\|\xi_i\| = 1$ for any $1 \leq i \leq n$.
- The eigenvectors satisfy (for $1 \leq i, j \leq n$)

$$\xi_i^T \xi_j = \begin{cases} 1 & \text{if } i = j, \\ 0 & \text{otherwise.} \end{cases} \tag{2.28}$$

  That is, the n eigenvectors form an orthogonal basis set of $\mathbb{R}^n$. Let E be an $n \times n$ matrix whose ith column is ξ_i, that is,

$$E = [\xi_1 | \xi_2 | \ldots | \xi_n].$$

  Then Eq. (2.28) is equivalent to

$$EE^T = E^T E = I. \tag{2.29}$$

- $\operatorname{rank}(E) = n$, because E is an orthogonal matrix. It is also easy to see that $|E| = \pm 1$ and $E^{-1} = E^T$.
- If we define a diagonal matrix $\Lambda = \operatorname{diag}(\lambda_1, \lambda_2, \ldots, \lambda_n)$, then the eigendecomposition of X is

$$X = E \Lambda E^T. \tag{2.30}$$

- The eigendecomposition can also be written in an equivalent form as

$$X = \sum_{i=1}^{n} \lambda_i \xi_i \xi_i^T, \tag{2.31}$$

  which is called the spectral decomposition. The spectral decomposition says that the matrix X equals a weighted sum of n matrices, each being the outer product between one eigenvector and itself, and weighted by the corresponding eigenvalue.

We will also encounter the generalized eigenvalue problem. Let A and B be two square matrices (and we assume they are real symmetric in this book). Then a vector $\boldsymbol{x}$ and a scalar λ that satisfy

$$A\boldsymbol{x} = \lambda B\boldsymbol{x}$$

are called, respectively, the generalized eigenvector and generalized eigenvalue of A *and* B. The generalized eigenvectors, however, are usually not normalized, and are not orthogonal.

2.1.8 Singular Value Decomposition

Eigendecomposition is related to the singular value decomposition (SVD). We will briefly introduce a few facts for real matrices.

Let X be an $m \times n$ matrix; the SVD of X is

$$X = U\Sigma V^T, \tag{2.32}$$

where U is an $m \times m$ matrix, Σ is an $m \times n$ matrix whose nondiagonal elements are all 0, and V is an $n \times n$ matrix.

If there are a scalar σ and two vectors $\boldsymbol{u} \in \mathbb{R}^m$ and $\boldsymbol{v} \in \mathbb{R}^n$ (both are unit vectors) that simultaneously satisfy

$$X\boldsymbol{v} = \sigma\boldsymbol{u} \quad \text{and} \quad X^T\boldsymbol{u} = \sigma\boldsymbol{v}, \tag{2.33}$$

we say that σ is a singular value of X, and $\boldsymbol{u}$ and $\boldsymbol{v}$ are its associated left- and right-singular vectors, respectively.

If $(\sigma, \boldsymbol{u}, \boldsymbol{v})$ satisfy the above equation, so do $(-\sigma, -\boldsymbol{u}, \boldsymbol{v})$. In order to remove this ambiguity, the singular value is always nonnegative (i.e., $\sigma \geq 0$).

The SVD finds all singular values and singular vectors. The columns of U are called the left-singular vectors of X, and the columns of V are the right-singular vectors. The matrices U and V are orthogonal. The diagonal entries in Σ are the corresponding singular values.

Because $XX^T = (U\Sigma V^T)(V\Sigma^T U^T) = U\Sigma\Sigma^T U^T$ and $\Sigma\Sigma^T$ is diagonal, we get that the left-singular vectors of X are the eigenvectors of XX^T, and similarly, the right-singular vectors of X are the eigenvectors of $X^T X$; the nonzero singular values of X (diagonal nonzero entries in Σ) are the square roots of the nonzero eigenvalues of XX^T and $X^T X$. A by-product is that the nonzero eigenvalues of XX^T and $X^T X$ are exactly the same.

This connection is helpful. When $m \gg n$ (e.g., $n = 10$ but $m = 100\,000$), the eigendecomposition of XX^T needs to perform eigendecomposition for a $100\,000 \times 100\,000$ matrix, which is infeasible or at least very inefficient. However, we can compute the SVD of X. The squared positive singular values and left-singular vectors are the positive eigenvalues and their associated eigenvectors of XX^T. The same trick also works well when $n \gg m$, in which the right-singular vectors are useful in finding the eigendecomposition of $X^T X$.

2.1.9 Positive (Semi)Definite Real Symmetric Matrices

We consider only real symmetric matrices and real vectors in this section, although the definitions of positive definite and positive semidefinite matrices are wider than that.

An $n \times n$ matrix A is positive definite if for any nonzero real vector $\boldsymbol{x}$ (i.e., $\boldsymbol{x} \in \mathbb{R}^n$ and $\boldsymbol{x} \neq \boldsymbol{0}$),

$$\boldsymbol{x}^T A \boldsymbol{x} > 0. \tag{2.34}$$

We say that A is positive semidefinite if $\boldsymbol{x}^T A \boldsymbol{x} \geq 0$ holds for any $\boldsymbol{x}$. The fact that matrix A is positive definite can be abbreviated as "A is PD" or in mathematical notation as $A \succ 0$. Similarly, A is positive semidefinite is equivalent to $A \succcurlyeq 0$ or "A is PSD."

The term

$$\boldsymbol{x}^T A \boldsymbol{x} = \sum_{i=1}^{n} \sum_{j=1}^{n} x_i x_j a_{ij} \tag{2.35}$$

is a real quadratic form, which will be frequently used in this book.

There is a simple connection between eigenvalues and PD (PSD) matrices. A real symmetric matrix is PD/PSD if and only if all its eigenvalues are positive/nonnegative.

One type of PSD matrix we will use frequently is of the form AA^T or $A^T A$, in which A is any real matrix. The proof is pretty simple: because

$$\boldsymbol{x}^T A A^T \boldsymbol{x} = \left(A^T \boldsymbol{x}\right)^T \left(A^T \boldsymbol{x}\right) = \|A^T \boldsymbol{x}\|^2 \geq 0,$$

AA^T is PSD, and similarly $A^T A$ is also PSD.

Now, for a PSD real symmetric matrix, we sort its eigenvalues as $\lambda_1 \geq \lambda_2 \geq \cdots \geq \lambda_n \geq 0$, in which the final ≥ 0 relationship is always true for PSD matrices, but not for all real symmetric matrices.

2.2 Probability

A random variable is usually denoted by an upper-case letter, such as X. A random variable is a variable that can take a value from a finite or infinite set. To keep things simple, we refrain from using the measure-theoretic definition of random variables and probabilities. We will use the terms *random variable* and *distribution* interchangeably.

2.2.1 Basics

If a random variable X can take a value from a finite or countably infinite set, it is called a discrete random variable. Suppose the outcome of a particular trial is either success or failure, and the chance of success is p ($0 \leq p \leq 1$). When multiple trials are tested, the chance of success in any one trial is not affected by any other trial (i.e., the trials are independent). Then we denote the number of trials that are required till we see the first successful outcome as X, which is a random variable that can take its value from the countably infinite set $\{1,2,3,\ldots\}$, hence is a discrete random variable. We say that X follows a geometric distribution with parameter p.[3]

A random variable is different from a usual variable: it may take different values with different likelihoods (or probabilities). Hence, a random variable is a function rather than a variable whose value can be fixed. Let the set $E = \{x_1, x_2, x_3, \ldots\}$ denote all values that a discrete random variable X can possibly take. We call each x_i an event. The number of events should be either finite or countably infinite, and the events are mutually exclusive; that is, if an event x_i happens, then any other event x_j ($j \neq i$) cannot happen in the same trial. Hence, the probability that either one of two events x_i or x_j happens equals the sum of the probability of the two events:

$$\Pr(X = x_1 \| X = x_2) = \Pr(X = x_1) + \Pr(X = x_2),$$

in which $\Pr(\cdot)$ means the probability and $\|$ is the logical or. The summation rule can be extended to a countable number of elements.

A discrete random variable is determined by a probability mass function (p.m.f.) $p(X)$. A p.m.f. is specified by the probability of each event: $\Pr(X = x_i) = c_i$ ($c_i \in \mathbb{R}$), and it is a valid p.m.f. if and only if

$$c_i \geq 0 \ (\forall x_i \in E) \quad \text{and} \quad \sum_{x_i \in E} c_i = 1. \tag{2.36}$$

For the geometric distribution, we have $\Pr(X = 1) = p$, $\Pr(X = 2) = (1-p)p$, and in general, $c_i = (1-p)^{i-1}p$. Since $\sum_{i=1}^{\infty} c_i = 1$, this is a valid p.m.f. And $\Pr(X \leq 2) = \Pr(X = 1) + \Pr(X = 2) = 2p - p^2$. The function

$$F(x) = \Pr(X \leq x) \tag{2.37}$$

is called the cumulative distribution function (c.d.f. or CDF).

If the set of possible values E is infinite and uncountable (for example and most likely, $\mathbb{R}$ or a subset of it), and in addition $\Pr(X = x) = 0$ for each possible $x \in E$, then we say that X is a continuous random variable or continuous distribution.[4]

As in the discrete case, the c.d.f. of X is still

$$F(x) = \Pr(X \leq x) = \Pr(X < x),$$

where the additional equality follows from $\Pr(X = x) = 0$. The corresponding function of the discrete p.m.f. is called the probability density function (p.d.f.) $p(x)$, which should satisfy

$$p(x) \geq 0 \quad \text{and} \quad \int_{-\infty}^{\infty} p(x)\,\mathrm{d}x = 1 \tag{2.38}$$

[3] Another definition of the geometric distribution defines it as the number of failures before the first success, and possible values are $\{0,1,2,\ldots\}$.

[4] In fact, if $\Pr(X = x) = 0$ for all $x \in E$, then E cannot be finite or countable.

to make $p(x)$ a valid p.d.f. In this book, we assume a continuous c.d.f. is differentiable; then

$$p(x) = F'(x), \tag{2.39}$$

where F' means the derivative of F.

The c.d.f. measures the accumulation of probability in both discrete and continuous domains. The p.d.f. $p(x)$ (which is the derivative of the c.d.f.) measures the rate of accumulation of probability—in other words, how dense X is at x. Hence, the higher $p(x)$ is, the larger the probability $\Pr(x - \varepsilon \le X \le x + \varepsilon)$ (but not a larger $\Pr(x)$, which is always 0).

A few statements about c.d.f. and p.d.f.:

- $F(x)$ is nondecreasing, and

$$F(-\infty) \triangleq \lim_{x \to -\infty} F(x) = 0,$$

$$F(\infty) \triangleq \lim_{x \to \infty} F(x) = 1,$$

  in which $\triangleq$ means "defined as." This property is true for both discrete and continuous distributions.
- $\Pr(a \le X \le b) = \int_a^b p(x)\,\mathrm{d}x = F(b) - F(a)$.
- Although the p.m.f. is always between 0 and 1, the p.d.f. can be any nonnegative value.
- If a continuous X takes values only in the range $E = [a,b]$, we can still say that $E = \mathbb{R}$, and let the p.d.f. $p(x) = 0$ for $x < a$ or $x > b$.

When there is more than one random variable, we will use a subscript to distinguish them—e.g., $p_Y(y)$ or $p_X(x)$. If Y is a continuous random variable and g is a fixed function (i.e., no randomness in the computation of g) and is monotonic, then $X = g(Y)$ is also a random variable, and its p.d.f. can be computed as

$$p_Y(y) = p_X(x)\left|\frac{\mathrm{d}x}{\mathrm{d}y}\right| = p_X(g(y))\left|g'(y)\right|, \tag{2.40}$$

in which $|\cdot|$ is the absolute value function.

2.2.2 Joint and Conditional Distributions, and Bayes' Theorem

In many situations we need to consider two or more random variables simultaneously. For example, let A be the age and I be the annual income in year 2016 (in RMB, the Chinese currency; using 10 000 as a step) for a person in China. Then the joint c.d.f. $\Pr(A \le a, I \le i)$ is the percentage of people in China whose age is not larger than a years old and whose income is not higher than i RMB in the year 2016. If we denote the random vector $X = (A, I)^T$ and $\boldsymbol{x} = (30, 80\,000)^T$, then $F(\boldsymbol{x}) = \Pr(X \le \boldsymbol{x}) = \Pr(A \le 30, I \le 80\,000)$ defines the c.d.f. of a joint distribution. This definition also applies to any number of random variables. The joint distribution can be discrete (if all random variables in it are discrete), continuous (if all random variables in it are continuous), or hybrid (if both discrete and continuous random variables exist). We will not deal with hybrid distributions in this book.

For the discrete case, a multidimensional p.m.f. $p(\boldsymbol{x})$ requires $p(\boldsymbol{x}) \geq 0$ for any $\boldsymbol{x}$ and $\sum_{\boldsymbol{x}} p(\boldsymbol{x}) = 1$. For the continuous case, we require the p.d.f. $p(\boldsymbol{x})$ to satisfy $p(\boldsymbol{x}) \geq 0$ for any $\boldsymbol{x}$ and $\int p(\boldsymbol{x})\,\mathrm{d}\boldsymbol{x} = 1$.

It is obvious that for a discrete p.m.f.,

$$p(\boldsymbol{x}) = \sum_{\boldsymbol{y}} p(\boldsymbol{x}, \boldsymbol{y})$$

when $\boldsymbol{x}$ and $\boldsymbol{y}$ are two random vectors (and one or both can be random variables—i.e., one-dimensional random vectors). In the continuous case,

$$p(\boldsymbol{x}) = \int_{\boldsymbol{y}} p(\boldsymbol{x}, \boldsymbol{y})\,\mathrm{d}\boldsymbol{y}.$$

The distributions obtained by summing or integrating one or more random variables out are called marginal distributions. The summation is taken over all possible values of $\boldsymbol{y}$ (the variable that is summed or integrated out).

Note that in general

$$p(\boldsymbol{x}, \boldsymbol{y}) \neq p(\boldsymbol{x})p(\boldsymbol{y}).$$

For example, let us guess $\Pr(A = 3) = 0.04$ and $\Pr(I = 80\,000) = 0.1$; i.e., in China the percentage of people aged 3 is 4%, and people with 80 000 yearly income is 10%. Then $\Pr(A = 3)\Pr(I = 80\,000) = 0.004$. However, we would expect $\Pr(A = 3, I = 80\,000)$ to be almost 0: How many 3-year-old children have 80 000 RMB yearly income?

In a random vector, if we know the value of one random variable for a particular example (or sample, or instance, or instantiation), it will affect our estimate of other random variable(s) in that sample. In the age–income hypothetic example, if we know $I = 80\,000$, then we know $A = 3$ is almost impossible for the same individual. Our estimate of the age will change to a new one when we know the income, and this new distribution is called the conditional distribution. We use $\boldsymbol{x}|Y = \boldsymbol{y}$ to denote the random vector (distribution) of $\boldsymbol{x}$ conditioned on $Y = \boldsymbol{y}$, and use $p(\boldsymbol{x}|Y = \boldsymbol{y})$ to denote the conditional p.m.f. or p.d.f. For conditional distributions we have

$$p(\boldsymbol{x}\,|\,\boldsymbol{y}) = \frac{p(\boldsymbol{x}, \boldsymbol{y})}{p(\boldsymbol{y})}, \tag{2.41}$$

$$p(\boldsymbol{y}) = \int_{\boldsymbol{x}} p(\boldsymbol{y}|\boldsymbol{x})p(\boldsymbol{x})\,\mathrm{d}\boldsymbol{x}. \tag{2.42}$$

In the discrete case, $\int$ in Eq. (2.42) is changed to $\sum$, and is called the law of total probability. Putting these two together, we get Bayes' theorem:[5]

[5] It is also called Bayes' rule or Bayes' law, named after Thomas Bayes, a famous British statistician and philosopher.

$$p(\boldsymbol{x}|\boldsymbol{y}) = \frac{p(\boldsymbol{y}|\boldsymbol{x})p(\boldsymbol{x})}{p(\boldsymbol{y})} = \frac{p(\boldsymbol{y}|\boldsymbol{x})p(\boldsymbol{x})}{\int_{\boldsymbol{x}} p(\boldsymbol{y}|\boldsymbol{x})p(\boldsymbol{x})\,\mathrm{d}\boldsymbol{x}}. \tag{2.43}$$

Let $\boldsymbol{y}$ be some random vectors we can observe (or measure) and $\boldsymbol{x}$ be the random variables that we cannot directly observe but want to estimate or predict. Then the known (observed) values of $\boldsymbol{y}$ are "evidence" that will make us update our estimate ("belief") of $\boldsymbol{x}$. Bayes' theorem provides a mathematically precise way to perform such updates, and we will use it frequently in this book.

2.2.3 Expectation and Variance/Covariance Matrices

The expectation (or mean, or average, or expected value) of a random vector X is denoted by $\mathbb{E}[X]$ (or EX, or $E(X)$, or $\mathcal{E}(X)$, etc.), and is computed as

$$\mathbb{E}[X] = \int_{\boldsymbol{x}} p(\boldsymbol{x})\boldsymbol{x}\,\mathrm{d}\boldsymbol{x}, \tag{2.44}$$

i.e., a weighted sum of $\boldsymbol{x}$, and the weights are the p.d.f. or p.m.f. (changing $\int$ to $\sum$ in the discrete case). Note that the expectation is a normal scalar or vector, which is not affected by randomness anymore (or at least not the randomness related to X). Two obvious properties of expectations are

- $\mathbb{E}[X+Y] = \mathbb{E}[X] + \mathbb{E}[Y]$;
- $\mathbb{E}[cX] = c\mathbb{E}[X]$ for a scalar c.

The expectation concept can be generalized. Let $g(\cdot)$ be a function; then $g(X)$ is a random vector, and its expectation is

$$\mathbb{E}[g(X)] = \int_{\boldsymbol{x}} p(\boldsymbol{x})g(\boldsymbol{x})\,\mathrm{d}\boldsymbol{x}. \tag{2.45}$$

Similarly, $g(X)|Y$ is also a random vector, and its expectation (the conditional expectation) is

$$\mathbb{E}[g(X)|Y=\boldsymbol{y}] = \int_{\boldsymbol{x}} p(\boldsymbol{x}|Y=\boldsymbol{y})g(\boldsymbol{x})\,\mathrm{d}\boldsymbol{x}. \tag{2.46}$$

And we can also write

$$h(\boldsymbol{y}) = \mathbb{E}[g(X)|Y=\boldsymbol{y}]. \tag{2.47}$$

Note that the expectation $\mathbb{E}[g(X)|Y=\boldsymbol{y}]$ is not dependent on X because it is integrated (or summed) out. Hence, $h(\boldsymbol{y})$ is a normal function of $\boldsymbol{y}$, which is not affected by the randomness caused by X anymore.

Now, in Eq. (2.45) we can specify

$$g(x) = (x - \mathbb{E}[X])^2,$$

in which $\mathbb{E}[X]$ is a completely determined scalar (if the p.m.f. or p.d.f. of X is known) and $g(x)$ is thus not affected by randomness. The expectation of this particular choice is called the variance (if X is a random variable) or covariance matrix (if X is a random vector) of X:

$$\mathrm{Var}(X) = \mathbb{E}[(X - \mathbb{E}[X])^2] \quad \text{or} \quad \mathrm{Cov}(X) = \mathbb{E}[(X - \mathbb{E}[X])(X - \mathbb{E}[X])^T]. \tag{2.48}$$

When X is a random variable, this expectation is called the variance and is denoted by $\mathrm{Var}(X)$. Variance is a scalar (which is always nonnegative), and its square root is called the standard deviation of X, denoted by σ_X.

When X is a random vector, this expectation is called the covariance matrix and is denoted by $\mathrm{Cov}(X)$. The covariance matrix for a d-dimensional random vector is a $d \times d$ real symmetric matrix, and is always positive semidefinite.

For a random variable X, it is easy to prove the following useful formula:

$$\mathrm{Var}(X) = \mathbb{E}[X^2] - (\mathbb{E}[X])^2. \tag{2.49}$$

Hence, the variance is the difference between two terms: the expectation of the squared random variable and the square of the mean. Because variance is nonnegative, we always have

$$\mathbb{E}[X^2] \geq (\mathbb{E}[X])^2.$$

A similar formula holds for random vectors:

$$\mathrm{Cov}(X) = \mathbb{E}[XX^T] - \mathbb{E}[X]\mathbb{E}[X]^T. \tag{2.50}$$

In a complex expectation involving multiple random variables or random vectors, we may specify which random variable (or vector) we want to compute the expectation for by adding a subscript. For example, $\mathbb{E}_X[g(X,Y)]$ computes the expectation of $g(X,Y)$ with respect to X.

One final note about expectation is that an expectation may not exist—e.g., if the integration or summation is undefined. The standard Cauchy distribution provides an example.[6] The p.d.f. of the standard Cauchy distribution is defined as

$$p(x) = \frac{1}{\pi(1+x^2)}. \tag{2.51}$$

Since $\int_{-\infty}^{\infty} \frac{1}{\pi(1+x^2)}\,\mathrm{d}x = \frac{1}{\pi}\left(\arctan(\infty) - \arctan(-\infty)\right) = 1$ and $p(x) \geq 0$, this is a valid p.d.f. The expectation, however, does not exist because it is the sum of two infinite values, which is not well defined in mathematical analysis.

2.2.4 Inequalities

If we are asked to estimate a probability $\Pr(a \leq X \leq b)$ but know nothing about X, the best we can say is that it is between 0 and 1 (including both ends). That is, if there is no information in, there is no information out—the estimation is valid for any distribution and is not useful at all.

[6] The Cauchy distribution is named, once again, after Augustin-Louis Cauchy.

If we know more about X, we can say more about probabilities involving X. Markov's inequality states that if X is a nonnegative random variable (or $\Pr(X < 0) = 0$) and $a > 0$ is a scalar, then

$$\Pr(X \geq a) \leq \frac{\mathbb{E}[X]}{a}, \tag{2.52}$$

assuming the mean is finite.[7]

Chebyshev's inequality depends on both the mean and the variance. For a random variable X, if its mean is finite and its variance is nonzero, then for any scalar $k > 0$,

$$\Pr\left(|X - \mathbb{E}[X]| \geq k\sigma\right) \leq \frac{1}{k^2}, \tag{2.53}$$

in which $\sigma = \sqrt{\mathrm{Var}(X)}$ is the standard deviation of X.[8]

There is also a one-tailed version of Chebyshev's inequality, which states that for $k > 0$,

$$\Pr(X - \mathbb{E}[X] \geq k\sigma) \leq \frac{1}{1+k^2}. \tag{2.54}$$

2.2.5 Independence and Correlation

Two random variables X and Y are independent if and only if the joint c.d.f. $F_{X,Y}$ and the marginal c.d.f. F_X and F_Y satisfy

$$F_{X,Y}(x,y) = F_X(x)F_Y(y) \tag{2.55}$$

for *any* x and y, or equivalently, if and only if the p.d.f. satisfies

$$f_{X,Y}(x,y) = f_X(x)f_Y(y). \tag{2.56}$$

When X and Y are independent, knowing the distribution of X does not give us any information about Y, and vice versa; in addition, $\mathbb{E}[XY] = \mathbb{E}[X]\mathbb{E}[Y]$. When X and Y are not independent, we say that they are dependent.

Another concept related to independence (or dependence) is correlatedness (or uncorrelatedness). Two random variables are said to be uncorrelated if their covariance is zero and correlated if their covariance is nonzero. The covariance between two random variables X and Y is defined as

$$\mathrm{Cov}(X,Y) = \mathbb{E}[XY] - \mathbb{E}[X]\mathbb{E}[Y], \tag{2.57}$$

which measures the level of linear relationship between them.

The range of $\mathrm{Cov}(X,Y)$ is not bounded. A proper normalization could convert it to a closed interval. Pearson's correlation coefficient is denoted by $\rho_{X,Y}$ or $\mathrm{corr}(X,Y)$,[9] and is defined as

[7] This inequality is named after Andrey (Andrei) Andreyevich Markov, a famous Russian mathematician.
[8] This inequality is named after Pafnuty Lvovich Chebyshev, another Russian mathematician.
[9] It is named after Karl Pearson, a famous British mathematician and biostatistician.

$$\rho_{X,Y} = \operatorname{corr}(X,Y) = \frac{\operatorname{Cov}(X,Y)}{\sigma_X \sigma_Y} = \frac{\mathbb{E}[XY] - \mathbb{E}[X]\mathbb{E}[Y]}{\sigma_X \sigma_Y}. \tag{2.58}$$

The range of Pearson's correlation coefficient is $[-1, +1]$. When the correlation coefficient is $+1$ or -1, X and Y are related by a perfect linear relationship $X = cY + b$; when the correlation coefficient is 0, they are uncorrelated.

When X and Y are random vectors (m- and n-dimensional, respectively), $\operatorname{Cov}(X,Y)$ is an $m \times n$ covariance matrix, and defined as

$$\operatorname{Cov}(X,Y) = \mathbb{E}\big[(X - \mathbb{E}[X])(Y - \mathbb{E}[Y])^T\big] \tag{2.59}$$

$$= \mathbb{E}\big[XY^T\big] - \mathbb{E}[X]\mathbb{E}[Y]^T. \tag{2.60}$$

Note that when $X = Y$, we get the covariance matrix of X (cf. Eq. 2.50).

Independence is a much stronger condition than uncorrelatedness:

$$X \text{ and } Y \text{ are independent} \Longrightarrow X \text{ and } Y \text{ are uncorrelated}, \tag{2.61}$$

$$X \text{ and } Y \text{ are uncorrelated} \not\Longrightarrow X \text{ and } Y \text{ are independent}. \tag{2.62}$$

2.2.6 The Normal Distribution

Among all distributions, the normal distribution is probably the most widely used. A random variable X follows a normal distribution if its p.d.f. is in the form

$$p(x) = \frac{1}{\sqrt{2\pi}\sigma} \exp\left(-\frac{(x-\mu)^2}{2\sigma^2}\right), \tag{2.63}$$

for some $\mu \in \mathbb{R}$ and $\sigma^2 > 0$. We can denote it as $X \sim N(\mu, \sigma^2)$ or $p(x) = N(x; \mu, \sigma^2)$. A normal distribution is also called a Gaussian distribution.[10] Note that the parameters that determine a normal distribution are (μ, σ^2), not (μ, σ).

A d-dimensional random vector is jointly normal (or has a multivariate normal distribution) if its p.d.f. is in the form

$$p(\boldsymbol{x}) = (2\pi)^{-d/2} |\Sigma|^{-1/2} \exp\left(-\tfrac{1}{2}(\boldsymbol{x} - \boldsymbol{\mu})^T \Sigma^{-1} (\boldsymbol{x} - \boldsymbol{\mu})\right), \tag{2.64}$$

for some $\boldsymbol{\mu} \in \mathbb{R}^d$ and positive semidefinite symmetric matrix Σ, and $|\cdot|$ is the determinant of a matrix. We can write this distribution as $X \sim N(\boldsymbol{\mu}, \Sigma)$ or $p(\boldsymbol{x}) = N(\boldsymbol{x}; \boldsymbol{\mu}, \Sigma)$.

Examples of the normal p.d.f. are shown in Figure 2.2. Figure 2.2a is a normal distribution with $\mu = 0$ and $\sigma^2 = 1$, and Figure 2.2b is a two-dimensional normal distribution with $\boldsymbol{\mu} = \boldsymbol{0}$ and $\Sigma = I_2$.

The expectation of single- and multivariate normal distributions are μ and $\boldsymbol{\mu}$, respectively. Their variance and covariance matrices are σ^2 and Σ, respectively. Hence, μ and σ^2 (not σ) are the counterparts of $\boldsymbol{\mu}$ and Σ, respectively.

We might remember $p(x) = \frac{1}{\sqrt{2\pi}\sigma} \exp\big(-\frac{(x-\mu)^2}{2\sigma^2}\big)$ very well, but be less familiar with the multivariate version $p(\boldsymbol{x})$. However, the one-dimensional distribution can

[10] It is named after Johann Carl Friedrich Gauss, a very influential German mathematician.

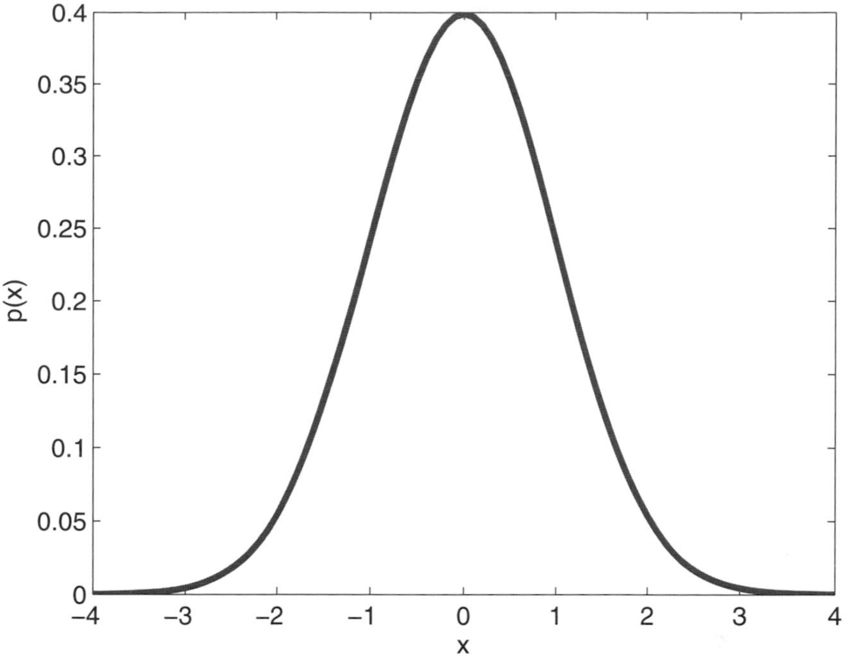

(a) One-dimensional normal

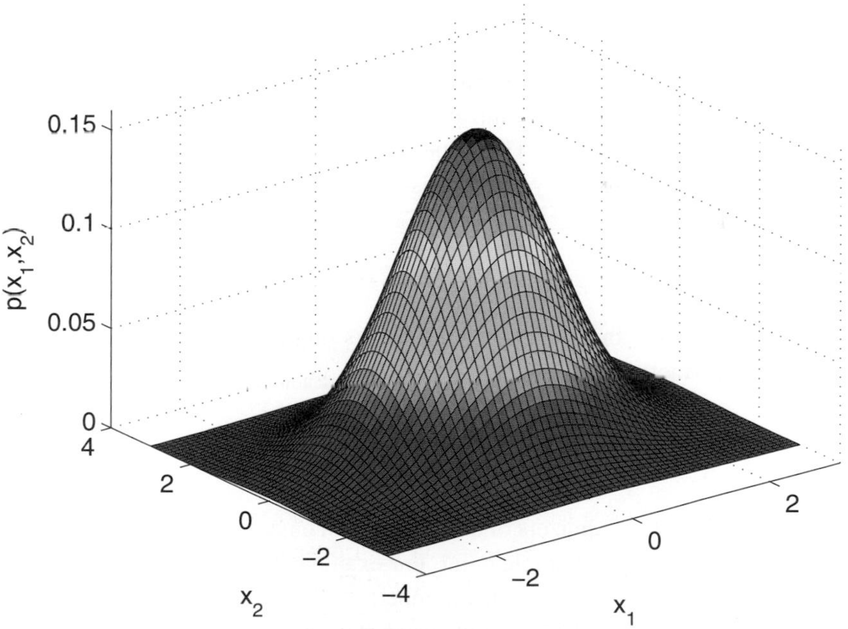

(b) Two-dimensional normal

Figure 2.2 Probability density function of example normal distributions. (A black and white version of this figure will appear in some formats. For the color version, please refer to the plate section.)

help us to remember the more complex multivariate p.d.f. If we rewrite the univariate normal density into an equivalent form

$$p(x) = (2\pi)^{-1/2}(\sigma^2)^{-1/2} \exp\left(-\tfrac{1}{2}(x-\mu)^T(\sigma^2)^{-1}(x-\mu)\right) \quad (2.65)$$

and change the dimensionality from 1 to d, the variance from σ^2 to the covariance matrix Σ or its determinant $|\Sigma|$, x to $\boldsymbol{x}$, and the mean from μ to $\boldsymbol{\mu}$, we get exactly the multivariate p.d.f.

$$p(\boldsymbol{x}) = (2\pi)^{-d/2}|\Sigma|^{-1/2} \exp\left(-\tfrac{1}{2}(\boldsymbol{x}-\boldsymbol{\mu})^T\Sigma^{-1}(\boldsymbol{x}-\boldsymbol{\mu})\right). \quad (2.66)$$

The Gaussian distribution has many nice properties, some of which can be found in Chapter 13, which is devoted to the properties of normal distributions. One particularly useful property is that if X and Y are jointly Gaussian and X and Y are uncorrelated, then they are independent.

2.3 Optimization and Matrix Calculus

Optimization will be frequently encountered in this book. However, details of optimization principles and techniques are beyond the scope of this book. We will touch only a little bit on this huge topic in this chapter.

Informally speaking, given a cost (or objective) function $f(\boldsymbol{x})\colon \mathcal{D} \mapsto \mathbb{R}$, the purpose of mathematical optimization is to find an $\boldsymbol{x}^\star$ in the domain $\mathcal{D}$, such that $f(\boldsymbol{x}^\star) \le f(\boldsymbol{x})$ for any $\boldsymbol{x} \in \mathcal{D}$. This type of optimization problem is called a minimization problem, and is usually denoted as

$$\min_{\boldsymbol{x}\in\mathcal{D}} f(\boldsymbol{x}). \quad (2.67)$$

A solution $\boldsymbol{x}^\star$ that makes $f(\boldsymbol{x})$ reach its minimum value is called a minimizer of f, and is denoted as

$$\boldsymbol{x}^\star = \arg\min_{\boldsymbol{x}\in\mathcal{D}} f(\boldsymbol{x}). \quad (2.68)$$

Note that the minimizers of a minimization objective can be a (possibly infinite) set of values rather than a single point. For example, the minimizers for $\min_{x\in\mathbb{R}} \sin(x)$ are a set containing infinitely many numbers: $-\frac{\pi}{2} + 2n\pi$ for any integer n. We are, however, in practice satisfied by any one of the minimizers in many applications.

In contrast, an optimization problem can also be maximizing a function $f(\boldsymbol{x})$, denoted as $\max_{\boldsymbol{x}\in\mathcal{D}} f(\boldsymbol{x})$. The maximizers are similarly denoted as $\boldsymbol{x}^\star = \arg\max_{\boldsymbol{x}\in\mathcal{D}} f(\boldsymbol{x})$. However, since maximizing $f(\boldsymbol{x})$ is equivalent to minimizing $-f(\boldsymbol{x})$, we often talk only about minimization problems.

2.3.1 Local Minimum, Necessary Condition, and Matrix Calculus

An $\boldsymbol{x}^\star \in \mathcal{D}$ that satisfies $f(\boldsymbol{x}^\star) \le f(\boldsymbol{x})$ for all $\boldsymbol{x} \in \mathcal{D}$ is called a global minimum. However, global minima are difficult to find in many (complex) optimization problems. In such cases, we are usually satisfied by a local minimum.

A local minimum, in layman's language, is some $\boldsymbol{x}$ that leads to the smallest objective value in its local neighborhood. In mathematics, $\boldsymbol{x}^\star$ is a local minimum if it belongs to the domain $\mathcal{D}$, and there exists some radius $r > 0$ such that for all $\boldsymbol{x} \in \mathcal{D}$ satisfying $\|\boldsymbol{x} - \boldsymbol{x}^\star\| \le r$, we always have $f(\boldsymbol{x}^\star) \le f(\boldsymbol{x})$.

There is one commonly used criterion for determining whether a particular point $\boldsymbol{x}$ is a candidate for being a minimizer of $f(\boldsymbol{x})$. If f is differentiable, then

$$\frac{\partial f}{\partial \boldsymbol{x}} = \boldsymbol{0} \tag{2.69}$$

is a *necessary* condition for $\boldsymbol{x}$ to be a local minimum (or a local maximum). In other words, for $\boldsymbol{x}$ to be either a minimum or a maximum point, the gradient at that point should be an all-zero vector. Note that this is only a necessary condition, but may not be sufficient. And we do not know whether an $\boldsymbol{x}$ satisfying this gradient test is a maximizer, a minimizer, or a saddle point (neither a maximum nor a minimum). Points with an all-zero gradient are also called stationary points or critical points.

The gradient $\frac{\partial f}{\partial \boldsymbol{x}}$ is defined in all undergraduate mathematics texts if $\boldsymbol{x} \in \mathbb{R}$, i.e., a scalar variable. In this case, the gradient is the derivative $\frac{\mathrm{d}f}{\mathrm{d}x}$. The gradient $\frac{\partial f}{\partial \boldsymbol{x}}$ for multivariate functions, however, is rarely included in these textbooks. These gradients are defined via matrix calculus as partial derivatives. For vectors $\boldsymbol{x}$, $\boldsymbol{y}$, scalars x, y, and matrix X, the matrix form is defined as

$$\left[\frac{\partial \boldsymbol{x}}{\partial y}\right]_i = \frac{\partial x_i}{\partial y}, \tag{2.70}$$

$$\left[\frac{\partial x}{\partial \boldsymbol{y}}\right]_i = \frac{\partial x}{\partial y_i}, \tag{2.71}$$

$$\left[\frac{\partial \boldsymbol{x}}{\partial \boldsymbol{y}}\right]_{ij} = \frac{\partial x_i}{\partial y_j} \quad \text{(which is a matrix)}, \tag{2.72}$$

$$\left[\frac{\partial y}{\partial X}\right]_{ij} = \frac{\partial y}{\partial x_{ij}}. \tag{2.73}$$

Using these definitions, it is easy to calculate some gradients (partial derivatives)—e.g.,

$$\frac{\partial \boldsymbol{x}^T \boldsymbol{y}}{\partial \boldsymbol{x}} = \boldsymbol{y}, \tag{2.74}$$

$$\frac{\partial \boldsymbol{a}^T X \boldsymbol{b}}{\partial X} = \boldsymbol{a}\boldsymbol{b}^T. \tag{2.75}$$

However, for more complex gradients—for example, those involving matrix inverse, eigenvalues, and matrix determinant—the solutions are not obvious. We recommend *The Matrix Cookbook* (Petersen & Pedersen 2012), which lists many useful results—e.g.,

$$\frac{\partial \det(X)}{\partial X} = \det(X) X^{-T}. \tag{2.76}$$

2.3.2 Convex and Concave Optimization

Some functions have nicer properties than others in the optimization realm. For example, when $f(\boldsymbol{x})$ is a *convex* function whose domain is $\mathbb{R}^d$, any local minimum is also a global minimum. More generally, a convex minimization problem is to minimize a convex objective on a convex set. In convex minimization, any local minimum must also be a global minimum.

In this book, we consider only subsets of $\mathbb{R}^d$. If $S \subseteq \mathbb{R}^d$, then S is a convex set if for any $\boldsymbol{x} \in S$, $\boldsymbol{y} \in S$ and $0 \le \lambda \le 1$,

$$\lambda \boldsymbol{x} + (1-\lambda)\boldsymbol{y} \in S$$

always holds. In other words, if we pick any two points from a set S and the line segment connecting them falls entirely inside S, then S is convex. For example, in two-dimensional space, all points inside a circle form a convex set, but the set of points outside that circle is not convex.

A function f (whose domain is S) is convex if for any $\boldsymbol{x}$ and $\boldsymbol{y}$ in S and any λ $(0 \le \lambda \le 1)$, we have

$$f(\lambda \boldsymbol{x} + (1-\lambda)\boldsymbol{y}) \le \lambda f(\boldsymbol{x}) + (1-\lambda) f(\boldsymbol{y}).$$

For example, $f(x) = x^2$ is a convex function. If we pick any two points $a < b$ on its curve, the line segment that connects them is above the $f(x) = x^2$ curve in the range (a,b), as illustrated in Figure 2.3.

If f is a convex function, we say that $-f$ is a concave function. Any local maximum of a concave function (on a convex domain) is also a global maximum.

Jensen's inequality shows that the constraints in the convex function definition can be extended to an arbitrary number of points. Let $f(\boldsymbol{x})$ be a convex function defined on a convex set S, and $\boldsymbol{x}_1, \boldsymbol{x}_2, \ldots, \boldsymbol{x}_n$ are points in S. Then, for weights $w_1, w_2, \ldots, w_n$ satisfying $w_i \ge 0$ (for all $1 \le i \le n$) and $\sum_{i=1}^n w_i = 1$, Jensen's inequality states that

$$f\left(\sum_{i=1}^n w_i \boldsymbol{x}_i\right) \le \sum_{i=1}^n w_i f(\boldsymbol{x}_i). \tag{2.77}$$

If $f(x)$ is a concave function defined on a convex set S, we have

$$f\left(\sum_{i=1}^n w_i \boldsymbol{x}_i\right) \ge \sum_{i=1}^n w_i f(\boldsymbol{x}_i). \tag{2.78}$$

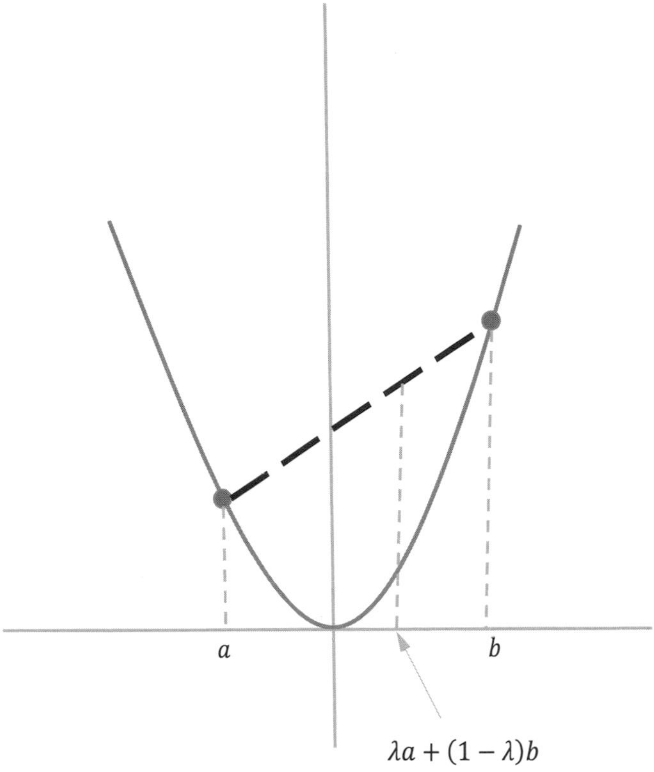

Figure 2.3 Illustration of a simple convex function.

If we assume $w_i > 0$ for all i, the equality holds if and only if $\boldsymbol{x}_1 = \boldsymbol{x}_2 = \cdots = \boldsymbol{x}_n$ or f is a linear function. If $w_i = 0$ for some i, we can remove these w_i and their corresponding $\boldsymbol{x}_i$ and apply the equality condition again.

A twice differentiable function is convex (concave) if its second derivative is non-negative (nonpositive). For example, $\ln(x)$ is concave on $(0, \infty)$ because $\ln''(x) = -\frac{1}{x^2} < 0$. Similarly, $f(x) = x^4$ is convex because its second derivative is $12x^2 \geq 0$. The same convexity test applies to a convex subset of $\mathbb{R}$—e.g., an interval $[a, b]$.

For a scalar-valued function involving many variables, if it is continuous and twice differentiable, its second-order partial derivatives form a square matrix, called the Hessian matrix, or simply the Hessian. Such a function is convex if the Hessian is positive semidefinite. For example, $f(\boldsymbol{x}) = \boldsymbol{x}^T A \boldsymbol{x}$ is convex if A is positive semidefinite.

A function f is *strictly* convex if for any $\boldsymbol{x} \neq \boldsymbol{y}$ in a convex domain S and any λ $(0 < \lambda < 1)$, we have $f(\lambda \boldsymbol{x} + (1 - \lambda)\boldsymbol{y}) < \lambda f(\boldsymbol{x}) + (1 - \lambda) f(\boldsymbol{y})$.[11]

A twice differentiable function is strictly convex if its second derivative is positive (or its Hessian is positive definite in the multivariate case). For example, $f(x) = x^2$

[11] Please pay attention to the three changes in this definition (compared to the convex function definition): $\boldsymbol{x} \neq \boldsymbol{y}$, $(0, 1)$ instead of $[0, 1]$, and $<$ instead of $\leq$.

is strictly convex, but any linear function is not. Hence, the equality condition for Jensen's inequality applied to a strictly convex function is $\boldsymbol{x}_i = \boldsymbol{c}$ if $w_i > 0$, in which $\boldsymbol{c}$ is a fixed vector.

For more treatments on convex functions and convex optimization, *Convex Optimization* (Boyd & Vandenberghe 2004) is an excellent textbook and reference.

2.3.3 Constrained Optimization and the Lagrange Multipliers

Sometimes, beyond the objective $f(\boldsymbol{x})$, we also require the variables $\boldsymbol{x}$ to satisfy some constraints. For example, we may require that $\boldsymbol{x}$ has unit length (which will appear quite frequently later in this book). For $\boldsymbol{x} = (x_1, x_2)^T$ and domain $\mathcal{D} = \mathbb{R}^2$, a concrete example is

$$\min \quad f(\boldsymbol{x}) = \boldsymbol{v}^T\boldsymbol{x} \tag{2.79}$$

$$\text{s.t.} \quad \boldsymbol{x}^T\boldsymbol{x} = 1, \tag{2.80}$$

in which $\boldsymbol{v} = \left[\begin{smallmatrix}1\\2\end{smallmatrix}\right]$ is a constant vector and "s.t." means "subject to," which specifies a constraint on $\boldsymbol{x}$. There can be more than one constraint, and the constraint can also be an inequality.

Let us focus on equality constraints for now. A minimization problem with only equality constraints is

$$\min \quad f(\boldsymbol{x}) \tag{2.81}$$

$$\text{s.t.} \quad g_1(\boldsymbol{x}) = 0, \tag{2.82}$$

$$\dots$$

$$g_m(\boldsymbol{x}) = 0. \tag{2.83}$$

The method of Lagrange multipliers is a good tool to deal with this kind of problem.[12] This method defines a Lagrange function (or Lagrangian) as

$$L(\boldsymbol{x}, \boldsymbol{\lambda}) = f(\boldsymbol{x}) - \boldsymbol{\lambda}^T\boldsymbol{g}(\boldsymbol{x}), \tag{2.84}$$

in which $\boldsymbol{\lambda} = (\lambda_1, \lambda_2, \dots, \lambda_m)^T$ are the m Lagrange multipliers, with the ith Lagrange multiplier λ_i associated with the ith constraint $g_i(\boldsymbol{x}) = 0$, and we use $\boldsymbol{g}(\boldsymbol{x})$ to denote $(g_1(\boldsymbol{x}), g_2(\boldsymbol{x}), \dots, g_m(\boldsymbol{x}))^T$, the values of all m constraints. Then L is an unconstrained optimization objective and

$$\frac{\partial L}{\partial \boldsymbol{x}} = 0, \tag{2.85}$$

$$\frac{\partial L}{\partial \boldsymbol{\lambda}} = 0 \tag{2.86}$$

are necessary conditions for $(\boldsymbol{x}, \boldsymbol{\lambda})$ to be a stationary point of $L(\boldsymbol{x}, \boldsymbol{\lambda})$. Note that the domain of the Lagrange multipliers is $\mathbb{R}^m$—i.e., without any restriction. Hence, we can also change the minus sign $(-)$ to a plus sign $(+)$ in the Lagrangian.

[12] This method is named after Joseph-Louis Lagrange, an Italian mathematician and astronomer.

The method of Lagrange multipliers states that if $\boldsymbol{x}_0$ is a stationary point of the original constrained optimization problem, there always exists a $\boldsymbol{\lambda}_0$ such that $(\boldsymbol{x}_0, \boldsymbol{\lambda}_0)$ is also a stationary point of the unconstrained objective $L(\boldsymbol{x}, \boldsymbol{\lambda})$. In other words, we can use Eqs. (2.85) and (2.86) to find all stationary points of the original problem.

If we move back to our example at the beginning of this section, its Lagrangian is

$$L(\boldsymbol{x}, \lambda) = \boldsymbol{v}^T\boldsymbol{x} - \lambda(\boldsymbol{x}^T\boldsymbol{x} - 1). \tag{2.87}$$

Setting $\frac{\partial L}{\partial \boldsymbol{x}} = \boldsymbol{0}$ leads to $\boldsymbol{v} = 2\lambda\boldsymbol{x}$, and setting $\frac{\partial L}{\partial \lambda} = \boldsymbol{0}$ gives us the original constraint $\boldsymbol{x}^T\boldsymbol{x} = 1$.

Because $\boldsymbol{v} = 2\lambda\boldsymbol{x}$, we have $\|\boldsymbol{v}\|^2 = \boldsymbol{v}^T\boldsymbol{v} = 4\lambda^2\boldsymbol{x}^T\boldsymbol{x} = 4\lambda^2$. Hence, $|\lambda| = \frac{1}{2}\|\boldsymbol{v}\|$, and the stationary point is $\boldsymbol{x} = \frac{1}{2\lambda}\boldsymbol{v}$.

Since $\boldsymbol{v} = (1,2)^T$ in our example, we have $\lambda^2 = \frac{1}{4}\|\boldsymbol{v}\|^2 = \frac{5}{4}$, or $\lambda = \pm\frac{\sqrt{5}}{2}$. Thus, $f(\boldsymbol{x}) = \boldsymbol{v}^T\boldsymbol{x} = 2\lambda\boldsymbol{x}^T\boldsymbol{x} = 2\lambda$. Hence, $\min f(\boldsymbol{x}) = -\sqrt{5}$ and $\max f(\boldsymbol{x}) = \sqrt{5}$. The minimizer is $-\frac{1}{\sqrt{5}}(1,2)^T$, and the maximizer is $\frac{1}{\sqrt{5}}(1,2)^T$.

These solutions are easily verified. Applying the Cauchy–Schwarz inequality, we know $|f(\boldsymbol{x})| = |\boldsymbol{v}^T\boldsymbol{x}| \le \|\boldsymbol{v}\|\,\|\boldsymbol{x}\| = \sqrt{5}$. That is, $-\sqrt{5} \le f(\boldsymbol{x}) \le \sqrt{5}$, and the equality is obtained when $\boldsymbol{v} = c\boldsymbol{x}$ for some constant c. Because $\|\boldsymbol{v}\| = \sqrt{5}$ and $\|\boldsymbol{x}\| = 1$, we know $c = \sqrt{5}$ and get the maximum and minimum points as above.

The handling of inequality constraints is more complex than equality constraints, and involves duality, saddle points, and duality gaps. The method of Lagrange multipliers can be extended to handle these cases, but are beyond the scope of this book. Interested readers are referred to the *Convex Optimization* book for more details.

2.4 Complexity of Algorithms

In the next chapter, we will discuss how modern algorithms and systems require a lot of computing and storage resources, in terms of the number of instructions to be executed by the CPU (central processing unit) and GPU (graphics processing unit), or the amount of data that need to be stored in main memory or hard disk. Of course, we prefer algorithms whose resource consumption (i.e., running time or storage complexity) is low.

In the theoretical analysis of an algorithm's complexity, we are often interested in how fast the complexity grows when the input size gets larger. The unit of such complexity, however, is usually variable. For example, when the complexity analysis is based on a specific algorithm's pseudocode, and we are interested in how many arithmetic operations are involved when the input size is 100, the running time complexity might evaluate to 50 000 arithmetic operations. If instead we are interested in the number of CPU instructions that are executed, the same algorithm may have a complexity of 200 000 in terms of CPU instructions.

Big-O notation ($\mathcal{O}$) is often used to analyze the theoretical complexity of algorithms, which measures how the running time or storage requirement grows when the size of the input increases. Note that the input size may be measured by more than one number—e.g., by both the number of training examples n and the length of the feature vector d.

When the input size is a single number n and the complexity is $f(n)$, we say that this algorithm's complexity is $\mathcal{O}(g(n))$ if and only if there exist a positive constant M and an input size n_0, such that when $n \geq n_0$, we always have

$$f(n) \leq Mg(n). \tag{2.88}$$

We assume that both f and g are positive in the above equation. With a slight abuse of notation, we can write the complexity as

$$f(n) = \mathcal{O}(g(n)). \tag{2.89}$$

Informally speaking, Eq. (2.89) states that $f(n)$ grows at most as fast as $g(n)$ after the problem size n is large enough.

An interesting observation can be made from Eq. (2.88). If this equation holds, then we should have $f(n) \leq cMg(n)$ when $c > 1$ too. That is, when $c > 1$, $f(n) = \mathcal{O}(g(n))$ implies $f(n) = \mathcal{O}(cg(n))$. In other words, a positive constant scalar will not change the complexity result in big-O notation. A direct consequence of this observation is that we do not need to be very careful in deciding the unit for our complexity result.

However, in a specific application, different constant scalars might have very different impacts. Both $f_1(n) = 2n^2$ and $f_2(n) = 20n^2$ are $\mathcal{O}(n^2)$ in big-O notation, but their running speed may differ by a factor of 10, and this speed variation makes a big difference in real-world systems.

Big-O notation can be generalized to scenarios when there are more variables involved in determining the input size. For example, the first pattern recognition system we introduce (cf. Chapter 3) has a complexity $f(n,d) = \mathcal{O}(nd)$ when there are n training examples and each training example is d-dimensional. This notation means that there exist numbers n_0 and d_0, and a positive constant M, such that when $n \geq n_0$ and $d \geq d_0$, we always have

$$f(n,d) \leq Mnd. \tag{2.90}$$

The generalization to more than two variables is trivial.

2.5 Miscellaneous Notes and Additional Resources

For detailed treatment of linear algebra materials, Strang (2018) is a good resource. Similarly, DeGroot & Schervish (2011) is an accessible textbook for basic probability and statistics.

To find more details and proofs of matrix computations such as singular value decomposition, please refer to Golub & van Loan (1996), which also provides pseudocode for many matrix computation algorithms. If you are interested in implementing such algorithms, Press et al. (1992) is an excellent tool. For readers who speak Chinese, Zhang (2013) is a good reference manual.

Many good books exist for both optimization theory and methods. To learn about linear, nonlinear, and convex optimization theory, Bertsimas & Tsitsiklis (1997), Bertsekas (2016), and Bertsekas (2009) are good textbooks. To learn how to mathematically model problems as convex optimization ones and to learn convex optimization methods, please refer to Boyd & Vandenberghe (2004). An accessible optimization textbook, Lange (2013), is also worth reading.

More details about big-O notation and analysis of algorithms can be found in Cormen et al. (2009).

Exercises

2.1 Let $\boldsymbol{x} = (\sqrt{3}, 1)^T$ and $\boldsymbol{y} = (1, \sqrt{3})^T$ be two vectors, and $\boldsymbol{x}_\perp$ be the projection of $\boldsymbol{x}$ onto $\boldsymbol{y}$.

(a) What is the value of $\boldsymbol{x}_\perp$?

(b) Prove that $\boldsymbol{y} \perp (\boldsymbol{x} - \boldsymbol{x}_\perp)$.

(c) Draw a graph to illustrate the relationship between these vectors.

(d) Prove that for any $\lambda \in \mathbb{R}$, $\|\boldsymbol{x} - \boldsymbol{x}_\perp\| \le \|\boldsymbol{x} - \lambda \boldsymbol{y}\|$. (Hint: The geometry between these vectors suggests that $\|\boldsymbol{x} - \boldsymbol{x}_\perp\|^2 + \|\boldsymbol{x}_\perp - \lambda \boldsymbol{y}\|^2 = \|\boldsymbol{x} - \lambda \boldsymbol{y}\|^2$.)

2.2 Let X be a 5×5 real symmetric matrix, whose eigenvalues are 1, 1, 3, 4, and x.

(a) Define a necessary and sufficient condition on x such that X is a positive definite matrix.

(b) If $\det(X) = 72$, what is the value of x?

2.3 Let $\boldsymbol{x}$ be a d-dimensional random vector, and $\boldsymbol{x} \sim N(\boldsymbol{\mu}, \Sigma)$.

(a) Let $p(\boldsymbol{x})$ be the probability density function for $\boldsymbol{x}$. What is the equation that defines $p(\boldsymbol{x})$?

(b) Write down the equation that defines $\ln p(\boldsymbol{x})$.

(c) If you have access to *The Matrix Cookbook* (Petersen & Pedersen 2012), which equation will you use to help you derive $\frac{\partial \ln p(\boldsymbol{x})}{\partial \boldsymbol{\mu}}$? What is your result?

(d) Similarly, if we treat Σ^{-1} as a variable (rather than Σ), which equation (or equations) will you use to help you derive $\frac{\partial \ln p(\boldsymbol{x})}{\partial \Sigma^{-1}}$, and what is the result?

2.4 (Schwarz inequality) Let X and Y be two random variables (discrete or continuous) and let $\mathbb{E}[XY]$ exist. Prove that

$$(\mathbb{E}[XY])^2 \le \mathbb{E}[X^2]\mathbb{E}[Y^2].$$

2.5 Prove the following equality and inequalities:

(a) Starting from the definition of the covariance matrix for a random vector X, prove

$$\operatorname{Cov}(X) = \mathbb{E}[XX^T] - \mathbb{E}[X]\mathbb{E}[X]^T.$$

(b) Let X and Y be two random variables. Prove that for any constant $u \in \mathbb{R}$ and $v \in \mathbb{R}$,

$$\operatorname{Cov}(X, Y) = \operatorname{Cov}(X + u, Y + v).$$

(c) Let X and Y be two random variables (discrete or continuous). Prove that the correlation coefficient $\rho_{X,Y}$ satisfies

$$-1 \le \rho_{X,Y} \le 1.$$

2.6 Answer the following questions related to the exponential distribution:
(a) Calculate the expectation and variance of the exponential distribution with p.d.f.

$$p(x) = \begin{cases} \beta e^{-\beta x} & \text{for } x \geq 0, \\ 0 & \text{for } x < 0 \end{cases}$$

(in which $\beta > 0$).

(b) What is the c.d.f. of this distribution?

(c) (Memoryless property) Let X denote a continuous exponential random variable. Prove that for any $a > 0$ and $b > 0$,

$$\Pr(X \geq a + b | X \geq a) = \Pr(X \geq b).$$

(d) Assume X, the lifetime of a light bulb, follows the exponential distribution with $\beta = 10^{-3}$. What is its expected lifetime? If a particular light bulb has worked for 2000 hours, what is the expectation of its remaining lifetime?

2.7 Suppose X is a random variable following the exponential distribution, whose probability density function is $p(x) = 3e^{-3x}$ for $x \geq 0$ and $p(x) = 0$ for $x < 0$.

(a) What are the values of $\mathbb{E}[X]$ and $\operatorname{Var}(X)$? Just give the results, no derivation is needed.

(b) Can we apply Markov's inequality to this distribution? If the answer is yes, what is the estimate for $\Pr(X \geq 1)$?

(c) Can we apply Chebyshev's inequality? If the answer is yes, what is the estimate for $\Pr(X \geq 1)$?

(d) The one-sided (or one-tailed) Chebyshev inequality states that if $\mathbb{E}[X]$ and $\operatorname{Var}(X)$ both exist, for any positive number $a > 0$ we have $\Pr(X \geq \mathbb{E}[X] + a) \leq \frac{\operatorname{Var}(X)}{\operatorname{Var}(X)+a^2}$ and $\Pr(X \leq \mathbb{E}[X] - a) \leq \frac{\operatorname{Var}(X)}{\operatorname{Var}(X)+a^2}$. Apply this inequality to estimate $\Pr(X \geq 1)$.

(e) What is the exact value for $\Pr(X \geq 1)$?

(f) Compare the four values: the estimate based on Markov's inequality, the estimate based on Chebyshev's inequality, the estimate based on the one-sided Chebyshev inequality, and the true value: What conclusion do you make?

2.8 Let A be a $d \times d$ real symmetric matrix, whose eigenvalues are sorted and denoted by $\lambda_1 \geq \lambda_2 \geq \cdots \geq \lambda_d$. The eigenvector associated with λ_i is $\boldsymbol{\xi}_i$. All the eigenvectors form an orthogonal matrix E, whose ith column is $\boldsymbol{\xi}_i$. If we denote $\Lambda = \operatorname{diag}(\lambda_1, \lambda_2, \ldots, \lambda_d)$, we have $A = E\Lambda E^T$.

(a) For any nonzero vector $\boldsymbol{x} \neq \boldsymbol{0}$, the term

$$\frac{\boldsymbol{x}^T A \boldsymbol{x}}{\boldsymbol{x}^T \boldsymbol{x}}$$

is called the *Rayleigh quotient*, denoted by $R(\boldsymbol{x}, A)$. Prove that for any $c \neq 0$,

$$R(\boldsymbol{x}, A) = R(c\boldsymbol{x}, A).$$

(b) Show that

$$\max_{\boldsymbol{x} \neq \boldsymbol{0}} \frac{\boldsymbol{x}^T A \boldsymbol{x}}{\boldsymbol{x}^T \boldsymbol{x}} = \max_{\boldsymbol{x}^T \boldsymbol{x} = 1} \boldsymbol{x}^T A \boldsymbol{x}.$$

(c) Show that any unit norm vector $\boldsymbol{x}$ (i.e., $\|\boldsymbol{x}\| = 1$) can be expressed as a linear combination of the eigenvectors, as $\boldsymbol{x} = E\boldsymbol{w}$, or equivalently,

$$\boldsymbol{x} = \sum_{i=1}^{d} w_i \xi_i,$$

where $\boldsymbol{w} = (w_1, w_2, \ldots, w_d)^T$, with $\|\boldsymbol{w}\| = 1$.

(d) Prove that

$$\max_{\boldsymbol{x}^T\boldsymbol{x}=1} \boldsymbol{x}^T A \boldsymbol{x} = \lambda_1,$$

i.e., the maximum value of the Rayleigh quotient $R(\boldsymbol{x}, A)$ is λ_1, the largest eigenvalue of A. What is the optimal $\boldsymbol{x}$ that achieves this maximum? (Hint: Express $\boldsymbol{x}$ as a linear combination of ξ_i.)

(e) Prove that

$$\min_{\boldsymbol{x}^T\boldsymbol{x}=1} \boldsymbol{x}^T A \boldsymbol{x} = \lambda_d,$$

i.e., the minimum value of the Rayleigh quotient $R(\boldsymbol{x}, A)$ is λ_d, the smallest eigenvalue of A. What is the optimal $\boldsymbol{x}$ that achieves this minimum? (Hint: Express $\boldsymbol{x}$ as a linear combination of ξ_i.)

2.9 Answer the following questions on the Cauchy distribution:

(a) Show that the Cauchy distribution is a valid continuous distribution.

(b) Show that the expectation of the Cauchy distribution does not exist.

2.10 Answer the following questions related to convex and concave functions:

(a) Show that $f(x) = e^{ax}$ is a convex function for any $a \in \mathbb{R}$.

(b) Show that $g(x) = \ln(x)$ is a concave function on $\{x \mid x > 0\}$.

(c) Show that $h(x) = x\ln(x)$ is a convex function on $\{x \mid x \geq 0\}$ (we define $0 \ln 0 = 0$).

(d) Given a discrete distribution with its p.m.f. $(p_1, p_2, \ldots, p_n)$ ($p_i \geq 0$), its *entropy* is defined as

$$H = -\sum_{l=1}^{n} p_i \log_2 p_i,$$

in which we assume $0 \ln 0 = 0$. Use the method of Lagrange multipliers to find which values of p_i will maximize the entropy.

2.11 Let X and Y be two random variables.

(a) Prove that if X and Y are independent, then they are uncorrelated.

(b) Let X be uniformly distributed on $[-1, 1]$, and $Y = X^2$. Show that X and Y are uncorrelated but not independent.

(c) Let X and Y be two discrete random variables whose values can be either 1 or 2. The joint probability is $p_{ij} = \Pr(X = i, Y = j)$ ($i, j \in \{1, 2\}$). Prove that if X and Y are uncorrelated, then they are independent too.

3 Overview of a Pattern Recognition System

The purpose of this chapter is to introduce a few components that are common to most (if not all) pattern recognition or machine learning systems, including a few key concepts and building blocks. Some commonly encountered issues are also discussed.

We will use face recognition as an example to introduce these components, and use the nearest neighbor classifier as a simple solution to the face recognition problem.

3.1 Face Recognition

You are working in a small start-up IT company, which uses a face recognition device to record its employees' attendance. In the morning (or noon since it is an IT company), you come into the office and look into this face recognition gadget. It will automatically take a picture of you, and it (successfully) recognizes your face. A welcome message "Morning John" is emitted by it and your attendance recorded. The synthesized speech is dumb; you think, "I will ask the CTO to change it!"

For now let us forget about the dumb voice of the device, and forget about why a start-up IT company needs an attendance recording system. You have just passed that face-recognition-based attendance-recording gadget, and cannot help thinking about this question: How is face recognition accomplished by this small device?

Your records must be prestored in that device. You do not need to be Sherlock Holmes to deduce this. How is it possible to recognize your face and your name if that is not the case? In fact, on your first day in this company, it was the same device that took your face pictures, and a guy also keyed in your name such that the device can associate these pictures with you. You were told that everybody has five pictures stored in that little thing. If you remember that the word "records" is used at the beginning of this paragraph, by "records" we are talking about these photos and their *associated* names.

Then things become trivial, you think. You are the latest employee and your ID is 24 in this company. You calculated it: 120 ($24 \times 5 = 120$ pictures) is even much smaller than the number of images stored in your mobile phone. The device just needs to find out which one of the 120 stored pictures is similar to the one that was taken 10 seconds ago. *Of course* it is one of your five pictures that is the most similar, so then the gadget knows your name. "That is so simple, and I am so smart."

Your smart solution is in fact a *nearest neighbor classifier*, which is a classic method in machine learning and pattern recognition. However, in order to turn your idea (which, as you will see, has many vague components) into precise algorithms and a working system, we need to first obtain a precise mathematical description of the task and your idea.

Face recognition is a typical application of nearest neighbor classification. Given an image that contains a human face, the task of face recognition is to find the identity of the human in the image. We are faced with two types of images or pictures. One type is called the training examples (like those five pictures of you taken on your first day), which have labels (your name) associated with them. We call the collection of this type of example the training set. In this task, the training set is composed of many face images and the identities associated with them.

The second type of examples are called the test examples (like the picture taken just 10 seconds back). It is obvious that the face recognition task is to find the correct label (i.e., name) of those test set images.

The procedure that finds the label for a test example is the central part of machine learning and pattern recognition, which can be abstracted as a mapping (recall this important mathematical concept?) from an input (test) example to its label. A computer vision, machine learning, or pattern recognition method or system needs to find a good *mapping* for a particular task, which can be described by algorithms and then implemented by various programming languages on different hardware platforms.

3.2 A Simple Nearest Neighbor Classifier

In order to achieve this, we need to formalize every concept described above using precise mathematical notation. Only with this formalization can we turn vague ideas into programmable solutions.

3.2.1 Training or Learning

Formally speaking, in order to learn this mapping, we have access to n pairs of entities $\boldsymbol{x}_i$ and y_i. The pair $(\boldsymbol{x}_i, y_i)$ include the ith *training example* ($\boldsymbol{x}_i$, also called the ith training instance) and its associated *label* (y_i). The set of all training instances and their associated labels forms the *training set*. The first stage in our task is called the *training* or *learning* stage, in which we need to find how we can deduce the label y for *any* example $\boldsymbol{x}$.

The examples $\boldsymbol{x}_i$ comprise the *features*. We can directly use raw input as features (e.g., directly use the face images captured by a camera) or use feature extraction techniques to process the raw input and obtain more abstract features (e.g., coordinates of various facial keypoints). In our example, $n = 24 \times 5 = 120$, and each $\boldsymbol{x}_i$ is a picture stored in the gadget. We can use the employee ID to denote the human identity. Hence, $y_i \in \{1, 2, \ldots, 24\}$, which has a one-to-one correspondence with the employee's name.

We can write the mapping formally as $f : \mathbb{X} \mapsto \mathbb{Y}$. The set $\mathbb{X}$ is the space in which all training instances reside—i.e., $\boldsymbol{x}_i \in \mathbb{X}$ for $1 \leq i \leq n$. If there are any additional training examples, we also require that they belong to $\mathbb{X}$. Furthermore, we assume that any instance or example in our specific task, no matter whether they are associated with labels (e.g., training instances) or not (e.g., test examples, which we will introduce soon), should also be in the set $\mathbb{X}$. Hence, given any example $\boldsymbol{x}$ in $\mathbb{X}$, we can apply the mapping f to output our best *guess* of its associated label, as $f(\boldsymbol{x})$.

3.2.2 Testing or Predicting

There are two main scenarios in applying the mapping f. Suppose we are given another set of examples $\boldsymbol{x}_i$, $n+1 \leq i \leq n+m$. If we do not have the labels associated with these new examples, we can apply the mapping to obtain $\hat{y}_i$ $(n+1 \leq i \leq n+m)$, and $\hat{y}_i$ is the prediction produced by the mapping f (which in turn is the product of the learning stage). We are, however, unaware of the quality of these predictions: Are they accurate or not?

In the second scenario of applying the learned mapping f, we are given the labels y_i, $n+1 \leq i \leq n+m$, that is, we know the *groundtruth* values of the labels. Then we can also estimate how accurate our learned mapping is, by comparing y_i and $\hat{y}_i$ for $n+1 \leq i \leq n+m$.

For example, the *accuracy* is measured as the percentage of cases when $y_i = \hat{y}_i$. Of course, we want the accuracy to be as high as possible. The process of estimating the quality of the learning mapping is often called *testing*, and the set of examples used for testing, $(\boldsymbol{x}_i, y_i)$ $(n+1 \leq i \leq n+m)$ is called the *test set*. Testing is often the second stage in our task.

If the quality of our mapping f is not satisfactory (e.g., its accuracy is too low), we need to improve it (e.g., by designing or learning better features, or by learning a better mapping). When the mapping has exhibited acceptable quality in the testing, it is ready to be shipped to its users (i.e., to run under the first scenario in applying the mapping f in which we no longer have the groundtruth labels). The deployment of the learned mapping can be considered as the third stage of our task.

Deployment may raise new issues and requirements, which often will require more iterations of training and testing. Although deployment is often ignored in a course (e.g., in this chapter and this book) and research activities, it is very important in real-world systems.

We want to emphasize that the labels of test examples are *strictly not allowed* to be used in the first stage (i.e., the training or learning phase). In fact, the test examples (including both the instances $\boldsymbol{x}$ and their groundtruth labels y) can *only* be used for testing.

An ideal scenario is to separate the training and testing stages to two groups of people. The first group of people have access to the training data but they have absolutely no access to the test data. After the first group of people learn a mapping f (e.g., implemented as a piece of software), the second group of people will test the performance of f using the test data.

This ideal scenario may be impractical in research activities or small companies, in which the two groups of people may reduce to a single person. However, even in this adverse setup, test examples (both instances $\boldsymbol{x}$ and labels y) are not allowed to be utilized in the learning phase.

3.2.3 A Nearest Neighbor Classifier

Although tons of details are still missing, we are closer to an algorithmic description of a face recognition method. We have n training examples $(\boldsymbol{x}_i, y_i)$, in which $\boldsymbol{x}_i$ $(1 \le i \le n)$ refers to one particular picture stored in the gadget and $n = 120$; $1 \le y_i \le 24$ and $y_i \in \mathbb{Z}$ records the employee ID associated with $\boldsymbol{x}_i$. Note that $\mathbb{Z}$ is the set of integers.

Given any picture taken by the gadget, we just need to find an i such that $\boldsymbol{x}_i$ is the *most similar* one to it. The question is how we decide the similarity between two pictures. We need to turn these words into formal mathematical descriptions that are both precise and *executable*.

The first obstacle is, in fact, how we represent a picture in $\boldsymbol{x}_i$. You may decide to use the simplest image representation in your first trial: using the pixel intensity values. An image with height H and width W has $H \times W$ pixels, and each pixel contains three channels (RGB) of values. To make the representation simpler, you decide to work with *grayscale* images, which collapse the color (RGB) into one single number (the pixel grayscale, or intensity). Hence, an image is coded as a matrix with H rows and W columns.

The matrix is an essential mathematical concept, and you know a lot of tricks to handle matrices. However, as you have seen (or will read from this book soon), most learning algorithms deal with *vector* data rather than matrices.

Hence you decide to convert the matrices into vectors. This is pretty simple—just "stretch" the matrix into a vector—i.e., a matrix $X \in \mathbb{R}^H \times \mathbb{R}^W$ is converted into a vector $\boldsymbol{x} \in \mathbb{R}^{HW}$, with

$$x_{(i-1)\times W+j} = X_{i,j} \quad \forall\, 1 \le i \le H,\ 1 \le j \le W. \tag{3.1}$$

This simple image representation strategy applies to all images in this face recognition setup, no matter whether they are training or test images.

The second question is, naturally, how we find the example in the training set $\boldsymbol{x}_i$ $(1 \le i \le n)$ that is the most similar to a new image $\boldsymbol{x}$. Now that we have represented these images as vectors, we can easily compute the distance between any two vectors using the classical Euclidean distance.

Suppose $\boldsymbol{x} \in \mathbb{R}^d$ and $\boldsymbol{y} \in \mathbb{R}^d$ are two vectors with the same dimensionality; the Euclidean distance between them is

$$d(\boldsymbol{x}, \boldsymbol{y}) = \|\boldsymbol{x} - \boldsymbol{y}\|. \tag{3.2}$$

It is natural to use distance as a measure of the dissimilarity—i.e., two vectors are dissimilar if the distance between them is large. Hence, the most similar training example can be chosen as the example that has the smallest distance to the new test example.

So now we have collected all necessary notation and algorithmic details to turn your vague idea into an operational algorithm, which is listed as Algorithm 1.

Algorithm 1 A simple nearest neighbor algorithm for face recognition

1: **Input:** A training set $(\boldsymbol{x}_i, y_i)$, $1 \leq i \leq n$. The ith training image is converted to the vector $\boldsymbol{x}_i$.

2: **Input:** A test example $\boldsymbol{x}$, which is converted from a test image.

3: Find the index of the nearest neighbor in the training set, as

$$\text{nn} = \underset{1 \leq i \leq n}{\arg\min} \|\boldsymbol{x} - \boldsymbol{x}_i\|. \tag{3.3}$$

4: **Output:** Return the predicted identity as

$$y_{\text{nn}}. \tag{3.4}$$

Is that fantastic? Your idea now is an executable algorithm, which is possibly the shortest nontrivial algorithm in machine learning and pattern recognition—its main body has only one line (Eq. 3.3), and the equation in that line also looks succinct and beautiful!

It is easy to understand Algorithm 1. Given any test image $\boldsymbol{x}$, you first compute the distance between it and every training example. The arg min operator finds which index corresponds to the smallest distance. For example, if $\boldsymbol{x}_{24}$ has the smallest distance to $\boldsymbol{x}$, Eq. (3.3) will assign 24 to nn. Then the algorithm terminates by returning the label (human identity) associated with $\boldsymbol{x}_{24}$, i.e., $y_{24} = y_{\text{nn}}$.

As simple as Algorithm 1 is, we have a working face recognition algorithm. Its core is Eq. (3.3), which finds the nearest neighbor of an example $\boldsymbol{x}$ in a set of training examples. We call this simple algorithm the nearest neighbor algorithm, abbreviated as the NN algorithm, or the nearest neighbor classification method. The operation in Eq. (3.3) is also called nearest neighbor search.

It is also obvious that the NN method can be used in many other tasks so long as the vectors $\boldsymbol{x}_i$ represent instances other than face images. In other words, although extremely simple, the nearest neighbor classifier is a neat and general learning method.

3.2.4 *k*-Nearest Neighbors

One variant of the NN algorithm is k-nearest neighbors (or k-NN). In k-NN, k is an integer value—e.g., $k = 5$. In the nearest neighbor search, k-NN returns the k nearest neighbors instead of the single nearest one.

The label that appears most frequently in the returned k examples is the prediction of the k-NN algorithm. For example, if $k = 5$ and the five nearest neighbors of your picture have labels 7, 24, 3, 24, 24, then the k-NN prediction is 24 (which is correct).

Although the label of the nearest example is 7, there are three examples out of the five nearest neighbors with the correct label (24).

The nearest neighbor algorithm is also called the 1-NN algorithm. When $k > 1$, k-NN may lead to higher accuracy than 1-NN because it can remove the effect of an incorrect nearest neighbor. For instance, in the above example, 1-NN will return 7, but 5-NN predicts the correct result.

3.3 The Ugly Details

Unfortunately, making a system that works well is never going to be neat. Many difficulties or caveats can be envisioned prior to the actual system building, but many more may appear at any point in a pattern recognition project. In the following we list a few typical difficulties, once again using nearest-neighbor-based face recognition as an example to illustrate them.

Some of these difficulties may be regarded as unimportant details at first sight. However, these details easily become ugly or even devastating if they are not taken good care of from the very beginning. The degradation in accuracy caused by any of these improperly handled details can be much larger than the performance drop caused by a bad learning algorithm (in comparison to a good one).

- **Noisy sensing data.** The raw data in both the training and test sets are mostly obtained from various sensors. Sensors, however, are subject to the effects of various internal and external noise.

  For example, a drop of water on the camera lens may cause out-of-focus or blurred face images; a defective camera lens or CCD component may cause pepper noise or other weird types of artifacts in the face images captured by this camera.

  There could also be occlusion in the face images. For example, people may wear sunglasses or scarfs. And, as we have discussed, the resolution of that camera may be too low for this specific application.
- **Noisy or wrong labels.** Likewise, the labels associated with training examples can also be noisy. The noise can be attributed to many factors—e.g., a typo can occur when the labels are keyed into the gadget.

  In tasks where the labels are difficult to obtain, the groundtruth labels (i.e., the labels that are considered correct) provided in a dataset might contain errors.

  For example, a doctor is often asked to determine whether a computed tomography (CT) image indicates a specific type of disease, but even experienced doctors (i.e., experts) can make wrong judgments.
- **Uncontrolled environment.** We are implicitly assuming some restrictions on the environment. For example, in the face recognition gadget we assume that any picture taken by the gadget will have one (and only one) face in it. We probably also require that the face will be at the center of the image, and its size will be proper. A missing face, or a face that is too large or too small, or two faces in the same picture will inevitably cause trouble for our simple algorithm.

Furthermore, we probably also must assume that anybody going through the gadget is an employee of your company (and his or her picture has already been stored in the gadget). We also have to assume that the employees are all prosaic enough that they will not put on an entire Spider-Man costume to test the limits of the poor gadget!

The list of potential assumptions can go on indefinitely. In short, we need many (either explicit or implicit) assumptions to make a system work.

- **Improper preprocessing.** Suppose the face images stored in the gadget are in 100×100 resolution, which means $\boldsymbol{x}_i \in \mathbb{R}^{10\,000}$ for $1 \le i \le n$. However, if the gadget takes your photo at resolution 200×200, Algorithm 1 is presented with an input $\boldsymbol{x} \in \mathbb{R}^{40\,000}$.

  This will render our algorithm invalid because Eq. (3.3) is not well defined if $\boldsymbol{x}$ has a different dimensionality from any $\boldsymbol{x}_i$. This issue can be easily solved though. We can resize the test image $\boldsymbol{x}$ to 100×100 using image processing routines, which can be regarded as a preprocessing of your data.

  In addition to the learning algorithms, many components in a complete system enforce various assumptions on your raw input data. Hence, the preprocessing step should understand and fulfill the requirements of all other modules in the system.
- **The existence of a semantic gap.** The numeric description and comparison of images are often far away from their meanings. For example, neither the pixel intensity values nor the Euclidean distance in Eq. (3.3) knows the existence of faces.

  The intensity values are integers between 0 and 255, and every pair of values is treated as independent of every other by the Euclidean distance measure. It is very possible that two images of the same person may have a Euclidean distance that is larger than that between images of two different persons.

  This phenomenon is called the *semantic gap*, referring to the vast difference between human and computer understanding and descriptions of the same input data. The semantic gap occurs not only in recognizing and understanding images. It is also a serious issue in methods and systems that deal with acoustic and many other raw input data.
- **Improper or failed feature extraction.** Feature extraction is the major step responsible for extracting features that (hopefully) describe the semantic information in the raw input data (e.g., "there is a cat lying on a white couch"). Features extracted in classic methods and systems, however, are some statistics of the raw input data (often simple statistics such as histograms), which are at best implicitly related to the useful semantic information.

  Domain experts may describe some semantic properties that are useful for certain tasks, and the feature extraction module will design features that may explicitly or implicitly describe such properties. An expert may list statistics that are useful for face recognition: the shape of the eyes, the shape of the face contour, the distance between the eyes, etc. The extraction of these properties requires the face contour and the eyes to be detected and precisely located in a face image. The detection of these facial features, however, may be a task that is more difficult than face recognition itself.

In short, proper feature extraction is a difficult problem. Furthermore, imperfect raw input can make the problem even more difficult. The input may be noisy or have missing values (e.g., a large area of the face is occluded by a scarf.)

- **Mismatch between your data and the algorithm.** We often apply restrictions to change the environment from uncontrolled wilderness to a more civilized one. These restrictions allow us to make some assumptions about the input data of our learning algorithms. As will soon be discussed, assumptions on the input data are essential to the success of learning algorithms and recognition systems.

  The *no free lunch* theorem for machine learning states that if no assumption is made about the data, any two machine learning algorithms (under rather weak requirements) will have exactly the same accuracy when averaged over all possible datasets. Hence, tasks with different data assumptions must be equipped with different learning algorithms that match these assumptions.

  The nearest neighbor method may be suitable for face recognition but inappropriate for searching time-series data (e.g., the stock price change pattern in a day). This is why so many machine learning algorithms have been proposed to date, because the characteristics of data appearing in different tasks vary a lot. A mismatch between the data and the learning algorithm may cause serious performance degradation.
- **Thirst for resources.** The above algorithm might work extremely well in your company (which has only 24 employees). But what will happen if it is migrated to a large company without modification?

  Let us suppose the face image resolution is 100×100 and there are 10 000 employees now (hence $d = 100 \times 100 = 10\,000$ and $n = 50\,000$ if every employee has five images stored in the gadget.) The gadget needs to store n d-dimensional vectors, which means that 500 megabytes are required to store the face images. And the gadget is forced to search the entire 500 megabytes to find a match of any test image—which means roughly 20 seconds for attendance recording for any single individual!

  Algorithms and systems become greedy, requesting huge amounts of CPU, storage, and time resources, when the quantity of data they handle becomes big. These requests are highly impractical in real-world systems. Energy is another type of resource that is essential for modern systems. A high energy consumption gadget is likely to be unwelcome in the market.
- **Improper objectives.** Many objectives should be set forth for a recognition system, including at least accuracy, running speed, and other resource requirements. If we are talking about objectives for a commercial system, many more can be added—e.g., system price, complexity of system deployment, and maintenance.

  Should we expect a system that is 100% correct, requires almost zero CPU/storage/power resources, is extremely inexpensive, and requires almost no effort in its maintenance? This type of system will be the star product on the market—so long as it exists! These requirements are contradictory to each other, and we must be careful to reach a satisfactory trade-off among all these factors.

For example, you may request three years and a one million dollar budget to develop a “perfect” face-recognition-based attendance gadget that is fast and highly accurate (e.g., with 99.99% accuracy). But your CEO approves only three months and 100K dollars. You have to compromise the gadget’s accuracy and speed.

Even with enough budget, manpower, and time, you may not reach the 99.99% accuracy objective either. We will show that a learning task has a theoretical upper bound on how accurate it can be (see Chapter 4). If that upper bound is 97% for your data, you will never reach the 99.99% accuracy target. Other factors (for example, running speed) may also force you to accept a lower recognition accuracy.

- **Improper post-processing or decision.** Making a prediction is probably the last step in many machine learning algorithms, but almost never the last step in a real-world system. We often need to make a decision or choice based on this prediction, and then react to the environment according to the decision.

  For example, what is a good reaction if the gadget determines that you are recording attendance twice within five minutes? It might be overreacting if it sounds an alarm and instructs the security guards to nab you, but it is also bad if it pretends that nothing unusual is happening.

  A more concrete example is in autonomous driving. What is the proper action to take if the autonomous driving system finds a car too close to you? Emergency braking, or a sudden lane change, or swerving to the road shoulder? An appropriate reaction may avoid a fatal accident, but a bad one may claim several lives.
- **Improper evaluation.** How do we decide whether an algorithm or system is good or bad? And how do we know that our decision is correct? Accuracy, the simple metric, is not always valid.

  For example, in an imbalanced binary classification problem in which one category has 9900 training examples but the other has only 100, accuracy is a wrong evaluation metric. A classifier can simply predict any example as belonging to class 1 (the class with 9900 training examples). Although its accuracy is pretty high (99%), this prediction rule may lead to great loss.

  Suppose the task is to approve or reject credit card applications, and the two classes correspond to safe and risky applicants, respectively. The simple classifier has 99% accuracy but will approve a credit card to any applicant that sends in an application form!

3.4 Making Assumptions and Simplifications

As shown by the above discussions, the performance of a learning or recognition system is determined by many factors. The quality of the raw input data is, however, arguably the most important single factor, and is beyond the control of the learning algorithm.

3.4.1 Engineering the Environment vs. Designing Sophisticated Algorithms

Hence, an essential step in building a recognition system is to engineer your environment (and subsequently the raw input data to your system). For example, it might be quite difficult to prevent fraudulent attendance recording if someone uses a three-dimensional printed face mask to cheat the system. A diligent security guard, however, can easily detect such unusual activities and stop someone wearing a mask from accessing the building so that they cannot even reach the gadget.

Let us compare two face-recognition-based attendance-recording gadgets. One gadget may allow a user to record attendance at any position around the gadget and use sophisticated face detection and face alignment techniques to correctly find and match the face. Because different locations may have varying illumination conditions, some preprocessing will have to compensate for this variation in different face images. This gadget (gadget A) might be advertised as high-tech, but will require many subsystems (detection, alignment, illumination handling, etc.) and use many computing resources.

As a comparison, another gadget (gadget B) might require a sign on the ground at a fixed location in front of it and require all users to stand on the sign and look toward the gadget. Furthermore, because the user's location is fixed, gadget B can ensure that the illumination conditions under which the face image is taken are consistent. Hence, gadget B may omit the detection and alignment modules and run much faster. Most probably, gadget B will have higher face recognition accuracy than gadget A because its raw input data are captured in a well-controlled situation.

In short, if it is at all possible, we want to engineer our data collection environment to ensure high-quality and easy-to-process raw input data. With appropriate constraints on the environment, we can assume that certain properties hold for the input data that our learning algorithm will process, which will greatly simplify the learning process and attain higher performance (e.g., both higher speed and higher accuracy).

Of course, some environments cannot be easily engineered. For example, for a robot that carries boxes around a storage house, it is reasonable and advantageous to assume that the ground is flat. This assumption can be easily implemented, but will greatly simplify the robot's locomotion components—two or four simple rolling wheels are sufficient. But the same assumption seriously breaks down for a battlefield robot, which unfortunately must move on any terrain that is in front of it. In that case, we have no choice and have to develop more complex theory and to design corresponding (hardware and software) systems and algorithms.

Autonomously moving a robot in difficult terrain is still an open problem, although some significant progress has been achieved—e.g., the BigDog robot. More information about the BigDog robot can be found at `https://en.wikipedia.org/wiki/BigDog`. And, to be precise, autonomously moving a robot is not a machine learning or pattern recognition task, although many machine learning and pattern recognition modules may be required in order to solve this task. We simply use this example to illustrate the difference between preparing the environment and not.

3.4.2 Assumptions and Simplifications

In fact, quite some assumptions have been made in our (somewhat informal) description of the training and testing stages, which will be recalled throughout this book. Similarly, quite some simplifications have also been made accordingly. In this section, we will discuss some commonly used assumptions and simplifications. We will also briefly mention some approaches to handling the difficulties listed above.

Note that this section provides a summary of the rest of the chapters in a different context from that in Chapter 1. In this section, instead of focusing on the contents of each chapter, we instead try to explain the logic behind why each chapter is presented and why the topic in it is important.

- If not otherwise specified, we assume the input data (or features extracted from them) are free of noise or other types of errors. This assumption, as you will soon see in later chapters, makes the design and analysis of algorithms and systems easier.

  Noise and errors are, however, always present in real-world data. Various methods have been developed to handle them, but they are beyond the scope of this introductory book.
- We also assume that the labels (for both training and test examples) are noise- and error-free.
- We assume that the groundtruth and predicted labels in a specific task (or equivalently, in the mapping f) belong to the same set $\mathbb{Y}$. Many practical applications are compatible with this assumption, which is also assumed throughout this book.

  For example, if only male and female appear as labels in a gender classification task's training set, we do not need to worry about a third type of gender emerging as the groundtruth label for a test example. However, the taxonomy of gender can be more complex than this simple dichotomy.

  One gender taxonomy uses the X and Y chromosomes, where most people are either XX (biological female) or XY (biological male). Other chromosome combinations such as XXY (Klinefelter syndrome) also exist. Hence, a gender classification system may not follow this assumption.

  Because XXY does not appear in the gender classification training set, we call it a *novel class* when an example from it appears in the test set. Novel class detection and handling is an advanced topic that will not be discussed in this book.
- We assume that for an example $\boldsymbol{x}$ and its corresponding label y, it is certain that there is a relationship that makes $\boldsymbol{x}$ and y correlated. If $\boldsymbol{x}$ and y are not related (or even are independent), no learning algorithm or recognition system can learn a meaningful mapping f that maps $\boldsymbol{x}$ to y.

  For example, if $\boldsymbol{x}$ is a digitized version of Claude Monet's famous painting *Impression, Sunrise* and y is tomorrow's NYSE (New York Stock Exchange) closing index value, we cannot build the mapping between them because these two variables are independent of each other.
- In the statistical machine learning formulation, we view $\boldsymbol{x}$ as a random vector and y as a random variable, and require that $\boldsymbol{x}$ and y are not independent. Let $p(\boldsymbol{x}, y)$

be the joint density for $\boldsymbol{x}$ and y. The most commonly used assumption is the i.i.d. (independent and identically distributed) assumption.

The i.i.d. assumption states that any example $(\boldsymbol{x}, y)$ is sampled from the same underlying distribution $p(\boldsymbol{x}, y)$ (i.e., *identically distributed*) and any two examples are *independently* sampled from the density (i.e., the generation of any two examples will not interfere with each other).

Note that this assumption states only the existence of the joint density, but does not tell us how to model or compute the joint density $p(\boldsymbol{x}, y)$. The i.i.d. assumption is assumed throughout this book, if not otherwise specified.

Many things can be derived from the i.i.d. assumption. We list a few related discussions below.

- To be more specific, the i.i.d. assumption assumes that the training and test data are sampled from exactly the same underlying distribution $p(\boldsymbol{x}, y)$. Hence, after we use a training set to learn a mapping f, this mapping can be safely applied to examples in the test set to obtain predictions.
- Another implication of the i.i.d. assumption is that the underlying distribution $p(\boldsymbol{x}, y)$ does not change. In some dynamic environments, the characteristics of the label y (and sometimes the raw input data $\boldsymbol{x}$ as well) may change.

  This phenomenon is termed *concept drift* (that is, the distribution $p(\boldsymbol{x}, y)$ is not stationary). Handling concept drifting is an important problem but will not be discussed in this book.
- To abide by the i.i.d. assumption requires the environment to be under control (at least under control in certain important aspects), which is not always possible.

  For example, a guest visiting your company may decide to try the gadget. Since his or her face images have not been stored in the gadget, this test example violates the i.i.d. assumption and is an *outlier* in the face recognition task.

  The detection and processing of outliers are also important issues in learning systems, although we will not elaborate on it.

• We will introduce three types of preprocessing techniques in this book.

  Principal component analysis (PCA) is good at reducing the effect of white noise (a special type of noise in the input data). It can also be viewed as a simple linear feature extraction method. Since PCA reduces the number of dimensions in the data, it is useful for reducing the CPU usage and memory footprint too. We have Chapter 5 specifically devoted to PCA.
  - Another simple but useful preprocessing technique is the normalization of features, which helps when the different dimensions in an example's feature vector have different scales. It is also useful when feature vectors of different examples have scale variations. Half of Chapter 9 discusses this topic.
  - The third type of preprocessing technique we introduce in this book is Fisher's linear discriminant (FLD), which is often used as a feature extraction method. We devote Chapter 6 to FLD.

- After the input data and labels have been fixed, the feature extraction module might be the most important for achieving highly accurate recognition results. Good features should be able to capture useful semantic information from the raw input data. However, extracting semantically meaningful features is very difficult due to the semantic gap.

  A classic approach is to interpret domain experts' knowledge and turn it into a feature extraction method. But this interpretation process is never easy. And a new feature extraction method is required whenever there is a novel task domain. The extracted features are then subject to the processing of other learning algorithms.

  A recent breakthrough in machine learning is the rise of deep learning methods. Deep learning is sometimes termed representation learning, because feature (or representation) learning is the core of deep learning.

  Deep learning is an advanced topic, and we have a chapter on deep learning at the end of this book (Chapter 15). In contrast to the separate feature extraction module preceding a machine learning module, deep learning methods are often *end-to-end*—i.e., the input of a deep learning method is the raw input data, while the output of it is the learning target. The feature extraction and learning modules are combined into one.
- The data we need to handle are complex and appear in different formats. Two types of formats are widely used: real numbers and categorical data.

  A real number is a value that represents a quantity along the real line—e.g., 3.14159 (an approximation of π). We can compare any two real numbers (e.g., $\pi > 3.14159$) and compute the distance between them (e.g., $|\pi - 3.14159| = 0.00000\,26535\,89793\,23846\ldots$).

  Categorical data refers to different categories, whose magnitudes cannot be compared. For example, we can use 1 and 2 to refer to two categories "apple" and "banana," respectively. However, we cannot say "apple (1)" is smaller than "banana (2)."

  When we encounter different types of data, we are dealing with different machine learning or pattern recognition tasks.

  - We assume the labels for both training and test examples $y \in \mathbb{Y}$. The task of learning the mapping f is called a regression task if $\mathbb{Y}$ is the set of real numbers $\mathbb{R}$ (or a subset of it); the task is called classification if $\mathbb{Y}$ is a set of categorical values. Face recognition is a classification task, in which $\mathbb{Y}$ is the set $\{1, 2, \ldots, 24\}$ in our attendance recording example.
  - Classification is a major task in learning and recognition research. Many algorithms have been proposed on this topic. We will introduce the support vector machine (SVM) and probabilistic classifiers (Chapters 7 and 8, respectively). These methods have their respective assumptions and are suitable for different tasks.

    The expectation maximization (EM) algorithm is a very important tool for probabilistic methods. The EM algorithm might seem slightly advanced for this introductory book, and we introduce it as an advanced topic in Chapter 14 in the final part of the book.

- The nearest neighbor algorithm uses the Euclidean distance to compute the distance between two faces. Because the Euclidean distance cannot handle categorical data, we need different tools when the input features are categorical. We will briefly introduce the decision tree classifier for this purpose. Decision trees are introduced in Chapter 10, sharing that chapter with a minimal introduction to information theory.
- Information theory formally studies how *information* can be quantized, stored, and transferred. Although these tasks are not the focus of this book, the mathematical tools developed in information theory have proved themselves very useful in describing various quantities in machine learning and pattern recognition. By viewing our real-valued and categorical data as (respectively) continuous and discrete random variables, we can use these tools to compare our data (e.g., to compute the distance between two sets of categorical feature values).
- Although we will not explicitly study the regression task in this book, many tasks we study have their output label y on the real line. Hence, they are in fact regression tasks. One example is the similarity computation task.

  When we compare two examples, we may prefer a numerical value (e.g., the similarity is 65% or 0.65) over binary answers (e.g., 0 for dissimilar and 1 for similar).

  Distance metric learning can learn a suitable similarity (or dissimilarity) metric specifically for a particular task. We introduce a few generalizations of the Euclidean distance, distance metric learning, and some feature normalization techniques in Chapter 9.
- We assume that the label y is always a real-valued or categorical variable in this book. However, we want to point out that more complex output formats are common in practical applications. The label y can be a vector (e.g., in multilabel classification or vector regression), a matrix of values (e.g., in semantic segmentation of images), a tree (e.g., in natural language analysis), etc.
- We assume that the label y is given for every training example. This is a *supervised* learning setting. *Unsupervised* learning is also widely studied, in which the labels are not available even for the training examples.

  Suppose you are given 120 images stored in the gadget (24 people, five images each) without their associated identity information (i.e., the labels are not present). It is possible to group these images into 24 groups, where the images belonging to the same employee in your company form one group. This process is called *clustering*, which is a typical unsupervised learning task. There are also other types of unsupervised learning tasks, but we will not cover unsupervised learning in this book.[1]

[1] However, one exercise problem in this chapter introduces K-means, a widely studied clustering problem.

  - We will also discuss three types of special data formats. In the nearest neighbor search algorithm, we assume the same number of dimensions for all examples $\boldsymbol{x}_i$, and the same dimension in all examples is associated with the same semantic meaning. However, some tasks have misaligned data.

    For example, one input data item might be a short video clip showing a golf swing action. Two people may use different speeds to carry out the swing. Hence, their corresponding videos will have different lengths, which means that there is no direct correspondence in the semantics in equivalent frames from the two different videos, and a simple distance metric (such as the Euclidean distance) is not applicable.

    In some other tasks, the data are inherently *sparse*, meaning many of their dimensions are zero. We will discuss misaligned data and sparse data in Chapter 11.
  - The third type of special data is time series data. In speech recognition, a person reads a sentence, and the signal is recorded as a time series of sensor inputs. The temporal relationship among these sensory recordings is vital for the speech recognition task and requires algorithms that explicitly model these temporal signals. The hidden Markov model (HMM) is such a tool, and we introduce its basic concepts and algorithms in Chapter 12.

- We will introduce the convolutional neural network (CNN), a representative example for deep learning, as an advanced topic in Chapter 15. CNN is particularly useful in analyzing images, which are the major sensory input for many recognition tasks.

  Compared to other methods we introduce in this book, CNN (and other deep learning methods) have many virtues: end-to-end (hence no need for manual feature extraction), handles big data, and very accurate.
- However, CNN also has its limitations. It requires a lot of training data (much more compared to other methods) and a lot of computing resources (CPU and/or GPU instructions, graphical and main memory and disk storage, and energy consumption). In a real system development, one should carefully consider all these factors and make compromises, including at least interactions between the pattern recognition module and other system modules and the relationship between overall system objectives and the pattern recognition module's objective.

  For example, approximate nearest neighbor (ANN) search is a good choice for the gadget if the company grows large and an exact NN search becomes too slow. ANN tries to greatly reduce the running time of NN search by tolerating small errors in the search results (hence the name "approximate").

  Hence, in an easy task (such as recognizing only 24 faces), CNN may not be the best choice. However, in the development and research efforts related to CNN, there has also been great progress on reducing the resource consumption of CNN models.
- The final aspect we want to discuss is how to evaluate a learning or recognition system. Is it accurate? How accurate can it be? Is method A better than method B? We will discuss these issues in the next chapter (Chapter 4).

3.5 A Framework

Till now, we have used the nearest neighbor search algorithm (and the face recognition method for the attendance-recording task) as an example to introduce some basic concepts and issues, some possible solutions, and some advanced topics. Before we finish this chapter, we want to revisit how the nearest neighbor algorithm was arrived at in this chapter.

To reach Algorithm 1, we went through the following steps (but some of these steps do not explicitly appear in Algorithm 1 because they are too simple).

- **Know your problem**. Try to understand the input, desired output, and potential difficulties in the task.
- **Make assumptions** and **formalize your problem**. Decide on some restrictions on your task's environment and convert them to assumptions on your input data. Try to use mathematical language to describe your problem and assumptions precisely.
- **Come up with a good idea**. How will you solve a particular task (or a module inside it)? You may have some intuition or ideas, either from studying the properties of your data or from observing how human experts solve these tasks.
- **Formalize the idea**. Turn this idea (or these ideas) into precise mathematical language. Often they end up as one or a few mathematical optimization problems. Try to make your equations (mathematical descriptions of the idea) as succinct as possible (cf. Eq. 3.3).

  In some cases you may find it difficult to write down your idea(s) mathematically, let alone to be succinct. In this case, you should probably go back and scrutinize that idea—maybe the idea is not good enough yet.
- **Start from the simple case**. You may find the mathematical optimization problem very difficult. It is indeed extremely difficult in some problems. In the other problems, however, you can try to simplify your setup (e.g., by making more restrictions and assumptions) *so long as these simplifications do not change the most important characteristic of your problem*. You will possibly find that the problem becomes much easier to solve. And you can solve the original problem by relaxing these simplifications later.
- **Solve it**.

The above overly simplified way of thinking has turned out to be useful in understanding (and inventing) many learning and recognition algorithms. We encourage you to *apply these steps to understand the algorithms in this book*. For example, PCA and SVM are two perfect examples to showcase the utility of these steps.

3.6 Miscellaneous Notes and Additional Resources

The face recognition example involves some basic digital image processing concepts, such as an image histogram or turning color images into grayscale ones. They can be found in the manual of every image processing software or digital image processing textbook such as Gonzalez & Woods (2017).

Face recognition in the real world is much more complex than Algorithm 1. A good summary of face recognition datasets and algorithms can be found in Zhao et al. (2003). However, in recent years, face recognition has often been solved using convolutional neural networks, e.g., in Schroff et al. (2015).

Details of the no free lunch theorem can be found in Wolpert (1996).

We provide a pointer to one implementation of approximate nearest neighbor in Exercise 3.1, whose technical details can be found in the paper Muja & Lowe (2014).

We also briefly mentioned some advanced research problems in this chapter, such as noise, concept drift, and outliers. Research papers aiming at solving these problems often appear in conference and journal papers in related subjects. At the end of this section, we list a few important conferences and journals, which are the best sources for learning state-of-the-art methods.

An incomplete list of related academic conferences includes

- International Conference on Machine Learning (ICML),
  `https://icml.cc/`
- Annual Conference on Neural Information Processing Systems (NIPS/NeurIPS),
  `https://nips.cc/`
- International Conference on Computer Vision (ICCV),
  `http://pamitc.org/`
- IEEE/CVF Conference on Computer Vision and Pattern Recognition (CVPR),
  `http://pamitc.org/`
- European Conference on Computer Vision (ECCV)
- International Joint Conference on Artificial Intelligence (IJCAI),
  `www.ijcai.org/`
- AAAI Conference on Artificial Intelligence (AAAI),
  `www.aaai.org/Conferences/`
- International Conference on Pattern Recognition (ICPR)
- International Conference on Learning Representations (ICLR),
  `https://iclr.cc/`

An incomplete list of related academic journals includes

- Journal of Machine Learning Research,
  `http://jmlr.org/`
- Machine Learning,
  `https://link.springer.com/journal/10994`
- IEEE Transactions on Pattern Analysis and Machine Intelligence,
  `http://computer.org/tpami`
- International Journal on Computer Vision,
  `https://link.springer.com/journal/11263`
- IEEE Transactions on Image Processing,
  `http://ieeexplore.ieee.org/servlet/opac?punumber=83`

- Artificial Intelligence,
  `www.journals.elsevier.com/artificial-intelligence/`
- Pattern Recognition,
  `www.journals.elsevier.com/pattern-recognition/`
- Neural Computation,
  `www.mitpressjournals.org/loi/neco`
- IEEE Transactions on Neural Networks and Learning Systems,
  `http://ieeexplore.ieee.org/servlet/opac?punumber=5962385`

Exercises

3.1 In this problem, we will have a taste of approximate nearest neighbor search. We use the ANN functions provided in the VLFeat software packages (`www.vlfeat.org/`). In order to understand how these functions work, please refer to Muja & Lowe (2014).

(a) Read the installation instructions and install the VLFeat software on your computer. Make sure your installation satisfies the following requirements: installed under the Linux environment; the MATLAB interface is installed;[2] the installation is compiled from the source code (rather than using the precompiled executables); and finally, before you start the installation, change the makefile to remove support for OpenMP.

(b) In MATLAB (or GNU Octave), use `x=rand(5000,10)` to generate your data: 5000 examples, each has 10 dimensions. Write a MATLAB (or GNU Octave) program to find the nearest neighbor of every example. You need to compute the distances between one example and *the rest* of the examples, and find the smallest distance. Record the time used to find all nearest neighbors. For every example, record the index of its nearest neighbor and the distance between them. Calculate the distances from scratch (i.e., do not use functions such as `pdist`), and avoid using multiple CPU cores in your computation.

(c) Use VLFeat functions to carry out the same task. Carefully read and understand the documents for `vl_kdtreebuild` and `vl_kdtreequery` in VLFeat. Set `NumTrees` to 1 and `MaxNumComparisons` to 6000, and then compare the running time of your program and the VLFeat functions. You need to exclude the running time of `vl_kdtreebuild` in the comparison.

(d) These two VLFeat functions provide an ANN method, which seeks approximate nearest neighbors. How can you reveal the error rate of these approximate nearest neighbors? What is the error rate in your experiment?

(e) When you choose different parameters in the VLFeat ANN functions, how do the error rate and running speed change?

(f) When the dataset size changes (e.g., from 5000 to 500 or 50 000), how do the error rate and running speed change?

[2] If you do not have access to the MATLAB software, you can use the GNU Octave interface as an alternative.

(g) From the VLFeat documentation, find the paper based on which these two functions are implemented. Carefully read the paper and understand the rationale behind these functions.

3.2 (K-means clustering) Clustering is a typical example of *unsupervised learning*, and K-means clustering is probably the most widely studied problem among the clustering tasks.

Given a set of samples $\{\boldsymbol{x}_1, \boldsymbol{x}_2, \ldots, \boldsymbol{x}_M\}$ in which $\boldsymbol{x}_j \in \mathbb{R}^d$ $(1 \le j \le M)$, the K-means clustering problem tries to group these M samples into K groups, where the samples inside each group are similar to each other (i.e., the distances between same-group pairs are small).

Let γ_{ij} $(1 \le i \le K, 1 \le j \le M)$ be the group indicator, that is, $\gamma_{ij} = 1$ if $\boldsymbol{x}_j$ is assigned to the ith group; otherwise $\gamma_{ij} = 0$. Note that

$$\sum_{i=1}^{K} \gamma_{ij} = 1$$

for any $1 \le j \le M$. Let $\boldsymbol{\mu}_i \in \mathbb{R}^d$ $(1 \le i \le K)$ be a representative of the ith group.

(a) Show that the following optimization formalizes the K-means goal:

$$\underset{\gamma_{ij}, \boldsymbol{\mu}_i}{\arg\min} \sum_{i=1}^{K} \sum_{j=1}^{M} \gamma_{ij} \|\boldsymbol{x}_j - \boldsymbol{\mu}_i\|^2. \tag{3.5}$$

(b) Finding assignments of γ_{ij} and $\boldsymbol{\mu}_i$ that are the global solution for Eq. (3.5) is NP hard. In practice, K-means solutions are often found by Lloyd's method. After γ_{ij} and $\boldsymbol{\mu}_i$ are initialized, this method iterates through two steps until convergence:

(i) Fix $\boldsymbol{\mu}_i$ (for all $1 \le i \le K$), then find γ_{ij} that minimizes the loss function. This step *reassigns every example to one of the groups*.

(ii) Fix γ_{ij} (for all $1 \le i \le K, 1 \le j \le M$), then find $\boldsymbol{\mu}_i$ that minimizes the loss function. This step *recomputes the representative of every group*.

Derive the rules to update γ_{ij} and $\boldsymbol{\mu}_i$ in these two steps, respectively. When $\boldsymbol{\mu}_i$ (for all $1 \le i \le K$) are fixed, you should find assignments for γ_{ij} that minimize Eq. (3.5), and vice versa.

(c) Show that Lloyd's method will converge.

4 Evaluation

It is very important to evaluate the performance of a learning algorithm or a recognition system. A systematic evaluation is often a comprehensive process, which may involve many aspects such as the speed, accuracy (or other accuracy-related evaluation metrics), scalability, and reliability. In this chapter, we focus on the evaluation of the accuracy and other accuracy-related evaluation metrics. We will also briefly discuss why perfect accuracy is impossible for many tasks, where the errors come from, and how confident we should be about the evaluation results.

4.1 Accuracy and Error in the Simple Case

Accuracy is a widely used evaluation metric in classification tasks, which we briefly mentioned in the previous chapter. In layman's language, accuracy is the percentage of examples that are correctly classified. The error rate is the percentage of examples that are wrongly (incorrectly) classified—i.e., 1 minus the accuracy. We use Acc and Err to denote accuracy and error rate, respectively. Note that both accuracy and error rate are between 0 and 1 (e.g., $0.49 = 49\%$). However, as mentioned in the previous chapter, we have to resort to some assumptions to make this definition crystal clear.

Suppose we are dealing with a classification task, which means that the labels of all examples are taken from a set of categorical values $\mathbb{Y}$. Similarly, the features of all examples are from the set $\mathbb{X}$. We want to evaluate the accuracy of a learned mapping

$$f\colon \mathbb{X} \mapsto \mathbb{Y}.$$

We obey the i.i.d. assumption—that is, any example $(\boldsymbol{x}, y)$ satisfies the conditions that $\boldsymbol{x} \in \mathbb{X}$, $y \in \mathbb{Y}$, and an example is drawn independently from the same underlying joint distribution $p(\boldsymbol{x}, y)$, written as

$$(\boldsymbol{x}, y) \sim p(\boldsymbol{x}, y).$$

The mapping is learned on a training set of examples D_{train}, and we also have a set of test examples D_{test} for evaluation purposes. Under these assumptions, we can define the following error rates:

- The *generalization* error. This is the expected error rate when we consider all possible examples that follow the underlying distribution, i.e.,

$$\mathrm{Err} = \mathbb{E}_{(\boldsymbol{x},y)\sim p(\boldsymbol{x},y)}\big[[\![f(\boldsymbol{x}) \neq y]\!]\big], \tag{4.1}$$

in which $[\![\cdot]\!]$ is the indicator function. If we know the underlying distribution *and* the examples and labels can be enumerated (e.g., the joint distribution is discrete) or analytically integrated (e.g., the joint distribution is a simple continuous one), the generalization error can be explicitly computed.

However, in almost all tasks, the underlying distribution is unknown. Hence, we often assume the generalization error exists as a fixed number between 0 and 1 but cannot be explicitly calculated. Our purpose is to provide a robust estimate of the generalization error.

- Approximate error. Because of the i.i.d. assumption, we can use a set of examples (denoted as D) to *approximate* the generalization error, *so long as D is sampled from the underlying distribution following the i.i.d. assumption*,

$$\mathrm{Err} \approx \frac{1}{|D|} \sum_{(\boldsymbol{x},y)\in D} [\![f(\boldsymbol{x}) \neq y]\!], \tag{4.2}$$

in which $|D|$ is the number of elements in the set D. It is easy to verify that Eq. (4.2) calculates the percentage of examples in D that are incorrectly classified $(f(\boldsymbol{x}) \neq y)$.

- The *training* and *test* error. The training set D_{train} and the test set D_{test} are two obvious candidates for the D set in Eq. (4.2). When $D = D_{\text{train}}$ the calculated error rate is called the training error, and when $D = D_{\text{test}}$ it is called the test error.

4.1.1 Training and Test Error

Why do we need a test set? The answer is simple: the training error is *not* a reliable estimate of the generalization error.

Consider the nearest neighbor classifier. It is easy to deduce that the training error will be 0 because the nearest neighbor of one training example must be itself.[1] However, we have good reason to believe that NN search will lead to errors in most applications (i.e., the generalization error is larger than 0). Hence, the training error is too optimistic for estimating the generalization error of the 1-NN classifier.

The NN example is only an extreme case. However, in most tasks we will find that the training error is an *overly optimistic* approximation of the generalization error. That is, it is usually smaller than the true error rate. Because the mapping f is learned to fit the characteristics of the training set, it makes sense that f will perform better on D_{train} than on examples not in the training set.

The solution is to use a separate test set D_{test}. Because D_{test} is sampled i.i.d., we expect the examples in D_{train} and D_{test} to be different from each other with high probability (especially when the space $\mathbb{X}$ is large). That is, it is unlikely that examples

[1] If two examples $(\boldsymbol{x}_1, y_1)$ and $(\boldsymbol{x}_2, y_2)$ are in the training set, with $\boldsymbol{x}_1 = \boldsymbol{x}_2$ but $y_1 \neq y_2$ due to label noise or other reasons, the training error of the nearest neighbor classifier will not be 0. A more detailed analysis of this kind of irreducible error will be presented later in this chapter. For now we assume that if $\boldsymbol{x}_1 = \boldsymbol{x}_2$ then $y_1 = y_2$.

in D_{test} have been utilized in learning f. Hence, the test error (which is calculated based on D_{test}) is a better estimate of the generalization error than the training error. In practice, we divide all the available examples into two *disjoint* sets, the training set and the test set, i.e.,

$$D_{\text{train}} \cap D_{\text{test}} = \emptyset.$$

4.1.2 Overfitting and Underfitting

Over- and underfitting are two adverse phenomena when learning a mapping f. We use a simple regression task to illustrate these two concepts and a commonly used evaluation metric for regression.

The regression mapping we study is $f\colon \mathbb{R} \mapsto \mathbb{R}$. In this simple task, the mapping can be written as $f(x)$, where the input x and output $f(x)$ are both real numbers. We assume the mapping f is a polynomial with degree d—i.e., the model is

$$y = f(x) + \epsilon = p_d x^d + p_{d-1} x^{d-1} + \cdots + p_1 x + p_0 + \epsilon. \tag{4.3}$$

This model has $d + 1$ *parameters* $p_i \in \mathbb{R}$ $(0 \leq i \leq d)$, and the random variable ϵ models the noise of the mapping—i.e.,

$$\epsilon = y - f(x).$$

The noise ϵ is *independent* of x. We then use a training set to learn these parameters.

Note that the polynomial degree d is not considered a parameter of $f(x)$, which is specified prior to the learning process. We call d a *hyperparameter*. After both the hyperparameter d and all the parameters p_i are specified, the mapping f is completely learned.

It is not difficult to find the optimal parameters for polynomial regression, which we leave as an exercise. In Figure 4.1, we show the fitted models for the same set of training data for different polynomial degrees. The data are generated by a degree 2 polynomial

$$y = 3(x - 0.2)^2 - 7(x - 0.2) + 4.2 + \epsilon, \tag{4.4}$$

in which ϵ is i.i.d. sampled from a standard normal distribution—i.e.,

$$\epsilon \sim N(0, 1). \tag{4.5}$$

In Figure 4.1, the x- and y-axes represent x and $y/f(x)$ values, respectively. One blue marker corresponds to one training example, and the purple curve is the fitted polynomial regression model $f(x)$. In Figure 4.1a, $d = 1$, and the fitted model is a linear one. It is easy to observe from the blue circles that the true relationship between x and y is nonlinear. Hence, the capacity or representation power of the model (degree 1 polynomial) is lower than the complexity in the data. This phenomenon is called *underfitting*, and we expect large errors when underfitting happens. As shown by the large discrepancy between the purple curve and the blue points, large regression errors do indeed occur.

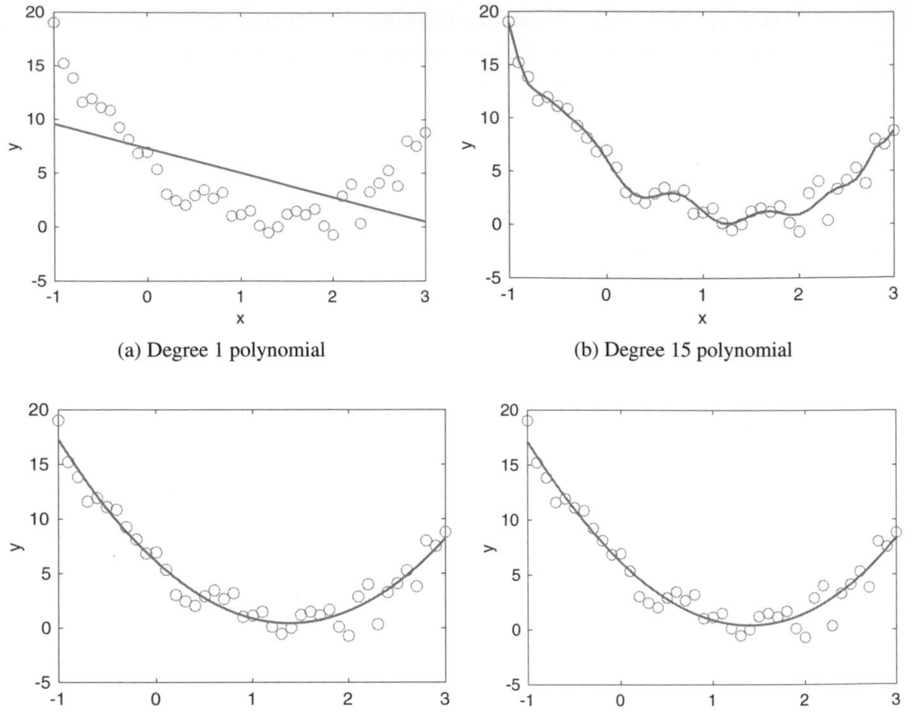

(a) Degree 1 polynomial

(b) Degree 15 polynomial

(c) Degree 2 polynomial

(d) Degree 3 polynomial

Figure 4.1 Fitting data with polynomials with different degrees of freedom. (A black and white version of this figure will appear in some formats. For the color version, please refer to the plate section.)

Now we move on to Figure 4.1b (with $d = 15$). The learned polynomial curve is a complex one, with many upward and downward transitions along the curve. We observe that most blue points are very close to the purple curve, meaning that the fitting error is very small *on the training set*. However, since the data are generated using a degree 2 polynomial, its generalization (or test) error will be large too. A higher-order polynomial has larger representation power than a lower-order one. The extra capacity is often used to model the noise in the examples (the normal noise ϵ in this case) or some peculiar property in the training set (which is not a property of the underlying distribution). This phenomenon is called *overfitting*.

Nowadays we are equipped with more computing resources, which means we can afford to use models with large capacity. Overfitting has become a more serious issue than underfitting in many modern algorithms and systems.

Figure 4.1c uses the correct polynomial degree ($d = 2$). It strikes a good balance between minimizing the training error and avoiding overfitting. As shown by this figure, most blue points are around the purple curve, and the curve is quite smooth. We expect it to also achieve small generalization error.

Table 4.1 True (first row) and learned (second and third rows) parameters of polynomial regression.

	p_3	p_2	p_1	p_0
True		3.0000	−8.2000	6.8000
$d = 2$		2.9659	−9.1970	6.1079
$d = 3$	0.0489	2.8191	−8.1734	6.1821

In Figure 4.1d we set $d = 3$, which is slightly larger than the correct value ($d = 2$). There are indeed differences between the curves in Figures 4.1c and 4.1d, although the differences are almost indistinguishable. We have also listed the true and learned parameter values in Table 4.1. Both learned sets of parameters match the true values quite well. The p_3 parameter for the degree 3 polynomial is close to 0, which indicates that the term p_3x^3 has limited impact for predicting y. In other words, when the model capacity is only slightly higher than the data's true complexity, a learning algorithm still has the potential to properly fit the data. However, when the gap between model and data complexity is large (cf. Figure 4.1b), overfitting will cause serious problems.

4.1.3 Choosing the Hyperparameter(s) Using Validation

Unlike the parameters, which can be learned based on the training data, hyperparameters are usually not learnable. Hyperparameters are often related to the capacity or representation power of the mapping f. A few examples are listed here.

- d in polynomial regression. It is obvious that a larger d is directly related to higher representation power.
- k in k-NN. A large k value can reduce the effect of noise, but may reduce the discriminative power in classification. For example, if k equals the number of training examples, the k-NN classifier will return the same prediction for any example.
- Bandwidth h in kernel density estimation (KDE). We will introduce KDE in the chapter on probabilistic methods (Chapter 8). Unlike in the above examples, there is a theoretical rule that guides the choice of optimal bandwidth.
- γ in the RBF (radial basis function) kernel for SVM. We will introduce the RBF kernel in the SVM chapter (Chapter 7). The choice of this hyperparameter, however, is neither learnable from data nor guided by a theoretical result.

Hyperparameters are often critical in a learning method. Wrongly changing the value of one hyperparameter (e.g., γ in the RBF kernel) may dramatically reduce the classification accuracy (e.g., from above 90% to less than 60%). We need to be careful about hyperparameters.

One widely adopted approach is to use a validation set. The validation set is provided in some tasks, in which we want to ensure that the training, validation, and test sets are *disjoint*. In scenarios where this split is not provided, we can randomly split the set of all available data into three disjoint sets: D_{train}, D_{val} (the validation set), and D_{test}.

Then we can list a set of representative hyperparameter values—e.g., $k \in \{1,3,5,7,9\}$ for k-NN—and train a classifier using the training set and one of the hyperparameter values. The resulting classifier can be evaluated using the *validation* set to obtain a validation error. For example, we will obtain five validation k-NN error rates, one for each hyperparameter value. The hyperparameter value that leads to the smallest validation error rate will be used as the chosen hyperparameter value.

In the last step, we train a classifier using D_{train} and the chosen hyperparameter value to train a classifier, and its performance can be evaluated using D_{test}. When there are ample examples, this strategy often works well. For example, we can use $\frac{n}{10}$ examples for testing when there are n examples in total *and* when n is large. In the remaining $\frac{9n}{10}$ examples, we can use $\frac{n}{10}$ for validation and the remaining $\frac{8n}{10}$ for training. The ratio of sizes between training/validation or training/testing is not fixed, but we usually set aside a large portion of examples for training. If a split between training and test examples has been prespecified, we can split the training set into a smaller training set and a validation set when necessary.

The validation set can be used for other purposes too. For example, the parameters of neural networks (including the convolutional neural network) are learned iteratively. The neural network model (i.e., the values of its parameters) is updated in every iteration. However, it is not trivial to determine when to stop the iterative updating procedure. Neural networks have very large capacity. Hence, the training error will continue to decrease even after many training iterations. But, after some number of iterations, the new updates may be mainly fitting the noise, which leads to overfitting, and the validation error will start to increase. Note that the validation and training sets are disjoint. Hence, both the validation error and the test error rates will increase if overfitting happens.

One useful strategy is to evaluate the model's validation error. The learning process can be terminated if the validation error becomes stable (not decreasing in a few consecutive iterations) or even starts to increase—that is, when it starts to continuously overfit. This strategy is called "early stopping" in the neural network community.

Figure 4.2 illustrates the interaction between training and validation error rates. Note that this is only a schematic illustration. In practice, although the overall trend is that the training error reduces when more iterations are updated, it can have small ups and downs in a short period. The validation error can also be (slightly) smaller than the training error before overfitting occurs. In this example, it is probably a good idea to stop the training process after six iterations.

4.1.4 Cross-Validation

The validation strategy works well when there are a large number of examples. For example, if one million ($n = 10^6$) examples are available, the validation set has 100 000 examples ($\frac{n}{10}$), which is enough to provide a good estimate of the generalization error. However, when n is small (e.g., $n = 100$), this strategy may cease to work if we use a small portion of examples for validation (e.g., $\frac{n}{10} = 10$). If we set

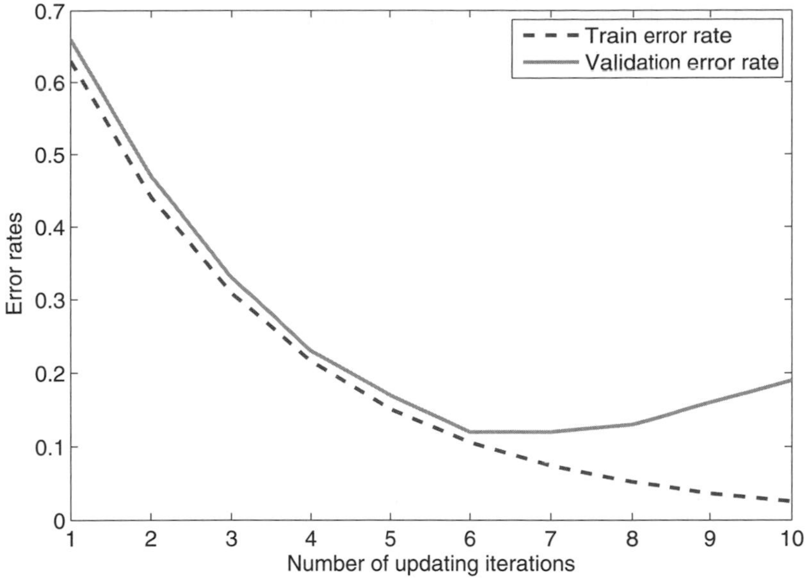

Figure 4.2 Illustration of the overfitting phenomenon. One unit in the x-axis can be one or more (e.g., 1000) updating iterations.

aside a large portion as the validation set (e.g., $\frac{n}{2} = 50$), the training set will be too small to learn a good classifier.

Cross-validation (CV) is an alternative strategy for small size tasks. A k-fold CV *randomly* divides the training set D_{train} into k (roughly) *even* and *disjoint* subsets $D_1, D_2, \ldots, D_k$, such that

$$\bigcup_{i=1}^{k} D_i = D_{\text{train}}, \tag{4.6}$$

$$D_i \cap D_j = \emptyset \quad \forall\, 1 \leq i \neq j \leq k, \tag{4.7}$$

$$|D_i| \approx \frac{|D_{\text{train}}|}{k} \quad \forall\, 1 \leq i \leq k. \tag{4.8}$$

The CV estimate of the error rate then operates following Algorithm 2.

In Algorithm 2, the learning algorithm is run k times. In the ith run, all examples except those in the ith subset D_i are used for training, while D_i is used to compute the validation error Err_i. After all the k runs, the cross-validation estimate is the average of k validation errors Err_i $(1 \leq i \leq k)$.

Note that every example is used *exactly once* to compute one of the validation error rates, and at the same time is used $k - 1$ times for training one of the k classifiers. In other words, the CV strategy makes good use of the small number of examples and hence may provide a reasonable estimate of the error rate.

Because the number of training examples is small, often a small k is used—e.g., $k = 10$ or $k = 5$. Although k classifiers have to be learned, the computational costs are still acceptable because $|D_{\text{train}}|$ is small.

Algorithm 2 Cross-validation estimate of the error rate

Input: k, D_{train}, a learning algorithm (with hyperparameters specified).
Randomly divide the training set into k subsets satisfying Eqs. (4.6)–(4.8).
for $i = 1, 2, \ldots, k$ **do**
  Construct a new training set, which consists of all the examples from $D_1, \ldots, D_{i-1}, D_{i+1}, \ldots, D_k$.
  Learn a classifier f_i using this training set and the learning algorithm.
  Calculate the error rate of f_i on D_i, denoted as Err_i.
end for
Output: Return the error rate estimated by cross-validation as

$$\text{Err}_{\text{CV}} = \frac{1}{k} \sum_{i=1}^{k} \text{Err}_i. \tag{4.9}$$

Furthermore, because there is randomness in the division of D_{train} into k subsets, different Err_{CV} will be returned if we run Algorithm 2 multiple times. The difference can be large if $|D_{\text{train}}|$ is really small (e.g., a few tens). In this case, we can run k-fold CV multiple times and return the average of their estimates. A commonly used CV schedule is a 10 times average of 10-fold cross-validation.

When the number of available examples is small, we may use all these examples as D_{train} (i.e., do not put aside examples as a separate test set). The cross-validation error rate can be used to evaluate classifiers in this case.

4.2 Minimizing the Cost/Loss

Based on the above analyses of error rates, it is a natural idea to formulate a learning task as an optimization problem which minimizes the error rate. We will use the classification task to illustrate this idea.

Given a training set consisting of n examples $(\boldsymbol{x}_i, y_i)$ $(1 \le i \le n)$, the training error rate of a mapping f is simply

$$\min_f \frac{1}{n} \sum_{i=1}^{n} [\![f(\boldsymbol{x}_i) \neq y_i]\!]. \tag{4.10}$$

In Eq. (4.10), the exact form of the mapping f and its parameters are not specified. After these components are fully specified, optimizing Eq. (4.10) will lead to an optimal (in the training error sense) mapping f.

However, the indicator function $[\![\cdot]\!]$ is not smooth—even not convex for most functional forms and parameterizations of f. Hence, as we discussed in Chapter 2, solving Eq. (4.10) will be very difficult. We may also have to require $f(\boldsymbol{x}_i)$ to be categorical (or integer) values, which makes designing the form of f more difficult.

When $[\![f(\boldsymbol{x}_i) \neq y_i]\!]$ is 1, the ith training example is wrongly classified by f, which means some *cost* or *loss* has been attributed to the mapping f with respect to the example $(\boldsymbol{x}_i, y_i)$, and Eq. (4.10) is minimizing the average loss on the training set. Hence, this type of learning is also called cost minimization or loss minimization.

A widely used strategy is to replace the difficult-to-optimize loss function $[\![\cdot]\!]$ with a new optimization-friendly loss function. For example, if the classification problem is binary—i.e., $y_i \in \{0, 1\}$ for all i—we can use the *mean squared error* (MSE) loss

$$\min_f \frac{1}{n} \sum_{i=1}^{n} (f(\boldsymbol{x}_i) - y_i)^2 . \tag{4.11}$$

A few properties of the MSE loss make it a good loss function:

- We can treat y_i as real values in MSE, and $f(\boldsymbol{x}_i)$ does *not* need to be categorical. During prediction, the output can be 1 if $f(\boldsymbol{x}_i) \geq 0.5$ and 0 otherwise.
- In order to minimize the loss, MSE encourages $f(\boldsymbol{x}_i)$ to be close to 0 if $y_i = 0$, and pushes $f(\boldsymbol{x}_i)$ to be around 1 if $y_i = 1$. In other words, the behavior of MSE mimics some *key characteristics* of the indicator function (the true loss function). We expect a classifier learned based on MSE to have a low training error rate too (even though it might not be the smallest possible).
- The square function is smooth, differentiable, and convex, which makes the minimization of MSE an easy task. Hence, in this formalization of loss minimization, we can treat the MSE as a simplification of the indicator function.

MSE is also a natural loss function for regression tasks (e.g., polynomial regression). In this book, we will encounter many other loss functions.

The above strategy replaces the mean indicator loss function with a mean squared error, which is called a *surrogate* loss function. If a surrogate loss is easier to minimize and its key characteristics mimic the original one, we can replace the original loss function with the surrogate to make the optimization tractable.

4.2.1 Regularization

As illustrated by Figure 4.1, both underfitting and overfitting are harmful. As we will show later in this book, a classifier with small capacity will have large *bias*, which constitutes part of the error rate. In contrast, a classifier with large capacity or representation power will have small bias but large *variance*, which is another major contributor to the error rate.

Since we do not know the inherent complexity in our task's examples, it is never easy to choose a classifier that has suitable capacity for a specific task. One commonly used strategy to deal with this difficulty is to use a mapping f with high capacity, but at the same time add a *regularization* term to it.

An ideal situation is that the bias will be small (because f is complex enough) and the variance may also be small (because the regularization term penalizes complex f). Let $\mathcal{R}(f)$ be a regularizer on f; the MSE minimization (Eq. 4.11) now becomes

$$\min_f \frac{1}{n}\sum_{i=1}^{n}(f(\boldsymbol{x}_i) - y_i)^2 + \lambda\mathcal{R}(f). \tag{4.12}$$

The hyperparameter $\lambda > 0$ is a trade-off parameter that controls the balance between a small training set cost $\frac{1}{n}\sum_{i=1}^{n}(f(\boldsymbol{x}_i) - y_i)^2$ and a small regularization cost $\mathcal{R}(f)$.

The regularization term (also called the regularizer) has different forms for different classifiers. Some regularizers will be introduced later in this book.

4.2.2 Cost Matrix

The simple accuracy or error rate criterion may work poorly in many situations. Indeed, as we have already discussed, minimizing the error rate in a severely imbalanced binary classification task may cause the classifier to classify all examples into the majority class.

Most imbalanced learning tasks are also *cost-sensitive*, meaning that different types of errors will incur losses that are also imbalanced. Let us consider the small start-up IT company with 24 employees once again. Company X has signed a contract with your company, and you (with your employee ID being 24) are assigned to this project. Company X produces part Y for a complex product Z, and decides to replace the quality inspector with an automatic system. The percentage of qualified parts is around 99% in company X, hence you have to deal with an imbalanced classification task. If a qualified part is predicted as defective, this part will be discarded, which will cost 10 RMB. In contrast, if a part is in fact defective but is predicted as qualified, it will be assembled into the final product Z and disable the entire product Z. Company X has to pay 1000 RMB for one such defective part. Hence, your problem is also obviously cost sensitive.

The cost minimization framework can be naturally extended to handle cost-sensitive tasks. Let $(\boldsymbol{x}, y)$ be an example and $f(\boldsymbol{x})$ be a mapping that predicts the label for $\boldsymbol{x}$. The groundtruth label for $\boldsymbol{x}$ is y, which is denoted as 0 if the part $\boldsymbol{x}$ is qualified and 1 if it is defective. For simplicity, we assume $f(\boldsymbol{x})$ is also binary (0 if it predicts $\boldsymbol{x}$ as qualified, and 1 for defective). We can define a 2×2 *cost matrix* to summarize the cost incurred in different cases:

$$\begin{bmatrix} c_{00} & c_{01} \\ c_{10} & c_{11} \end{bmatrix} = \begin{bmatrix} 0 & 10 \\ 1000 & 10 \end{bmatrix}. \tag{4.13}$$

In Eq. (4.13), c_{ij} is the cost incurred when the groundtruth label y is i and the prediction $f(\boldsymbol{x})$ is j.

Note that even a correct prediction can incur certain cost. For example, $c_{11} = 10$ because a defective part will cost 10 RMB even if it is correctly detected as a defective one.

With an appropriate cost matrix, Eq. (4.10) becomes

$$\min_f \frac{1}{n} \sum_{i=1}^{n} c_{y_i, f(\boldsymbol{x}_i)}, \tag{4.14}$$

which properly handles different costs.

Cost-sensitive learning is an important topic in learning and recognition. Although we will not cover its details in this book, we want to present a few notes on the cost matrix.

- Minimizing the error rate can be considered as a special case of cost minimization, in which the cost matrix is $\begin{bmatrix} 0 & 1 \\ 1 & 0 \end{bmatrix}$.
- It is, however, difficult to determine appropriate c_{ij} values in many real-world applications.
- The cost matrix can be easily extended to multiclass problems. In an m class classification problem, the cost matrix is of size $m \times m$, and c_{ij} is the cost when the groundtruth label is i but the prediction is j.

4.2.3 Bayes Decision Theory

Bayes decision theory minimizes the cost function in the probabilistic sense. Assume the data $(\boldsymbol{x}, y)$ is a random vector, and the joint probability is $\Pr(\boldsymbol{x}, y)$; Bayes decision theory seeks to minimize the *risk*, which is the expected loss with respect to the joint density:

$$\sum_{\boldsymbol{x}, y} c_{y, f(\boldsymbol{x})} \Pr(\boldsymbol{x}, y). \tag{4.15}$$

Here we are using the notation for discrete random variables. If continuous or hybrid random distributions are involved, integrations (or a combination of summations and integrations) can be used to replace the summations.

The risk is the average loss over the true underlying probability, which can also be succinctly written as

$$\mathbb{E}_{(\boldsymbol{x}, y)}[c_{y, f(\boldsymbol{x})}]. \tag{4.16}$$

By picking the mapping $f(\boldsymbol{x})$ that minimizes the risk, Bayes decision theory is optimal under these assumptions in the minimum cost sense.

4.3 Evaluation in Imbalanced Problems

Error rate is not a good evaluation metric in imbalanced or cost-sensitive tasks. It is also difficult to determine the cost (c_{ij}) values in Eq. (4.13). In practice, we use another set of evaluation metrics (such as *precision* and *recall*) for these tasks.

In this section, we will consider binary classification tasks only. Following the commonly used terminology, we call the two classes *positive* and *negative*, respectively.

Table 4.2 Possible combinations for the groundtruth and the predicted label. (A black and white version of this figure will appear in some formats. For the color version, please refer to the plate section.)

	Prediction $f(\boldsymbol{x}) = +1$	Prediction $f(\boldsymbol{x}) = -1$
True label $y = +1$	True positive	False negative
True label $y = -1$	False positive	True negative

The positive class often happens to be the minority class, that is, the class with fewer examples (e.g., defective parts). The negative class often happens to be the majority class, that is, the class with more examples (e.g., qualified parts). We use $+1$ and -1 to denote positive and negative classes, respectively.

4.3.1 Rates inside Individual Class

There are four possible combinations of the groundtruth label y and the prediction $f(\boldsymbol{x})$ for one example $\boldsymbol{x}$, which are summarized in Table 4.2.

We use two words to pinpoint one of these four possible cases, such as true positive or false negative. In each possible case, the second word refers to the predicted label (which is shown in red in Table 4.2). The first word describes whether the prediction is correct or not. For example, *false positive* indicates the predicted label is "positive" $(+1)$ and this prediction is wrong ("false"); hence, the true label is "negative" (-1). We use the initials as abbreviations for these four cases: TP, FN, FP, TN.

Given a test set with number of examples TOTAL, we also use these abbreviations to denote the number of examples falling into each of the four cases. For example, TP $= 37$ means that 37 examples in the test set are true positives. The following quantities are defined based on TP, FN, FP, and TN:

- The total number of examples:

$$\text{TOTAL} = \text{TP} + \text{FN} + \text{FP} + \text{TN}.$$

- The total number of positive examples (whose true label is $+1$):

$$P = \text{TP} + \text{FN}.$$

- The total number of negative examples (whose true label is -1):

$$N = \text{FP} + \text{TN}.$$

- Accuracy:

$$\text{Acc} = \frac{\text{TP} + \text{TN}}{\text{TOTAL}}.$$

- Error rate:

$$\text{Err} = \frac{\text{FP} + \text{FN}}{\text{TOTAL}} = 1 - \text{Acc}.$$

- True positive rate:

$$\mathrm{TPR} = \frac{\mathrm{TP}}{P},$$

which is the ratio between the number of true positives and the total number of positive examples.
- False positive rate:

$$\mathrm{FPR} = \frac{\mathrm{FP}}{N},$$

which is the ratio between the number of false positives and the total number of negative examples.
- True negative rate:

$$\mathrm{TNR} = \frac{\mathrm{TN}}{N},$$

which is the ratio between the number of true negatives and the total number of negative examples.
- False negative rate:

$$\mathrm{FNR} = \frac{\mathrm{FN}}{P},$$

which is the ratio between the number of false negatives and the total number of positive examples.

To help remember the last four rates, we note that the denominator can be deduced from the numerator in the definitions. For example, in $\mathrm{FPR} = \frac{\mathrm{FP}}{N}$, the numerator says "false positive" (whose true label is negative), which determines the denominator as N, the total number of negative examples.

These rates have been defined in different areas (such as statistics) and have different names. For example, TPR is also called *sensitivity* and FNR the *miss rate*.

One simple way to understand these rates is to treat them as evaluation results only on examples of *single* class. For example, if we use instances from only the positive class ($y = +1$) to evaluate $f(\boldsymbol{x})$, the obtained accuracy and error rate are TPR and FNR, respectively. If only the negative class is used, the accuracy and error are TNR and FPR, respectively.

4.3.2 Area under the ROC Curve

FPR and FNR calculate the error rates in two classes *separately*, which will not be affected by the class imbalance issue. However, we usually prefer one single number to describe the performance of one classifier, rather than two or more rates.

What is more, in most classifiers we can obtain many pairs of different (FPR, FNR) values. Suppose

$$f(\boldsymbol{x}) = 2\left(\llbracket \boldsymbol{w}^T \boldsymbol{x} > b \rrbracket - 0.5\right),$$

that is, the prediction is positive (+1) if $w^T x > b$ (-1 if $w^T x \leq b$). The parameters of this classifier include both w and b. After we obtain the optimal w parameters, we may utilize the freedom in the value of b to gradually change its value:

- When $b = -\infty$, the prediction is always $+1$ regardless of the values in x. That is, FPR is 1 and FNR is 0.
- When b gradually increases, some test examples will be classified as negative. If the true label for one such example is positive, a false negative is created, hence the FNR will increase; if the true label for this example is negative, then when $b = -\infty$ it is a false positive, hence, the FPR will be reduced. In general, when b increases, FPR will gradually decrease and FNR will gradually increase.
- Finally when $b = \infty$, the prediction is always -1. Hence, FPR $= 0$ and FNR $= 1$.

The receiver operating characteristics (ROC) curve records the process of these changes in a curve. The name ROC was first invented to describe the performance of finding enemy targets by radar, whose original meaning is not very important in our usage of this curve.

As shown in Figure 4.3, the x-axis is the false positive rate FPR and the y-axis is the true positive rate TPR. Because (why?)

$$\text{TPR} = 1 - \text{FNR},$$

when b sweeps from ∞ to $-\infty$ by gradually decreasing b, the (FPR, TPR) pair will move from the coordinate $(0, 0)$ to $(1, 1)$, and the curve is nondecreasing.

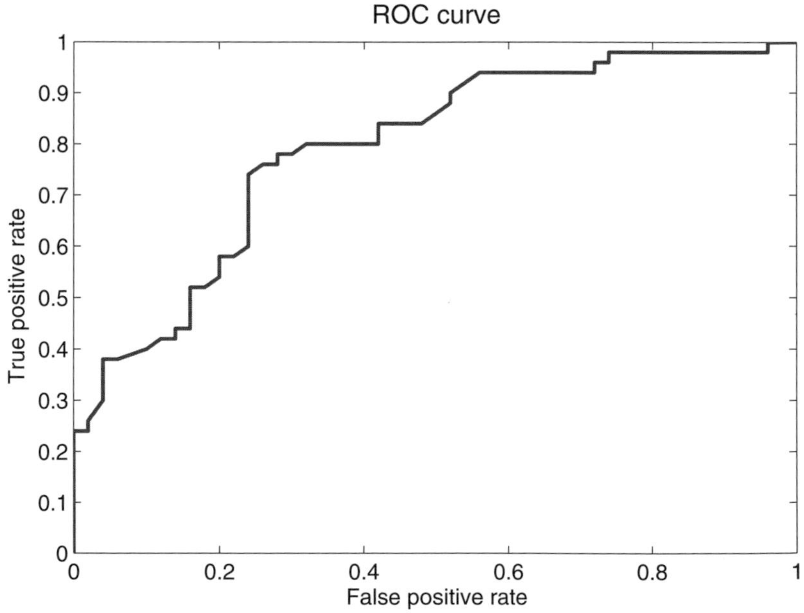

Figure 4.3 One example of the receiver operating characteristics (ROC) curve.

Because the ROC curve summarizes the classifier's performance over the entire operational range (by changing the value of b), we can use the area under the ROC curve (called the AUC-ROC) as a single-number metric for its evaluation, which is also suitable in imbalanced tasks. In a classifier other than the linear classifier $\boldsymbol{w}^T\boldsymbol{x}+b$, we often can find another parameter that acts as a decision threshold (similar to b), and then can generate the ROC by altering this parameter.

The ROC of a classifier that randomly guesses its answer should be a line segment that connects $(0,0)$ and $(1,1)$ (i.e., the diagonal), and its AUC-ROC is 0.5. Hence, we expect any reasonable classifier to have its AUC-ROC larger than 0.5 in a binary classification problem.

The best ROC consists of two line segments: a vertical one from $(0,0)$ to $(0,1)$ followed by a horizontal one from $(0,1)$ to $(1,1)$. The classifier corresponding to this ROC always correctly classifies all test examples. Its AUC-ROC is 1.

4.3.3 Precision, Recall, and F-Measure

Precision and recall are two other measures suitable for evaluating imbalanced tasks. They are defined as

$$\text{precision} = \frac{\text{TP}}{\text{TP}+\text{FP}}, \tag{4.17}$$

$$\text{recall} = \frac{\text{TP}}{P}. \tag{4.18}$$

Note that the recall measure is simply another name for the true positive rate.

Consider an image retrieval application. The test set has 10 000 images in total, in which 100 are related to *Nanjing University* (which we treat as positive class examples). When you type "Nanjing University" as the retrieval request, the retrieval system returns 50 images to you, which are those predicted as related to Nanjing University (i.e., predicted as positive). The returned results contain some images that indeed are related to Nanjing University (TP), but some are irrelevant (FP). Two measures are important when you evaluate the retrieval system:

- Are the returned results precise? You want most (if not all) returned images to be positive/related to Nanjing University. This measure is the *precision*, the percentage of true positives among those that are predicted as positive—i.e., $\frac{\text{TP}}{\text{TP}+\text{FP}}$.
- Are all positive examples recalled? You want most (if not all) positive images to be included in the returned set. This measure is the *recall* (or TPR), the percentage of true positives among all positive images in the entire test set—i.e., $\frac{\text{TP}}{P}$.

It is not difficult to observe that these two performance measures are still meaningful in imbalanced tasks.

There are two widely used ways to summarize precision and recall into one number. Similar to the ROC curve, we can alter the threshold parameter in a classifier or a retrieval system and generate many pairs of (precision, recall) values, which form the

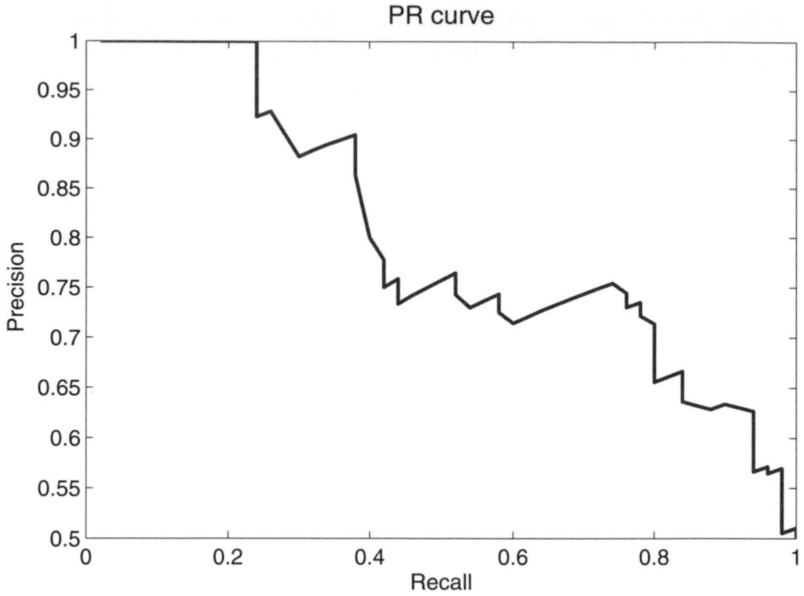

Figure 4.4 One example of the precision–recall (PR) curve.

precision–recall (PR) curve. Then we can use the AUC-PR (area under the precision–recall curve) as the evaluation metric. Figure 4.4 shows one example PR curve.

One notable difference between the PR and ROC curves is that the PR curve is no longer nondecreasing. In most tasks, we will observe PR curves that zigzag, like the one in Figure 4.4.

The AUC-PR measure is more discriminating than AUC-ROC. One may observe AUC-ROC scores that are very close to each other for many classifiers. In this case, AUC-PR may be a better evaluation metric.

The second way to combine precision and recall is the F-measure, which is defined as

$$\mathrm{F} = \frac{2 \cdot \text{precision} \cdot \text{recall}}{\text{precision} + \text{recall}}. \tag{4.19}$$

The F-measure is the harmonic mean of precision and recall, which is always between 0 and 1. A higher F-measure indicates a better classifier. It is also easy to see that

$$\mathrm{F} = \frac{2\mathrm{TP}}{2\mathrm{TP} + \mathrm{FP} + \mathrm{FN}}. \tag{4.20}$$

The F-measure treats precision and recall equally. An extension of the F-measure is defined for a fixed $\beta > 0$, as

$$\mathrm{F}_\beta = (1 + \beta^2) \cdot \frac{\text{precision} \cdot \text{recall}}{\beta^2 \cdot \text{precision} + \text{recall}}. \tag{4.21}$$

Either the precision or the recall is considered more important than the other, depending on the value of β. Note that the F-measure is a special case of F_β when $\beta = 1$.

An intuitive way to understand the relative importance between precision and recall is to consider extreme β values. If $\beta \to 0$, $F_\beta \to$ precision—that is, precision is more important for small β values. If $\beta \to \infty$, $F_\beta \to$ recall—that is, recall is more important for large β. When $\beta = 1$, the F-measure is symmetric about precision and recall—i.e., $F_1(\text{precision}, \text{recall}) = F_1(\text{recall}, \text{precision})$. Hence, they are equally important when $\beta = 1$. More properties and implications of F_β will be discussed in the exercises.

4.4 Can We Reach 100% Accuracy?

Till now, we have introduced ways to evaluate a system's accuracy or error in a few different tasks. What we really want is, in fact, a learning algorithm or recognition system that has *no* error. Can we implement such a system with 100% accuracy?

The answer to this question hinges on the data in your task. In the probabilistic interpretation, the data are expressed as random variables $(\boldsymbol{x}, y)$, and the examples are sampled i.i.d. from an underlying distribution $\Pr(\boldsymbol{x}, y)$ (or use the density $p(\boldsymbol{x}, y)$ for continuous random variables). If there exists an instance $\boldsymbol{x}^1$ and two different values of y (y^1 and y^2, and $y^1 \neq y^2$), such that $\Pr(\boldsymbol{x}^1, y^1) > 0$ and $\Pr(\boldsymbol{x}^1, y^2) > 0$, then a classifier with 100% (generalization) accuracy is impossible. If this classifier correctly classifies the example $(\boldsymbol{x}^1, y^1)$, it will err on $(\boldsymbol{x}^1, y^2)$, and vice versa.

4.4.1 Bayes Error Rate

We assume any classifier $f(\boldsymbol{x})$ is a valid function, which can map $\boldsymbol{x}$ only to a single fixed element y—that is, $f(\boldsymbol{x}^1) = y^1$ and $f(\boldsymbol{x}^1) = y^2$ cannot both happen if $y^1 \neq y^2$. This assumption is a valid one because in a classifier, we expect a deterministic answer. Hence, in either the training or test set, any instance $\boldsymbol{x}$ will be assigned only one groundtruth label y, and the prediction is also unique.

Now we can consider three cases for the above example.

- The true label for the instance $\boldsymbol{x}^1$ is set to be y^1. Then the example $(\boldsymbol{x}^1, y^2)$ is considered an error. Because $\Pr(\boldsymbol{x}^1, y^2) > 0$, this example will contribute at least $\Pr(\boldsymbol{x}^1, y^2)$ to the generalization error. That is, no matter what classifier is used, $(\boldsymbol{x}^1, y^2)$ will contribute $\Pr(\boldsymbol{x}^1, y^2)$ to this classifier's generalization error.
- The true label for the instance $\boldsymbol{x}^1$ is set to be y^2. Then the example $(\boldsymbol{x}^1, y^1)$ is considered an error. Because $\Pr(\boldsymbol{x}^1, y^1) > 0$, this example will contribute at least $\Pr(\boldsymbol{x}^1, y^1)$ to the generalization error. That is, no matter what classifier is used, $(\boldsymbol{x}^1, y^1)$ will contribute $\Pr(\boldsymbol{x}^1, y^1)$ to this classifier's generalization error.
- The true label for the instance $\boldsymbol{x}^1$ is set to be neither y^1 nor y^2. Then both examples $(\boldsymbol{x}^1, y^1)$ and $(\boldsymbol{x}^1, y^2)$ are errors. Because both $\Pr(\boldsymbol{x}^1, y^1) > 0$ and $\Pr(\boldsymbol{x}^1, y^2) > 0$,

these two examples will contribute at least $\Pr(\boldsymbol{x}^1, y^1) + \Pr(\boldsymbol{x}^1, y^2)$ to the generalization error of any possible classifier.

These three cases exhaust all possible cases for $(\boldsymbol{x}^1, y^1)$ and $(\boldsymbol{x}^1, y^2)$. If there are more than two y values that make $\Pr(\boldsymbol{x}^1, y) > 0$, analyses can be made in the same way. Hence, we reach the following conclusions:

- Errors are inevitable if there exist $\boldsymbol{x}^1$ and y^1, y^2 $(y^1 \neq y^2)$ such that $\Pr(\boldsymbol{x}^1, y^1) > 0$ and $\Pr(\boldsymbol{x}^1, y^2) > 0$. Note that this statement is classifier agnostic—it is true regardless of the classifier.
- If a nondeterministic label is inevitable for an instance $\boldsymbol{x}^1$ (as in this particular example), we will compare the two probabilities $\Pr(\boldsymbol{x}^1, y^1)$ and $\Pr(\boldsymbol{x}^1, y^2)$. If $\Pr(\boldsymbol{x}^1, y^1) > \Pr(\boldsymbol{x}^1, y^2)$, we set the groundtruth label for $\boldsymbol{x}^1$ to y^1 so that its contribution of unavoidable error $\Pr(\boldsymbol{x}^1, y^2)$ is small (compared to the case when the groundtruth label is set to y^2). If $\Pr(\boldsymbol{x}^1, y^2) > \Pr(\boldsymbol{x}^1, y^1)$, we must set the groundtruth label to y^2.
- Let us consider the general situation. There are m classes $(m \geq 2)$, which are denoted by $y = i$ $(1 \leq i \leq m)$ for the ith class. For any instance $\boldsymbol{x}$, we should set its groundtruth label as

$$y^\star = \arg\max_y \Pr(\boldsymbol{x}, y)$$

to obtain the smallest unavoidable error, which is

$$\sum_{y \neq y^\star} \Pr(\boldsymbol{x}, y)$$

for $\boldsymbol{x}$.

If we repeat the above analyses for all possible instances $\boldsymbol{x} \in \mathbb{X}$, the generalization error of any classifier has a lower bound, as

$$\sum_{\boldsymbol{x} \in \mathbb{X}} \sum_{y \neq y^\star(\boldsymbol{x})} \Pr(\boldsymbol{x}, y) = 1 - \sum_{\boldsymbol{x} \in \mathbb{X}} \Pr(\boldsymbol{x}, y^\star(\boldsymbol{x})), \tag{4.22}$$

in which $y^\star(\boldsymbol{x}) = \arg\max_y \Pr(\boldsymbol{x}, y)$ is the class index that makes $\Pr(\boldsymbol{x}, y)$ the largest for $\boldsymbol{x}$.

Equation (4.22) defines the *Bayes error rate*, which is a theoretical bound of the smallest error rate that *any* classifier can attain. Comparing Eqs. (4.16) and (4.22), it is easy to see that the loss incurred by Bayes decision theory is exactly the Bayes error rate if the cost matrix is $\left[\begin{smallmatrix} 0 & 1 \\ 1 & 0 \end{smallmatrix}\right]$.

4.4.2 Groundtruth Labels

The Bayes error rate is a theoretical bound, which assumes that the joint density $p(\boldsymbol{x}, y)$ or joint probability $\Pr(\boldsymbol{x}, y)$ is known and can be analytically computed or exhaustively enumerated. The underlying distribution, however, is unknown in almost all real-world tasks. How then have the groundtruth labels been decided?

In some applications, labels of training examples are accessible. For example, you try to predict day $t+1$'s NYSE closing index value based on the previous n days' closing NYSE index values, which is a regression task. On day $t+2$, you have observed the label of this regression task for day $t+1$. Hence, you can collect the training instances and labels using NYSE history data. A model learned from the history data can be used to predict the next day's trading trend, although that prediction may be highly inaccurate—suppose a parallel universe does exist and our universe is split into two different parallel ones after the New York stock exchange closes on day $t+1$: the closing NYSE index values may be dramatically different in the two universes.

In most cases, the groundtruth labels are not observable and are obtained via human judgments. An expert in the task domain will manually specify labels for instances. For example, an experienced doctor will look at a patient's bone X-ray image and decide whether a bone injury exists or not. This type of human annotation is the major labeling method.

Human annotations are susceptible to errors and noise. In some difficult cases, even an expert will have difficulty in determining an accurate groundtruth label. An exhausted expert may make mistakes during labeling, especially when many examples need to be labeled. The labeling process can be extremely time consuming, which also leads to high financial pressure—imagine you have to hire a top-notch doctor for 100 business days to label your data! In cases where both $\Pr(\boldsymbol{x}^1, y^1) > 0$ and $\Pr(\boldsymbol{x}^1, y^2) > 0$, the expert has to choose from y^1 or y^2, which may be difficult in some applications.

In summary, the labels can be a categorical value (for classification), a real number (for regression), a vector or matrix of real numbers, or even more complex data structures. The groundtruth labels may also contain uncertainty, noise, or error.

In this introductory book, we will focus on simple classification and regression tasks, and assume that the labels are error- and noise-free *unless otherwise specified* (mainly because methods that explicitly handle label errors are advanced and beyond the scope of this book).

4.4.3 Bias–Variance Decomposition

Now that the error is inevitable, it is helpful to study what components contribute to it. Hopefully, this understanding will help us in reducing the part of the error that is larger than the Bayes error rate. We will use regression as an example to illustrate the *bias–variance decomposition*. Similar decompositions also exist for classifiers, but are more complex.

We need many assumptions to set up the stage for bias–variance decomposition. First, we have a function $F(\boldsymbol{x}) \in \mathbb{R}$, which is the function that generates our training data. However, the training data are susceptible to noise. A training example $(\boldsymbol{x}, y)$ follows

$$y = F(\boldsymbol{x}) + \epsilon, \tag{4.23}$$

in which $\epsilon \sim N(0, \sigma^2)$ is Gaussian random noise, which is *independent* of $\boldsymbol{x}$.

Next we can sample (i.i.d.) from Eq. (4.23) to generate different training sets, which may contain different numbers of training examples. We use a random variable D to represent the training set.

Third, we have a regression model f, which will generate a mapping $f(\boldsymbol{x}; D)$ by learning from the training set D, and will predict $f(\boldsymbol{x}; D)$ for any instance $\boldsymbol{x}$. We put D in prediction notation to emphasize that the prediction is based on the mapping learned from D. When different samples of D (different training sets) are used, we expect different prediction results for the same $\boldsymbol{x}$.

However, we assume that the regression method is deterministic. That is, given the same training set many times, it will produce the same mapping and predictions.

Finally, because of the i.i.d. sampling assumption, we need to consider just one specific instance $\boldsymbol{x}$ and examine the sources of error in predicting the regression output for $\boldsymbol{x}$.

An important note about these assumptions: since the underlying function F, the regression learning process, and $\boldsymbol{x}$ are deterministic, the randomness comes solely from the training set D. For example, $F(\boldsymbol{x})$ is deterministic, but $f(\boldsymbol{x}; D)$ is a random variable since it depends on D. For notational simplicity, we will simplify $\mathbb{E}_D[f(\boldsymbol{x}; D)]$ as $\mathbb{E}[f(\boldsymbol{x})]$, but it is essential to remember that the expectation is with respect to the distribution of D, and $f(\boldsymbol{x})$ means $f(\boldsymbol{x}; D)$.

Now we have all the tools to study $\mathbb{E}[(y - f(\boldsymbol{x}))^2]$, the generalization error in the squared error sense. Because we consider only one fixed example $\boldsymbol{x}$, we will write $F(\boldsymbol{x})$ as F and $f(\boldsymbol{x})$ as f. Note that F is deterministic (hence $\mathbb{E}[F] = F$), and $\mathbb{E}[f]$ means $\mathbb{E}_D[f(\boldsymbol{x}; D)]$ (which is also a fixed value).

The error is then

$$\mathbb{E}[(y - f)^2] = \mathbb{E}[(F - f + \epsilon)^2].$$

Because the noise ϵ is independent of all other random variables, we have

$$\begin{aligned} \mathbb{E}[(y - f)^2] &= \mathbb{E}[(F - f + \epsilon)^2] && (4.24) \\ &= \mathbb{E}\big[(F - f)^2 + \epsilon^2 + 2(F - f)\epsilon\big] && (4.25) \\ &= \mathbb{E}[(F - f)^2] + \sigma^2. && (4.26) \end{aligned}$$

Note that

$$\mathbb{E}[\epsilon^2] = (\mathbb{E}[\epsilon])^2 + \mathrm{Var}(\epsilon) = \sigma^2,$$

and

$$\mathbb{E}[(F - f)\epsilon] = \mathbb{E}[F - f]\mathbb{E}[\epsilon] = 0$$

because of the independence.

We can further expand $\mathbb{E}[(F - f)^2]$ as

$$\mathbb{E}[(F - f)^2] = (\mathbb{E}[F - f])^2 + \mathrm{Var}(F - f). \quad (4.27)$$

For the first term on the right-hand side of Eq. (4.27), because $\mathbb{E}[F - f] = F - \mathbb{E}[f]$, we have

$$(\mathbb{E}[F - f])^2 = (F - \mathbb{E}[f])^2.$$

For the second term, because F is deterministic, we have

$$\mathrm{Var}(F - f) = \mathrm{Var}(-f) = \mathrm{Var}(f) = \mathbb{E}\left[(f - \mathbb{E}[f])^2\right],$$

i.e., it equals the variance of $f(\boldsymbol{x}; D)$.

Putting all these results together we have

$$\mathbb{E}[(y - f)^2] = (F - \mathbb{E}[f])^2 + \mathbb{E}\left[(f - \mathbb{E}[f])^2\right] + \sigma^2, \tag{4.28}$$

which is the bias–variance decomposition for regression. This decomposition states that the generalization error for any example $\boldsymbol{x}$ comes from three parts: the squared *bias*, the *variance*, and the noise.

- $F - \mathbb{E}[f]$ is called the bias and has exact notation

$$F(\boldsymbol{x}) - \mathbb{E}_D[f(\boldsymbol{x}; D)]. \tag{4.29}$$

  Because an expectation is taken on $f(\boldsymbol{x}; D)$, the bias is not dependent on a training set. Hence, it is determined by the regression model—e.g., are you using a degree 2 or degree 15 polynomial? After we fix the form of our regression model, the bias is fixed too.
- $\mathbb{E}\left[(f - \mathbb{E}[f])^2\right]$ is the variance of the regression *with respect to the variation in the training set*. The exact notation for the variance is

$$\mathbb{E}_D\left[\,(f(\boldsymbol{x}; D) - \mathbb{E}_D[f(\boldsymbol{x}; D)])^2\,\right]. \tag{4.30}$$

- σ^2 is the variance of the noise, which is irreducible (cf. the Bayes error rate in the classification). Even if we know the underlying function $F(\boldsymbol{x})$ exactly and set $f = F$, the generalization error is still $\sigma^2 > 0$.
- This decomposition can be applied to any $\boldsymbol{x}$. Although we omitted $\boldsymbol{x}$ from the notation in Eq. (4.28), the bias and variance will have different values when $\boldsymbol{x}$ changes.

For the regression task in Eq. (4.4), we can compute the bias and variance for any x, and the results are shown in Figure 4.5. Three regression models are considered: degree 1, 2, and 15 polynomials. In Figure 4.5, F is shown as the blue curve, $\mathbb{E}[f]$ is the black curve, and the two purple curves are above and below $\mathbb{E}[f]$ by one standard deviation of f, respectively. Hence, the difference between the black and blue curves equals the bias, and the squared difference between the black and purple curves equals the variance at every x-coordinate. In order to compute $\mathbb{E}[f]$ and $\mathrm{Var}(f)$, we i.i.d. sampled 100 training sets with the same size.

When the model has enough capacity (e.g., degree 2 or 15 polynomials), the bias can be very small. The black and blue curves in Figures 4.5b and 4.5c are almost

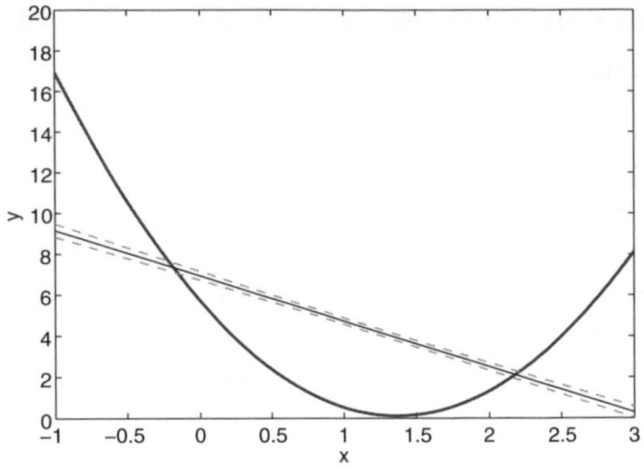

(a) Degree 1 polynomial

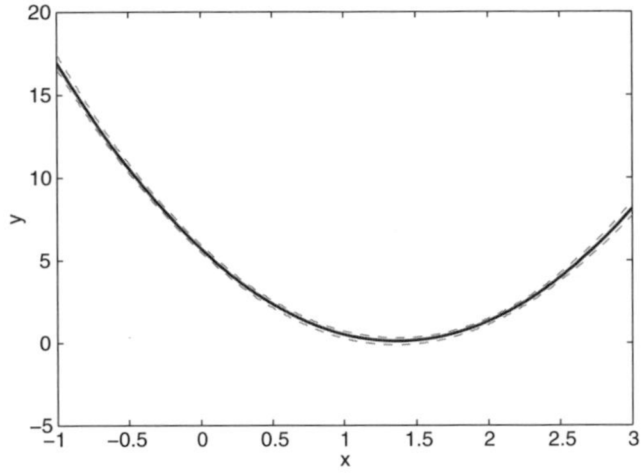

(b) Degree 2 polynomial

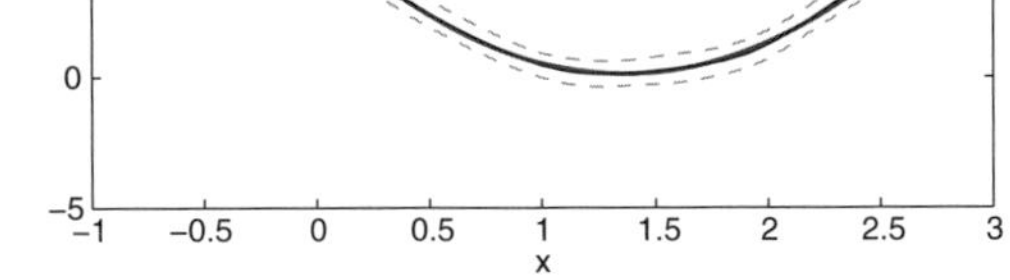

(c) Degree 15 polynomial

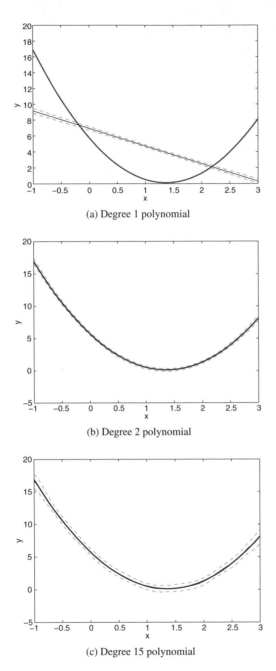

Figure 4.5 Illustration of bias and variance in a simple polynomial regression task. The blue curve is the groundtruth, the black curve is the mean of 100 regression models learned from different training sets, and the two purple curves are the mean plus/minus one standard deviation of the regression models. (A black and white version of this figure will appear in some formats. For the color version, please refer to the plate section.)

identical. However, the linear (degree 1 polynomial) model is too simple for this task, and its bias is huge: the distance between the black and blue curves is very large at most points.

Also note that the bias and variance are not constant when x changes. In Figure 4.5a the bias term changes quickly when x changes, while in Figure 4.5c the variance is largest when x is close to both ends of the exhibited x range.

However, we do not want the model to be too complex. Although Figures 4.5c and 4.5b both exhibit small distances between the black and blue curves (biases), the degree 15 polynomial model in Figure 4.5c shows quite large variances. That is, a slight change in the training set can lead to large variations in the learned regression results. We call this type of model *unstable*. In short, we want a learning model that has enough capacity (to have small bias) and is stable (to have small variance).

These requirements are contradictory to each other in most cases. For example, the linear model (cf. Figure 4.5a) is stable but its capacity is low. Adding regularization to complex models is one viable approach. Averaging many models (i.e., model ensemble) is also widely used.

4.5 Confidence in the Evaluation Results

At the end of this chapter, we briefly discuss the following question: After you have obtained an estimate of your classifier's error rate, how confident are you about this estimation?

One factor that affects the confidence is the size of your test or validation set. In some tasks such as the ImageNet image classification challenge, the test or validation set size is large (50 000 images in its validation set).[2] Researchers use the test or validation error rate with high confidence.

In some other problems with moderate numbers of examples, we can randomly divide all available examples into a training set and a test set. This split will be repeated k times (with $k = 10$ being a typical value), and the error rates evaluated in all k splits are averaged. The sample standard deviations (standard deviations computed from the k error rates) are almost always reported along with the average error rates.

When there are even fewer (e.g., a few hundred) examples, within each of the k splits, cross-validation is used to calculate the cross-validation error rate in each split. The average and sample standard deviation of the k splits are reported.

4.5.1 Why Averaging?

As shown by the bias–variance decomposition, the bias will not change after the classifier has been fixed. Hence, the error rate's variations are caused by different training and test sets. By reducing this variation we have more confidence in the error rate estimate.

[2] `www.image-net.org/`

Let E be a random variable corresponding to the error rate. Let $E_1, E_2, \ldots, E_k$ be k samples of E, computed from i.i.d. sampled training and test sets (with the same training and test set size). The error rate is often modeled as a normal distribution—i.e., $E \sim N(\mu, \sigma^2)$. It is easy to verify that the average

$$\bar{E} = \frac{1}{k}\sum_{j=1}^{k} E_j \sim N\left(\mu, \frac{\sigma^2}{k}\right), \tag{4.31}$$

that is, the average of multiple *independent* error rates, will reduce the variance by a factor of k. This fact means that averaging can reduce the variance of the error rate estimates.

However, if we split a set of examples k times, the k training and k test sets cannot be independent because they are split from the same set of examples. Hence, we expect the average $\bar{E}$ to have a smaller variance than E, but not as small as $\frac{\sigma^2}{k}$. The smaller variance is still useful in providing a better estimate than using a single train/test split.

4.5.2 Why Report the Sample Standard Deviation?

If we know both $\bar{E}$ and σ (the population/true standard deviation, not the sample standard deviation), we can deduce how confident we are about $\bar{E}$.

Because $\bar{E} \sim N\left(\mu, \frac{\sigma^2}{k}\right)$, we have

$$\frac{\bar{E} - \mu}{\sigma/\sqrt{k}} \sim N(0,1).$$

In Figure 4.6 we show the p.d.f. of the standard normal $N(0,1)$. The area of the green region is the probability $\Pr(|X| \leq 1)$ if $X \sim N(0,1)$, which is 0.6827; the area of the green plus the two blue regions is the probability $\Pr(|X| \leq 2)$ if $X \sim N(0,1)$, which is 0.9545.

Because $\frac{\bar{E}-\mu}{\sigma/\sqrt{k}} \sim N(0,1)$, we have $\Pr\left(\left|\frac{\bar{E}-\mu}{\sigma/\sqrt{k}}\right| \leq 2\right) = 0.9545$, or

$$\Pr\left(\bar{E} - \frac{2\sigma}{\sqrt{k}} \leq \mu \leq \bar{E} + \frac{2\sigma}{\sqrt{k}}\right) > 0.95. \tag{4.32}$$

That is, although we do *not* know the generalization error μ, a pretty confident (95%) estimate can be provided by $\bar{E}$ and σ. We know it is very likely (95% confident) that μ will be in the interval

$$\left[\bar{E} - \frac{2\sigma}{\sqrt{k}}, \bar{E} + \frac{2\sigma}{\sqrt{k}}\right].$$

A smaller variance σ^2 means the confidence interval is smaller. Hence, it is useful to report the variance (or standard deviation).

However, two caveats exist about this interpretation. First, we do not know the true population standard deviation σ, which will be replaced by the sample standard deviation computed from the k splits. Hence, Eq. (4.32) will not be correct anymore.

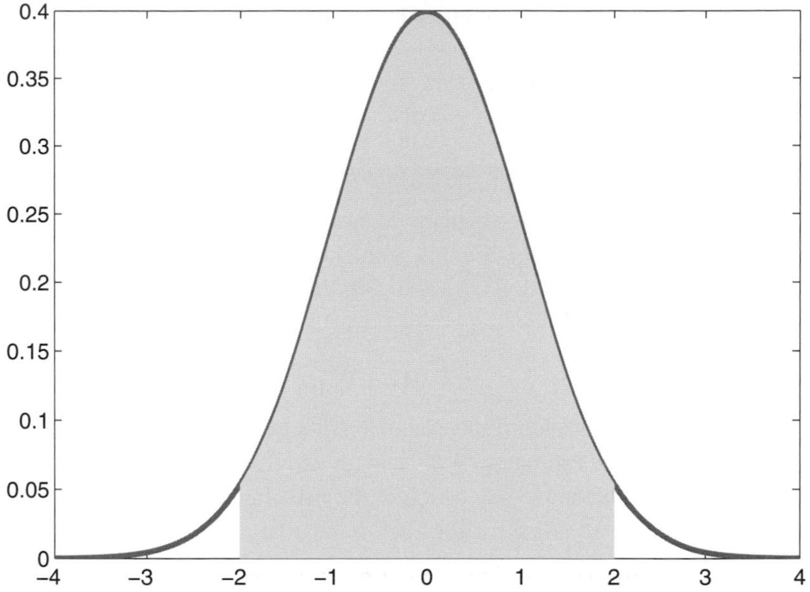

Figure 4.6 The standard normal probability density function and the one- and two-sigma ranges. The one-sigma range has an area of 0.6827, and the two-sigma range has an area of 0.9545. (A black and white version of this figure will appear in some formats. For the color version, please refer to the plate section.)

Fortunately, the distribution after using the sample standard deviation has a closed form: Student's t-distribution. We will discuss the t-distribution further soon.

Second, $\bar{E}$ is a random variable in Eq. (4.32). In practice, we need to replace it with the sample mean $\bar{e}$ computed from the k splits in one experiment. However, the interval

$$\left[\bar{e} - \frac{2\sigma}{\sqrt{k}}, \bar{e} + \frac{2\sigma}{\sqrt{k}}\right]$$

is deterministic, hence does *not* have a probability associated with it. Now, a 95% confidence means the following:

In one experiment, we will split the data k times, computing one $\bar{e}$ and one confidence interval accordingly. We will obtain 100 *values of $\bar{e}$ and* 100 *confidence intervals in* 100 *experiments. Then, among the* 100 *experiments, around* 95 *times μ will fall into the respective intervals, but around* 5 *times it may not.*

4.5.3 Comparing Two Classifiers

We have two classifiers f_1 and f_2, and we want to evaluate which is better for a problem based on a set of examples D. We may evaluate f_1 and f_2, and estimate the error rate for f_1 as 0.08 ± 0.002 (meaning that the sample mean and standard deviation for the error of f_1 are 0.08 and 0.002, respectively). Similarly, the evaluation result for f_2 is 0.06 ± 0.003. Now because

$$\frac{0.08 - 0.06}{0.002 + 0.003} = 4, \tag{4.33}$$

we know that the distance between the two sample means is very large compared to the sum of the two sample standard deviations.[3] We are confident enough ($> 99\%$) to say that f_2 is better than f_1 on this problem.

However, if f_1 is 0.08 ± 0.01 and f_2 is evaluated as 0.06 ± 0.012, we have

$$\frac{0.08 - 0.06}{0.012 + 0.01} = 0.91,$$

that is, the one-standard-deviation confidence intervals (whose confidence is < 0.6827) of the estimates of f_1 and f_2 overlap with each other. Hence, there is not enough confidence to say which of the two classifiers is better.

Student's t-test[4] is useful for such comparisons. A full description of the t-test involves many different cases and details. In this chapter, we only introduce an application of the paired t-test, which can be used to compare two classifiers on a wide range of problems.

Suppose we evaluate f_1 and f_2 on n datasets, yielding errors E_{ij} where $i \in \{1,2\}$ is the classifier index and j ($1 \le j \le n$) is the index to the datasets. Individually, E_{1j} and E_{2j} may not be confidently compared for most of the j values/datasets. However, this is a *paired* comparison because for any j, the same dataset is used by f_1 and f_2. Hence, we can study the properties of $E_{1j} - E_{2j}$ for all $1 \le j \le n$. Furthermore, we assume the datasets are not dependent on each other, thus different j values lead to *independent* $E_{1j} - E_{2j}$ random variables. Because the sum of two normally distributed variables has once again a normal distribution, we also assume $E_{1j} - E_{2j}$ is *normally distributed.*

For notational simplicity, we denote

$$X_j = E_{1j} - E_{2j}, \quad 1 \le j \le n.$$

Under the above assumptions, we know that X_j are i.i.d. samples from

$$X \sim N(\mu, \sigma^2),$$

but the parameters μ and σ are unknown. The average

$$\bar{X} = \frac{1}{n} \sum_{j=1}^{n} X_j \sim N\left(\mu, \frac{\sigma^2}{n}\right).$$

[3] The rationale behind Eq. (4.33) will be made clear in Chapter 6.

[4] William Sealy Gosset designed this test's statistics, and published his results under the pen name "Student."

Hence,

$$\frac{\bar{X}-\mu}{\sigma/\sqrt{n}} \sim N(0,1).$$

Note that a particular parameter value $\mu = 0$ is of special interest to us. When $\mu = 0$, we have $\mathbb{E}[\bar{X}] = \mathbb{E}[X_j] = \mathbb{E}[E_{1j} - E_{2j}] = 0$, that is, on average f_1 and f_2 have the same error rate. When $\mu > 0$ the error of f_1 is higher than that of f_2, and smaller than that of f_2 if $\mu < 0$.

The t-test answers the following question: Do f_1 and f_2 have different error rates? The *null hypothesis* is that $\mu = 0$, meaning that there is no significant difference between f_1 and f_2. If f_1 is a new algorithm proposed by you and f_2 is a method in the literature, you may want the null hypothesis to be *rejected* (i.e., with enough evidence to believe it is not true) because you hope your new algorithm is better.

How can we confidently reject the null hypothesis? We can define a *test statistic* T, whose distribution can be derived *by assuming the null hypothesis is true* (i.e., when $\mu = 0$). For example, assuming $\mu = 0$, σ is known, and $T = \frac{\bar{X}}{\sigma/\sqrt{n}}$, we know that the distribution of T is the standard normal $N(0,1)$.

In the next step, you can compute the value of the statistic T based on your data, denoted as t, and say $t = 3.1$. Because T is a standard normal, we have $\Pr(|T| > 3) = 0.0027$, or 0.27%: it is a *small probability event* to observe $t = 3.1$ in one experiment—either something must have gone wrong or you are extremely unlucky.

The only thing that can be wrong is the assumption that "the null hypothesis is true." Hence, when we observe unusual or extreme values for t, we have confidence to reject the null hypothesis.

Precisely speaking, we can specify a *significance level* α, which is a small number between 0 and 1. When assuming that the null hypothesis is true, but the probability of observing an extreme value $T = t$ is smaller than α—i.e.,

$$\Pr(|T| > t) < \alpha,$$

we conclude that we are rejecting the null hypothesis at confidence level α.

In practice, σ is unknown. Let e_{ij} and x_j be samples for E_{ij} and X_j in one experiment, respectively. We can compute the sample mean and sample standard deviation for X as

$$\bar{x} = \frac{1}{n}\sum_{j=1}^{n} x_j, \tag{4.34}$$

$$s = \sqrt{\frac{1}{n-1}\sum_{j=1}^{n}(x_j - \bar{x})^2}, \tag{4.35}$$

which correspond to random variables $\bar{X}$ and S, respectively. Note that $\frac{1}{n-1}$ is used instead of $\frac{1}{n}$.

The new paired t-test statistic is

$$T = \frac{\bar{X}}{S/\sqrt{n}}, \tag{4.36}$$

which replaces σ with S. Consequently, T is no longer the standard normal distribution. Fortunately, we know that T follows Student's t-distribution with number of degrees of freedom $\nu = n - 1$. Note that the number of degrees of freedom is *not* n.

A t-distribution has one integer parameter: the number of degrees of freedom ν. Its p.d.f. is

$$p(t) = \frac{\Gamma(\frac{\nu+1}{2})}{\sqrt{\nu\pi}\Gamma(\frac{\nu}{2})}\left(1 + \frac{t^2}{\nu}\right)^{-\frac{\nu+1}{2}}, \tag{4.37}$$

in which Γ is the gamma function defined as

$$\Gamma(t) = \int_0^\infty x^{t-1} e^{-x}\, dx.$$

As shown in Figure 4.7, the t-distribution is symmetric about 0 and looks like the standard normal distribution. However, the t-distribution has more density at its tails than the standard normal distribution. As the number of degrees of freedom ν grows, the t-distribution gets closer to $N(0, 1)$. When $\nu \to \infty$, the t-distribution converges to the standard normal distribution.

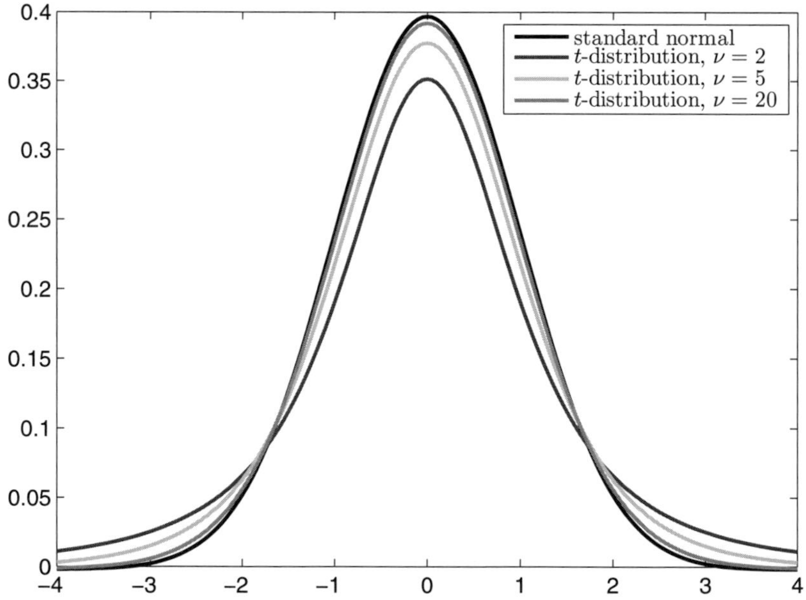

Figure 4.7 Probability density function of Student's t-distribution with different degrees of freedom. (A black and white version of this figure will appear in some formats. For the color version, please refer to the plate section.)

Often the number of degrees of freedom is small. For one fixed value of ν and a given significance level α, a critical value $c_{\nu,\alpha/2} > 0$ can be found in statistical tables, satisfying

$$\Pr(|T| > c_{\nu,\alpha/2}) = \alpha.$$

Because the t-distribution is symmetric and the region of extremal values can be at either side with equal probability, $\alpha/2$ is used in finding the critical value.

Hence, for one experiment, we can compute the sample statistic

$$t = \frac{\bar{x}}{s/\sqrt{n}},$$

and reject the null hypothesis if

$$|t| > c_{\nu,\alpha/2}.$$

The paired t-test for comparing two classifiers is summarized in Algorithm 3.

Algorithm 3 The paired t-test for comparing two classifiers

Input: Two classifiers f_1 and f_2, whose error rate estimates on n datasets are e_{ij} $(i \in \{1,2\};\ 1 \le j \le n)$.
Choose a significance level α (widely used values are 0.05 and 0.01).
Find the critical value $c_{n-1,\alpha/2}$.
$x_j \leftarrow e_{1j} - e_{2j}$, for $1 \le j \le n$.
$\bar{x} \leftarrow \frac{1}{n}\sum_{j=1}^{n} x_j$, $s \leftarrow \sqrt{\frac{1}{n-1}\sum_{j=1}^{n}(x_j - \bar{x})^2}$.
$t \leftarrow \frac{\bar{x}}{s/\sqrt{n}}$.
if $|t| > c_{n-1,\alpha/2}$ **then**
    We believe that f_1 and f_2 have different error rates. (The null hypothesis is rejected at confidence level α.)
else
    We do not believe there is significant difference between the error rates of f_1 and f_2.
end if

Note that the paired t-test requires that

- the errors e_{ij} are paired;
- the errors are independent for different j; and
- the difference x_j is normally distributed.

Although slight or moderate violation of the third assumption is usually acceptable, the first two (paired and independent) assumptions cannot be violated.

Algorithm 3 specifies a *two-tailed* test, which cares only about whether f_1 and f_2 have the same/similar error rates or not. In many scenarios we need a *one-tailed* version of the test—for example, if you want to show that your new algorithm f_1 is better than f_2.

In the one-tailed test, if you want to show that the error rate of f_1 is smaller than that of f_2, you need to change the critical value to $c_{n-1,\alpha}$ and further require $t < -c_{n-1,\alpha}$. If you want to show that f_2 is better than f_1, you need to have $t > c_{n-1,\alpha}$.

If statistical tables are not handy but you have a computer at your disposal (which happens to have a suitable software package installed on it), you can compute the critical value by one line of code in your favorite software. For example, let us compute the two-tailed critical value for the paired t-test, with $\nu = 6$ and $\alpha = 0.05$.

Because the t-distribution is symmetric, we have

$$\Pr(T > c_{\nu,\alpha/2}) = \alpha/2.$$

Let Φ denote the c.d.f. of a t-distribution with ν degrees of freedom; we have

$$\Phi(c_{\nu,\alpha/2}) = 1 - \alpha/2.$$

Hence,

$$c_{\nu,\alpha/2} = \Phi^{-1}(1 - \alpha/2),$$

in which $\Phi^{-1}(\cdot)$ is the inverse c.d.f. function.

The MATLAB/GNU Octave function `tinv(p,ν)` calculates the inverse c.d.f. value for probability `p` and degrees of freedom ν. One single MATLAB/GNU Octave command

```
tinv(1-0.05/2,6)
```

tells us that the critical value for a two-tailed, six degrees of freedom, significance level 0.05, paired t-test is 2.4469. Similarly, for the one-tailed test, we have the critical value computed as

```
tinv(1-0.05,6),
```

which is 1.9432.

The t-test is a relatively simple statistical test that can be adopted to compare classification methods (or other learning algorithms/systems). Many other tests (e.g., various rank tests) are useful in this respect too. We hope that its introduction in this chapter will help readers in understanding other statistical tests, but will not go into details of these tests.

One final note: whenever you want to apply a statistical test to your data, the first thing to check is whether your data satisfy the assumptions of that particular test!

4.6 Miscellaneous Notes and Additional Resources

A good pointer to various resources related to imbalanced learning is He & Garcia (2009), and an interesting paper about cost-sensitive learning, Elkan (2001), is a good starting point for studying this topic.

In Exercise 4.5 we provide a concrete example to explain the details of how AUC-PR and average precision (AP) are computed. For more information about various evaluation metrics, please refer to Manning & Schütze (1999). The harmonic mean will be further discussed in Chapter 9.

For various definitions and studies on the bias–variance decomposition for classifiers, please refer to Geman et al. (1992), Kohavi & Wolpert (1996), Breiman (1996b), and Domingos (2000).

Various aspects of ensemble learning can be found in Zhou (2012).

For more details of various statistical tests, tables, and distributions (including the t-distribution), please refer to DeGroot & Schervish (2011).

For applying appropriate statistical tests to compare classifiers, please refer to Dietterich (1998) and Demšar (2006).

Exercises

4.1 In a binary classification problem, we know $P = N = 100$ (i.e., there are 100 positive and 100 negative examples in the test set). If FPR $= 0.3$ and TPR $= 0.2$, then what are the precision, recall, and F_1 score? What are its accuracy and error rate?

4.2 (Linear regression) Consider a set of n examples $(\boldsymbol{x}_i, y_i)$ $(1 \le i \le n)$ where $\boldsymbol{x}_i \in \mathbb{R}^d$ and $y_i \in \mathbb{R}$. A *linear regression* model assumes

$$y = \boldsymbol{x}^T \boldsymbol{\beta} + \epsilon$$

for any example $(\boldsymbol{x}, y)$, where ϵ is a random variable modeling the regression error and $\boldsymbol{\beta} \in \mathbb{R}^d$ are the parameters of this model. For the ith example, we have $\epsilon_i = y_i - \boldsymbol{x}_i^T \boldsymbol{\beta}$.

(a) Express the linear regression task as an optimization problem over the training set, using the training examples, the parameters $\boldsymbol{\beta}$, and the squared error ($\sum_{i=1}^n \epsilon_i^2$, which is the MSE times the number of examples).

(b) We can organize the training examples $\boldsymbol{x}_i$ into an $n \times d$ matrix X, whose ith row is the vector $\boldsymbol{x}_i^T$. Similarly, we can organize y_i into a vector $\boldsymbol{y} \in \mathbb{R}^n$, with y_i in the ith row. Rewrite the optimization problem in (a) using X and $\boldsymbol{y}$.

(c) Find the optimal values for $\boldsymbol{\beta}$. For now, assume that $X^T X$ is invertible. This solution is called the *ordinary linear regression* solution.

(d) When there are more dimensions than examples—i.e., when $d > n$—will $X^T X$ be invertible?

(e) If we add a regularizer

$$\mathcal{R}(\boldsymbol{\beta}) = \boldsymbol{\beta}^T \boldsymbol{\beta}$$

with a trade-off parameter λ ($\lambda > 0$) to a linear regression, what effect will that regularizer have? Linear regression with this regularizer is called the *ridge regression*, and this regularizer is a special case of the *Tikhonov regularization*.

(f) Express the optimization problem in ridge regression using X, $\boldsymbol{y}$, $\boldsymbol{\beta}$, and λ. Find the solution.

(g) Ordinary linear regression will encounter difficulties when $X^T X$ is not invertible. How will ridge regression help in this aspect?

(h) What will the ridge regression solution be if $\lambda = 0$? What if $\lambda = \infty$?

(i) Can we learn a good λ value by treating λ as a regular parameter (instead of a hyperparameter)—that is, by minimizing the ridge regression loss function jointly over λ and $\boldsymbol{\beta}$ on the training set (without using a validation set)?

4.3 (Polynomial regression) The polynomial regression model $y = f(x) + \epsilon$ assumes that the mapping f is a polynomial. A degree d polynomial is of the form

$$f(x) = \sum_{i=0}^{d} p_i x^i, \tag{4.38}$$

with $d + 1$ parameters p_i $(0 \le i \le d)$. Use ordinary linear regression to find the optimal parameters for polynomial regression. (Hint: Set the parameters of the linear regression to $\boldsymbol{\beta} = (p_0, p_1, \ldots, p_d)^T$.)

4.4 (F_β measure) Answer the following two questions about the F_β measure:

(a) Prove that $0 \le \mathrm{F}_\beta \le 1$ for any $\beta \ge 0$.

(b) When β takes different values, the F_β measure places different relative importance on the precision and recall. Which one (precision or recall) is more important if $\beta > 1$? Which one is more important if $0 \le \beta < 1$? (Hint: What is the speed of change of F_β when the precision or recall changes?)

4.5 (AUC-PR and AP) We have not discussed the details of how the AUC-PR measurement is calculated. For a binary classification task, we assume that every example $\boldsymbol{x}$ has a score $f(\boldsymbol{x})$, and sort the test examples into descending order of these scores. Then, for every example, we set the classification threshold as the current example's score (i.e., only this example and the examples before it are classified as positive). A pair of precision and recall values are computed at this threshold. The PR curve is drawn by connecting nearby points using line segments. Then AUC-PR is the area under the PR curve.

Let (r_i, p_i) denote the ith recall and precision rates ($i = 1, 2, \ldots$). When computing the area, the contribution between r_i and r_{i-1} is calculated using the *trapezoidal* interpolation $(r_i - r_{i-1})\frac{p_i + p_{i-1}}{2}$, in which $r_i - r_{i-1}$ is the length on the x-axis, and p_i and p_{i-1} are the lengths of two vertical lines on the y-axis. Summing over all i values, we obtain the AUC-PR score. Note that we assume the first pair $(r_0, p_0) = (0, 1)$, which is a pseudopair corresponding to the threshold $+\infty$.

(a) For the test set with 10 examples (indexed from 1 to 10) in Table 4.3, calculate the precision (p_i) and recall (r_i) when the threshold is set as the current example's $f(x_i)$ value. Use class 1 as positive, and fill in these values in Table 4.3. Put the trapezoidal approximation $(r_i - r_{i-1})\frac{p_i + p_{i-1}}{2}$ in the "AUC-PR" column for the ith row, and fill in their sum in the final row.

(b) *Average precision* (AP) is another way to summarize the PR curve into one number. Similar to AUC-PR, AP approximates the contribution between r_i and r_{i-1} using a rectangle, as $(r_i - r_{i-1})p_i$. Fill in this approximation in the "AP" column for the ith row, and put their sum in the final row. Both AUC-PR and AP summarize the PR curve, hence they should be similar to each other. Are they?

Table 4.3 Calculation of AUC-PR and AP.

Index	Label	Score	Precision	Recall	AUC-PR	AP
0			1.0000	0.0000	—	—
1	1	1.0				
2	2	0.9				
3	1	0.8				
4	1	0.7				
5	2	0.6				
6	1	0.5				
7	2	0.4				
8	2	0.3				
9	1	0.2				
10	2	0.1				
					(?)	(?)

(c) Both AUC-PR and AP are sensitive to the order of labels. If the labels of the ninth and the tenth rows are exchanged, what are the new AUC-PR and AP?

(d) Write a program to calculate both AUC-PR and AP based on the labels, scores, and the positive class. Validate your program's correctness using the example test set in Table 4.3.

4.6 We can use the k-NN method for regression. Let $D = \{\boldsymbol{x}_i, y_i\}_{i=1}^n$ be a training set, where the labels $y \in \mathbb{R}$ are generated by $y = F(\boldsymbol{x}) + \epsilon$, in which the true regression function F is contaminated by noise ϵ to generate the labels y. We assume that the random noise ϵ is independent of anything else, $\mathbb{E}[\epsilon] = 0$, and $\mathrm{Var}(\epsilon) = \sigma^2$.

For any test example $\boldsymbol{x}$, the k-NN method finds its k (k is a positive integer) nearest neighbors in D, denoted by $\boldsymbol{x}_{\mathrm{nn}(1)}, \boldsymbol{x}_{\mathrm{nn}(2)}, \ldots, \boldsymbol{x}_{\mathrm{nn}(k)}$, where $1 \le \mathrm{nn}(i) \le n$ is the index of the ith nearest neighbor. Then the prediction for $\boldsymbol{x}$ is

$$f(\boldsymbol{x}; D) = \frac{1}{k} \sum_{i=1}^{k} y_{\mathrm{nn}(i)}.$$

(a) What is the bias–variance decomposition for $\mathbb{E}[(y - f(\boldsymbol{x}; D))^2]$, in which y is the label for $\boldsymbol{x}$? Do not use abbreviations (Eq. (4.28) uses abbreviations, e.g., $\mathbb{E}[f]$ should be $\mathbb{E}_D[f(\boldsymbol{x}; D)]$.) Use $\boldsymbol{x}$, y, F, f, D, and σ to express the decomposition.

(b) Use $f(\boldsymbol{x}; D) = \frac{1}{k} \sum_{i=1}^{k} y_{\mathrm{nn}(i)}$ to compute $\mathbb{E}[f]$ (abbreviations can be used from here on).

(c) Replace the f term in the decomposition by using $\boldsymbol{x}$ and y.

(d) What is the variance term? How will it change when k changes?

(e) What is the squared bias term? How will it change with k? (Hint: Consider $k = n$.)

4.7 (Bayes decision theory) Consider a binary classification task, in which the label $y \in \{1, 2\}$. If an example $x \in \mathbb{R}$ belongs to class 1, it is generated by the class conditional p.d.f. $p(x|y = 1) = N(-1, 0.25)$, and a class 2 example is sampled from the class conditional distribution $p(x|y = 2) = N(1,0.25)$. Suppose $\Pr(y = 1) = \Pr(y = 2) = 0.5$.

(a) What is the p.d.f. $p(x)$?

(b) Let us use the cost matrix $\left[\begin{smallmatrix} 0 & 1 \\ 1 & 0 \end{smallmatrix}\right]$. Show that for any x, if we choose $f(x) = \arg\max_y p(y|x)$ to be our prediction for x, the cost $\mathbb{E}_{(x,y)}[c_{y,f(x)}]$ is minimized, and hence it is the optimal solution. Is this rule optimal if $y \in \{1,2,\ldots,C\}$ $(C > 2)$ (i.e., in a multiclass classification problem)?

(c) Using the cost matrix $\left[\begin{smallmatrix} 0 & 1 \\ 1 & 0 \end{smallmatrix}\right]$ and Bayes decision theory, which classification strategy will be optimal for this task? What is the Bayes risk in this example?

(d) If the cost matrix is $\left[\begin{smallmatrix} 0 & 10 \\ 1 & 0 \end{smallmatrix}\right]$ (i.e., when the true label is 1 but the prediction is 2, the cost is increased to 10), what is the new decision rule?

4.8 (Stratified sampling) Let D be a training set with only 10 examples, whose labels are 1, 1, 2, 2, 2, 2, 2, 2, 2, 2, respectively. This dataset is both small in size and imbalanced. We need cross-validation during evaluation, and 2-fold CV seems a good choice.

(a) Write a program to *randomly* split this dataset into two subsets, with five examples in each subset. Repeat this random split 10 times. The histogram of class 1 examples in these two subsets can be $(0,2)$ or $(1,1)$—one subset has zero (two) and the other has two (zero) class 1 examples, or every subset has exactly one class 1 example. In your 10 splits, how many times does $(0,2)$ appear? (Note: This number can be different if you perform the experiments multiple times.)

(b) What is the probability that $(0,2)$ will appear in one random split of these 10 examples?

(c) In your 2-fold CV evaluation, if the split's class 1 distribution in the two subsets is $(0,2)$, how will it affect the evaluation?

(d) One commonly used way to avoid this issue to use *stratified sampling*. In stratified sampling, we perform the train/test split for *every* class separately. Show that if stratified sampling is used, the distribution of class 1 examples will always be $(1,1)$.

4.9 (Confusion matrix) In a classification problem with K classes, the cost matrix is $K \times K$ matrix $C = [c_{ij}]$ in which c_{ij} is the cost when one example belongs to class i but is predicted to be in class j. Similarly, a confusion matrix is a $K \times K$ matrix $A = [a_{ij}]$, in which a_{ij} is the number of class i examples that are classified as belonging to class j.

Let the confusion matrix be computed based on a test set with N examples. We often normalize the confusion matrix to obtain $\hat{A}$, by $\hat{a}_{ij} = a_{ij} / \sum_{k=1}^{K} a_{ik}$. Hence, the sum of all elements in any row of $\hat{A}$ equals 1. We call $\hat{A}$ the normalized confusion matrix.

(a) Prove that the total cost for the test set equals $\operatorname{tr}(C^T A)$.

(b) In an imbalanced classification problem, do you prefer the confusion matrix or the normalized one? Why?

4.10 (McNemar's test) Find resources about McNemar's test.[5] *Carefully* read through these resources until you believe you have understood when this test can be applied and how to apply it to compare two classifiers.

[5] For example, in your school's library or search on the internet.

Part II

Domain-Independent Feature Extraction

5 Principal Component Analysis

In this chapter, we will introduce the principal component analysis (PCA) technique. The key focus of this chapter is comprehensibility. We focus on the motivation and ideas behind PCA, rather than the mathematical details. However, we will maintain correctness of the equations. The goal is that an average non-math-major student with undergraduate mathematical background in linear algebra and some basic probability will read through this chapter without any difficulty. And we will start from the motivation.

5.1 Motivation

PCA is a linear feature extraction method, and at the same time a linear *dimensionality reduction* technique too. Hence, let us start from an examination of various aspects of the dimensionality of our data.

5.1.1 Dimensionality and Inherent Dimensionality

Let us consider some data that are two-dimensional, and we will use (x, y) to denote one such data point. Hence, the (natural) dimensionality of our data is 2. In different scenarios, we will also encounter data that exhibit different properties, which we illustrate in Figure 5.1. We discuss these examples one by one.

- The dataset has two degrees of freedom. As illustrated by those points in Figure 5.1a, we need exactly two values (x, y) to specify any single data point in this case. Hence, we say that the dataset has an *inherent dimensionality* of 2, which is the same as its natural dimensionality.

  In fact, the data points in this figure are generated in a way that makes y independent of x, as shown in Table 5.1, if we consider x and y as random variables. We cannot find a relationship among the ten two-dimensional data points in this figure.
- The world, however, usually generates data that are not independent. In other words, x and y are dependent in most cases, especially considering those data we need to deal with in machine learning or pattern recognition. In our examples, we expect that x and y are usually correlated with each other. Figure 5.1b exhibits a special

Table 5.1 MATLAB/GNU Octave code to generate the data points in Figure 5.1.

Generating x	`x = 1:10;`
Generating y for Figure 5.1a	`y = rand(1,10) * 30;`
Generating y for Figure 5.1b	`y = 3 * x - 2;`
Generating y for Figure 5.1c	`y = 3 * x - 2; y = y + randn(size(y)) * 2;`
Generating y for Figure 5.1d	`y = 3 * x - 2; y(7) = 5;`

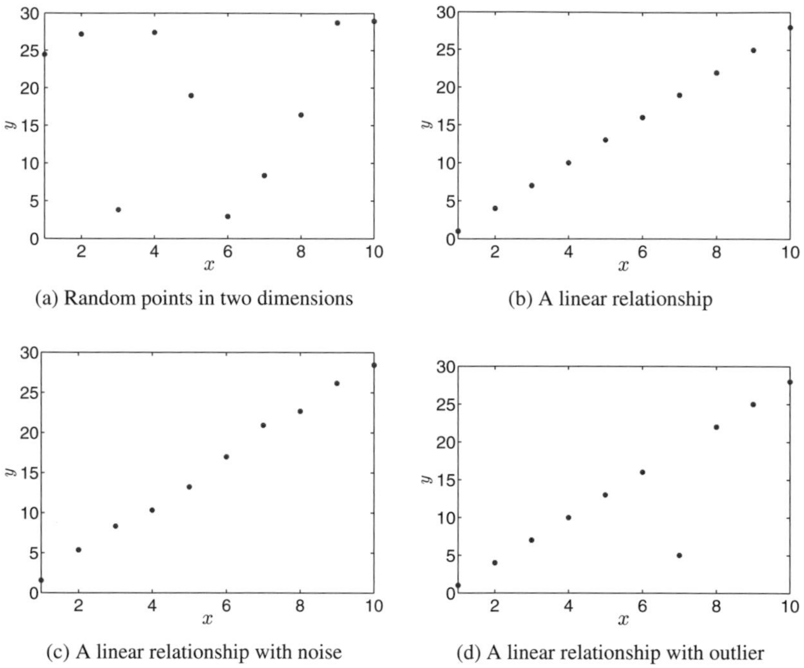

(a) Random points in two dimensions

(b) A linear relationship

(c) A linear relationship with noise

(d) A linear relationship with outlier

Figure 5.1 Illustration of various types of relationships between dimensions.

type of correlation: linear correlation. As shown by the data generation command in Table 5.1, y is a linear function of x.

Hence, in this figure, there is only one degree of freedom—once we know x, we can immediately determine the value of y, and vice versa. We need only one value to *completely* specify a pair (x, y), which could be x, y, or even a *linear combination of* x *and* y. Hence, we say that the inherent dimensionality of the data in this figure is 1, which is obviously smaller than its natural dimensionality. In the figure, the 10 points are aligned on one line, $y = 3x - 2$. In fact, as we will soon see, a linear combination of the original dimensions is the central part of PCA.

- The world, once again, is not as benign as what is shown in Figure 5.1b. In many cases, there exist obvious correlations among dimensions of the original data. However, the correlation is rarely a perfect linear relationship. As shown in Figure 5.1c, many people will agree that x and y are roughly related by a linear relationship (i.e., the 10 points are roughly aligned in a line), but with noticeable deviations.

As shown in Table 5.1, there is indeed the same linear relationship between x and y as the one in Figure 5.1b, but in addition this is affected by Gaussian noise. The noise is usually not welcome and we want to get rid of it. Hence, it is still reasonable to say that the data in Figure 5.1c have an inherent dimensionality of 1, because the number of meaningful degrees of freedom is still 1.

- The world could be even more hostile to us, as shown by the example in Figure 5.1d. If we remove the seventh data point, we get a perfect linear relationship. This point is significantly different than the others, and we call it an *outlier*. It is difficult to say that the dataset in Figure 5.1d has an inherent dimensionality of 1, given the existence of the outlier.

  In other words, outliers seem more difficult to handle than noise. However, if we are able to remove the outlier using some sophisticated techniques, the inherent dimensionality of the remaining points is still 1.

5.1.2 Dimensionality Reduction

In these four examples, we may safely conclude that the inherent dimensionality in both Figures 5.1b and 5.1c is 1. In other words, we require only one variable, z, to represent such data points. Finding a lower-dimensional representation of the original (relatively) higher-dimensional vector is called *dimensionality reduction*. In spite of the fact that fewer dimensions are used, we expect the dimensionality reduction process to keep the useful information in the original data.

The potential benefits of dimensionality reduction can be manyfold, with a few listed below.

- Lower resource requirements. A direct consequence of lower dimensionality is that less memory is needed to store the data, either in the main memory or on disk. An equally obvious benefit is that fewer CPU cycles are required.
- Removal of noise. As shown in Figure 5.1c, we can recover the linear relationship and reduce the dimensionality to 1. However, a benign side effect is that the noise may well be removed from the data in this process, which happens in PCA in many problems. Less noisy data usually leads to higher accuracy.
- Explanation and understanding. If the outcomes of dimensionality reduction happen to coincide well with the underlying hidden factors that generate the original data, the new lower-dimensional representation will be helpful in explaining how the data are generated and in understanding their properties.

  In addition, when we come across a new dataset, we can reduce it to two or three dimensions (by PCA or other methods). A visualization of the dimensionality reduced data will give us some hints on the properties of that dataset.

5.1.3 PCA and Subspace Methods

As far as we know, there is no precise definition for the inherent dimensionality of a dataset or a data generation process/distribution in general. In the above examples, we use the degrees of freedom of the data generation processes to describe their inherent dimensionality. Data generation, however, could be nonlinear, which will be more complex than the linear relationship shown in Figure 5.1. But since PCA considers only linear relationships, we will ignore nonlinear relationships or nonlinear dimensionality reduction methods in this chapter.

Now consider a vector $\boldsymbol{x} \in \mathbb{R}^D$. A linear relationship among its components can be expressed as a simple equation

$$\boldsymbol{x}^T \boldsymbol{w} + b = 0. \tag{5.1}$$

From basic linear algebra, we know that any $\boldsymbol{x}$ that satisfies Eq. (5.1) resides in a subspace of $\mathbb{R}^D$ whose dimensionality is $D-1$. If there are more linear constraints on $\boldsymbol{x}$, then $\boldsymbol{x}$ will reside in a subspace with even lower dimensionality.

Hence, the problem of linear dimensionality reduction can be seen as finding the linear constraints or finding the lower-dimensional subspace of $\mathbb{R}^D$, which are also called subspace methods. Subspace methods differ from each other in how they find the constraints or subspaces. They have different evaluation metrics (e.g., which subspace is considered the best) or assumptions (e.g., whether we know the category label of $\boldsymbol{x}$).

PCA is possibly the simplest subspace method, which we will introduce in the coming sections.

5.2 PCA to Zero-Dimensional Subspace

Let us start from an extreme case. What if the lower-dimensional subspace is only a single point? In other words, what if its dimensionality is 0?

Suppose we are given a set of instantiations of $\boldsymbol{x}$,

$$X = \{\boldsymbol{x}_1, \boldsymbol{x}_2, \ldots, \boldsymbol{x}_N\},$$

which form the training set for us to learn PCA parameters. Note that there is a slight abuse of notation here. The symbol $\boldsymbol{x}$ may refer to a single data point. However, it may also be used to refer to the underlying distribution (or random variable) that generates the training set.

If there is no noise and a zero-dimensional subspace exists to represent this set, the only possibility is that

$$\boldsymbol{x}_1 = \boldsymbol{x}_2 = \cdots = \boldsymbol{x}_N.$$

We can use $\boldsymbol{x}_1$ to represent any example in X without requiring any additional information. Storing $\boldsymbol{x}_1$ requires D dimensions. However, the average number of dimensions needed for every $\boldsymbol{x}_i$ is only $\frac{D}{N}$. Because $\lim_{N\to\infty} \frac{D}{N} = 0$, it is reasonable to say that this is a zero-dimensional representation.

But, if noise exists, there will be $1 \le i < j \le N$ such that $\boldsymbol{x}_i \neq \boldsymbol{x}_j$. How will we find the *best* zero-dimensional representation in the presence of noise? We still need to find a vector $\boldsymbol{m}$ that represents every element in X. The key issue is how we will decide the optimality.

5.2.1 The Idea–Formalization–Optimization Approach

The *idea* can be inspired by the noise-free case. If we assume that the noise scale is small, we want to find an $\boldsymbol{m}$ that is *close to all the elements in* X. This choice has two nice properties. First, it coincides well with our intuition. Second, when the noise scale is 0, "close to" can be changed to "equal to," and it degenerates to the noise-free case.

The next step is to *formalize* this idea. It is natural to translate "close to" as "small distance," and translate "distance to all elements in X is small" to "the sum of distances to all elements in X is small." If the sum is small, of course every individual distance must be small.

Hence, we can write our idea precisely in mathematical language as

$$\boldsymbol{m}^\star = \underset{\boldsymbol{m}}{\arg\min} \frac{1}{N} \sum_{i=1}^{N} \|\boldsymbol{x}_i - \boldsymbol{m}\|^2, \tag{5.2}$$

where the right-hand side is an optimization problem, and $\boldsymbol{m}^\star$ is the parameter that solves the optimization problem (which is the best $\boldsymbol{m}$ we seek).

The final step is how to get $\boldsymbol{m}^\star$, or how to optimize Eq. (5.2).

5.2.2 A Simple Optimization

With some background in vector calculus, it is easy to solve Eq. (5.2). We can denote

$$J = \frac{1}{N} \sum_{i=1}^{N} \|\boldsymbol{x}_i - \boldsymbol{m}\|^2 = \frac{1}{N} \sum_{i=1}^{N} (\boldsymbol{x}_i - \boldsymbol{m})^T (\boldsymbol{x}_i - \boldsymbol{m}), \tag{5.3}$$

and get

$$\frac{\partial J}{\partial \boldsymbol{m}} = \frac{2}{N} \sum_{i=1}^{N} (\boldsymbol{m} - \boldsymbol{x}_i), \tag{5.4}$$

where the partial derivative rules can be found in *The Matrix Cookbook* (Petersen & Pedersen 2012). Setting this term to 0 gives us the following optimality condition:

$$\boldsymbol{m} = \frac{1}{N} \sum_{i=1}^{N} \boldsymbol{x}_i \triangleq \bar{\boldsymbol{x}}. \tag{5.5}$$

That is, the best zero-dimensional representation is the average of all the training examples, which we denote by $\bar{\boldsymbol{x}}$.

5.2.3 A Few Comments

In spite of its simplicity, we have a few comments on the zero-dimensional reduction.

- When we encounter a new problem, the *idea–formalization–optimization* process can be very helpful. We first inspect the problem (maybe with some initial trials or visualization to understand the data property), which gives us some ideas to its solution.

  We then define proper notation and convert our ideas into a precise mathematical form, which often appears in an optimization problem format. The final step is to solve it, either by ourselves or by using the abundant tools that are available.
- It is also worth noting that Eq. (5.2) is in fact slightly different from our idea. First, it is the squared distances that are summed, rather than the distances. Second, the term $\frac{1}{N}$ converts the sum into an average.

  The term $\frac{1}{N}$ will not change the optimization's solution. It is introduced following the tradition in the literature, and sometimes it helps to simplify the optimization or to reduce numerical difficulties. The change from distance to squared distance, as shown in the optimization, makes the optimization much easier. In addition, a small squared distance implies a small distance. Hence, our idea is still valid.

  It is always good to *tune the mathematical translation* so long as the tuning still matches our idea and makes the optimization easier to do.
- Although our idea starts from the assumption that the elements in X are the same data point subject to different noise, this assumption is *not* used at all in the formalization or optimization step.

  Thus, for *any* dataset X, we can *generalize* and say that its average is the best zero-dimensional representation (under the sum of squared distance evaluation metric).

5.3 PCA to One-Dimensional Subspace

Now we are ready to move one step further to the one-dimensional subspace, where we can use one additional value to represent each $\boldsymbol{x}_i$ in addition to $\bar{\boldsymbol{x}}$.

5.3.1 New Formalization

Any element $\boldsymbol{x} \in \mathbb{R}^D$ in a one-dimensional subspace can be represented as

$$\boldsymbol{x} = \boldsymbol{x}_0 + a\boldsymbol{w}$$

for some $a \in \mathbb{R}$, $\boldsymbol{x}_0 \in \mathbb{R}^D$, and $\boldsymbol{w} \in \mathbb{R}^D$, and vice versa, in which $\boldsymbol{x}_0$ and $\boldsymbol{w}$ are determined by the subspace and a is determined by the element $\boldsymbol{x}$ (recall your linear algebra and note that a one-dimensional subspace means a line!).

Now that we already have the zero-dimensional representation, we should set

$$\boldsymbol{x}_0 = \bar{\boldsymbol{x}}.$$

Hence, for any $\boldsymbol{x}_i$, the new one-dimensional representation is a_i. Using this new representation, we can find an approximation of $\boldsymbol{x}_i$ as

$$\boldsymbol{x}_i \approx \bar{\boldsymbol{x}} + a_i \boldsymbol{w},$$

and the difference (or residue),

$$\boldsymbol{x}_i - (\bar{\boldsymbol{x}} + a_i \boldsymbol{w}),$$

is considered to be caused by noise, which we want to minimize. Note that now we do *not* need to require that $\boldsymbol{x}_i$ resides in a one-dimensional subspace.

The parameters we need to find are a_i $(1 \le i \le N)$ and $\boldsymbol{w}$. We denote

$$\boldsymbol{a} = (a_1, a_2, \ldots, a_N)^T,$$

and define an objective J to minimize the average squared distance:

$$J(\boldsymbol{w}, \boldsymbol{a}) = \frac{1}{N} \sum_{i=1}^{N} \|\boldsymbol{x}_i - (\bar{\boldsymbol{x}} + a_i \boldsymbol{w})\|^2 \tag{5.6}$$

$$= \frac{1}{N} \sum_{i=1}^{N} \|a_i \boldsymbol{w} - (\boldsymbol{x}_i - \bar{\boldsymbol{x}})\|^2 \tag{5.7}$$

$$= \sum_{i=1}^{N} \frac{a_i^2 \|\boldsymbol{w}\|^2 + \|\boldsymbol{x}_i - \bar{\boldsymbol{x}}\|^2 - 2a_i \boldsymbol{w}^T (\boldsymbol{x}_i - \bar{\boldsymbol{x}})}{N}. \tag{5.8}$$

5.3.2 Optimality Condition and Simplification

Now we calculate the partial derivatives, and set them to 0, as

$$\frac{\partial J}{\partial a_i} = \frac{2}{N} \left(a_i \|\boldsymbol{w}\|^2 - \boldsymbol{w}^T (\boldsymbol{x}_i - \bar{\boldsymbol{x}}) \right) = 0 \quad \forall i, \tag{5.9}$$

$$\frac{\partial J}{\partial \boldsymbol{w}} = \frac{2}{N} \sum_{i=1}^{N} \left(a_i^2 \boldsymbol{w} - a_i (\boldsymbol{x}_i - \bar{\boldsymbol{x}}) \right) = 0. \tag{5.10}$$

Equation (5.9) gives us the solution for a_i as

$$a_i = \frac{\boldsymbol{w}^T (\boldsymbol{x}_i - \bar{\boldsymbol{x}})}{\|\boldsymbol{w}\|^2} = \frac{(\boldsymbol{x}_i - \bar{\boldsymbol{x}})^T \boldsymbol{w}}{\|\boldsymbol{w}\|^2}. \tag{5.11}$$

Note that the projection of $\boldsymbol{x}_i - \bar{\boldsymbol{x}}$ onto $\boldsymbol{w}$ is $\frac{(\boldsymbol{x}_i - \bar{\boldsymbol{x}})^T \boldsymbol{w}}{\|\boldsymbol{w}\|^2} \boldsymbol{w}$; we conclude that the optimal a_i can be viewed as the signed length of $\boldsymbol{x}_i - \bar{\boldsymbol{x}}$ projected onto $\boldsymbol{w}$. When the angle between $\boldsymbol{x}_i - \bar{\boldsymbol{x}}$ and $\boldsymbol{w}$ is larger than 90°, $a_i \le 0$.

Before proceeding to process Eq. (5.10), a further examination of $a_i \boldsymbol{w}$ shows that

$$a_i \boldsymbol{w} = \frac{\boldsymbol{w}^T (\boldsymbol{x}_i - \bar{\boldsymbol{x}}) \boldsymbol{w}}{\|\boldsymbol{w}\|^2} = \frac{(c\boldsymbol{w})^T (\boldsymbol{x}_i - \bar{\boldsymbol{x}})(c\boldsymbol{w})}{\|c\boldsymbol{w}\|^2} \tag{5.12}$$

for any nonzero scalar value $c \in \mathbb{R}$. In other words, we have the freedom to specify that

$$\|\boldsymbol{w}\| = 1, \tag{5.13}$$

and this additional constraint will not change the optimization problem's solution!

We choose $\|\boldsymbol{w}\| = 1$ because this choice greatly simplifies our optimization problem. Now we have

$$a_i = \boldsymbol{w}^T(\boldsymbol{x}_i - \bar{\boldsymbol{x}}) = (\boldsymbol{x}_i - \bar{\boldsymbol{x}})^T\boldsymbol{w}. \tag{5.14}$$

Plugging it back into the optimization objective we get a much simplified version

$$J(\boldsymbol{w},\boldsymbol{a}) = \frac{1}{N}\sum_{i=1}^{N}\left[\|\boldsymbol{x}_i - \bar{\boldsymbol{x}}\|^2 - a_i^2\right] \tag{5.15}$$

by noting that $a_i\boldsymbol{w}^T(\boldsymbol{x}_i - \bar{\boldsymbol{x}}) = a_i^2$ and $a_i^2\|\boldsymbol{w}\|^2 = a_i^2$.

Hence, we know the optimal parameters are obtained via *maximizing*

$$\frac{1}{N}\sum_{i=1}^{N} a_i^2 \tag{5.16}$$

because $\|\boldsymbol{x}_i - \bar{\boldsymbol{x}}\|^2$ does not depend on either $\boldsymbol{w}$ or $\boldsymbol{a}$.

One note we want to add is that various transformations can greatly simplify our optimization problem, and it is worthwhile paying attention to such simplification opportunities. In fact, in this derivation we could specify the constraint $\|\boldsymbol{w}\| = 1$ *before* finding the optimality conditions.

It is easy to observe that

$$J(\boldsymbol{w},\boldsymbol{a}) = J\left(c\boldsymbol{w}, \frac{1}{c}\boldsymbol{a}\right) \tag{5.17}$$

for any $c \neq 0$, and there is no constraint on $\boldsymbol{w}$ or $\boldsymbol{a}$ in the original formulation. Hence, if $(\boldsymbol{w}^\star, \boldsymbol{a}^\star)$ is an optimal solution that minimizes J, so will be $(c\boldsymbol{w}^\star, \frac{1}{c}\boldsymbol{a}^\star)$ for any $c \neq 0$. That is, for an optimal solution $(\boldsymbol{w}^\star, \boldsymbol{a}^\star)$, $\left(\frac{1}{\|\boldsymbol{w}^\star\|}\boldsymbol{w}^\star, \|\boldsymbol{w}^\star\|\boldsymbol{a}^\star\right)$ will also be an optimal solution.

Obviously the norm of $\frac{1}{\|\boldsymbol{w}^\star\|}\boldsymbol{w}^\star$ is 1. Hence, we can specify $\|\boldsymbol{w}\| = 1$ without changing the optimization objective, but this will greatly simplify the optimization from the very beginning. It is always beneficial to find such simplifications and transformations before we attempt to solve the optimization task.

5.3.3 The Eigen-Decomposition Connection

Now we turn our attention to Eq. (5.10), which tells us that

$$\frac{1}{N}\left(\sum_{i=1}^{N} a_i^2\right)\boldsymbol{w} = \frac{1}{N}\sum_{i=1}^{N} a_i(\boldsymbol{x}_i - \bar{\boldsymbol{x}}). \tag{5.18}$$

And plugging a_i into Eq. (5.18), we can simplify its right-hand side as

$$\frac{1}{N}\sum_{i=1}^{N} a_i(\boldsymbol{x}_i - \bar{\boldsymbol{x}}) = \frac{1}{N}\sum_{i=1}^{N}(\boldsymbol{x}_i - \bar{\boldsymbol{x}})a_i \tag{5.19}$$

$$= \frac{\sum_{i=1}^{N}(\boldsymbol{x}_i - \bar{\boldsymbol{x}})(\boldsymbol{x}_i - \bar{\boldsymbol{x}})^T \boldsymbol{w}}{N} \tag{5.20}$$

$$= \operatorname{Cov}(\boldsymbol{x})\boldsymbol{w}, \tag{5.21}$$

in which

$$\operatorname{Cov}(\boldsymbol{x}) = \frac{1}{N}\sum_{i=1}^{N}(\boldsymbol{x}_i - \bar{\boldsymbol{x}})(\boldsymbol{x}_i - \bar{\boldsymbol{x}})^T$$

is the covariance matrix of $\boldsymbol{x}$ computed from the training set X.

Hence, Eq. (5.18) now gives us

$$\operatorname{Cov}(\boldsymbol{x})\boldsymbol{w} = \frac{\sum_{i=1}^{N} a_i^2}{N}\boldsymbol{w}, \tag{5.22}$$

which immediately reminds us of the eigen-decomposition equation—this equation tells us that the optimal $\boldsymbol{w}$ must be an eigenvector of $\operatorname{Cov}(\boldsymbol{x})$, and $\frac{1}{N}\sum_{i=1}^{N} a_i^2$ is the corresponding eigenvalue!

The constraint in Eq. (5.13) also fits this eigen-decomposition interpretation, because eigenvectors are also constrained to have unit ℓ_2 norm.

5.3.4 The Solution

The covariance matrix $\operatorname{Cov}(\boldsymbol{x})$ has many eigenvectors and corresponding eigenvalues. However, Eq. (5.16) reminds us that we want to maximize $\frac{1}{N}\sum_{i=1}^{N} a_i^2$, while Eq. (5.22) tells us that $\frac{1}{N}\sum_{i=1}^{N} a_i^2$ is the eigenvalue corresponding to $\boldsymbol{w}$. Hence, it is trivial to choose among all the eigenvectors—choose the one that corresponds to the largest eigenvalue!

Now we have everything to compute the one-dimensional reduction. From X we can compute the covariance matrix $\operatorname{Cov}(\boldsymbol{x})$, and we set $\boldsymbol{w}^\star = \boldsymbol{\xi}_1$, where $\boldsymbol{\xi}_1$ is the eigenvector of $\operatorname{Cov}(\boldsymbol{x})$ that corresponds to the largest eigenvalue. The optimal new one-dimensional representation for $\boldsymbol{x}_i$ is then

$$a_i^\star = \boldsymbol{\xi}_1^T(\boldsymbol{x}_i - \bar{\boldsymbol{x}}). \tag{5.23}$$

Given the one-dimensional representation, the original input $\boldsymbol{x}$ is approximated as

$$\boldsymbol{x} \approx \bar{\boldsymbol{x}} + (\boldsymbol{\xi}_1^T(\boldsymbol{x}_i - \bar{\boldsymbol{x}}))\boldsymbol{\xi}_1. \tag{5.24}$$

Because $(\boldsymbol{\xi}_1^T(\boldsymbol{x}_i - \bar{\boldsymbol{x}}))\boldsymbol{\xi}_1$ equals the projection of $\boldsymbol{x}_i - \bar{\boldsymbol{x}}$ onto $\boldsymbol{\xi}_1$,[1] we also call $\boldsymbol{\xi}_1$ the first *projection direction*, and call $\boldsymbol{\xi}_1^T(\boldsymbol{x}_i - \bar{\boldsymbol{x}})$ the projected value of $\boldsymbol{x}_i$ onto this direction.

[1] Note that the projection of $\boldsymbol{x}$ onto $\boldsymbol{y}$ is $\frac{\boldsymbol{x}^T\boldsymbol{y}}{\|\boldsymbol{y}\|^2}\boldsymbol{y}$, and $\|\boldsymbol{\xi}_1\| = 1$.

5.4 PCA for More Dimensions

Now we generalize PCA to two or more dimensions, thanks to the spectral decomposition of the covariance matrix.

It is obvious that $\text{Cov}(\boldsymbol{x})$ is a real symmetric matrix, and furthermore it is a positive semidefinite matrix. According to matrix analysis theory, $\text{Cov}(\boldsymbol{x})$ has D eigenvectors $\boldsymbol{\xi}_1, \boldsymbol{\xi}_2, \ldots, \boldsymbol{\xi}_D$ whose elements are all real numbers. And the eigenvalues corresponding to them are $\lambda_1, \lambda_2, \ldots, \lambda_D$, which are all real numbers satisfying $\lambda_1 \geq \lambda_2 \geq \cdots \geq \lambda_D \geq 0$. The spectral decomposition states that

$$\text{Cov}(\boldsymbol{x}) = \sum_{i=1}^{D} \lambda_i \boldsymbol{\xi}_i \boldsymbol{\xi}_i^T. \tag{5.25}$$

The eigenvectors of real symmetric matrices satisfy that for any $i \neq j$, $\boldsymbol{\xi}_i^T \boldsymbol{\xi}_j = 0$ and $\|\boldsymbol{\xi}_i\| = 1$ for $1 \leq i \leq D, 1 \leq j \leq D$. Hence, if we construct a $D \times D$ matrix E, whose ith column is formed by $\boldsymbol{\xi}_i$, we have

$$EE^T = E^T E = I. \tag{5.26}$$

Then we can show that

$$\begin{aligned} \boldsymbol{x} &= \bar{\boldsymbol{x}} + (\boldsymbol{x} - \bar{\boldsymbol{x}}) && (5.27)\\ &= \bar{\boldsymbol{x}} + EE^T(\boldsymbol{x} - \bar{\boldsymbol{x}}) && (5.28)\\ &= \bar{\boldsymbol{x}} + (\boldsymbol{\xi}_1^T(\boldsymbol{x} - \bar{\boldsymbol{x}}))\boldsymbol{\xi}_1 + (\boldsymbol{\xi}_2^T(\boldsymbol{x} - \bar{\boldsymbol{x}}))\boldsymbol{\xi}_2 + \cdots + (\boldsymbol{\xi}_D^T(\boldsymbol{x} - \bar{\boldsymbol{x}}))\boldsymbol{\xi}_D, && (5.29) \end{aligned}$$

for any $\boldsymbol{x} \in \mathbb{R}^D$, even if $\boldsymbol{x}$ does not follow the same relationships inside the training set X (in other words, being an outlier!).

Comparing Eq. (5.24) with Eq. (5.29), a guess of PCA with more dimensions naturally comes to us: $\boldsymbol{\xi}_i$ should be the ith projection direction, and the coefficient is $\boldsymbol{\xi}_i^T(\boldsymbol{x} - \bar{\boldsymbol{x}})$.

This conjecture is correct, and is easy to prove following the procedure in Section 5.3. We will omit the details here, but leaving them to the reader.

5.5 The Complete PCA Algorithm

The complete principal component analysis algorithm is described in Algorithm 4.

Let E_d be the $D \times d$ matrix that consists of the first d columns in E; the new lower-dimensional representation can be succinctly written as

$$\boldsymbol{y} = E_d^T(\boldsymbol{x} - \bar{\boldsymbol{x}}), \tag{5.30}$$

and the approximation is

$$\boldsymbol{x} \approx \bar{\boldsymbol{x}} + E_d E_d^T(\boldsymbol{x} - \bar{\boldsymbol{x}}). \tag{5.31}$$

Algorithm 4 The PCA algorithm

1: **Input**: A D-dimensional training set $X = \{\boldsymbol{x}_1, \boldsymbol{x}_2, \ldots, \boldsymbol{x}_N\}$ and the new (lower) dimensionality d (with $d < D$).

2: Compute the mean

$$\bar{\boldsymbol{x}} = \frac{1}{N}\sum_{i=1}^{N} \boldsymbol{x}_i .$$

3: Compute the covariance matrix

$$\operatorname{Cov}(\boldsymbol{x}) = \frac{1}{N}\sum_{i=1}^{N} (\boldsymbol{x}_i - \bar{\boldsymbol{x}})\,(\boldsymbol{x}_i - \bar{\boldsymbol{x}})^T .$$

4: Find the spectral decomposition of $\operatorname{Cov}(\boldsymbol{x})$, obtaining the eigenvectors $\boldsymbol{\xi}_1, \boldsymbol{\xi}_2, \ldots, \boldsymbol{\xi}_D$ and their corresponding eigenvalues $\lambda_1, \lambda_2, \ldots, \lambda_D$. Note that the eigenvalues are sorted, such that $\lambda_1 \geq \lambda_2 \geq \cdots \geq \lambda_D \geq 0$.

5: For any $\boldsymbol{x} \in \mathbb{R}^D$, its new lower-dimensional representation is

$$\boldsymbol{y} = \left(\boldsymbol{\xi}_1^T(\boldsymbol{x} - \bar{\boldsymbol{x}}), \boldsymbol{\xi}_2^T(\boldsymbol{x} - \bar{\boldsymbol{x}}), \ldots, \boldsymbol{\xi}_d^T(\boldsymbol{x} - \bar{\boldsymbol{x}})\right)^T \in \mathbb{R}^d, \tag{5.32}$$

and the original $\boldsymbol{x}$ can be approximated by

$$\boldsymbol{x} \approx \bar{\boldsymbol{x}} + (\boldsymbol{\xi}_1^T(\boldsymbol{x} - \bar{\boldsymbol{x}}))\boldsymbol{\xi}_1 + (\boldsymbol{\xi}_2^T(\boldsymbol{x} - \bar{\boldsymbol{x}}))\boldsymbol{\xi}_2 + \cdots + (\boldsymbol{\xi}_d^T(\boldsymbol{x} - \bar{\boldsymbol{x}}))\boldsymbol{\xi}_d . \tag{5.33}$$

Dimensions of the new representation are called the *principal components*, hence the name principal component analysis (PCA). Sometimes a typo will happen that spells PCA as princip<u>le</u> component analysis, but that is not correct.

5.6 Variance Analysis

Note that we have used $\boldsymbol{y}$ to denote the new lower-dimensional representation in Algorithm 4. Let y_i be the ith dimension of $\boldsymbol{y}$; we can compute its expectation:

$$\mathbb{E}[y_i] = \mathbb{E}\left[\boldsymbol{\xi}_i^T(\boldsymbol{x} - \bar{\boldsymbol{x}})\right] = \boldsymbol{\xi}_i^T\,\mathbb{E}\left[\boldsymbol{x} - \bar{\boldsymbol{x}}\right] = \boldsymbol{\xi}_i^T\boldsymbol{0} = 0, \tag{5.34}$$

where $\boldsymbol{0}$ is a vector whose elements are all zero.

We can further calculate its variance:

$$\begin{aligned}
\operatorname{Var}(y_i) &= \mathbb{E}[y_i^2] - (\mathbb{E}[y_i])^2 && (5.35)\\
&= \mathbb{E}[y_i^2] && (5.36)\\
&= \mathbb{E}\left[\boldsymbol{\xi}_i^T(\boldsymbol{x} - \bar{\boldsymbol{x}})\boldsymbol{\xi}_i^T(\boldsymbol{x} - \bar{\boldsymbol{x}})\right] && (5.37)\\
&= \mathbb{E}\left[\boldsymbol{\xi}_i^T(\boldsymbol{x} - \bar{\boldsymbol{x}})(\boldsymbol{x} - \bar{\boldsymbol{x}})^T\boldsymbol{\xi}_i\right] && (5.38)\\
&= \boldsymbol{\xi}_i^T\operatorname{Cov}(\boldsymbol{x})\boldsymbol{\xi}_i && (5.39)
\end{aligned}$$

$$= \xi_i^T \left[\operatorname{Cov}(\boldsymbol{x})\xi_i\right] \tag{5.40}$$

$$= \xi_i^T \left(\lambda_i \xi_i\right) \tag{5.41}$$

$$= \lambda_i \xi_i^T \xi_i \tag{5.42}$$

$$= \lambda_i . \tag{5.43}$$

Hence, y_i has zero mean and its variance is λ_i.

Equation (5.22) tells us that for the first new dimension,

$$\frac{\sum_{i=1}^N a_i^2}{N} = \lambda_1 \tag{5.44}$$

and Eq. (5.15) tells us that

$$J(\xi_1) = \frac{1}{N} \sum_{i=1}^N \left[\|\boldsymbol{x}_i - \bar{\boldsymbol{x}}\|^2 - a_i^2\right] = \frac{\sum_{i=1}^N \|\boldsymbol{x}_i - \bar{\boldsymbol{x}}\|^2}{N} - \lambda_1 . \tag{5.45}$$

That is, $\frac{1}{N} \sum_{i=1}^N \|\boldsymbol{x}_i - \bar{\boldsymbol{x}}\|^2$ is the average squared distance for the zero-dimensional representation, and λ_1 is the part of the cost that is reduced by introducing the ξ_1 projection direction as a new dimension. It is also easy to prove that

$$J(\xi_1, \xi_2, \ldots, \xi_k) = \frac{\sum_{i=1}^N \|\boldsymbol{x}_i - \bar{\boldsymbol{x}}\|^2}{N} - \lambda_1 - \lambda_2 - \cdots - \lambda_k \tag{5.46}$$

for $1 \le k \le D$ and

$$J(\xi_1, \xi_2, \ldots, \xi_D) = 0. \tag{5.47}$$

Hence, every new dimension is responsible for reducing the reconstruction distance between any point $\boldsymbol{x}$ and its approximation $\bar{\boldsymbol{x}} + \sum_{i=1}^k (\xi_i^T (\boldsymbol{x} - \bar{\boldsymbol{x}}))\xi_i$. And we know that the ith new dimension reduces the expected squared distance by λ_i, and that distance will reduce to 0 if all eigenvectors are used. From these observations, we obtain the following properties:

- If all eigenvectors are used, PCA is simply a shift plus a *rotation*, because

  $$\boldsymbol{y} = E^T(\boldsymbol{x} - \bar{\boldsymbol{x}})$$

  for any $\boldsymbol{x}$, and E is an orthogonal matrix. We also know that in this case the norm is unchanged:

  $$\|\boldsymbol{y}\| = \|\boldsymbol{x} - \bar{\boldsymbol{x}}\|.$$

- We know that the larger an eigenvalue, the more its associated eigenvector (projection direction) will reduce the approximation error.
- We also know that the eigenvalue λ_i is the expectation of the square of the ith new dimension (cf. Eq. 5.43). Hence, we will expect the average scale of y_i (the ith dimension in $\boldsymbol{y}$) to be larger than that of y_j if $i < j$.

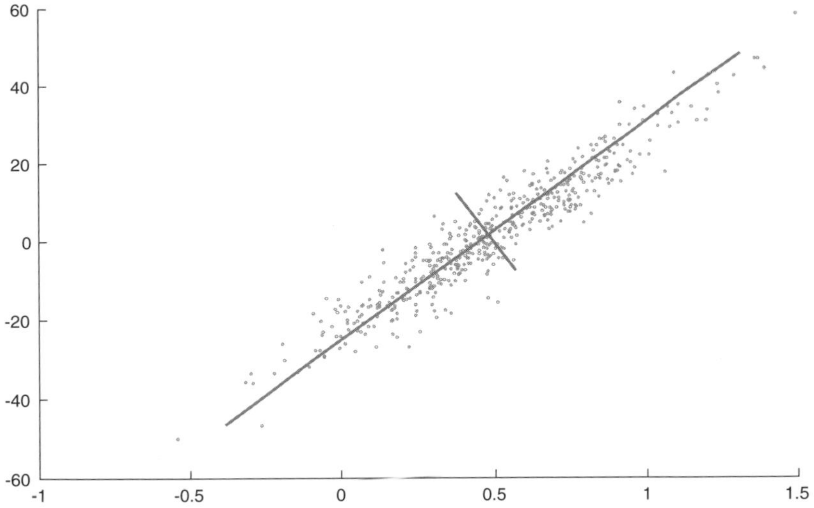

Figure 5.2 Variance of projected values. (A black and white version of this figure will appear in some formats. For the color version, please refer to the plate section.)

5.6.1 PCA from Maximization of Variance

Based on the above observations, we can also interpret PCA as maximizing the variance of the projected values onto a certain direction based on Eq. (5.43). This perspective is illustrated in Figure 5.2.

The two red lines show the two eigenvectors of the covariance matrix. It is not surprising that the long red line has the highest variance of its projected values. In other words, PCA can also be derived by maximizing the variance of the projected values onto a projection direction, and the optimal solution of this formulation must be the same as we obtain from the minimization of average squared distances.

Hence, we can use the following terms interchangeably because they are *equivalent in the context of PCA*: variance (of projected values), eigenvalue, and reduction in approximation error.

5.6.2 A Simpler Derivation

Let us work out just the first projection direction that maximizes the variance of the projected values. Given any projection direction $\boldsymbol{w}$, the projected point of a data point $\boldsymbol{x}$ onto $\boldsymbol{w}$ will be (cf. footnote 1 on page 109)

$$\frac{\boldsymbol{x}^T \boldsymbol{w}}{\|\boldsymbol{w}\|^2} \boldsymbol{w} = \boldsymbol{x}^T \boldsymbol{w} \boldsymbol{w}. \tag{5.48}$$

In the above formula, we assume $\|\boldsymbol{w}\| = 1$. In the minimal reconstruction error formulation, we add this restriction because the norm of $\boldsymbol{w}$ does not change our optimization.

Here, $\boldsymbol{w}$ is a projection *direction*, and hence its length is irrelevant. We can then add the same constraint $\|\boldsymbol{w}\| = 1$. Hence, the projected value for $\boldsymbol{x}$ is $\boldsymbol{x}^T\boldsymbol{w}$. The mean of all projected values is

$$\mathbb{E}[\boldsymbol{x}^T\boldsymbol{w}] = \bar{\boldsymbol{x}}^T\boldsymbol{w}.$$

Next we compute the variance of all projected values as

$$\begin{aligned}\operatorname{Var}(\boldsymbol{x}^T\boldsymbol{w}) &= \mathbb{E}\left[(\boldsymbol{x}^T\boldsymbol{w} - \bar{\boldsymbol{x}}^T\boldsymbol{w})^2\right] && (5.49)\\ &= \boldsymbol{w}^T\mathbb{E}\left[(\boldsymbol{x}-\bar{\boldsymbol{x}})(\boldsymbol{x}-\bar{\boldsymbol{x}})^T\right]\boldsymbol{w} && (5.50)\\ &= \boldsymbol{w}^T\operatorname{Cov}(\boldsymbol{x})\boldsymbol{w}. && (5.51)\end{aligned}$$

This is the second time we have seen this optimization problem:

$$\begin{aligned}\max_{\boldsymbol{w}} &\quad \boldsymbol{w}^T\operatorname{Cov}(\boldsymbol{x})\boldsymbol{w} && (5.52)\\ \text{s.t.} &\quad \|\boldsymbol{w}\| = 1. && (5.53)\end{aligned}$$

This is sufficient evidence that the variance maximization perspective leads to exactly the same PCA solution as the one we just obtained by minimizing the approximation error. The variance perspective, however, is much easier for deriving the PCA solution. The approximation perspective, although requiring a little more effort, reveals more properties of PCA, such as the relationship between the eigenvalue, approximation error, and variance. Hence, we started from the approximation perspective in this chapter.

5.6.3 How Many Dimensions Do We Need?

The equivalence of these terms also gives us hints on how to choose d, the number of dimensions in the new representation.

If one eigenvalue is 0, then its corresponding eigenvector (projection direction) is not useful in keeping information of the original data distribution at all. All data points that have the same characteristic as the training set will have a constant projected value for this eigenvector because the variance of the projected values equals the eigenvalue, which is 0. Hence, this eigenvalue and its associated eigenvector can be safely removed.

When an eigenvalue is quite small, there is good reason to conjecture that this particular projection direction does not contain useful information either. Rather, it could be there due to white (or other types of) noise, as illustrated in the example of Figure 5.1c. Hence, removing such directions is usually encouraged and in many cases will increase the accuracy of our new representation in subsequent classification systems (or other tasks).

We want to keep a reasonably large portion of the variance, such that the rest of the eigenvalues/variance are small enough and likely caused by noise. Hence, the rule of thumb is often to choose to cut off if the accumulated eigenvalues have exceeded 90%

of the sum of all eigenvalues. In other words, we choose d to be the first integer that satisfies

$$\frac{\lambda_1 + \lambda_2 + \cdots + \lambda_d}{\lambda_1 + \lambda_2 + \cdots + \lambda_D} > 0.9. \tag{5.54}$$

Although 0.9 seems to be the widely used cutoff threshold, other values (such as 0.85 or 0.95) can also be used.

5.7 When to Use or Not to Use PCA?

Discussions on this question will end this chapter's presentation on PCA. And before we tackle this tough question, we start with a simpler one: How will PCA affect $\boldsymbol{x}$ if the latter follows a normal distribution?

5.7.1 PCA for Gaussian Data

Let us suppose $\boldsymbol{x} \sim N(\boldsymbol{\mu}, \Sigma)$. Usually we do not know the exact value of the mean $\boldsymbol{\mu}$ or the covariance matrix Σ. However, the maximum likelihood estimation of these terms can be obtained as $\bar{\boldsymbol{x}}$ and $\operatorname{Cov}(\boldsymbol{x})$, respectively.[2]

Let Λ denote the diagonal matrix consisting of the eigenvalues of $\operatorname{Cov}(\boldsymbol{x})$, i.e.,

$$\Lambda = \operatorname{diag}(\lambda_1, \lambda_2, \ldots, \lambda_D).$$

Following the properties of normal distributions,[3] it is easy to verify that the new PCA representation $\boldsymbol{y}$ is also normally distributed, with parameters estimated as

$$\boldsymbol{y} \sim N(\mathbf{0}, \Lambda), \tag{5.55}$$

if all projection directions are used. That is, PCA performs a translation with respect to $\bar{\boldsymbol{x}}$, followed by a rotation such that the axes of the normal distribution are parallel to the coordinate system's axes.

A direct consequence of this result is that different components of $\boldsymbol{y}$ are *independent* of each other because different dimensions of an ellipsoidal normal distribution are independent.

If only the first d eigenvectors are used, then we can define a $d \times d$ matrix Λ_d such that $\Lambda_d = \operatorname{diag}(\lambda_1, \lambda_2, \ldots, \lambda_d)$, and

$$\boldsymbol{y}_d \sim N(\mathbf{0}, \Lambda_d). \tag{5.56}$$

The projected dimensions are independent of each other too. Figure 5.3 shows an example, in which Figure 5.3a contains 2000 normally distributed two-dimensional data points, generated in MATLAB/GNU Octave by `x=randn(2000,2)*[2 1; 1 2]`. After the PCA operation, Figure 5.3b shows that these data points are rotated back to follow an ellipsoidal normal distribution (i.e., one whose covariance matrix is diagonal).

2 We will discuss maximum likelihood estimation in Chapter 8.
3 See Chapter 13 for more details.

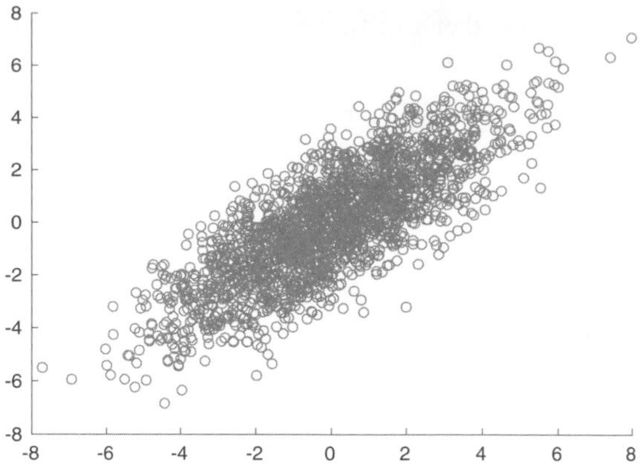

(a) Input data

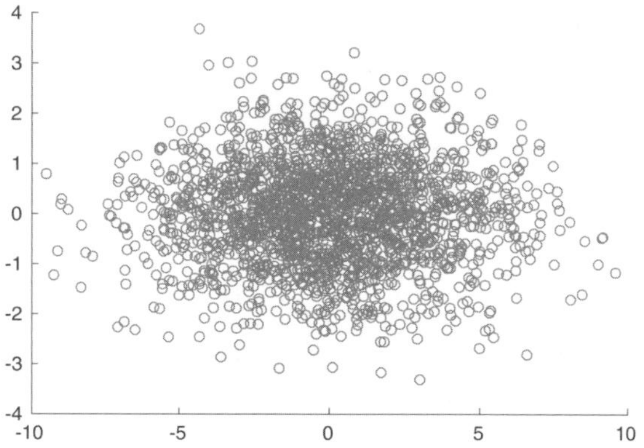

(b) PCA

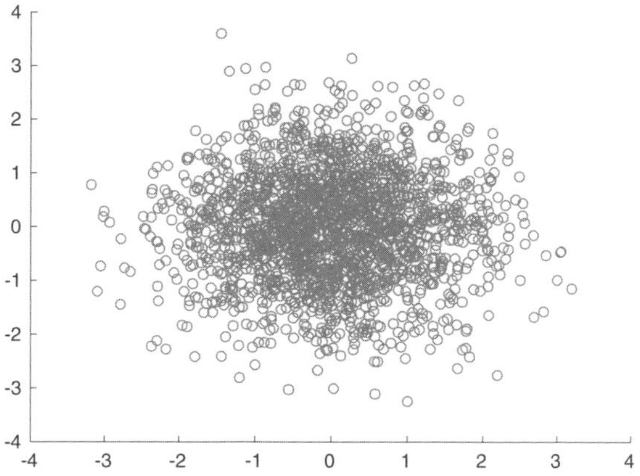

(c) Whitening

Figure 5.3 PCA and the whitening transform applied to Gaussian data. Figure 5.3a is the two-dimensional input data. After PCA, the data are rotated such that the two major axes of the data are parallel to the coordinate system's axes in Figure 5.3b (i.e., the normal distribution becomes an ellipsoidal one). After the whitening transform, the data has the same scale in the two major axes in Figure 5.3c (i.e., the normal distribution becomes a spherical one). Note that the x- and y-axes in the different subfigures have different scales.

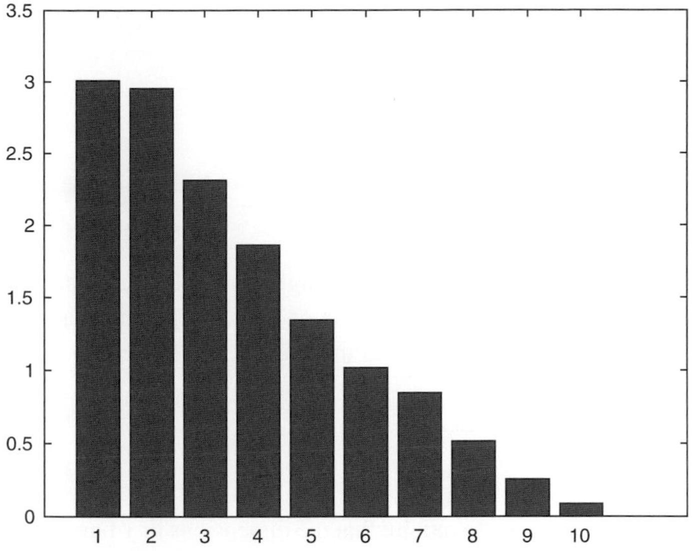

Figure 5.4 Eigenvalues shown in decreasing order.

5.7.2 PCA for Non-Gaussian Data

We will, however, expect many non-Gaussian datasets. Figure 5.4 shows the eigenvalue distribution of a non-Gaussian dataset.

We observe an *exponential* trend in how the eigenvalues decrease. Because of this exponential decay trend, the first few eigenvalues may quickly accumulate a high proportion of the total variance (or, sum of eigenvalues). Hence, when the eigenvalues show an exponential decay trend, the last few dimensions may be noise, and it is reasonable to apply PCA to such data.

In Figure 5.4, the last three eigenvalues account for only 6% of the total variance. We can safely set $d = 7$ in this example (where $D = 10$).

If the data are not Gaussian, $\boldsymbol{y}$ will have mean $\mathbf{0}$ and covariance matrix Λ (or Λ_d) after PCA. Thus, we know the dimensions in $\boldsymbol{y}$ are not correlated. However, they are not necessarily independent because $\boldsymbol{y}$ is not a multivariate normal distribution if $\boldsymbol{x}$ is non-Gaussian.

5.7.3 PCA for Data with Outliers

Outliers can cause serious trouble for PCA. We compute PCA for the data used in Figure 5.1. In Table 5.2, we listed the PCA results for the data in the last three subfigures of Figure 5.1.

When there is no noise, PCA successfully estimates the major projection direction as (3, 1), which fits Figure 5.1b. The white noise is applied to every data point in Figure 5.1c. However, it only slightly increases λ_2, from 0 to 0.75, and slightly changes the

Table 5.2 PCA outcome for data in Figure 5.1b, 5.1c, and 5.1d.

Data source	λ_1	λ_2	Projection direction
Figure 5.1b	82.5	0	(3.00, 1)
Figure 5.1c	77.0	0.75	(2.90, 1)
Figure 5.1d	85.9	16.43	(3.43, 1)

projection direction to $(2.9, 1)$. But one single outlier in the data of Figure 5.1d significantly changes the projection direction to $(3.43, 1)$ and leads to a large λ_2 (16.43). Overall, PCA is not effective in the existence of outliers.

5.8 The Whitening Transform

Sometimes we have reasons to require that the dimensions in $\boldsymbol{y}$ have roughly the same scale. However, PCA ensures that

$$\mathbb{E}[y_1^2] \geq \mathbb{E}[y_2^2] \geq \cdots \geq \mathbb{E}[y_d^2].$$

The whitening transform is a simple variation of PCA, and can achieve this goal.

The whitening transform derives the new lower-dimensional representation as

$$\boldsymbol{y} = (E_d \Lambda_d^{-1/2})^T (\boldsymbol{x} - \bar{\boldsymbol{x}}). \tag{5.57}$$

This equation differs from Eq. (5.30) by an additional term $\Lambda_d^{-1/2}$, which guarantees that

$$\mathbb{E}[y_1^2] = \mathbb{E}[y_2^2] = \cdots = \mathbb{E}[y_d^2]$$

after the whitening transform. However, we have to remove any projection direction whose corresponding eigenvalue is 0 in the whitening transform.

As shown in Figure 5.3c, after the whitening transform the dataset follows a spherical normal distribution.

5.9 Eigen-Decomposition vs. SVD

When either the number of data points N or the dimensionality D is large, especially when D is large, eigen-decomposition could be computationally very expensive. Singular value decomposition (SVD) is usually used to replace eigen-decomposition in this scenario.

The covariance matrix $\text{Cov}(\boldsymbol{x})$ does not need to be explicitly computed. Simply using the data matrix X, SVD can compute the (left and right) singular vectors and singular values. Depending on whether $N > D$ or $D > N$, the eigenvectors of $\text{Cov}(\boldsymbol{x})$

will match either the left or right singular vectors. And the singular values, when squared, will match the eigenvalues.

5.10 Miscellaneous Notes and Additional Resources

We will introduce some methods that are useful in computing the eigen-decomposition in the exercise problems for this chapter. However, for efficient and accurate eigen-decomposition implementations, please refer to Press et al. (1992) and Golub & van Loan (1996).

An interesting extension of the PCA method is to make it probabilistic. More details of probabilistic principal component analysis can be found in Tipping & Bishop (1999). A more comprehensive treatment of PCA and its generalization is Vidal et al. (2016).

PCA is very useful in visualizing a dataset with low inherent dimensionality (e.g., 2 or 3). However, in order to visualize a dataset that is more complex (e.g., with higher inherent dimensionality or a nonlinear relationship among the dimensions), advanced tools such as t-SNE (van der Maaten & Hinton 2008) are required.

Typical examples of nonlinear dimensionality reduction include LLE (Roweis & Saul 2000) and Isomap (Tenenbaum et al. 2000). And we will present LLE as Exercise 9.2 in Chapter 9.

Exercises

5.1 Let X be an $m \times n$ matrix with singular value decomposition

$$X = U\Sigma V^T,$$

where $\Sigma = \operatorname{diag}(\sigma_1, \sigma_2, \ldots, \sigma_{\min(m,n)})^T$ contains the singular values of X.

(a) What are the eigenvalues and eigenvectors of XX^T?

(b) What are the eigenvalues and eigenvectors of $X^T X$?

(c) What is the relationship between the eigenvalues of XX^T and $X^T X$?

(d) What is the relationship between the singular values of X and the eigenvalues of XX^T $(X^T X)$?

(e) If $m = 2$ and $n = 100\,000$, how will you compute the eigenvalues of $X^T X$?

5.2 We study the effect of the average vector in PCA in this problem. Use the following MATLAB/GNU Octave code to generate a dataset with 5000 examples and compute their eigenvectors. If we forget to transform the data by minus the average vector from every example, is there a relationship between the first eigenvector (i.e., the one associated with the largest eigenvalue) and the average vector?

Observe these vectors while changing the value of `scale` in the set

$$\{1, 0.5, 0.1, 0.05, 0.01, 0.005, 0.001, 0.0005, 0.0001\}.$$

What is the correct eigenvector (in which the average vector is removed from every example) if `scale` changes?

```
% set the random number seed to 0 for reproducibility
rand('seed',0);
avg = [1 2 3 4 5 6 7 8 9 10];
scale = 0.001;
% generate 5000 examples, each 10 dim
data = randn(5000,10)+repmat(avg*scale,5000,1);

m = mean(data);  % average
m1 = m / norm(m); % normalized average

% do PCA, but without centering
[~, S, V] = svd(data);
S = diag(S);
e1 = V(:,1); % first eigenvector, not minus mean vector
% do correct PCA with centering
newdata = data - repmat(m,5000,1);
[U, S, V] = svd(newdata);
S = diag(S);
new_e1 = V(:,1); % first eigenvector, minus mean vector

% correlation between first eigenvector (new & old) and mean
avg = avg - mean(avg);
avg = avg / norm(avg);
e1 = e1 - mean(e1);
e1 = e1 / norm(e1);
new_e1 = new_e1 - mean(new_e1);
new_e1 = new_e1 / norm(new_e1);
corr1 = avg*e1
corr2 = e1'*new_e1
```

5.3 Complete the following experiments using MATLAB or GNU Octave. Write your own code to implement both PCA and whitening—you can use functions such as `eig` or `svd`, but do not use functions that directly complete the task for you (e.g., the `princomp` function).

(a) Generate 2000 examples using `x=randn(2000,2)*[2 1;1 2]`, in which the examples are two-dimensional. Use the `scatter` function to plot these 2000 examples.

(b) Perform the PCA operation on these examples and keep both dimensions. Use the `scatter` function to plot the examples after PCA.

(c) Perform the whitening operation on these examples and keep both dimensions. Use the `scatter` function to plot the examples after PCA.

(d) Why is PCA a rotation (after the translation operation) of the data if all dimensions are kept in the PCA operation? Why is this operation useful?

5.4 (Givens rotations) Givens rotations (which are named after James Wallace Givens, Jr., a US mathematician) are useful in setting certain elements in a vector to 0. A Givens rotation involves two indexes i, j and an angle θ, which generate a matrix of the form

$$G(i,j,\theta) = \begin{bmatrix} 1 & \cdots & 0 & \cdots & 0 & \cdots & 0 \\ \vdots & \ddots & \vdots & & \vdots & & \vdots \\ 0 & \cdots & c & \cdots & s & \cdots & 0 \\ \vdots & & \vdots & \ddots & \vdots & & \vdots \\ 0 & \cdots & -s & \cdots & c & \cdots & 0 \\ \vdots & & \vdots & & \vdots & \ddots & \vdots \\ 0 & \cdots & 0 & \cdots & 0 & \cdots & 1 \end{bmatrix} \tag{5.58}$$

in which $c = \cos\theta$ and $s = \sin\theta$. The diagonal entries in the matrix $G(i,j,\theta)$ are all 1, except for $G(i,j,\theta)_{i,i} = G(i,j,\theta)_{j,j} = c$. Most of the off-diagonal entries are 0, except for $G(i,j,\theta)_{i,j} = s$ and $G(i,j,\theta)_{j,i} = -s$. Let $G(i,j,\theta)$ be of size $m \times m$ and $\boldsymbol{x} \in \mathbb{R}^m$.

(a) What is the effect of left multiplying $\boldsymbol{x}$ by $G(i,j,\theta)^T$? That is, what is the difference between $\boldsymbol{x}$ and $\boldsymbol{y} = G(i,j,\theta)^T\boldsymbol{x}$?

(b) If we want to enforce $y_j = 0$, what is your choice of θ (or equivalently, of c and s values)?

(c) Evaluation of trigonometric functions or their inverse functions is expensive. Without using trigonometric functions, how could you determine the matrix $G(i,j,\theta)$? That is, how could the values c and s be determined?

(d) If $G(i,j,\theta)^T$ left multiplies a matrix A of size $m \times n$, how does it alter A? How can we use a Givens rotation to change one entry of a matrix A to 0? What is the computational complexity of applying this transformation?

(e) (QR decomposition) Let A be a real matrix of size $m \times n$. Then there exists an orthogonal real matrix Q (of size $m \times m$) and an upper triangular real matrix R (of size $m \times n$),[4] such that

$$A = QR.$$

This decomposition for any real matrix A is called the *QR decomposition*. How would you make use of Givens rotations to produce a QR decomposition?

5.5 (Jacobi method) One method to calculate the principal components is Jacobi's approach, invented by and named after Carl Gustav Jacob Jacobi, a German mathematician.

Let X be a real symmetric matrix of size $n \times n$.

(a) If G is an orthogonal $n \times n$ real matrix and $\boldsymbol{x} \in \mathbb{R}^n$, prove that $\|\boldsymbol{x}\| = \|G\boldsymbol{x}\|$ and $\|\boldsymbol{x}\| = \|G^T\boldsymbol{x}\|$ (i.e., a rotation will not change the length of a vector).

(b) The Frobenius norm of an $m \times n$ matrix A is defined as

$$\|A\|_F = \sqrt{\sum_{i=1}^{m}\sum_{j=1}^{n} a_{i,j}^2} = \sqrt{\operatorname{tr}(AA^T)}.$$

[4] R is an upper triangular matrix if all entries below the main diagonal are 0, i.e., $R_{ij} = 0$ so long as $i > j$.

If G is an orthogonal $n \times n$ real matrix, and X is any real matrix of size $n \times n$, prove that

$$\|X\|_F = \|G^T X G\|_F.$$

(c) For a real symmetric matrix X, Jacobi defined a loss function for it as the Frobenius norm of the off-diagonal elements in X—i.e.,

$$\texttt{off}(X) = \sqrt{\sum_{i=1}^{n} \sum_{j=1, j \neq i}^{n} x_{i,j}^2}.$$

The basic building block in the Jacobi method for eigen-decomposition is to find an orthogonal matrix J such that

$$\texttt{off}(J^T X J) < \texttt{off}(X).$$

Explain why this basic step is useful in finding the eigenvectors and eigenvalues of X.

(d) How do you choose an orthogonal matrix J such that the (i, j)th and (j, i)th entries in $J^T X J$ are both zero $(i \neq j)$? (Hint: Let $J(i, j, \theta)$ be a Givens rotation matrix.)

(e) The classic Jacobi method iterates between the following steps:

(i) Find one off-diagonal entry in X that has the largest absolute value—i.e.,

$$|x_{pq}| = \max_{i \neq j} |x_{ij}|.$$

(ii) $X \leftarrow J(p, q, \theta)^T X J(p, q, \theta)$.

This process converges if $\texttt{off}(X)$ is smaller than a predefined threshold ϵ. Prove that one iteration will not increase $\texttt{off}(X)$.

(f) Given the specific choice in the classic Jacobi method, prove that it always converges.

6 Fisher's Linear Discriminant

Fisher's linear discriminant (FLD), which is also a linear dimensionality reduction method, extracts lower-dimensional features utilizing linear relationships among the dimensions of the original input. It is natural to ask what makes FLD different from PCA, and why do we still need FLD when we have PCA handy?

A short answer is that FLD is supervised, but PCA is unsupervised. We illustrate their differences using a somewhat extreme example in Figure 6.1.

Suppose we are to deal with a binary classification problem. We are given a set of input vectors $\boldsymbol{x} \in \mathbb{R}^D$ (which is two-dimensional in Figure 6.1), and need to sort them into two classes. The class label y can take a value in the set $\{1,2\}$. In Figure 6.1, we are given 200 examples with $y = 1$ and 200 examples with $y = 2$. These 400 examples form our training set for this binary classification problem. The positive examples (with $y = 1$) are denoted by the red $\circ$ sign, and negative examples ($y = 2$) are denoted by the blue $+$ sign in Figure 6.1.

In this example, the two classes have special properties: the inherent dimensionality of each seems to be 1. In fact, these data points are generated using the following MATLAB commands:

```
n1 = 200;
n2 = 200;
rot = [1 2; 2 4.5];
data1 = randn(n1,2) * rot;
data2 = randn(n2,2) * rot + repmat([0 5],n2,1);
```

In other words, we generate two very thin Gaussians and shift one of them to separate them.

Visual inspection tells us that it is easy to classify these examples into two classes if we project any $\boldsymbol{x}$ into the projection direction labeled "FLD" (the solid green line). After the projection, the positive class examples clump into a small range of values, as do the negative examples. However, the two ranges of projected values almost never overlap with each other. That is, a proper linear dimensionality reduction makes our binary classification problem trivial to solve.

But if we compute the PCA solution using all 400 training examples, the first eigenvector generates the black dashed line (with the label "PCA" in Figure 6.1).

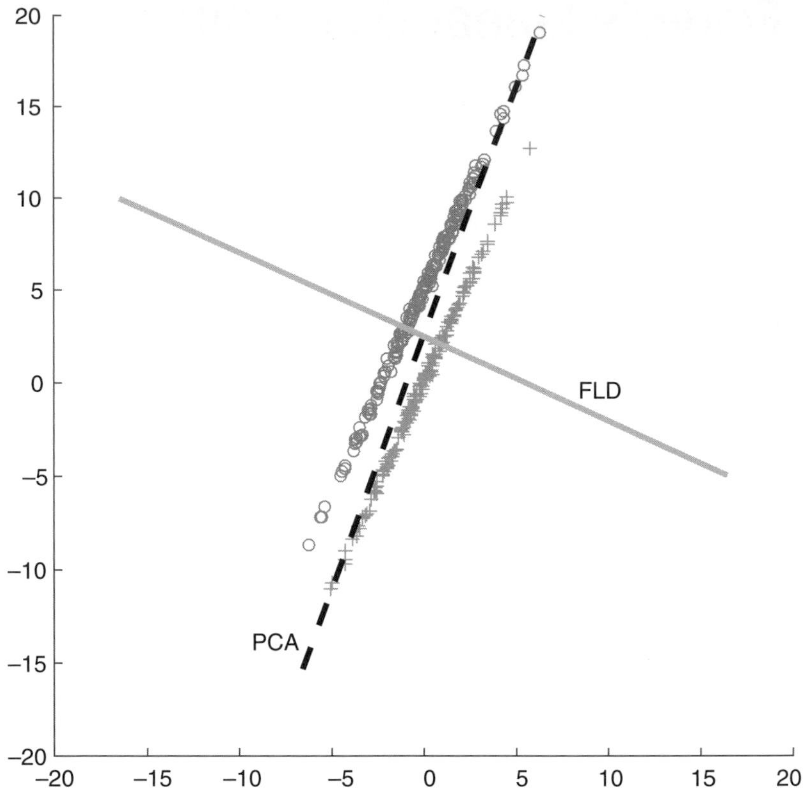

Figure 6.1 FLD vs. PCA. (A black and white version of this figure will appear in some formats. For the color version, please refer to the plate section.)

The PCA projection direction is surprisingly bad for the classification. The ranges of projection values are almost identical for the positive and the negative class—that is, this direction is almost useless for classification.

What makes PCA so unsuitable in this example? PCA is an unsupervised method, which does not consider any label information. It tries to eliminate the projection direction that corresponds to small variance (which is the FLD projection direction). However, in this example, the labels tell us that it is this specific direction that separates the two classes!

Hence, when we are given labels of examples in a classification task, it is essential to take these labels into consideration when we perform linear dimensionality reduction. FLD is such a supervised dimensionality reduction method, and we will start the introduction of FLD from the simple binary classification setup again.

The example in Figure 6.1 is rather contrived and extreme. In real applications, both PCA and FLD are useful, and they can be combined to produce better linear dimensionality reduction results. PCA+FLD has been a very successful method in face recognition.

6.1 FLD for Binary Classification

The example in Figure 6.1 also gives us some hints on how to incorporate the labels. Given any projection direction $\boldsymbol{w}$ ($\|\boldsymbol{w}\| = 1$), we can compute the projected values as $\boldsymbol{w}^T\boldsymbol{x}$, and require that projected values from the positive and the negative classes are *far apart* from each other.

6.1.1 Idea: What Is Far Apart?

But how do we translate the phrase "two sets of values are far apart from each other" into precise mathematical expressions? That is, we need a way to measure the level of separation between two sets of values. There are many different ways to compare the distance between two sets of values, and we will introduce only the FLD approach in this chapter.

Figure 6.2 shows the histograms (with 10 bins) of the projected values for the data in Figure 6.1, when the PCA or FLD projection directions are used. A plot that shows all the projected values might be too cluttered to reflect any valuable information. A histogram succinctly captures the distribution properties of the projected values, and hence is a useful tool in various studies.

Let us look first at the FLD figure (Figure 6.2b). The histograms of both classes are sharp, meaning that the projected values of the positive examples are in a small range, as are those of the negative examples. In this case, we can use the mean of each class to represent that class. And the level of separation between these two classes can be measured by the distance between the two mean values. In this example, the two mean values are 0.0016 and 2.0654, respectively. The distance between them is 2.0638.

However, if we apply this measure of separation, we will encounter difficulty when we move to the PCA projection direction, whose histogram is shown in Figure 6.2a. The two mean values are -2.2916 and 2.2916, respectively. The distance, 4.5832, is even larger than that in the FLD case (2.0638). Note that the scale of the x-axis is different in Figures 6.2b and 6.2a.

This does not mean that the PCA projection direction is better, though. As shown in Figure 6.2a, the two histograms overlap seriously, meaning that the level of separation is low. This paradox (i.e., PCA has larger distance between projected mean values, but worse separation) appears because the *shapes* of the histograms are not taken into account. The FLD histograms are sharp and have small variances (or standard deviations). The distance between mean values is very large compared to *both* standard deviations. Hence, the two histograms do not overlap with each other.

In the PCA case, the distance between mean values is smaller than both standard deviations. Hence, the two histograms significantly overlap with each other, which means low separation ability.

Putting these facts together, it is the *ratio* between

- the distance between the two mean values and
- the two standard deviations

that decides separability, not the distance alone. We want to maximize this ratio.

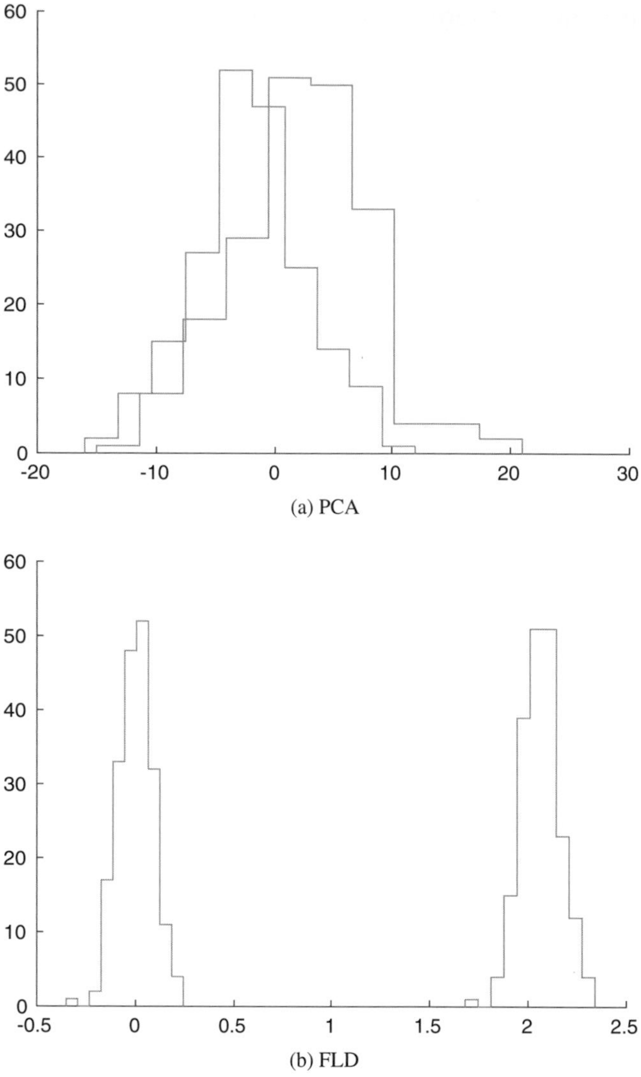

Figure 6.2 Histograms of projected values of the dataset in Figure 6.1 along the PCA (Figure 6.2a) or FLD (Figure 6.2b) direction. Please note that the scales in the x-axis are *different* in these figures. (A black and white version of this figure will appear in some formats. For the color version, please refer to the plate section.)

6.1.2 Translation into Mathematics

Let us define our notation first. One training example for FLD will be a pair $(\boldsymbol{x}_i, y_i)$ instead of a single vector $\boldsymbol{x}_i$, in which $\boldsymbol{x}_i \in \mathbb{R}^D$ is the original input vector that describes the ith example in the training set, and $y_i \in \{1, 2\}$ is a label that specifies to which class $\boldsymbol{x}_i$ belongs. Hence, a training set X with N such pairs can be written as $\{(\boldsymbol{x}_i, y_i)\}_{i=1}^N$, which is an abbreviation for the set $\{(\boldsymbol{x}_1, y_1), (\boldsymbol{x}_2, y_2), \ldots, (\boldsymbol{x}_N, y_N)\}$.

Because there are two categories, we can collect all positive examples to form a subset of X as

$$X_1 = \{\boldsymbol{x}_i \mid 1 \le i \le N,\ y_i = 1\},$$

and $N_1 = |X_1|$ is the size of this subset, which is also the number of positive examples in X. Similarly, we define

$$X_2 = \{\boldsymbol{x}_i \mid 1 \le i \le N,\ y_i = 2\}$$

and $N_2 = |X_2|$. Note that we do not include the labels y_i in X_1 or X_2, because the labels of examples in them can be easily deduced.

The means of vectors in these subsets are also easy to define, as

$$\boldsymbol{m}_1 = \frac{1}{N_1} \sum_{\boldsymbol{x} \in X_1} \boldsymbol{x}, \tag{6.1}$$

$$\boldsymbol{m}_2 = \frac{1}{N_2} \sum_{\boldsymbol{x} \in X_2} \boldsymbol{x}, \tag{6.2}$$

respectively. Later, we will find these two pieces of notation very useful, and it is convenient to define them early. Similarly, the covariance matrices are

$$C_1 = \frac{1}{N_1} \sum_{\boldsymbol{x} \in X_1} (\boldsymbol{x} - \boldsymbol{m}_1)(\boldsymbol{x} - \boldsymbol{m}_1)^T, \tag{6.3}$$

$$C_2 = \frac{1}{N_2} \sum_{\boldsymbol{x} \in X_2} (\boldsymbol{x} - \boldsymbol{m}_2)(\boldsymbol{x} - \boldsymbol{m}_2)^T, \tag{6.4}$$

respectively.

Given any projection direction $\boldsymbol{w}$, as in the PCA case we can safely assume $\|\boldsymbol{w}\| = 1$. Hence, the projected value for $\boldsymbol{x}_i$ is $\boldsymbol{x}_i^T \boldsymbol{w}$. The means of projected values for the two classes are

$$m_1 = \boldsymbol{m}_1^T \boldsymbol{w}, \tag{6.5}$$

$$m_2 = \boldsymbol{m}_2^T \boldsymbol{w}, \tag{6.6}$$

respectively.

The variance for projected positive examples is

$$\frac{1}{N_1} \sum_{\boldsymbol{x} \in X_1} \left(\boldsymbol{x}^T \boldsymbol{w} - \boldsymbol{m}_1^T \boldsymbol{w}\right)^2 \tag{6.7}$$

$$= \boldsymbol{w}^T \left(\frac{1}{N_1} \sum_{\boldsymbol{x} \in X_1} (\boldsymbol{x} - \boldsymbol{m}_1)(\boldsymbol{x} - \boldsymbol{m}_1)^T \right) \boldsymbol{w} \tag{6.8}$$

$$= \boldsymbol{w}^T C_1 \boldsymbol{w}, \tag{6.9}$$

and the standard deviation is

$$\sigma_1 = \sqrt{\boldsymbol{w}^T C_1 \boldsymbol{w}}. \tag{6.10}$$

Similarly, the variance and standard deviation for the negative examples are

$$\boldsymbol{w}^T C_2 \boldsymbol{w} \tag{6.11}$$

$$\text{and} \quad \sigma_2 = \sqrt{\boldsymbol{w}^T C_2 \boldsymbol{w}}, \tag{6.12}$$

respectively.

The ratio we want to maximize can be translated into different forms, e.g.,

$$\frac{|m_1 - m_2|}{\sigma_1 + \sigma_2} \tag{6.13}$$

or

$$\frac{|m_1 - m_2|}{\sqrt{\sigma_1^2 + \sigma_2^2}}. \tag{6.14}$$

Both equations are referred to as Fisher's linear discriminant by some authors. However, the classic FLD has a slightly different form, which we will introduce soon. We want to point out that the solution of these two equations should also give reasonable projection directions for binary problems because they share the same intuition with FLD.

6.1.3 Scatter vs. Covariance Matrix

Maximizing Eq. (6.14) does not seem convenient. The absolute value and the square root both complicate the optimization. However, we can maximize the alternative objective function

$$\frac{(m_1 - m_2)^2}{\sigma_1^2 + \sigma_2^2}, \tag{6.15}$$

because maximizing this equation is obviously equivalent to maximizing Eq. (6.14).

The projection $\boldsymbol{w}$ is only implicitly embedded in Eq. (6.15). Plugging in the expressions for m_1, m_2, σ_1^2, and σ_2^2, we get the following objective, which is explicit in $\boldsymbol{w}$:

$$\frac{\boldsymbol{w}^T(\boldsymbol{m}_1 - \boldsymbol{m}_2)(\boldsymbol{m}_1 - \boldsymbol{m}_2)^T \boldsymbol{w}}{\boldsymbol{w}^T(C_1 + C_2)\boldsymbol{w}}. \tag{6.16}$$

The term $C_1 + C_2$ uses the covariance matrix statistics of X_1 and X_2 to measure how *scattered* they are. Other than covariance matrices, the *scatter matrix* is another interesting statistic to measure how scattered a set of points is. The scatter matrix for a set of points $z_1, z_2, \ldots, z_n$ is defined as

$$S = \sum_{i=1}^{n} (z_i - \bar{z})(z_i - \bar{z})^T, \tag{6.17}$$

where $\bar{z}$ is the mean of these points, defined as

$$\bar{z} = \frac{1}{n}\sum_{i=1}^{n} z_i.$$

It is obvious that these two statistics are related to each other. Let us denote the scatter matrix for X_1 and X_2 as S_1 and S_2, respectively. Then

$$S_1 = N_1 C_1, \tag{6.18}$$

$$S_2 = N_2 C_2. \tag{6.19}$$

They are equivalent to each other, modulo the slight difference in multiplying by the number of points or not.

Traditionally, the scatter matrix is used in FLD, not the covariance matrix. That is, the FLD objective is

$$\frac{\boldsymbol{w}^T(\boldsymbol{m}_1 - \boldsymbol{m}_2)(\boldsymbol{m}_1 - \boldsymbol{m}_2)^T \boldsymbol{w}}{\boldsymbol{w}^T(S_1 + S_2)\boldsymbol{w}}. \tag{6.20}$$

However, we want to point out that the solutions for both forms should be similar to each other qualitatively. When the numbers of examples in all classes are the same, these two should give the same answer.

6.1.4 The Two Scatter Matrices and the FLD Objective

In FLD (for binary problems), two additional symbols are introduced:

$$S_B = (\boldsymbol{m}_1 - \boldsymbol{m}_2)(\boldsymbol{m}_1 - \boldsymbol{m}_2)^T, \tag{6.21}$$

$$S_W = S_1 + S_2, \tag{6.22}$$

in which S_B is called the between-class scatter matrix, and S_W is the within-class scatter matrix (both are $D \times D$ in size). The matrix S_W measures how *scattered* the original input dataset is *within* each class, whereas S_B measures the scatter caused by the two class means, which measures how scattered it is *between* different classes.

Now we can formally define the FLD objective as

$$J = \frac{\boldsymbol{w}^T S_B \boldsymbol{w}}{\boldsymbol{w}^T S_W \boldsymbol{w}}. \tag{6.23}$$

In other words, this optimization aims at finding a projection direction that makes the *between-class scatter much larger than the within-class scatter.*

A side note will be useful soon when we deal with multiclass problems. In Eq. (6.21), one class is approximately represented by its mean (as $\boldsymbol{m}_1$ and $\boldsymbol{m}_2$, respectively). This is a reasonable simplification, especially when the scatter within each class is not large.

However, if one mean vector acts as a surrogate for all examples in its respective class, we would expect that the *scatter matrix of the set of mean vectors* to be the between-class scatter—i.e., we should expect that

$$\sum_{i=1}^{2}(\boldsymbol{m}_i - \bar{\boldsymbol{m}})(\boldsymbol{m}_i - \bar{\boldsymbol{m}})^T \tag{6.24}$$

is the between-class scatter, rather than S_B. In Eq. (6.24),

$$\bar{\boldsymbol{m}} = \frac{\boldsymbol{m}_1 + \boldsymbol{m}_2}{2}.$$

These two terms (Eqs. 6.24 and 6.21) are not exactly the same; however, it is easy to verify that

$$\frac{1}{2} S_B = \sum_{i=1}^{2} (\boldsymbol{m}_i - \bar{\boldsymbol{m}})(\boldsymbol{m}_i - \bar{\boldsymbol{m}})^T. \tag{6.25}$$

Hence, it is reasonable to define S_B in the form of Eq. (6.21) because a constant factor $\frac{1}{2}$ will not change the optimal solution for Eq. (6.23).

6.1.5 The Optimization

The right-hand side of Eq. (6.23) is called the generalized Rayleigh quotient, or the Rayleigh–Ritz ratio, whose maximization is not only useful in computer science (e.g., in FLD), but also in other subjects (such as physics).

Finding the derivative of J with respect to $\boldsymbol{w}$ and setting that to $\boldsymbol{0}$, we get

$$\frac{\partial J}{\partial \boldsymbol{w}} = \frac{2\left((\boldsymbol{w}^T S_W \boldsymbol{w}) S_B \boldsymbol{w} - (\boldsymbol{w}^T S_B \boldsymbol{w}) S_W \boldsymbol{w}\right)}{(\boldsymbol{w}^T S_W \boldsymbol{w})^2} = \boldsymbol{0}. \tag{6.26}$$

Hence, one necessary condition for optimality is

$$S_B \boldsymbol{w} = \frac{\boldsymbol{w}^T S_B \boldsymbol{w}}{\boldsymbol{w}^T S_W \boldsymbol{w}} S_W \boldsymbol{w}. \tag{6.27}$$

Noticing that $\frac{\boldsymbol{w}^T S_B \boldsymbol{w}}{\boldsymbol{w}^T S_W \boldsymbol{w}}$ is a scalar value, this condition states that $\boldsymbol{w}$ should be a *generalized eigenvector of S_B and S_W*, with $\frac{\boldsymbol{w}^T S_B \boldsymbol{w}}{\boldsymbol{w}^T S_W \boldsymbol{w}}$ being its corresponding generalized eigenvalue!

Since $J = \frac{\boldsymbol{w}^T S_B \boldsymbol{w}}{\boldsymbol{w}^T S_W \boldsymbol{w}}$ is both the generalized eigenvalue and the optimization objective, we should use the generalized eigenvector of S_B and S_W whose corresponding generalized eigenvalue is the largest; this gives the optimal parameter $\boldsymbol{w}^\star$ that maximizes J.

6.1.6 Wait, We Have a Shortcut!

Although there are efficient routines to find generalized eigenvalues and eigenvectors, there is an easier way to solve FLD for a binary problem—if we look carefully we will find it.

Some small tweaking to Eq. (6.27) tells us that

$$S_W \boldsymbol{w} = \frac{\boldsymbol{w}^T S_W \boldsymbol{w}}{\boldsymbol{w}^T S_B \boldsymbol{w}} S_B \boldsymbol{w} \tag{6.28}$$

$$= \frac{\boldsymbol{w}^T S_W \boldsymbol{w}}{\boldsymbol{w}^T S_B \boldsymbol{w}} (\boldsymbol{m}_1 - \boldsymbol{m}_2)(\boldsymbol{m}_1 - \boldsymbol{m}_2)^T \boldsymbol{w} \tag{6.29}$$

$$= \frac{\boldsymbol{w}^T S_W \boldsymbol{w}}{\boldsymbol{w}^T S_B \boldsymbol{w}} (\boldsymbol{m}_1 - \boldsymbol{m}_2)^T \boldsymbol{w} (\boldsymbol{m}_1 - \boldsymbol{m}_2) \tag{6.30}$$

$$= c(\boldsymbol{m}_1 - \boldsymbol{m}_2), \tag{6.31}$$

in which we define

$$c \triangleq \frac{\boldsymbol{w}^T S_W \boldsymbol{w}}{\boldsymbol{w}^T S_B \boldsymbol{w}} (\boldsymbol{m}_1 - \boldsymbol{m}_2)^T \boldsymbol{w},$$

and c is a scalar value. Hence, this optimality condition directly leads to the optimal projection direction:

$$S_W^{-1}(\boldsymbol{m}_1 - \boldsymbol{m}_2). \tag{6.32}$$

Then by normalizing this direction to make its ℓ_2 norm equal 1, we get the optimal $\boldsymbol{w}$. In the above equation, we have omitted the factor c because it will disappear anyway in the normalization process. More details of data normalization will be discussed in Chapter 9.

6.1.7 The FLD Method for Binary Problems

Algorithm 5 describes the steps to find the FLD projection direction for a binary classification problem.

Algorithm 5 The FLD algorithm for a binary problem

1: **Input**: A D dimensional binary training set $\{(\boldsymbol{x}_i, y_i)\}_{i=1}^N$.

2: Compute $\boldsymbol{m}_1$, $\boldsymbol{m}_2$, and S_W following the equations in this chapter.

3: Compute

$$\boldsymbol{w} \leftarrow S_W^{-1}(\boldsymbol{m}_1 - \boldsymbol{m}_2).$$

4: Normalize:

$$\boldsymbol{w} \leftarrow \frac{\boldsymbol{w}}{\|\boldsymbol{w}\|}.$$

The idea of FLD was originally described by Ronald Fisher, a famous statistician and biologist. This method is named after him, as *Fisher's linear discriminant*, abbreviated as FLD. This name is sometimes used interchangeably with LDA (which stands for linear discriminant analysis). LDA, however, is often used to refer to any linear discriminant function, including FLD but not limited to it.

6.1.8 A Caveat: What If S_W Is Not Invertible?

There is an obvious shortcoming of Algorithm 5: it is not well defined if S_W is not invertible.

If there are more positive (or negative) examples than the number of dimensions—i.e., if $N_1 > D$ or $N_2 > D$—then S_W will be invertible with high probability. However, if S_W^{-1} does not exist in some cases, we can use the Moore–Penrose (or MP for short) pseudoinverse to replace the inverse. Detailed coverage of the Moore–Penrose pseudoinverse is beyond the scope of this book: we will only briefly explain how to compute it for S_W.

Instead of the $^{-1}$ superscript, the Moore–Penrose pseudoinverse is usually denoted by a $^+$ superscript. It is easy to compute the MP pseudoinverse for a 1×1 matrix—i.e., a scalar $x \in \mathbb{R}$—following the rule

$$x^+ = \begin{cases} 0 & \text{if } x = 0, \\ \dfrac{1}{x} & \text{otherwise.} \end{cases} \tag{6.33}$$

Then a diagonal matrix

$$\Lambda = \operatorname{diag}(\lambda_1, \lambda_2, \ldots, \lambda_D)$$

has its MP pseudoinverse as

$$\Lambda^+ = \operatorname{diag}(\lambda_1^+, \lambda_2^+, \ldots, \lambda_D^+). \tag{6.34}$$

Note that when Λ is invertible (i.e., when $\lambda_i \neq 0$ for $1 \leq i \leq D$), the MP pseudoinverse is the same as the usual matrix inverse.

Since S_W is the sum of two covariance matrices, it is positive semidefinite. Hence, we can find its spectral decomposition as

$$S_W = E \Lambda E^T,$$

where the diagonal matrix Λ contains the eigenvalues of S_W and the columns of the orthogonal matrix E contain the eigenvectors of S_W. The Moore–Penrose pseudoinverse of S_W is then

$$S_W^+ = E \Lambda^+ E^T. \tag{6.35}$$

Note that when S_W is invertible, $S_W^+ = S_W^{-1}$.

6.2 FLD for More Classes

When our data are multiclass—i.e., when there are more than two possible labels—we need to extend Algorithm 5 to handle this situation.

We still have a training set $\{(\boldsymbol{x}_i, y_i)\}_{i=1}^N$. However, y_i now has a different domain. Let $\mathcal{Y} = \{1, 2, \ldots, K\}$ denote the K possible labels in a K-class problem, and $y_i \in \mathcal{Y}$ for all $1 \leq i \leq N$.

The idea of letting the projection values of examples in these K classes be far apart from each other still makes sense in this more complex setting. But it is more difficult to translate this idea into precise mathematics.

In the binary case, we maximize $\frac{\boldsymbol{w}^T S_B \boldsymbol{w}}{\boldsymbol{w}^T S_W \boldsymbol{w}}$ (cf. Eq. 6.23), whose meaning is to make the between-class variance (or scatter) much larger than the within-class variance (or scatter). This intuition may still be valid in multiclass problems. However, the key issue becomes how to define these two variances (or scatter) when we have $K > 2$ classes (i.e., how do we define S_B and S_W for this new setup?).

6.2.1 Slightly Modified Notation and S_W

The within-class scatter matrix S_W can be easily extended to multiclass while keeping its semantic meaning. We just need to modify the notation a bit.

Let N_k, $\boldsymbol{m}_k$, C_k, and S_k be the size, mean, covariance matrix, and scatter matrix, respectively, of the subset X_k of X that belongs to the kth class, $1 \le k \le K$—i.e.,

$$X_k = \{\boldsymbol{x}_i \mid y_i = k\}, \tag{6.36}$$

$$N_k = |X_k|, \tag{6.37}$$

$$\boldsymbol{m}_k = \frac{1}{N_k} \sum_{\boldsymbol{x} \in X_k} \boldsymbol{x}, \tag{6.38}$$

$$C_k = \frac{1}{N_k} \sum_{\boldsymbol{x} \in X_k} (\boldsymbol{x} - \boldsymbol{m}_k)(\boldsymbol{x} - \boldsymbol{m}_k)^T, \tag{6.39}$$

$$S_k = N_k C_k = \sum_{\boldsymbol{x} \in X_k} (\boldsymbol{x} - \boldsymbol{m}_k)(\boldsymbol{x} - \boldsymbol{m}_k)^T. \tag{6.40}$$

The within-class scatter is then simply the sum of the scatter matrices of the K subsets, which measures the overall within-class scatter of the multiclass training set,

$$S_W = \sum_{k=1}^{K} S_k. \tag{6.41}$$

6.2.2 Candidates for S_B

It is, however, not trivial to extend the between-class scatter matrix S_B to multiclass in a natural way. A straightforward extension might be

$$\sum_{i=1}^{K} \sum_{j=1}^{K} (\boldsymbol{m}_i - \boldsymbol{m}_j)(\boldsymbol{m}_i - \boldsymbol{m}_j)^T, \tag{6.42}$$

which mimics Eq. (6.21). But this equation requires the creation of K^2 matrices of size $D \times D$, and also the sum of them. Hence, it is not very attractive in terms of computational efficiency.

Equation (6.25) may lead to another possible extension,

$$\sum_{k=1}^{K}(\boldsymbol{m}_k - \bar{\boldsymbol{m}})(\boldsymbol{m}_k - \bar{\boldsymbol{m}})^T, \tag{6.43}$$

where

$$\bar{\boldsymbol{m}} = \frac{1}{K}\sum_{k=1}^{K}\boldsymbol{m}_k. \tag{6.44}$$

Equation (6.43) is the scatter of the K mean vectors, which fits our intuition of the between-class scatter and is also fast to compute.

However, researchers have found another definition, which makes even more sense.

6.2.3 A Tale of Three Scatter Matrices

Note that we can compute the scatter matrix for the entire training set regardless of the class labels. We denote it as S_T, with

$$S_T = \sum_{i=1}^{N}(\boldsymbol{x}_i - \boldsymbol{m})(\boldsymbol{x}_i - \boldsymbol{m})^T, \tag{6.45}$$

where

$$\boldsymbol{m} = \frac{1}{N}\sum_{i=1}^{N}\boldsymbol{x}_i \tag{6.46}$$

is the mean of all training points. Note that Eq. (6.46) (for $\boldsymbol{m}$) is different from Eq. (6.44) (for $\bar{\boldsymbol{m}}$).

We call S_T the *total scatter* matrix. It is interesting to see what the difference is between the total and within-class scatter, and some algebraic manipulation gives us

$$S_T - S_W = \sum_{k=1}^{K} N_k(\boldsymbol{m}_k - \boldsymbol{m})(\boldsymbol{m}_k - \boldsymbol{m})^T. \tag{6.47}$$

The right-hand side of Eq. (6.47) closely resembles the scatter matrix in Eq. (6.43), with only two slight exceptions. First, $\boldsymbol{m}$ replaces $\bar{\boldsymbol{m}}$; second, each term in the summation is multiplied by N_k.

In FLD, the between-class scatter is defined as

$$S_B = \sum_{k=1}^{K} N_k(\boldsymbol{m}_k - \boldsymbol{m})(\boldsymbol{m}_k - \boldsymbol{m})^T. \tag{6.48}$$

We want to point out that when the classes have equal sizes—i.e., when $N_i = N_j$ for any i and j—the above two deviations are trivial. In that case, $\boldsymbol{m} = \bar{\boldsymbol{m}}$ and Eq. (6.48) differs from Eq. (6.43) only by the constant multiplier $\frac{K}{N}$.

Furthermore, these changes are effective in imbalanced problems. Consider an imbalanced problem where $N_i \gg N_j$ for some i and j. We expect $\boldsymbol{m}_i$ to be more important than $\boldsymbol{m}_j$. Both Eqs. (6.46) and (6.48) put more weight on $\boldsymbol{m}_i$ than $\boldsymbol{m}_j$, while they are treated equally in Eqs. (6.44) and (6.43).

Finally, it makes sense if the sum of between- and within-class scatter matrices equals the total scatter matrix, in which case we have an easy-to-remember and reasonable equation that describes the tale of three scatter matrices:

$$S_T = S_B + S_W. \tag{6.49}$$

We also point out that when $K = 2$, Eq. (6.48) is different from Eq. (6.21). When we are dealing with an imbalanced binary problem (e.g., when the negative class has many more examples than the positive class), it might help if we define S_B following Eq. (6.48) even in the binary setup.

6.2.4 The Solution

Since S_B is not a rank 1 matrix in multiclass problems, Algorithm 5 is not applicable. However, we can still find the optimal projection direction by solving a generalized eigenvalue problem

$$S_B\boldsymbol{w} = \lambda S_W \boldsymbol{w}.$$

When S_W is invertible, the generalized eigenvalue problem is equivalent to an eigenvalue problem

$$S_W^{-1} S_B \boldsymbol{w} = \lambda \boldsymbol{w}.$$

However, directly solving the generalized eigenvalue problem is more efficient. For example, in MATLAB we can obtain the solution using a simple command `eig(A,B)`, where $A = S_B$ and $B = S_W$, and retrieve the generalized eigenvector associated with the largest generalized eigenvalue.

6.2.5 Finding More Projection Directions

As in PCA, we can find more projection directions for multiclass FLD: just use the generalized eigenvectors associated with the top $K-1$ largest generalized eigenvalues.

For a K-class problem we can extract at most $K-1$ meaningful features (i.e., projected values). We will leave the proof of this statement to the reader as an exercise problem.

The generalized eigenvectors are not necessarily ℓ_2 normalized or perpendicular to each other.

6.3 Miscellaneous Notes and Additional Resources

In this chapter, we did not explain how the generalized eigenvectors are computed or why there are at most $K-1$ meaningful FLD features. The exercise problems for this chapter are designed to explain these slightly more advanced topics. These problems cover concepts such as matrix rank, matrix norm, matrix factorization (LU, LDL, and Cholesky). Putting these concepts and related algorithms together, one can come up with an FLD solver for the multiclass case. We also introduce the condition number. For details that are important in implementing these algorithms, please refer to Press et al. (1992) and Golub & van Loan (1996).

One important application of FLD (and PCA) is face recognition, which is briefly introduced as a programming problem. More details of Fisherfaces (which uses both PCA and FLD for face recognition) can be found in Belhumeur et al. (1997).

For comparing two sets of values, the Hausdorff distance is widely used, e.g., to compare images (Huttenlocher et al. 1993). In a machine learning paradigm called multi-instance learning, a set of values are combined to form a bag, and bags can be efficiently compared (Wei et al. 2017b).

Details and more theoretical treatments of the generalized inverse can be found in Ben-Israel & Greville (2003).

Exercises

6.1 (Matrix rank) Let A be a real matrix of size $m \times n$. Its rank, denoted as $\operatorname{rank}(A)$, is defined as the maximal number of linearly independent rows in A, which is also called the row rank. Similarly, the column rank is the maximal number of linearly independent columns in A.

(a) Prove that the row rank is equal to the column rank. Hence,

$$\operatorname{rank}(X) = \operatorname{rank}(X^T).$$

(b) Prove that

$$\operatorname{rank}(A) \le \min(m,n).$$

(c) Let X and Y be two matrices of the same size. Show that

$$\operatorname{rank}(X+Y) \le \operatorname{rank}(X) + \operatorname{rank}(Y).$$

(d) Show that

$$\operatorname{rank}(XY) \le \min(\operatorname{rank}(X), \operatorname{rank}(Y))$$

so long as the matrix multiplication is well defined.

(e) A matrix X of size $m \times n$ is called *full rank* if

$$\operatorname{rank}(X) = \min(m,n).$$

Prove that if X is full rank, then

$$\operatorname{rank}(X) = \operatorname{rank}(XX^T) = \operatorname{rank}(X^TX).$$

(f) Let $\boldsymbol{x}$ be a vector; what is the rank of $\boldsymbol{x}\boldsymbol{x}^T$? Show that the rank of a real symmetric matrix X equals its number of nonzero eigenvalues. This is the way we used to define matrix rank in Chapter 2.

6.2 (Matrix norm) Similar to vectors norms, various matrix norms can be defined. By definition, $f\colon \mathbb{R}^{m\times n} \mapsto \mathbb{R}$ is a matrix norm if it satisfies the following conditions:

(i) $f(X) \geq 0$ for any $X \in \mathbb{R}^{m\times n}$;
(ii) $f(X) = 0$ if and only if X is a zero matrix;
(iii) $f(X+Y) \leq f(X) + f(Y)$ for $X, Y \in \mathbb{R}^{m\times n}$;
(iv) $f(cX) = |c| f(X)$ for $c \in \mathbb{R}$ and $X \in \mathbb{R}^{m\times n}$.

(a) Prove that

$$\|X\|_2 = \max_{\|\boldsymbol{v}\|=1} \|X\boldsymbol{v}\|$$

is a valid matrix norm (which is called the 2-norm). The vector norm considered here is the vector 2-norm $\|\boldsymbol{x}\| = \sqrt{\boldsymbol{x}^T\boldsymbol{x}}$.

(b) Let $\sigma_{\max}(X)$ denote the largest singular value of a matrix X. Prove that if X and Y are of the same size, then

$$\sigma_{\max}(X) + \sigma_{\max}(Y) \geq \sigma_{\max}(X+Y).$$

(Hint: What is the relationship between $\sigma_{\max}(X)$ and $\|X\|_2$?)

6.3 (Condition number) Given any matrix norm $\|\cdot\|$, a corresponding *condition number* can be defined for a nonsingular real square matrix. The condition number of a matrix X is defined as

$$\kappa(X) = \|X\|\,\|X^{-1}\|.$$

One frequently used condition number is the 2-norm condition:

$$\kappa_2(X) = \|X\|_2\|X^{-1}\|_2.$$

A matrix is called *ill conditioned* if its condition number is large.

(a) If you already know the singular values of X as $\sigma_1 \geq \sigma_2 \geq \cdots \geq \sigma_n$, what is the condition number $\kappa_2(X)$?

(b) Let f be a function from a set $\mathbb{X}$ to a set $\mathbb{Y}$. Suppose $f(\boldsymbol{x}) = \boldsymbol{y}$ and $f(\boldsymbol{x}+\Delta\boldsymbol{x}) = \boldsymbol{y}+\Delta\boldsymbol{y}$. We call f *ill conditioned* if a small $\Delta\boldsymbol{x}$ leads to a large $\Delta\boldsymbol{y}$. Let A be a square full-rank matrix (i.e., invertible matrix) in $\mathbb{R}^{n\times n}$ and $\boldsymbol{b} \in \mathbb{R}^n$, and we are interested in solving $A\boldsymbol{x} = \boldsymbol{b}$. Show that this linear system is ill conditioned if $\kappa_2(A)$ is large. (You are not required to prove this conclusion. Just give some intuition as to why an ill-conditioned matrix A is bad.)

(c) Show that an orthogonal matrix is well conditioned (i.e., has a small condition number).

6.4 (LU, LDL, and Cholesky factorizations) In this exercise we study various factorizations that are useful in computing the generalized eigenvalue problem.

(a) Show that

$$\begin{bmatrix} 1 & 2 & 3 \\ 2 & 3 & 4 \\ 3 & 4 & 6 \end{bmatrix} = \begin{bmatrix} 1 & 0 & 0 \\ 2 & 1 & 0 \\ 3 & 0 & 1 \end{bmatrix} \begin{bmatrix} 1 & 2 & 3 \\ 0 & -1 & -2 \\ 0 & -2 & -3 \end{bmatrix}.$$

(b) (Gauss transformation) In a more general form, let $\boldsymbol{v}$ be a vector in $\mathbb{R}^n$ and $v_k \neq 0$. Then the *Gauss transformation* M_k is an $n \times n$ lower triangular matrix of the form

$$M_k = \begin{bmatrix} 1 & \cdots & 0 & 0 & \cdots & 0 \\ \vdots & \ddots & \vdots & \vdots & \ddots & \vdots \\ 0 & \cdots & 1 & 0 & \cdots & 0 \\ 0 & \cdots & -\frac{v_{k+1}}{v_k} & 1 & \cdots & 0 \\ \vdots & \ddots & \vdots & \vdots & \ddots & \vdots \\ 0 & \cdots & -\frac{v_n}{v_k} & 0 & \cdots & 1 \end{bmatrix}. \tag{6.50}$$

That is, entries in M_k are all 0 except for those on the diagonals and those in the kth column. The diagonals are all 1s. In the kth column, the first $k-1$ entries are 0, the kth entry is 1, and the ith entry ($i > k$) is $-\frac{v_i}{v_k}$. What is the result of left-multiplying $\boldsymbol{v}$ by M_k?

(c) For an $n \times n$ matrix A, what is the effect of running the following algorithm?

```
A^(1) = A.
for k = 1, 2, ..., n − 1 do
    Let v = A^(k)_{:k} (i.e., the kth column of A^(k)), and compute the Gauss transforma-
    tion M_k based on v.
    A^(k+1) ← M_k A^(k).
end for
```

In the above algorithm, we assume $a_{kk}^{(k)} \neq 0$ for $1 \leq k \leq n-1$.

(d) Show that $\det(M_k) = 1$ for all $1 \leq k < n$. If $L = M_{n-1}M_{n-2}\dots M_1$, prove that L is lower triangular and its determinant is 1.

(e) (LU factorization) Let $A \in \mathbb{R}^{n \times n}$. And, for $1 \leq k \leq n-1$, the leading principal submatrix $A_{1:k,\,1:k}$ is nonsingular. Prove that there exists a decomposition

$$A = LR,$$

where $L \in \mathbb{R}^{n \times n}$ is lower triangular with its diagonal entries all being 1, and $U \in \mathbb{R}^{n \times n}$ is upper triangular. If A is furthermore nonsingular, prove that the LU decomposition is *unique*.

(f) (LDL factorization) We turn our attention to the LDL factorization of a real symmetric and positive definite matrix. If A is such a matrix, prove that there exist a *unique* lower triangular real matrix L (with its diagonal entries all being 1) and a diagonal matrix D such that

$$A = LDL^T.$$

(g) (Cholesky factorization) Let A be a real symmetric positive definite matrix. Then prove that there exists a *unique* real lower triangular matrix G such that

$$A = GG^T,$$

and the diagonal entries in G are all positive. This matrix decomposition is called the *Cholesky* factorization or Cholesky decomposition, named after the French mathematician André-Louis Cholesky.

6.5 (Solving FLD) Consider a C ($C > 2$) class FLD problem, in which there are N examples of D dimensions.

(a) If $N < D$, will S_W be invertible?

(b) Prove that at most $C-1$ generalized eigenvectors can be obtained. (Hint: What is the rank of S_B?)

(c) Explain why S_W is very probably invertible if $N > D$, especially if $N \gg D$.

(d) The generalized eigenvalue problem $S_B\boldsymbol{w} = \lambda S_W\boldsymbol{w}$ is equivalent to $S_W^{-1}S_B\boldsymbol{w} = \lambda\boldsymbol{w}$ when S_W is invertible. However, in practice we do not solve $S_W^{-1}S_B\boldsymbol{w} = \lambda\boldsymbol{w}$. One algorithm for computing the FLD solution is as follows.

First, assuming S_W is positive definite, the Cholesky factorization finds a G such that $S_W = GG^T$.

Second, compute $C = G^{-1}S_BG^{-T}$.

Third, diagonalize C such that there is an orthogonal matrix Q and Q^TCQ is a diagonal matrix.

Finally, let $X = G^{-T}Q$.

Prove that X^TS_BX is diagonal and X^TS_WX is the identity matrix. Show that the generalized eigenvectors are in the columns of X and the generalized eigenvalues are in the diagonal entries of X^TS_BX. Are the generalized eigenvectors computed in this way unit norm or orthogonal?

6.6 (PCA+FLD face recognition) Both PCA and FLD are useful in the face recognition application.

(a) The ORL dataset is an early dataset for face recognition. Download the ORL dataset from `www.cl.cam.ac.uk/research/dtg/attarchive/facedatabase.html`. Read the instructions on that page to understand the format of this dataset.

(b) OpenCV is an open source computer vision library, which provides many functions useful for various computer vision applications. Download the library from `http://opencv.org/`. Learn OpenCV basics from `http://docs.opencv.org/`.

(c) There is an OpenCV tutorial on face recognition, which is available at `http://docs.opencv.org/2.4/modules/contrib/doc/facerec/facerec_tutorial.html`. Try to understand every line of code in the tutorial, especially those on Eigenfaces (PCA) and Fisherfaces (FLD). Run experiments on the ORL dataset to analyze the differences between the recognition results of these methods.

(d) In the Eigenface experiment, you can reconstruct an approximate face image using the eigenfaces (i.e., eigenvectors). Modify the source code in the OpenCV tutorial, and observe the visualization using different numbers of eigenfaces. How many eigenfaces are required if you want the face reconstructed from the eigenfaces to be visually indistinguishable from the original input face image?

Part III

Classifiers and Tools

7 Support Vector Machines

Support vector machines (SVMs) are a family of widely applied classification methods that have exhibited excellent accuracy in various classification problems. Complex mathematics is involved in various aspects of SVMs—e.g., proof of their generalization bounds, their optimization, and designing and proving the validity of various nonlinear kernels. We will, however, not focus on the mathematics. The main purpose of this chapter is to introduce how the ideas in SVMs are formulated, why are they reasonable, and how various simplifications are useful in shaping the SVM primal form.

We will not touch on any generalization bounds of SVMs, although this is an area that has attracted intensive research effort. We will not talk about how the optimization problem in SVMs can be solved or approximately solved (for efficiency and scalability). These choices enable us to focus on the key ideas that lead to SVMs and the strategies in SVMs that may be helpful in other domains. We encourage readers also to pay attention to these aspects of SVMs while reading this chapter.

7.1 The Key SVM Idea

How will we accomplish a classification task? In Chapter 4 we discussed the Bayes decision theory, which suggests that we can estimate the probability distribution $\Pr(\boldsymbol{x}, y)$ or the density function $p(\boldsymbol{x}, y)$ using the training data. With these distributions, the Bayes decision theory will guide us on how to classify a new example. These types of probabilistic methods are called generative methods. An alternative type of method is the discriminative method, which directly estimates the probability $\Pr(y|\boldsymbol{x})$ or $p(y|\boldsymbol{x})$.

In SVMs we do not model either the generative or the discriminative distributions based on the training data. Instead, the SVM seeks to directly find the best classification boundary that divides the domain of $\boldsymbol{x}$ into different regions. Examples falling in one region all belong to one category, and different regions correspond to different categories or classes.

The rationale behind this choice is that the estimation of probability distributions or densities is a difficult task, which might be even more difficult than the classification task itself, especially when there are only a few training examples.[1] In other words, classification based on density estimation might be taking a detour. Then why not directly estimate the classification boundaries? As illustrated by Figure 7.2, it might be a much easier task to estimate the boundary in some scenarios.

Then the natural question is which classification boundary is considered good or even the best?

7.1.1 Simplify It, Simplify It, Simplify It!

One key to answering this question is actually to simplify the problem, in order to find out in which scenarios it will be easy to determine a good classification boundary. The heading says "simplify it" three times—this is not only because it is important (so must be repeated three times), but also because we are making three simplifying assumptions.

Given datasets (or classification problems) such as those appearing in Figure 7.1, it is difficult to figure out which classifier is good. In Figure 7.1a, the two classes (whose examples are denoted by black squares and red circles, respectively) cannot be classified by any linear boundary. Using a complex curve (i.e., a nonlinear boundary), we can separate these two classes with zero training error. However, it is not obvious either how to compare two complex nonlinear classification boundaries. Hence, we make the first two assumptions:

- *linear boundary* (or linear classifier); and
- *separable* (i.e., linear classifiers can achieve 100% accuracy on the training set).

These two are usually combined to require a *linearly separable* problem.

The problem in Figure 7.1b is in fact linearly separable: the four classes can be divided into nonoverlapping regions by linear boundaries—e.g., the three lines that enclose the red class examples. However, it is not easy to judge whether one triplet of lines is better than another triplet. And there are many other possible linear boundaries beyond triplets that would enclose the red examples. Hence, we make a third assumption:

- The problem is *binary*.

Putting all the assumptions together, we start by considering only *linearly separable binary* classification problems.

We want to emphasize that *these simplifications are reasonable*—i.e., they will not change the essence of the classification problem. As we will introduce in this chapter, all these assumptions will be relaxed and taken care of in SVM. Hence, reasonable simplifying assumptions help us find ideas and good solutions to a complex problem, and we have the option to reconsider these assumptions later such that our method has the potential to solve complex tasks too. However, if an assumption changes some basic characteristics of our problem, it is better avoided.

[1] We will discuss density estimation in the next chapter.

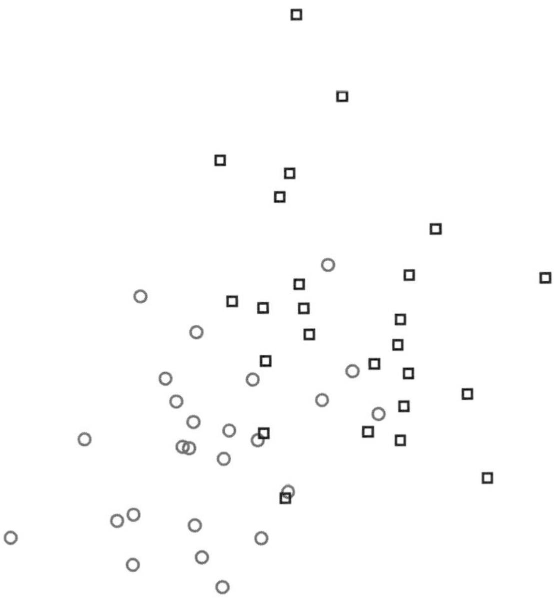

(a) Inseparable data are messy

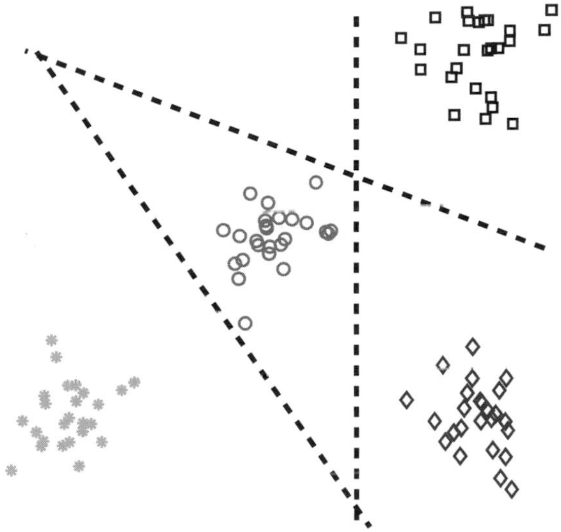

(b) Multiclass data are complex

Figure 7.1 Illustration of complex classification problems. (A black and white version of this figure will appear in some formats. For the color version, please refer to the plate section.)

7.1.2 Finding a Max (or Large) Margin Classifier

Figure 7.2 shows a linearly separable binary problem. It is clear that any line between the cluster of red circles and the cluster of black squares can separate them perfectly. In Figure 7.2a three example boundaries are illustrated: the solid blue line, the red dashed line, and the black dotted line.

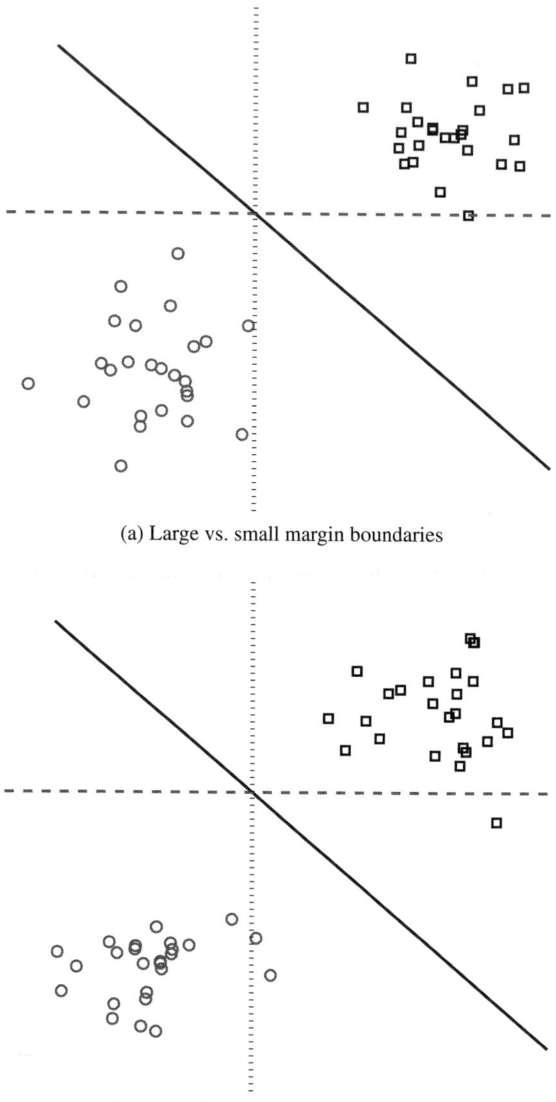

(a) Large vs. small margin boundaries

(b) A small margin can cause problems

Figure 7.2 Illustration of the large margin idea. (A black and white version of this figure will appear in some formats. For the color version, please refer to the plate section.)

Furthermore, it becomes easier to determine which classifier is better (or the best) in this linearly separable binary example. Most people will agree that the classification boundary determined by the solid blue line is better than the other two. The other two boundaries are too close to the examples, leaving very little (almost no) room for variations or noise. The examples in Figures 7.2a and 7.2b are generated using the same underlying distribution and contain the same number of training examples.

However, because of the randomness, in Figure 7.2b two red circles appear on the right-hand side of the black dotted line, and one black square appears below the red dashed line. These examples are errors for the two boundaries, respectively.

The solid blue line, however, correctly classifies all examples in Figure 7.2b. The reason for this robustness is that this boundary is far away from all training examples; hence, when variations or noise are in effect, this classifier has the *margin* to accommodate these changes since the scale of such changes is usually small. As shown in Figure 7.2, the margin of a classifier is the distance from it to the training examples that are the closest to it.

Hence, the margin of one example (with respect to a classification boundary) is the distance from that point to the boundary. Naturally, the margin of a dataset is the minimum of the margins of all its samples.

Because a large margin is beneficial for classification, some classifiers directly maximize the margin; these are called *max-margin classifiers*. Some classifiers seek a compromise between a large margin and other properties, and are called *large margin classifiers*. The SVM is a max-margin classifier.

And, of course, the next task after having had the max-margin idea is how to translate the max-margin idea into operational procedures. First we need to formalize the max-margin idea.

7.2 Visualizing and Calculating the Margin

Given a linear classification boundary and a point $\boldsymbol{x}$, how do we calculate the margin of $\boldsymbol{x}$? We know that in a d-dimensional space, a linear classification boundary is a hyperplane. An illustration such as Figure 7.3 is helpful.

7.2.1 Visualizing the Geometry

We have two ways to specify a vector $\boldsymbol{x}$ in an illustration. One way is to draw an arrow from the origin (O) to the coordinates specified by the elements of $\boldsymbol{x}$. We use this way to draw $\boldsymbol{x}$, $\boldsymbol{x}_\perp$, and $\boldsymbol{x}_0$ in Figure 7.3 (denoted by dashed arrows, but the arrow for $\boldsymbol{x}_0$ is omitted to preserve the illustration's clarity). Another way is to use two endpoints to specify a vector, such that the vector is the difference between the two points. For example, $\boldsymbol{z} = \boldsymbol{x} - \boldsymbol{x}_\perp$ (denoted by the solid black arrow) and two vectors involving $\boldsymbol{x}_0$ (denoted by dotted arrows) are shown in this manner. The vectors $\boldsymbol{w}$ and $-\boldsymbol{w}$ are also specified in this way.

All points in a hyperplane in d-dimensional space are specified by an equation

$$f(\boldsymbol{x}) = \boldsymbol{w}^T\boldsymbol{x} + b = 0,$$

where $\boldsymbol{w}$ determines the direction of the hyperplane. The direction of $\boldsymbol{w}$ (i.e., $\frac{\boldsymbol{w}}{\|\boldsymbol{w}\|}$) is called the normal vector of the hyperplane. A hyperplane is perpendicular to its

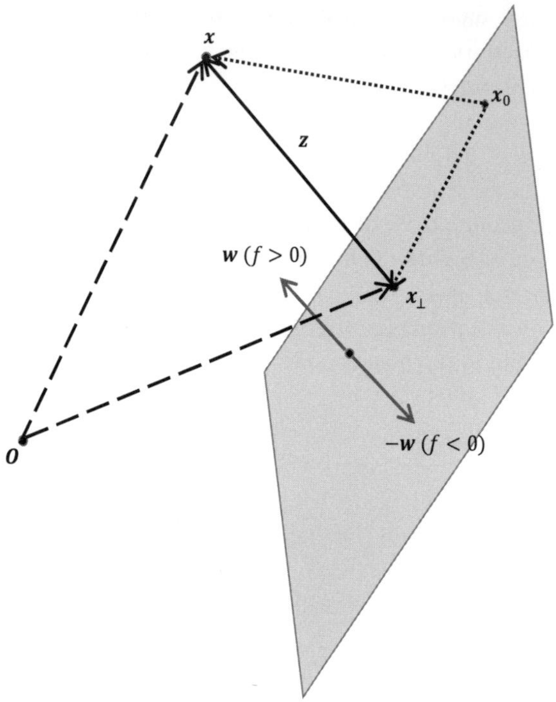

Figure 7.3 Illustration of projection, margin, and normal vector. (A black and white version of this figure will appear in some formats. For the color version, please refer to the plate section.)

normal vector. In other words, if $\boldsymbol{x}_1$ and $\boldsymbol{x}_2$ are two different points on the hyperplane (i.e., satisfying $f(\boldsymbol{x}_1) = f(\boldsymbol{x}_2) = 0$ and $\boldsymbol{x}_1 \neq \boldsymbol{x}_2$), we always have

$$\boldsymbol{w}^T(\boldsymbol{x}_1 - \boldsymbol{x}_2) = 0.$$

If $\boldsymbol{x}$ is on the hyperplane, then $f(\boldsymbol{x}) = 0$; if $\boldsymbol{x}$ is not on the hyperplane, but in the same direction as $\boldsymbol{w}$ with respect to the hyperplane, then $f(\boldsymbol{x}) > 0$, and $f(\boldsymbol{x}) < 0$ holds for points in the opposite direction (cf. the solid red arrows).

In Figure 7.3, $\boldsymbol{x}_\perp$ is the projection of $\boldsymbol{x}$ onto the hyperplane. That is, $\boldsymbol{x}$ is decomposed as

$$\boldsymbol{x} = \boldsymbol{x}_\perp + \boldsymbol{z}.$$

Given any point $\boldsymbol{x}_0$ ($\neq \boldsymbol{x}_\perp$) on the hyperplane, we always have

$$\boldsymbol{z} \perp (\boldsymbol{x}_\perp - \boldsymbol{x}_0).$$

However, $\boldsymbol{x}_\perp$ is not perpendicular to z if $b \neq 0$. This geometry tells us that $\|z\|$ is the distance we are looking for. Hence, a visualization with proper notation helps us translate the description "distance" into precise mathematics.

7.2.2 Calculating the Margin as an Optimization

Even better, the visualization also hints at how to calculate the distance. Since $z \perp (\boldsymbol{x}_\perp - \boldsymbol{x}_0)$, we know $\|z\| \leq \|\boldsymbol{x} - \boldsymbol{x}_0\|$ for any $\boldsymbol{x}_0$ on the hyperplane because of the Pythagorean theorem, which also holds in a space $\mathbb{R}^d$ whose dimensionality is higher than 2 ($d > 2$). That is, $\boldsymbol{x}_\perp$ is the solution of the following optimization problem:

$$\operatorname*{arg\,min}_{\boldsymbol{y}} \quad \|\boldsymbol{x} - \boldsymbol{y}\|^2 \tag{7.1}$$

$$\text{s.t.} \quad f(\boldsymbol{y}) = 0. \tag{7.2}$$

This is an optimization problem with one equality constraint. The Lagrangian is

$$L(\boldsymbol{y}, \lambda) = \|\boldsymbol{x} - \boldsymbol{y}\|^2 - \lambda(\boldsymbol{w}^T \boldsymbol{y} + b).$$

Setting $\frac{\partial L}{\partial \boldsymbol{y}} = \boldsymbol{0}$ gives $2(\boldsymbol{y} - \boldsymbol{x}) = \lambda \boldsymbol{w}$. That is,

$$\boldsymbol{y} = \boldsymbol{x} + \frac{\lambda}{2}\boldsymbol{w}.$$

Plugging it into $f(\boldsymbol{y}) = 0$, we get $\frac{\lambda}{2}\boldsymbol{w}^T\boldsymbol{w} + f(\boldsymbol{x}) = 0$, hence

$$\lambda = -\frac{2f(\boldsymbol{x})}{\boldsymbol{w}^T\boldsymbol{w}}.$$

Then the projection is

$$\boldsymbol{x}_\perp = \boldsymbol{x} + \frac{\lambda}{2}\boldsymbol{w} = \boldsymbol{x} - \frac{f(\boldsymbol{x})}{\boldsymbol{w}^T\boldsymbol{w}}\boldsymbol{w}.$$

Now it is easy to obtain

$$z = \boldsymbol{x} - \boldsymbol{x}_\perp = \frac{f(\boldsymbol{x})}{\boldsymbol{w}^T\boldsymbol{w}}\boldsymbol{w},$$

hence the distance (and the margin of $\boldsymbol{x}$) is

$$\left\| \frac{f(\boldsymbol{x})}{\boldsymbol{w}^T\boldsymbol{w}}\boldsymbol{w} \right\| = \left| \frac{f(\boldsymbol{x})}{\|\boldsymbol{w}\|^2} \right| \|\boldsymbol{w}\| = \frac{|f(\boldsymbol{x})|}{\|\boldsymbol{w}\|}. \tag{7.3}$$

There are simpler ways to find the margin than what is presented here. However, in this section we familiarized ourselves with the geometry useful for SVM, found the actual value of $\boldsymbol{x}_\perp$, exercised the process of formalization and optimization, and applied the method of Lagrange multipliers. These are all fruitful outcomes.

7.3 Maximizing the Margin

The SVM tries to maximize the margin of the dataset—i.e., the smallest margin of all training points.

7.3.1 The Formalization

Let us denote the training set as $\{(\boldsymbol{x}_i, y_i)\}_{i=1}^n$, where $\boldsymbol{x}_i \in \mathbb{R}^d$ is an example, and $y \in \mathcal{Y}$. For a binary problem, $\mathcal{Y} = \{1,2\}$. To maximize the margin of this dataset with respect to a linear boundary $f(\boldsymbol{x}) = \boldsymbol{w}^T\boldsymbol{x} + b$ means to solve the following optimization problem:

$$\max_{\boldsymbol{w},b} \min_{1 \le i \le n} \frac{|f(\boldsymbol{x}_i)|}{\|\boldsymbol{w}\|}, \tag{7.4}$$

with the additional constraint that $f(\boldsymbol{x})$ can classify all training examples correctly. Hence, we also need to mathematically describe "correctly classified."

This is quite simple if we change the definition of $\mathcal{Y}$ slightly. If we set $\mathcal{Y} = \{+1, -1\}$, the meaning of it will not change—the two numbers refer to the labels of the two classes, and the specific values of them are not relevant (e.g., 2 vs. -1), so long as the two values are different. However, with this slight change, the following statement holds:

$$\begin{aligned} &f(\boldsymbol{x}) \text{ correctly classifies all training examples} \\ &\text{if and only if } y_i f(\boldsymbol{x}_i) > 0 \text{ for all } 1 \le i \le n. \end{aligned}$$

When $y_i = 1$ (i.e., a positive example), $y_i f(\boldsymbol{x}_i) > 0$ means $f(\boldsymbol{x}_i) > 0$, thus the prediction is also positive. When $y_i = -1$, $f(\boldsymbol{x}_i) < 0$ and it predicts $\boldsymbol{x}_i$ as negative.

The SVM then optimizes the following problem for a binary linearly separable dataset:

$$\max_{\boldsymbol{w},b} \quad \min_{1 \le i \le n} \frac{|f(\boldsymbol{x}_i)|}{\|\boldsymbol{w}\|} \tag{7.5}$$

$$\text{s.t.} \quad y_i f(\boldsymbol{x}_i) > 0, \quad 1 \le i \le n. \tag{7.6}$$

7.3.2 The Simplifications

The constraints can be handled by a Lagrangian. However, the objective contains a fraction, an absolute value, a vector norm and the maximization of a minimum, all of which are hostile to optimization. Fortunately, by looking at this objective more carefully, there exist ways to avoid all these difficulties.

Our assumption ensures that $y_i f(\boldsymbol{x}_i) > 0$ for all $1 \le i \le n$—that is, we always have

$$y_i f(\boldsymbol{x}_i) = |f(\boldsymbol{x}_i)|$$

because $|y_i| = 1$. Hence, the objective can be rewritten as

$$\min_{1\le i\le n} \frac{|f(\boldsymbol{x}_i)|}{\|\boldsymbol{w}\|} = \min_{1\le i\le n} \frac{y_i f(\boldsymbol{x}_i)}{\|\boldsymbol{w}\|} \tag{7.7}$$

$$= \frac{1}{\|\boldsymbol{w}\|} \min_{1\le i\le n} \left(y_i(\boldsymbol{w}^T\boldsymbol{x}_i + b)\right). \tag{7.8}$$

This type of objective (as a ratio) has appeared many times (e.g., in PCA). If $(\boldsymbol{w}^\star, b^\star)$ is a maximizer of the above objective, so will $(c\boldsymbol{w}^\star, cb^\star)$ be for any nonzero constant $c \in \mathbb{R}$. However, since this is a constrained optimization problem, $c \le 0$ will make all the constraints invalid. When $c > 0$, $(c\boldsymbol{w}^\star, cb^\star)$ will not change the objective, and all constraints remain satisfied. That is, we have the freedom to choose any $c > 0$. In the past, we have chosen a c such that $\|\boldsymbol{w}\| = 1$. If we use this same assumption, the optimization becomes

$$\max_{\boldsymbol{w},b} \quad \min_{1\le i\le n} y_i f(\boldsymbol{x}_i) \tag{7.9}$$

$$\text{s.t.} \quad y_i f(\boldsymbol{x}_i) > 0, \quad 1 \le i \le n, \tag{7.10}$$

$$\boldsymbol{w}^T\boldsymbol{w} = 1. \tag{7.11}$$

The objective is still a maximization of a minimum. And this optimization problem is still difficult to solve.

However, note that $y_i f(\boldsymbol{x}_i)$ appears in both the objective and the constraints; there is a clever trick to further simplify it. If $(\boldsymbol{w}^\star, b^\star)$ is a maximizer of the original objective $\min_{1\le i\le n} \frac{|f(\boldsymbol{x}_i)|}{\|\boldsymbol{w}\|}$, we choose

$$c = \min_{1\le i\le n} y_i((\boldsymbol{w}^\star)^T\boldsymbol{x} + b^\star).$$

Obviously $c > 0$, hence $\frac{1}{c}(\boldsymbol{w}^\star, b^\star)$ is also a maximizer of the original problem.

Let us consider this particular choice of c, which leads to

$$\min_{1\le i\le n} y_i \left(\left(\frac{1}{c}\boldsymbol{w}^\star\right)^T \boldsymbol{x} + \frac{1}{c}b^\star \right) = 1 > 0.$$

Hence, we can add the following constraint to our optimization problem without changing the optimal objective value:

$$\min_{1\le i\le n} y_i(\boldsymbol{w}^T\boldsymbol{x}_i + b) = 1, \tag{7.12}$$

or equivalently

$$y_i(\boldsymbol{w}^T\boldsymbol{x}_i + b) \ge 1 (> 0), \tag{7.13}$$

for all $1 \le i \le n$—which means all constraints in the original problem are automatically satisfied!

To be precise, $\min_{1\le i\le n} y_i(\boldsymbol{w}^T\boldsymbol{x}_i + b) = 1$ is not equivalent to $y_i(\boldsymbol{w}^T\boldsymbol{x}_i + b) \ge 1$ for all i. When $y_i(\boldsymbol{w}^T\boldsymbol{x}_i + b) \ge 1$, it is possible that $\min_{1\le i\le n} y_i(\boldsymbol{w}^T\boldsymbol{x}_i + b) > 1$; for example, it is possible that $\min_{1\le i\le n} y_i(\boldsymbol{w}^T\boldsymbol{x}_i + b) = 2$. However, since in an SVM the objective is to minimize $\frac{1}{2}\boldsymbol{w}^T\boldsymbol{w}$, the constraints $y_i(\boldsymbol{w}^T\boldsymbol{x}_i + b) \ge 1$ altogether imply

$\min_{1\le i\le n} y_i(\boldsymbol{w}^T\boldsymbol{x}_i + b) = 1$ in the optimal solution. The proof of this fact is pretty simple, and is left to the reader.

In other words, we can convert the original problem into the following equivalent one:

$$\max_{\boldsymbol{w},b} \quad \frac{\min_{1\le i\le n} y_i(\boldsymbol{w}^T\boldsymbol{x} + b)}{\|\boldsymbol{w}\|} = \frac{1}{\|\boldsymbol{w}\|} \tag{7.14}$$

$$\text{s.t.} \quad y_i f(\boldsymbol{x}_i) \ge 1, \quad 1 \le i \le n. \tag{7.15}$$

A final step is to change the maximization of $\frac{1}{\|\boldsymbol{w}\|}$ to the minimization of $\|\boldsymbol{w}\|$ and furthermore (equivalently) to the minimization of $\boldsymbol{w}^T\boldsymbol{w}$ and $\frac{1}{2}\boldsymbol{w}^T\boldsymbol{w}$, which leads to

$$\min_{\boldsymbol{w},b} \quad \frac{1}{2}\boldsymbol{w}^T\boldsymbol{w} \tag{7.16}$$

$$\text{s.t.} \quad y_i f(\boldsymbol{x}_i) \ge 1, \quad 1 \le i \le n. \tag{7.17}$$

The additional term $\frac{1}{2}$ will make later derivations easier.

In this series of transformations and simplifications, we get a series of *equivalent* problems and hence will get the same optimal objective value as that of the original problem. The new constraints are very similar to the original ones (and are handled by the method of Lagrange multipliers in the same manner). However, the objective is now a quadratic form ($\frac{1}{2}\boldsymbol{w}^T\boldsymbol{w}$), and very amenable to optimization.

We will work (a little bit) on the optimization of Eqs. (7.16) and (7.17); they are called the primal form of the SVM formulation, or simply a primal SVM.

7.4 The Optimization and the Solution

We use the method of Lagrange multipliers to handle the n inequality constraints and state the necessary and sufficient conditions for the minimizers of the primal SVM. The proof is beyond the scope of this book and is thus omitted. With these conditions, the primal form turns into an equivalent dual form.

7.4.1 The Lagrangian and the KKT Conditions

We still define one Lagrange multiplier α_i for each constraint, and the constraints $y_i f(\boldsymbol{x}_i) \ge 1$ are rewritten as $y_i f(\boldsymbol{x}_i) - 1 \ge 0$. The Lagrangian is

$$L(\boldsymbol{w}, b, \boldsymbol{\alpha}) = \frac{1}{2}\boldsymbol{w}^T\boldsymbol{w} - \sum_{i=1}^{n} \alpha_i \big(y_i(\boldsymbol{w}^T\boldsymbol{x}_i + b) - 1\big) \tag{7.18}$$

$$\text{s.t.} \quad \alpha_i \ge 0, \quad 1 \le i \le n, \tag{7.19}$$

in which

$$\boldsymbol{\alpha} = (\alpha_1, \alpha_2, \ldots, \alpha_n)^T$$

is the vector of Lagrange multipliers.

For inequality constraints, however, the multipliers are not free anymore—they are required to be nonnegative. If one constraint is violated—i.e., if $y_i f(\boldsymbol{x}_i) - 1 < 0$ for some i—we have $-\alpha_i\left(y_i(\boldsymbol{w}^T\boldsymbol{x}_i + b) - 1\right) > 0$, meaning that a punishment term is added to $L(\boldsymbol{w}, b, \boldsymbol{\alpha})$. Hence, setting $\alpha_i \geq 0$ for all i is somehow enforcing the ith constraint. Also, if

$$\alpha_i \left(y_i(\boldsymbol{w}^T\boldsymbol{x}_i + b) - 1\right) = 0 \tag{7.20}$$

for all $1 \leq i \leq n$, then $L(\boldsymbol{w}, b, \boldsymbol{\alpha}) = \frac{1}{2}\boldsymbol{w}^T\boldsymbol{w}$ matches the primal objective. Later we will show that the optimality condition indeed specifies $\alpha_i\left(y_i(\boldsymbol{w}^T\boldsymbol{x}_i + b) - 1\right) = 0$ for all $1 \leq i \leq n$.

As usual, we compute the gradients and set them to $\boldsymbol{0}$ or 0, respectively:

$$\frac{\partial L}{\partial \boldsymbol{w}} = \boldsymbol{0} \quad \Longrightarrow \quad \boldsymbol{w} = \sum_{i=1}^{n} \alpha_i y_i \boldsymbol{x}_i, \tag{7.21}$$

$$\frac{\partial L}{\partial b} = 0 \quad \Longrightarrow \quad \sum_{i=1}^{n} \alpha_i y_i = 0. \tag{7.22}$$

The above three equality conditions, the original inequality constraints, and the constraints on the Lagrange multipliers form the Karush–Kuhn–Tucker (KKT) conditions for the primal SVM optimization problem:

$$\boldsymbol{w} = \sum_{i=1}^{n} \alpha_i y_i \boldsymbol{x}_i, \tag{7.23}$$

$$\sum_{i=1}^{n} \alpha_i y_i = 0, \tag{7.24}$$

$$\alpha_i \left(y_i(\boldsymbol{w}^T\boldsymbol{x}_i + b) - 1\right) = 0, \quad i = 1, 2, \ldots, n, \tag{7.25}$$

$$\alpha_i \geq 0, \quad i = 1, 2, \ldots, n, \tag{7.26}$$

$$y_i(\boldsymbol{w}^T\boldsymbol{x}_i + b) \geq 1, \quad i = 1, 2, \ldots, n. \tag{7.27}$$

These KKT conditions are not necessary and sufficient in general. However, for the primal SVM problem, these conditions are both necessary and sufficient to specify optimal solutions.

Equation (7.23) states that the optimal solution $\boldsymbol{w}$ can be represented by a weighted combination of the training examples; the signs of the weights are determined by the labels of the examples, and the magnitudes of these weights are the Lagrange multipliers. In more general large margin learning, the *representer theorem* ensures this weighted average representation is still valid in many other situations–e.g., in kernel SVMs.

Equation (7.24) states that these weights are *balanced* in the two classes. If we sum the Lagrange multipliers for all positive training examples, this must equal the sum of weights for all negative training examples. Because these Lagrange multipliers can be considered as weights for positive and negative examples, one way to interpret

Eq. (7.24) is that an SVM has an internal mechanism to balance weights between the positive and negative examples, which might be useful in handling imbalanced datasets so long as the level of imbalance is not large.

Equation (7.25) is called the *complementary slackness* property, which is important in SVMs, and we will soon discuss this property in more depth. The other two conditions are the nonnegative constraints for the Lagrange multipliers and the original constraints.

7.4.2 The Dual SVM Formulation

Equations (7.23) and (7.24) allow us to remove the original parameters $(\boldsymbol{w}, b)$ from the Lagrangian. Note that

$$\frac{1}{2}\boldsymbol{w}^T\boldsymbol{w} = \frac{1}{2}\sum_{i=1}^{n}\sum_{j=1}^{n}\alpha_i\alpha_j y_i y_j \boldsymbol{x}_i^T\boldsymbol{x}_j, \tag{7.28}$$

$$\sum_{i=1}^{n}\alpha_i y_i \boldsymbol{w}^T\boldsymbol{x}_i = \boldsymbol{w}^T\boldsymbol{w} = \sum_{i=1}^{n}\sum_{j=1}^{n}\alpha_i\alpha_j y_i y_j \boldsymbol{x}_i^T\boldsymbol{x}_j, \tag{7.29}$$

$$\sum_{i=1}^{n}\alpha_i y_i b = \left(\sum_{i=1}^{n}\alpha_i y_i\right) b = 0, \tag{7.30}$$

when the KKT conditions hold. Hence, the Lagrangian becomes

$$-\frac{1}{2}\sum_{i=1}^{n}\sum_{j=1}^{n}\alpha_i\alpha_j y_i y_j \boldsymbol{x}_i^T\boldsymbol{x}_j + \sum_{i=1}^{n}\alpha_i, \tag{7.31}$$

which does not involve $\boldsymbol{w}$ or b anymore. Putting the constraints on α_i in, we get

$$\max_{\boldsymbol{\alpha}} \quad \sum_{i=1}^{n}\alpha_i - \frac{1}{2}\sum_{i=1}^{n}\sum_{j=1}^{n}\alpha_i\alpha_j y_i y_j \boldsymbol{x}_i^T\boldsymbol{x}_j \tag{7.32}$$

$$\text{s.t.} \quad \alpha_i \geq 0, \quad i = 1, 2, \ldots, n, \tag{7.33}$$

$$\sum_{i=1}^{n}\alpha_i y_i = 0, \tag{7.34}$$

which is called the *dual SVM formulation*, or simply the *dual*.

In more detail, the above choices for $\boldsymbol{w}$ and b lead to

$$g(\boldsymbol{\alpha}) = \inf_{(\boldsymbol{w}, b)} L(\boldsymbol{w}, b, \boldsymbol{\alpha}),$$

in which inf means the infimum (i.e., greatest lower bound) and g is called the Lagrange dual function, which is always concave. The *maximization* of g with respect to $\boldsymbol{\alpha}$ is always smaller than or equal to the minimization of the original (primal) problem, and the difference between them is called the duality gap. When the duality gap is 0, we can maximize the dual instead of solving the original minimization problem.

One notable difference between the dual and the primal SVM is that in the dual, the training data never appear alone (as in the primal), but instead they *always appear in a pair as a dot product* $\boldsymbol{x}_i^T \boldsymbol{x}_j$.

In general, the optimal objective value of the primal and dual forms of an optimization problem are not equal (i.e., there exists a duality gap). In SVMs the duality gap is 0—the dual and the primal forms will lead to the same optimal value. We will not talk about the optimization techniques in this chapter, which are beyond the scope of this book. However, many high-quality optimization toolboxes (including those specifically designed for SVMs) are available to solve either the primal or the dual SVM optimization.

One can solve the SVM optimization using the primal form and obtain $(\boldsymbol{w}^\star, b^\star)$ directly; one can also solve the dual form and obtain the optimal Lagrange multipliers $\boldsymbol{\alpha}^\star$, and Eq. (7.23) will give us the optimal $\boldsymbol{w}^\star$.

7.4.3 The Optimal b Value and Support Vectors

To obtain the optimal value for b is a little more tricky in the dual form, which hinges on the complementary slackness property:

$$\alpha_i \big(y_i(\boldsymbol{w}^T \boldsymbol{x}_i + b) - 1\big) = 0, \quad i = 1, 2, \ldots, n. \tag{7.35}$$

Based on complementary slackness, if we find one constraint whose corresponding Lagrange multiplier is positive (i.e., $\alpha_i > 0$), then we must have $y_i(\boldsymbol{w}^T \boldsymbol{x}_i + b) - 1 = 0$. Hence

$$b^\star = y_i - \left(\boldsymbol{w}^\star\right)^T \boldsymbol{x}_i \tag{7.36}$$

for this particular i. This solution is easy to derive. Because

$$y_i b = 1 - y_i \boldsymbol{w}^T \boldsymbol{x}_i \tag{7.37}$$

when $\alpha_i > 0$, and noting that $y_i^2 = 1$, we can multiply both sides of Eq. (7.37) by y_i and obtain Eq. (7.36).

The optimal b value obtained in this manner may not be very reliable because some numerical errors can reduce its accuracy. Hence, we can also find all those examples whose corresponding α_i is nonzero, compute b from them individually, and then use their average as $b^\star$.

Those examples that are useful for computing $b^\star$, whose corresponding Lagrange multipliers are positive, are special in the training set. They are called the *support vectors*, and consequently the classification method is called the support vector machine.

When $\alpha_i > 0$ we know $y_i(\boldsymbol{w}^T \boldsymbol{x}_i + b) - 1 = 0$, which means that the ith constraint has to be active—i.e., the margin of the training example $\boldsymbol{x}_i$ must be 1, as shown in Figure 7.4. In the figure, examples in two classes are denoted by blue circles and orange squares, respectively; the black line is the classification boundary $f(\boldsymbol{x}) = 0$, while the red lines correspond to $f(\boldsymbol{x}) = \pm 1$—i.e., all examples whose margin $y_i f(\boldsymbol{x}_i)$ is 1 (remember that in the SVM formulation we assume $y_i = \pm 1$ and the smallest margin of all training examples is 1). The three examples (two filled

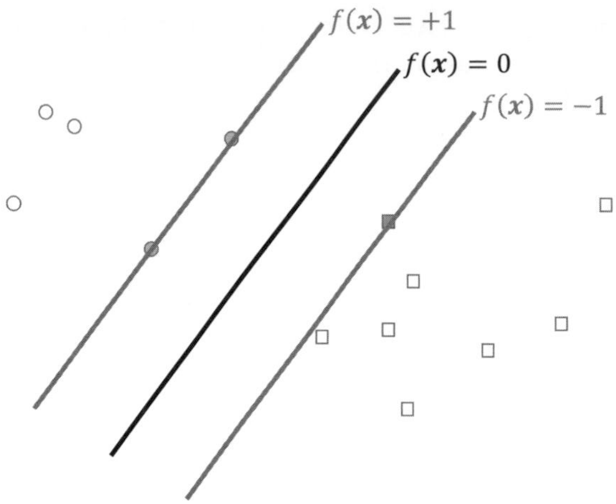

Figure 7.4 Illustration of support vectors. (A black and white version of this figure will appear in some formats. For the color version, please refer to the plate section.)

circles and one filled square) are the support vectors, with corresponding $\alpha_i > 0$ and $y_i f(\boldsymbol{x}_i) = 1$.

The classification boundary $f(\boldsymbol{x}) = \boldsymbol{w}^T\boldsymbol{x} + b$ is a line in linear SVMs. Hence, we can explicitly compute $\boldsymbol{w} = \sum_{i=1}^{n} \alpha_i y_i \boldsymbol{x}_i \in \mathbb{R}^d$, and consequently it is very efficient to compute the decision value $f(\boldsymbol{x})$, which requires only one dot-product computation. The linear SVM is hence both accurate and efficient. However, the derivation of decision values for more complex SVM classifiers—e.g., nonlinear SVMs—requires a lot of computation.

The prediction (after the decision value $f(\boldsymbol{x})$ is computed) is a simple task. As illustrated in Figure 7.4, the prediction is simply $\text{sign}(f(\boldsymbol{x}))$, in which sign is the sign function:

$$\text{sign}(x) = \begin{cases} +1 & \text{if } x > 0, \\ -1 & \text{if } x < 0, \\ 0 & \text{if } x = 0. \end{cases} \tag{7.38}$$

When a test example $\boldsymbol{x}$ happens to have $f(\boldsymbol{x}) = 0$, the above sign function returns 0, which is not suitable for our classification problem. We can output a prediction of either $+1$ or -1 in an ad-hoc manner; we can also randomly assign a label for these special (and rare) testing examples.

7.4.4 Looking at the Primal and the Dual Simultaneously

Since the primal and the dual give the same answer in SVMs, we can look at them simultaneously. After the optimal primal and dual variables are obtained, they guarantee that the margin of all training examples is ≥ 1, that is, the distance between any positive and negative training examples is ≥ 2. This observation provides a lower bound for the distance between examples from different classes.

The objective $\boldsymbol{w}^T\boldsymbol{w}$ is equal to $\sum_{i=1}^n \sum_{j=1}^n \alpha_i\alpha_j y_i y_j \boldsymbol{x}_i^T\boldsymbol{x}_j$. The primal and dual parameters in this section refer to the optimal ones. However, we omit the * superscript to make the notation simpler. Let us define some more notation:

$$\alpha_+ = \sum_{y_i=+1} \alpha_i, \tag{7.39}$$

$$\alpha_- = \sum_{y_i=-1} \alpha_i, \tag{7.40}$$

$$\boldsymbol{s}_+ = \sum_{y_i=+1} \alpha_i\boldsymbol{x}_i, \tag{7.41}$$

$$\boldsymbol{s}_- = \sum_{y_i=-1} \alpha_i\boldsymbol{x}_i \tag{7.42}$$

are the sums of Lagrange multipliers (weights) for all positive examples and negative examples and the weighted sums of all positive examples and all negative examples, respectively.

Equation (7.24) leads to

$$\alpha_+ = \alpha_-,$$

and Eq. (7.23) shows

$$\boldsymbol{w} = \boldsymbol{s}_+ - \boldsymbol{s}_-.$$

Hence, the primal objective is to minimize $\|\boldsymbol{s}_+ - \boldsymbol{s}_-\|^2$, which is also equivalent to

$$\left\| \frac{\boldsymbol{s}_+}{\alpha_+} - \frac{\boldsymbol{s}_-}{\alpha_-} \right\|, \tag{7.43}$$

where $\frac{\boldsymbol{s}_+}{\alpha_+}$ ($\frac{\boldsymbol{s}_-}{\alpha_-}$) is the weighted average of all positive (negative) examples. Hence, the distance between them must be ≥ 2, and equality can happen only if $\alpha_i = 0$ for all training examples whose margin is > 1.

If any training example $\boldsymbol{x}_i$ has a margin $y_i f(\boldsymbol{x}_i) > 1$ and $\alpha_i > 0$, then $\frac{\boldsymbol{s}_+}{\alpha_+}$ or $\frac{\boldsymbol{s}_-}{\alpha_-}$ will not reside on the two lines whose margin is 1 (cf. the red lines in Figure 7.4) and the distance between them will be > 2.

Hence, in the linearly separable case, all support vectors reside on these two lines and are sparse (i.e., the number of support vectors is only a small fraction of the number of all training examples, as shown in Figure 7.4).

7.5 Extensions for Linearly Inseparable and Multiclass Problems

We have made three assumptions in the above derivation: linear classifier, separable, and binary problems. These assumptions (and restrictions) have to be relaxed now that we already have a solution for the simplified problem. In this section, we deal with the nonseparable case (still with linear classifiers), and the extension to multiclass problems. Nonlinear classifiers will be discussed in the next section.

7.5.1 Linear Classifiers for Nonseparable Problems

In some binary problems, the training set is not linearly separable—i.e., there is no single line that can perfectly separate examples in the two classes. However, as in the example of Figure 7.1a, a linear classifier still seems the best model we can find using our eyes and brains. In other words, the positive and negative examples are roughly linearly separable.

In fact, the two classes in Figure 7.1a are generated by two Gaussians with the same covariance matrix and equal prior, and the optimal classification boundary (in the minimum cost sense) is indeed a linear one. This statement will become obvious after we discuss probabilistic methods in the next chapter.

The linear SVM classifier can be extended to handle such roughly linearly separable problems for real-world tasks, using a trick called *slack variables*. The current constraint, $y_i f(\boldsymbol{x}_i) \geq 1$, means that not only is the ith example correctly classified, but its distance to the linear boundary is also relatively far (> 1), leaving room to accommodate possible variations in test examples.

However, must we strictly maintain this constraint? Maybe we can achieve a much larger margin of the dataset[2] at the cost of only slightly violating this single constraint (e.g., $y_i f(\boldsymbol{x}_i) = 0.9 < 1$). So long as $y_i f(\boldsymbol{x}_i) > 0$ (e.g., 0.9), this particular training example $\boldsymbol{x}_i$ is still correctly classified, but larger margins are made possible for other examples.

At another extreme, there may be one outlier $\boldsymbol{x}_i$ in the training set, e.g., $y_i = +1$, but it is in a cluster of negative examples. If we want to strictly maintain the constraint associated with $\boldsymbol{x}_i$, we must pay the price that the problem is not solvable or that the margins of other examples are greatly reduced. We need a mechanism to allow this outlier to be wrongly classified—i.e., to allow $y_i f(\boldsymbol{x}_i) \leq 0$ in a few cases.

These exceptions (either $0 < y_i f(\boldsymbol{x}_i) < 1$ or $y_i f(\boldsymbol{x}_i) \leq 0$), however, cannot happen too frequently. We also need a mechanism to specify that the total price (cost) we pay for such relatively rare or extreme cases is small. In SVMs, a slack variable ξ_i is introduced as the price we pay for $\boldsymbol{x}_i$, and its associated constraint is changed to two constraints:

$$y_i f(\boldsymbol{x}_i) \geq 1 - \xi_i, \tag{7.44}$$

$$\xi_i \geq 0. \tag{7.45}$$

There can be three possible cases for ξ_i:

- When $\xi_i = 0$ for an $\boldsymbol{x}_i$, the original constraint is maintained, and no price is paid.
- When $0 < \xi_i \leq 1$, this example is still correctly classified, but the margin is $1 - \xi_i < 1$, hence the price is ξ_i.
- When $\xi_i > 1$, this example is wrongly classified, and the price is still ξ_i.

[2] In the SVM formulation, this is equivalent to reducing $\boldsymbol{w}^T \boldsymbol{w}$ by a large amount while fixing the margin to 1.

Hence, the total price is

$$\sum_{i=1}^{n} \xi_i .$$

To require the total price to be small, we just add this term to the (minimization) objective as a *regularizer*, and the primal linear SVM formulation becomes

$$\min_{w,b} \quad \frac{1}{2}w^T w + C\sum_{i=1}^{n} \xi_i \tag{7.46}$$

$$\text{s.t.} \quad y_i f(x_i) \geq 1 - \xi_i, \quad 1 \leq i \leq n, \tag{7.47}$$

$$\xi_i \geq 0, \quad 1 \leq i \leq n. \tag{7.48}$$

In the above SVM formulation, a new symbol C is introduced where $C > 0$ is a scalar that determines the relative importance between a large margin (minimizing $w^T w$) and paying a small total price ($\sum_{i=1}^{n} \xi_i$). When C is large the small total price part is more important, and when $C \to \infty$ the margin requirement is completely ignored. When $C < 1$ the large margin requirement is emphasized, and when $C \to 0$ no price is paid at all. Hence, in problems showing different properties, C values have to be tuned to seek the best accuracy.

Using almost the same procedure as in the linearly separable case, we obtain the new dual form

$$\max_{\alpha} \quad \sum_{i=1}^{n} \alpha_i - \frac{1}{2}\sum_{i=1}^{n}\sum_{j=1}^{n} \alpha_i \alpha_j y_i y_j x_i^T x_j \tag{7.49}$$

$$\text{s.t.} \quad C \geq \alpha_i \geq 0, \quad i = 1,2,\ldots,n, \tag{7.50}$$

$$\sum_{i=1}^{n} \alpha_i y_i = 0. \tag{7.51}$$

Note that the only difference between this formulation and the one for linearly separable SVMs is in the constraints on dual variables: $\alpha_i \geq 0$ is changed to $0 \leq \alpha_i \leq C$, which hardly increases the difficulty of solving the dual problem, but the capacity of our SVM formulation has been greatly extended.

We can also view the new objective from a different perspective. The total cost $\sum_{i=1}^{n} \xi_i$ can be seen as minimizing the cost over the training set—i.e., the empirical cost (or empirical loss). The term $w^T w$ can alternatively be viewed as a regularization term, which encourages linear classification boundaries that are less complex because the large components in w allow larger variations in it and are hence more complex.

Since $\xi_i \geq 0$ and $\xi_i \geq 1 - y_i f(x_i)$ (based on Eqs. 7.44 and 7.45), we can combine them as

$$\xi_i = (1 - y_i f(x_i))_+ , \tag{7.52}$$

in which x_+ is called the *hinge loss* for x; also, $x_+ = x$ if $x \geq 0$, and $x_+ = 0$ if $x < 0$. It is obvious that

$$x_+ = \max(0, x).$$

The hinge loss incurs no penalty if $y_i f(\boldsymbol{x})_i \geq 1$—i.e., when the margin for $\boldsymbol{x}_i$ is larger than 1. Only when the margin is small ($0 < y_i f(\boldsymbol{x}_i) < 1$) or $\boldsymbol{x}_i$ is wrongly classified ($y_i f(\boldsymbol{x}_i) < 0$) is the loss $1 - y_i f(\boldsymbol{x}_i)$ incurred. Using the hinge loss, we can rewrite the primal SVM as

$$\min_{\boldsymbol{w},b} \quad \frac{1}{2}\boldsymbol{w}^T\boldsymbol{w} + C\sum_{i=1}^{n}\xi_i \tag{7.53}$$

$$\text{or} \quad \min_{\boldsymbol{w},b} \quad \frac{1}{2}\boldsymbol{w}^T\boldsymbol{w} + C\sum_{i=1}^{n}(1 - y_i f(\boldsymbol{x}_i))_+ . \tag{7.54}$$

In this formulation, the constraints are implicitly encoded in the hinge loss and do not appear as constraints anymore.

One practical question is how to find the optimal C value for this trade-off parameter. We will leave this to later sections.

7.5.2 Multiclass SVMs

There are two main strategies to handle multiclass problems in the SVM literature: one is to combine multiple binary SVMs to solve the multiclass one, and the other is to extend the max-margin idea and its mathematics into multiclass using similar techniques, then to solve the multiclass problem using a single optimization. We will introduce the first strategy. In fact, this strategy is not only valid for SVM classifiers, but also effective for extending many binary classification methods to the multiclass case.

The one-vs.-rest (or one-versus-all, or OvA) method trains m binary SVM classifiers for an m-class problem. In training the ith binary SVM, examples belonging to the ith class are used as the positive class examples in the binary problem, and all other training examples are used as the negative class examples. Let us denote this binary SVM classifier as $f_i(\boldsymbol{x})$. In the binary case, when an example is far away from the classification boundary (i.e., with a large margin), there is good reason to believe it will be more tolerant of variations in the distribution of examples. In other words, we are more *confident* about our prediction if it has a large margin.

In the multiclass case, if $f_i(\boldsymbol{x})$ is large (and positive), we can also say with high confidence that $\boldsymbol{x}$ belongs to the ith class. Hence, the m binary classifiers $f_i(\boldsymbol{x})$ ($1 \leq i \leq m$) give us m confidence scores, and our prediction for $\boldsymbol{x}$ is simply the class having the highest confidence. That is, the predicted class for a test example $\boldsymbol{x}$ is

$$\operatorname*{arg\,max}_{1\leq i\leq m} f_i(\boldsymbol{x}) \tag{7.55}$$

in the OvA method.

The one-vs.-one (or one-versus-one, or OvO) method trains $\binom{m}{2} = \frac{m(m-1)}{2}$ binary SVM classifiers. For any pair (i, j) satisfying $1 \leq i < j \leq m$, we can use the examples in the ith class as positive ones, and those in the jth class as negative ones; all other training examples are ignored for this pair. The trained classifier $f_{i,j}(\boldsymbol{x})$ (after the sign function) determines whether $\boldsymbol{x}$ should be assigned to the ith or jth class—although it is possible that $\boldsymbol{x}$ is neither in the ith nor the jth class—and we say that the ith or jth class receives one vote.

For any test example $\boldsymbol{x}$, it will receive $\binom{m}{2}$ votes, distributed among the m classes. If the groundtruth class for $\boldsymbol{x}$ is k ($1 \le k \le m$), we expect that the kth class will receive the largest number of votes. Hence, in the OvO method, the prediction for any example $\boldsymbol{x}$ is the class that receives the most votes.

There have been empirical comparisons between the OvA and OvO methods. In terms of classification accuracy, there is no obvious winner. Hence, both methods are applicable when m is not large.

However, for problems with a large number of classes—e.g., when $m = 1000$—the number of binary SVM classifiers to be trained in OvO is $\binom{m}{2}$ (499 500 if $m = 1000$). To train a large number of classifiers requires an excessively long time, and to store and apply all these trained models is also prohibitively expensive. Hence, the OvA method is more popular when m is large.

7.6 Kernel SVMs

The final major missing block is a nonlinear SVM in which the classification boundary is made up not of lines but of complex curves such as those in Figure 7.5. Figure 7.5a shows a problem with 200 training examples while Figure 7.5b has 2000. The blue hyperbolic curves form the groundtruth decision boundary that separates the two classes, and the green curves are decision boundaries constructed by an SVM using the nonlinear RBF kernel, which we will explain in this section. As shown in these figures, the kernel (or nonlinear) SVM can approximate the groundtruth decision boundary well, especially in regions where many training examples are available.

Kernel methods are a class of methods that are popular in nonlinear learning, and SVMs are a typical example of kernel methods.

7.6.1 The Kernel Trick

First, let us consider and reexamine the second term in the SVM dual objective,

$$\sum_{i=1}^{n}\sum_{j=1}^{n} \alpha_i \alpha_j y_i y_j \boldsymbol{x}_i^T \boldsymbol{x}_j .$$

Inside the summations is an inner product between $\alpha_i y_i \boldsymbol{x}_i$ and $\alpha_j y_j \boldsymbol{x}_j$—i.e., an inner product between two training examples whose signs are determined by the labels and the weights by the dual variables.

It is well known that the dot product between two vectors can be treated as a measure of their similarity.[3] If both vectors are unit vectors, the dot product equals

[3] We will discuss similarity and dissimilarity metrics in more detail in Chapter 9.

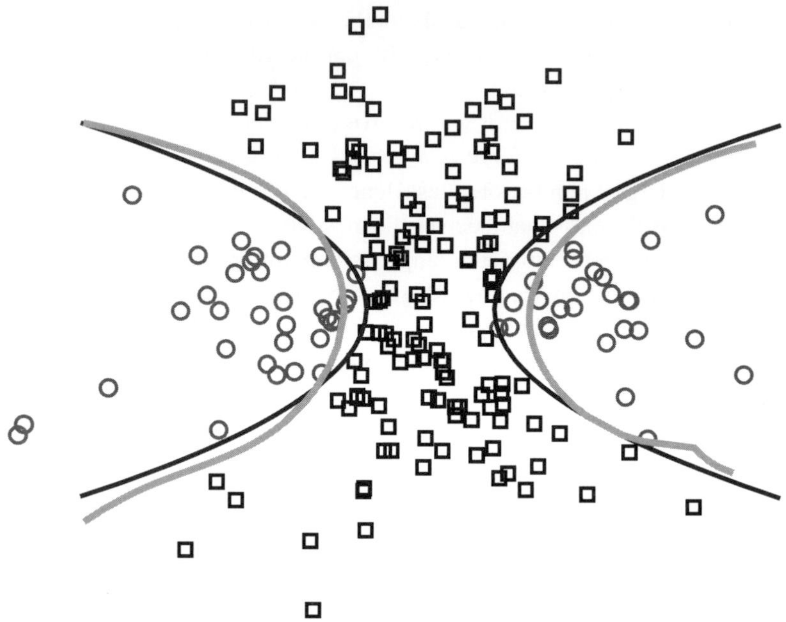

(a) 200 training examples

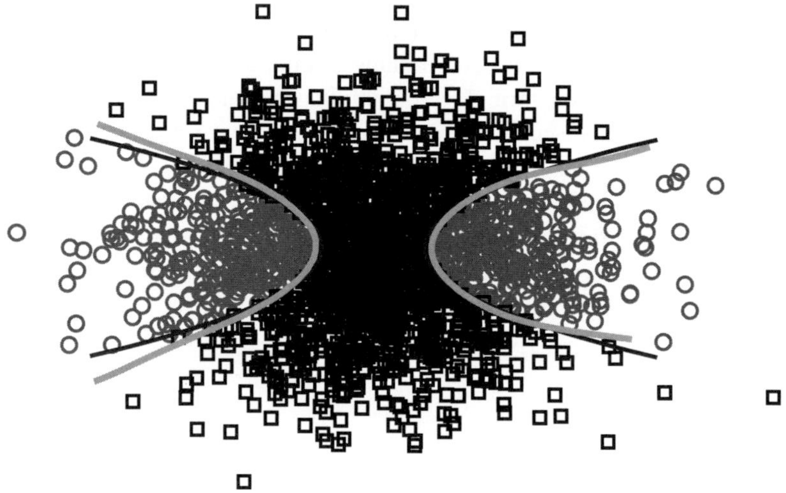

(b) 2000 training examples

Figure 7.5 Illustration of nonlinear classifiers. (A black and white version of this figure will appear in some formats. For the color version, please refer to the plate section.)

the cosine of the angle between these two vectors. A small dot-product value means that the angle is close to 90° and the two vectors are far away from each other; a large positive dot-product result means that the angle is close to 0° and the two vectors are close to each other; and a large negative dot product means that the angle is close to 180° and the two vectors are almost the farthest apart possible on a unit hypersphere.

Hence, it is natural to guess that *if we replace the dot product with some other nonlinear similarity metric, we may be able to get a nonlinear boundary better than a line.* This guess seems viable because in the dual SVM formulation, as we have observed, the training examples always appear as dot products (or loosely speaking, always as similarity comparisons!).

Some theories (unfortunately beyond the scope of this book) endorse the above guess, but the nonlinear similarity measure must satisfy a certain condition (called Mercer's condition). Let κ be a nonlinear function satisfying Mercer's condition; then the nonlinear dual SVM formulation is

$$\max_{\alpha} \quad \sum_{i=1}^{n} \alpha_i - \frac{1}{2}\sum_{i=1}^{n}\sum_{j=1}^{n} \alpha_i \alpha_j y_i y_j \kappa(\boldsymbol{x}_i, \boldsymbol{x}_j) \tag{7.56}$$

$$\text{s.t.} \quad C \geq \alpha_i \geq 0, \quad i = 1, 2, \ldots, n, \tag{7.57}$$

$$\sum_{i=1}^{n} \alpha_i y_i = 0. \tag{7.58}$$

The optimization is the same as in the linear case, just replacing the (constant) values $\boldsymbol{x}_i^T \boldsymbol{x}_j$ by $\kappa(\boldsymbol{x}_i, \boldsymbol{x}_j)$.

7.6.2 Mercer's Condition and Feature Mapping

To introduce Mercer's condition, we need to define the quadratically integrable (or square integrable) function concept. A function $g\colon \mathbb{R}^d \mapsto \mathbb{R}$ is square integrable if

$$\int_{-\infty}^{\infty} g^2(\boldsymbol{x})\, \mathrm{d}\boldsymbol{x} < \infty. \tag{7.59}$$

A function $\kappa(\cdot,\cdot)\colon \mathbb{R}^d \times \mathbb{R}^d \mapsto \mathbb{R}$ satisfies Mercer's condition if for *any* square integrable function $g(\boldsymbol{x})$, the following inequality is always true:

$$\iint \kappa(\boldsymbol{x}, \boldsymbol{y}) g(\boldsymbol{x}) g(\boldsymbol{y})\, \mathrm{d}\boldsymbol{x}\, \mathrm{d}\boldsymbol{y} \geq 0, \tag{7.60}$$

and it is symmetric, i.e.,

$$\kappa(\boldsymbol{x}, \boldsymbol{y}) = \kappa(\boldsymbol{y}, \boldsymbol{x}).$$

In the context of SVMs, Mercer's condition translates to another way to check whether κ is a valid kernel (i.e., it meets Mercer's condition or not). For a symmetric function $\kappa(\cdot,\cdot)$ and a set of examples $\boldsymbol{x}_1, \boldsymbol{x}_2, \ldots, \boldsymbol{x}_n \in \mathbb{R}^d$, one can define a matrix $K \in \mathbb{R}^n \times \mathbb{R}^n$, with

$$[K]_{ij} = \kappa(\boldsymbol{x}_i, \boldsymbol{x}_j)$$

for $1 \leq i, j \leq n$. If the matrix K is positive semidefinite for an *arbitrary* integer $n > 0$ and an *arbitrary* set of examples $\boldsymbol{x}_1, \boldsymbol{x}_2, \ldots, \boldsymbol{x}_n$, then κ is a valid kernel function. When κ is a valid kernel, K is called the kernel matrix (induced by κ).

When κ is a valid kernel, then there exists a mapping $\phi\colon \mathbb{R}^d \mapsto \mathcal{X}$ that maps the input $\boldsymbol{x}$ from the input space to a *feature space* $\mathcal{X}$ and satisfies

$$\kappa(\boldsymbol{x}, \boldsymbol{y}) = \phi(\boldsymbol{x})^T \phi(\boldsymbol{y}) \tag{7.61}$$

for *any* $\boldsymbol{x}, \boldsymbol{y} \in \mathbb{R}^d$. Although in many cases we do not know how to compute this mapping associated with κ, its existence has been rigorously proved. When we cannot explicitly spell out ϕ, we call it an implicit mapping.

The feature space $\mathcal{X}$ is usually high-dimensional. Its dimensionality is often much larger than d, and for many kernels is infinite! Although we skip the advanced concepts (e.g., reproducing kernel Hilbert space), we want to assure the reader that so long as an infinite-dimensional space satisfies certain conditions (such as the mappings in kernel SVMs), the inner product between any two vectors in it is well defined.

Conceptually, the kernel method has *turned a nonlinear classification problem (in the input space) into an equivalent linear classification problem in the (usually much higher-dimensional) feature space*, as shown by the dual formulation for kernel SVMs. In the feature space, the linear boundary enjoys the same max-margin benefit. Fortunately, because of the kernel trick, we do not need to compute the dot product explicitly: $\kappa(\boldsymbol{x}, \boldsymbol{y})$ replaces $\phi(\boldsymbol{x})^T \phi(\boldsymbol{y})$.

The representer theorem once again gives us

$$\boldsymbol{w} = \sum_{i=1}^{n} \alpha_i y_i \phi(\boldsymbol{x}_i).$$

However, $\boldsymbol{w}$ can be infinite-dimensional too. Hence, the prediction is performed through the kernel trick, as

$$f(\boldsymbol{x}) = \boldsymbol{w}^T \phi(\boldsymbol{x}) + b \tag{7.62}$$

$$= \sum_{i=1}^{n} \alpha_i y_i \phi(\boldsymbol{x}_i)^T \phi(\boldsymbol{x}) + b \tag{7.63}$$

$$= \sum_{i=1}^{n} \alpha_i y_i \kappa(\boldsymbol{x}_i, \boldsymbol{x}) + b. \tag{7.64}$$

This computation, however, is much more expensive than that in linear SVMs. Assuming that the complexity of $\kappa(\boldsymbol{x}_i, \boldsymbol{x})$ is $\mathcal{O}(d)$, predicting one example may take $\mathcal{O}(nd)$ steps. When the number of training examples is large (e.g., $n = 1\,000\,000$), kernel SVM prediction is very slow and we need to store all training examples in the SVM model, which incurs very high storage costs.

The actual SVM prediction cost, however, is lower than $\mathcal{O}(nd)$. If a training example $\boldsymbol{x}_i$ is not a support vector, then its Lagrange multiplier α_i is 0, and is useless in the above summation. Hence, *only support vectors are used in prediction and are stored in the SVM model.*

The Lagrange multipliers are sparse—i.e., many α_i are 0. Let n' denote the number of support vectors, usually $n' \ll n$, and the kernel SVM prediction complexity $\mathcal{O}(n'd)$ is much lower than nd.

7.6.3 Popular Kernels and the Hyperparameters

Commonly used kernel functions include

$$\text{linear:} \quad \kappa(\boldsymbol{x}, \boldsymbol{y}) = \boldsymbol{x}^T \boldsymbol{y}, \tag{7.65}$$

$$\text{RBF:} \quad \kappa(\boldsymbol{x}, \boldsymbol{y}) = \exp(-\gamma \|\boldsymbol{x} - \boldsymbol{y}\|^2), \tag{7.66}$$

$$\text{polynomial:} \quad \kappa(\boldsymbol{x}, \boldsymbol{y}) = (\gamma \boldsymbol{x}^T \boldsymbol{y} + c)^D. \tag{7.67}$$

The RBF (radial basis function) kernel is sometimes called the Gaussian kernel. Some of these kernels are parameterized—e.g., the RBF kernel has a parameter $\gamma > 0$, and the polynomial kernel has three parameters γ, c, and D (D is a positive integer, called the degree of the polynomial).

We can examine a special case of the polynomial kernel when $\gamma = 1$, $c = 1$, and $D = 2$. With these parameters, the polynomial kernel is

$$\kappa(\boldsymbol{x}, \boldsymbol{y}) = (1 + \boldsymbol{x}^T \boldsymbol{y})^2.$$

If we assume the examples are in the two-dimensional space—i.e., $\boldsymbol{x} = (x_1, x_2)^T$, $\boldsymbol{y} = (y_1, y_2)^T$—then

$$\begin{aligned}
\kappa(\boldsymbol{x}, \boldsymbol{y}) &= (1 + x_1 y_1 + x_2 y_2)^2 && (7.68)\\
&= 1 + 2x_1 y_1 + 2x_2 y_2 + x_1^2 y_1^2 + x_2^2 y_2^2 + 2x_1 x_2 y_1 y_2 && (7.69)\\
&= \begin{bmatrix} 1 \\ \sqrt{2}x_1 \\ \sqrt{2}x_2 \\ x_1^2 \\ x_2^2 \\ \sqrt{2}x_1 x_2 \end{bmatrix}^T \begin{bmatrix} 1 \\ \sqrt{2}y_1 \\ \sqrt{2}y_2 \\ y_1^2 \\ y_2^2 \\ \sqrt{2}y_1 y_2 \end{bmatrix} && (7.70)\\
&= \phi(\boldsymbol{x})^T \phi(\boldsymbol{y}). && (7.71)
\end{aligned}$$

Hence, for the degree 2 polynomial kernel, we can explicitly write down its mapping from the input space to the feature space, as

$$\phi(\boldsymbol{x}) = (1, \sqrt{2}x_1, \sqrt{2}x_2, x_1^2, x_2^2, \sqrt{2}x_1 x_2)^T.$$

The feature space is six-dimensional in this particular example, which is three times that of the input space.

The trade-off parameter C in the SVM formulation and the kernel parameters γ, c, and D are hyperparameters. Note that different hyperparameters lead to different kernels and different SVM solutions, even if the same training set is used!

However, there is very little theoretical work to guide us on how to choose hyperparameters. In practice, the most commonly used method is to use cross-validation to choose them. For example, we can try a few candidate values for C in the set

$$\{2^{-10},2^{-8},2^{-6},2^{-4},2^{-2},2^{0},2^{2},2^{4},2^{6},2^{8},2^{10}\}.$$

Using the training set, we can obtain the cross-validation error rate *on the training set* using each of these values. The C value that achieves the smallest cross-validation error rate is chosen.

This strategy, however, is very time consuming. Assuming an m class problem and a K-fold cross-validation, $K \times \binom{m}{2}$ binary SVM classifiers are required to obtain a single cross-validation error rate if the OvO method is used. If there are two hyperparameters (e.g., C and γ if the RBF kernel is used), and K_1 and K_2 candidate values exist for them, respectively, then the total number of binary SVMs to train is $KK_1K_2\binom{m}{2}$, which is very large.

7.6.4 SVM Complexity, Trade-off, and More

In the early days, the popular SVM solver was the SMO (sequential minimal optimization) method, whose complexity is rather difficult to estimate precisely. Empirical evaluations usually show complexity higher than $\mathcal{O}(n^{2.5}d)$, where n and d are the number and dimensionality of training examples, respectively. This complexity is too high for large-scale problems.

For linear SVMs, however, many fast methods have been proposed, which can complete the learning in $\mathcal{O}(nd)$ steps, using techniques such as column generation, stochastic gradient descent, and coordinate descent. These new methods enable the training of linear SVMs for large problems—e.g., with millions of examples and/or millions of dimensions.

Although there are also acceleration techniques for nonlinear SVM learning, its training complexity is still much higher than that of linear SVMs. The same also applies to the testing complexity. Linear SVM testing requires only a single dot product in a binary problem, while nonlinear SVM testing is much slower.

Nonlinear SVMs, if they can be trained in viable time for a problem, can usually achieve higher (and significantly higher in some problems) accuracy than linear ones. Hence, there is a trade-off between the accuracy and complexity of SVM classifiers. Nonlinear SVMs are a good choice when the dataset is small or medium sized, and linear SVMs are a good option for large problems, particularly when there are many feature dimensions.

For some special kernels, such as the power mean kernels, algorithms specifically designed for them can obtain both fast speed and highly accurate models.

High-quality SVM solvers for both general nonlinear and fast linear kernels are available. Examples include the LIBSVM package (for general nonlinear SVMs) and LIBLINEAR (for fast linear SVMs). We will discuss more details of these topics in the exercise problems.

SVMs can also be extended to handle regression problems, called support vector regression (SVR), which is also implemented in many software packages, including both LIBSVM and LIBLINEAR.

7.7 Miscellaneous Notes and Additional Resources

Scholkopf & Smola (2002) is an excellent resource for advanced materials that are mentioned but not discussed in this chapter. An incomplete list of these advanced materials includes kernel methods, Mercer's condition, reproducing kernel Hilbert space, feature space, representer theorem, conditional positive definiteness. Exercise 7.3 briefly introduces the conditional positive definiteness concept. The tutorial in Burges (1998) is also an excellent document that covers important aspects of SVMs.

To understand the statistical learning theory behind SVMs, please refer to the classic work Vapnik (1999).

For duality, the Lagrange multiplier method for inequality constraints, duality gap, and KKT conditions, Boyd & Vandenberghe (2004) is an excellent resource, which is both rigorous and accessible.

A popular solver for nonlinear (kernel) SVMs is the SMO method, whose details can be found in Platt (1998). In Exercise 7.5 we ask readers to try LIBSVM (Chang & Lin 2011), which is popular SVM solver software, based on the SMO method.

For linear (or dot-product kernel) SVMs, many fast algorithms have been proposed. The training complexity is often $\mathcal{O}(nd)$, and their training speed can be many orders of magnitude faster than that of nonlinear SVMs. Yuan et al. (2012) is a summary of advancements in linear SVMs and other linear classification methods. In Exercise 7.5 we introduce one such algorithm (Hsieh et al. 2008), which is integrated as part of the LIBLINEAR software package (Fan et al. 2008).

For multiclass SVMs, the OvO and OvA strategies have been empirically compared in Hsu & Lin (2002). An alternative multiclass large margin classification strategy is called DAGSVM (Platt et al. 2000). The Crammer–Singer formulation (Crammer & Singer 2001) solves multiclass SVMs in one large optimization problem instead of many smaller ones as in OvO or OvA.

A migration of SVM to regression tasks is support vector regression, for which Smola & Scholkopf (2004) provides a good tutorial.

Additive kernels and power mean kernels (Wu 2012b) are also introduced in the exercise problems for this chapter.

Exercises

7.1 LIBSVM is a widely used software package for learning kernel SVM classifiers and regressors. In this problem, we will experiment with this software. LIBSVM also has an accompanying page that collects datasets.

(a) Download the LIBSVM software package from `www.csie.ntu.edu.tw/~cjlin/libsvm/`. Read the instructions and compile the software from the source code.

(b) Download the `svmguide1` dataset from the LIBSVM datasets page (`www.csie.ntu.edu.tw/~cjlin/libsvmtools/datasets/`).

For each of the following setups, train SVM model(s) using the training set, and compare the accuracy on the test set under different setups.

(i) Use the default parameters (i.e., $C = 1$ and the RBF kernel).

(ii) Use the `svm-scale` utility to normalize the features. Make sure your scaling operation is *proper*: use the parameters from the training set to normalize the test set data. Read the instructions for this utility program carefully.

(iii) Use the linear kernel instead of the RBF kernel.

(iv) Use $C = 1000$ and the RBF kernel.

(v) Use the `easy.py` utility to determine hyperparameters C and γ in the RBF kernel.

What have you learned from these experiments?

(c) Play with the datasets in the LIBSVM datasets page. Can you find an imbalanced dataset? The LIBSVM parameter `-wi` is useful in handling imbalanced data. Try this parameter for the imbalanced dataset you have found. Is it helpful?

7.2 (Additive kernels) A kernel is called additive if it has the form

$$\kappa(\boldsymbol{x}, \boldsymbol{y}) = \sum_{i=1}^{d} \kappa(x_i, y_i)$$

for two d-dimensional vectors $\boldsymbol{x}$ and $\boldsymbol{y}$. Note that we used the same symbol κ to denote the kernel for comparing two vectors and two scalars.

(a) The *histogram intersection kernel* is a widely used additive kernel, which is defined *for vectors with only nonnegative values*, as

$$\kappa_{\mathrm{HI}}(\boldsymbol{x}, \boldsymbol{y}) = \sum_{i=1}^{d} \min(x_i, y_i).$$

Show that if $\kappa_{\mathrm{HI}}(x, y) = \min(x, y)$, for nonnegative scalars x and y, is a valid kernel then κ_{HI} is a valid kernel for nonnegative vectors $\boldsymbol{x}$ and $\boldsymbol{y}$.

(b) Now we consider κ_{HI} for scalars. For *any* set of nonnegative scalar values $x_1, x_2, \ldots, x_n$, the kernel matrix formed by these values is

$$[X]_{ij} = \min(x_i, x_j)$$

for $1 \le i, j \le n$, in which n is an arbitrary positive integer. Let $y_1, y_2, \ldots, y_n$ be a *permutation* of $x_1, x_2, \ldots, x_n$ such that $y_1 \le y_2 \le \cdots \le y_n$, and similarly define an $n \times n$ matrix Y with

$$y_{ij} = \min(y_i, y_j) = y_{\min(i,j)}.$$

Prove that X is positive (semi)definite if and only if Y is positive (semi)definite.

(c) For any set of values $0 \le x_1 \le x_2 \le \cdots \le x_n$, prove that the kernel matrix X with

$$x_{ij} = \min(x_i, x_j) = x_{\min(i,j)}$$

is positive semidefinite. (Hint: What is the LDL factorization of X?)

Note that combining the above results has proved that κ_{HI} is a valid kernel for nonnegative vectors.

(d) The χ^2 *kernel* (chi-square kernel) is another widely used additive kernel defined for positive data, which is defined as

$$\kappa_{\chi^2}(\boldsymbol{x}, \boldsymbol{y}) = \sum_{i=1}^{d} \frac{2x_i y_i}{x_i + y_i}.$$

For positive data, this kernel is positive definite (see the next problem for a proof). Prove that

$$\kappa_{\mathrm{HI}}(\boldsymbol{x}, \boldsymbol{y}) \leq \kappa_{\chi^2}(\boldsymbol{x}, \boldsymbol{y}).$$

(e) *Hellinger's kernel* is defined for nonnegative data as

$$\kappa_{\mathrm{HE}}(\boldsymbol{x}, \boldsymbol{y}) = \sum_{i=1}^{d} \sqrt{x_i y_i}.$$

Prove that this is a valid kernel and that

$$\kappa_{\mathrm{HE}}(\boldsymbol{x}, \boldsymbol{y}) \geq \kappa_{\chi^2}(\boldsymbol{x}, \boldsymbol{y})$$

for positive data.

(f) Additive kernels are particularly effective when the feature vector is a *histogram*. A histogram (which is not normalized) contains natural numbers (i.e., zero or positive integers). Write out an explicit mapping for the histogram intersection kernel when the features are all natural numbers.

7.3 (Power mean kernels) In this problem we introduce the *power mean kernels*, which are a family of additive kernels and are closely related to the *generalized mean* in mathematics.

(a) Read the information on the page `https://en.wikipedia.org/wiki/Generalized_mean`. When we consider only the power mean of two *positive* numbers x and y, what are $M_0(x, y)$, $M_{-1}(x, y)$, and $M_{-\infty}(x, y)$?

(b) The power mean kernels are a family of additive kernels, each indexed by a *negative or zero* real number p. For two positive vectors $\boldsymbol{x}$ and $\boldsymbol{y}$ with $x_i, y_i > 0$ $(1 \leq i \leq d)$, the power mean kernel M_p is defined as

$$M_p(\boldsymbol{x}, \boldsymbol{y}) = \sum_{i=1}^{d} M_p(x_i, y_i) = \sum_{i=1}^{d} \left(\frac{x^p + y^p}{2} \right)^{1/p}.$$

Power mean kernels were proposed in Wu (2012b). Show that the three additive kernels discussed in the previous problem (histogram intersection, χ^2, and Hellinger's) are all special cases of the power mean kernels.

(c) (Conditionally positive definite kernel) A function κ is called a *conditionally positive definite kernel* if for an arbitrary positive integer n and any $c_1, c_2, \ldots, c_n \in \mathbb{R}$ that satisfies

$$\sum_{i=1}^{n} c_i = 0,$$

the inequality

$$\sum_{i=1}^{n} \sum_{j=1}^{n} c_i c_j \kappa(x_i, x_j) \geq 0$$

holds for *arbitrary* $x_1, x_2, \ldots, x_n \in \mathbb{R}$. Prove that

$$-\frac{x^p + y^p}{2}$$

is conditionally positive definite for positive data.

(c) Use the following theorem to prove that power mean kernels are positive definite kernels when $-\infty \leq p \leq 0$—i.e., they satisfy Mercer's condition.

If a kernel κ is conditionally positive definite and negative valued, then $\frac{1}{(-\kappa)^\delta}$ is positive definite for all $\delta \geq 0$.

(d) When we use the power mean kernel $M_{-\infty}$ to replace the histogram intersection kernel in a programming environment, we have to use a p value that is far away from the zero value to replace $-\infty$. For example, we can use $p = -32$—i.e., using M_{-32} to approximate $M_{-\infty}/\kappa_{\text{HI}}$.

Write a simple MATLAB or GNU Octave program to evaluate the largest absolute error and relative error between $M_{-32}(x, y)$ and $M_{-\infty}(x, y)$, where x and y are generated by the command `x=0.01:0.01:1` and `y=0.01:0.01:1`, respectively. Is M_{-32} a good approximation for κ_{HI}? That is, compare $\kappa_{\text{HI}}(x, y)$ and $M_{-32}(x, y)$ for the 10 000 pairs of x and y values.

(e) To illustrate the effectiveness of power mean kernels, visit `https://sites.google.com/site/wujx2001/home/power-mean-svm` and read the instructions there for installation and usage instructions. Use the resources on this page to generate training and testing data for the Caltech 101 dataset. When you generate the data, use `K = 100` rather than `K = 2000`. Try different p values, and apply the PmSVM software to this dataset. Use the LIBSVM software and the RBF kernel on the same dataset. Which one has higher accuracy on this dataset (whose feature vectors are histograms)? Note that if you use the tool provided in LIBSVM to choose optimal C and gamma hyperparameter values, it will take a very long time to finish. Which software has higher training and testing speed?

7.4 (SVMs without bias) In the linear SVM formulation, we assume a classification boundary of the form $\boldsymbol{w}^T\boldsymbol{x} + b$, which includes a bias term $b \in \mathbb{R}$. However, it is also possible to learn a linear SVM classifier *without* the bias term—i.e., using $\boldsymbol{w}^T\boldsymbol{x}$ as the classification boundary.

(a) Without the bias term, what is the optimization problem in the primal space? Use the notation in this chapter.

(b) Without the bias term, show that the dual form is

$$\min_{\boldsymbol{\alpha}} \quad f(\boldsymbol{\alpha}) = \frac{1}{2}\sum_{i=1}^{n}\sum_{j=1}^{n} \alpha_i \alpha_j y_i y_j \boldsymbol{x}_i^T \boldsymbol{x}_j - \sum_{i=1}^{n} \alpha_i \tag{7.72}$$

$$\text{s.t.} \quad 0 \le \alpha_i \le C, \quad i = 1, 2, \ldots, n. \tag{7.73}$$

If the solution for $\boldsymbol{\alpha}$ is $\boldsymbol{\alpha}^\star$, how do you find the optimal decision boundary $\boldsymbol{w}^\star$?

(c) When a bias is preferred, this formulation (without bias) can still be useful. Given a training dataset $(\boldsymbol{x}_i, y_i)$ $(1 \le i \le n)$, one can convert any $\boldsymbol{x} \in \mathbb{R}^d$ into $\hat{\boldsymbol{x}}$ in $\mathbb{R}^{d+1}$ by adding an extra dimension to $\boldsymbol{x}$. The added dimension always has constant value 1. Suppose $\boldsymbol{\alpha}^\star$ is the optimal solution for the dual formulation, and suppose the classification boundary is $\boldsymbol{w}^T\boldsymbol{x} + b$; what is the optimal b value?

7.5 (Dual coordinate descent) In this problem, we introduce the *dual coordinate descent* algorithm for solving a linear SVM without the bias term in the dual space.

(a) Using the notation in the previous problem, find $\frac{\partial f}{\partial \alpha_i}$. Find a way to calculate $\frac{\partial f}{\partial \alpha_i}$ in $\mathcal{O}(d)$ steps. We use $f'(\boldsymbol{\alpha})$ to denote the partial derivative of f with respect to $\boldsymbol{\alpha}$—i.e., $f'(\boldsymbol{\alpha})_i = \frac{\partial f}{\partial \alpha_i}$.

(b) The dual coordinate descent (DCD) algorithm was proposed in Hsieh et al. (2008). Among the n Lagrange multipliers α_i $(1 \le i \le n)$, DCD updates one multiplier at a time. One training epoch updates $\alpha_1, \alpha_2, \ldots, \alpha_n$ sequentially one by one. The DCD algorithm was proved to converge, and in practice it often converges in a few epochs.

Now suppose we fix $\alpha_1, \ldots, \alpha_{i-1}$ and $\alpha_{i+1}, \ldots, \alpha_n$, and want to find a better value for α_i. Denote the set of Lagrange multipliers after this update as $\boldsymbol{\alpha}'$, in which $\alpha_i' = \alpha_i + d$ and $\alpha_j' = \alpha_j$ for $j \ne i$. Show that

$$f(\boldsymbol{\alpha}') - f(\boldsymbol{\alpha}) = \frac{1}{2}\|\boldsymbol{x}_i\|^2 d^2 + f'(\boldsymbol{\alpha})d.$$

(c) Remember that α_i and α_i' should both be between 0 and C. Then what is the optimal value for α_i'?

(d) A practical implementation of the DCD algorithm needs to pay attention to a lot of implementation details—e.g., randomize the order of updating for different α_i values in different epochs. Read the DCD paper and understand which details are important. This paper also provides a proof of DCD's convergence.

A C++ implementation is provided at `www.csie.ntu.edu.tw/~cjlin/liblinear/`. Download this software and learn how to use it. This software has different solvers for linear classification and regression problems and several parameters. How do you specify parameters to perform classification in Eqs. (7.72) and (7.73)?

(e) Download the `rcv1.binary` training set from the LIBSVM data page (`www.csie.ntu.edu.tw/~cjlin/libsvmtools/datasets/`).

Use 5-fold cross-validation and obtain the training time and the cross-validation accuracy. Compare LIBSVM and LIBLINEAR on this task: use the linear kernel in LIBSVM, and in LIBLINEAR use the problem specified by Eqs. (7.72) and (7.73). Set $C = 4$ in these experiments.

8 Probabilistic Methods

We will discuss a few probabilistic methods in this chapter. As the name suggests, we estimate probability functions (p.m.f. or p.d.f.) in such models, and use these probability functions to guide our decisions (e.g., classification).

This is a huge topic and a great many methods exist within this category. We will touch only the most basic concepts and methods, and provide only brief introductions (perhaps one or two sentences) to some other methods. The main purpose of this chapter is to introduce the terminology, a few important concepts and methods, and the probabilistic approach to inference and decision making.

8.1 The Probabilistic Way of Thinking

The first thing to do is to introduce the terminology, which is a little different from that used in other parts of this book.

8.1.1 Terminology

Suppose we are given a training set $\{(\boldsymbol{x}_i, y_i)\}_{i=1}^n$ with training examples $\boldsymbol{x}_i$ and their associated labels y_i for all $1 \le i \le n$. Our task is to find a mapping $f: \mathcal{X} \mapsto \mathcal{Y}$, in which $\mathcal{X}$ is the input domain, $\boldsymbol{x}_i \in \mathcal{X}$, $\mathcal{Y}$ is the domain for labels or predictions, and $y_i \in \mathcal{Y}$. During the testing phase, we are given any example $\boldsymbol{x} \in \mathcal{X}$, and need to predict a value $y \in \mathcal{Y}$ for it.

In the probabilistic world, we use random variables (or random vectors) X and Y to denote the above-mentioned input examples and labels. The training examples $\boldsymbol{x}_i$ are treated as samples drawn from the random vector X, and in most cases, these examples are considered to be sampled i.i.d. (independent and identically distributed) from X. In other words, one can treat each $\boldsymbol{x}_i$ as a random variable, but they follow the same distribution as X and are independent of each other. This view is useful in analyzing probabilistic models and their properties. However, in this chapter we can simply treat $\boldsymbol{x}_i$ as an example (or instantiation) drawn from the distribution following X in the i.i.d. manner. The same applies to any test example $\boldsymbol{x}$.

Since we are given (i.e., have access to, or can observe) the values of $\boldsymbol{x}_i$, the random vector X is called an observable or observed. When we use diagrams or graphs to illustrate probabilistic models, an observable random variable is often drawn as a filled circle.

Similarly, the labels y_i or predictions y are samples drawn from Y. Because they are the variable(s) we want to predict (i.e., have no access to, or cannot directly observe), they are called hidden or latent variables, and are drawn as circled nodes.

The values of random variables can be of different types. For example, the label Y can be categorical. A categorical variable is also called a nominal variable, and can take a value from various (two or more) categories. For example, if $\mathcal{Y} = \{$"male","female"$\}$, then Y is categorical, with "male" and "female" denoting the two categories. It is important to remember that these categories are orderless—that is, you cannot find a natural or intrinsic ordering of these categories. When Y is categorical, we say the task is *classification*, and the mapping f is a classification model (or a classifier).

Alternatively, Y can be real valued—e.g., $\mathcal{Y} = \mathbb{R}$. In this case the task is called *regression* and the mapping f is called a regression model. In statistical regression, the X are also called the independent variables, and Y the dependent variable.

It is also possible that Y is a random vector, which may comprise both discrete and continuous random variables. However, in this book, we focus on the classification task. Hence, Y is always a discrete random variable and is always categorical (except in rare cases where Y is explicitly specified differently).

8.1.2 Distributions and Inference

Let $p(X,Y)$ be the *joint* distribution of X and Y. Since we assume that Y can be somehow predicted based on X, there must be some relationship between X and Y. In other words, X and Y cannot be independent—which means that we should expect that

$$p_{X,Y}(X,Y) \neq p_X(X)p_Y(Y). \tag{8.1}$$

If instead we have

$$p_{X,Y}(X,Y) = p_X(X)p_Y(Y),$$

then knowing X is not helpful for predicting Y at all and we cannot learn any meaningful model.

The marginal distribution $p_X(x)$ is measuring the density of data X without considering the effect of Y (or having the effect of Y integrated out from the joint).[1] It is called the *marginal likelihood*.

The marginal distribution $p_Y(y)$ is the *prior* distribution of Y when X is not considered (or not observed yet). It reflects the prior knowledge we have about Y (e.g., through domain knowledge) before any input is observed.

[1] In the Bayesian perspective, this is the likelihood of the observed data marginalized over the parameters. We will postpone our brief introduction of the Bayesian view to a later section.

After we observe X, because of the relationship between X and Y we can estimate the value of Y more precisely. That is, $p_{Y|X}(Y|X)$ (or simply $p(Y|X)$ when the meaning can be safely deduced from its context) is a better estimate of Y than $p_Y(Y)$. This distribution is called the *posterior* distribution. When given more *evidence* (samples of X), we can update our *belief* about Y. The updated belief—i.e., the posterior or the conditional distribution $p(Y|X)$—acts as the best estimate we have for Y given X.

The procedure of updating the belief (i.e., updating the posterior distribution) using the evidence is called probabilistic *inference*. We also need to decide what we can do after obtaining the posterior, hence the *decision* process follows. Classification is a typical type of decision.

8.1.3 Bayes' Theorem

Inference can be performed through Bayes' theorem (or Bayes' rule)

$$p(Y|X) = \frac{p(X|Y)p(Y)}{p(X)}. \tag{8.2}$$

The term $p(X|Y)$ is called the *likelihood*. It is also a conditional distribution. If we know $Y = y$, then the distribution of X will be different from its prior $p(X)$. For example, if we want to decide the gender of a person from their height, then the distribution (likelihood) of males $p(\text{height}|Y = \text{“male”})$ or females $p(\text{height}|Y = \text{“female”})$ will definitely be different from the distribution (marginal likelihood) of all people $p(\text{height})$.

Since we consider only the classification problem, $p(X|Y)$ are also the *class conditional* distributions. In short, Bayes' theorem states that

$$\text{posterior} = \frac{\text{likelihood} \times \text{prior}}{\text{marginal likelihood}}. \tag{8.3}$$

One thing is worth mentioning about Bayes' rule. Since the denominator $p(X)$ does not depend on Y, we can write

$$p(Y|X) \propto p(X|Y)p(Y) \tag{8.4}$$

$$= \frac{1}{Z}p(X|Y)p(Y), \tag{8.5}$$

in which $\propto$ means “proportional to” and $Z = p(X) > 0$ is a normalization constant that makes $p(Y|X)$ a valid probability distribution.

8.2 Choices

Now it seems that we just need to estimate $p(Y|X)$, and that distribution alone will give us sufficient information to make decisions relevant to Y (given the evidence from X). There are, however, several questions remaining, such as the following:

- Shall we estimate $p(Y|X)$ using Bayes' theorem—i.e., by first estimating $p(X|Y)$ and $p(Y)$? This is equivalent to estimating the joint $p(X,Y)$. Is there any other way?
- How do we represent the distributions?
- How do we estimate the distributions?

At first glance, these questions may seem unnecessary or even trivial. However, different answers to these questions lead to different solutions or decisions, or even different conceptions of the world.

Next we will discuss a few important options for these questions. No matter which option is chosen, parameter estimation is the key in probabilistic methods. When the considered distribution is continuous, we use the phrase *density estimation* to refer to the estimation of the continuous distribution's density function.

8.2.1 Generative vs. Discriminative Models

If one directly models the conditional/posterior distribution $p(Y|X)$, this is a *discriminative model*. Discriminative models, however, cannot draw (or generate) a sample pair $(\boldsymbol{x}, y)$ that follows the underlying joint distribution. Generating a sample is important in some applications. Hence, one can also model the joint distribution $p(X,Y)$, which leads to a *generative model*.

In terms of classification, usually the prior distribution $p(Y)$ and the class conditional distribution $p(X|Y)$ are modeled instead. This is equivalent to modeling $p(X,Y)$, as

$$p(X,Y) = p(Y)p(X|Y).$$

When the capability to sample from the joint (i.e., to generate instances from the joint) is not important, a discriminative model is applicable, and it usually has higher classification accuracy than a generative model in practice. However, if the goal is to model the data generation process rather than classification, a generative model is necessary.

There are other options too. We do not necessarily need to interpret the world probabilistically. To find the classification boundary (which is also called the discriminant functions) directly without considering probabilities sometimes leads to better results than even the discriminative model.

8.2.2 Parametric vs. Nonparametric

A natural way to represent a distribution is to assume that it has a specific parametric form. For example, if we assume that a distribution is a normal distribution, then the p.d.f. has a fixed functional form

$$p(\boldsymbol{x}) = \frac{1}{(2\pi)^{d/2}|\Sigma|^{1/2}} \exp\left(-\frac{1}{2}(\boldsymbol{x}-\boldsymbol{\mu})^T\Sigma^{-1}(\boldsymbol{x}-\boldsymbol{\mu})\right), \tag{8.6}$$

and is completely specified by two parameters: the mean $\boldsymbol{\mu}$ and the covariance matrix Σ. Hence, estimating the distribution means estimating its parameters.

Given a dataset $D = \{\boldsymbol{x}_1, \boldsymbol{x}_2, \ldots, \boldsymbol{x}_n\}$ and assuming a multivariate normal distribution, we will soon show that the best maximum likelihood (ML) estimates of the parameters are

$$\boldsymbol{\mu}_{\text{ML}} = \frac{1}{n}\sum_{i=1}^{n} \boldsymbol{x}_i, \tag{8.7}$$

$$\Sigma_{\text{ML}} = \frac{1}{n}\sum_{i=1}^{n} (\boldsymbol{x}_i - \boldsymbol{\mu}_{\text{ML}})(\boldsymbol{x}_i - \boldsymbol{\mu}_{\text{ML}})^T. \tag{8.8}$$

There are, however, different criteria for the "best" estimation. For example, when the maximum a posteriori (MAP) estimation is used, the best estimation of $\boldsymbol{\mu}$ and Σ will be different. We will discuss ML and MAP estimations later in this chapter. These methods can also be used to estimate the parameters of discrete distributions—i.e., to estimate the probability mass functions.

This family of methods for density estimation are called the *parametric* methods, because we assume specific functional forms (e.g., normal or exponential p.d.f.) and only estimate the parameters in these functions. Parametric estimation is a powerful tool when domain knowledge can suggest the particular form of a p.d.f.

When the functional form of a continuous distribution is unknown, we can use a GMM (Gaussian mixture model) instead:

$$p(\boldsymbol{x}) = \sum_{i=1}^{K} \alpha_i N(\boldsymbol{x}; \boldsymbol{\mu}_i, \Sigma_i), \tag{8.9}$$

in which $\alpha_i \geq 0$ $(1 \leq i \leq K)$ are the mixing weights satisfying $\sum_{i=1}^{K} \alpha_i = 1$, and $N(\boldsymbol{x}; \boldsymbol{\mu}_i, \Sigma_i)$ is the ith component multivariate Gaussian with mean $\boldsymbol{\mu}_i$ and covariance matrix Σ_i. This GMM distribution is a valid continuous distribution.

So long as we can use as many Gaussian components as we require, the GMM is a universal approximator in the sense that it can accurately approximate any continuous distribution with high accuracy. In practice, however, it is never easy to estimate the parameters in a GMM (the α_i, $\boldsymbol{\mu}_i$, Σ_i parameters). This is a nonconvex problem and we can find only a local minimum in the ML or MAP estimation.[2] A more serious problem is that an accurate enough estimation may require a large K, which is computationally infeasible and requires too many training examples. And we do not know what value of K fits a particular density estimation problem.

Another family of density estimation methods are called the *nonparametric* methods, because no specific functional form is assumed for the density function. Nonparametric methods use the training examples to estimate the density at any particular point of the domain. Note that the word "nonparametric" means that no parameterized functional form is assumed, but does *not* mean parameters are not

[2] For example, use the EM method, which will be discussed in Chapter 14.

needed. In fact, all training examples are parameters in such methods in addition to other possible parameters, and the number of parameters can grow toward infinity in nonparametric models.

The number of parameters in a nonparametric model usually increases when the number of training examples increases. Hence, we do not need to manually control the model complexity (such as choosing a proper K value in a GMM model). Nonparametric methods, however, usually suffer from high computational cost. We will present a simple nonparametric method in this chapter: kernel density estimation.

8.2.3 What Is a Parameter?

When we say that the ML estimate of a Gaussian's mean is $\frac{1}{n}\sum_{i=1}^{n}\boldsymbol{x}_i$, we have an implicit assumption (or we view the parameter $\boldsymbol{\mu}$ in this way): the parameter $\boldsymbol{\mu}$ is a vector whose values are fixed (i.e., without randomness), but we do not know the exact values. Hence, the maximum likelihood method uses the training data to find this set of fixed but unknown parameter values. The same interpretation applies to the MAP estimation method. This view is associated with the *frequentist view of probability*. The estimation result of these methods is a fixed point (without randomness) in the space of possible parameter values, and is called a *point estimate*.

The *Bayesian interpretation of probability* interprets parameters and parameter estimation in a different manner. The parameters (e.g., $\boldsymbol{\mu}$) are also considered as random variables (or random vectors). Hence, what we should estimate are not a fixed set of values, but distributions.

Since $\boldsymbol{\mu}$ is also a random vector, it must have a prior distribution (before we observe the training set). If that prior distribution is a multivariate Gaussian, Bayes' rule leads to a Bayesian estimation of $\boldsymbol{\mu}$, which is an *entire Gaussian distribution* $N(\boldsymbol{\mu}_n, \Sigma_n)$, rather than a single fixed point. Bayesian estimation is a complex topic. We will introduce only a very simple example of Bayesian estimation in this chapter. The focus, however, is not the technique itself, but the different interpretations of these two lines of methods.

8.3 Parametric Estimation

Since parameter estimation is the key in all sorts of parametric methods, in this section we introduce three types of parameter estimation methods: ML, MAP, and Bayesian. We mainly use simple examples to introduce the ideas. Interested readers can refer to advanced textbooks for more technical details.

8.3.1 Maximum Likelihood

The maximum likelihood (ML) estimation method is probably the simplest parameter estimation method.

Suppose we have a set of scalar training examples $D = \{x_1, x_2, \ldots, x_n\}$. Furthermore, we assume that they are drawn i.i.d. from a normal distribution $N(\mu, \sigma^2)$. The parameters to be estimated are denoted as $\boldsymbol{\theta}$, where $\boldsymbol{\theta} = (\mu, \sigma^2)$. The ML method estimates the parameters depending on the answer to this question:

Given two parameters $\boldsymbol{\theta}_1 = (\mu_1, \sigma_1^2)$ and $\boldsymbol{\theta}_2 = (\mu_2, \sigma_2^2)$, how do we judge whether $\boldsymbol{\theta}_1$ is better than $\boldsymbol{\theta}_2$ (or the reverse)?

A concrete example is as follows. If

$$D = \{5.67, 3.79, 5.72, 6.63, 5.49, 6.03, 5.73, 4.70, 5.29, 4.21\}$$

follows the normal distribution with $\sigma^2 = 1$, and $\mu_1 = 0$, $\mu_2 = 5$, which one is a better choice for the μ parameter?

For a normal distribution, we know that the probability of a point bigger than 3σ plus the mean is less than 0.0015.[3] Hence, if $\mu = \mu_1 = 0$, then the probability we observe any single point in D (which are all more than 3σ away from the mean) is less than 0.0015. Because these points are i.i.d. sampled, assuming $\mu = 0$, the chance or *likelihood* that we will observe D is extremely small: smaller than $0.0015^{10} < 5.8 \times 10^{-29}$!

For another candidate $\mu = \mu_2 = 5$, we see that all values in D are around 5, and we will compute a much higher likelihood of observing D if $\mu = 5$. Hence, it is natural to determine that $\mu_2 = 5$ is better than $\mu_1 = 0$ when we are given the dataset D and $\sigma^2 = 1$.

Formally, given a training set D and a parametric density p, we define

$$p(D|\boldsymbol{\theta}) = \prod_{i=1}^{n} p(x_i|\boldsymbol{\theta}). \tag{8.10}$$

In our normal distribution example, we further have

$$p(D|\boldsymbol{\theta}) = \prod_{i=1}^{n} \frac{1}{\sqrt{2\pi}\sigma} \exp\left(-\frac{(x_i - \mu)^2}{2\sigma^2}\right). \tag{8.11}$$

The term $p(D|\boldsymbol{\theta})$ is called the likelihood (of observing the training data D when the parameter value is fixed at $\boldsymbol{\theta}$).

However, because $\boldsymbol{\theta}$ is not a random vector, $p(D|\boldsymbol{\theta})$ is *not* a conditional distribution. This notation can be a little confusing in some cases. Hence, it is common to define a *likelihood function* $\ell(\boldsymbol{\theta})$:

$$\ell(\boldsymbol{\theta}) = \prod_{i=1}^{n} p(x_i|\boldsymbol{\theta}), \tag{8.12}$$

[3] Let Φ be the c.d.f. of the standard normal distribution ($\mu = 0$ and $\sigma^2 = 1$). Then this probability is

$$1 - \Phi(3) \approx 0.0013,$$

because we consider the one-sided range $(\mu + 3\sigma, \infty)$ only.

which clearly indicates that the likelihood is a function of $\boldsymbol{\theta}$. Because the function exp is involved in many densities, the logarithm of $\ell(\boldsymbol{\theta})$ is very useful. It is called the log-likelihood function, and defined as

$$\ell\ell(\boldsymbol{\theta}) = \ln \ell(\boldsymbol{\theta}) = \sum_{i=1}^{n} \ln p(x_i \mid \boldsymbol{\theta}). \tag{8.13}$$

If the observations are vectors, we can use the notation $\boldsymbol{x}_i$ to replace x_i.

As its name suggests, the maximum likelihood estimation solves the following optimization:

$$\boldsymbol{\theta}_{\text{ML}} = \arg\max_{\boldsymbol{\theta}} \ell(\boldsymbol{\theta}) = \arg\max_{\boldsymbol{\theta}} \ell\ell(\boldsymbol{\theta}). \tag{8.14}$$

The logarithm function is a monotonically increasing function, so applying it to $\ell(\boldsymbol{\theta})$ will not change the optimal estimation.

Returning to our normal distribution example, it is easy to solve the above optimization by setting the partial derivatives to 0, and get

$$\mu_{\text{ML}} = \frac{1}{n} \sum_{i=1}^{n} x_i, \tag{8.15}$$

$$\sigma_{\text{ML}}^2 = \frac{1}{n} \sum_{i=1}^{n} (x_i - \mu_{\text{ML}})^2. \tag{8.16}$$

Generalizing this to the multivariate normal distribution, Eqs. (8.7) and (8.8) are the ML estimates for $\boldsymbol{\mu}$ and Σ, respectively.

However, the optimization in ML estimation is not always as easy as in the above example. The ML estimation for a GMM model, for example, is nonconvex and difficult. Advanced techniques such as expectation-maximization (EM), which we introduce in Chapter 14, have to be adopted.

8.3.2 Maximum A Posteriori

The ML estimate can be accurate if we have enough examples. However, when there are only a small number of training examples, the ML estimate might suffer from inaccurate results. One remedy is to incorporate our domain knowledge about the parameters.

For example, if we know that the mean μ should be around 5.5, this knowledge can be translated into a prior distribution[4]

$$p(\boldsymbol{\theta}) = p(\mu, \sigma) = \frac{1}{\sqrt{2\pi}\sigma_0} \exp\left(-\frac{(\mu - 5.5)^2}{2\sigma_0^2}\right),$$

[4] The phrases *a priori* and *a posteriori* are two Latin phrases, meaning conclusions that come before and after we sense observations, respectively. In probability, our belief before sensing observations is encoded in the *prior* distribution, and the belief is updated to form the *posterior* distribution after the observations are factored in.

in which σ_0 is a relatively large number. In this example, we assume no prior knowledge about σ, and assume a priori that μ follows a Gaussian distribution whose mean is 5.5 and the variance σ_0^2 is large (i.e., the prior distribution is flat.)

The maximum a posteriori (MAP) estimation then solves

$$\arg\max_{\boldsymbol{\theta}} p(\boldsymbol{\theta})\ell(\boldsymbol{\theta}) = \arg\max_{\boldsymbol{\theta}} \{\ln p(\boldsymbol{\theta}) + \ell\ell(\boldsymbol{\theta})\} . \tag{8.17}$$

The optimization is similar to what is in the ML estimate.

MAP takes into account both the prior knowledge and training data. When the size (n) of the training dataset is small, the prior $\ln p(\boldsymbol{\theta})$ may play an important role, especially when the sampled examples are unluckily not a representative set of samples from $p(\boldsymbol{x};\boldsymbol{\theta})$. However, when there are a large number of training examples, $\ell\ell(\boldsymbol{\theta})$ will be much larger than $\ln p(\boldsymbol{\theta})$, and the effect of the prior knowledge is diluted.

Both ML and MAP are point estimation methods, which return one single optimal value for $\boldsymbol{\theta}$. In a generative model, after estimating the parameters of the joint distribution $p(\boldsymbol{x},\boldsymbol{y};\boldsymbol{\theta})$, we are able to calculate $p(\boldsymbol{y}|\boldsymbol{x};\boldsymbol{\theta})$ and make decisions about $\boldsymbol{y}$. In a discriminative model, after estimating the parameters of the distribution $p(\boldsymbol{y}|\boldsymbol{x};\boldsymbol{\theta})$, we can also make decisions based on $p(\boldsymbol{y}|\boldsymbol{x};\boldsymbol{\theta})$. Note that in $p(\boldsymbol{y}|\boldsymbol{x};\boldsymbol{\theta})$, the inclusion of $\boldsymbol{\theta}$ after the "|" sign indicates only that this density function is computed using the estimated parameter value $\boldsymbol{\theta}$, but $\boldsymbol{\theta}$ is not a random variable. Hence, $\boldsymbol{\theta}$ is put after a ";" sign.

8.3.3 Bayesian

In the Bayesian point of view and the Bayesian parameter estimation method, $\boldsymbol{\theta}$ is a random variable (or random vector), which means that its best estimate is no longer a fixed value (vector), but an entire distribution. Hence, the output of the Bayesian estimation is $p(\boldsymbol{\theta}|D)$. Now this *is* a valid p.d.f. because both $\boldsymbol{\theta}$ (the parameters) and D (with one instance sampled from D being the training set) are random vectors.

Bayesian estimation is a complex topic and we work on a simplified example only.

Given a dataset $D = \{x_1, x_2, \ldots, x_n\}$, it is interpreted as there being n random variables $X_1, X_2, \ldots, X_n$ that are i.i.d., and x_i is sampled from X_i. Hence, D is one sample of an array of random variables. If we assume that X_i is normally distributed, these random variables will follow the same normal distribution $N(\mu,\sigma^2)$. To simplify the problem, we assume that σ is *known* and we need to estimate only μ. Hence, $\boldsymbol{\theta} = \mu$.

Because $\boldsymbol{\theta}$ (or μ) is a random variable, it should have a prior distribution, which we assume is

$$p(\mu) = N(\mu;\mu_0,\sigma_0^2).$$

To further simplify our introduction, we assume that both μ_0 and σ_0 are *known*. Usually σ_0 is set to a large value because the prior knowledge cannot be very certain.

We need to estimate $p(\mu|D)$. As the name suggests, Bayes' rule is key to this estimate:

$$p(\mu|D) = \frac{p(D|\mu)p(\mu)}{\int p(D|\mu)p(\mu)\,\mathrm{d}\mu} \tag{8.18}$$

$$= \alpha p(D|\mu)p(\mu) \tag{8.19}$$

$$= \alpha \prod_{i=1}^{n} p(x_i|\mu)p(\mu), \tag{8.20}$$

in which $\alpha = 1/\int p(D|\mu)p(\mu)\,\mathrm{d}\mu$ is a normalization constant that does not depend on μ.

This estimate involves the product of several normal p.d.f.s. According to the properties of normal distributions, we have[5]

$$p(\mu|D) = N(\mu_n, \sigma_n^2), \tag{8.21}$$

in which

$$\left(\sigma_n^2\right)^{-1} = \left(\sigma_0^2\right)^{-1} + \left(\frac{\sigma^2}{n}\right)^{-1}, \tag{8.22}$$

$$\mu_n = \frac{\sigma^2/n}{\sigma_0^2 + \sigma^2/n}\mu_0 + \frac{\sigma_0^2}{\sigma_0^2 + \sigma^2/n}\mu_{\mathrm{ML}}. \tag{8.23}$$

The reciprocal of σ_n^2 is the sum of two terms: the reciprocal of the variance (uncertainty) in the prior (σ_0^2) and a weighted version of the uncertainty in the distribution ($\frac{1}{n} \times \sigma^2$). It is equivalent to

$$\sigma_n^2 = \frac{\sigma_0^2 \times (\sigma^2/n)}{\sigma_0^2 + (\sigma^2/n)}. \tag{8.24}$$

When there are only a few examples, the prior plays an important role; however, when $n \to \infty$, we have $(\sigma^2/n) \to 0$ and $\sigma_n^2 < (\sigma^2/n) \to 0$; i.e., as we have more training examples, the uncertainty about μ is reduced toward 0.

Furthermore, μ_n is also a weighted average of the prior mean μ_0 and the sample mean μ_{ML}, and the weights are the two uncertainties: σ^2/n for μ_0 and σ_0^2 for μ_{ML}. When n is small, both the prior and the data are important components of the estimation; however, when $n \to \infty$, $(\sigma^2/n) \to 0$ and the effect of the prior disappears.

Hence, these Bayesian estimates at least match our intuition: when there are only a few training examples, a proper prior distribution is helpful; when there are enough examples, the prior distribution can be safely disregarded.

An example of Bayesian estimation is shown in Figure 8.1. In this example we estimate the μ parameter of a normal distribution whose $\sigma^2 = 4$. The prior for μ is $N(7, 25)$, i.e., $\mu_0 = 7$, $\sigma_0 = 5$. The training data D are generated using $\mu = 5$, and contain n examples.

[5] Please refer to Chapter 13 for details of this derivation.

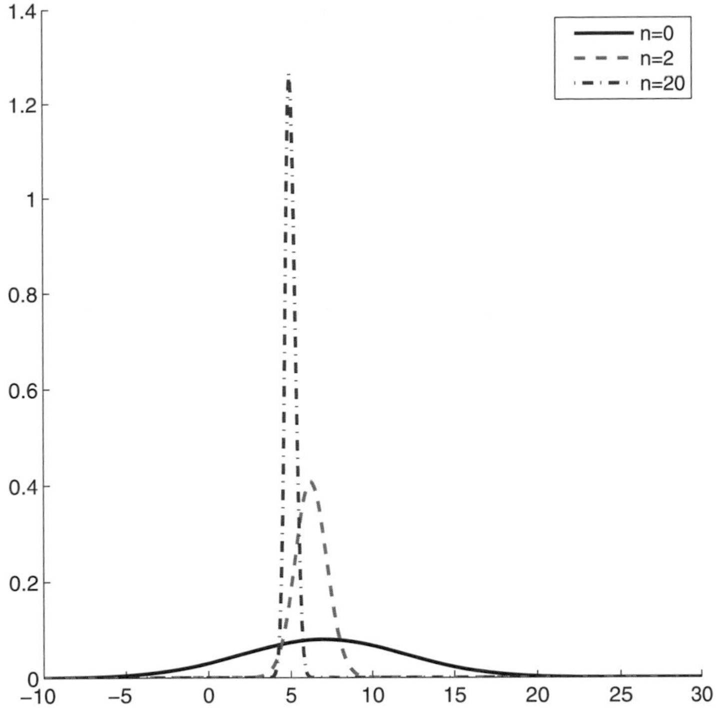

Figure 8.1 An illustration of the Bayesian parameter estimation. The solid black curve is the prior distribution for μ. The red dashed curve is the Bayesian estimation when $n = 2$. The blue dash-dotted curve is the Bayesian estimation when $n = 20$. (A black and white version of this figure will appear in some formats. For the color version, please refer to the plate section.)

As shown in Figure 8.1, when $n = 20$ the Bayesian estimation is quite accurate: its mode is close to 5 and the variance is small. However, when $n = 2$ the estimated density has a mean that is almost the same as that of the prior. These observations match the intuition from the equations.

A lot can be said about Bayesian estimation. However, we discuss a few issues only qualitatively because more detailed explanations are beyond the scope of this book.

- In the above example, when $p(D|\mu)$ is a normal distribution, we *choose* the prior for μ to be a normal distribution; then the posterior $p(\mu|D)$ is also a normal distribution, i.e., in the same functional form as the prior. This fact makes our derivation easier.

  In general, when the likelihood function $p(D|\boldsymbol{\theta})$ follows a particular distribution A and the prior $p(\boldsymbol{\theta})$ follows distribution B (which could be the same as A or different), then if the posterior $p(\boldsymbol{\theta}|D)$ is also in the distribution family B (i.e., has the same functional form as the prior), we say that B is a *conjugate prior* for the likelihood function A. For example, the conjugate prior of a Gaussian is again a Gaussian.

- Bayesian estimation has nice theoretical underpinnings, and the mathematics involved is usually beautiful. However, its derivation is usually much more complex than point estimation methods such as ML and MAP. Although the conjugate priors of some likelihood distributions are known, it is hard to find the conjugate prior for an arbitrary density function.
- Integration is involved in Bayesian estimation. When closed-form solutions are not available as a proper conjugate prior, the integration has to be done numerically or through methods such as MCMC (Markov chain Monte Carlo), which is computationally very expensive. This fact limits the scale of problems that Bayesian estimation can handle.
- When Bayesian estimation is used in a decision process, we need to find $p(\boldsymbol{y}|D)$, which means another integration over $\boldsymbol{\theta}$ is required. Hence, it is not as convenient as the decision process using point estimation methods.

  Note that $p(\boldsymbol{y}|D)$ is a distribution (called the posterior predicative distribution). Then $\mathbb{E}[p(\boldsymbol{y}|D)]$ can be used to guide the decision process. In some cases, the uncertainty of our decision is also required, and can be measured by $\sqrt{\mathrm{Var}(p(\boldsymbol{y}|D))}$.
- In the Bayesian view of probability, parameters of the prior (such as μ_0 and σ_0) are also random variables. Sometimes it is necessary to define prior distributions for these parameters, and these prior distributions will in turn have parameters that have to be modeled. Hence, a Bayesian model can be hierarchical and rather complex.
- Bayesian estimation and decisions are very useful when there are a small number of training examples. When we have ample training examples, its performance (e.g., accuracy in a classification problem) is usually lower than other methods (such as a discriminant function).
- Sometimes the prior distribution can be an *uninformative distribution*, which does not carry useful information in it. For example, if we know that μ is between 0 and 10 (but know no further information beyond that), the prior of μ can be a uniform distribution on $[0, 10]$ (i.e., $p(\mu) = 0.1$ for $\mu \in [0, 10]$ and $p(\mu) = 0$ for $\mu < 0$ and $\mu > 10$), which does not favor any particular point in this range.

  One extreme situation is that we know nothing about μ, and set $p(\mu) = \text{const}$. This type of prior assumes a uniform distribution in $\mathbb{R}$, but is not a valid probability density function; hence, it is called an *improper prior*.

8.4 Nonparametric Estimation

Nonparametric estimation does not assume any functional form of the density. Different ideas and intuition can lead to different nonparametric estimation approaches. In this section, we talk about only classic nonparametric density estimation, and the more advanced nonparametric Bayesian concept will not be touched.

We introduce nonparametric estimation for continuous distributions, and start from the simple one-dimensional distribution case.

8.4.1 A One-Dimensional Example

Given a set of scalar values $D = \{x_1, x_2, \ldots, x_n\}$ drawn i.i.d. from a random variable X with an underlying density $p(x)$, we want to estimate this density function.

The histogram is an excellent visualization tool that helps us to examine the distribution of values in one-dimensional space. We draw 400 examples from the two-component Gaussian mixture model (GMM)

$$0.25N(x;0,1) + 0.75N(x;6,4), \tag{8.25}$$

and compute three histograms with 10, 20, and 40 bins, respectively, as shown in Figure 8.2.

The first step to building a histogram is to find the data range. Let us denote the minimum value in D as a, and the maximum value as b. Then we can use the range $[a,b]$ as the range of possible values. We can also extend the range to $[a-\epsilon, b+\epsilon]$ to allow for possible variations in the data, where ϵ is a small positive number.

In the second step, we need to determine the number of bins in the histogram. If m bins are used, the range $[a,b]$ is then divided into m nonoverlapping subranges

$$\left[a + (i-1)\frac{b-a}{m}, \quad a + i\frac{b-a}{m}\right), \quad 1 \le i \le m-1,$$

and final subrange

$$\left[a + (m-1)\frac{b-a}{m}, \quad b\right].$$

In fact, the assignment of the values $a + i\frac{b-a}{m}$ to either the left-hand or the right-hand subrange is not important. We choose the right-hand subrange.

Each subrange defines a histogram bin, and we use $\text{Bin}(i)$ to denote the ith bin and its associated subrange. The length of these subranges, $\frac{b-a}{m}$, is the bin *width*. An m-bin histogram is a vector $\boldsymbol{h} = (h_1, h_2, \ldots, h_m)^T$, and h_i is the number of elements in D that fall in the ith bin, i.e.,

$$h_i = \sum_{j=1}^{n} [\![x_j \in \text{Bin}(i)]\!], \tag{8.26}$$

in which $[\![\cdot]\!]$ is the indicator function. Hence,

$$\sum_{i=1}^{m} h_i = n.$$

Sometimes we ℓ_1 normalize the histogram by $h_i \leftarrow \frac{h_i}{n}$ such that $\sum_{i=1}^{m} h_i = 1$ after the normalization. More details on normalization will be introduced in Chapter 9.

In Figure 8.2, we use stairs instead of bars to draw the histograms, which make the histograms look more similar to the true p.d.f. curve. As the figures show, although the histograms are not smooth and are different from the p.d.f. at almost every single point, the difference between the histograms and the p.d.f. is not large. In other words, the histogram is a good approximation of the p.d.f.

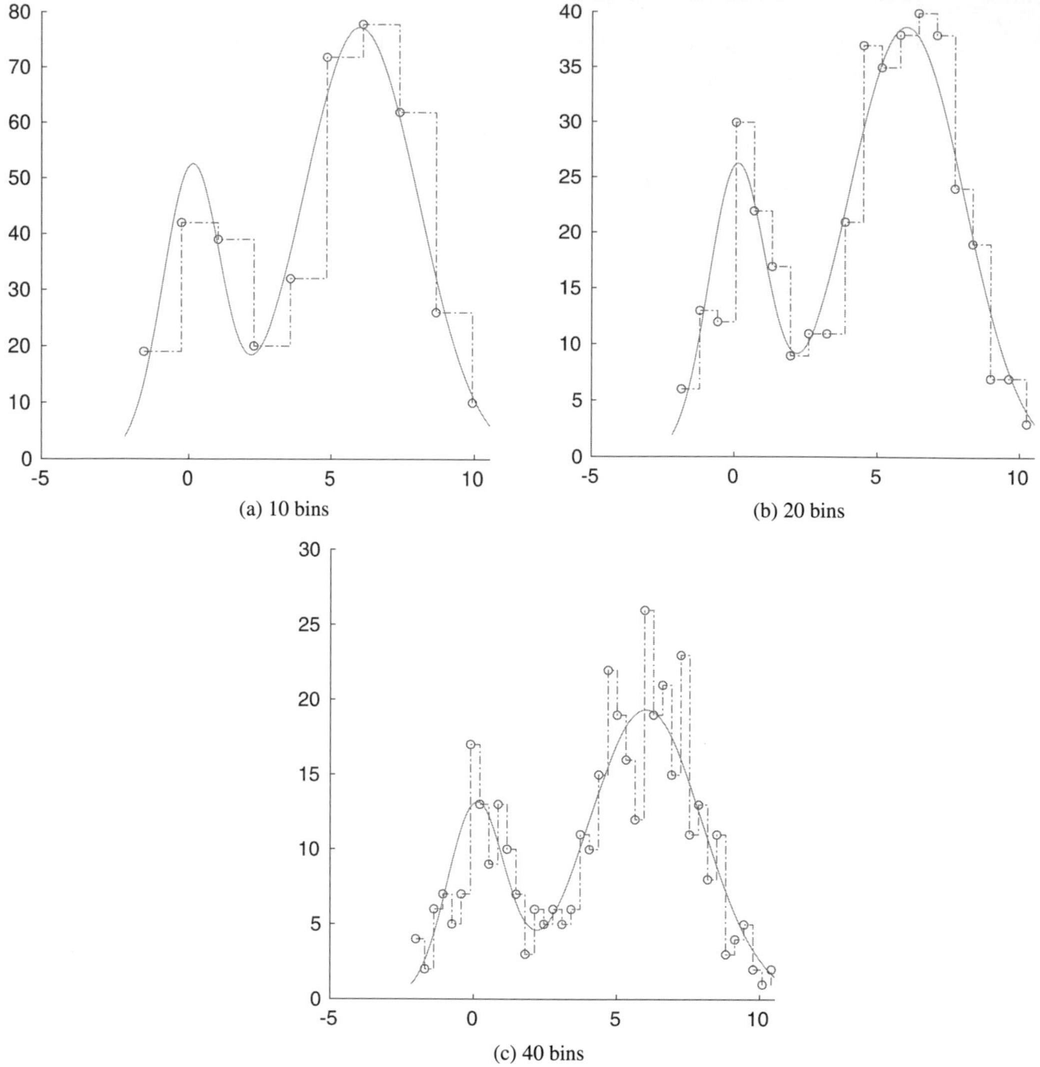

Figure 8.2 Histograms with different numbers of bins. The red dash-dotted curves are the histograms calculated from 400 examples. The three figures contain histograms with 10, 20, and 40 bins, respectively. The solid curve shows the distribution that generates the 400 data points. The solid curves are scaled to match the magnitude of the dash-dotted curves in each figure. (A black and white version of this figure will appear in some formats. For the color version, please refer to the plate section.)

For example, given a value x, we can first find which bin it belongs to. Denote the bin that x falls into by $\text{id}(x)$; we can approximate $p(x)$ as

$$p_{\text{hist}}(x) \propto h_{\text{id}(x)}, \tag{8.27}$$

in which $\propto$ means proportional to. This equation is correct no matter whether ℓ_1 normalization is used or not.

8.4.2 Problems with the Histogram Approximation

The histogram approximation has quite a number of problems. The following are a few important ones.

- No continuous estimation. Estimation directly from a histogram is not continuous, leaving discontinuities at the boundary of two bins. Inside each bin, a constant value represents the entire range, which leads to large errors. Furthermore, if we need to estimate $p(x)$ but x is beyond the range of the histogram, the estimation will be 0, which is not suitable.
- Curse of dimensionality. When there are multiple dimensions, we divide each dimension into bins individually. However, suppose each dimension is divided into m bins; a distribution with d dimensions has m^d bins in total! If $m = 4$ (which is smaller than most typical m values) and $d = 100$ (which is also smaller than typical dimensionality for modern features), the number of bins is $4^{100} \approx 1.6 \times 10^{60}$.

  In other words, we need this huge number of values to describe the 100-dimensional histogram. Since 10^{60} far exceeds the number of training examples, most of the bins will be empty, and their corresponding estimation is 0. This phenomenon is called the *curse of dimensionality*. As the number of dimensions increases linearly, the complexity of the model (e.g., histogram) increases exponentially, which makes histogram-based estimation impossible because we will never have enough training examples or computing resources to learn these values.
- The need to find a suitable bin width (or equivalently, number of bins). Figure 8.2 clearly illustrates this issue. When the number of bins $m = 20$, the histogram in Figure 8.2b matches the true p.d.f. closely. However, when $m = 10$, the histogram in Figure 8.2a has clear discrepancies with the p.d.f. The complexity of the model (i.e., histogram) is lower than that of the data (i.e., the p.d.f.). Underfitting leads to inferior approximation.

  In Figure 8.2c, $m = 40$ leads to an overly complex histogram, which has more peaks and valleys than the p.d.f. exhibits. It is obvious that the complex model is overfitting peculiar properties of the samples D, but not the p.d.f.

  The bin width (or number of bins) in a histogram model is a hyperparameter. It significantly affects the model's success, but there is no good theory to guide its choice.

In low-dimensional problems, however, the histogram is a good tool to model and visualize our data. For example, if $d = 1$ or $d = 2$, the curse of dimensionality is not a problem. A histogram with a properly chosen bin width can approximate a continuous distribution fairly accurately. One additional benefit is that we do not need to store the dataset D—storing the histogram $\boldsymbol{h}$ is enough.

8.4.3 Making Your Examples Far Reaching

There is another perspective of histograms to consider. The histogram counts h_i reflect the accumulated contributions of all training examples in D. If we single out one particular example x_i (which falls into a bin with index $\mathrm{id}(x_i)$), its contribution to the entire domain ($\mathbb{R}$ in one dimension) is a function $h^{x_i}(x)$:

$$h^{x_i}(x) = \begin{cases} 1 & \text{if } \mathrm{id}(x) = \mathrm{id}(x_i), \\ 0 & \text{otherwise,} \end{cases} \tag{8.28}$$

and obviously the histogram estimate $p_{\mathrm{hist}}(x)$ (cf. Eq. 8.27) can be computed as

$$p_{\mathrm{hist}}(x) \propto \sum_{i=1}^{n} h^{x_i}(x). \tag{8.29}$$

Every training example contributes to the estimate individually and independently. The manner of their contribution, however, is problematic:

- Not symmetric. There is no reason to guess that the distribution to the left of x_i is more important than the distribution to its right, or vice versa. However, if a bin is defined as the range $[1,2)$ and $x_i = 1.9$, then only a small range of the right-hand side of x_i receives its contribution ($[1.9,2)$, whose length is 0.1), but on the left a large range is the beneficiary of x_i ($[1,1.9)$, whose length is 0.9).
- Finite support. As shown in the above example, only samples in the range $[1,2)$ receive contributions from x_i, a fact that leads to the discontinuous estimate.
- Uniform radiation. In the finite range that x_i affects, the effect is uniform. No matter whether x is far away from or close to x_i, it receives the same contribution from x_i. This is somehow counterintuitive. We usually agree that x_i has large impact on its near neighbors, but its effect should fade as the distance grows (and gradually reduce to 0 if the distance grows to infinity).

In other words, we want to replace $h^{x_i}(x)$ with a continuous, symmetric function (centered at x_i) whose support is the entire domain (i.e., the impact of any example is far reaching) and whose magnitude reduces along with increasing distance to its center. And of course, the contribution function must be nonnegative. In some cases, the infinite support condition can be changed to a limited but sufficiently large support condition.

8.4.4 Kernel Density Estimation

Formally, the kernel density estimation (KDE) method satisfies all these expectations. Let K be a *kernel* function that is nonnegative ($K(x) \ge 0$ for any $x \in \mathbb{R}$) and integrates to 1 ($\int K(x)\,\mathrm{d}x = 1$). In addition, we also require that $\int x K(x)\,\mathrm{d}x = 0$. Then the kernel density estimator is

$$p_{\mathrm{KDE}}(x) = \frac{1}{n} \sum_{i=1}^{n} \frac{1}{h} K\left(\frac{x - x_i}{h}\right). \tag{8.30}$$

A few points are worth pointing out about KDE.

- The word *kernel* has a different meaning from the word *kernel* in kernel methods (such as SVM), although some functions are valid kernels in both cases (such as the RBF/Gaussian kernel).
- The parameter $h > 0$ plays a similar role to the bin width in histogram estimation. This parameter is called the *bandwidth* in KDE. The same symbol has different meanings in these two settings (bin counts vs. bandwidth), but the context should make the distinction clear.
- Since $\int K(x)\,\mathrm{d}x = 1$, we have $\int K\left(\frac{x-x_i}{h}\right)\mathrm{d}x = h$ for any $h > 0$, $x_i \in \mathbb{R}$, and $\int \frac{1}{h}K\left(\frac{x-x_i}{h}\right)\mathrm{d}x = 1$. Because $K(x) \geq 0$, we know $p_{\mathrm{KDE}}(x) \geq 0$ and $\int p_{\mathrm{KDE}}(x)\,\mathrm{d}x = 1$, hence the kernel density estimator is a valid p.d.f.

The Epanechnikov kernel has been proved to be the optimal kernel in the sense of least squared error, and is defined as

$$K(x) = \begin{cases} \dfrac{3}{4\sqrt{5}}\left(1 - \dfrac{x^2}{5}\right) & \text{if } |x| < \sqrt{5}, \\ 0 & \text{otherwise}. \end{cases} \tag{8.31}$$

This kernel has finite support.

The Gaussian kernel is probably more popular in practice; it has infinite support, as

$$K(x) = \frac{1}{\sqrt{2\pi}} \exp\left(-\frac{x^2}{2}\right)$$

for $-\infty < x < \infty$. When the bandwidth is h, the KDE is

$$p_{\mathrm{KDE}}(x) = \frac{1}{n}\sum_{i=1}^{n} \frac{1}{\sqrt{2\pi}h} \exp\left(-\frac{(x-x_i)^2}{2h^2}\right). \tag{8.32}$$

8.4.5 Bandwidth Selection

Bandwidth selection turns out to be much more important than kernel selection. Even though the Gaussian kernel is suboptimal, when the bandwidth h is chosen carefully the difference in errors between the Gaussian and the Epanechnikov kernels is small. When an incorrect bandwidth is used, however, either underfitting (if h is too large) or overfitting (if h is too small) will lead to poor estimation of the density. Fortunately, for KDE both theoretical and practical guidelines exist for the choice of the bandwidth.

Under rather weak assumptions on the density to be estimated (i.e., p) and the kernel (i.e., K), the theoretically optimal bandwidth is

$$h^\star = \frac{c_1^{-2/5} c_2^{1/5} c_3^{-1/5}}{n^{1/5}}, \tag{8.33}$$

in which $c_1 = \int x^2 K(x)\,\mathrm{d}x$, $c_2 = \int K^2(x)\,\mathrm{d}x$, and $c_3 = \int (p''(x))^2\,\mathrm{d}x$.

Note that c_3 is difficult to estimate reliably. However, if $p(x)$ is a normal distribution, a practical rule is to use

$$h^\star \approx \left(\frac{4\hat{\sigma}^5}{3n}\right)^{1/5} \approx 1.06\hat{\sigma}n^{-1/5}, \tag{8.34}$$

in which $\hat{\sigma}$ is the standard deviation estimated from the training set.

But when the data are not similar to a Gaussian (e.g., with two or more modes), Eq. (8.34) may lead to very poor density estimation quality. In that case, the cross-validation strategy may be used to estimate the bandwidth.

KDE is continuous, has nonuniform infinite (or enough) support for each training example, is symmetric, and has guided bandwidth selection under some situations. Hence, KDE is a nice method for density estimation in one dimension. The training examples, however, have to be stored in the KDE model, and to compute p_{KDE} requires many computations.

8.4.6 Multivariate KDE

The extension of KDE to more dimensions—i.e., multivariate KDE—is not trivial. Let $D = \{\boldsymbol{x}_1,\boldsymbol{x}_2,\ldots,\boldsymbol{x}_n\}$ be the training set and $\boldsymbol{x}_i \in \mathbb{R}^d$. The bandwidth h now becomes H, a $d \times d$ bandwidth matrix, which is required to be symmetric positive definite—i.e., $H = H^T$ and $H \succ 0$. The kernel function K is centered and symmetric. Hence, we expect $K(\boldsymbol{x} - \boldsymbol{x}_i)$ to be the largest when $\boldsymbol{x} = \boldsymbol{x}_i$, and its value will decrease symmetrically (i.e., at the same speed in all directions) when $\|\boldsymbol{x} - \boldsymbol{x}_i\|$ increases.

If H is not diagonal, then applying the bandwidth matrix H will change the speed of decrease in different directions. The bandwidth matrix is applied as

$$|H|^{-1/2}K\left(H^{-1/2}\boldsymbol{x}\right), \tag{8.35}$$

in which $|\cdot|$ is the determinant of a matrix.[6] This transformation is performing a rotation and a scaling of the dimensions (determined by H) in d-dimensional space. For example, if we use a multivariate Gaussian kernel, we have

$$p_{\text{KDE}}(\boldsymbol{x}) = \frac{1}{n}\sum_{i=1}^{n}\frac{1}{(2\pi)^{d/2}|H|^{1/2}}\exp\left(-\frac{1}{2}(\boldsymbol{x}-\boldsymbol{x}_i)^T H^{-1}(\boldsymbol{x}-\boldsymbol{x}_i)\right). \tag{8.36}$$

In other words, it is a Gaussian mixture model with n components. The ith component is centered at $\boldsymbol{x}_i$, and all component Gaussians share the same covariance matrix (the bandwidth matrix H).

To find the optimal H, however, is not as easy as in the one-dimensional case, even though it is theoretically viable. Furthermore, the computation of $p_{\text{KDE}}(\boldsymbol{x})$ is prohibitively expensive when n is large. Hence, in practice, one usually assumes a diagonal bandwidth matrix $H = \text{diag}(d_1,d_2,\ldots,d_n)$.

[6] A similar transformation is used in Chapter 13 on properties of normal distributions, when we transit from the single variable normal distribution to the multivariate one.

Diagonal GMMs are also very powerful models—in fact, they are universal approximators for continuous distributions. Hence, we expect that a diagonal H matrix will also lead to an accurate (or at least reasonable) approximation of the underlying density $p(\boldsymbol{x})$. The computation of a diagonal multivariate KDE is also lighter—e.g., in the Gaussian kernel it becomes

$$p_{\mathrm{KDE}}(\boldsymbol{x}) = \frac{1}{n}\sum_{i=1}^{n} \frac{1}{(2\pi)^{d/2}\prod_{j=1}^{d} h_j} \prod_{j=1}^{d} \exp\left(-\frac{(x_j - x_{i,j})^2}{2h_j^2}\right), \tag{8.37}$$

in which x_j is the jth dimension of a new example $\boldsymbol{x}$, and $x_{i,j}$ is the jth dimension of the ith training example $\boldsymbol{x}_i$.

Advanced algorithms can greatly accelerate the computations in KDE and multivariate KDE, but that is beyond the scope of this book.

8.5 Making Decisions

The estimated densities are used to make decisions—e.g., to determine the class label for a test example. In this section, we consider only a simple scenario where point estimation methods are used to estimate $p(\boldsymbol{x}|y = i; \boldsymbol{\theta})$ and $p(y = i)$, in which $1 \le i \le m$ is one label in an m-class classification problem.

Under the 0–1 loss, the optimal strategy is to choose the class with highest posterior probability $p(y|\boldsymbol{x}; \boldsymbol{\theta})$ for a test example $\boldsymbol{x}$, i.e.,

$$y^\star = \operatorname*{arg\,max}_{1\le i\le m} p(y = i|\boldsymbol{x}; \boldsymbol{\theta}). \tag{8.38}$$

We can define m discriminant functions for $1 \le i \le m$ as

$$g_i(\boldsymbol{x}) = p(y = i|\boldsymbol{x}; \boldsymbol{\theta}) = \frac{p(\boldsymbol{x}|y = i; \boldsymbol{\theta})p(y = i)}{p(\boldsymbol{x}; \boldsymbol{\theta})}. \tag{8.39}$$

Because $p(\boldsymbol{x}; \boldsymbol{\theta})$ has nothing to do with y, we can alternatively define the discriminant function as

$$g_i(\boldsymbol{x}) = p(\boldsymbol{x}|y = i; \boldsymbol{\theta})p(y = i). \tag{8.40}$$

One further simplification is to take the logarithm, as

$$g_i(\boldsymbol{x}) = \ln\left(p(\boldsymbol{x}|y = i; \boldsymbol{\theta})\right) + \ln(p(y = i)), \tag{8.41}$$

which is useful for simplifying the equations when $p(\boldsymbol{x}|y = i; \boldsymbol{\theta})$ is in the exponential family (e.g., Gaussian). The prior for y is a discrete distribution and estimated as the percentage of examples in different classes, which is easy to handle.

8.6 Miscellaneous Notes and Additional Resources

For a more in-depth introduction to probabilistic methods for pattern recognition and machine learning, please refer to Bishop (2006) and Murphy (2012). For example, Bishop (2006) contains many probabilistic and Bayesian interpretations of methods that are not introduced from a probabilistic perspective in this book. Murphy (2012) contains more advanced material, such as the exponential family and conjugate priors. We will also briefly introduce the exponential family in the exercise problems for Chapter 13.

For more details of the Epanechnikov kernel, please refer to Wasserman (2003), which is a good reference manual for statistics. A similar reference also exists for nonparametric statistics (Wasserman 2007).

The selection of bandwidth in KDE is discussed in detail in Silverman (1986), and a thorough introduction to KDE can be found in Scott (2015), which also contains more details about the universal approximation property of GMM.

GMM parameters are approximately learned using expectation-maximization (EM). Chapter 14 is devoted to this advanced topic. Another widely used family of parameter estimation methods is variational inference, for which the readers may refer to the tutorial Fox & Roberts (2011) or the more advanced monograph Wainwright & Jordan (2008). In Exercise 8.5, we design an experiment for the readers to understand the motivation of variational inference.

Exercises

8.1 Let $\mathcal{D} = \{x_1, x_2, \ldots, x_n\}$ be i.i.d. samples from an exponential distribution whose p.d.f. is

$$p(x) = \lambda \exp(-\lambda x)[\![x \geq 0]\!] = \begin{cases} \lambda \exp(-\lambda x) & \text{if } x \geq 0, \\ 0 & \text{if } x < 0, \end{cases} \tag{8.42}$$

in which $\lambda > 0$ is a parameter and $[\![\cdot]\!]$ is the indicator function. Find the maximum likelihood estimate for λ.

8.2 (Pareto distribution) The Pareto distribution is defined by the p.d.f.

$$p(x) = \frac{\alpha x_m^\alpha}{x^{\alpha+1}}[\![x \geq x_m]\!] = \begin{cases} \frac{\alpha x_m^\alpha}{x^{\alpha+1}}, & x \geq x_m, \\ 0, & x < x_m, \end{cases} \tag{8.43}$$

in which $[\![\cdot]\!]$ is the indicator function. There are two parameters: a scale parameter $x_m > 0$ and a shape parameter $\alpha > 0$. We denote such a Pareto distribution as $\text{Pareto}(x_m, \alpha)$.

(a) Let X be a random variable with p.d.f.

$$p_1(x) = \frac{c_1}{x^{\alpha+1}}[\![x \geq x_m]\!],$$

in which $x_m > 0$, $\alpha > 0$, and we constrain $c_1 > 0$ so that it does *not* depend on x. Show that X follows Pareto(x_m, α). You will find this observation useful in later tasks.

(b) Let $\mathcal{D} = \{x_1, x_2, \ldots, x_n\}$ be i.i.d. samples from Pareto(x_m, α). Find the maximum likelihood estimation for α and x_m.

(c) Let us consider a uniform distribution in the range $[0, \theta]$ with $p(x) = \frac{1}{\theta}[\![0 \le x \le \theta]\!]$. We want to provide a Bayesian estimate for θ. We use a set of i.i.d. examples $\mathcal{D} = \{x_1, x_2, \ldots, x_n\}$ to estimate θ. Show that uniform and Pareto are conjugate distributions—that is, when the prior for θ is $p(\theta|x_m, k) = \text{Pareto}(x_m, k)$, show that the posterior $p(\theta|\mathcal{D})$ is a Pareto distribution too. What are the parameters for the posterior distribution?

To avoid confusion in the notation, we assume $m > n$. However, we want to emphasize that the notation x_m as a whole is a parameter for the Pareto prior, and does not mean the mth element in the dataset $\mathcal{D}$.

8.3 Prove that the Epanechnikov kernel satisfies the conditions to be used in KDE—that is, nonnegative, zero mean, and the integral is 1.

8.4 (KDE) In this problem, we use the MATLAB function `ksdensity` to obtain first-hand experience with kernel density estimation.

(a) Find appropriate function(s) in MATLAB to generate 1000 i.i.d. samples from the log-normal distribution. The log-normal distribution is defined by the p.d.f.

$$p(x) = \begin{cases} \dfrac{1}{\sqrt{2\pi}\sigma x} \exp\left(-\dfrac{(\ln(x) - \mu)^2}{2\sigma^2} \right) & \text{if } x > 0, \\ 0 & \text{otherwise.} \end{cases} \tag{8.44}$$

Use $\mu = 2$ and $\sigma = 0.5$ to generate your samples.

(b) Use the `ksdensity` function to perform KDE, then draw the true log-normal p.d.f. and the KDE estimation results in one figure. This function automatically chooses a bandwidth. What is the bandwidth value?

(c) In the `ksdensity` function, set the bandwidth to 0.2 and 5 and run KDE for each. Draw these two additional curves and compare them with the previous ones. What causes the differences among these curves (i.e., KDE estimation quality differences)?

(d) If you use 10 000 and 100 000 samples in the `ksdensity` function, what are the automatically chosen bandwidth values? What is the trend for the bandwidth? Explain this trend.

8.5 (Mean field approximation) In Eq. (8.37) we observe that the multivariate Gaussian kernel (Eq. 8.36) is replaced (or approximated) by a diagonal multivariate Gaussian, which is computationally much more attractive.

This type of approximation can be generalized. Let $\boldsymbol{X} = (X_1, X_2, \ldots, X_d)$ be a multivariate distribution whose joint p.d.f. is complex. The *mean field approximation* approximates $p_X(\boldsymbol{x})$ using another random vector $\boldsymbol{Y} = (Y_1, Y_2, \ldots, Y_d)$ whose components are independent—that is,

$$p_X(\boldsymbol{x}) \approx p_Y(\boldsymbol{y}|\boldsymbol{\theta}) = \prod_{i=1}^{d} p_{Y_i}(y_i|\boldsymbol{\theta}),$$

in which $\boldsymbol{\theta}$ are the parameters for describing Y. The task of mean field approximation is to find an optimal set of parameters $\boldsymbol{\theta}^\star$ such that $p_X(\boldsymbol{x})$ and $\prod_{i=1}^{d} p_{Y_i}(y_i|\boldsymbol{\theta}^\star)$ are as close to each other as possible.

This strategy is widely used in *variational inference methods* in Bayesian inference, because $p_Y(\boldsymbol{y}|\boldsymbol{\theta}) = \prod_{i=1}^{d} p_{Y_i}(y_i|\boldsymbol{\theta})$ is easy to compute even when the computing of $p_X(\boldsymbol{x})$ is intractable.

We will not introduce any variational inference details in this introductory book. However, in this problem, we try to empirically answer the following question: Is the mean field approximation good enough?

(a) Use the following MATLAB/GNU Octave code to generate a two-dimensional normal density that is nondiagonal. Read and try to understand what this code is doing.

```
iSigma = inv([2 1; 1 4]);
pts = -5:0.1:5;
l = length(pts);
GT = zeros(l);
for i=1:l
    for j=1:l
        temp = [pts(i) pts(j)];
        % manually compute the probablity density
        GT(i,j)=exp(-0.5*temp*iSigma*temp'); %#ok<MINV>
    end
end
GT = GT / sum(GT(:)); % make it a discrete distribution
```

Note that the density is computed on a grid of points, and the last line discretizes the density into a discrete joint p.m.f.

(b) Suppose there are two independent normal random variables. They potentially have different standard deviations, but both their mean values equal 0. We can use the product of their p.d.f.s to approximate the nondiagonal complex Gaussian density. To do so, we discretize the density of the product on the same grid of points. Write your own code to finish these tasks.

(c) To find the best mean field approximation, we search through possible standard deviations. Try the range 0.05 to 3 (with step size 0.05) as the search range for the two independent normal random variables. One pair of standard deviation candidates should generate a discrete joint p.m.f., denoted by `MF`. We use the following code to compute the distance between it and the distribution `GT`:

```
error = 1 - sum(min(GT(:),MF(:)));
```

Write your own code to finish the search process. What are the optimal values for the two standard deviations? What is the distance at these optimal values? Is this distance small enough such that the mean field approximation is useful?

Note that the purpose of this problem is to intuitively illustrate the usefulness of mean field approximation. In practice there are more advanced methods to find the optimal parameters than grid search.

8.6 In a binary classification problem, let the two class conditional distributions be $p(\boldsymbol{x}|y = i) = N(\boldsymbol{\mu}_i, \Sigma)$, $i \in \{1,2\}$. That is, the two classes are both Gaussian and share the same covariance matrix. Let $\Pr(y = 1) = \Pr(y = 2) = 0.5$, and the 0–1 loss is used. Then the prediction is given by Eq. (8.38).

Show that the prediction rule can be rewritten in the following equivalent form:

$$y^\star = \begin{cases} 1 & \text{if } \boldsymbol{w}^T\boldsymbol{x} + b > 0, \\ 2 & \text{if } \boldsymbol{w}^T\boldsymbol{x} + b \le 0. \end{cases} \tag{8.45}$$

Give the expressions for $\boldsymbol{w}$ and b in terms of $\boldsymbol{\mu}_1$, $\boldsymbol{\mu}_2$, and Σ.

9 Distance Metrics and Data Transformations

In this chapter, we deal with two seemingly disjoint topics: distance metrics and similarity measures, and data transformation and normalization. We will see, however, that these topics are in fact related to each other.

In fact, in order for distance metrics to make sense, good data transformation or normalization is required. And in the design of many data transformation equations and normalization methods, the objective is usually to ensure that the computed distance metric or similarity measure will reflect the inherent distance or similarity of the data.

9.1 Distance Metrics and Similarity Measures

The task we have dealt with in this book so far is to learn a mapping $f\colon \mathcal{X} \mapsto \mathcal{Y}$ with a set of training examples $\{\boldsymbol{x}_i, y_i\}_{i=1}^n$. In the problems we have studied up to now, $y_i \in \mathcal{Y}$ is categorical and $\boldsymbol{x}_i \in \mathcal{X}$ are always real vectors—i.e., $\mathcal{X} \subseteq \mathbb{R}^d$.

It is vital to measure whether two examples $\boldsymbol{x}$ and $\boldsymbol{y}$ are similar or not, and the preferred answer to this question is a real number. In k-nearest neighbor, principal component analysis, and Fisher's linear discriminant, we use *distance* as a measure for the dissimilarity, while in support vector machines and kernel density estimation we use the dot product or other kernels (such as the Gaussian kernel) as a measure for the similarity between any two vectors $\boldsymbol{x}, \boldsymbol{y} \in \mathbb{R}^d$. All these similarity and dissimilarity measures return a real number whose magnitude is associated with the level of similarity or dissimilarity.

These two concepts, similarity and dissimilarity, are closely related: if similarity is high then dissimilarity is low, and vice versa. The RBF (Gaussian) kernel is a typical example of this relationship: the similarity is measured by a decreasing function of the dissimilarity (which is the Euclidean distance):

$$K_{\text{RBF}}(\boldsymbol{x}, \boldsymbol{y}) = \exp(-\gamma \|\boldsymbol{x} - \boldsymbol{y}\|^2), \tag{9.1}$$

in which the decreasing function is

$$g(d) = \exp(-\gamma d^2)$$

with $\gamma > 0$. Other types of decreasing functions, such as

$$g(d) = \frac{1}{d},$$

can also be used. The exponential function, however, has the additional benefit that its range (i.e., computed similarity) is between 0 and 1, which fits our intuition about similarity. For example, when $K_{\text{RBF}}(\boldsymbol{x}, \boldsymbol{y}) = 0.99$, it is reasonable to say that the similarity between $\boldsymbol{x}$ and $\boldsymbol{y}$ is 99%.

9.1.1 Distance Metrics

We turn our attention first to the distances, or how to measure the dissimilarity. Formally speaking, a metric is a function $\mathcal{X} \times \mathcal{X} \mapsto \mathbb{R}_+$, in which $\mathbb{R}_+$ is the set of nonnegative real numbers, i.e.,

$$\mathbb{R}_+ = \{x \mid x \geq 0\}.$$

A metric is also called a distance function or simply a distance. The most commonly used distance metric is the Euclidean distance, which is defined for two vectors $\boldsymbol{x} = (x_1, x_2, \ldots, x_d)^T$ and $\boldsymbol{y} = (y_1, y_2, \ldots, y_d)^T$ as

$$d(\boldsymbol{x}, \boldsymbol{y}) = \|\boldsymbol{x} - \boldsymbol{y}\| = \sqrt{\sum_{i=1}^{d} (x_i - y_i)^2}. \tag{9.2}$$

The Euclidean distance has all the following properties for any $\boldsymbol{x}, \boldsymbol{y}, \boldsymbol{z} \in \mathcal{X}$:

$$\begin{aligned} &\text{(i)}\ d(\boldsymbol{x}, \boldsymbol{y}) \geq 0 && \text{(nonnegativity)}, \\ &\text{(ii)}\ d(\boldsymbol{x}, \boldsymbol{y}) = d(\boldsymbol{y}, \boldsymbol{x}) && \text{(symmetry)}, \\ &\text{(iii)}\ d(\boldsymbol{x}, \boldsymbol{y}) = 0 \Leftrightarrow \boldsymbol{x} = \boldsymbol{y} && \text{(identity of indiscernibles)}, \\ &\text{(iv)}\ d(\boldsymbol{x}, \boldsymbol{z}) \leq d(\boldsymbol{x}, \boldsymbol{y}) + d(\boldsymbol{y}, \boldsymbol{z}) && \text{(triangle inequality)}. \end{aligned} \tag{9.3}$$

These four properties specify that a distance should be nonnegative (i.e., distance is always ≥ 0), symmetric (i.e., inward and outward trips should have the same distance), be 0 if and only if the two vectors are exactly the same (i.e., we did not move at all), and satisfy the triangle inequality (i.e., the shortest distance between two points is the length of the line segment connecting them)—these equations formalize our (maybe vague) intuition of what a distance should be.

These formal descriptions also generalize the concept *distance*. Any mapping $f: \mathcal{X} \times \mathcal{X} \mapsto \mathcal{Y}$ satisfying all these four conditions is called a *metric*, which can be considered as a generalization (or more abstract version) of the distance concept. In addition to the Euclidean distance, in this chapter we will also introduce two other metrics: the discrete metric and the ℓ_p metric.

The discrete metric is useful for comparing two categorical values. It is defined as

$$\rho(x, y) = \begin{cases} 1 & \text{if } x \neq y, \\ 0 & \text{if } x = y, \end{cases} \tag{9.4}$$

which indicates simply whether two categorical values are the same or not. It is easy to prove that ρ is a valid metric—i.e., it satisfies all four conditions for metrics.

9.1.2 Vector Norm and Metric

It is obvious that the Euclidean distance is closely related to the vector norm, because $d(\boldsymbol{x}, \boldsymbol{y}) = \|\boldsymbol{x} - \boldsymbol{y}\|$. In linear algebra, a vector norm is defined more generally than $\|\boldsymbol{x}\| = \sqrt{\boldsymbol{x}^T\boldsymbol{x}}$.

If we restrict our attention to real-valued vectors, a function $f\colon \mathbb{R}^d \mapsto \mathbb{R}_+$ is a *vector norm* if it satisfies the following three properties for all $\boldsymbol{x}, \boldsymbol{y} \in \mathbb{R}^d$ and any value $c \in \mathbb{R}$:

$$\begin{aligned} &\text{(i)}\ f(c\boldsymbol{x}) = |c| f(\boldsymbol{x}) && \text{(absolute scalability)},\\ &\text{(ii)}\ f(\boldsymbol{x}) = 0 \Leftrightarrow \boldsymbol{x} = \boldsymbol{0} && \text{(separates points)},\\ &\text{(iii)}\ f(\boldsymbol{x} + \boldsymbol{y}) \le f(\boldsymbol{x}) + f(\boldsymbol{y}) && \text{(triangle inequality)}. \end{aligned} \tag{9.5}$$

It is easy to show that

$$f(\boldsymbol{0}) = f(0\boldsymbol{x}) = 0 f(\boldsymbol{x}) = 0, \tag{9.6}$$

$$f(-\boldsymbol{x}) = f(-1 \times \boldsymbol{x}) = |-1| f(\boldsymbol{x}) = f(\boldsymbol{x}) \tag{9.7}$$

for an arbitrary vector $\boldsymbol{x}$ in $\mathbb{R}^d$. Hence, these properties not only imply symmetry, but also nonnegativity: because

$$0 = f(\boldsymbol{0}) = f(\boldsymbol{x} + (-\boldsymbol{x})) \le f(\boldsymbol{x}) + f(-\boldsymbol{x}) = 2f(\boldsymbol{x})$$

for arbitrary $\boldsymbol{x}$, we always have

$$f(\boldsymbol{x}) \ge 0.$$

That is, the vector norm is always nonnegative.

Simulating the Euclidean distance, if we define a mapping $\mathcal{X} \times \mathcal{X} \mapsto \mathbb{R}_+$ as $f(\boldsymbol{x} - \boldsymbol{y})$ for any vector norm f, it is trivial to verify that $f(\boldsymbol{x} - \boldsymbol{y})$ satisfies all the conditions for a metric. In other words, whenever we have a valid vector norm, we automatically obtain a corresponding metric. We say that this metric is induced by the norm.

9.1.3 The ℓ_p Norm and ℓ_p Metric

In this section, we focus on the ℓ_p vector norm and its induced ℓ_p metric. The ℓ_p norm (or simply p-norm) is well defined for $p \ge 1$ in $\mathbb{R}^d$ as

$$\|\boldsymbol{x}\|_p = \left(\sum_{i=1}^{d} |x_i|^p\right)^{1/p}, \tag{9.8}$$

in which the ℓ_p norm of $\boldsymbol{x}$ is denoted as $\|\boldsymbol{x}\|_p$. When p is an irrational number and x is negative, x^p is not defined. Hence, the absolute value operator in $|x_i|$ cannot be omitted in this definition.

We usually omit the subscript for the ℓ_2 norm, simply writing $\|\boldsymbol{x}\|$ if $p = 2$. It is easy to prove that $\|\boldsymbol{x}\|_p$ satisfies properties (i) and (ii) in Eq. (9.5). Property (iii) is guaranteed by the Minkowski inequality, whose proof is omitted.[1] The Minkowski inequality states that for real numbers $x_i, y_i \geq 0$, $i = 1, 2, \ldots, d$, and $p > 1$,

$$\left(\sum_{i=1}^{d}(x_i + y_i)^p\right)^{1/p} \leq \left(\sum_{i=1}^{d} x_i^p\right)^{1/p} + \left(\sum_{i=1}^{d} y_i^p\right)^{1/p}. \tag{9.9}$$

The equality holds if and only if there exists a $\lambda \in \mathbb{R}$ such that $x_i = \lambda y_i$ for all $1 \leq i \leq d$.

Why do we specify $p \geq 1$ in the definition? Considering two unit vectors $\boldsymbol{x} = (1, 0, 0, \ldots, 0)^T$ and $\boldsymbol{y} = (0, 1, 0, \ldots, 0)^T$, we have $\|\boldsymbol{x} + \boldsymbol{y}\|_p = 2^{1/p}$ and $\|\boldsymbol{x}\|_p = \|\boldsymbol{y}\|_p = 1$. Hence, the triangle inequality requires $2^{1/p} \leq 2$, which specifies $p \geq 1$. When $0 < p < 1$, $\|\boldsymbol{x}\|_p$ is not a norm, but we can still use $\|\boldsymbol{x}\|_p$ to represent the mapping in Eq. (9.8).

In Figure 9.1, we show the contours formed by points with $\|\boldsymbol{x}\|_p = 1$ for different p values. As shown by these figures, when $p \geq 1$ the regions enclosed by the contours (i.e., all points with $\|\boldsymbol{x}\|_p \leq 1$) are convex and $\|\boldsymbol{x}\|_p$ is a norm; when $0 < p < 1$, the regions are nonconvex and $\|\boldsymbol{x}\|_p$ is not a norm.

Figure 9.1 also suggests that the limit when $p \to \infty$ exists. When $p \to \infty$, we have

$$\ell_\infty \triangleq \lim_{p\to\infty} \|\boldsymbol{x}\|_p = \max\{|x_1|, |x_2|, \ldots, |x_d|\}. \tag{9.10}$$

When $p \to 0$, $\|\boldsymbol{x}\|_0$ is *not* a norm. However, in areas such as sparse learning methods, researchers use the term ℓ_0 *norm* to mean the *number of nonzero elements* in $\boldsymbol{x}$. We want to emphasize that this is not a valid norm. Sometimes quotation marks are added to emphasize this fact (i.e., ℓ_0 "norm").

When $p \geq 1$, the ℓ_p norm induces an ℓ_p metric (which we denote as d_p)

$$d_p(\boldsymbol{x}, \boldsymbol{y}) = \|\boldsymbol{x} - \boldsymbol{y}\|_p. \tag{9.11}$$

We also call the ℓ_p metric the ℓ_p distance. It is obvious that the ℓ_2 distance is the Euclidean distance.

The ℓ_1 distance and associated ℓ_1 norm are also widely used (e.g., in sparse learning methods). The ℓ_1 distance is also called the Manhattan distance or the city block distance, computed as

$$d_1(\boldsymbol{x}, \boldsymbol{y}) = \sum_{i=1}^{d} |x_i - y_i|. \tag{9.12}$$

In a city whose roads form a regular grid (such as those in Manhattan, New York City), the distance between two locations is the number of blocks that are between them, as shown in Figure 9.2, no matter whether the red or the blue path (or any other route along the roads) is followed.

[1] The Minkowski inequality is named after Hermann Minkowski, a Lithuanian–German mathematician.

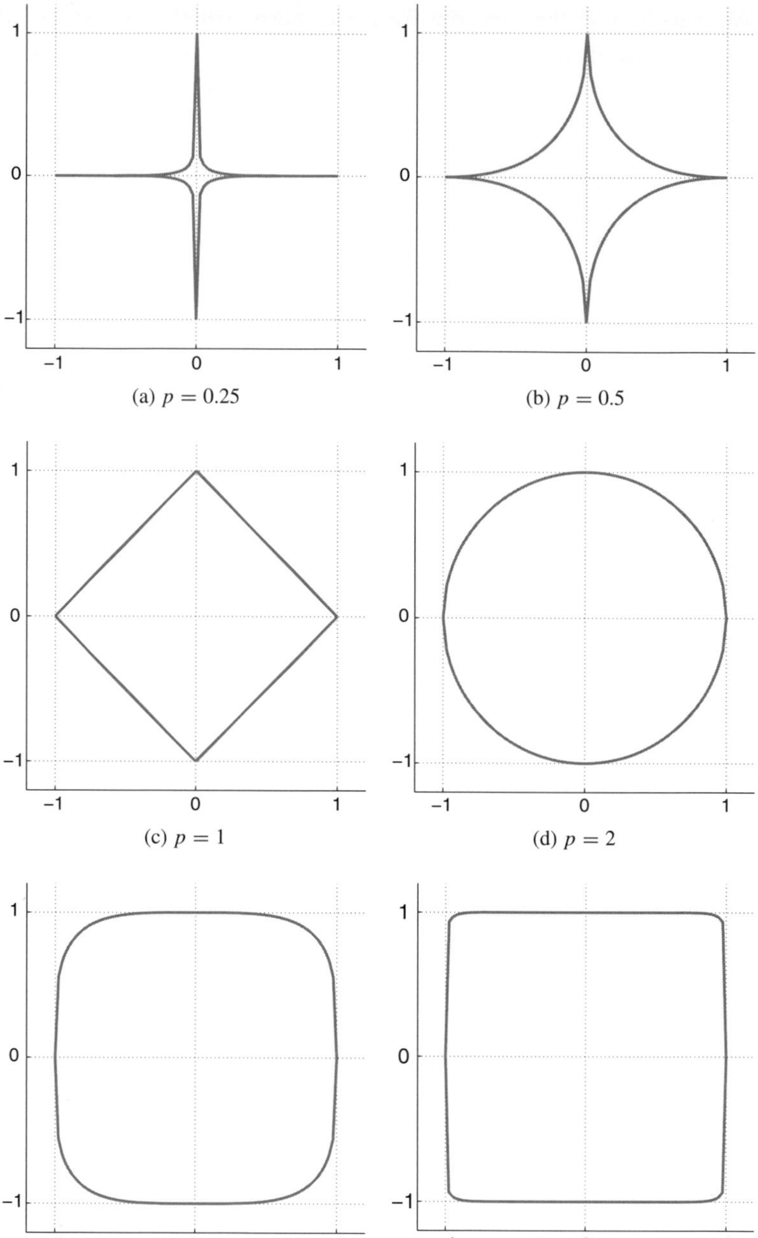

(a) $p = 0.25$ (b) $p = 0.5$ (c) $p = 1$ (d) $p = 2$ (e) $p = 4$ (f) $p = 16$

Figure 9.1 Illustration of two-dimensional points that satisfy $\|\boldsymbol{x}\|_p = 1$.

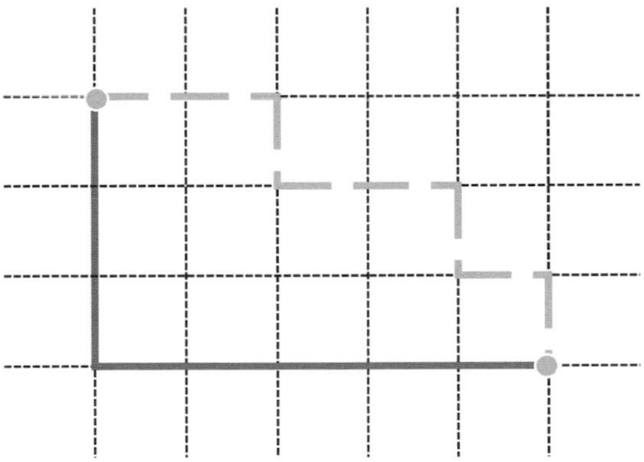

Figure 9.2 The Manhattan (city block) distance. (A black and white version of this figure will appear in some formats. For the color version, please refer to the plate section.)

The ℓ_∞ distance measures the largest distance in any single dimension:

$$d_\infty(\boldsymbol{x}, \boldsymbol{y}) = \max\{|x_1 - y_1|, |x_2 - y_2|, \dots, |x_d - y_d|\}.$$

When $p > q > 0$, we have

$$\|\boldsymbol{x}\|_p \le \|\boldsymbol{x}\|_q. \tag{9.13}$$

In other words, as p increases, the ℓ_p norm will decrease or remain unchanged. We leave the proof of this inequality as an exercise.

9.1.4 Distance Metric Learning

Another type of vector-norm-induced metric is widely used. Let $\boldsymbol{x} \in \mathbb{R}^d$ and G be any $d \times d$ positive definite matrix; then the mapping

$$f(\boldsymbol{x}) = \|G\boldsymbol{x}\| \tag{9.14}$$

defines a valid vector norm. The distance metric associated with it is $\|G(\boldsymbol{x} - \boldsymbol{y})\|$. However, the squared distance is often used:

$$d_A^2(\boldsymbol{x}, \boldsymbol{y}) = (\boldsymbol{x} - \boldsymbol{y})^T A(\boldsymbol{x} - \boldsymbol{y}), \tag{9.15}$$

in which $A = G^T G$ is a $d \times d$ positive definite square matrix.

This kind of distance is called the (squared) Mahalanobis distance. If our data follow a Gaussian distribution $N(\boldsymbol{\mu}, \Sigma)$ and $\Sigma \neq I_d$, then it is inappropriate to use $\|\boldsymbol{x}_1 - \boldsymbol{x}_2\|$ to represent the distance between $\boldsymbol{x}_1$ and $\boldsymbol{x}_2$. If both points are on the major axis (corresponding to the largest eigenvalue λ_1 of Σ, say $\lambda_1 = 100$), $\|\boldsymbol{x}_1 - \boldsymbol{x}_2\| = 1$ indicates that the points are close to each other (roughly only 10% of the standard deviation in that direction). However, if these points are on the minor axis (corresponding to the smallest eigenvalue—e.g., $\lambda_d = 0.01$), $\|\boldsymbol{x}_1 - \boldsymbol{x}_2\| = 1$ in fact means a 10 times standard deviation distance in that direction!

We know that the whitening transform $\Sigma^{-1/2}(\boldsymbol{x} - \bar{\boldsymbol{x}})$ translates, rotates, and scales the distribution, such that it becomes a spherical Gaussian. In other words, all dimensions are independent and at the same scale. Hence, the squared Euclidean distance in the transformed space is a good distance metric, which is exactly the squared Mahalanobis distance, with $G = \Sigma^{-1/2}$ and $A = \Sigma^{-1}$.

The squared Mahalanobis distance is a special case of the squared distance in Eq. (9.15), with A fixed to Σ^{-1}. When the data are not Gaussian, however, using the inverse covariance matrix is not optimal. Hence, *distance metric learning* tries to learn a good A matrix from the training data. In this case, we use $\|\boldsymbol{x} - \boldsymbol{y}\|_A$ to denote the learned distance between $\boldsymbol{x}$ and $\boldsymbol{y}$, i.e.,

$$\|\boldsymbol{x} - \boldsymbol{y}\|_A^2 = (\boldsymbol{x} - \boldsymbol{y})^T A(\boldsymbol{x} - \boldsymbol{y}).$$

If we are given a training set $\{(\boldsymbol{x}_i, y_i)\}_{i=1}^n$ in a binary classification problem, we can learn a good distance metric by optimizing the following problem:

$$\min_{A \in \mathbb{R}^d \times \mathbb{R}^d} \quad \sum_{\substack{1 \le i < j \le n \\ y_i = y_j}} \|\boldsymbol{x}_i - \boldsymbol{x}_j\|_A^2 \tag{9.16}$$

$$\text{s.t.} \quad \sum_{\substack{1 \le i < j \le n \\ y_i \neq y_j}} \|\boldsymbol{x}_i - \boldsymbol{x}_j\|_A^2 \ge 1, \tag{9.17}$$

$$A \succeq 0. \tag{9.18}$$

The learned distance metric should make the distances between examples in the same class as small as possible (via minimizing the objective), while keeping the distances between examples in different classes large (via the first constraint.) Hence, the learned optimal distance metric (or equivalently, the optimal positive semidefinite matrix A) is useful for classification of the two classes.

In distance metric learning, A is required to be positive semidefinite, rather than positive definite. With this relaxation, $\|\boldsymbol{x} - \boldsymbol{y}\|_A$ is no longer a metric in the strict sense because $\|\boldsymbol{x} - \boldsymbol{y}\|_A = 0$ is possible even if $\boldsymbol{x} \neq \boldsymbol{y}$. However, this relaxation allows us to learn inherently lower-dimensional representations. For example, if $G \in \mathbb{R}^k \times \mathbb{R}^d$ and $k < d$, then $A = G^T G$ is positive semidefinite but not positive definite, and $G\boldsymbol{x}$ has fewer dimensions than $\boldsymbol{x}$.

9.1.5 The Mean as a Similarity Measure

Now we turn our attention to similarity measures. We have seen different similarity measures—e.g., the dot product and those transformed from a distance metric (such as the RBF kernel). Another group of similarity measures are in fact the average values (i.e., the mean). For example, if we want to find the similarity of two *distributions*, as illustrated in Figure 9.3, a natural idea is to use the area of their common region (i.e., the blue region) as a numerical similarity measure. Because the area under each distribution is 1 ($\int p(x)\,\mathrm{d}x = 1$ for a valid distribution $p(x)$), the similarity will always be between 0 and 1, which fits our intuition well.

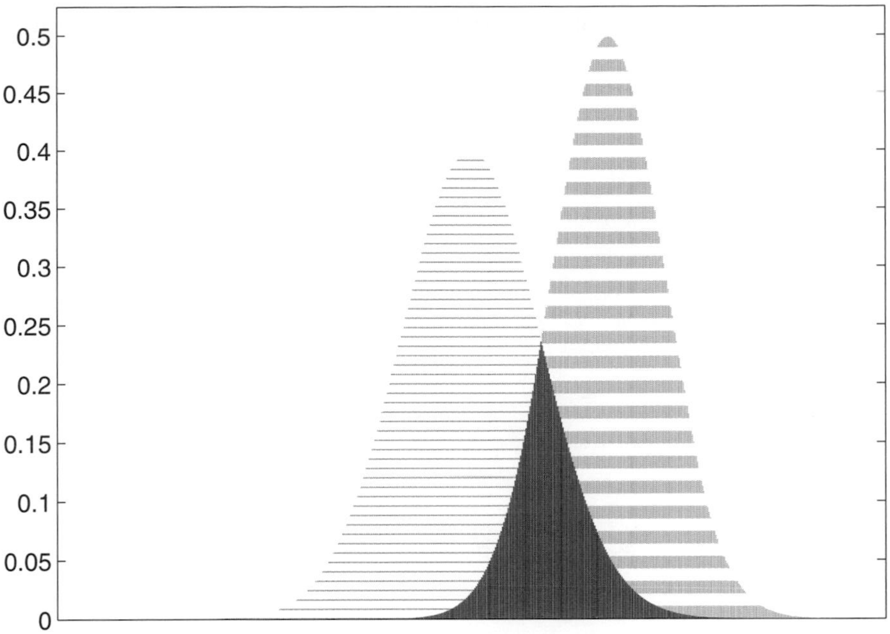

Figure 9.3 Illustration of the similarity of two distributions. (A black and white version of this figure will appear in some formats. For the color version, please refer to the plate section.)

Given two distributions $p_X(x)$ and $p_Y(y)$, a particular value v will contribute

$$\min(p_X(v), p_Y(v))$$

to the similarity in Figure 9.3, which means the similarity is

$$\int \min(p_X(v), p_Y(v))\, \mathrm{d}v.$$

The minimum between two nonnegative values, $\min(x, y)$, is in fact a special type of mean value between x and y, called the generalized mean.

The generalized mean (also called the power mean) with exponent p of a set of *positive* values $x_1, x_2, \ldots, x_n$ is defined as

$$M_p(x_1, x_2, \ldots, x_n) = \left(\frac{1}{n} \sum_{i=1}^{n} x_i^p \right)^{1/p}. \tag{9.19}$$

The power mean is very similar to the p-norm (Eq. 9.8). However, there are a few important differences.

- First, the power mean requires x_i to be positive but the p-norm uses the absolute value of x_i.
- Second, the $\frac{1}{n}$ term in the power mean does *not* appear in the p-norm.
- More importantly, the power mean is well defined for all real numbers, while the p-norm requires $p \geq 1$!

The power means for the following special p values are given their designated names:

$$M_{-\infty}(x_1,\ldots,x_n) = \lim_{p\to-\infty} M_p(x_1,\ldots,x_n) = \min\{x_1,\ldots,x_n\} \quad \text{(minimum value)}, \tag{9.20}$$

$$M_{-1}(x_1,\ldots,x_n) = \frac{n}{x_1^{-1}+\cdots+x_n^{-1}} \quad \text{(harmonic mean)}, \tag{9.21}$$

$$M_0(x_1,\ldots,x_n) = \lim_{p\to 0} M_p(x_1,\ldots,x_n) = \sqrt[n]{\prod_{i=1}^{n} x_i} \quad \text{(geometric mean)}, \tag{9.22}$$

$$M_1(x_1,\ldots,x_n) = \frac{x_1+\cdots+x_n}{n} \quad \text{(arithmetic mean)}, \tag{9.23}$$

$$M_2(x_1,\ldots,x_n) = \sqrt{\frac{x_1^2+\cdots+x_n^2}{n}} \quad \text{(square mean)}, \tag{9.24}$$

$$M_{\infty}(x_1,\ldots,x_n) = \lim_{p\to\infty} M_p(x_1,\ldots,x_n) = \max\{x_1,\ldots,x_n\} \quad \text{(maximum value)}. \tag{9.25}$$

The minimum, geometric, and maximum mean values are defined using limits. The harmonic mean has been used previously: the F1 score is the harmonic mean of precision and recall. The arithmetic mean is the most commonly used mean value.

The power mean with exponent p and the p-norm differ only by a factor $n^{1/p}$. This slight difference, however, leads to very different properties. When $p_1 < p_2$, we have

$$M_{p_1}(x_1,x_2,\ldots,x_n) \le M_{p_2}(x_1,x_2,\ldots,x_n), \tag{9.26}$$

that is, M_p is a nondecreasing function of p in the entire real domain. The equality holds if and only if $x_1 = x_2 = \cdots = x_n$. In contrast, $\|\boldsymbol{x}\|_p \ge \|\boldsymbol{x}\|_q$ if $0 < p < q$!

Figure 9.4 illustrates various power mean values for two positive numbers a and b, which clearly shows that

$$M_{-\infty} < M_{-1} < M_0 < M_1 < M_2 < M_{\infty}$$

when $a \ne b$.

9.1.6 Power Mean Kernel

Some similarity functions, such as the dot product or RBF, can be used as kernel functions in kernel methods. The same argument also applies to the power mean, but *only* when $p \le 0$. Given two *nonnegative*[2] vectors $\boldsymbol{x} = (x_1,x_2,\ldots,x_d)^T$ and $\boldsymbol{y} = (y_1,y_2,\ldots,y_d)^T$ in which $x_i, y_i \ge 0$ for all $1 \le i \le d$, the power mean kernel is defined (for $p \le 0$) as

$$M_p(\boldsymbol{x},\boldsymbol{y}) = \sum_{i=1}^{d} M_p(x_i,y_i). \tag{9.27}$$

[2] We assume $0^p = 0$ even for $p \le 0$.

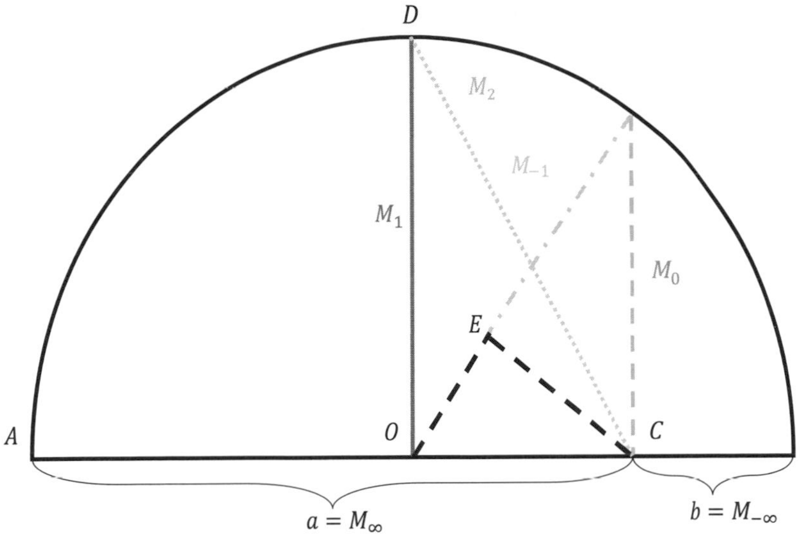

Figure 9.4 Illustration of different power mean values. (A black and white version of this figure will appear in some formats. For the color version, please refer to the plate section.)

When we want to compare two distributions—e.g., when the two distributions are represented as two histograms whose values are nonnegative—the power mean kernel family usually produces better similarity measures than commonly used kernels such as the dot product, RBF, or polynomial. A few special p values in the power mean kernel family also lead to kernels that are defined in statistics:

$$
\begin{aligned}
M_0(\boldsymbol{x}, \boldsymbol{y}) &= \sum_{i=1}^{d} \sqrt{x_i y_i} && \text{(Hellinger's kernel)}, \\
M_{-1}(\boldsymbol{x}, \boldsymbol{y}) &= \sum_{i=1}^{d} \frac{2x_i y_i}{x_i + y_i} && (\chi^2 \text{ kernel}), \\
M_{-\infty}(\boldsymbol{x}, \boldsymbol{y}) &= \sum_{i=1}^{d} \min(x_i, y_i) && \text{(histogram intersection kernel)}.
\end{aligned}
\tag{9.28}
$$

Hellinger's kernel is the similarity measure corresponding to the Hellinger distance (also called the Bhattacharyya distance), which is an established measure for quantifying the distance (or dissimilarity) between two distributions. The χ^2 kernel is closely related to the χ^2-squared test (or written as chi-squared test) and the χ^2-distance, which is a widely used measure to quantify the difference between two distributions. And the histogram intersection kernel (HIK), as we mentioned above, is an intuitive way to measure the similarity between two distributions, which is illustrated in Figure 9.3.

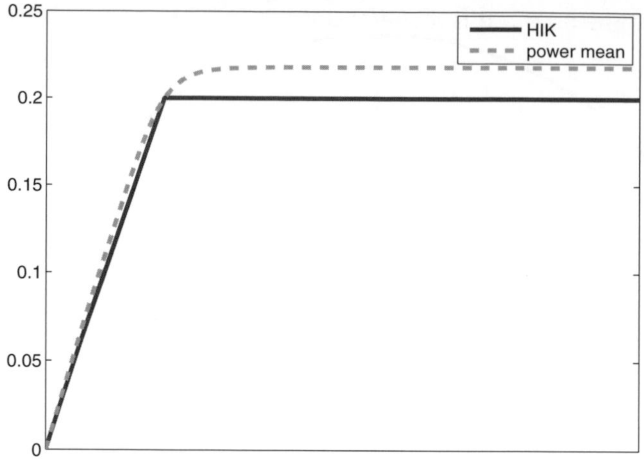

(a) $p = -8$

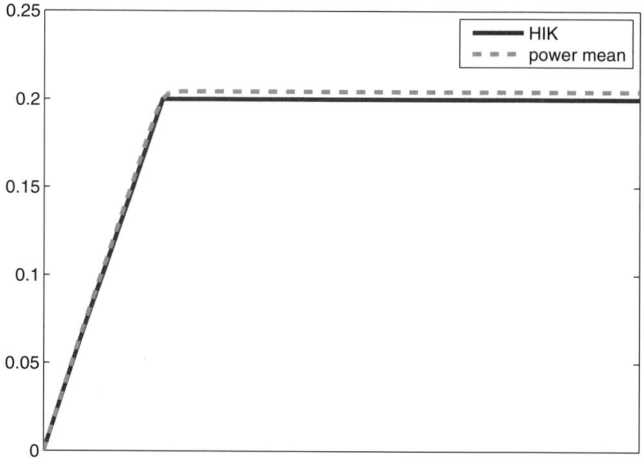

(b) $p = -32$

Figure 9.5 Use the power mean kernel to approximate the histogram intersection kernel. (A black and white version of this figure will appear in some formats. For the color version, please refer to the plate section.)

The power mean kernel family is a generalization of all these special kernels, which are suitable for the comparison of distributions (or histograms). One benefit of the power mean kernel is that there are efficient algorithms for learning and testing the entire power mean family, and it can also provide smooth alternatives to the histogram intersection kernel (which is in fact not differentiable).

Figure 9.5a shows the curve for $M_{-\infty}(0.2, x)$ (i.e., the HIK between x and a fixed value 0.2) and $M_{-8}(0.2, x)$, while Figure 9.5b shows the power mean approximation of the HIK when $p = -32$. When $p = -32$, the power mean approximation to the HIK is already fairly accurate.

9.2 Data Transformation and Normalization

When we seek a mapping $f: \mathcal{X} \mapsto \mathcal{Y}$ and $\mathcal{Y} = \mathbb{R}$, the task is called regression. Although we will not introduce regression methods in detail, let us motivate the need for data transformation and normalization using linear regression as an example.

In a regression task, we are given a set of training examples $\{(\boldsymbol{x}_i, y_i)\}_{i=1}^n$ where $\boldsymbol{x}_i \in \mathbb{R}^d$ and $y_i \in \mathbb{R}$. We want to find a function f such that for any point $(\boldsymbol{x}, y)$ sampled from the same distribution as the training set, $f(\boldsymbol{x}) \approx y$. This approximation is usually performed by minimizing the residue $f(\boldsymbol{x}) - y$—e.g., by minimizing $\mathbb{E}[(f(\boldsymbol{x}) - y)^2]$.

9.2.1 Linear Regression

In linear regression, we assume that f approximates y using a linear combination of components of $\boldsymbol{x}$, i.e.,

$$y_i = \boldsymbol{x}_i^T \boldsymbol{\beta} + \epsilon_i, \tag{9.29}$$

in which $\boldsymbol{\beta} \in \mathbb{R}^d$ is the parameter of linear regression and ϵ_i is the residue from approximating y_i using $\boldsymbol{x}_i$. Hence, the training objective is to minimize the residues, by

$$\boldsymbol{\beta}^\star = \operatorname*{arg\,min}_{\boldsymbol{\beta}} \sum_{i=1}^{n} \left(\boldsymbol{x}_i^T \boldsymbol{\beta} - y_i\right)^2. \tag{9.30}$$

This objective can be further simplified using matrix notation. Using block matrix notation we define

$$X = \begin{bmatrix} \boldsymbol{x}_1^T \\ \hline \boldsymbol{x}_2^T \\ \hline \vdots \\ \hline \boldsymbol{x}_n^T \end{bmatrix} \in \mathbb{R}^n \times \mathbb{R}^d, \quad \boldsymbol{y} = \begin{bmatrix} y_1 \\ y_2 \\ \vdots \\ y_n \end{bmatrix} \in \mathbb{R}^n, \tag{9.31}$$

and the linear regression optimization becomes

$$\boldsymbol{\beta}^\star = \operatorname*{arg\,min}_{\boldsymbol{\beta}} \|\boldsymbol{y} - X\boldsymbol{\beta}\|^2 = \operatorname*{arg\,min}_{\boldsymbol{\beta}} \left(\boldsymbol{\beta}^T X^T X \boldsymbol{\beta} - 2\boldsymbol{y}^T X \boldsymbol{\beta}\right). \tag{9.32}$$

In the last equality we have dropped the term $\boldsymbol{y}^T\boldsymbol{y}$ because it does not depend on $\boldsymbol{\beta}$.

Because $\frac{\partial\left(\boldsymbol{\beta}^T X^T X \boldsymbol{\beta} - 2\boldsymbol{y}^T X \boldsymbol{\beta}\right)}{\partial \boldsymbol{\beta}} = 2X^T X \boldsymbol{\beta} - 2X^T \boldsymbol{y}$, we know that

$$X^T X \boldsymbol{\beta} = X^T \boldsymbol{y} \tag{9.33}$$

is a necessary condition for the optimal value. Hence, the solution to the linear regression is

$$\boldsymbol{\beta}^\star = (X^T X)^{-1} X^T \boldsymbol{y}. \tag{9.34}$$

When the matrix $X^T X$ is not invertible, a practical approach is to use

$$\boldsymbol{\beta}^\star = X^+ \boldsymbol{y},$$

in which X^+ is the Moore–Penrose pseudoinverse of X. Given any testing example $\boldsymbol{x}$, its associated y is approximated as

$$y \approx \boldsymbol{x}^T \boldsymbol{\beta}^\star. \tag{9.35}$$

Now we consider a problem with 10 examples in two dimensions: $\boldsymbol{x} = (x_1, x_2)^T$. The two dimensions correspond to the height and the waist circumference of a male person. The heights (x_1) are measured in centimeters, and the 10 heights are generated as

$$x_{i,1} = 169 + i, \quad 1 \le i \le 10.$$

The waist-to-height ratio for a healthy adult man is considered to be in the range $[0.43, 0.52]$. Hence, we generate the waist circumference (x_2) as

$$x_{i,2} = (0.46 + 0.02v)x_{i,1},$$

where the variation $v \sim N(0,1)$ is randomly sampled for each example independently. We expect the waist-to-height ratio to be between 0.40 and 0.52 (i.e., within the "3σ" range).

The labels y are generated using $\boldsymbol{\beta} = (1,1)^T$ and a white noise $0.0001N(0,1)$, that is,

$$y_i = x_{i,1} + x_{i,2} + \epsilon_i, \tag{9.36}$$

$$\epsilon_i \sim 0.0001N(0,1). \tag{9.37}$$

The estimated $\boldsymbol{\beta}$ will be slightly different from run to run because of the noise. However, because the label noise $0.0001N(0,1)$ is very small compared to the scale of x_1 and x_2, the estimation is fairly accurate—e.g., $\boldsymbol{\beta}^\star = (0.9999, 1.0197)^T$ in one of our runs.

Suppose, however, that the waist circumference and the height are measured by two different individuals, one using centimeters for heights and the other using meters for waist circumference. Then an example (x_1, x_2) becomes $(x_1, 0.01x_2)$. The linear regression model has much larger estimation errors, and $\boldsymbol{\beta}^\star = (0.9992, 1.1788)^T$ is one example. We want to point out that even though the second dimension is now much smaller than the first, it is still 50 to 100 times larger than the noise $0.0001N(0,1)$. Hence, the wrong scales for some feature dimensions may cause serious problems in machine learning and pattern recognition if the difference in scale is not underpinned by certain properties in their data generation process.

9.2.2 Feature Normalization

Data normalization can solve this problem. We first find the minimum and maximum value of the jth dimension ($1 \le j \le d$) in the training set—that is,

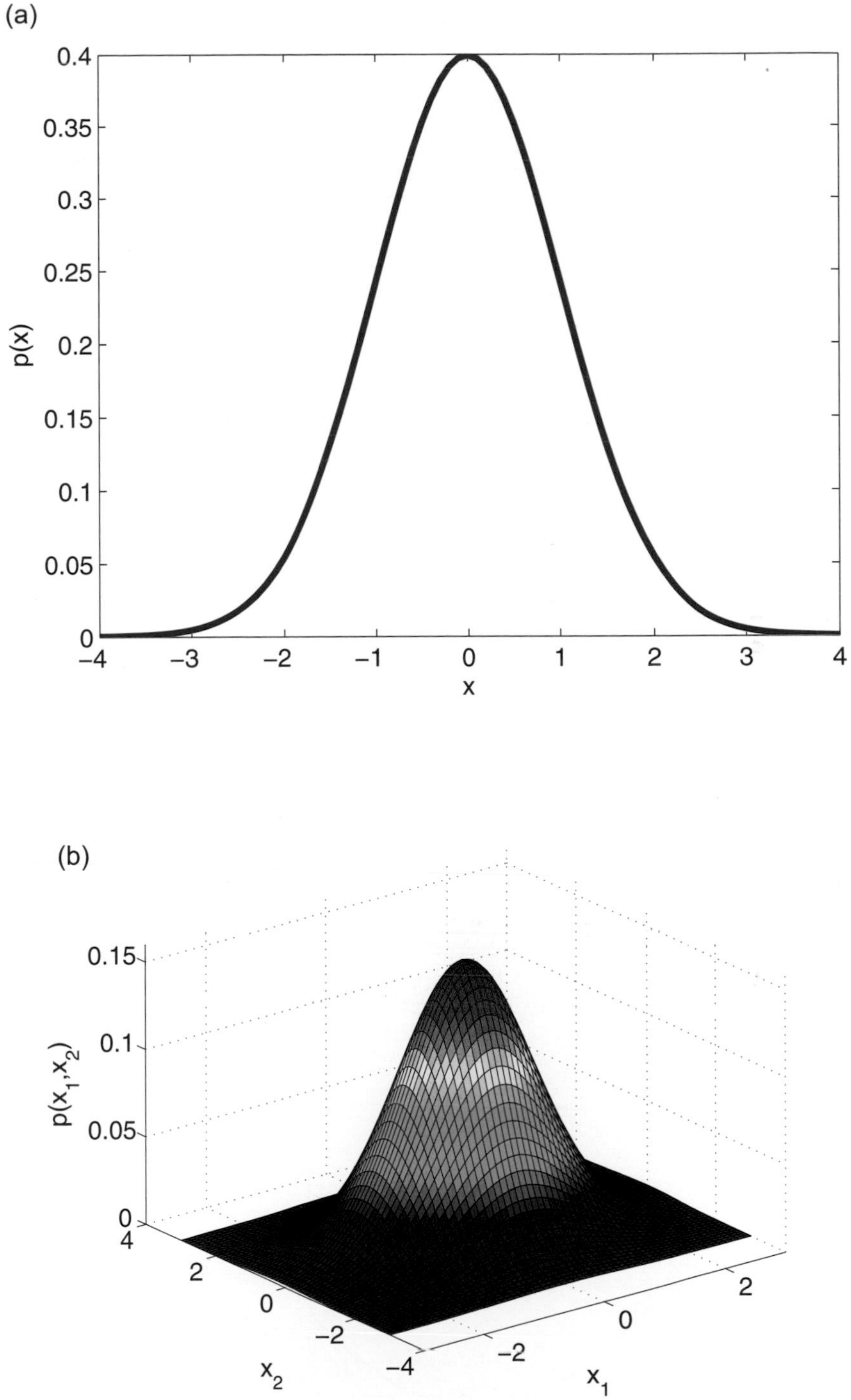
(a)
0.4
0.35
0.3
0.25
0.2
0.15
0.1
0.05
0
p(x)
−4
−3
−2
−1
0
1
2
3
4
x
(b)
0.15
0.1
0.05
0
p(x1,x2)
4
2
0
−2
−4
x2
−2
0
2
x1

Figure 2.2

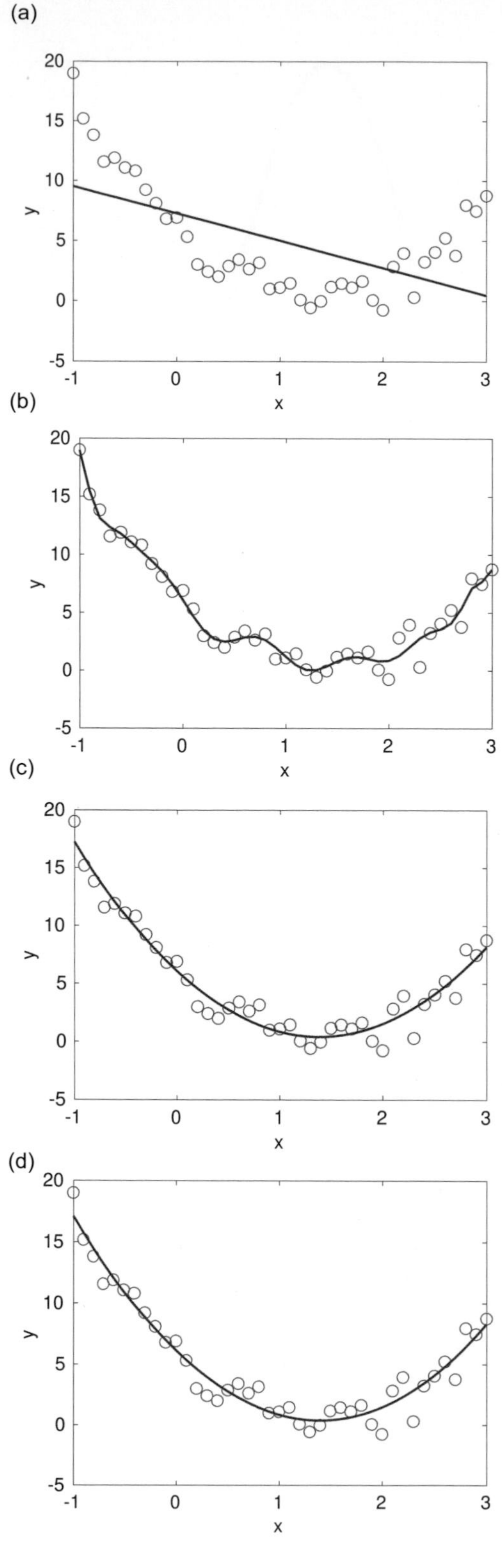

Figure 4.1

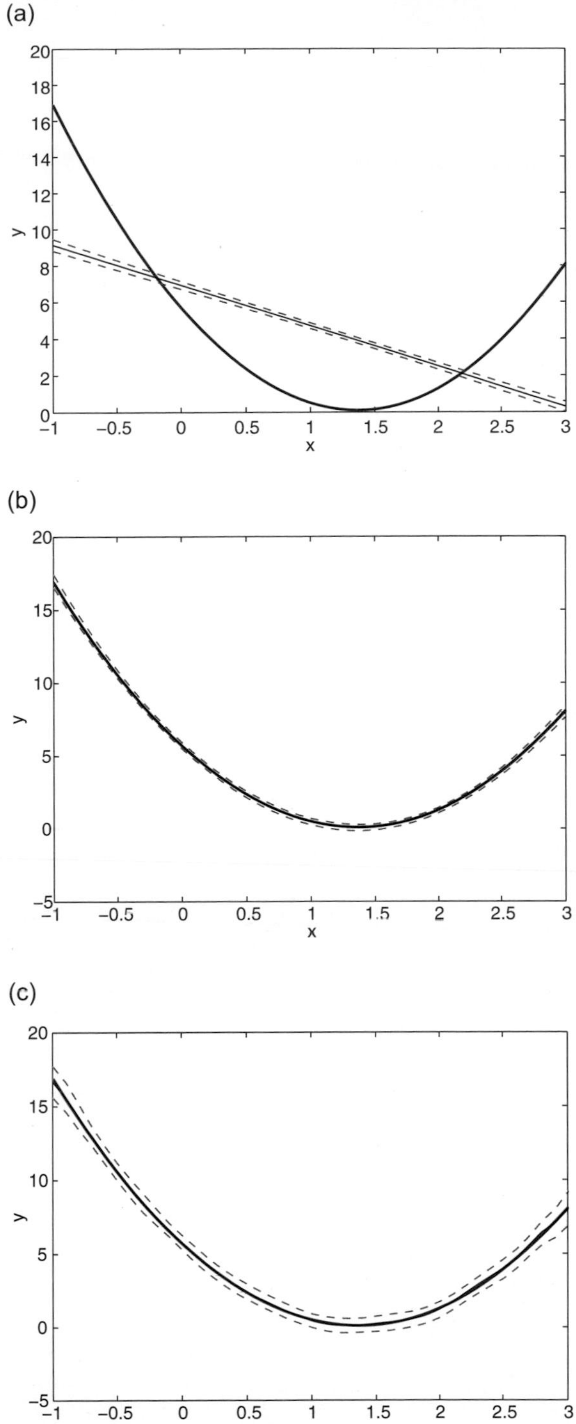
(a)
20
18
16
14
12
10
8
6
4
2
0
−1
−0.5
0
0.5
1
1.5
2
2.5
3
x
y
(b)
20
15
10
5
0
−5
−1
−0.5
0
0.5
1
1.5
2
2.5
3
x
y
(c)
20
15
10
5
0
−5
−1
−0.5
0
0.5
1
1.5
2
2.5
3
x
y

Figure 4.5

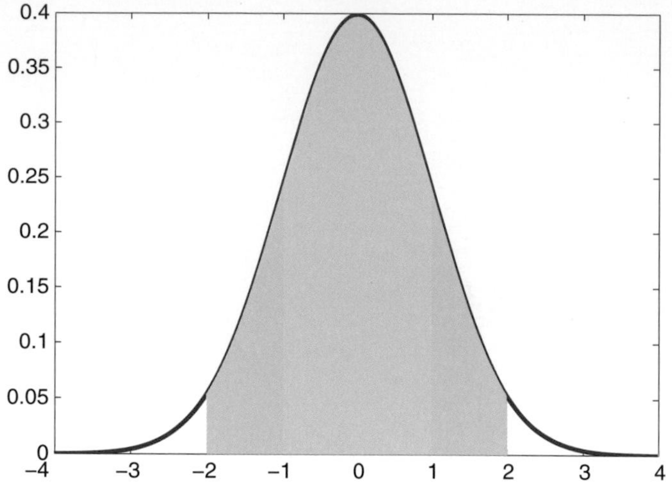

Figure 4.6

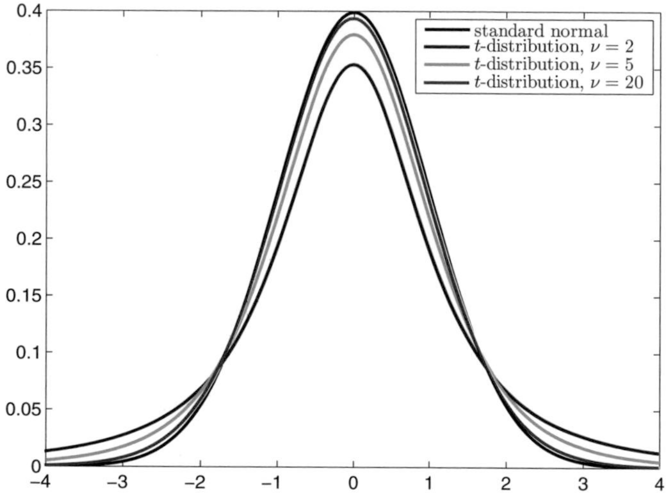

Figure 4.7

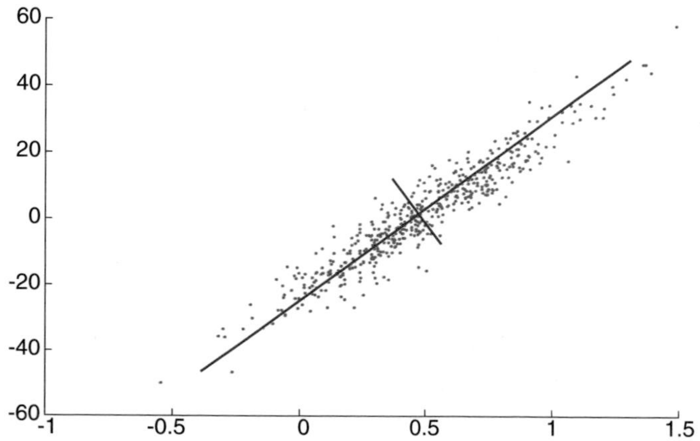

Figure 5.2

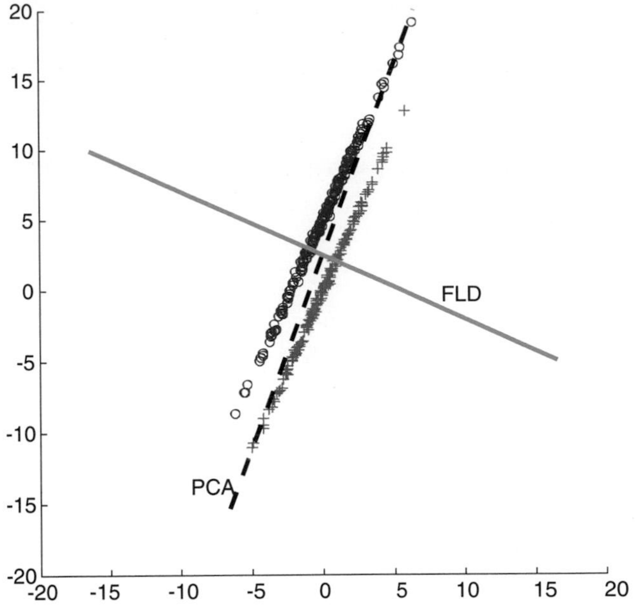

Figure 6.1

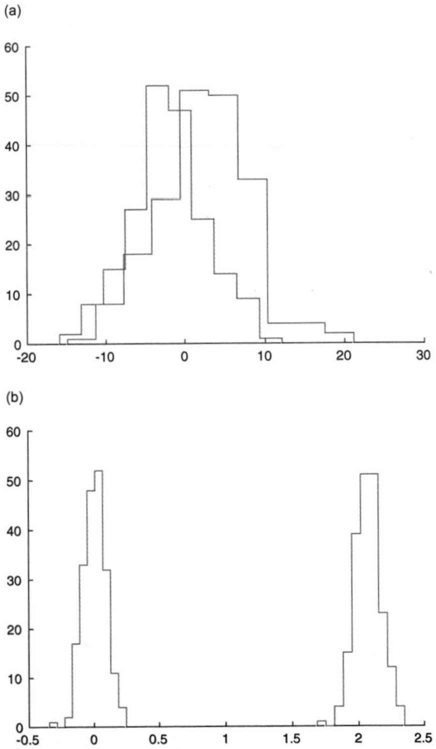

Figure 6.2

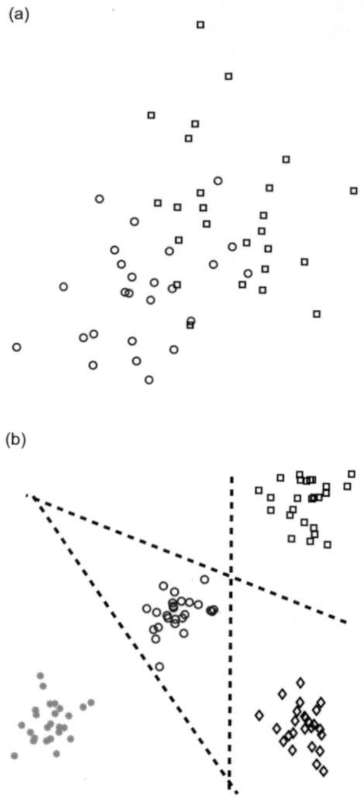

Figure 7.1

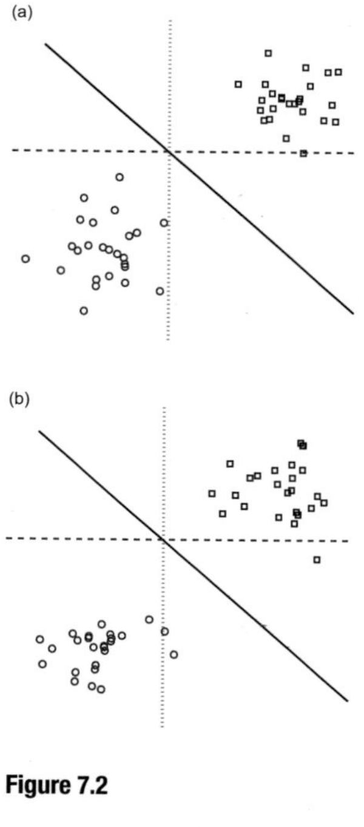

Figure 7.2

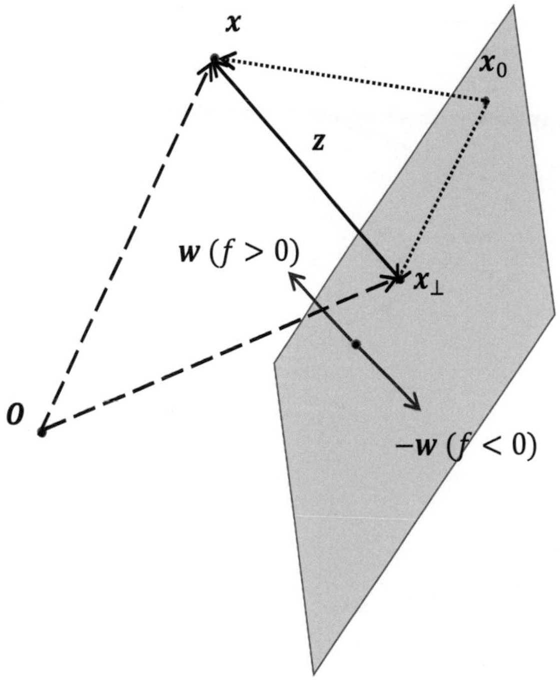

Figure 7.3

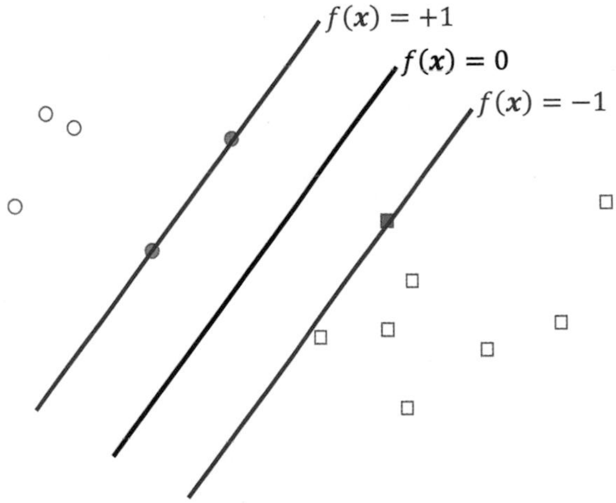

Figure 7.4

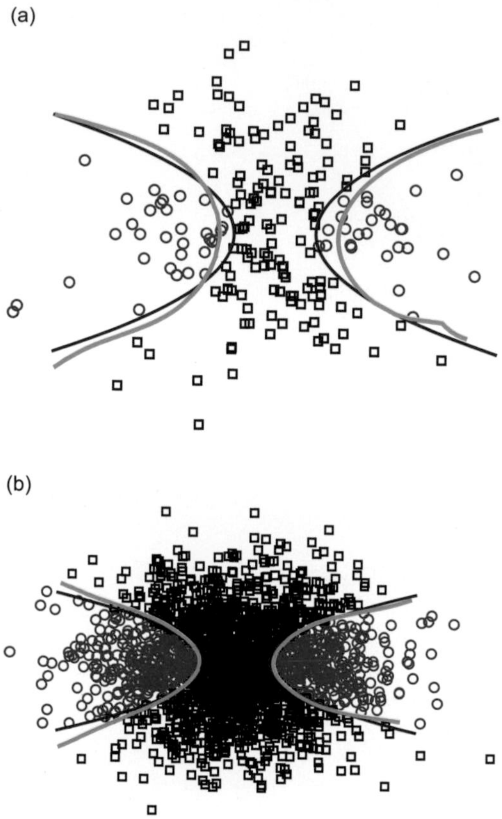

Figure 7.5

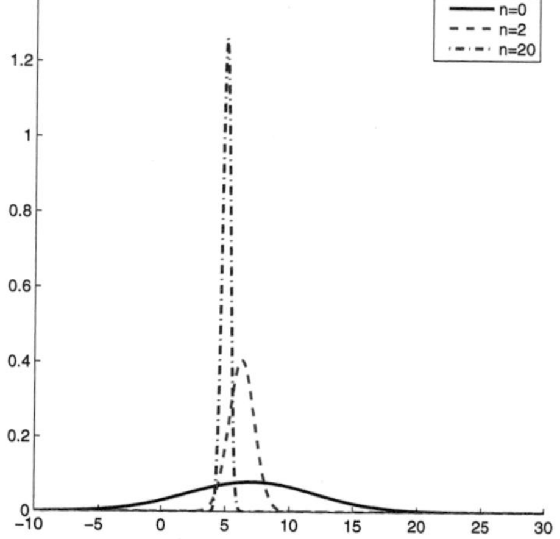

Figure 8.1

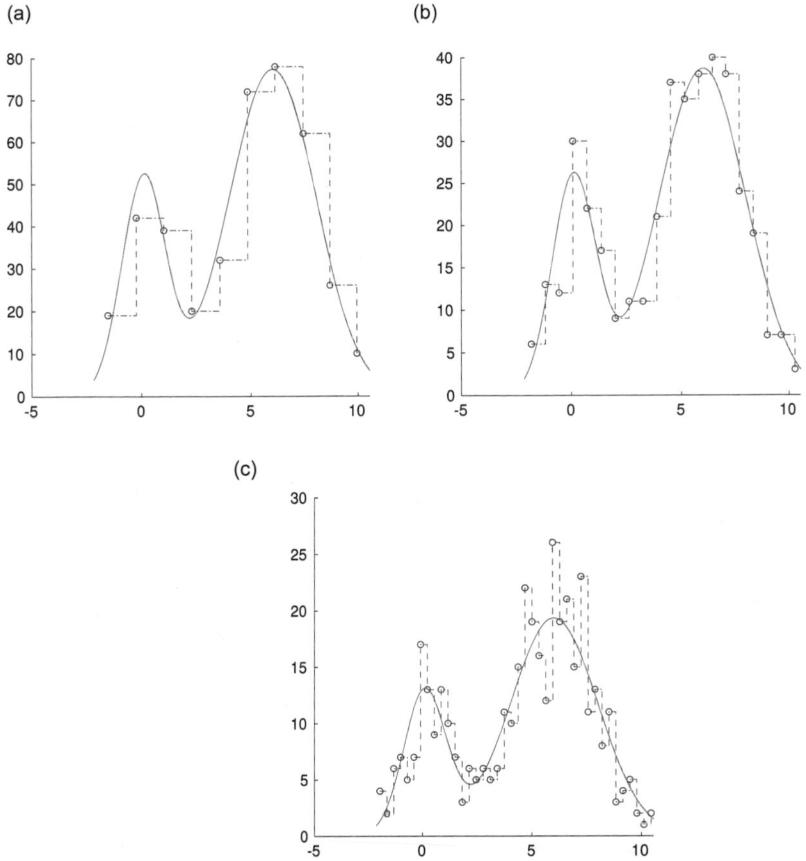

Figure 8.2

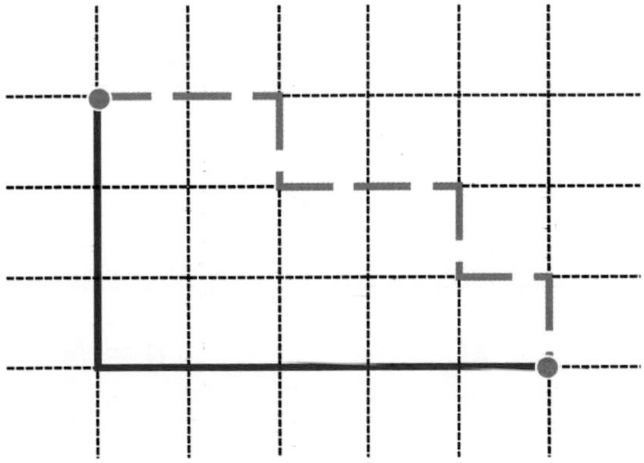

Figure 9.2

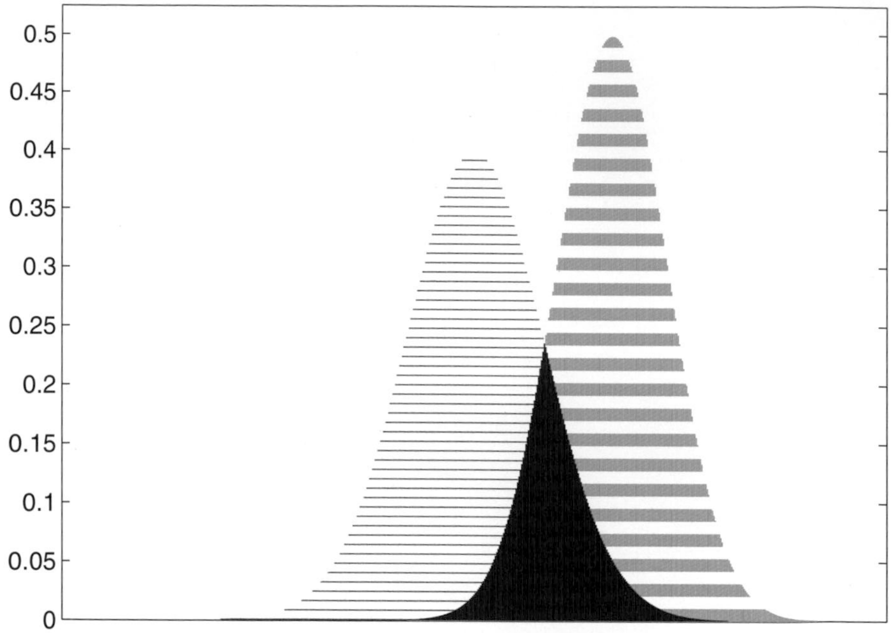

Figure 9.3

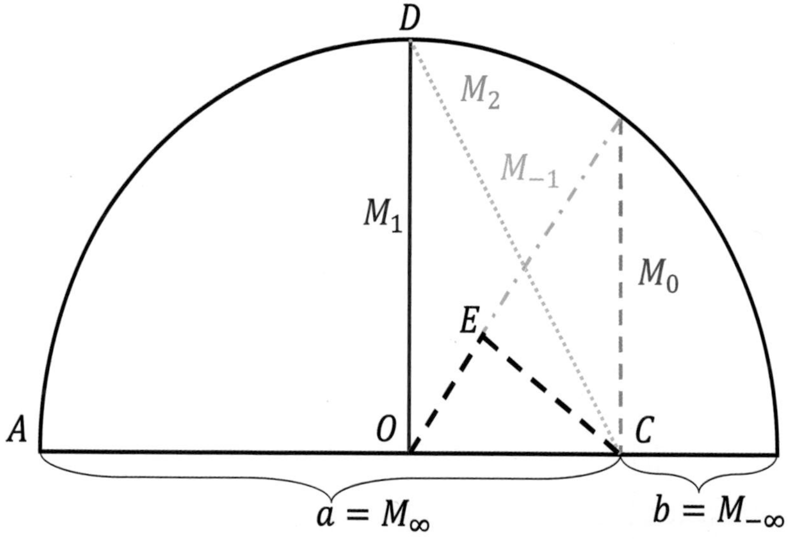

Figure 9.4

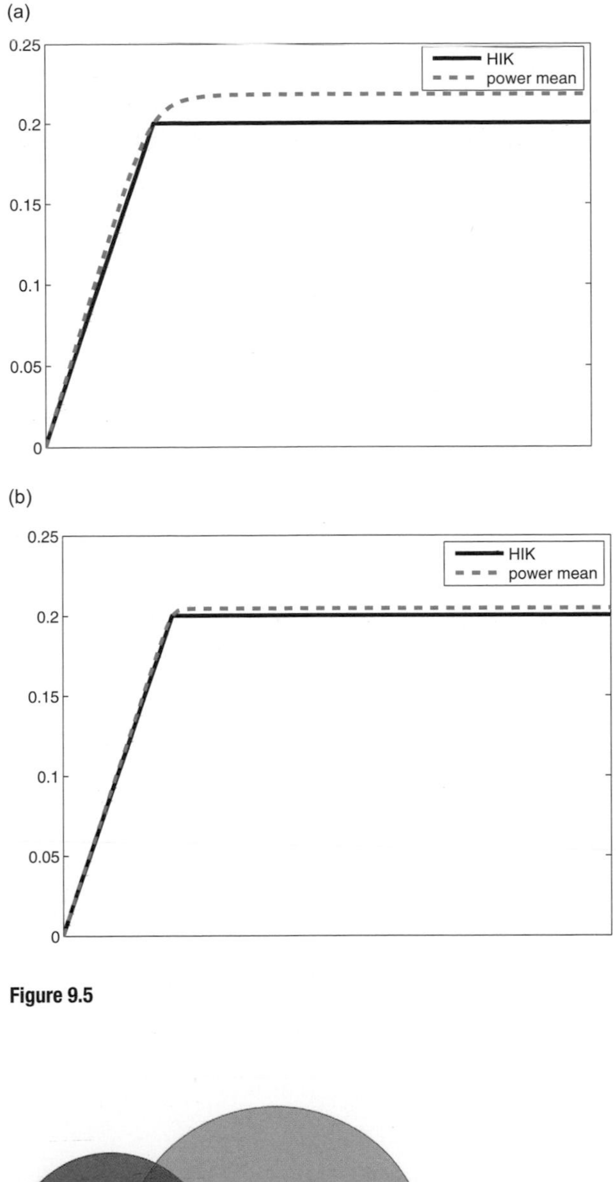

Figure 9.5

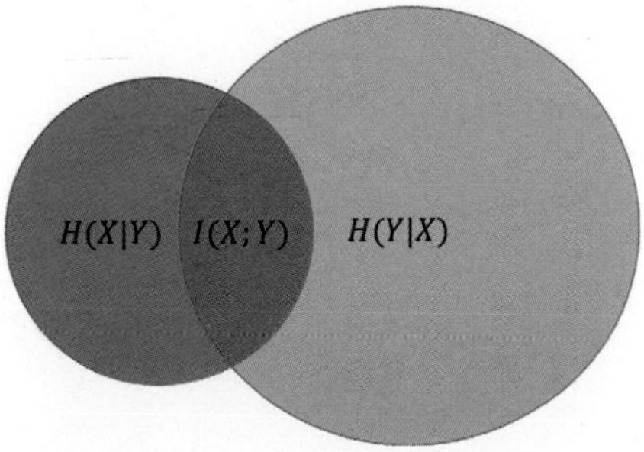

Figure 10.2

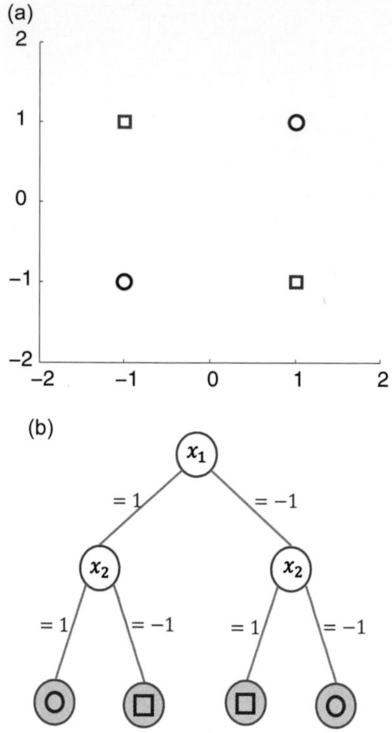

Figure 10.3

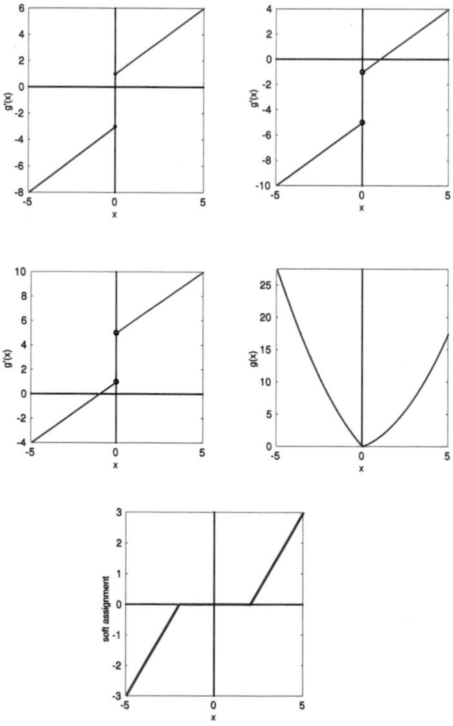

Figure 11.1

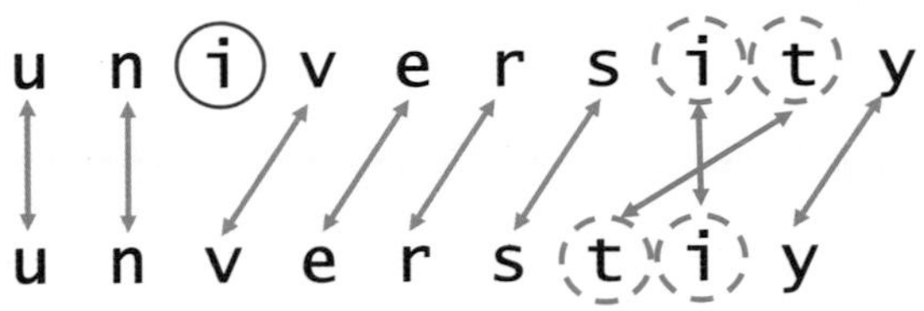

Figure 11.2

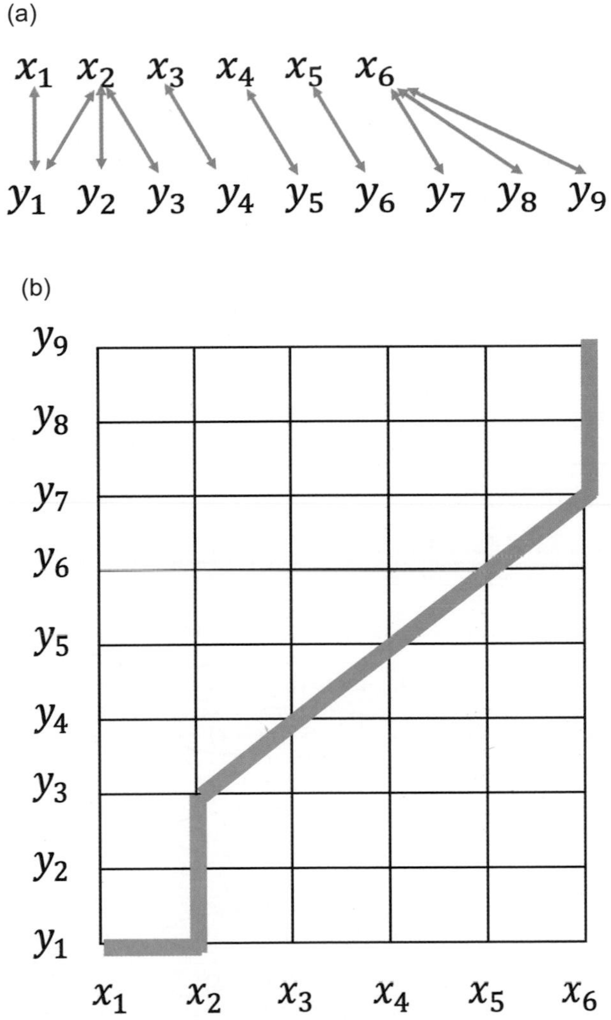

Figure 11.3

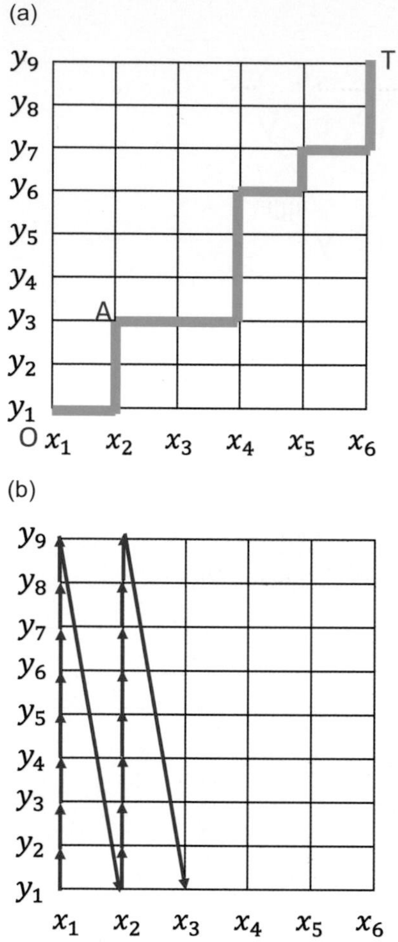

Figure 11.4

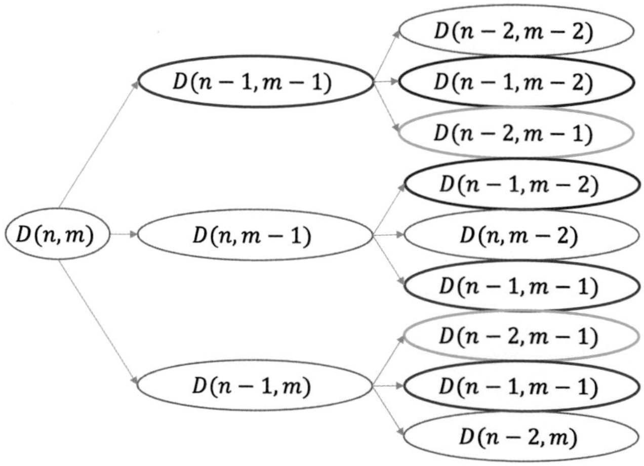

Figure 11.5

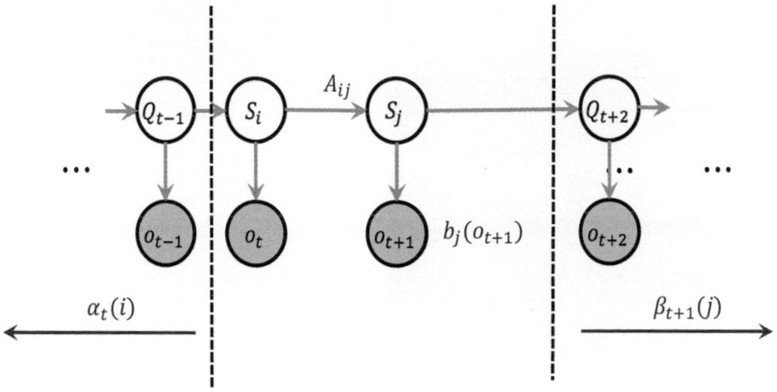

Figure 12.5

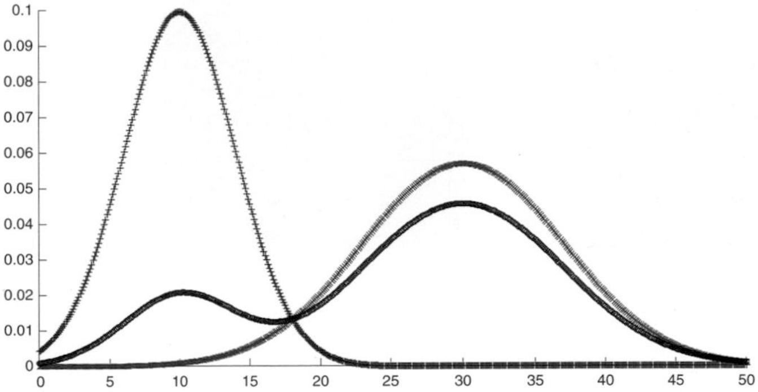

Figure 14.1

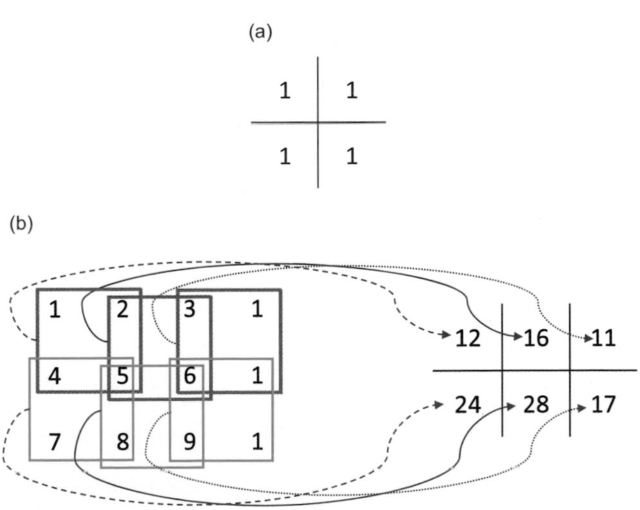

Figure 15.3

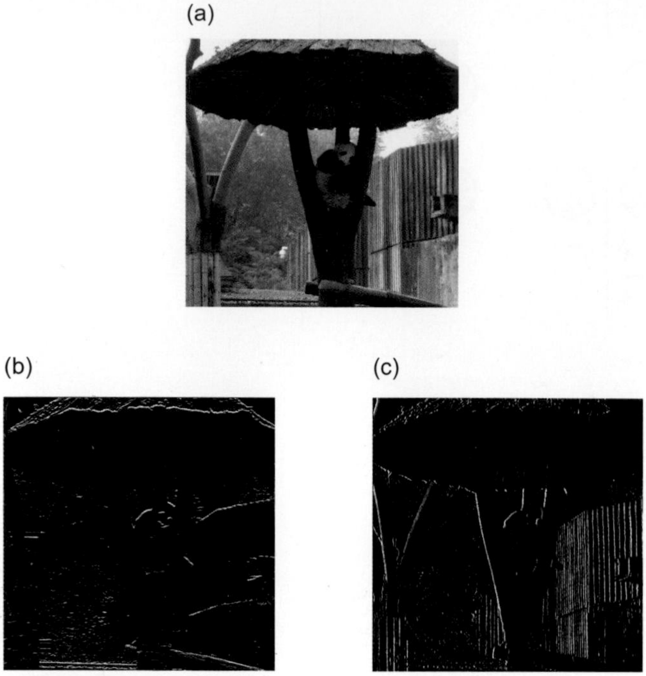

Figure 15.4

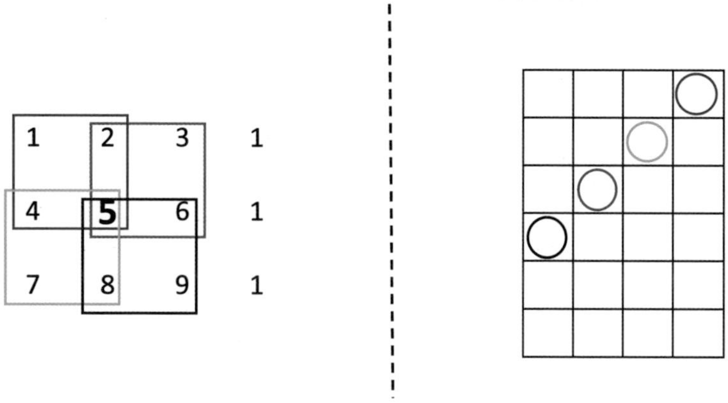

Figure 15.5

Table 4.2

	Prediction $f(\boldsymbol{x}) = +1$	Prediction $f(\boldsymbol{x}) = -1$
True label $y = +1$	True positive	False negative
True label $y = -1$	False positive	True negative

$$x_{\min, j} = \min_{1 \le i \le n} x_{i,j} \quad \text{and} \quad x_{\max, j} = \max_{1 \le i \le n} x_{i,j}. \tag{9.38}$$

Then we can normalize the range of the jth dimension to $[0, 1]$ by

$$\hat{x}_{i,j} = \frac{x_{i,j} - x_{\min, j}}{x_{\max, j} - x_{\min, j}}. \tag{9.39}$$

Note that $\min_{1 \le i \le n} \hat{x}_{i,j} = 0$ and $\max_{1 \le i \le n} \hat{x}_{i,j} = 1$.

This per-dimension normalization is also a learning process because it learns how to preprocess the data using the training set. Hence, we need to retain this model for normalization, which includes $x_{\min, j}$ and $x_{\max, j}$ for all $1 \le j \le d$—i.e., $2d$ numbers as the normalization model's parameters. Finally, the normalized data are used to learn a model f for classification, regression, or other tasks.

When a test example $\boldsymbol{x}$ is presented to us, we first use the normalization parameters to convert $\boldsymbol{x}$ to the normalized version $\hat{\boldsymbol{x}}$, and then output the prediction using $f(\hat{\boldsymbol{x}})$. A commonly occurring error for novices is to learn the maximum and minimum values for dimensions in the test set, and use these values to normalize the test examples. Test data cannot be used apart from when being tested.

Similarly, in a cross-validation process we learn the normalization parameters for each fold separately. The available examples are divided into different training and validation sets in different folds. In one fold, we learn the normalization parameters using the training set for this fold and apply it to all examples. We have to learn different normalization parameters in different folds.

This seemingly trivial normalization trick has more factors to consider.

- If we want a range different from $[0, 1]$—e.g., $[-1, +1]$—this is also possible, by

$$\hat{x}_{i,j} = 2\left(\frac{x_{i,j} - x_{\min, j}}{x_{\max, j} - x_{\min, j}} - 0.5\right). \tag{9.40}$$

  In fact, we can stretch the feature values to any range $[a, b]$ ($a < b$).
- If $x_{\max, j} = x_{\min, j}$ for some dimension j, it means that all values in this dimension are the same and the normalization equation is not well defined. However, a constant dimension means a useless one. Hence, we can simply discard all such dimensions.
- A vector is called *sparse* if many of its dimensions are zeros. A sparse dataset not only has many zeros in every row, it will also have many zeros in each dimension (column in X). Equation (9.39) will normalize a zero value to

$$-\frac{x_{\min, j}}{x_{\max, j} - x_{\min, j}},$$

  which is nonzero if $x_{\min, j} \neq 0$. However, if a zero value in the original data means "null" or "no information" based on its data generation process, this normalization is not welcome. In that case, we can specify that 0 is always normalized to 0.
- After normalization, the values in test examples could be smaller than 0 or larger than 1. In some problems the $[0, 1]$ range is required by the algorithm to learn f—e.g., the power mean kernels require all feature values to be nonnegative. We can

set all negative values to 0 and all values larger than 1 to 1. We can still use this strategy if the learning algorithm does not require a strict $[0, 1]$ range. However, we can also leave these values as they are.

If there is a reason to believe that a dimension j is a Gaussian, then it is probably better to normalize that dimension to a standard normal distribution, rather than to the range $[0, 1]$. We can first find μ_j and σ_j as the mean and standard deviation of that dimension based on the training set, and normalize it as

$$\hat{x}_{i,j} = \frac{x_{i,j} - \mu_j}{\sigma_j}. \tag{9.41}$$

Of course, we will use the μ_j and σ_j computed from the training set to normalize all examples, including the test ones. We have seen this type of normalization done implicitly in the whitening transform.

In some applications, we have reasons to require the scale of examples $\boldsymbol{x}$ to be roughly equal, rather than requiring the scale of feature dimensions to match. The ℓ_2 normalization normalizes any (training or test) example $\boldsymbol{x}$ to be a unit vector, that is,

$$\hat{\boldsymbol{x}} = \frac{\boldsymbol{x}}{\|\boldsymbol{x}\|}. \tag{9.42}$$

Another commonly used per-example normalization is the ℓ_1 normalization, which is

$$\hat{\boldsymbol{x}} = \frac{\boldsymbol{x}}{\|\boldsymbol{x}\|_1}. \tag{9.43}$$

After the ℓ_1 normalization, the dimensions of every example will sum to 1 if the values are nonnegative. It is a good idea to normalize a histogram using the ℓ_1 normalization. If necessary, other ℓ_p norms can be used to normalize our data too.

In short, proper normalization is essential in many learning and recognition methods and systems, no matter whether they are deep or not. But which type of normalization is the most suitable for a particular dataset or problem? There is no silver bullet in making this choice. Visualizing and studying the properties (e.g., distributions) of your input, interim, and output data should be a useful strategy in general. After properly understanding your data's properties, you will be able to find a matching normalization strategy for them.

9.2.3 Data Transformation

Feature normalization is a type of data transformation. Converting a distance metric to a similarity measure is also a transformation. In this section, we briefly introduce another type of transformation that converts arbitrary real numbers into a limited range. This type of transformation is useful in various methods—e.g., to convert the value of a discriminant function (which is a real number) to $[0, 1]$, allowing us to interpret the transformed value as a probability.

One type of conversion can convert a categorical dimension to a vector, such that the Euclidean distance on the vector is proportional to the discrete distance on the categorical data. For example, say a categorical dimension has three possible values a, b, c. Then we can transform a to a short vector $\boldsymbol{t}_a = (1,0,0)$, b to $\boldsymbol{t}_b = (0,1,0)$, and c to $\boldsymbol{t}_c = (0,0,1)$. In other words, $\boldsymbol{t}_x$ is the histogram of a singleton set {x}, which contains only one element x.

It is easy to prove that $\rho(\mathrm{x},\mathrm{y}) = \frac{1}{\sqrt{2}}\|\boldsymbol{t}_x - \boldsymbol{t}_y\|$, where $\mathrm{x},\mathrm{y} \in \{\mathtt{a},\mathtt{b},\mathtt{c}\}$, and

$$1 - \rho(\mathrm{x},\mathrm{y}) = \boldsymbol{t}_x^T \boldsymbol{t}_y.$$

For example, if a problem has both categorical and real-valued features, we can convert every categorical dimension to a short vector, and the SVM method can be applied on the transformed data for both training and testing.

To convert a set of values to another set of values that could form a probability mass function, the *softmax* transform is popular. The softmax transformation is in fact a nonlinear normalization too. Given a vector of arbitrary values $\boldsymbol{x} = (x_1, x_2, \ldots, x_d)^T$, the softmax function converts it to another d-dimensional vector $\boldsymbol{z}$. Components of the new vector are nonnegative and sum to 1, hence could be interpreted as probabilities $\Pr(y = i|\boldsymbol{x})$. The softmax transformation is defined as

$$z_i = \frac{\exp(x_i)}{\sum_{j=1}^{d} \exp(x_j)}. \tag{9.44}$$

The data could be scaled to form a better probability distribution, e.g.,

$$z_i = \frac{\exp(\gamma x_i)}{\sum_{j=1}^{d} \exp(\gamma x_j)}, \quad \gamma > 0.$$

To convert one value to another value in a limited range, there is also the logistic sigmoid function

$$\sigma(x) = \frac{1}{1 + e^{-x}}, \tag{9.45}$$

which is illustrated in Figure 9.6. Its range is $(0, +1)$ since $\sigma(\infty) = \lim_{x\to\infty} \sigma(x) = 1$ and $\sigma(-\infty) = \lim_{x\to -\infty} \sigma(x) = 0$.

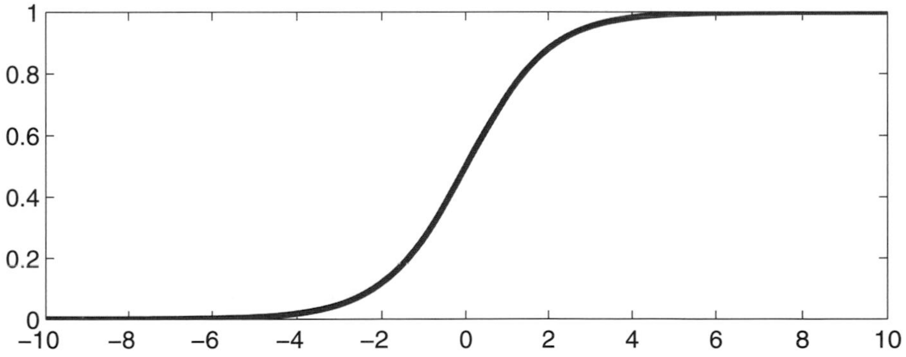

Figure 9.6 The logistic sigmoid function.

The logistic sigmoid function σ is a special case of the logistic function family, which has the form

$$f(x) = \frac{L}{1 + e^{-k(x - x_0)}}, \tag{9.46}$$

where L, k, and x_0 are the maximum value, steepness (of the logistic curve), and midpoint, respectively.

A transformation similar to the logistic sigmoid function is the hyperbolic tangent function tanh,

$$\tanh(x) = \frac{e^x - e^{-x}}{e^x + e^{-x}}. \tag{9.47}$$

The curve of tanh is similar to that of the logistic sigmoid. However, its range is $(-1, +1)$. Both the logistic sigmoid and hyperbolic tangent have been widely used in neural network models.

In linear regression, if we transform the linear combination $\boldsymbol{x}^T\boldsymbol{\beta}$ using a logistic function, we arrive at a commonly used classification model in statistics, called the logistic regression.[3] Unlike linear regression, logistic regression finds nonlinear classification boundaries.

In a binary problem, we assume the probability of $\boldsymbol{x}$ belonging to the positive class has the form

$$\Pr(y = 1|\boldsymbol{x}) \approx f(\boldsymbol{x}) = \frac{1}{1 + e^{-\boldsymbol{x}^T\boldsymbol{\beta}}}, \tag{9.48}$$

and use methods such as maximum likelihood estimation to find a good $\boldsymbol{\beta}$ value. It is convenient to use $\mathcal{Y} = \{0, 1\}$ in logistic regression because we can write the objective as maximizing

$$\prod_{i=1}^{n} f(\boldsymbol{x}_i)^{y_i} (1 - f(\boldsymbol{x}_i))^{1-y_i}, \tag{9.49}$$

in which $\Pr(y_i = 0|\boldsymbol{x}_i) = 1 - \Pr(y_i = 1|\boldsymbol{x}_i) \approx 1 - f(\boldsymbol{x}_i)$.

Considering the ith training example $(\boldsymbol{x}_i, y_i)$, the above objective says that if $y_i = 1$ we want $\Pr(y_i = 1|\boldsymbol{x}_i) \approx f(\boldsymbol{x}_i)$ to be large, and when $y_i = 0$ we want $\Pr(y_i = 0|\boldsymbol{x}_i) = 1 - \Pr(y_i = 1|\boldsymbol{x}_i) \approx 1 - f(\boldsymbol{x}_i)$ to be large. Overall, we want the probability distribution predicted by our model to match the distribution computed from the training set. In the next chapter, we will also very briefly introduce multinomial logistic regression, which extends the logistic regression model to multiclass classification problems.

Logistic regression is a representative *discriminative* probabilistic model, because it directly models the posterior distribution $\Pr(y|\boldsymbol{x})$.

To solve logistic regression optimization is beyond the scope of this book. However, before we conclude this chapter, we want to add that logistic regression is a popular approach in classification, especially when probability estimates are required.

[3] Although the word "regression" is used in its name, logistic regression is a classification method.

Through some transformations, other classifiers such as SVM can also output a probability estimation, but that estimation is usually inferior to the probability estimated by logistic regression.

9.3 Miscellaneous Notes and Additional Resources

The proof of the Minkowski inequality can be found in many resources, e.g., on the Wikipedia page https://en.wikipedia.org/wiki/Minkowski_inequality.

There are many research papers on distance metric learning, e.g., Xing et al. (2003) and Weinberger & Saul (2009). We will discuss LLE (locally linear embedding), a nonlinear method in Exercise 9.2.

More information on various linear regression methods can be found in Montgomery et al. (2007).

We will see how the sigmoid function is used in neural networks in Chapter 15.

More information on the χ^2 distribution and distance can be found in DeGroot & Schervish (2011).

Exercises

9.1 Principal component analysis (PCA) transforms a vector $\boldsymbol{x} \in \mathbb{R}^D$ to a lower-dimensional vector $\boldsymbol{y} \in \mathbb{R}^d$ $(d < D)$ using

$$\boldsymbol{y} = E_d^T(\boldsymbol{x} - \bar{\boldsymbol{x}}),$$

in which $\bar{\boldsymbol{x}}$ is the sample mean of $\boldsymbol{x}$, and E_d is a $D \times d$ matrix formed by the top d eigenvectors of the sample covariance matrix of $\boldsymbol{x}$ (cf. Chapter 5).

Let $\boldsymbol{x}_1$ and $\boldsymbol{x}_2$ be any two samples of $\boldsymbol{x}$, and $\boldsymbol{y}_1$ and $\boldsymbol{y}_2$ be the PCA-transformed version of them. Show that

$$d_A^2(\boldsymbol{x}_1, \boldsymbol{x}_2) = \|\boldsymbol{y}_1 - \boldsymbol{y}_2\|_2^2$$

is a valid distance metric in the family defined by Eq. (9.15). What should be assigned to be the matrix A?

9.2 (Locally linear embedding) PCA is a *linear* transformation that approximately keeps the dissimilarity (aka distance) between any two data points: $\|\boldsymbol{y}_1 - \boldsymbol{y}_2\|_2^2 \approx \|\boldsymbol{x}_1 - \boldsymbol{x}_2\|_2^2$ because $E_d^T E_d \approx I$. It is particularly useful when *all* data points approximately lie on a linear subspace of $\mathbb{R}^D$ (i.e., a global subspace).

However, the global linear subspace assumption often breaks down in real-world data that are complex in nature. In this case, it is reasonable to assume *local* linear relationships and use these relationships for dimensionality reduction or a better similarity (dissimilarity) measure. Locally linear embedding (LLE), proposed in Roweis & Saul (2000), is one such method.

(a) **Local geometry.** The local geometry around an example $\boldsymbol{x}_i$ is represented by a local linear reconstruction. Let there be n examples $\boldsymbol{x}_1, \boldsymbol{x}_2, \ldots, \boldsymbol{x}_n$. For any example $\boldsymbol{x}_i$, LLE first finds the nearest neighbors of $\boldsymbol{x}_i$, and uses a linear combination of these nearest neighbors to reconstruct $\boldsymbol{x}_i$. That is, for $\boldsymbol{x}_i$, LLE wants to minimize the reconstruction error

$$e_i = \left\| \boldsymbol{x}_i - \sum_{j=1}^{n} w_{ij} \boldsymbol{x}_j \right\|^2, \tag{9.50}$$

in which w_{ij} is the linear weight for $\boldsymbol{x}_j$ in the reconstruction. Note that $w_{ij} = 0$ if $\boldsymbol{x}_j$ is not among the nearest neighbors of $\boldsymbol{x}_i$ (hence $w_{ii} = 0$). An additional constraint is that

$$\sum_{j=1}^{n} w_{ij} = 1 \tag{9.51}$$

for any $1 \le i \le n$. This constraint makes the solution for w unique.

On the entire dataset, LLE seeks a matrix W (with $[W]_{ij} = w_{ij}$) that both satisfies all these constraints and minimizes the total error $\sum_{i=1}^{n} e_i$. Suppose K nearest neighbors are used; find the optimal solution for w_{ij} $(1 \le i, j \le n)$.

(b) **Invariance.** We can apply the same operation to all examples in the dataset.

(i) *Rotation*: $\boldsymbol{x}_i \leftarrow Q\boldsymbol{x}_i$ with $QQ^T = Q^TQ = I$ for all $1 \le i \le n$.

(ii) *Translation*: $\boldsymbol{x}_i \leftarrow \boldsymbol{x}_i + \boldsymbol{t}$ with $\boldsymbol{t} \in \mathbb{R}^D$ for all $1 \le i \le n$.

(iii) *Scaling*: $\boldsymbol{x}_i \leftarrow s\boldsymbol{x}_i$ with $s \ne 0$ for all $1 \le i \le n$.

Show that the optimal solution for w_{ij} is invariant to any one of these three operations.

(c) **New representation: formulation.** In the next step, LLE seeks a shorter vector $\boldsymbol{y}_i \in \mathbb{R}^d$ with $d \ll D$ as a new representation for $\boldsymbol{x}_i$. The main purpose is to reduce unnecessary degrees of freedom in the new representation while preserving the local geometry (i.e., w_{ij}). To find the optimal $\boldsymbol{y}_i$, the following optimization is solved:

$$\operatorname*{arg\,min}_{\boldsymbol{y}_1, \boldsymbol{y}_2, \ldots, \boldsymbol{y}_n} \quad \sum_{i=1}^{n} \left\| \boldsymbol{y}_i - \sum_{j=1}^{n} w_{ij} \boldsymbol{y}_j \right\|^2 \tag{9.52}$$

$$\text{s.t.} \quad \sum_{i=1}^{n} \boldsymbol{y}_i = \boldsymbol{0}, \tag{9.53}$$

$$\sum_{i=1}^{n} \boldsymbol{y}_i \boldsymbol{y}_i^T = I, \tag{9.54}$$

in which $\boldsymbol{0}$ is a vector of all 0s, I is an identity matrix with appropriate dimensions, and w_{ij} are the optimal values learned in the previous step.

Explain (intuitively) why this optimization keeps the local geometry, and what the effects of the two conditions are. In terms of rotation, translation, and scaling, which of these degrees of freedom are eliminated? If there are some degrees of freedom still in effect, do they adversely affect the new representation?

(d) **New representation: simplification.** Let W be an $n \times n$ matrix with $[W]_{ij} = w_{ij}$, and let M be an $n \times n$ matrix defined by $M = (I - W)^T(I - W)$. Show that the above optimization objective is equivalent to

$$\sum_{i=1}^{n}\sum_{j=1}^{n} M_{ij}\boldsymbol{y}_i^T\boldsymbol{y}_j. \tag{9.55}$$

(e) **New representation: solution.** First, show that M is positive semidefinite, and then that $\mathbf{1}$ is an eigenvector of M.

Then let $\boldsymbol{\xi}_1, \boldsymbol{\xi}_2, \ldots$ be eigenvectors of M sorted in *ascending* order of their corresponding eigenvalues, and let E_d be an $n \times d$ matrix defined by $E_d = [\boldsymbol{\xi}_2|\boldsymbol{\xi}_3|\ldots|\boldsymbol{\xi}_{d+1}]$. Matrix analysis results tell us that if we set $\boldsymbol{y}_i$ to be the ith row of E_d, the objective is minimized (which is easy to prove). Hence, the ith eigenvector contains the $(i-1)$th dimension of the new representation for all n examples.

Show that the two constraints are satisfied, hence the rows in E_d are indeed the optimal solutions for $\boldsymbol{y}_i$. Why is $\boldsymbol{\xi}_1$ discarded?

(f) The page `www.cs.nyu.edu/~roweis/lle/` lists some useful resources for LLE, including publications, code, visualizations, and demonstrations. Browse the resources on this page and play with the code and demos.

9.3 In this exercise, we prove that $\|\boldsymbol{x}\|_p$ $(p > 0)$ is a nonincreasing function of p. In other words, if $0 < p < q$, prove

$$\left(|x_1|^p + |x_2|^p + \cdots + |x_d|^p\right)^{1/p} \geq \left(|x_1|^q + |x_2|^q + \cdots + |x_d|^q\right)^{1/q}. \tag{9.56}$$

(a) Show that proving Eq. (9.56) is equivalent to proving

$$\left(x_1^p + x_2^p + \cdots + x_d^p\right)^{1/p} \geq \left(x_1^q + x_2^q + \cdots + x_d^q\right)^{1/q} \tag{9.57}$$

under the additional constraint $x_i \geq 0$ for all $1 \leq i \leq d$.

(b) Denote $r = \frac{q}{p}$ $(0 < p < q)$ and assume $x_i \geq 0$ for all $1 \leq i \leq d$; prove that Eq. (9.57) is equivalent to

$$(y_1 + y_2 + \cdots + y_d)^r \geq \left(y_1^r + y_2^r + \cdots + y_d^r\right), \tag{9.58}$$

in which $y_i = x_i^p$.

(c) Prove that Eq. (9.58) holds when $r > 1$ and $y_i \geq 0$ $(i = 1, 2, \ldots, d)$. (Hint: Use Taylor's expansion for $d = 2$ and mathematical induction for $d > 2$.)

(d) The above three steps prove Eq. (9.56). Note that one simplification (assuming nonnegative numbers) and one change of variables transformation $(y_i = x_i^p)$ are used in this proof. Neither simplification changes the properties of the original problem. After the simplifications, Eq. (9.58) is easy (if not trivial) to prove. Try to prove Eq. (9.56) without using these simplifications—e.g., by showing

$$\frac{\mathrm{d}\|\boldsymbol{x}\|_p}{\mathrm{d}p} \leq 0$$

when $p > 0$ and $d \geq 1$. How would you compare the level of difficulty of these two different proof approaches?

9.4 Prove $\|Gx\|$ ($x \in \mathbb{R}^d$) is a valid vector norm when $G \in \mathbb{R}^d \times \mathbb{R}^d$ is a positive definite matrix.

9.5 (Ridge regression) In this problem, we consider linear regression models. The model produced by Eq. (9.34) is called the *ordinary least squares* (OLS) model. This solution method, however, is problematic when noise exists in the data or the labels, as shown by the example below.

We use the MATLAB/GNU Octave command

```
x = -7:1:7;
```

to generate 15 one-dimensional examples, and the linear regression model is

$$y = 0.3x + 0.2.$$

In order to handle the bias term (i.e., 0.2), we use the command

```
xb = [x; ones(size(x))];
```

to transform the input x to two dimensions, where the second dimension is constant and will handle the bias term. We suppose the labels are corrupted by white noise, as

```
rng(0) % make it repeatable          (9.59)
noise = randn(size(y))*0.2;          (9.60)
z = y + noise;                       (9.61)
```

(a) We want to use x (or xb) and z to estimate a linear model such that $z = wx + b$, in which the true values are $w = 0.3$ and $b = 0.2$. Write a program to find the ordinary least square estimation for w and b. Are there errors in these estimations? Are the estimations for w and b equally accurate? What causes the errors in the OLS estimation?

(b) The loss function in ordinary linear regression is shown in Eq. (9.30) as

$$\arg\min_{\beta} \sum_{i=1}^{n} \left(x_i^T \beta - y_i\right)^2,$$

in which x_i and y_i are the ith training feature and label, respectively. An alternative linear regression method, *ridge regression*, minimizes the objective

$$\arg\min_{\beta} \sum_{i=1}^{n} \left(x_i^T \beta - y_i\right)^2 + \lambda \|\beta\|^2, \tag{9.62}$$

in which $\lambda > 0$ is a hyperparameter. The regularization term $\lambda\|\beta\|^2$ will change the solution of OLS. What is the effect of this regularization term?

(c) Now try ridge regression with $\lambda = 9.3$. What are the estimates in this setup? Are these estimates better or worse than the OLS ones?

(d) Try different λ values, and enter the ridge regression estimates into Table 9.1. What have you learned from this table?

Table 9.1 Ridge regression under different λ values.

λ	10^{-2}	10^{-1}	10^{0}	10^{1}	10^{2}
w					
b					

9.6 In this problem, we will use the LIBLINEAR software and try one particular data transformation.

(a) Download the LIBLINEAR software (`www.csie.ntu.edu.tw/~cjlin/liblinear/`) and learn how to use it. You can also use the MATLAB/GNU Octave binding and use it along with MATLAB/GNU Octave.

(b) Download the MNIST dataset from `www.csie.ntu.edu.tw/~cjlin/libsvmtools/datasets/multiclass.html#mnist`. Use the nonscaled version, which includes a training set and a test set. Using the default parameters of LIBLINEAR, what is the accuracy?

(c) For every feature value (including those for both training and test examples), perform the following data transformation:

$$x \leftarrow \sqrt{x}.$$

What is the new accuracy rate after this transformation?

(d) Why does the square root transformation change the accuracy in this way?

9.7 (Sigmoid) The logistic sigmoid function has been widely used in machine learning and pattern recognition, especially in the neural networks community. Let

$$\sigma(x) = \frac{1}{1+e^{-x}}$$

denote the logistic sigmoid function. In this exercise we study this function.

(a) Prove that $1 - \sigma(x) = \sigma(-x)$.

(b) Prove that $\sigma'(x) = \sigma(x)(1-\sigma(x))$, in which $\sigma'(x)$ means $\frac{\mathrm{d}}{\mathrm{d}x}\sigma(x)$. Draw a figure to show the curves of $\sigma(x)$ and $\sigma'(x)$ simultaneously.

(c) A neural network is often a layer-by-layer processing machine. For example, the output $\boldsymbol{y}$ for an input $\boldsymbol{x}$ can be produced as

$$\boldsymbol{y} = f^{(L)}\left(f^{(L-1)}\left(\cdots f^{(2)}\left(f^{(1)}(\boldsymbol{x})\right)\right)\right),$$

in which $f^{(i)}$ is a mathematical function describing the ith layer of processing. When the number of processing layers L is large, it is called a deep neural network (cf. Chapter 15).

Stochastic gradient descent is often the choice of optimization algorithm for neural networks. Let $\boldsymbol{\theta}$ be the current values of all parameters in the network, and $\boldsymbol{g}$ the gradients of the loss function with respect to $\boldsymbol{\theta}$; then $\boldsymbol{\theta}$ is updated as

$$\boldsymbol{\theta}^{\text{new}} \leftarrow \boldsymbol{\theta} - \lambda \boldsymbol{g}, \tag{9.63}$$

in which λ is a positive learning rate.

The gradients $\boldsymbol{g}$ are computed using a chain rule. Let $\boldsymbol{\theta}^{(i)}$ be the parameters in the ith layer, and $\boldsymbol{y}^{(i)}$ be the output after the first i layers. Then

$$\frac{\partial \ell}{\partial (\boldsymbol{\theta}^{(i)})^T} = \frac{\partial \ell}{\partial (\boldsymbol{y}^{(i)})^T} \frac{\partial \boldsymbol{y}^{(i)}}{\partial (\boldsymbol{\theta}^{(i)})^T}, \tag{9.64}$$

in which ℓ is the overall loss function to be minimized. This computation is called *error back-propagation*, because the errors in ℓ propagate from the last layer toward the first layer in backward order.

This learning strategy, however, often suffers from the *diminishing gradient* problem, which means that for some i, the gradient of this layer $\frac{\partial \ell}{\partial (\boldsymbol{\theta}^{(i)})^T}$ becomes very small, or $\left\| \frac{\partial \ell}{\partial (\boldsymbol{\theta}^{(i)})^T} \right\| \to 0$ quickly when i moves from L toward 1. The sigmoid function $\sigma(x)$ was popular in neural networks. Several layers $f^{(i)}$ apply the sigmoid function individually to every element in its input.

Show that the sigmoid function easily leads to the vanishing gradient difficulty. (Hint: You can look at just one element in the gradient. Refer to the figure you created for the last subproblem.)

10 Information Theory and Decision Trees

In this chapter, we introduce two topics: a few basic concepts and results from information theory and a very simple decision tree model. We have put these two things together because the specific decision tree model we introduce here is based on entropy, the core concept in information theory. We will also mention in passing applications of information theory in pattern recognition and machine learning—e.g., in feature selection and neural network learning.

10.1 Prefix Code and Huffman Tree

We will use the Huffman code as an example to motivate information theory. Suppose we want to count the number of different trees in a garden. You are given a hand-held smart device that can automatically transmit its GPS coordinates (i.e., the location) to a server. The device automatically recognizes the species of the tree in front of it using some pattern recognition techniques, and also transmits this to the same server. There are only five different types of trees in the garden, denoted by the symbols `a`, `b`, `c`, `d`, and `e`, respectively. By proportion, 50% (or $\frac{1}{2}$) of the trees in the garden are of type `a`, and the other four types each represent 12.5% (or $\frac{1}{8}$) of the trees.

A simple idea is to represent these symbols as five binary codes:

`000, 001, 010, 011, 100.`

Hence, we need to transmit three bits for each tree's identity. For some reason, the hand-held device has extremely limited transmission bandwidth, and we want to use the *minimum number of bits* to code these tree types.

The Huffman code is such a code. It uses different numbers of bits to code the symbols:

`a:0, b:100, c:101, d:110, e:111.`

Hence, the average number of bits per tree is

$$\frac{1}{2} \times 1 + \frac{1}{8} \times 3 + \frac{1}{8} \times 3 + \frac{1}{8} \times 3 + \frac{1}{8} \times 3 = 2,$$

which is smaller than 3. If there are 1000 trees in the garden, 1000 bits of bandwidth have been saved by using the Huffman code.

The Huffman code is a *prefix* code, meaning that the code for any symbol will not be the prefix of any other code. For example, $\{$`0,100,010`$\}$ is not a prefix code because `0` is the prefix of `010`. The five symbols in our garden example also form a prefix code.

For a prefix code, we do not need any marker to separate two symbols. For example, `11111001000101` is decoded as `111/110/0/100/0/101`, or `edabac`, without using additional information.

The Huffman code is an optimal prefix code, and it is built using the Huffman tree. Given a set of m discrete symbols $s_1, s_2, \ldots, s_m$, we assume that each symbol s_i is associated with an occurrence probability a_i ($a_i \geq 0$ and $\sum_{i=1}^{m} a_i = 1$). The Huffman tree is built using the following steps.

- Build a priority queue with m nodes, where each node s_i has weight a_i.
- Remove the two nodes with the smallest weights from the priority queue.
- Create a new node, whose weight is the sum of the weights of the two removed nodes, and place these two nodes as its children. Put the new node into the priority queue.
- Repeat the previous two steps until the priority queue is empty.

The Huffman tree is a binary tree. Figure 10.1 is the Huffman tree for our garden example. We label the edge connecting a node to its left and right children with

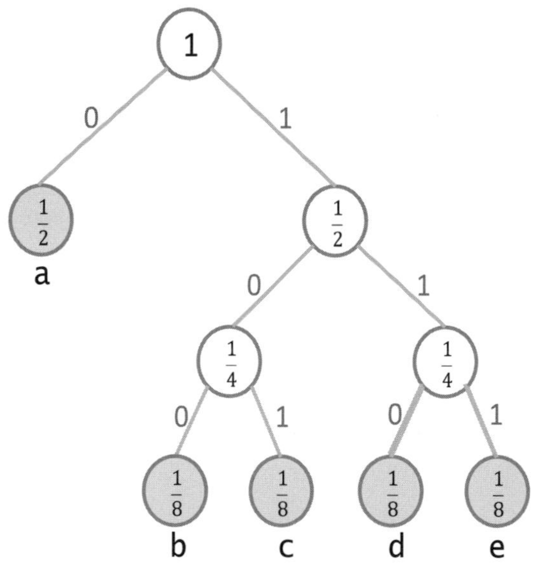

Figure 10.1 An example Huffman tree. Filled nodes are the symbols and the others are internal nodes.

`0` and `1`, respectively. The Huffman code for a symbol is the concatenation of the labels of all edges in the path from the root to that symbol.

From the tree building process, we observe that symbols appearing frequently (e.g., `a`) have short codes, and rare symbols have longer codes.

10.2 Basics of Information Theory

The average length of the binary string (or average number of bits) per symbol is closely related to the uncertainty in the symbols. To transmit a symbol over a communication channel, the binary codes must fully specify or describe the symbol. Let X be a discrete random variable, and $p(X = s_i) = a_i$ $(1 \le i \le m)$ be the probability mass function. Now let us consider an extreme case, in which $a_1 = 1$ and $a_i = 0$ for $i > 1$ (i.e., only s_1 will occur). There is no uncertainty at all in this case. In order to transmit n symbols, we need to transmit just the integer n once, and the receiver understands that this means a sequence with n symbols (which are all s_1). In other words, the number of bits per symbol is $\frac{1}{n}$, or 0 when $n \to \infty$. The least uncertainty leads to the shortest possible codes.

In another extreme, we consider the most uncertain case. Intuitively, the uniform distribution (i.e., $a_i = \frac{1}{m}$) is the most uncertain case, in which we cannot favor any particular symbol. It is obvious that the Huffman code requires $\lceil \log_2 m \rceil$ bits for every symbol, in which $\lceil \cdot \rceil$ is the ceiling function. Because for any p.m.f. we can encode all symbols by using $\lceil \log_2 m \rceil$ bits, the most uncertain p.m.f. leads to the longest possible codes.

Entropy is the core concept in *information theory*.[1] Entropy is a measure of uncertainty (or unpredictability) of information content, and technically it provides a theoretically unbreakable limit on the shortest possible binary codes, if the symbols to be transmitted are not approximated (i.e., it is a lossless code) and is not compressed. Although this book is not on computer communication, Shannon entropy is now widely used in machine learning and pattern recognition because it can measure the *information content* of a distribution, which is very useful in our subject.

10.2.1 Entropy and Uncertainty

Formally, the entropy of a discrete random variable X with p.m.f. $p_i = p(X = s_i) = a_i$ $(1 \le i \le m)$ is

$$H(X) = -\sum_{i=1}^{m} p_i \log_2 p_i, \tag{10.1}$$

[1] Entropy also refers to an important concept in thermodynamics. We say "Shannon entropy" to specifically refer to entropy in information theory. Claude Elwood Shannon is an American mathematician, electrical engineer, and cryptographer, in particular "the father of information theory."

and the unit for entropy is the *bit*. It is obvious that $H(X) = 0$ when $p_i = 1$ for some i, and $H(X) = \log_2 m$ when X is a discrete uniform distribution, which meets our expectations that $H(X)$ is the shortest possible average (or expected) code length.[2] We can also write the entropy as an expectation:

$$H(X) = -\mathbb{E}_X[\log_2 p(X)], \tag{10.2}$$

where p is the p.m.f. of X.

10.2.2 Joint and Conditional Entropy

Given two discrete random variables X and Y, their joint entropy is

$$H(X,Y) = -\sum_x \sum_y p(x,y) \log_2 p(x,y) = -\mathbb{E}_{(X,Y)}[\log_2 p(X,Y)], \tag{10.3}$$

in which we have omitted the domain for $X(x)$ and $Y(y)$ and the subscript of the p.m.f. (which is clear from the variables). The joint entropy can be extended to more than two variables.

When $X = x$, the notation $Y|X = x$ denotes another random variable (Y conditioned on a specific value of $X = x$), and it has an entropy

$$H(Y|X = x) = -\sum_y p_{Y|X=x}(y|x) \log_2 p_{Y|X=x}(y|x), \tag{10.4}$$

or $H(Y|X=x) = -\sum_y p(y|x) \log_2 p(y|x)$. The conditional entropy $H(Y|X)$ is defined as

$$H(Y|X) = \sum_x p(x) H(Y|X = x) = -\sum_{x,y} p(x,y) \log_2 p(y|x), \tag{10.5}$$

which is the weighted average of $H(Y|X = x)$ for all x. The conditional entropy can also be written as

$$-\mathbb{E}_{(X,Y)}[\log_2 p(Y|X)]$$

because of the last equality.

With some simple manipulation we have

$$H(X,Y) = H(X) + H(Y|X). \tag{10.6}$$

That is, the conditional entropy $H(Y|X)$ is the difference between the information contained in the joint random vector (X,Y) and the random variable X. We can roughly interpret this equality: the information content in (X,Y) is the sum of the information in X and in the part of Y that is not dependent on X (i.e., the information in Y with the effect of X removed).

[2] Note that the length must be an integer in real-world communication channels, hence $\lceil \log_2 m \rceil$. Other bases (such as e and 10) are also used in entropy calculation.

10.2.3 Mutual Information and Relative Entropy

The conditional distribution is not symmetric; hence in general

$$H(Y|X) \neq H(X|Y).$$

However, since $H(X,Y) = H(X) + H(Y|X) = H(Y) + H(X|Y)$, we always have

$$H(X) - H(X|Y) = H(Y) - H(Y|X). \tag{10.7}$$

We can roughly interpret this equality: the difference between the amounts of information in X and $X|Y$ (distribution of X if we know Y) equals the difference between the amounts of information in Y and $Y|X$ (distribution of Y if we know X). Thus, this difference can be naturally treated as the information content that is common to both X and Y. The *mutual information* between X and Y is defined as

$$I(X;Y) = \sum_{x,y} p(x,y) \log_2 \frac{p(x,y)}{p(x)p(y)} \tag{10.8}$$

$$= \mathbb{E}_{(X,Y)}\left[\log_2 \frac{p(X,Y)}{p(X)p(Y)}\right] \tag{10.9}$$

$$= I(Y;X). \tag{10.10}$$

Please note there is *no* negative sign before the expectation. Mutual information is symmetric, and it is easy to verify that

$$I(X;Y) = H(X) - H(X|Y) \tag{10.11}$$

$$= H(Y) - H(Y|X) \tag{10.12}$$

$$= H(X) + H(Y) - H(X,Y). \tag{10.13}$$

The equality

$$I(X;X) = H(X)$$

holds because $I(X;X) = H(X) - H(X|X)$ and $H(X|X) = 0$. Hence, $H(X)$ is the mutual information between X and itself, and sometimes the entropy $H(X)$ is called the *self-information*.

The definition of mutual information shows that it measures the difference in the amount of information in the joint $p(X,Y)$ and in the two marginals $p(X)$ and $p(Y)$. The difference (or "distance") between two distributions is measured by the Kullback–Leibler divergence (or KL distance). For two p.m.f.s $p(x)$ and $q(x)$ (defined on the same domain), the KL divergence is

$$\mathrm{KL}(p\|q) = \sum_{x} p(x) \log_2 \frac{p(x)}{q(x)}. \tag{10.14}$$

Note that there is no negative sign before the summation. Hence,

$$I(X;Y) = \mathrm{KL}\left(p(x,y)\|p(x)p(y)\right). \tag{10.15}$$

The KL divergence is also called the *relative entropy*. When $p(x) = 0$ or $q(x) = 0$ for some x, we assume $0 \log_2 \frac{0}{q(x)} = 0$, $p(x) \log_2 \frac{p(x)}{0} = \infty$, and $0 \log_2 \frac{0}{0} = 0$.

The KL "distance" is not symmetric. Neither does it satisfy the triangle inequality. Hence, it is *not* a distance metric. However, it is indeed nonnegative, and $\mathrm{KL}(p(x)\|q(x)) = 0$ implies $p(x) = q(x)$ for any x.

10.2.4 Some Inequalities

The nonnegativity of the KL distance is proved using Jensen's inequality. We have

$$-\mathrm{KL}(p\|q) = \sum_{x:p(x)>0} p(x) \log_2 \frac{q(x)}{p(x)} \leq \log_2 \left(\sum_{x:p(x)>0} p(x) \frac{q(x)}{p(x)} \right)$$

because $\log_2(x)$ is a concave function and $\sum_x p(x) = 1$, $p(x) \geq 0$. Then

$$-\mathrm{KL}(p\|q) \leq \log_2 \sum_{x:p(x)>0} q(x) \leq \log_2 \sum_x q(x) = \log_2 1 = 0.$$

Hence, the KL distance is always nonnegative.

The KL distance reaches 0 if and only if (1) for any x with $p(x) > 0$, $\frac{p(x)}{q(x)} = c$ is a constant (the equality condition of Jensen's inequality) and (2) $\sum_{x:p(x)>0} q(x) = \sum_x q(x) = 1$. Condition (2) means that $q(x) = 0$ when $p(x) = 0$. Hence, $p(x) = cq(x)$ holds for any x. Because $\sum_x p(x) = \sum_x q(x) = 1$, we have $c = 1$—that is, *the KL distance is* 0 *if and only if for any* x, $p(x) = q(x)$.

The nonnegativity of the KL distance has many implications and corollaries:

- The mutual information $I(X;Y)$ is nonnegative. It is 0 if and only if X and Y are independent.
- Let U be the discrete uniform distribution with m events—i.e., $p_U(u) = \frac{1}{m}$ for any u. Then $\mathrm{KL}(X\|U) = \sum_x p(x) \log_2 \frac{p(x)}{1/m} = \log_2 m - H(X)$. Hence, for any X, we have

$$H(X) = \log_2 m - \mathrm{KL}(X\|U), \tag{10.16}$$

$$0 \leq H(X) \leq \log_2 m. \tag{10.17}$$

  That is, $\log_2 m$ is indeed the upper bound of the uncertainty and $\lceil \log_2 m \rceil$ is the longest average length of binary codes. The equality holds only if the distribution is a uniform one.
- $H(X) \geq H(X|Y)$. In other words, knowing additional information (Y) about a random variable (X) will not increase our uncertainty. The proof is simple: $H(X) - H(X|Y) = I(X;Y) \geq 0$. Hence, the equality holds if and only if X and Y are independent. That is, knowing Y will reduce the uncertainty about X, unless they are independent.
- $H(X)+H(Y) \geq H(X,Y)$, and the equality holds if and only if they are independent. The proof is trivial, because $I(X;Y) = H(X) + H(Y) - H(X,Y) \geq 0$.

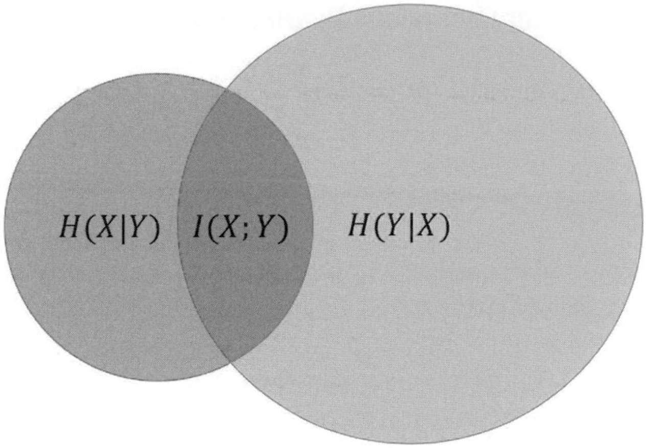

Figure 10.2 Relationships between entropy, conditional entropy, and mutual information. (A black and white version of this figure will appear in some formats. For the color version, please refer to the plate section.)

Figure 10.2 summarizes these relationships. The smaller, red circle is $H(X)$, which is decomposed into two parts: $I(X;Y)$ which is the common information between X and Y (the purple region), and $H(X|Y)$ which is the part of the information about X that is independent of Y. The larger, blue circle is $H(Y)$, composed of two parts $I(X;Y)$ and $H(Y|X)$. The union of the two circles is the entropy of the joint $H(X,Y)$.

The purple area is nonempty if X and Y are dependent—that is, $I(X;Y) > 0$. If X and Y are independent, the two circles do not overlap. In this figure, the region corresponding to $H(X|Y)$ is inside that corresponding to $H(X)$, hence $H(X|Y) \le H(X)$. Similarly, $H(Y|X) \le H(Y)$.

The purple area also indicates $I(X;Y) = I(Y;X)$. However, the two circles are of different sizes, indicating that $H(X|Y) \neq H(Y|X)$ in general.

10.2.5 Entropy of Discrete Distributions

To end this section, we introduce the entropy of some commonly used discrete distributions:

- The entropy of an m-event discrete uniform random variable is $\log_2 m$.
- The entropy of a Bernoulli distribution with success rate $0 < p < 1$ ($p_1 = p$ and $p_2 = 1 - p$) is $-p \log_2 p - (1-p)\log_2(1-p)$.
- The geometric distribution with success rate $0 < p \le 1$ has a p.m.f. $p_i = (1-p)^{i-1}p$, and its entropy is

$$\frac{-(1-p)\log_2(1-p) - p\log_2 p}{p},$$

which is $\frac{1}{p}$ times the entropy of a Bernoulli distribution with the same parameter.

10.3 Information Theory for Continuous Distributions

Entropy can also be computed for continuous random variables, by replacing the summations with integrals.

10.3.1 Differential Entropy

Given a continuous random variable X with p.d.f. $p(x)$, its differential entropy (or simply entropy) is defined as

$$h(X) = -\int p(x) \ln p(x) \,\mathrm{d}x. \tag{10.18}$$

Note that we use the natural logarithm and use h instead of H (and the unit of differential entropy is the *nat*). The integration is supposed to happen only for those x with $p(x) > 0$. In the continuous case, the integration can be infinite, though. Since the definition depends only on the p.d.f., we can also write the differential entropy as $h(p)$.

Let us take the normal distribution as an example. Let $p(x) = N(x; \mu, \sigma^2)$ be a normal p.d.f.; its differential entropy is

$$h(X) = -\int p(x) \left(-\frac{1}{2} \ln(2\pi\sigma^2) - \frac{(x-\mu)^2}{2\sigma^2} \right) \mathrm{d}x \tag{10.19}$$

$$= \frac{1}{2} \ln(2\pi\sigma^2) + \frac{\mathrm{Var}(X)}{2\sigma^2} \tag{10.20}$$

$$= \frac{1}{2} \ln(2\pi e\sigma^2). \tag{10.21}$$

In the above calculation, we used the fact that $\int p(x)\,\mathrm{d}x = 1$ and $\mathrm{Var}(x) = \int p(x)(x-\mu)^2\,\mathrm{d}x = \sigma^2$. The entropy of a standard normal distribution $N(0,1)$ is $\frac{1}{2}\ln(2\pi e)$.

Note that the differential entropy can be zero or negative, which is different from the entropy for discrete random variables. If $\sigma \ll 1$, then the entropy of $N(0,\sigma^2)$ is negative. More precisely, the entropy is negative if $\sigma^2 < \frac{1}{2\pi e} = 0.0585$, or $\sigma < 0.2420$.

The joint entropy of (X, Y) is defined as

$$h(X,Y) = -\int p(x,y) \ln p(x,y) \,\mathrm{d}x\,\mathrm{d}y, \tag{10.22}$$

and can be extended to more random variables. Similarly, the conditional differential entropy is defined as

$$h(X|Y) = -\int p(x,y) \ln p(x|y) \,\mathrm{d}x\,\mathrm{d}y. \tag{10.23}$$

The following equation also holds for conditional entropies:

$$h(X|Y) = h(X,Y) - h(Y) \quad \text{and} \quad h(Y|X) = h(X,Y) - h(X). \tag{10.24}$$

The mutual information between X and Y is

$$I(X;Y) = \int p(x,y) \ln \frac{p(x,y)}{p(x)p(y)} \, dx \, dy, \tag{10.25}$$

and we still have

$$\begin{aligned} I(X;Y) &= h(X) - h(X|Y) & (10.26)\\ &= h(Y) - h(Y|X) & (10.27)\\ &= h(X) + h(Y) - h(X,Y). & (10.28) \end{aligned}$$

Figure 10.2 is still valid if we replace all H with h.

The KL distance (or KL divergence, or relative entropy) for two p.d.f.s $f(x)$ and $g(x)$ defined on the same domain is defined as

$$\mathrm{KL}(f\|g) = \int f(x) \ln \frac{f(x)}{g(x)} \, dx, \tag{10.29}$$

and we still have $\mathrm{KL}(f\|g) \geq 0$, $I(X;Y) \geq 0$, and $h(X|Y) \leq h(X)$. The equality in the last two inequalities holds when X and Y are independent. The equality condition for $\mathrm{KL}(f\|g) \geq 0$ is a little more complex, and requires $f = g$ *almost everywhere*.[3]

- If $p(x)$ is the p.d.f. of a uniform distribution on the range $[a,b]$, its entropy is $\ln(b-a)$.
- If $p(x)$ is the p.d.f. of a normal distribution $N(\mu,\sigma^2)$, then its entropy is $\frac{1}{2}\ln(2\pi e\sigma^2)$.
- If $p(x)$ is the p.d.f. of an exponential distribution—i.e., $p(x) = \lambda e^{-\lambda x}$ for $x \geq 0$ ($\lambda > 0$) and $p(x) = 0$ for $x < 0$—its entropy is $1 - \ln(\lambda)$.
- If $p(x)$ is the p.d.f of a Laplace distribution, i.e.,

  $$p(x) = \frac{1}{2b} \exp\left(-\frac{|x-\mu|}{b}\right), \quad b > 0,$$

  its entropy is $1 + \ln(2b)$.
- If $X > 0$ is a random variable and $\ln(X)$ follows a normal distribution $N(\mu,\sigma^2)$, then X is called a log-normal distribution. Its entropy is $\frac{1}{2}\ln(2\pi e\sigma^2) + \mu$—that is, the entropy of a log-normal random variable X is μ plus the entropy of $\ln(X)$.

10.3.2 Entropy of a Multivariate Gaussian

In this section, we compute the entropy of the d-dimensional multivariate normal distribution

$$p(\boldsymbol{x}) = N(\boldsymbol{x};\boldsymbol{\mu},\Sigma) = (2\pi)^{-\frac{d}{2}}|\Sigma|^{-\frac{1}{2}} \exp\left(-\frac{1}{2}(\boldsymbol{x}-\boldsymbol{\mu})^T\Sigma^{-1}(\boldsymbol{x}-\boldsymbol{\mu})\right)$$

using a series of simplifications.

[3] To fully specify the precise meaning of "almost everywhere" requires knowledge from measure theory, which is beyond the scope of this book. In fact, "$f = g$ almost everywhere" means that the set of elements satisfying $f \neq g$ is of measure zero. For the continuous distributions that we encounter in this book, we can treat it as approximately meaning that the number of elements satisfying $f \neq g$ is at most countably infinite.

First, let the transformation $\boldsymbol{y} = \boldsymbol{x} - \boldsymbol{\mu}$ define another random vector Y. The Jacobian of this transformation is $\frac{\partial \boldsymbol{y}}{\partial \boldsymbol{x}} = I_d$, and its determinant is 1. So, $p_Y(\boldsymbol{y}) = p_X(\boldsymbol{x} - \boldsymbol{\mu})$, and $\mathrm{d}\boldsymbol{y} = \mathrm{d}\boldsymbol{x}$. We have

$$\int p(\boldsymbol{x}) \ln p(\boldsymbol{x})\, \mathrm{d}\boldsymbol{x} = \int p(\boldsymbol{y}) \ln p(\boldsymbol{y})\, \mathrm{d}\boldsymbol{y}. \tag{10.30}$$

In other words, *translating a distribution does not change the differential entropy.* Hence, we need to compute the entropy of just the centered normal $p(\boldsymbol{y}) = N(\boldsymbol{y}; \boldsymbol{0}, \Sigma)$, or $h(Y)$.

Second, we apply the whitening transform to $\boldsymbol{y}$—i.e., $\boldsymbol{z} = \Lambda^{-\frac{1}{2}} U \boldsymbol{y}$ in which $\Sigma = U^T \Lambda U$, U is an orthogonal matrix, Λ is a (positive definite) diagonal matrix, and the new random vector

$$Z \sim N(\boldsymbol{0}, I_d).$$

The Jacobian of this transformation is

$$\frac{\partial \boldsymbol{z}}{\partial \boldsymbol{y}} = \Lambda^{-\frac{1}{2}} U,$$

and the determinant of it is $|\Lambda^{-\frac{1}{2}} U| = |\Lambda|^{-\frac{1}{2}} |U| = |\Lambda|^{-\frac{1}{2}} = |\Sigma|^{-\frac{1}{2}}$ (because $|U| = 1$ and $|\Sigma| = |\Lambda|$). How will this transformation affect $h(Y)$?

Let $Z = AY$, where A is a fixed square positive definite matrix and Y is a random vector. Hence, $Y = A^{-1}Z$. The Jacobian of this transformation is A. Since A is positive definite, its determinant $|A|$ is positive. In other words, $|A|$ and $|\det(A)| = \det(A)$ mean the same thing. So, $p_Z(\boldsymbol{z}) = \frac{1}{|A|} p_Y(A^{-1}\boldsymbol{z})$, and $\mathrm{d}\boldsymbol{z} = |A|\, \mathrm{d}\boldsymbol{y}$. Thus, we have

$$h(Z) = -\int p_Z(\boldsymbol{z}) \ln p_Z(\boldsymbol{z})\, \mathrm{d}\boldsymbol{z} \tag{10.31}$$

$$= -\int \frac{1}{|A|} p_Y(A^{-1}\boldsymbol{z}) \ln \left(\frac{1}{|A|} p_Y(A^{-1}\boldsymbol{z}) \right) \mathrm{d}\boldsymbol{z} \tag{10.32}$$

$$= -\int p_Y(\boldsymbol{y}) \left(\ln \frac{1}{|A|} + \ln p_Y(\boldsymbol{y}) \right) \mathrm{d}\boldsymbol{y} \tag{10.33}$$

$$= -\int p_Y(\boldsymbol{y}) \ln p_Y(\boldsymbol{y})\, \mathrm{d}\boldsymbol{y} + \ln |A| \int p_Y(\boldsymbol{y})\, \mathrm{d}\boldsymbol{y} \tag{10.34}$$

$$= h(Y) + \ln |A|. \tag{10.35}$$

Hence, for a linear transformation $Z = AY$ ($A \succ 0$), we always have

$$h(Z) = h(Y) + \ln |A|. \tag{10.36}$$

Applying this rule to the transformation $\boldsymbol{z} = \Lambda^{-\frac{1}{2}} U \boldsymbol{y}$ (and noting that $|\Lambda^{-\frac{1}{2}} U| = |\Sigma|^{-\frac{1}{2}}$), we get

$$h(Z) = h(Y) + \ln |\Sigma|^{-\frac{1}{2}}.$$

The final step is to compute the entropy $h(Z)$, where Z is a centered spherical normal distribution $N(\mathbf{0}, I_d)$. For independent random variables, the entropy of the joint is the sum of the entropies of the individual random variables. We have computed the entropy of a standard normal distribution as $\frac{1}{2}\ln(2\pi e)$. Thus,

$$h(Z) = \frac{d}{2}\ln(2\pi e).$$

Finally, we have

$$\begin{aligned} h(X) &= h(Y) && (10.37)\\ &= h(Z) - \ln|\Sigma|^{-1/2} && (10.38)\\ &= h(Z) + \ln|\Sigma|^{1/2} && (10.39)\\ &= \frac{d}{2}\ln(2\pi e) + \frac{1}{2}\ln|\Sigma| && (10.40)\\ &= \frac{1}{2}\ln\left((2\pi e)^d|\Sigma|\right). && (10.41) \end{aligned}$$

Through a series of simplifications, we have arrived at a neat conclusion: the entropy of a multivariate normal distribution $X \sim N(\boldsymbol{\mu}, \Sigma)$ is

$$h(X) = \frac{1}{2}\ln\left((2\pi e)^d|\Sigma|\right). \qquad (10.42)$$

10.3.3 The Gaussian as the Maximum Entropy Distribution

Now we are ready to show that the multivariate Gaussian distribution $N(\boldsymbol{\mu}, \Sigma)$ has the largest entropy among distributions whose *mean and entropy exist*, and whose *covariance matrix is* Σ.

Because a translation does not change the entropy, we can assume that the multivariate Gaussian X has a p.d.f.

$$p(\boldsymbol{x}) = (2\pi)^{-\frac{d}{2}}|\Sigma|^{-\frac{1}{2}}\exp\left(-\frac{1}{2}\boldsymbol{x}^T\Sigma^{-1}\boldsymbol{x}\right).$$

Let q be the p.d.f. of another d-dimensional random vector Y; we can assume $\mathbb{E}[\boldsymbol{y}] = \mathbf{0}$, and $\text{Var}(Y) = \mathbb{E}[\boldsymbol{y}\boldsymbol{y}^T] = \Sigma\ (= U^T\Lambda U)$.

One further simplification (which we are familiar with) is to remove the effect of the covariance matrix. Let us define two new random vectors X' and Y' with

$$\boldsymbol{x}' = \Lambda^{-\frac{1}{2}}U\boldsymbol{x}, \quad \boldsymbol{y}' = \Lambda^{-\frac{1}{2}}U\boldsymbol{y}.$$

Then $X' \sim N(\mathbf{0}, I_d)$, $\mathbb{E}[\boldsymbol{y}'] = \mathbf{0}$, and $\text{Var}(Y') = I_d$. We use p' and q' to denote their p.d.f.s, respectively. The entropy of X' is $\frac{1}{2}\ln\left((2\pi e)^d\right)$.

In the above, we have proved $h(X') = h(X) + \ln|\Sigma|^{-\frac{1}{2}}$ and $h(Y') = h(Y) + \ln|\Sigma|^{-\frac{1}{2}}$. Hence, to prove that X is the maximum entropy distribution, we need just to show $h(X') \geq h(Y')$.

We start from $\mathrm{KL}(q'\|p') \geq 0$, because that is the inequality we are familiar with:

$$0 \leq \mathrm{KL}(q'\|p') \tag{10.43}$$

$$= \int q'(\boldsymbol{x}) \ln \frac{q'(\boldsymbol{x})}{p'(\boldsymbol{x})} \,\mathrm{d}\boldsymbol{x} \tag{10.44}$$

$$= \int q'(\boldsymbol{x}) \ln q'(\boldsymbol{x}) \,\mathrm{d}\boldsymbol{x} - \int q'(\boldsymbol{x}) \ln p'(\boldsymbol{x}) \,\mathrm{d}\boldsymbol{x} \tag{10.45}$$

$$= -h(Y') - \int q'(\boldsymbol{x}) \ln p'(\boldsymbol{x}) \,\mathrm{d}\boldsymbol{x}. \tag{10.46}$$

We can pause here and take a closer look at the term

$$-\int q'(\boldsymbol{x}) \ln p'(\boldsymbol{x}) \,\mathrm{d}\boldsymbol{x}.$$

This term is called the *cross entropy* between q' and p'. For two p.d.f.s p and q defined on the same domain, the cross entropy is defined for continuous and discrete distributions as[4]

$$\mathrm{CE}(p,q) = -\int p(\boldsymbol{x}) \ln q(\boldsymbol{x}) \,\mathrm{d}\boldsymbol{x}, \tag{10.47}$$

$$\mathrm{CE}(p,q) = -\sum_{x} p(\boldsymbol{x}) \log_2 q(\boldsymbol{x}), \tag{10.48}$$

respectively. Note that cross entropy is not symmetric. We have

$$\mathrm{CE}(q,p) = h(q) + \mathrm{KL}(q\|p) \quad \text{and} \quad \mathrm{CE}(p,q) = h(p) + \mathrm{KL}(p\|q) \tag{10.49}$$

for any two p.d.f.s p and q. These equalities also hold for discrete random vectors by changing h to H.

Later we will show that cross entropy is very useful for machine learning and pattern recognition. However, for now, if we can show $\mathrm{CE}(q',p') = h(p')$ (when p' is $N(\mathbf{0}, I_d)$ and q' has equal covariance matrix to p'), the proof is finished. Under these assumptions, we expand the cross entropy:

$$-\int q'(\boldsymbol{x}) \ln p'(\boldsymbol{x}) \,\mathrm{d}\boldsymbol{x} = -\int q'(\boldsymbol{x}) \left(\ln((2\pi)^{-\frac{d}{2}}) - \frac{1}{2}\boldsymbol{x}^T\boldsymbol{x} \right) \mathrm{d}\boldsymbol{x} \tag{10.50}$$

$$= \frac{1}{2} \ln\left((2\pi)^d\right) \int q'(\boldsymbol{x}) \,\mathrm{d}\boldsymbol{x} + \frac{1}{2} \int q'(\boldsymbol{x})\boldsymbol{x}^T\boldsymbol{x} \,\mathrm{d}\boldsymbol{x}. \tag{10.51}$$

Note that $\int q'(\boldsymbol{x}) \,\mathrm{d}\boldsymbol{x} = 1$ (since q' is a p.d.f.), and

$$\int q'(\boldsymbol{x})\boldsymbol{x}^T\boldsymbol{x} \,\mathrm{d}\boldsymbol{x} = \sum_{i=1}^{d} \int q'(\boldsymbol{x}) x_i^2 \,\mathrm{d}\boldsymbol{x}$$

[4] There does not seem to be widely accepted notation for cross entropy. We use CE in this book.

in which $\boldsymbol{x} = (x_1, x_2, \ldots, x_d)^T$ and $\int q'(\boldsymbol{x}) x_i^2 \, d\boldsymbol{x}$ is the (i,i)th entry in the covariance matrix of Y', i.e.,

$$\int q'(\boldsymbol{x}) x_i^2 \, d\boldsymbol{x} = 1.$$

Hence, the cross entropy equals

$$-\int q'(\boldsymbol{x}) \ln p'(\boldsymbol{x}) \, d\boldsymbol{x} = \frac{1}{2} \ln\left((2\pi)^d\right) + \frac{d}{2} = \frac{1}{2} \ln\left((2\pi e)^d\right), \tag{10.52}$$

which is exactly $h(X')$. In other words, if a distribution has bounded mean value and the same covariance as a Gaussian, then the cross entropy between this distribution and the multivariate normal distribution equals the entropy of the Gaussian.

Putting all these equations together, we have $0 \le -h(Y') + h(X')$. Hence, $h(Y') \le h(X')$ and consequently $h(Y) \le h(X)$, which finishes the proof of the Gaussian's maximum entropy property.

10.4 Information Theory in ML and PR

After introducing some basic concepts and facts in information theory, in this section we describe some applications of information theory in machine learning and pattern recognition, but will refrain from diving into their technical details.

10.4.1 Maximum Entropy

We know that the maximum entropy distribution is the distribution with the highest uncertainty under certain assumptions, or without commitment to or favoring any particular point in the space of all distributions that follow these assumptions. For example, the continuous uniform distribution in the range $[a,b]$ treats all points in this range equally.

Sometimes our prior knowledge or training data specifies some constraints. The principle of maximum entropy states that we should seek a distribution that

- satisfies these constraints and
- has maximum entropy

among all distributions that satisfy the constraints. The principle of maximum entropy is widely used in natural language processing.

Let us assume that we need to build a probability mass function p that will translate a Chinese word into English with some randomness. We have a large corpus and know that there are four possible candidates a, b, c, d. Hence, we have a constraint $p(\texttt{a}) + p(\texttt{b}) + p(\texttt{c}) + p(\texttt{d}) = 1$. We also require $p(\texttt{a}) \ge 0$ (and similarly for b, c, and d). From the corpus we observe that the translations a or c appear roughly once every three times, which leads to another constraint: $p(\texttt{a}) + p(\texttt{c}) = \frac{1}{3}$. Then the translation probability p can be any p.m.f. that satisfies these six constraints. However, the maximum entropy solution will find a p.m.f. that has the largest entropy. Maximum entropy leads to translations that vary and may be more attractive to the readers.

A similar situation occurs in specifying prior distributions. In MAP or Bayesian learning, the prior distribution should encode our knowledge about the parameters (e.g., range of values, approximate mean values). However, we do not want to introduce any bias apart from the prior knowledge. Hence, the one with maximum entropy is often used—for example, the uninformative prior (uniform distribution in a range) or a normal prior (which is the maximum entropy prior when the variance is fixed).

10.4.2 Minimum Cross Entropy

In a multiclass classification problem, if the logistic regression model is used, the classification model is called the multinomial logistic regression (which is an extension of the logistic regression method) or softmax regression. In an m-class problem, m linear directions $\boldsymbol{\beta}_j$ $(1 \le j \le m)$ are learned, each corresponding to one class. For any example $\boldsymbol{x}$, the values $\boldsymbol{x}^T \boldsymbol{\beta}_j$ are processed by the softmax transformation and form a probability estimate, i.e.,

$$\Pr(y = j|\boldsymbol{x}) \approx f^j(\boldsymbol{x}) = \frac{\exp(\boldsymbol{x}^T \boldsymbol{\beta}_j)}{\sum_{j'=1}^{m} \exp(\boldsymbol{x}^T \boldsymbol{\beta}_{j'})}, \tag{10.53}$$

in which $f^j(\boldsymbol{x})$ is the estimated probability for $\boldsymbol{x}$ belonging to the jth class. In a problem with n training examples $(\boldsymbol{x}_i, y_i)$ $(1 \le i \le n,\ y_i \in \mathcal{Y} = \{1,2,\ldots,m\})$, softmax regression maximizes the objective

$$\sum_{i=1}^{n} \sum_{j=1}^{m} [\![y_i = j]\!] \log_2 f^j(\boldsymbol{x}_i), \tag{10.54}$$

in which $[\![\cdot]\!]$ is the indicator function. Similarly to what we have analyzed for logistic regression, softmax regression aims at making the estimated probabilities $f^j(\boldsymbol{x}_i)$ compatible with the training set. In logistic regression, the objective is to maximize $\prod_{i=1}^{n} f(\boldsymbol{x}_i)^{y_i} (1 - f(\boldsymbol{x}_i))^{1-y_i}$ $(y_i \in \{0,1\})$, which is a special case of Eq. (10.54) if we take a base-2 logarithm.

Now consider two distributions p and q, where p is the probability observed from the training set $p_{ij} = [\![y_i = j]\!]$ and q is the probability estimated by our model $q_{ij} = f^j(\boldsymbol{x}_i)$. Then maximizing the above objective is equivalent to minimizing

$$\mathrm{CE}(p,q) = -\sum_{i=1}^{n} \sum_{j=1}^{m} p_{ij} \log_2 q_{ij}. \tag{10.55}$$

Hence, multinomial logistic regression seeks to minimize the cross entropy.

In general, if we have a target distribution p (e.g., based on the training set) and a learned estimate q, minimizing the cross entropy will force the estimate q to simulate the target p. Hence, the cross entropy between target and estimated distributions is called the *cross entropy loss*.

The cross entropy loss is popular in neural network learning. For example, a deep learning classification model can have m nodes as the output, estimating the probability of an example belonging to each of the m classes, respectively. When an example $\boldsymbol{x}_i$ belongs to the jth class (i.e., $y_i = j$), the target distribution is a length m vector whose entries are all 0 except for the jth entry (whose value is 1). The loss incurred by $(\boldsymbol{x}_i, y_i)$ is the cross entropy between this target distribution and the output of the network.

Since $\mathrm{CE}(p,q) = H(p) + \mathrm{KL}(p\|q)$ and $H(p)$ (entropy of the target distribution) is constant, minimizing the cross entropy is equivalent to minimizing the Kullback–Leibler divergence. This fact matches our intuition: to make q similar to p, we simply minimize the "distance" between them.

10.4.3 Feature Selection

Mutual information is widely used in feature selection. Given D-dimensional examples $\boldsymbol{x}$, we treat each dimension as a feature. There might be ample reason to reduce it to d-dimensional ($d \leq D$ and usually $d \ll D$). For example, some dimensions could be noise, or D might be so large that the CPU and memory costs are too high to process the problem on ordinary computers. Dimensionality reduction techniques such as PCA or FLD use all D dimensions to generate d new features (i.e., feature *extraction*). Instead, we may also choose a subset of d dimensions from the original number D, which is feature *selection*.

Suppose the original feature set is indexed by $O = \{1,2,\dots,D\}$ and $S \subseteq O$ is a subset of O. We use $f_1, f_2, \dots, f_D$ to denote the original feature dimensions, and $f_S = \{f_i | i \in S\}$ is the subset of features in S. If $\varphi(S)$ measures the fitness of S for our task, feature selection then seeks to maximize the fitness, as

$$\operatorname*{arg\,max}_{S \subseteq O} \varphi(S). \tag{10.56}$$

For example, if y represents the labels of training examples in a classification problem, we can set

$$\varphi_1(S) = I(f_S; y)$$

to be the fitness measure. If $I(f_S; y)$ is high, this means that f_S contains a large amount of information to describe the label y; hence mutual information is a suitable fitness measure for feature selection.

There is one major issue with this simple fitness measure: the complexity of estimating $I(f_S; y)$ grows exponentially with $|S|$, the size of S. The curse of dimensionality makes estimating $I(f_S; y)$ impractical. One idea is to use the marginal distributions to replace the joint distribution of f_S, that is,

$$\varphi_2(S) = \sum_{i \in S} I(f_i; y).$$

The complexity now grows linearly with $|S|$.

However, another problem will occur: the selected features may be redundant. In an extreme example, if all dimensions in a problem are exactly the same, then all D dimensions will be selected. But any single dimension will give the same classification accuracy as the accuracy using all dimensions. Hence, *redundant* features are not welcome in feature selection. One obvious treatment is to require the selected features to have minimal redundancy among themselves.

The redundancy between two selected features f_i and f_j can be measured as $I(f_i; f_j)$. To avoid the curse of dimensionality, we can use these pairwise redundancy numbers to measure the redundancy in a set S:

$$\sum_{i \in S, j \in S} I(f_i; f_j).$$

Hence, the overall objective can be a mix of $\sum_{i \in S} I(f_i; y)$ (to be maximized) and $\sum_{i \in S, j \in S} I(f_i; f_j)$ (to be minimized).

Now we have all necessary components to introduce the mRMR (minimum redundancy–maximum relevance) feature selection method. We introduce D binary variables $\boldsymbol{s} = (s_1, s_2, \ldots, s_D)^T$, $s_i \in \{0, 1\}$, where $s_i = 1$ means that the ith dimension is selected and $s_i = 0$ means that it is not. The mRMR method is

$$\max_{s \in \{0,1\}^D} \left(\frac{\sum_{i=1}^n s_i I(f_i; y)}{\sum_{i=1}^D s_i} - \frac{\sum_{i=1}^D \sum_{j=1}^D s_i s_j I(f_i; f_j)}{\left(\sum_{i=1}^D s_i\right)^2} \right). \tag{10.57}$$

Note that the selected subset S is formed by those i with $s_i = 1$.

Since $\boldsymbol{s} \in \{0, 1\}^D$ has 2^D candidates, the above optimization is difficult to solve. Various approaches are used in feature selection methods to handle this type of difficulty. A greedy method can first select one single feature with the largest fitness, then add features one by one. The added feature maximizes the difference between two of the terms: its own fitness and the sum of its pairwise relevance with features that are already chosen. The greedy method is suboptimal, and leads the optimization process to a local minimum.[5] We can also solve the optimization problem approximately using advanced algorithms.

Feature selection is a huge subject, and we have only introduced one feature selection method in this section. There are many research papers, software packages, and surveys available for feature selection.

10.5 Decision Trees

The decision tree is an important method in machine learning and pattern recognition. We will introduce the decision tree model, but only one component is introduced in detail: node splitting using the information gain criterion.

[5] However, for a certain class of functions, called submodular functions, the greedy algorithm works fine. We can treat the minimization of submodular functions as roughly the counterpart of convex optimization in the discrete space.

10.5.1 The XOR Problem and Its Decision Tree Model

The exclusive OR gate (XOR) problem is famous for being *linearly inseparable*. As shown in Figure 10.3a, four points $(1,1)$, $(1,-1)$, $(-1,1)$ and $(-1,-1)$ belong to two classes (blue circle and red square).[6] It is obvious that given a point (x_1,x_2), it belongs to the positive class (denoted by blue circles) if $x_1x_2 = 1$, and the negative class (denoted by red squares) if $x_1x_2 = -1$. It is also obvious that no single line can separate examples of the two classes perfectly—e.g., linear SVM. Although we can use more complex classifiers such as kernel SVM to solve the XOR problem, the decision tree is a conceptually simple method to solve it (and many other problems).

Figure 10.3b shows the decision tree model for the XOR problem. The model is organized in a tree structure. Given an example $(x_1,x_2) = (1,-1)$, we start from the root of the tree. The root node depends on x_1, and is split into two subtrees depending on whether the value of x_1 is 1 or -1. In our example, $x_1 = 1$ and we traverse to the left-hand subtree. This node depends on x_2. Since $x_2 = -1$ in our example, we traverse to its right-hand subtree. The right-hand subtree is a single node, which provides a decision (red square, or negative). Hence, our example is classified as negative by the decision tree model.

A decision tree has internal nodes and leaf nodes. An internal node depends on an attribute, which is usually one dimension in the input feature vector but can also be a function of several dimensions. Based on the value of an example, an internal node can route the decision to one of the child subtrees. An internal node can have two or more subtrees. If the root of the selected subtree is still an internal node, the routing process is iterated until the example reaches a leaf node, which gives a prediction.

Given a training set $\{(\boldsymbol{x}_i, y_i)\}_{i=1}^n$, the root node will process all n training examples. Depending on the evaluation result on the root node, training examples will be routed to different subtrees, until they reach leaf nodes. If a leaf node has n' training examples, they will jointly determine the prediction of this leaf node—e.g., by voting on these n' examples. Suppose a decision tree is a perfect binary tree (i.e., every node has two subtrees and all leaf nodes have the same depth D); then the number of leaf nodes is 2^{D-1}. Hence decision trees can model complex nonlinear decisions. And if the evaluations at internal nodes depend on a single feature, the prediction of a decision tree model is very fast. Furthermore, decision tree algorithms can naturally deal with categorical data.

However, we also anticipate many issues in decision tree learning, including the following examples:

- How should we choose the split criterion for an internal node?
- When should we stop splitting? We can split an internal node if there are two or more training examples associated with it. However, if a leaf node has only one training example, its prediction may be heavily affected by small amounts of noise

[6] The original XOR problem uses coordinates 1 and 0, not 1 and -1. However, the problem shown in Figure 10.3a is equivalent to the original XOR problem.

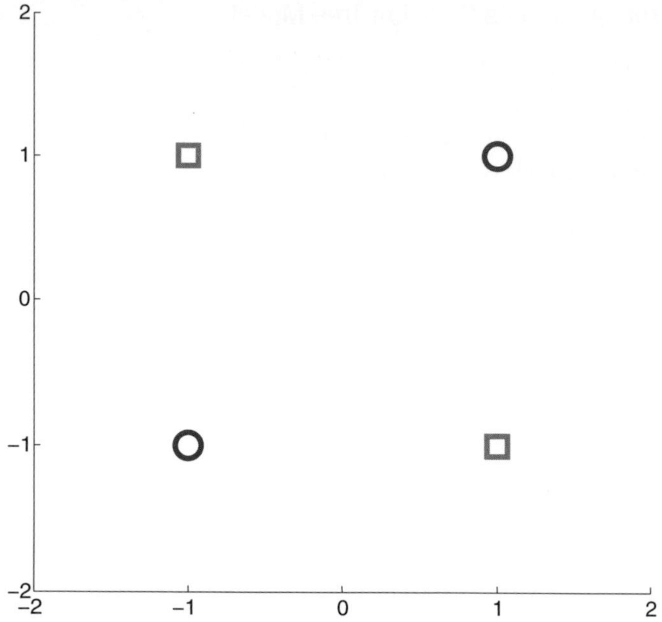

(a) The XOR problem

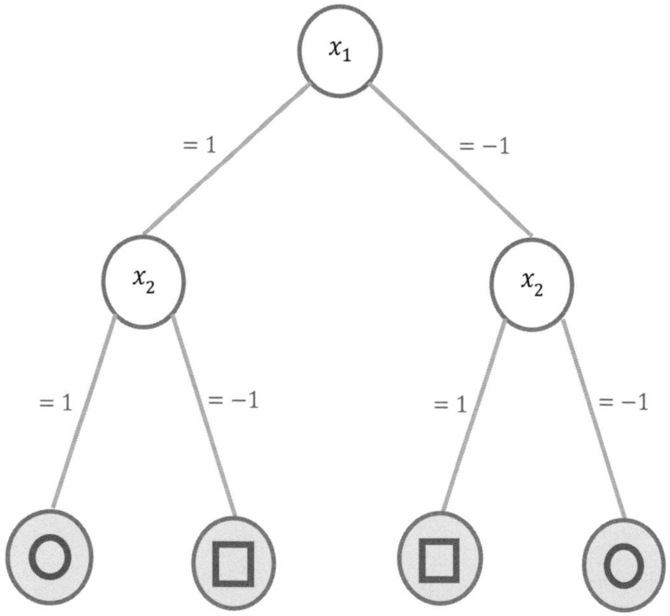

(b) The XOR decision tree

Figure 10.3 The XOR problem and its decision tree model. (A black and white version of this figure will appear in some formats. For the color version, please refer to the plate section.)

in the training data. That is, if the tree depth is too large, the decision tree will overfit. Similarly, a tree that is too shallow may underfit.

- How can a decision tree deal with real-valued variables?
- If the input feature vector has many dimensions and every dimension is only marginally useful for classification, a decision tree using one dimension for node split is inefficient.
- There exist problems that are difficult for a single decision tree to handle.

We will discuss only one proposal for the first issue: use information gain to decide the routing/splitting strategy for one node when the features are all categorical. In the decision tree literature, many proposals have been made to solve these issues. For example, one can create a deep tree and prune nodes that may cause overfitting. There are also ways to split nodes using real-valued features and the combination of a set of features. When a problem is difficult for a single tree, the ensemble of many trees (i.e., a decision forest) usually has higher accuracy than a single tree. Readers interested in decision trees can find more details in the literature.

10.5.2 Information-Gain-Based Node Split

Let us examine a hypothetical example. Suppose 30 male and 60 female students are in a classroom, and we want to predict their gender based on some feature values. If we use height as the root node's attribute and use 170 cm as a threshold, we get the two subtrees in Figure 10.4.

The root node is split into two new nodes, which seems more friendly for gender classification. For example, if we set the right-hand child node as a leaf node and predict all examples in that node as female, the error rate is only $\frac{3}{57} \approx 5\%$. The left-hand child node, if predicted as male, has the relatively higher error rate of $\frac{6}{33} = 18\%$,

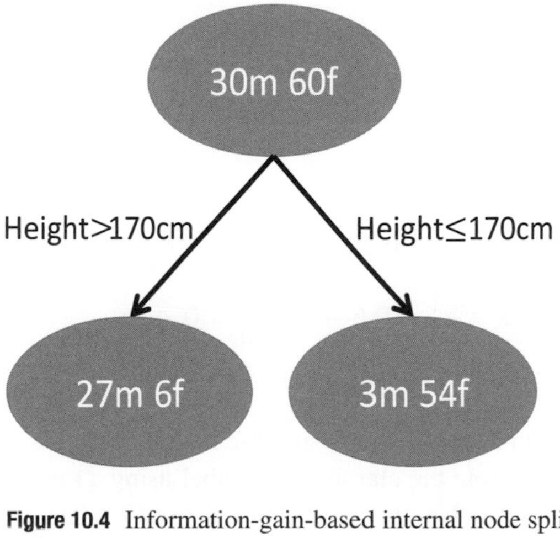

Figure 10.4 Information-gain-based internal node split.

which may require further splitting. In the root node, the best possible error rate is $\frac{30}{90} \approx 33\%$, which is higher than that of both its children.

The classification error is reduced after a node split, because the new nodes are more *pure*—i.e., the distribution of labels of training examples becomes more concentrated. In information theory, we can say that the entropies of the new nodes are both smaller than the root node. Hence, the information gain criterion tries to find a split that will make the difference in the entropies greatest.

Let us suppose that an internal node is associated with a set of training examples T. It is split based on a categorical feature, which has K possible values. There are K new nodes, each associated with a set of training examples T_i, where $\bigcup_{k=1}^{K} T_i = T$ and $T_i \cap T_j = \emptyset$ if $i \neq j$ (in which $\emptyset$ is the empty set). The proportion of examples in T_i with respect to T is

$$w_i = \frac{|T_i|}{\sum_{k=1}^{K} |T_k|},$$

and $\sum_{k=1}^{K} w_k = 1$. The *information gain* measures the reduction in uncertainty of our prediction, defined as

$$H(T) - \sum_{k=1}^{K} w_i H(T_i), \tag{10.58}$$

in which $H(T)$ is the entropy of labels in the set T.

In our hypothetical example,

$$H(T) = -\frac{1}{3}\log_2\frac{1}{3} - \frac{2}{3}\log_2\frac{2}{3} = 0.9183.$$

The left-hand child has $w_1 = \frac{33}{90}$ and

$$H(T_1) = -\frac{27}{33}\log_2\frac{27}{33} - \frac{6}{33}\log_2\frac{6}{33} = 0.6840.$$

Similarly, the right-hand child has $w_2 = \frac{57}{90}$ and

$$H(T_2) = -\frac{3}{57}\log_2\frac{3}{57} - \frac{54}{57}\log_2\frac{54}{57} = 0.2975.$$

Hence, the information gain is

$$\begin{aligned} & H(T) - w_1 H(T_1) - w_2 H(T_2) \\ &= 0.9183 - \frac{33}{90} \times 0.6840 - \frac{57}{90} \times 0.2975 \\ &= 0.4793. \end{aligned}$$

At an internal node, we can test all features and use the one with the greatest information gain to split it. If we denote the classification label using a random variable L and the feature that is used to calculate the information gain as F, then $\sum_{k=1}^{K} w_i H(T_i)$

is in fact the conditional entropy $H(L|F)$ computed using the training set. Hence, the information gain is

$$H(L) - H(L|F) = I(L;F),$$

or in other words, the uncertainty in L that is reduced by knowing F. Hence it is reasonable to choose the feature that leads to the largest reduction in uncertainty, which equals the mutual information. Because $I(L;F) \geq 0$, the information gain is always nonnegative.

Of course, we can also find the feature that minimizes $w_i H(T_i)$, because $H(T)$ does not change when different features are used.

10.6 Miscellaneous Notes and Additional Resources

For more results on information theory, please refer to the classic textbook Cover & Thomas (2006). MacKay (2003) is another accessible classic book on this topic.

For detailed treatment of priority queues and the proof of the optimality of Huffman code, please refer to Cormen et al. (2009).

We briefly mentioned natural language processing in this chapter, for which a good starting point is Manning & Schütze (1999).

The learning algorithms of logistic or multinomial logistic (softmax) regression are beyond the scope of this book. Interested readers may refer to Bishop (2006, Chapter 4).

Pointers to various feature selection resources can be found in the survey Guyon & Elisseeff (2003). The mRMR feature selection framework was proposed in Peng et al. (2005).

Submodular functions are very important in combinatorial optimization, and Lee (2004) can be a good starting point on this topic.

Also, there are ample resources for decision trees (Quinlan 1992, Breiman et al. 1984, Safavian & Landgrebe 1991) and (random) decision forests (Breiman 2001, Criminisi et al. 2012).

Exercises

10.1 (Huffman tree for Fibonacci numbers) The Fibonacci numbers are a sequence of numbers F_n $(n \geq 1)$, defined by

$$F_n = F_{n-1} + F_{n-2} \quad \forall n > 2 \in \mathbb{N}, \tag{10.59}$$

$$F_1 = F_2 = 1. \tag{10.60}$$

(a) Write out the first six Fibonacci numbers.

(b) Prove that for any positive integer n,

$$F_n = \frac{\alpha^n - \beta^n}{\sqrt{5}} = \frac{\alpha^n - \beta^n}{\alpha - \beta},$$

in which $\alpha = \frac{1+\sqrt{5}}{2} \approx 1.618$ and $\beta = \frac{1-\sqrt{5}}{2} \approx -0.618$.

(c) Prove that

$$\sum_{i=1}^{n} F_i = F_{n+2} - 1.$$

Hence, $\frac{F_i}{F_{n+2}-1}$ $(1 \le i \le n)$ forms the p.m.f. of a valid discrete distribution.

(d) Prove that

$$\sum_{i=1}^{n} i F_i = n F_{n+2} - F_{n+3} + 2.$$

(e) The p.m.f. of a discrete distribution is formed by $\frac{F_i}{F_7-1}$ $(1 \le i \le 5)$. Draw the Huffman tree for this distribution. In a more general case, what will the Huffman tree be for the distribution $\frac{F_i}{F_{n+2}-1}$ $(1 \le i \le n)$?

(f) Prove that the average number of required bits for the tree corresponding to $\frac{F_i}{F_{n+2}-1}$ $(1 \le i \le n)$ is

$$B_n = \frac{F_{n+4} - (n+4)}{F_{n+2} - 1}.$$

(g) What is $\lim_{n\to\infty} B_n$? That is, if n is large, how many bits will the Huffman tree use to encode the distribution $\frac{F_i}{F_{n+2}-1}$ $(1 \le i \le n)$?

10.2 Answer the following questions.

(a) For a function d to be a distance metric, what are the properties that d must satisfy?

(b) Is the KL divergence a valid distance metric? Use the following example to illustrate which properties are satisfied (or not satisfied) by the KL divergence.

In this example, we consider three discrete distributions that have only two possible outcomes. The p.m.f.s of these three distributions are specified by

$$A = \left(\frac{1}{2}, \frac{1}{2}\right), \tag{10.61}$$

$$B = \left(\frac{1}{4}, \frac{3}{4}\right), \tag{10.62}$$

$$C = \left(\frac{1}{8}, \frac{7}{8}\right). \tag{10.63}$$

Use pen and paper to check each of the properties on this example.

(c) Write a program to verify your calculations. Be succinct in writing the program.

10.3 Prove that

$$\mathrm{CE}(p,q) \ge h(p).$$

When will the equality hold? (Hint: Use the fact $\mathrm{CE}(p,q) = h(p) + \mathrm{KL}(p\|q)$.)

10.4 (Log sum inequality) In this problem, we will prove the log sum inequality and show some of its applications to information theory.

(a) Prove that $f(x) = x \log_2 x$ $(x > 0)$ is strictly convex.

(b) Let us define $0 \log_2 0 = 0$, $0 \log_2 \frac{0}{0} = 0$, and $x \log_2 \frac{x}{0} = \infty$ for $x > 0$. These definitions are reasonable. For example, because $\lim_{x \to 0^+} x \log_2 x = 0$, it makes sense to define $0 \log_2 0 = 0$.

Consider two sequences of nonnegative numbers $a_1, a_2, \ldots, a_n$ and $b_1, b_2, \ldots, b_n$. Prove

$$\sum_{i=1}^{n} a_i \log_2 \frac{a_i}{b_i} \geq \left(\sum_{i=1}^{n} a_i \right) \log_2 \left(\frac{\sum_{i=1}^{n} a_i}{\sum_{i=1}^{n} b_i} \right). \tag{10.64}$$

This inequality is called the *log sum inequality*. Although we use $\log_2$ here, any other base can be used in the logarithm. Show that the equality holds if and only if there exists a constant c such that $a_i = b_i c$ for all $1 \leq i \leq n$.

(c) (Gibbs' inequality) *Gibbs' inequality* is named after the American scientist Josiah Willard Gibbs. It states that for any two distributions p and q, the entropy of p is less than or equal to the cross entropy $\mathrm{CE}(p,q)$, and the equality holds if and only if $p = q$. That is,

$$H(p) \leq \mathrm{CE}(p,q). \tag{10.65}$$

We have already proved this fact in the previous problem by using (i) $\mathrm{CE}(p,q) = H(p) + \mathrm{KL}(p\|q)$ and (ii) $\mathrm{KL}(p\|q) \geq 0$.

Now, use the log sum inequality to prove Gibbs' inequality. Note that this provides another way to prove $\mathrm{KL}(p\|q) \geq 0$.

10.5 In this problem, we present yet another way to prove the nonnegative property of the Kullback–Leibler distance.

(a) Prove that for any $x > 0$, we have $\ln x \leq x - 1$. When will the equality hold?

(b) Use this result to prove $\mathrm{KL}(p\|q) \geq 0$ and that the equality holds if and only if $p = q$. You can limit your proof to the discrete random variable case.

10.6 Let X be a continuous random variable with a p.d.f. $q(x)$. Suppose $q(x) > 0$ when $x \geq 0$, and $q(x) = 0$ for $x < 0$. Furthermore, suppose the mean of X is $\mu > 0$ and its entropy exists.

Show that the exponential distribution with parameter $\lambda = \frac{1}{\mu}$ is the maximum entropy distribution under these constraints.

Part IV

Handling Diverse Data Formats

11 Sparse and Misaligned Data

In the learning and recognition methods we have introduced so far, we have not made strong assumptions about the data: nearest neighbor, SVM, distance metric learning, normalization, and decision trees do not explicitly assume distributional properties of the data; PCA and FLD are optimal solutions under certain data assumptions, but they work well in many other situations too; parametric probabilistic models assume certain functional forms of the underlying data distribution, but GMM and nonparametric probabilistic methods relax these assumptions.

Many types of data in the real world, however, exhibit strong characteristics that cannot be ignored. On the one hand, some data properties (such as sparsity) are helpful to obtain better representation and accuracy if they are properly utilized. On the other hand, some data properties are adversarial—they will seriously hurt a pattern recognition system if they are not appropriately handled (such as misaligned data).

In this chapter, we will discuss two examples that handle such good or bad data characteristics: sparse machine learning and dynamic time warping (DTW).

11.1 Sparse Machine Learning

As previously mentioned, a vector is *sparse* if many of its dimensions are zero. If a vector is not sparse, we say it is *dense*. However, in sparse machine learning, we usually do not mean that the input features are sparse when we say that some data exhibit the sparse property. Given an input vector $\boldsymbol{x}$, sparse machine learning often transforms $\boldsymbol{x}$ into a new *representation* $\boldsymbol{y}$, and the learning process ensures that the new representation $\boldsymbol{y}$ is sparse.

11.1.1 Sparse PCA?

Given a training set $\{\boldsymbol{x}_i\}$ ($\boldsymbol{x}_i \in \mathbb{R}^D$, $1 \le i \le n$), let the new representation for $\boldsymbol{x}_i$ be $\boldsymbol{y}_i \in \mathbb{R}^d$.[1] For example, in principal component analysis, $\boldsymbol{y}_i = E_d^T(\boldsymbol{x}_i - \bar{\boldsymbol{x}}) \in \mathbb{R}^d$, in which E_d is comprised of the eigenvectors of the covariance matrix of $\boldsymbol{x}$, corresponding to the d largest eigenvalues. The PCA parameters E_d are learned such that $\|\boldsymbol{y}_i - E_d^T(\boldsymbol{x}_i - \bar{\boldsymbol{x}})\|^2$ is smallest in the average squared error sense.

[1] For now we do not consider the labels for $\boldsymbol{x}_i$.

The new PCA representation $\boldsymbol{y}_i$, however, is not sparse. In order to make $\boldsymbol{y}_i$ sparse, a regularization term is needed. For example, to learn a sparse representation for $\boldsymbol{x}_i$, we can solve the optimization

$$\min_{\boldsymbol{y}_i} \|\boldsymbol{y}_i - E_d^T(\boldsymbol{x}_i - \bar{\boldsymbol{x}})\|^2 + \lambda \|\boldsymbol{y}_i\|_0, \tag{11.1}$$

where $\lambda > 0$ is a trade-off parameter between small reconstruction error and the sparsity of $\boldsymbol{y}_i$, and $\|\cdot\|_0$ is the ℓ_0 "norm." Because $\|\boldsymbol{y}_i\|_0$ is the number of nonzero elements in $\boldsymbol{y}_i$, minimizing this term encourages the solution to have many zero elements—i.e., to be sparse.

There are at least two issues with this formulation. First, the ℓ_0 "norm" is not continuous (let alone differentiable), which makes the optimization very difficult. Second, since E_d is proven to result in the smallest reconstruction error, enforcing sparsity in $\boldsymbol{y}_i$ probably will lead to large reconstruction error because obviously a sparse $\boldsymbol{y}_i$ will be significantly different from $E_d^T(\boldsymbol{x} - \bar{\boldsymbol{x}})$.

There are established solutions to these problems: use the ℓ_1 norm to replace the ℓ_0 "norm," and learn a good *dictionary* from the training data to replace E_d. We will introduce these two methods in the next two subsections. To learn a sparse PCA, we will replace E_d with a dictionary D and learn it using the training data; and we need to replace $\|\boldsymbol{y}_i\|_0$ with $\|\boldsymbol{y}_i\|_1$.

11.1.2 Using the ℓ_1 Norm to Induce Sparsity

A regularizer $\|\boldsymbol{x}\|_1$ will also encourage the elements of the solution $\boldsymbol{x}^\star$ to be zero. Hence we often *relax* an ℓ_0 constraint to the ℓ_1 constraint.

The ℓ_1 norm is defined as

$$\|\boldsymbol{x}\| = \sum_{i=1}^{d} |x_i|,$$

in which x_i is the ith element in $\boldsymbol{x}$. This function is convex, which is easy to verify. It is also a continuous function, and its gradients exist except when $x_i = 0$ for at least one i. Overall, the ℓ_1 norm is friendly to optimization and a good *surrogate* for the ℓ_0 "norm."

But why does $\|\boldsymbol{x}\|_1$ as a regularizer lead to sparse solutions? We show some of the intuition using a simple example.

Consider a minimization objective

$$f(x) = \frac{1}{2}x^2 - cx,$$

in which $c \in \mathbb{R}$ is a constant. If we add a regularizer $\lambda|x|$ ($\lambda\|x\|_1 = \lambda|x|$) to $f(x)$ and denote it by $g(x)$, the optimization problem becomes

$$x^\star = \arg\min_x g(x) \tag{11.2}$$
$$= \arg\min_x f(x) + \lambda|x| \tag{11.3}$$
$$= \arg\min_x \frac{1}{2}x^2 - cx + \lambda|x|, \tag{11.4}$$

in which $\lambda > 0$. It is obvious that $g(-\infty) = \infty$, $g(\infty) = \infty$, and $g(0) = 0$. Because $|c| < \infty$ and $\lambda > 0$, there does not exist an x such that $g(x) = -\infty$. Hence, there is a global minimum for $g(x) = f(x) + \lambda|x|$.

Note that $g(x)$ is differentiable except at $x = 0$. Its derivative is $x - c - \lambda$ when $x < 0$, and $x - c + \lambda$ when $x > 0$. When $x = 0$, the left derivative is $-c - \lambda$ and its right derivative is $-c + \lambda$. Hence, the optimal value $x^\star$ can happen in one of only two cases:

- $x^\star$ is at the nondifferentiable point—i.e., $x^\star = 0$, or
- one of the two gradient formulas is zero—i.e., $x^\star = c + \lambda$ or $x^\star = c - \lambda$.

Because $\lambda > 0$, the point $P_1 = (0, -c + \lambda)$ is always above the point $P_2 = (0, -c - \lambda)$. There are three possible scenarios for the derivatives:

- P_1 is above or on the x-axis but P_2 is on or below it, as shown in Figure 11.1a. This can happen only when $-c + \lambda \geq 0$ and $-c - \lambda \leq 0$, i.e., if $|c| \leq \lambda$.
- Both P_1 and P_2 are below the x-axis, as shown in Figure 11.1b. This can happen only when $-c + \lambda < 0$, or $c > \lambda > 0$.
- Both P_1 and P_2 are above the x-axis, as shown in Figure 11.1c. This can happen only when $-c - \lambda > 0$, or $c < -\lambda < 0$.

In the first case, the only possible solution is $x^\star = 0$ and $g(x^\star) = 0$. Figure 11.1d shows an example curve of $g(x)$ when $|c| \leq \lambda$.

In the second case, the line $x - c + \lambda$ has an intersection with the x-axis at $c - \lambda$ (which is positive)—i.e., $g'(c - \lambda) = 0$. Simple calculations show that

$$g(c - \lambda) = -\frac{1}{2}(c - \lambda)^2 < 0 = g(0).$$

Hence, when $c > \lambda$, $x^\star = c - \lambda$.

In the final case, the line $x - c - \lambda$ has an intersection with the x-axis at $c + \lambda$ (which is negative)—i.e., $g'(c + \lambda) = 0$. Simple calculations show that

$$g(c + \lambda) = -\frac{1}{2}(c + \lambda)^2 < 0 = g(0).$$

Hence, when $c < -\lambda$, $x^\star = c + \lambda$.

Putting these three cases together, the optimal x is determined by the *soft thresholding* formula[2]

$$x^\star = \operatorname{sign}(c)\,(|c| - \lambda)_+, \tag{11.5}$$

[2] Soft thresholding is an essential part of FISTA, an efficient sparse learning solver. We will discuss more about FISTA in the exercise problems.

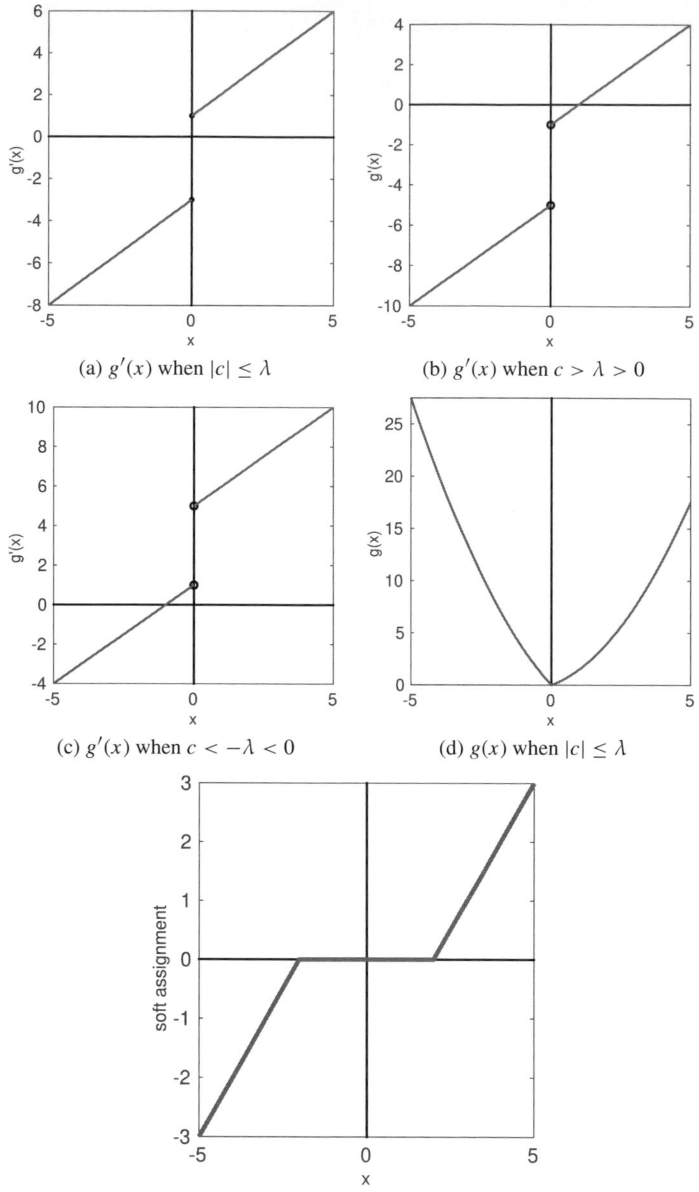

(a) $g'(x)$ when $|c| \leq \lambda$

(b) $g'(x)$ when $c > \lambda > 0$

(c) $g'(x)$ when $c < -\lambda < 0$

(d) $g(x)$ when $|c| \leq \lambda$

(e) Soft thresholding

Figure 11.1 The soft thresholding solution. The first three plots are different cases for the gradient $g'(x)$, and the fourth is the illustration of the function $g(x)$ when $|c| \leq \lambda$. The last figure shows the soft thresholding solution. (A black and white version of this figure will appear in some formats. For the color version, please refer to the plate section.)

in which $\text{sign}(\cdot)$ is the sign function and $x_+ = \max(0, x)$ is the hinge loss, which equals x if $x \geq 0$ and is always 0 if $x < 0$.

The soft thresholding solutions are shown in Figure 11.1e. Note that the $x^\star$ for $c \in [-\lambda, \lambda]$ are all 0! However, without the regularizer $|x|$, if $x^\star = 0$ for $f(x) = \frac{1}{2}x^2 - cx$, the only possible case is $c = 0$ because $f(x) = \frac{1}{2}(x-c)^2 - \frac{1}{2}c^2$ attains its minimum at $x^\star = c$. That is, adding the ℓ_1 regularizer makes $x^\star = 0$ in many more cases. Hence, the ℓ_1 regularizer is indeed sparsity inducing. When $\boldsymbol{x}$ is a vector, we have reason to expect that the simple ℓ_1 regularization $\|\boldsymbol{x}\|_1$ is effective in making many elements of $\boldsymbol{x}^\star$ be 0.

We can also take a second look at the SVM primal problem, which is

$$\min_{\boldsymbol{w},b} \frac{1}{2}\boldsymbol{w}^T\boldsymbol{w} + C\sum_{i=1}^{n} \xi_i, \tag{11.6}$$

where

$$\xi_i = (1 - y_i f(\boldsymbol{x}_i))_+ = \left(1 - y_i(\boldsymbol{w}^T\boldsymbol{x}_i + b)\right)_+ \tag{11.7}$$

is a function of $\boldsymbol{w}$.

Because $\xi_i \geq 0$, we have $\sum_{i=1}^{n} \xi_i = \|\boldsymbol{\xi}\|_1$, where $\boldsymbol{\xi} = (\xi_1, \xi_2, \ldots, \xi_m)^T$. Hence, the ℓ_1 regularization is also in effect in SVM learning. And the optimal solution is indeed sparse—$\xi_i \neq 0$ means $\boldsymbol{x}_i$ is a support vector, and support vectors are sparse!

In this SVM example, we observe that instead of directly using $\|\boldsymbol{x}\|_1$ as a regularizer, we can use $\|h(\boldsymbol{x})\|_1$, in which $h(\boldsymbol{x})$ is a function of $\boldsymbol{x}$. Another example of enforcing a sparsity constraint on transformed variables is *structured sparsity*. Suppose X is an $m \times n$ matrix,

$$s_i = \sqrt{\sum_{j=1}^{n} x_{ij}^2}, \quad 1 \leq i \leq m$$

is the ℓ_2 norm of its ith row, and

$$\boldsymbol{s} = (s_1, s_2, \ldots, s_m)^T.$$

Then the regularizer $\|\boldsymbol{s}\|_1$ makes $\boldsymbol{s}$ sparse. That is, many rows in the optimal X will be all 0s, because $s_i = 0$ forces $x_{ij} = 0$ for $1 \leq j \leq n$! If we use $\boldsymbol{x}_{i:}$ to denote the ith row, the mixed $\ell_{2,1}$ norm of the matrix X is

$$\sum_{i=1}^{m} \|\boldsymbol{x}_{i:}\|, \tag{11.8}$$

and a mixed $\ell_{2,1}$ regularization will encourage many rows of X to be $\boldsymbol{0}^T$. More generally, the mixed $\ell_{\alpha,\beta}$ norm of X is

$$\left(\sum_{i=1}^{m} \|\boldsymbol{x}_{i:}\|_\alpha^\beta\right)^{1/\beta}, \tag{11.9}$$

in which $\alpha \geq 1, \beta \geq 1$. We can also use the mixed $\ell_{\infty,1}$ norm to replace the $\ell_{2,1}$ norm.

If we know that one row in X contains grouped variables that change simultaneously, the $\ell_{2,1}$ regularizer encourages sparsity in terms of the groups of variables rather than individual variables. Similarly, the regularizer

$$\sum_{j=1}^{n} \|\boldsymbol{x}_{:j}\|_2$$

is useful when every column is a group, in which $\boldsymbol{x}_{:j}$ is the jth column. In addition to the row and column structures in a matrix, one can arbitrarily define structures in a vector or matrix by grouping variables together. These generalized sparsity constraints are called *group sparsity* or structured sparsity.

11.1.3 Using an Overcomplete Dictionary

Sparse machine learning covers diverse topics. In this section we introduce the formulation of the dictionary learning and sparse coding problem, which is also called compressive sensing or compressed sensing.

Consider the case where an input vector $\boldsymbol{x}$ is approximately connected to its new representation $\boldsymbol{\alpha}$ by a linear relationship. That is,

$$\boldsymbol{x} \approx D\boldsymbol{\alpha}, \tag{11.10}$$

in which $\boldsymbol{x} \in \mathbb{R}^p$, $D \in \mathbb{R}^p \times \mathbb{R}^k$, and $\boldsymbol{\alpha} \in \mathbb{R}^k$. If we denote D in block matrix form, it can be written as

$$D = [\boldsymbol{d}_1|\boldsymbol{d}_2|\dots|\boldsymbol{d}_k],$$

where $\boldsymbol{d}_i$ is the ith column in D, which has the same length as $\boldsymbol{x}$. Then we have

$$\boldsymbol{x} \approx \sum_{i=1}^{k} \alpha_i \boldsymbol{d}_i,$$

in which α_i is the ith element in $\boldsymbol{\alpha}$. In other words, $\boldsymbol{x}$ is approximated by a linear combination of the columns of D.

Given a training dataset $\{\boldsymbol{x}_i\}_{i=1}^n$, we can organize all training examples in a $p \times n$ matrix as

$$X = [\boldsymbol{x}_1|\boldsymbol{x}_2|\dots|\boldsymbol{x}_n].$$

We denote the new representation for $\boldsymbol{x}_i$ as $\boldsymbol{\alpha}_i$, and they also form a matrix

$$A = [\boldsymbol{\alpha}_1|\boldsymbol{\alpha}_2|\dots|\boldsymbol{\alpha}_n] \in \mathbb{R}^k \times \mathbb{R}^n.$$

The errors in this linear approximation for all n examples form a matrix $X - DA$ (with size $p \times n$).

To measure the approximation error, we can compute

$$\sum_{i=1}^{p}\sum_{j=1}^{n} [X - DA]_{ij}^2,$$

which can be written as $\|X - DA\|_F^2$. The subscript F denotes the Frobenius norm of a matrix—for an $m \times n$ matrix X,

$$\|X\|_F = \sqrt{\sum_{i=1}^{m}\sum_{j=1}^{n} x_{ij}^2} = \sqrt{\operatorname{tr}(XX^T)}.$$

If D is known and we want the reconstruction to be sparse—i.e., $\boldsymbol{\alpha}_i$ is sparse—we can solve the following problem:

$$\min_{\boldsymbol{\alpha}_i} \|\boldsymbol{x}_i - D\boldsymbol{\alpha}_i\|^2 + \lambda \|\boldsymbol{\alpha}_i\|_1.$$

However, in many applications D is unknown and has to be learned using the data X.

In this context, D is called the dictionary—i.e., we approximate any example using a weighted combination of dictionary items.[3] When $p > k$, there are more feature dimensions than dictionary items, and the dictionary is called undercomplete because it is not enough to fully describe $\boldsymbol{x}_i$ if X is full rank. For example, the E_d matrix in PCA is undercomplete and is not a suitable dictionary.

An overcomplete dictionary (i.e., $p < k$) is often used. For example, let X consist of frontal face images (stretched to a long vector using the "vec" operation) of 1000 different individuals, and let each individual have 100 images taken under different poses, illumination conditions, and facial expressions; hence $n = 100\,000$. If we use X itself as the dictionary (i.e., $D = X$, which is used in many face recognition sparse learning methods), we have $k = 100\,000$. Suppose the face images are resized to 100×100 for recognition; they have 10 000 pixels, and each image is stretched to a vector with $p = 10\,000$. The dictionary is then an overcomplete one.

During face recognition, we are presented with a testing example $\boldsymbol{x}$, which is taken from individual `id`, under pose `p`, illumination condition `i`, and expression `e`. It is natural to guess that $\boldsymbol{x}$ can be approximated by a sparse linear combination of images from the same identity, pose, illumination, and expression in X, and this guess has been proved by face recognition experiments! In an extreme situation, if $\boldsymbol{x}$ is in the training set X (and hence in the dictionary D), its corresponding $\boldsymbol{\alpha}$ needs just one nonzero entry (itself), and the reconstruction error is 0.

In other words, if we enforce sparsity on the reconstruction coefficient $\boldsymbol{\alpha}$ for $\boldsymbol{x}$, we expect only a few nonzero entries in α_i, and further expect the identity of these nonzero dictionary items (also training images because $D = X$ in this application) to be the same as $\boldsymbol{x}$. Hence, face recognition might, for example, be done by a voting of these nonzero entries. That is, sparse machine learning is useful in both learning representations and recognition.

In many applications, we cannot simply set $D = X$, but have to learn a good dictionary. The dictionary learning problem can be formulated as

$$\min_{D,A} \sum_{i=1}^{n} \left(\|\boldsymbol{x}_i - D\boldsymbol{\alpha}_i\|_F^2 + \lambda\|\boldsymbol{\alpha}_i\|_1\right) \tag{11.11}$$

$$\text{s.t.} \quad \|\boldsymbol{d}_j\| \le 1 \quad \forall 1 \le j \le k. \tag{11.12}$$

[3] Because D is used to denote the dictionary, we do not use D or d to denote the feature dimensionality in this section, but instead use p for this purpose.

As in PCA, we cannot let the dictionary item go unbounded; hence the constraint $\|\boldsymbol{d}_j\| \le 1$ (or $\|\boldsymbol{d}_j\| = 1$) is added. It is also worthwhile noting that although the optimal $\boldsymbol{\alpha}_i$ can be found for different i independently when D is fixed, the dictionary D has to been learned using all training examples altogether. Let vec(A) be the result of vectorizing the matrix A, i.e.,

$$[\text{vec}(A)]_{i\times n+j} = A_{ij} \in \mathbb{R}^{kn};$$

we can also write this optimization as

$$\min_{D,A} \quad \|X - DA\|_F^2 + \lambda\|\text{vec}(A)\|_1 \tag{11.13}$$

$$\text{s.t.} \quad \|\boldsymbol{d}_j\| \le 1 \quad \forall\, 1 \le j \le k. \tag{11.14}$$

Dictionary learning is difficult because its objective is nonconvex. We will not introduce its optimization process in detail. However, ample sparse learning packages are publicly available.

11.1.4 A Few Other Related Topics

A problem whose formulation is simpler than sparse coding is the lasso (least absolute shrinkage and selection operator) problem. The lasso is a linear regression model, but requires the regression parameters to be sparse. Given the training dataset $\{\boldsymbol{x}_i\}_{i=1}^n$ with $\boldsymbol{x}_i \in \mathbb{R}^p$ and organized into a matrix $X = [\boldsymbol{x}_1|\boldsymbol{x}_2|\ldots|\boldsymbol{x}_n]$, and the regression target values $\{y_i\}_{i=1}^n$ with $y_i \in \mathbb{R}$ and organized into a vector $\boldsymbol{y}$, the lasso aims to learn regression parameters $\boldsymbol{\beta}$ such that $X\boldsymbol{\beta}$ approximates $\boldsymbol{y}$, and $\boldsymbol{\beta}$ is sparse. This objective is described as the mathematical optimization problem

$$\min_{\boldsymbol{\beta}} \frac{1}{n}\|\boldsymbol{y} - X^T\boldsymbol{\beta}\|_2^2 + \lambda\|\boldsymbol{\beta}\|_1, \tag{11.15}$$

in which λ is a hyperparameter that determines the trade-off between approximation quality and sparsity.

The LARS (least-angle regression) solver for the lasso generates a complete regularization path—i.e., optimization results for a set of λ values in the reasonable range. The regularization path facilitates the choice of the hyperparameter λ.

A sparse linear learner (e.g., the lasso) has an additional benefit: if a dimension in the linear boundary $\boldsymbol{w}$ is zero (nonzero), we can interpret this fact as this feature being useless (useful). Hence, a sparse linear classifier can also be used as a feature selection mechanism. For example, we can add the sparse-inducing regularizer $\|\boldsymbol{w}\|_1$ to logistic regression or linear SVM.

Previously, we established that we can write the binary SVM problem as an unconstrained optimization problem

$$\min_{\boldsymbol{w},b} \frac{1}{2}\boldsymbol{w}^T\boldsymbol{w} + C\sum_{i=1}^{n}\big(1 - y_i(\boldsymbol{w}^T\boldsymbol{x}_i + b)\big)_+. \tag{11.16}$$

Note that $y_i \in \{+1, -1\}$. We can replace $\boldsymbol{w}^T\boldsymbol{w} = \|\boldsymbol{w}\|^2$ by $\|\boldsymbol{w}\|_1$, which leads to the sparse support vector classification

$$\min_{\boldsymbol{w},b} \|\boldsymbol{w}\|_1 + C\sum_{i=1}^{n}\left(1 - y_i(\boldsymbol{w}^T\boldsymbol{x}_i + b)\right)_+^2. \tag{11.17}$$

Note that the sparse support vector classification has changed the empirical loss from $\left(1 - y_i(\boldsymbol{w}^T\boldsymbol{x}_i + b)\right)_+$ to $\left(1 - y_i(\boldsymbol{w}^T\boldsymbol{x}_i + b)\right)_+^2$. This sparse linear classifier formulation can be used as a feature selection tool.

We have used $y_i \in \{0,1\}$ to denote the labels in logistic regression. If we use $y_i \in \{+1, -1\}$, then logistic regression estimates the probability

$$\Pr(y_i = 1|\boldsymbol{x}_i) \approx \frac{1}{1 + \exp(-\boldsymbol{x}^T\boldsymbol{w})}$$

and

$$\Pr(y_i = -1|\boldsymbol{x}_i) \approx 1 - \frac{1}{1 + \exp(-\boldsymbol{x}^T\boldsymbol{w})} = \frac{\exp(-\boldsymbol{x}^T\boldsymbol{w})}{1 + \exp(-\boldsymbol{x}^T\boldsymbol{w})}.$$

When $y_i = 1$, the negative log-likelihood of $\boldsymbol{x}_i$ is

$$\ln(1 + \exp(-\boldsymbol{x}^T\boldsymbol{w})),$$

which approximates $-\ln\left(\Pr(y_i = 1|\boldsymbol{x}_i)\right)$; when $y_i = -1$, the negative log-likelihood is

$$-\ln\left(1 - \frac{1}{1 + \exp(-\boldsymbol{x}^T\boldsymbol{w})}\right) = \ln(1 + \exp(\boldsymbol{x}^T\boldsymbol{w})).$$

Then the negative log-likelihood in these two cases can be unified as

$$\ln(1 + \exp(-y_i\boldsymbol{x}^T\boldsymbol{w})).$$

The maximum likelihood estimation for $\boldsymbol{w}$ can be achieved by minimizing the negative log-likelihood, and adding a sparse regularizer leads to the sparse logistic regression problem

$$\min_{\boldsymbol{w}} \|\boldsymbol{w}\|_1 + C\sum_{i=1}^{n}\ln\left(1 + \exp(-y_i\boldsymbol{x}_i^T\boldsymbol{w})\right). \tag{11.18}$$

Sparse logistic regression is also useful for feature selection.

A lot more can be said about sparse learning methods. For example, in sparse PCA (cf. Section 11.1.1) we require that D is sparse (while sparse coding requires that A is sparse); when our data are matrices, low rank is the corresponding concept to sparsity in vectors. There are many works on how to optimize sparse learning problems. However, as this is an introductory book, we will stop here.

11.2 Dynamic Time Warping

From now on, we will move away from the scenario in which a feature vector is a real-valued vector and the same dimension always has the same meaning in different feature vectors. In real-world applications, the raw data are usually more complex than this simple setup. For example, temporal or spatial relationships can be important. In face recognition, even though we can stretch a face image into a vector, the pixel at a given face location—e.g., nose tip—will appear at different vector locations because of the variations in face shape, pose, expression, etc. Another example is stock price progression. We can sample the price of one particular stock in a day using a fixed time step, such that we represent the price change of this stock as a fixed length vector per day. However, it is hard to say that the same dimensions in two different days' data (i.e., two days' feature vectors) mean the same thing.

Deep neural networks are very effective in dealing with these relationships. The convolutional neural network (CNN) is a very popular deep learning method and is to be introduced in Chapter 15. In this chapter, we discuss mainly types of data that can be aligned—i.e., after the alignment operation, the same dimensions in any two vectors do mean (or, approximately mean) the same thing. After the alignment, we can compute the similarity or distance between two examples as usual, and can apply our favorite learning and recognition methods.

Sometimes images require alignments. For example, if we want to compute the similarity or distance between two face images, they should be aligned frontal faces. If one face is slightly turned to the left and another has the head lifted, directly calculating distances between pixels at the same location is problematic—we may compare eyebrow pixels with forehead pixels, or cheek pixels with nose pixels. Alignment, however, usually requires domain knowledge about the data, and different alignment techniques are required for different types of data.

Mainly, we discuss the alignment of sequential data. Note that not all sequential data can be aligned—e.g., it seems very difficult (if not impossible) to align stock price data.

11.2.1 Misaligned Sequential Data

By sequential data, we mean a type of data that is comprised of an array of *ordered* elements. In a linear SVM classifier, if we rearrange the dimensions of every example and the classification boundary in the same way, the classification result will not change. For example, if we denote $\boldsymbol{x} = (x_1, x_2, x_3, x_4)^T$, $\boldsymbol{w} = (w_1, w_2, w_3, w_4)^T$, $\boldsymbol{x}' = (x_3, x_1, x_4, x_2)^T$, and $\boldsymbol{w}' = (w_3, w_1, w_4, w_2)^T$, we will always have $\boldsymbol{x}^T\boldsymbol{w} = \boldsymbol{x}'^T\boldsymbol{w}'$. Hence, the feature dimensions for SVM (and nearest neighbor, logistic regression, etc.) are unordered.

In the real world, many data are ordered. For example, an English word `university` is different from the word `unverstiy`, and the second one is in fact a typo. This typo (or, misalignment) is easy to fix (or, align), and our brain can immediately produce the alignment shown in Figure 11.2.

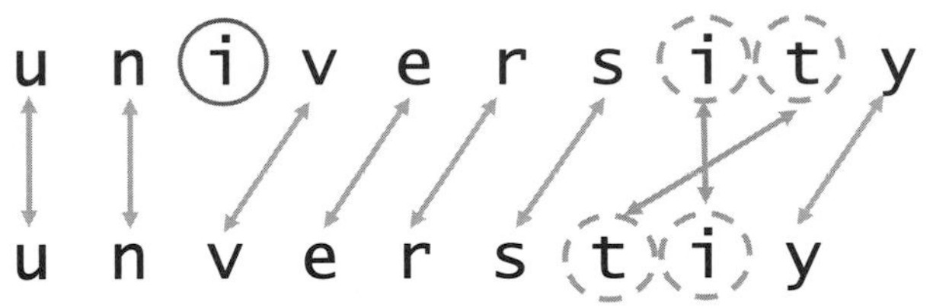

Figure 11.2 Alignment for `university` vs. `unverstiy`. (A black and white version of this figure will appear in some formats. For the color version, please refer to the plate section.)

We use red and green circles to denote mismatches of characters—i.e., misalignments in Figure 11.2. If an alignment can be established between the typo `unverstiy` and any other word—e.g., `universe`—we can use the number of misalignments as a measure of distance. For this example, the word `university` is the one with the smallest distance, and spell-checking software can then remind the writer to correct this typo.

The dynamic time warping (DTW) algorithm to be introduced in this section is a good tool to handle such misalignments: when the few misalignments are corrected by DTW, we can find a one-to-one correspondence between two sequences, and can use the usual distance metrics or similarity measures to compare the aligned sequences. For example, the discrete metric is used in the above spell checker example, which returns 1 if two characters are different and 0 if they are the same.

Before we introduce the details of DTW, we want to note that comparing two text sequences (i.e., strings) has wider application than building a spell checker. For example, string matching is very important in bioinformatics research.

The structure of DNA comprises four bases: thymine (T), adenine (A), cytosine (C), and guanine (G), and DNA sequencing determines their ordering—e.g., being sequenced as ATGACGTAAATG.... String matching is important in DNA sequencing and its applications, such as molecular biology and medicine. Many algorithms and systems (e.g., parallel design and implementation of these algorithms) have been produced for string matching.

11.2.2 The Idea (or Criteria)

DTW is a simple algorithm if one understands the dynamic programming strategy. What we want to emphasize in this chapter is, however, the way the method is formulated and solved.

One major scenario where DTW is useful is when speed is involved in generating the sequences. Two people can finish a golf swing at different speeds, hence taking different times. The same action will result in video clips of different lengths, meaning the input to action recognition is a sequence of frames with variable length. The same also happens in speech recognition, because humans speak at different speeds. However, we expect the same action or same speech to be similar even if they are produced by different people—i.e., they *can be aligned*.

Let $\boldsymbol{x} = (x_1, x_2, \ldots, x_n)$ and $\boldsymbol{y} = (y_1, y_2, \ldots, y_m)$. A few things are worth mentioning about this notation. First, sequences do not necessarily have the same length—i.e., $n \neq m$ is possible. Second, x_i $(1 \leq i \leq n)$ or y_j $(1 \leq j \leq m)$ can be a categorical value, a real value, an array, a matrix, or an even more complex data type. For example, if $\boldsymbol{x}$ is a video clip, x_i is a video frame, which is a matrix of pixel values (and a pixel can be a single value or an RGB triplet). Third, we assume that there is a distance metric that compares any x_i and y_j as $d(x_i, y_j)$. Hence, after $\boldsymbol{x}$ and $\boldsymbol{y}$ are aligned, we can compute the distance between them as the sum of distances of all matched elements in $\boldsymbol{x}$ and $\boldsymbol{y}$. For example, $d(x_i, y_j)$ can be the sum of Euclidean distances between all matched pixel pairs if x_i and y_j are frames in two videos.

What is a good match? Based on Figure 11.2, the following assumptions can be made:

(1) If x_i is matched to y_j, then $d(x_i, y_j)$ should be small.
(2) Some elements in $\boldsymbol{x}$ and/or $\boldsymbol{y}$ can be skipped in the matching process—e.g., the character `i` in the red circle in Figure 11.2.
(3) We will choose the match that leads to the smallest total distance.

However, these criteria are not suitable for an optimization. First, if every element is skipped, the total distance is zero, but this matching is obviously nonoptimal. The DTW remedy to this issue is to request that every element in $\boldsymbol{x}$ ($\boldsymbol{y}$) has a matched element in $\boldsymbol{y}$ ($\boldsymbol{x}$). Second, if two pairs of matched elements are out of order, the optimization will have a large search space and hence be very difficult. For example, if $x_i \leftrightarrow y_j$ (where $\leftrightarrow$ means a matched pair) and $x_{i+1} \leftrightarrow y_k$, but $j > k$, then these lead to an out-of-order match (as with the two green lines shown in Figure 11.2). In order to avoid this difficulty, DTW forbids out-of-order matched elements. In short, DTW uses the following two criteria to replace the second criterion in the above list:

(2.1) Every x_i $(1 \leq i \leq n)$ and y_j $(1 \leq j \leq m)$ has to have a matched element.
(2.2) The matching has to be in order—i.e., if $x_i \leftrightarrow y_j$ and $x_{i+1} \leftrightarrow y_k$, then $j \leq k$.

Note that we use $j \leq k$ instead of $j < k$ in criterion (2.2) because when $m \neq n$, there must be an element matched to more than one element.

11.2.3 Visualization and Formalization

Visualization is a good tool to intuitively understand these criteria. In the visualization in Figure 11.3, the matching in Figure 11.3a is translated into the blue path in Figure 11.3b.

In fact, we can translate the criteria for the match into requirements for the path, where a path is fully described by a series of coordinates (r_k, t_k) $(k = 1, 2, \ldots, K)$:

- "Every element is in the match" is partly translated into "the first coordinate is $(1, 1)$—i.e., $r_1 = 1$ and $t_1 = 1$—and the last coordinate is (n, m)—i.e., $r_K = n$ and $t_K = m$."

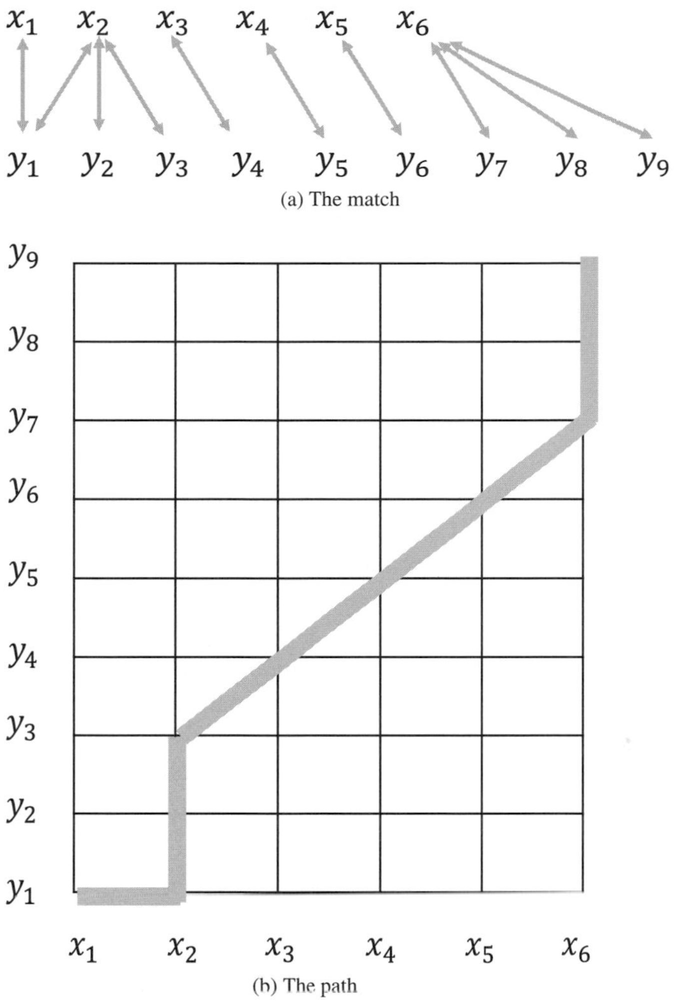

Figure 11.3 Visualizing a match between two sequences as a path. (A black and white version of this figure will appear in some formats. For the color version, please refer to the plate section.)

- "Matching is in order" plus "every element is in the match" is translated into a constraint between (r_k, t_k) and (r_{k+1}, t_{k+1}). There are only three possible cases:

$$\#1.\ r_{k+1} = r_k, \qquad t_{k+1} = t_k + 1 \quad \text{(the path moves upward)}, \tag{11.19}$$

$$\#2.\ r_{k+1} = r_k + 1, \qquad t_{k+1} = t_k \quad \text{(the path moves rightward)}, \tag{11.20}$$

$$\#3.\ r_{k+1} = r_k + 1, \qquad t_{k+1} = t_k + 1 \quad \text{(the path moves diagonally)}. \tag{11.21}$$

- The translation of "choose the path with the smallest total distance" requires some more notation. We denote $\boldsymbol{r} = (r_1, r_2, \ldots, r_K)$, $\boldsymbol{t} = (t_1, t_2, \ldots, t_K)$, and a path by $(\boldsymbol{r}, \boldsymbol{t})$. Let Ω be the set of all paths that satisfy these translated criteria; then minimizing the total matching distance is translated as

$$D(n,m) = \min_{(\boldsymbol{r},\boldsymbol{t})\in\Omega} \sum_{k=1}^{K_{(\boldsymbol{r},\boldsymbol{t})}} d(x_{r_k}, y_{t_k}). \qquad (11.22)$$

Note that for different paths, K may have different values; hence we use the notation $K_{(\boldsymbol{r},\boldsymbol{t})}$. The smallest total matching distance is $D(n,m)$.

11.2.4 Dynamic Programming

The number of paths that satisfy these constraints is enormous. If we allow moving rightward or upward only, as illustrated in Figure 11.4a, the number of paths is

$$\binom{n+m-2}{n-1} = \binom{n+m-2}{m-1},$$

the proof of which we leave as an exercise. When n or m is not too small (e.g., when $n \approx m$), this number increases exponentially with n (or m). Hence, it is not feasible to enumerate all paths and find the best one.

The *divide and conquer* strategy is useful in reducing the complexity for DTW. As illustrated in Figure 11.4a, if an oracle tells us that node $A = (x_2, y_3)$ is in the optimal path, then the optimal total distance is the sum of distances of the optimal path from O to A and the optimal path from A to T. The original large problem is split into two smaller ones, and smaller problems are usually easier to solve than bigger ones. For example, in the fast Fourier transform (FFT) algorithm, a size n problem is divided into two smaller problems with size $\frac{n}{2}$, whose solutions can be combined to solve the original problem. We can also use this strategy in DTW.

There are, however, two issues remaining for solving DTW using divide and conquer. First, we do not have an oracle to tell us "A is in the optimal path (or not in the optimal path)." Second, it is not clear how we should divide a large problem into smaller ones. The *dynamic programming* strategy solves the first issue by *enumerating all candidates for* A, and the second issue (usually) by splitting a large problem into a very small problem (which is trivial to solve) and another one.

In DTW, if we want to compute the optimal $D(n,m)$, there are three candidates for the intermediate point A when the path from A to T contains only one movement:

- $A = (x_{n-1}, y_{m-1})$ and the movement is upright (i.e., diagonal). Then we have

  $$D(n,m) = D(n-1, m-1) + d(x_n, y_m),$$

  in which $D(n-1, m-1)$ is the optimal distance from O to (x_{n-1}, y_{m-1}).
- $A = (x_n, y_{m-1})$ and the movement is upward. Then we have

  $$D(n,m) = D(n, m-1) + d(x_n, y_m).$$

- $A = (x_{n-1}, y_m)$ and the movement is rightward. Then we have

  $$D(n,m) = D(n-1, m) + d(x_n, y_m).$$

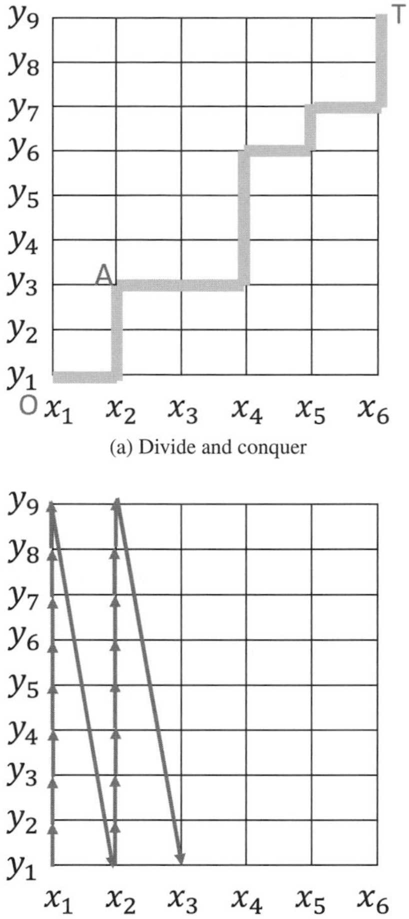

(a) Divide and conquer

(b) Dynamic programming

Figure 11.4 The dynamic programming strategy for DTW. (A black and white version of this figure will appear in some formats. For the color version, please refer to the plate section.)

To combine these three cases, we need just to find the smallest value among $D(n-1, m-1)$, $D(n,m-1)$, and $D(n-1,m)$. In other words, for any integer $1 < u \le n$ and $1 < v \le m$, we have

$$D(u,v) = d(x_u, y_v) + \min\{D(u-1,v), D(u,v-1), D(u-1,v-1)\}\,. \tag{11.23}$$

Equation (11.23) is a *recursive* relationship between a large problem and two smaller problems. One smaller problem is trivial to solve ($d(x_u, y_v)$), and there are three candidates for the other smaller problem. This kind of recursive relationship is the key in all dynamic programming methods. In order to find $D(n,m)$, we need to find three other optimal values $D(n-1,m-1)$, $D(n,m-1)$, and $D(n-1,m)$.

To find $D(n-1,m-1)$, we need to find three more optimal values $D(n-2,m-2)$, $D(n-1,m-2)$, and $D(n-2,m-1)$. And $D(n-1,m-2)$, $D(n,m-2)$, $D(n-1,m-1)$

are requested to find $D(n,m-1)$. We have the following observations for this recursive expansion:

- We can write a simple recursive program to compute $D(n,m)$—e.g., in C++ —as

```
double D(int n, int m, const double **dist)
{
  if (m == 1 && n == 1) return dist[1][1];
  if (n == 1)  return dist[n][m] + D(n, m-1, dist);
  if (m == 1)  return dist[n][m] + D(n-1, m, dist);

  return dist[n][m] +
         min( min(D(n-1, m-1, dist), D(n, m-1, dist)),
              D(n-1, m, dist));
}
```

  in which `dist` is a two-dimensional array, and `dist(i,j)` $= d(x_i, y_j)$. The number of function evaluations increases exponentially with n or m. We can build an expansion tree to illustrate the recursive computation, as illustrated in Figure 11.5. It is obvious that many computations are *redundant*—e.g., $D(n-1,m-1)$ is repeated three times, and $D(n-1,m-2)$ and $D(n-2,m-1)$ twice in the partial expansion of Figure 11.5.
- To compute $D(n,m)$ we need to compute all $D(u,v)$ for $1 \le u \le n$ and $1 \le v \le m$ in the expansion tree. There are in total nm optimal values to compute, including $D(n,m)$.

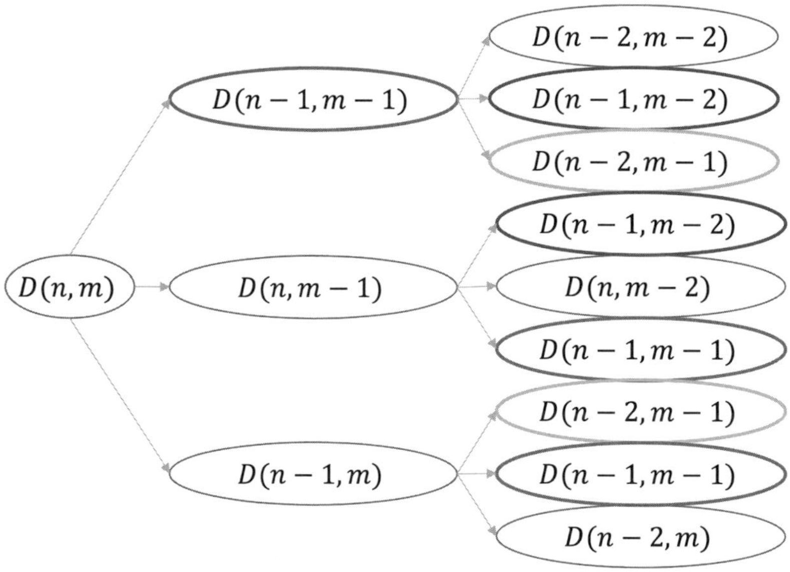

Figure 11.5 The (partial) expansion tree for recursive DTW computations. (A black and white version of this figure will appear in some formats. For the color version, please refer to the plate section.)

In fact, we need to compute just nm such $d(\cdot,\cdot)$ values if a proper evaluation order is designed. A good evaluation order should satisfy that $D(u-1,v-1)$, $D(u,v-1)$, and $D(u-1,v)$ have already been computed when we compute $D(u,v)$. Figure 11.4b specifies such an order: start from $(1,1)$ and move upward as far as $(1,m)$; then move to the next column $(2,1)$ and finish the second column up to $(2,m)$; then move to the next column, and so on. Finally, when the last column is traversed, we have computed $D(n,m)$ successfully. Now we have all the components of the DTW algorithm, which is described in Algorithm 6. Note that $D(i,j)$ in Algorithm 6 is the (i,j)th element in the two-dimensional array D, which is no longer a function call.

Algorithm 6 The dynamic time warping method

Input: Two sequences $\boldsymbol{x} = (x_1, x_2, \ldots, x_n)$ and $\boldsymbol{y} = (y_1, y_2, \ldots, y_m)$.
$D(1,1) = d(x_1, y_1)$.
for $j = 2$ to m **do**
    $D(1,j) = d(x_1, y_j) + D(1, j-1)$.
end for
for $i = 2$ to n **do**
    $D(i,1) = d(x_i, y_1) + D(i-1, 1)$.
    for $j = 2$ to m **do**
        $D(i,j) = d(x_i, y_j) + \min\{D(i-1, j-1), D(i, j-1), D(i-1, j)\}$.
    end for
end for

It is obvious that $d(x_i, y_j)$ is evaluated nm times in Algorithm 6, which is more efficient than the recursive code. The reason is that all redundant computations have been eliminated by a proper evaluation order. Algorithm 6 evaluates $D(u,v)$ in a column-based ordering. Other orderings are also possible. For example, we can evaluate the first row, then the second row, until $D(n,m)$ is computed. Note that with this ordering, when we need to compute $D(i,j)$, the values in $D(x,y)$ $(1 \le x \le i,\ 1 \le y \le j)$ have all been computed.

In Algorithm 6 there are two special cases: the first column $D(1,j)$ and the first row $D(i,1)$. We can pad a column to the left of the first column, and pad a row under the first row with appropriate values (0 or ∞). Then we can use Eq. (11.23) to process all of $D(u,v)$ in a unified way.

One frequently appearing characteristic of dynamic programming is that instead of computing one single optimal value (e.g., $D(n,m)$), dynamic programming methods compute the optimal values of many more problems (e.g., $D(u,v)$ for $1 \le u \le n$ and $1 \le v \le m$). These additional problems, however, lead to the efficient solution of the original problem.

Dynamic programming has a wide range of applications, and the recursive relationships may be much more complex than Eq. (11.23). The way to split a large problem into smaller ones has a lot of variations, and the number of smaller problems can be two, three, or even more. The order of evaluation does not necessarily start from the smallest problem. In more complex problems, the recursive relationship may involve two (or even more) sets of variables. We will see more examples of dynamic programming in the hidden Markov model (HMM), a tool to handle another type of nonvector data. The basics of the HMM will be introduced in the next chapter.

11.3 Miscellaneous Notes and Additional Resources

We did not introduce a sparse learning algorithm in this chapter. However, the first three exercises for this chapter describe FISTA (Beck & Teboulle 2009), an efficient sparse learning algorithm. More can be found in Vidal et al. (2016, Chapter 8).

Sparse learning theoretical results can be found in classic statistics papers, e.g., Donoho (2006) and Candès et al. (2006). Face recognition is a very successful application of sparse learning (Wright et al. 2009b). And K-SVD, a typical dictionary learning method, was introduced in Aharon et al. (2006).

Group sparsity often appear in advanced research papers, e.g., Bengio et al. (2009) and Huang et al. (2011). And when moving from one- to two-dimensional data, sparse vectors can be replaced by low-rank matrices, which are described in detail in Vidal et al. (2016).

More on the lasso and LARS can be found in Tibshirani (1996).

To have hands-on experience with sparse SVM and sparse LR, please refer to the LIBLINEAR software (Fan et al. 2008).

An in-depth introduction to dynamic programming algorithms (such as FFT) and applications can be found in Bellman & Dreyfus (2015) and Cormen et al. (2009).

Real-time face detection using integral images, or summed area tables (Crow 1984) can be found in Viola & Jones (2004).

Exercises

11.1 (Soft thresholding) Let $\lambda > 0$. Show that the solution for

$$\arg\min_{\boldsymbol{x}} \|\boldsymbol{x} - \boldsymbol{y}\|^2 + \lambda \|\boldsymbol{x}\|_1 \tag{11.24}$$

is the soft thresholding strategy applied to every dimension of $\boldsymbol{y}$ with a shrinkage parameter $\frac{\lambda}{2}$. That is,

$$\boldsymbol{x}^\star = \operatorname{sign}(\boldsymbol{y}) \left(|\boldsymbol{y}| - \frac{\lambda}{2} \right)_+, \tag{11.25}$$

in which the sign function, the absolute value function, the minus operation, the $(\cdot)_+$ thresholding function, and the multiplication are all applied elementwise. If we denote the shrinkage-thresholding operator as

$$\mathcal{T}_\lambda(\boldsymbol{x}) = \operatorname{sign}(\boldsymbol{x})\,(|\boldsymbol{x}| - \lambda)_+, \tag{11.26}$$

the solution can be represented as $\boldsymbol{x}^\star = \mathcal{T}_{\frac{\lambda}{2}}(\boldsymbol{y})$.

11.2 (ISTA) ISTA, or *iterative shrinkage-thresholding algorithms*, are a family of methods that can solve the following problem when the dictionary D and $\boldsymbol{x}$ are known:

$$\arg\min_{\boldsymbol{\alpha}} \|\boldsymbol{x} - D\boldsymbol{\alpha}\|^2 + \lambda\|\boldsymbol{\alpha}\|_1.$$

Let $f(\boldsymbol{\alpha})$ and $g(\boldsymbol{\alpha})$ be two functions of $\boldsymbol{\alpha}$, in which f is a smooth convex function and g is a continuous convex function. However, g is not necessarily smooth, which makes the optimization of $\min_{\boldsymbol{\alpha}} f(\boldsymbol{\alpha}) + g(\boldsymbol{\alpha})$ difficult.

ISTA solves $\min_{\boldsymbol{\alpha}} f(\boldsymbol{\alpha}) + g(\boldsymbol{\alpha})$ in an iterative manner, and each iteration is a shrinkage-thresholding step. Hence, it is called the iterative shrinkage-thresholding algorithm (ISTA). In this problem, we consider only the simple case of $f(\boldsymbol{\alpha}) = \|\boldsymbol{x} - D\boldsymbol{\alpha}\|^2$ and $g(\boldsymbol{\alpha}) = \lambda\|\boldsymbol{\alpha}\|_1$ ($\lambda > 0$).

(a) One additional requirement in ISTA is that f is continuously differentiable with Lipschitz continuous gradient $L(f)$—i.e., there exists an f-dependent constant $L(f)$, such that for any $\boldsymbol{\alpha}_1$ and $\boldsymbol{\alpha}_2$,

$$\|\nabla f(\boldsymbol{\alpha}_1) - \nabla f(\boldsymbol{\alpha}_2)\| \leq L(f)\|\boldsymbol{\alpha}_1 - \boldsymbol{\alpha}_2\|, \tag{11.27}$$

in which ∇f is the gradient of f.

For our choice of f, show that its corresponding $L(f)$ (abbreviated simply as L) is double the largest eigenvalue of $D^T D$, which is called the *Lipschitz constant* of ∇f.

(b) ISTA first initializes $\boldsymbol{\alpha}$ (e.g., by ignoring $g(\boldsymbol{\alpha})$ and solving the ordinary least square regression). Then in each iteration the following problem is solved:

$$p_L(\boldsymbol{\beta}) \overset{\text{def}}{=} \arg\min_{\boldsymbol{\alpha}} g(\boldsymbol{\alpha}) + \frac{L}{2}\left\|\boldsymbol{\alpha} - \left(\boldsymbol{\beta} - \frac{1}{L}\nabla f(\boldsymbol{\beta})\right)\right\|^2, \tag{11.28}$$

in which L is the Lipschitz constant and $\boldsymbol{\beta}$ is a parameter. In the tth iteration, ISTA updates the solution by

$$\boldsymbol{\alpha}_{t+1} = p_L(\boldsymbol{\alpha}_t).$$

Solve this optimization problem for our choice of f and g. Explain why sparsity is induced by every step in ISTA.

11.3 (FISTA) FISTA, which stands for fast ISTA, is an improved ISTA method. The FISTA method is shown as pseudocode in Algorithm 7. In terms of algorithmic details, the difference between FISTA and ISTA is the introduction of an intermediate variable $\boldsymbol{\beta}$ and a variable t that controls the update of $\boldsymbol{\alpha}$. These simple changes, however, greatly improve the convergence speed of ISTA (hence the name FISTA).

Use the following sample MATLAB/GNU Octave code to generate a dictionary D with 300 items (each being 150-dimensional). One example $\boldsymbol{x}$ is generated by a linear combination of 40 dictionary items (out of 300, hence it is sparse). Given a noise contaminated example $\boldsymbol{x}$, we will use the simple FISTA algorithm in Algorithm 7 to find an $\boldsymbol{\alpha}$, such that $\|\boldsymbol{x} - D\boldsymbol{\alpha}\|^2 + \lambda\|\boldsymbol{\alpha}\|_1$ is minimized. We use $\lambda = 1$.

```
p = 150; % dimensions
k = 300; % dictionary size
D = randn(p,k); % dictionary
```

Algorithm 7 FISTA: A fast iterative shrinkage-thresholding algorithm

1: {This version has a constant step size when the Lipschitz constant $L = \nabla f$ is known.}
2: {$\boldsymbol{\alpha}_0$ is the initial value for $\boldsymbol{\alpha}$, which can be obtained, e.g., through OLS.}
3: **Initialization:** $t \leftarrow 1$, $\boldsymbol{\alpha} \leftarrow \boldsymbol{\alpha}_0$, $\boldsymbol{\beta} \leftarrow \boldsymbol{\alpha}$.
4: **Iterate**: Repeat the following steps until convergence.

$$\boldsymbol{\alpha}' \leftarrow p_L(\boldsymbol{\beta}), \tag{11.29}$$

$$t' \leftarrow \frac{1+\sqrt{1+4t^2}}{2}, \tag{11.30}$$

$$\boldsymbol{\beta} \leftarrow \boldsymbol{\alpha}' + \left(\frac{t-1}{t'}\right)(\boldsymbol{\alpha}' - \boldsymbol{\alpha}), \tag{11.31}$$

$$\boldsymbol{\alpha} \leftarrow \boldsymbol{\alpha}', \tag{11.32}$$

$$t \leftarrow t'. \tag{11.33}$$

```
% normalize dictionary item
for i=1:k
    D(:,i) = D(:,i)/norm(D(:,i));
end
% x is a linear reconstruction of 40 dictionary items
truealpha = zeros(k,1);
truealpha(randperm(k,40)) = 30 * (rand(40,1)-0.5);
% add noise, and generate x
noisealpha = truealpha + .1*randn(size(truealpha));
x = D * noisealpha;
% set lambda=1
lambda = 1;
```

(a) Find the ordinary least square optimal solution (i.e., as if $\lambda = 0$). How many nonzero entries are there in the solution for $\boldsymbol{\alpha}$? Is it sparse?

(b) Write a MATLAB/GNU Octave program to implement Algorithm 7. Run 100 iterations before termination. Use the OLS solution to initialize (i.e., as $\boldsymbol{\alpha}_0$). Is the FISTA solution sparse? In the FISTA solution, how many of its nonzero entries happen to be nonzero in the true $\boldsymbol{\alpha}$ vector that is used to generate the data $\boldsymbol{x}$ (i.e., the `truealpha` variable)? Do you think FISTA gives a good solution?

(c) If you wanted the solution to be sparser (or denser), how would you change λ? Explain your choice and make your argument based specifically on the FISTA method.

Finally, we want to add a note of caution. The FISTA method is more complex than Algorithm 7. For example, it may be computationally infeasible to find the Lipschitz constant, and the termination criterion may be very complex. Algorithm 7 is only an illustration of the simplest possible implementation of FISTA. Albeit simple, it retains the core idea in FISTA.

11.4 Given an $n \times m$ grid, find the number of paths that move from the bottom-left corner to the top-right corner. A movement in the path can be only rightward or

Table 11.1 An example of the integral image: A is the input image and B is the integral image.

$\begin{pmatrix} 1 & 1 & -1 \\ 2 & 3 & 1 \\ 3 & 4 & 6 \end{pmatrix}$	$\Longrightarrow$	$\begin{pmatrix} \; & \; & \; \\ \; & \; & \; \\ \; & \; & \; \end{pmatrix}$
A		B

upward, and one move can traverse only one cell in the grid. An example is the blue path shown in Figure 11.4a, which contains 5 rightward and 8 upward movements.

11.5 (Integral image) The *integral image* is a data structure that has wide usage in computer vision, especially in applications that require fast processing speed—e.g., real-time face detection. It has appeared under other names in earlier literature, and as the *summed area table* in the computer graphics community.

(a) Let A be an $n \times m$ single-channel image (or equivalently, an $n \times m$ matrix). We denote the integral image of A as B, which has the same size as A. For any $1 \leq i \leq n$ and $1 \leq j \leq m$, $B(i,j)$ is defined as

$$B(i,j) = \sum_{u=1}^{i} \sum_{v=1}^{j} A(u,v). \tag{11.34}$$

On the left of Table 11.1, an example input image A is shown as a 3×3 matrix. Fill the values of B into the right-hand side of Table 11.1.

(b) Find a method to compute B from A, whose complexity is $\mathcal{O}(nm)$—i.e., linear in the number of pixels. (Hint: Use dynamic programming.)

(c) The main usage of an integral image B is to find the sum of all elements in *any* rectangular image patch inside A. Let (i_1, j_1) and (i_2, j_2) be two coordinates in the image ($1 \leq i_1 < i_2 \leq n$, $1 \leq j_1 < j_2 \leq m$), which defines the top-left and bottom-right corners of a rectangle. The task is to compute the rectangular sum

$$S = \sum_{i_1 \leq u \leq i_2} \sum_{j_1 \leq v \leq j_2} A(u,v).$$

Let B be the integral image of A. Show that any such rectangular sum can be computed in $\mathcal{O}(1)$ time.

12 Hidden Markov Model

In this chapter, we will introduce the basic concepts in the hidden Markov model (HMM) and a few important HMM learning algorithms.

12.1 Sequential Data and the Markov Property

The hidden Markov model deals with sequential data too. However, unlike in dynamic time warping, we do not assume the sequential data can be aligned. In the HMM, the data are supposed to possess the Markov property. We will first have a closer look at various types of sequential data, and then introduce the Markov property and HMM.

12.1.1 Various Sequential Data and Models

Depending on their properties and our objectives, sequential data have been modeled in different ways. As has been introduced, if the sequential data can be aligned, dynamic time warping and other related algorithms (e.g., string matching methods) can be applied to handle them.

However, there are many types of sequential data that cannot be aligned—e.g., stock price data. A great many methods have been proposed to handle sequential data. We introduce a small subset of these methods very briefly in this section, but will avoid going into details.

If dependencies in the sequence are not long term, it is possible to use short-term history data to predict the next element in a sequence. For example, let $x_1, x_2, \dots, x_t$ be an input sequence, and let the objective be to predict x_{t+1} based on the existing sequence. We can extract the most recent history data in a short time period or time window, e.g.,

$$(x_{t-k+1}, x_{t-k+2}, \dots, x_t)$$

is a time window with k readings in k time steps. Since we assume that the dependencies among sequential data have short range, a reasonably large k should provide enough information to predict x_{t+1}. In addition, since the size of the time window is fixed (e.g., k), we can use all sorts of machine learning methods to predict x_{t+1} using the fixed length vector $(x_{t-k+1}, x_{t-k+2}, \dots, x_t)$. If a linear relationship is considered, the moving average (MA) and autoregressive (AR) models are two example models popularly used in the statistical analysis of time series (aka, sequential data), but different assumptions on noise and linear relationships are utilized in these two models. AR and MA can be combined to form the autoregressive-moving-average (ARMA) model.

Statistical models (e.g., ARMA) have been thoroughly analyzed, and many theoretical results are available. However, linear relationships are usually insufficient to model sequential data, and the assumptions of these statistical methods are often broken in the real world. We also want to deal with variable length input in many situations, rather than a fixed length time window. The recurrent neural network (RNN) can handle these complex situations.

Figure 12.1a shows a simple RNN architecture. At time step t, the input is a vector $\boldsymbol{x}_t$, and the simple RNN also maintains a *state* vector $\boldsymbol{s}_t$ (which is updated at every

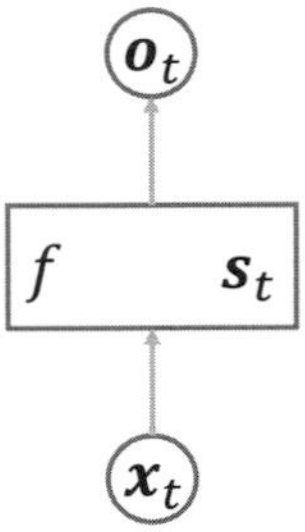

(a) Simple RNN

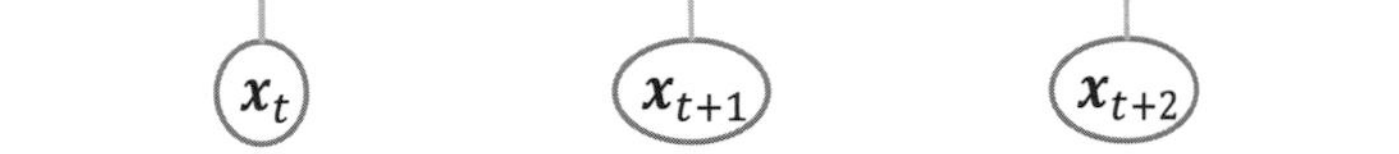

(b) RNN unfolded

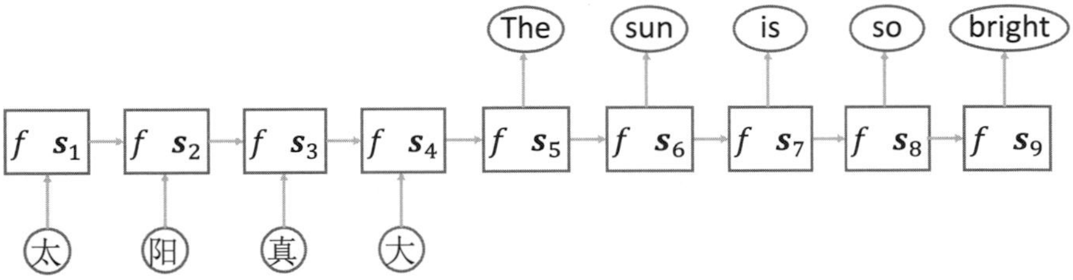

(c) RNN translation

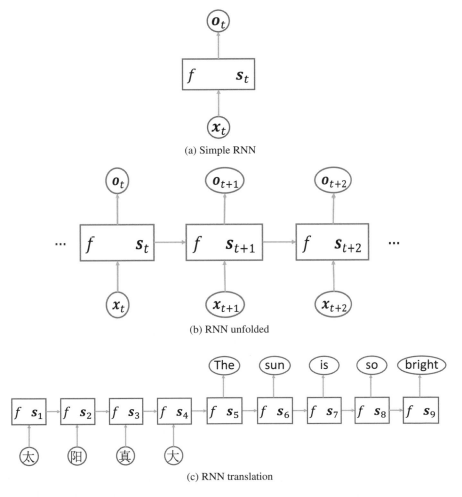

Figure 12.1 A simple RNN hidden unit, its unfolded version, and its application in language translation.

time step). The state vector is to be learned using the training data, and is taught by the training data to encode useful knowledge for fulfilling the learning objective included in the inputs till now: $(\boldsymbol{x}_1, \boldsymbol{x}_2, \ldots, \boldsymbol{x}_{t-1})$.

After observing $\boldsymbol{x}_t$, the hidden state vector should be updated at time $t+1$, given the current state vector $\boldsymbol{s}_t$ and input $\boldsymbol{x}_t$. A simple RNN updates the state using an affine transform and a nonlinear activation function, e.g.,

$$\boldsymbol{s}_{t+1} = f(W_x \boldsymbol{x}_t + W_s \boldsymbol{s}_t + \boldsymbol{b}_s), \tag{12.1}$$

in which W_x, W_s, and $\boldsymbol{b}_s$ are parameters of the affine transform, and f is the nonlinear activation function (e.g., the logistic sigmoid function).

A simple RNN hidden unit may have an optional output vector $\boldsymbol{o}_t$. For example, if we want to choose a word from a dictionary, one possible way is to calculate $W_o \boldsymbol{s}_t + \boldsymbol{b}_o$ to obtain a score for each word, in which W_o is a parameter matrix, with the same number of rows as there are words in the dictionary, and $\boldsymbol{b}_o$ is the bias parameter. Then a softmax transformation will turn these scores into a probability distribution, and we can sample from this distribution to determine which word will be the output at time t.

The same hidden unit architecture (Figure 12.1a) is used for $t = 1, 2, \ldots,$ in which the parameters remain unchanged but there are different values of the input, state, and output vectors. We can treat an RNN with T time steps as a network with T layers: the hidden unit with the input, state, and output vectors for the tth time step is the tth layer in the network. One way to understand its data flow is to *unfold* these units along the time axis, as shown in Figure 12.1b. After an RNN is unfolded, it can be viewed as a *deep* network with many layers. Although these layers have different input, state, and output vectors, they share the *same* set of parameter values (e.g., W_x, W_s, $\boldsymbol{b}_s$, W_o, and $\boldsymbol{b}_o$). Methods for training deep neural networks (e.g., stochastic gradient descent) can be adopted to learn the parameters of an RNN in the unfolded network.

One application of RNN is machine translation, which is illustrated in Figure 12.1c. Given one sentence in the source language (e.g., Chinese), an RNN (with parameters already learned from training data) reads it in as a sequence of words. No output is given before the sentence is completely read and processed. After that, no input is needed for subsequent layers (time steps), and the translation to the target language (e.g., English) is given by the output nodes as another sequence of words.

Note that this figure is only for illustrative purposes. An RNN for real-world translation (or other tasks) will be much more complex. For example, when long sequences are presented, a simple RNN will have difficulty in learning the parameters due to a problem called the *vanishing gradient* or *exploding gradient*. Also, a simple RNN is incapable of learning dependencies between inputs that are far apart. More complex hidden recurrent units have been proposed to deal with these difficulties—e.g., the long-short term memory (LSTM) hidden unit, the gated recurrent unit (GRU), and the minimal gated unit (MGU).

12.1.2 The Markov Property

The HMM, unlike RNNs, handles only data with the Markov property, which is a property for some stochastic processes. A stochastic process (or random process) is a sequence of ordered random variables, which can be treated as the evolution of states of a random system over time. Hence, unlike the RNN, which does not explicitly impose assumptions on the sequential data, the HMM interprets the sequential data from a probabilistic point of view. If $\boldsymbol{x}_1, \boldsymbol{x}_2, \ldots, \boldsymbol{x}_t$ is a sequence, then each $\boldsymbol{x}_i$ is considered a random vector (or its instantiation). We use $\boldsymbol{x}_{1:t}$ as an abbreviation of the entire sequence.

Let $\boldsymbol{x}_t$ be the coordinates of an autonomous driving car at time t, the precise values of which are essential in autonomous driving. However, we do not have a precise way to directly observe this variable. Some measurements that can be directly observed at time t—e.g., GPS readings and the video frame taken by a video camera—are collectively denoted by $\boldsymbol{o}_t$ and are useful for us to estimate $\boldsymbol{x}_t$.

Uncertainty exists in the observations. The GPS readings are not robust, and the car's coordinates may jump frequently even in a short time period. Cameras can help to reduce uncertainty in GPS readings, but scenes at different locations may look alike (e.g., imagine driving in the Great Sandy desert in Australia or the Taklamakan desert in Xinjiang, China). Hence, we need to use probabilistic methods to handle such uncertainties—i.e., our estimate of $\boldsymbol{x}_t$ is a distribution (instead of a single value).

When we move on from time $t-1$ to t, we can have an initial estimate of $\boldsymbol{x}_t$ based on (1) the distribution of $\boldsymbol{x}_{t-1}$ and (2) the driving speed and direction of the car (i.e., based on the dynamic model). After taking into account the new observation $\boldsymbol{o}_t$, we can update our belief in $\boldsymbol{x}_t$ based on this evidence. The Kalman filter is one of the popular tools to estimate $\boldsymbol{x}_t$ in this setup.[1]

More technical details of the Kalman filter can be found in Chapter 13. In this chapter, we want to emphasize that in the stochastic process we have just described, the estimation of $\boldsymbol{x}_t$ requires only two things: $\boldsymbol{x}_{t-1}$ and $\boldsymbol{o}_t$—any previous hidden state ($\boldsymbol{x}_{1:t-2}$) or previous observation ($\boldsymbol{o}_{1:t-1}$) is not needed at all!

This is not surprising in our setup. Since $\boldsymbol{x}_{t-1}$ is a random vector, its estimation is an entire distribution. If the probability estimate for $\boldsymbol{x}_{t-1}$ has included all information in $\boldsymbol{x}_{1:t-2}$ and $\boldsymbol{o}_{1:t-1}$, we no longer need this so long as we have already estimated the distribution of $\boldsymbol{x}_{t-1}$. This kind of "memoryless" property is called the *Markov property*, which states that the future evolution of a stochastic process depends only on the current state, and not on any preceding ones. It is obvious that the Kalman filter makes the Markov assumption—i.e., the Markov property is assumed in Kalman filtering.

[1] Rudolf Emil Kalman, the primary co-inventor of this method, is an American electrical engineer and mathematician.

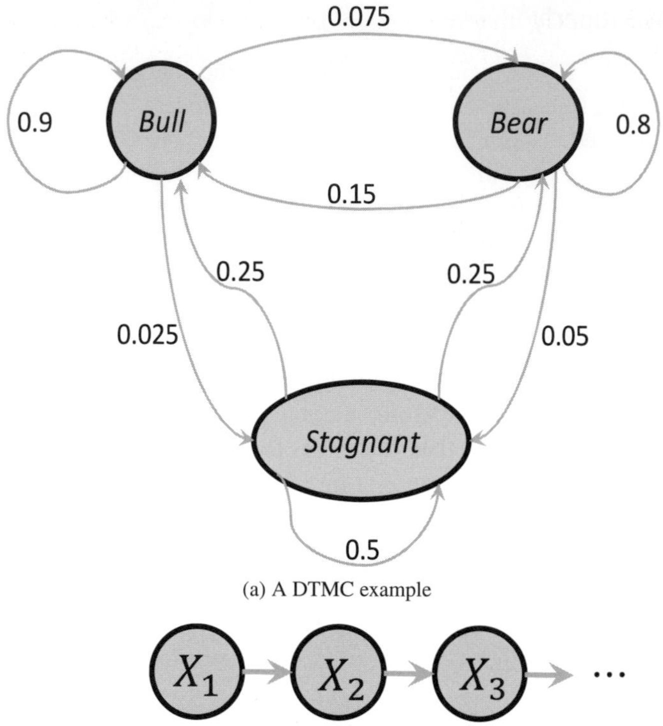

(a) A DTMC example

(b) DTMC graphical model

Figure 12.2 A discrete-time Markov chain example and its graphical model illustration.

We have used the natural numbers $1, 2, \ldots$ to denote discrete time steps. A discrete-time stochastic process satisfying the Markov property is known as a Markov chain (also called the DTMC, or discrete-time Markov chain).[2]

12.1.3 Discrete-Time Markov Chain

Figure 12.2a specifies the evolution of an example DTMC. It models a hypothetical and overly simplified stock market. The random variable in consideration (X) has three possible states: bull market, bear market, and stagnant market, which are the three filled nodes. Arcs denote transitions between different states, and numbers around arcs are the transition probabilities. For example, the arc from the "Bull" node to itself means that a bull market has a 90% chance to remain in the next time step (but also has a 7.5% probability to transit to a bear market and 2.5% to a stagnant one).

[2] Both the Markov property and Markov chain are named after Andrey Andreyevich Markov, a Russian mathematician. Markov's inequality, which is reviewed in Chapter 2, is also named after him.

If we ignore the transition probabilities and specific state symbols, the evolution process can be succinctly depicted as the graphical model in Figure 12.2b.[3] Note that random variables are considered observable in a DTMC, and are drawn as filled circle nodes in graphical models.

Suppose X is discrete and has N possible values, denoted by symbols $S_1, S_2, \ldots, S_N$. To study how X evolves, we first need to observe X_1 at the first time step. Before we observe its value, there is a prior distribution to specify X. We denote the prior distribution by $p(X_1)$, and its p.m.f. is specified by a vector

$$\pi = (\pi_1, \pi_2, \ldots, \pi_N)^T,$$

with $\pi_i = \Pr(X_1 = S_i)$, $\pi_i \geq 0$ $(1 \leq i \leq N)$, and $\sum_{i=1}^{N} \pi_i = 1$.

Because the evolution of X follows a DTMC, X_t depends only on X_{t-1} and not on $X_{1:t-2}$. The transition from X_{t-1} to X_t is stochastic (i.e., probabilistic), and fully specified by a *state transition probability matrix* A, which is an $N \times N$ matrix, with

$$A_{ij} = \Pr(X_t = S_j | X_{t-1} = S_i). \tag{12.2}$$

Because X_t must be one of the N states, we know

$$\begin{aligned} \sum_{j=1}^{N} A_{ij} &= 1 \quad \text{for any } 1 \leq i \leq N, \\ A_{ij} &\geq 0 \quad \text{for any } 1 \leq i, j \leq N. \end{aligned} \tag{12.3}$$

That is, every row of a transition matrix sums to 1. Hence, the numbers around all arcs emitting from any node in Figure 12.2a should sum to 1 (e.g., $0.5+0.25+0.25 = 1$ for the stagnant market node). We call a matrix satisfying these constraints a stochastic matrix. More precisely, it is a right stochastic matrix. A real matrix whose entries are nonnegative and every column sums to 1 is called a left stochastic matrix.

One key benefit of the Markov property is that it greatly reduces the model complexity. If the Markov assumption is invalid, we need to estimate X_t using all previous states $X_{1:t-1}$. Hence, the parameters of $p(X_t | X_{1:t-1})$ require N^t numbers to completely specify it. This exponential increase of model complexity (aka, the curse of dimensionality) makes such a model intractable. Assuming that A remains constant in different time steps, the two parameters (π, A) fully specify a DTMC because of the Markov assumption. Hence, we need only $N^2 - 1$ numbers to specify the parameters of a DTMC (cf. Exercise 12.1.) For notational simplicity, we use λ to denote the set of all parameters—i.e., $\lambda = (\pi, A)$.

[3] A graphical model (or probabilistic graphical model) uses nodes to represent random variables and arcs to denote probabilistic dependence among nodes. Arcs are replaced by lines in undirected graphical models. The Markov chain and HMM are both conveniently represented as graphical models. More complex graphical models and their inference algorithms are not discussed in this introductory book because they are advanced topics. Graphical models are important tools for learning and recognition.

With a set of known parameters λ, we can *generate* a sequence for this DTMC (i.e., *simulating* how X evolves or to *sample* from it). To generate a sequence, we first sample from π and get an instantiation of X_1, say $X_1 = S_{q_1}$. Then we sample from the row corresponding to X_1 (i.e., the q_1th row) in A and get an instantiation of X_2. The sampling process can continue for any number of time steps, and can generate an arbitrary length sequence whose distribution follows the DTMC.

12.1.4 Hidden Markov Models

A sequence generated (sampled) from a DTMC depends only on probabilistic transitions, which may generate strange sequences. For example, a series of transitions "bull–bear–bull–bear" can be sampled from the DTMC in Figure 12.2a, but this sequence is in general unlikely if the unit of a time step is a day instead of a year. In the autonomous driving car example, if observations $\boldsymbol{o}_t$ are not considered, we may find our car in Nanjing, China at time t (seconds), but in New York City, USA at time $t+1$ (seconds), which is impossible because teleportation has yet to be invented.

Observations are useful in dramatically reducing this kind of impossible or unreasonable transition between states. The GPS readings may be off by 10 meters, but will not locate a car at a site in New York if the real location is in Nanjing. A hidden Markov model uses observations and states simultaneously: the state is what we want to estimate (e.g., the car's precise location) but is not directly observable (i.e., is hidden); the observations can be observed, and we can estimate the hidden states using these observations.

The hidden Markov model is illustrated in Figure 12.3 as a graphical model. We use Q_t to denote the state random variable at time t, and O_t the observation random variable. To fully specify an HMM, we need the following five items:

- N: the number of possible states. We use N symbols $S_1, S_2, \ldots, S_N$ to denote them.
- M: the number of possible observations if we assume that observations are discrete too. Often, M is determined by or derived from domain knowledge. We use M symbols $V_1, V_2, \ldots, V_M$ to denote possible observations. The observation O_t

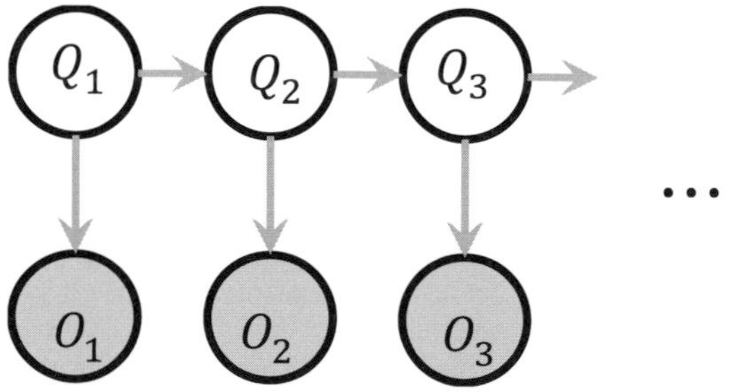

Figure 12.3 The hidden Markov model.

depends only on Q_t, but Q_t does not depend on O_t. Hence, HMM is a directed graphical model.

The observation in an HMM can be, e.g., a normal distribution or even a GMM. In this book, we focus only on the simple scenario where the observation is a discrete random variable.

- π: the prior (initial) state distribution. The vector $\pi = (\pi_1, \pi_2, \ldots, \pi_N)$ and $\pi_i = \Pr(Q_1 = S_i)$.
- A: the state transition matrix. The matrix entry $A_{ij} = \Pr(Q_t = S_j | Q_{t-1} = S_i)$ is the probability of the next state being S_j if the current one is S_i, $1 \le i, j \le N$. Note that we assume A does not change when t changes.
- B: the observation probability matrix. Instead of denoting one probability as B_{jk}, we use $b_j(k) = \Pr(O_t = V_k | Q_t = S_j)$ to denote the probability of the observation being V_k when the state is S_j, $1 \le j \le N$, $1 \le k \le M$. And we assume that B does not change when t changes.

The numbers N and M determine the architecture or structure of a hidden Markov model, and π, A, and B are parameters of the HMM. For notational simplicity, we also use

$$\lambda = (\pi, A, B)$$

to denote all the parameters of an HMM. Although we can manually design the state space for an HMM (or even manually set the values in A and B), it is convenient to specify the structure (N and M) and let an HMM learn its set of states and parameters from the training data.

The Markov property is translated in HMM notation as

$$\Pr(Q_t | Q_{1:t-1}, O_{1:t-1}) = \Pr(Q_t | Q_{t-1}) \tag{12.4}$$

for any t. HMM is a generative model. After the structure and parameters are fixed, we can easily compute the joint probability of T hidden states $q_{1:T}$ (where q_t is the index of the state at time t, $1 \le q_t \le N$ for $1 \le t \le T$) and T observations $o_{1:T}$ (where o_t is index of the observation at time t, $1 \le o_t \le M$):

$$\Pr(Q_1 = S_{q_1}, O_1 = V_{o_1}, \ldots, Q_T = S_{q_T}, O_T = V_{o_T}) \tag{12.5}$$

$$= \pi_{q_1} b_{q_1}(o_1) A_{q_1 q_2} b_{q_2}(o_2) A_{q_2 q_3} b_{q_3}(o_3) \cdots A_{q_{T-1} q_T} b_{q_T}(o_T) \tag{12.6}$$

$$= \pi_{q_1} b_{q_1}(o_1) \prod_{t=2}^{T} A_{q_{t-1} q_t} b_{q_t}(o_t). \tag{12.7}$$

In other words, because of the conditional independence (Q_t is conditionally independent of $Q_{1:t-2}$ and $O_{1:t-1}$ if Q_{t-1} is known), the joint probability is the product of a series of probabilities, whose computations never involve the joint of more than two random variables. For notational simplicity, we abbreviate the joint probability as $\Pr(q_{1:T}, o_{1:T})$.

Based on this joint probability mass function, we can sample from the HMM to generate an arbitrary length sequence of hidden states and observations. To generate a length T sequence, we use the following procedure:

1. $t \leftarrow 1$.
2. Sample $Q_1 = S_{q_1}$ from π.
3. Sample the observation $O_1 = V_{o_1}$ using the p.m.f. which is in the q_1th row of B.
4. If the current time $t = T$, terminate; otherwise, sample the next state $Q_{t+1} = S_{q_{t+1}}$ using the p.m.f. that is in the q_tth row of A.
5. Sample the observation $O_{t+1} = o_{t+1}$ using the p.m.f. that is in the q_{t+1}th row of B.
6. $t \leftarrow t + 1$, and go to line 4.

12.2 Three Basic Problems in HMM Learning

There are three basic learning problems in HMMs, whose definitions follow that in Rabiner (1989). In all three problems, we assume that the HMM structure (i.e., N and M) has been fixed. The first basic problem is to evaluate the probability of an observation sequence $o_{1:T}$ when the model parameters are fixed—i.e., to calculate $\Pr(o_{1:T}|\lambda)$. This *evaluation* problem, as will be shown soon, is relatively simple to solve among the three basic problems. However, the evaluation problem has many important applications in HMMs.

For example, given a fixed set of parameters λ and two sequences $o_{1:T}$ and $o'_{1:T}$, the evaluated sequence probability will tell us which sequence has a higher chance of being observed. Probably a more important usage of the evaluation problem is model selection. If we have an observation sequence $o_{1:T}$ and two sets of parameters λ_1 and λ_2 (which are, e.g., learned using different methods), it is reasonable to conjecture that the model with a larger probability of observing this sequence is a better fit to the observations. Note that when we allow the parameters λ to change, the probability of observing $o_{1:T}$ given parameters λ is the *likelihood* of the parameters. Given a training sequence $o_{1:T}$, maximum likelihood estimation will find a parameter set that maximizes this likelihood (which is the third basic problem).

The second basic problem is the *decoding* problem. When we are given a fixed parameter set λ and an observation sequence $o_{1:T}$, what is the best hidden state sequence corresponding to these observations? As we have illustrated using the autonomous driving car example, it is usually the hidden states (rather than the observations) that are useful for an application. Hence, decoding an optimal hidden state sequence from the observation sequence is a very important problem in HMM learning.

However, it is not always easy to define what *best* or *optimal* means in the decoding problem. As will be shown, different optimality criteria have been proposed and different answers to the decoding problem will be given accordingly. In addition to finding the best sequence of hidden states, the decoding problem has other applications in

HMM. For example, suppose we have learned an HMM model with a large N, but the decoding procedure has found that many symbols (in $S_1, S_2, \dots, S_N$) have never appeared in the decoded optimal sequences. This fact suggests that N is too big for our problem at hand (i.e., many state symbols are wasted), and we may need to learn a new model with a smaller N.

The third and final basic problem in HMM is to *learn* the optimal parameters for an HMM. We have assumed the HMM model—i.e., the parameters $\lambda = (\pi, A, B)$—have been given or assigned optimal values in the first two basic problems. In real-world applications, however, we have to learn these parameters for ourselves.

As mentioned before, the basic idea is to find the parameters that have the largest likelihood. That is, given N, M, and the training sequence $o_{1:T}$, we want to find the parameter set λ that maximizes the likelihood function $\Pr(o_{1:T}|\lambda)$. Note that in this maximum likelihood estimation, λ is not a random vector. Its appearance after the conditional probability symbol ("|") is only to indicate that the involved probability is computed using λ as the parameter values, and to be consistent with notation in the literature.

The training data for HMM learning, however, is different from those in methods we have seen (e.g., SVM). If T is large enough, one training sequence $o_{1:T}$ might be sufficient to learn a good HMM model. Of course, we can also use multiple training sequences to learn HMM parameters.

The key strategy for solving the first two basic problems is dynamic programming, which we experienced in the dynamic time warping method in the previous chapter. The third basic HMM problem can be solved by using the expectation-maximization (EM) algorithm. We will introduce the details of the solutions to these problems in the rest of this chapter.

12.3 α, β, and the Evaluation Problem

Given N, M, λ, and $o_{1:T}$, the evaluation problem tries to compute $\Pr(o_{1:T}|\lambda)$. The law of total probability gives a way to compute it:

$$\Pr(o_{1:T}|\lambda) = \sum_{q_{1:T}\in\Omega} \Pr(o_{1:T}, q_{1:T}|\lambda) \tag{12.8}$$

$$= \sum_{q_{1:T}\in\Omega} \Pr(o_{1:T}|q_{1:T}, \lambda) \Pr(q_{1:T}|\lambda), \tag{12.9}$$

in which Ω is the space of all possible sequences of hidden states. Note that $\Pr(o_{1:T}|q_{1:T}, \lambda)$ means $\Pr(O_{1:T} = V_{o_{1:T}}|Q_{1:T} = S_{q_{1:T}}, \lambda)$. When the meaning is obvious from the symbols and contexts, we will omit the random variable names in equations.

It is obvious that

$$\Pr(o_{1:T}|q_{1:T}, \lambda) = \prod_{t=1}^{T} \Pr(o_t|q_t, \lambda) = \prod_{t=1}^{T} b_{q_t}(o_t)$$

and

$$\Pr(q_{1:T}|\lambda) = \pi_{q_1} \prod_{t=2}^{T} A_{q_{t-1}q_t}.$$

In other words, in order to use the law of total probability to compute $\Pr(o_{1:T}|\lambda)$, we need to generate $|\Omega|$ sequences of hidden states and observations. Because each state can take the values of N possible symbols and there are T time steps, $|\Omega| = N^T$, which means Eq. (12.9) is not tractable.

The complexity of Eq. (12.9) comes from variations in the states $Q_{1:T}$. Because the states are hidden, we have to enumerate all possibilities and compute the expectation, which leads to the exponentially increasing complexity. However, the Markov assumption says that given $Q_t = S_{q_t}$, Q_{t+1} is independent of $Q_{1:t-1}$ and $O_{1:t-1}$. In addition, O_t depends only on Q_t. In other words, we can divide the calculation $\Pr(o_{1:T}|\lambda)$ into two smaller problems: $\Pr(o_{1:T-1}|\lambda)$ and $\Pr(o_T|\lambda)$, and combine them by enumerating all possible states of Q_{T-1} and Q_T (whose complexity is $N \times N = N^2$). Similarly, the calculation of $\Pr(o_{1:T-1}|\lambda)$ can be further divided into $\Pr(o_{1:T-2}|\lambda)$ and $\Pr(o_{T-1}|\lambda)$—a typical dynamic programming formulation!

12.3.1 The Forward Variable and Algorithm

The law of total probability tells us

$$\Pr(o_{1:T}|\lambda) = \sum_{i=1}^{N} \Pr(o_{1:T}, Q_T = S_i|\lambda) \tag{12.10}$$

$$= \sum_{i=1}^{N} \Pr(o_{1:T-1}, Q_T = S_i|\lambda) b_i(o_T), \tag{12.11}$$

and then we need to compute $\Pr(o_{1:T-1}, Q_T = S_i|\lambda)$. Using the law of total probability again we have

$$\Pr(o_{1:T-1}, Q_T = S_i|\lambda) \tag{12.12}$$

$$= \sum_{j=1}^{N} \Pr(o_{1:T-1}, Q_T = S_i, Q_{T-1} = S_j|\lambda) \tag{12.13}$$

$$= \sum_{j=1}^{N} \Pr(o_{1:T-1}, Q_{T-1} = S_j|\lambda) \Pr(Q_T = S_i|o_{1:T-1}, Q_{T-1} = S_j, \lambda) \tag{12.14}$$

$$= \sum_{j=1}^{N} \Pr(o_{1:T-1}, Q_{T-1} = S_j|\lambda) \Pr(Q_T = S_i|Q_{T-1} = S_j, \lambda) \tag{12.15}$$

$$= \sum_{j=1}^{N} \Pr(o_{1:T-1}, Q_{T-1} = S_j|\lambda) A_{ji}. \tag{12.16}$$

Note that in the above derivation, we have implicitly used *conditional independence* among variables without a proof. In the exercise problems for this chapter, we will describe the d-separation method, which can precisely reveal such conditional independence.

The recursion from $T-1$ to T is not obvious yet. However, because

$$\Pr(o_{1:T-1}|\lambda) = \sum_{j=1}^{N} \Pr(o_{1:T-1}, Q_{T-1} = S_j|\lambda), \tag{12.17}$$

if we can compute $\Pr(o_{1:T-1}, Q_{T-1} = S_j|\lambda)$ for *all* $1 \le j \le N$, we can evaluate $\Pr(o_{1:T-1}|\lambda)$, and similarly $\Pr(o_{1:T}|\lambda)$ for time T.

Hence, in a dynamic programming solution for the HMM evaluation problem, the quantity to be evaluated is $\Pr(o_{1:t}, Q_t = S_i|\lambda)$ for all $1 \le t \le T$ and $1 \le i \le N$. The *forward algorithm* (or forward procedure) defines this quantity as the forward variable $\alpha_t(i)$:

$$\alpha_t(i) = \Pr(o_{1:t}, Q_t = S_i|\lambda), \tag{12.18}$$

which is the probability that at time t, the hidden state is S_i and the observation history till time t is $o_{1:t}$. The recursion between forward variables in two consecutive time steps is

$$\alpha_{t+1}(i) = \left(\sum_{j=1}^{N} \alpha_t(j) A_{ji}\right) b_i(o_{t+1}), \tag{12.19}$$

which is easy to prove using Eqs. (12.12) and (12.16).

It is obvious that when $t = 1$ we have

$$\alpha_1(i) = \pi_i b_i(o_1).$$

Hence, we can start the recursion from $t = 1$, and move from left to right (i.e., t increases) until $t = T$ (hence this method is called the forward algorithm). The forward algorithm is described in Algorithm 8.

Algorithm 8 The forward algorithm

1: **Initialization**: $\alpha_1(i) = \pi_i b_i(o_1)$ for all $1 \le i \le N$.

2: **Forward recursion**: For $t = 1, 2, \ldots, T-2, T-1$ and all $1 \le i \le N$,

$$\alpha_{t+1}(i) = \left(\sum_{j=1}^{N} \alpha_t(j) A_{ji}\right) b_i(o_{t+1}).$$

3: **Output**:

$$P(o_{1:T}|\lambda) = \sum_{i=1}^{N} \alpha_T(i). \tag{12.20}$$

It is obvious that the complexity of the forward algorithm is $\mathcal{O}(TN^2)$, which is efficient and much faster than N^T. Dynamic programming has once again proved itself to be an effective strategy in removing redundant computations.

12.3.2 The Backward Variable and Algorithm

We can interpret the $\alpha_t(i)$ variable as the following: one person stands at time t and looks back; $\alpha_t(i)$ is the probability of this person observing state symbol S_i and the history observation sequence $o_{1:t}$. After obtaining $\alpha_t(i)$, if this person turns around and looks into the future, which information is still missing? We *have observed the state* $Q_t = S_i$ and observations $o_{1:t}$, and still have to observe $o_{t+1:T}$! Hence, the backward variable $\beta_t(i)$ is defined as

$$\beta_t(i) = \Pr(o_{t+1:T} | Q_t = S_i, \lambda), \tag{12.21}$$

i.e., $\beta_t(i)$ is the probability of observing future output sequence $o_{t+1:T}$ if the hidden state is S_i at time t.

It is easy to derive the recursive relationship for $\beta_t(i)$, which is

$$\beta_t(i) = \sum_{j=1}^{N} A_{ij} b_j(o_{t+1}) \beta_{t+1}(j). \tag{12.22}$$

It is obvious that the recursive updates move backward (i.e., use time $t+1$ probabilities to calculate those at time t). Hence, the backward algorithm (the backward procedure) must be initialized with $t = T$, and $\beta_T(i)$ is the probability of observing nothing after time T given the current state $Q_T = S_i$, which is 1. Finally, we have

$$\Pr(o_{1:T} | \lambda) = \sum_{i=1}^{N} \pi_i b_i(o_1) \beta_1(i). \tag{12.23}$$

The proofs of the above two equations are left as exercises. Putting these facts together, we have come up with the backward algorithm in Algorithm 9.

Algorithm 9 The backward algorithm

1: **Initialization**: $\beta_T(i) = 1$ for all $1 \le i \le N$.

2: **Backward recursion**: For $t = T-1, T-2, \ldots, 2, 1$ and all $1 \le i \le N$,

$$\beta_t(i) = \sum_{j=1}^{N} A_{ij} b_j(o_{t+1}) \beta_{t+1}(j).$$

3: **Output**:

$$\Pr(o_{1:T} | \lambda) = \sum_{i=1}^{N} \pi_i b_i(o_1) \beta_1(i). \tag{12.24}$$

```
iter = 1;
for iter = 1:1000
    N = 3;   % number of states
    Pi = rand(1,N); Pi = Pi / sum(Pi); % prior distribution
    A = rand(N,N); % state transition matrix
    A(1,3) = 0; % cannot have a transition from state 1 to 3
    for i=1:N     A(i,:) = A(i,:) / sum(A(i,:));    end
    M = 3; % number of outputs
    B = rand(N,M); % output probability matrix
    for i=1:N     B(i,:) = B(i,:) / sum(B(i,:));    end
    T = 5; % number of time steps
    O = randi(M, 1, T); % outputs

    Alpha = zeros (T, N); % alpha
    Beta = ones (T, N);   % beta
    % Compute Alpha
    Alpha(1,:) = Pi .* B(:, O(1))';
    for t = 2:T
        Alpha(t,:) = (Alpha(t-1,:) * A) .* B(:,O(t))';
    end
    % Compute Beta
    for t = (T-1):-1:1
        Beta(t,:) = A * (B(:,O(t+1)) .* Beta(t+1,:)');
    end
    Gamma = Alpha.*Beta; % (unnormalized) gamma
    % two ways to compute the sequence probablity
    p1 = sum(Alpha(end,:));
    p2 = sum(Gamma(1,:));
    assert(abs(p1-p2)<1e-12);
    % can we find an invalid transition from state 1 to 3?
    [~,I]=max(Gamma');
    for i=1:T-1
        if I(i)==1 && I(i+1)==3
            disp(['1-->3␣at␣iteration␣' num2str(iter) '!'])
            return
        end
    end
end
```

Figure 12.4 Sample code to compute α, β, and (unnormalized) γ variables. Note that this code is only for illustrative purposes—it is not practical for solving real-world HMM problems.

The forward and backward procedures must give the same answer because they are computing the same probability. Figure 12.4 includes MATLAB/GNU Octave code to evaluate $\Pr(o_{1:T}|\lambda)$, whose results show that the forward and backward algorithms indeed return the same answer to the evaluation problem.

However, the code in Figure 12.4 is listed only for illustrative purposes. When T is a large number, the computed probability will be a very small number (e.g., $< 10^{-400}$), so $\Pr(o_{1:T}|\lambda)$ may be smaller than the minimum floating point number that can be represented by a `float` (single precision) or `double` (double precision) type in a computer system. Numerical errors (such as rounding errors) will also quickly accumulate. Hence, implementing algorithms in hidden Markov models is complex and tricky. We will not dive into HMM implementation details, but interested readers can refer to publicly available HMM implementation source code such as the HTK package.[4]

12.4 γ, δ, ψ, and the Decoding Problem

Now we move on to the second basic problem: decoding. As we have discussed, given an observation sequence $o_{1:T}$, one major question is what the criterion to determine the best (or optimal) hidden state sequence is.

12.4.1 γ and the Independently Decoded Optimal States

One straightforward idea is to use a simple criterion: find the maximum likelihood state for each time step independently. That is, for any $1 \le t \le T$, we can compute $\Pr(Q_t = S_i | o_{1:T}, \lambda)$ for all $1 \le i \le N$, and set Q_t to the one leading to the maximum probability.

To solve this problem, we can define the γ variables as

$$\gamma_t(i) = \Pr(Q_t = S_i | o_{1:T}, \lambda), \tag{12.25}$$

and set

$$q_t = \underset{1 \le i \le N}{\arg\max}\, \gamma_t(i) \tag{12.26}$$

for all $1 \le t \le T$. We can then decode the hidden state Q_t as S_{q_t}.

The variable $\gamma_t(i)$ is the probability of Q_t being S_i when we have observed the complete observation sequence $o_{1:T}$. In fact, we do not need to design a new algorithm to compute this variable: it can easily be computed from $\alpha_t(i)$ and $\beta_t(i)$.

Because $O_{1:t}$ and $O_{t+1:T}$ are independent of each other if Q_t is known, we have

$$\begin{aligned}
\Pr(Q_t = S_i, o_{1:T} | \lambda) &= \Pr(o_{1:t}, o_{t+1:T} | Q_t = S_i, \lambda) \Pr(Q_t = S_i | \lambda) && (12.27)\\
&= \Pr(o_{1:t} | Q_t = S_i, \lambda) \Pr(o_{t+1:T} | Q_t = S_i, \lambda) \Pr(Q_t = S_i | \lambda) && (12.28)\\
&= \Pr(o_{t+1:T} | Q_t = S_i, \lambda) \Pr(Q_t = S_i, o_{1:t} | \lambda) && (12.29)\\
&= \alpha_t(i)\beta_t(i). && (12.30)
\end{aligned}$$

Then we can compute $\gamma_t(i)$ as

$$\begin{aligned}
\gamma_t(i) &= \frac{\Pr(Q_t = S_i, o_{1:T} | \lambda)}{\Pr(o_{1:T} | \lambda)} && (12.31)\\
&= \frac{\Pr(Q_t = S_i, o_{1:T} | \lambda)}{\sum_{j=1}^N \Pr(Q_t = S_j, o_{1:T} | \lambda)} && (12.32)\\
&= \frac{\alpha_t(i)\beta_t(i)}{\sum_{j=1}^N \alpha_t(j)\beta_t(j)}. && (12.33)
\end{aligned}$$

[4] http://htk.eng.cam.ac.uk/

To compute the γ variables, we can first set $\gamma_t(i) = \alpha_t(i)\beta_t(i)$, and then ℓ_1 normalize the γ values for every time step t. Note that we can find q_t by finding the maximum element in the unnormalized γ values (i.e., $\alpha_t(i)\beta_t(i)$) without the normalization, because the normalization constant $\Pr(o_{1:T}|\lambda)$ will not change the index of the largest γ value at time t.

One by-product of this derivation is that now we have three equivalent ways to solve the evaluation problem: using α, β, and $\alpha\beta$. Based on the above derivation, we have

$$\Pr(o_{1:T}|\lambda) = \sum_{i=1}^{N} \alpha_t(i)\beta_t(i) \tag{12.34}$$

for *any* time t!

This criterion finds the best state for each time t independently, which may lead to state sequences that should not appear. For example, in Figure 12.4, we have set the transition probability from S_1 to S_3 as 0—i.e., this transition must never happen. However, if we use γ to decode hidden states independently, running that piece of code shows that this impossible transition indeed happens in the decoded state sequences. Hence, this criterion (Eq. 12.26) has serious problems in some applications.

12.4.2 δ, ψ, and the Jointly Decoded Optimal States

To eliminate impossible state transitions, one possible solution is to jointly decode the entire optimal state sequence:

$$q_{1:T} = \arg\max_{Q_{1:T}} \Pr(Q_{1:T}|o_{1:T}, \lambda) \tag{12.35}$$

$$= \arg\max_{Q_{1:T}} \Pr(Q_{1:T}, o_{1:T}|\lambda). \tag{12.36}$$

The key to its solution is once again dynamic programming. The recursive relationship is as follows. Given $o_{1:t}$, it is very useful if we know the optimal paths for N subproblems:

$$\max_{Q_{1:t-1}} \Pr(Q_{1:t-1}, o_{1:t}, Q_t = S_i|\lambda), \quad 1 \le i \le N.$$

These subproblems are similar to the objective in Eq. (12.36), but with an additional constraint $Q_t = S_i$ for the ith subproblem. We can solve at least the following two problems using the answers to these N subproblems:

- The optimal state sequence till time t. If a subproblem $i^\star$ has the largest probability among all N subproblems, then the optimal parameter of this subproblem ($q_{1:t-1}$) plus $q_t = i^\star$ is the optimal hidden state sequence for observations $o_{1:t}$.
- The optimal $q_{1:t+1}$ for $o_{1:t+1}$ can be divided into three parts: $q_{1:t-1}$, q_t, and q_{t+1}. If an oracle tells us $q_t = i^\star$, the $q_{1:t-1}$ part can be found by the $i^\star$th subproblem. Because of the Markov assumption, we need to consider only N possible transitions $S_{q_t} \to S_{q_{t+1}}$ to decide which state is optimal for Q_{t+1}. Although we do not have

access to an oracle, we can try all N subproblems (i.e., $i^\star = 1, 2, \ldots, N$), which is still tractable.

The objectives of these subproblems are denoted by a new variable

$$\delta_t(i) = \max_{Q_{1:t-1}} \Pr(Q_{1:t-1}, o_{1:t}, Q_t = S_i | \lambda). \tag{12.37}$$

The recursive relationship is also obvious (by translating the above description into mathematics):

$$\delta_{t+1}(i) = \max_{1 \le j \le N} \left(\delta_t(j) A_{ji} b_i(o_{t+1}) \right), \tag{12.38}$$

in which $\delta_t(j)$ is the probability of the jth subproblem, A_{ji} transits from S_j (at time t) to S_i (at time $t+1$), and $b_i(o_{t+1})$ is the probability of observing $V_{o_{t+1}}$ when the state is S_i; i.e., $\delta_t(j) A_{ji} b_i(o_{t+1})$ is the probability of the optimal state sequence when an oracle tells us $Q_t = S_j$ for an observation sequence $o_{1:t+1}$. This recursive relationship is a forward one. Hence, we should start the recursion from $t = 1$.

After the δ variables are computed, it is easy to find q_T, by

$$q_T = \arg\max_{1 \le i \le N} \delta_T(i). \tag{12.39}$$

According to Eq. (12.38), if we know that the optimal state at time $t+1$ is q_{t+1}, we just need to find which j leads to the largest $\delta_t(j) A_{ji} b_i(o_{t+1})$; then S_j is the optimal state for Q_t. That is, we need to record the optimal transitions from time t to $t+1$. Using $\psi_{t+1}(i)$ to denote the optimal state at time t if the optimal state is i at time $t+1$, we have

$$\psi_{t+1}(i) = \arg\max_{1 \le j \le N} \left(\delta_t(j) A_{ji} b_i(o_{t+1}) \right) \tag{12.40}$$

$$= \arg\max_{1 \le j \le N} \left(\delta_t(j) A_{ji} \right). \tag{12.41}$$

The initialization should start at $t = 1$. According to the definition of the δ variables, we have

$$\delta_1(i) = \pi_i b_i(o_1)$$

for $1 \le i \le N$. Putting the initialization, recursion, and state tracking equations together, we get the Viterbi algorithm for decoding the optimal hidden state that is the solution of Eq. (12.36). The Viterbi algorithm is shown in Algorithm 10.[5]

Note that the initialization $\psi_1(i) = 0$ is in fact not used at all in the Viterbi algorithm. The complexity of Viterbi decoding is $\mathcal{O}(TN^2)$.

Equations (12.42) and (12.43) involve the sum or maximization of several probabilities. As $\delta_t(j)$ and A_{ji} form two discrete distributions when j varies from 1 to N, we can treat them as *messages* passing between Q_t and Q_{t+1}. Message passing algorithms (such as sum-product and max-product) can solve many inference problems in

[5] Andrew James Viterbi is an American electrical engineer and businessman. He is a cofounder of Qualcomm Inc. He proposed the Viterbi decoding algorithm in 1967, but did not patent it.

Algorithm 10 Viterbi decoding

1: **Initialization**: $\delta_1(i) = \pi_i b_i(o_1)$, $\psi_1(i) = 0$ for all $1 \le i \le N$.

2: **Forward recursion**: For $t = 2, 3, \ldots, T-2, T-1$ and all $1 \le i \le N$,

$$\delta_{t+1}(i) = \max_{1 \le j \le N} \left(\delta_t(j) A_{ji} b_i(o_{t+1}) \right), \tag{12.42}$$

$$\psi_{t+1}(i) = \arg\max_{1 \le j \le N} \left(\delta_t(j) A_{ji} \right). \tag{12.43}$$

3: **Output**: The optimal state q_T is determined by

$$q_T = \arg\max_{1 \le i \le N} \delta_T(i), \tag{12.44}$$

and the rest of the optimal path is determined by

$$q_t = \psi_{t+1}(q_{t+1}) \quad \text{for } t = T-1, T-2, \ldots, 2, 1. \tag{12.45}$$

graphical models, with the forward, backward, and Viterbi algorithms all as special cases in the message passing family.

12.5 ξ and Learning HMM Parameters

Given N, M, and a training sequence $o_{1:T}$, to learn the optimal parameters $\lambda = (\pi, A, B)$ is the most difficult among the three basic problems. The classic algorithm is called the Baum–Welch algorithm.[6] Baum–Welch is a maximum likelihood (ML) estimation algorithm, which maximizes the likelihood of λ for the observation sequence $o_{1:T}$:

$$\lambda^\star = \arg\max_{\lambda} \Pr(o_{1:T} | \lambda). \tag{12.46}$$

Note that we assume that only one training sequence is used, but the generalization of Baum–Welch to multiple training sequences is easy.

Baum–Welch is an iterative algorithm. With initial (e.g., randomly initialized or by clustering the training sequence) parameters $\lambda^{(1)}$, we can compute its likelihood $\ell^{(1)} = \Pr(o_{1:T} | \lambda^{(1)})$. Then we can find a new set of parameters $\lambda^{(2)}$ such that its likelihood $\ell^{(2)} = \Pr(o_{1:T} | \lambda^{(2)})$ is higher than $\ell^{(1)}$ (or at least the same). We can then move on to find the next set of better parameters $\lambda^{(3)}$, $\lambda^{(4)}$ and so on, until the likelihood converges.

Baum–Welch is in fact a special case of the more general expectation-maximization (EM) algorithm for maximum likelihood estimation. Hence, it is guaranteed to converge to a local maximum of the likelihood function. For more details of the EM

[6] This algorithm is named after Leonard Esau Baum and Lloyd Richard Welch, two American mathematicians.

algorithm, please refer to Chapter 14. In that chapter, there is also an exercise problem that derives Baum–Welch updating equations from the EM perspective.

12.5.1 Baum–Welch: Updating λ as Expected Proportions

The Baum–Welch algorithm uses a new variable ξ and a few simple equations to update $\lambda^{(r+1)}$ based on $\lambda^{(r)}$, in which r is the iteration number. In this chapter, we will ignore the proof that Baum–Welch always increases or keeps the same likelihood. Instead, we will focus on the intuition behind the ξ variables and the updating equations.

The ξ variable involves three other values: t (the time) and (i, j), which are state indexes:

$$\xi_t(i,j) = \Pr(Q_t = S_i, Q_{t+1} = S_j | o_{1:T}, \lambda). \tag{12.47}$$

The term $\xi_t(i,j)$ is the conditional probability of the states for t and $t+1$ being S_i and S_j, respectively, when the observation sequence $o_{1:T}$ is presented. In other words, $\xi_t(i,j)$ is the *expected proportion* of transition from S_i (at time t) to S_j (at time $t+1$). Based on this interpretation, it is natural to use $\xi_t(i,j)$ (computed based on the parameters $\lambda^{(r)}$) to update the value for A_{ij} in $\lambda^{(r+1)}$!

For example, if there are three states $\{S_1, S_2, S_3\}$ and $\sum_{t=1}^{T-1} \xi_t(2,1) = 100$, this means there are 100 (expected) transitions from S_2 to S_1 in the entire training sequence. Suppose $\sum_{t=1}^{T-1} \xi_t(2,2) = 150$ and $\sum_{t=1}^{T-1} \xi_t(2,3) = 250$. Then it is natural to update A_{21} as

$$\frac{100}{100 + 150 + 250} = 0.2,$$

because this is the expected proportion of transitions from S_2 to S_1. Similarly, A_{22} and A_{23} can be updated by their estimated proportions 0.3 and 0.5, respectively. The same idea can be used to update π and B.

12.5.2 How to Compute ξ

Using the definition of conditional probabilities, we have

$$\xi_t(i,j) \Pr(o_{1:T}|\lambda) = \Pr(Q_t = S_i, Q_{t+1} = S_j, o_{1:T}|\lambda). \tag{12.48}$$

Hence we can find the probability $\Pr(Q_t = S_i, Q_{t+1} = S_j, o_{1:T}|\lambda)$ and use it to compute $\xi_t(i,j)$. This probability can be factored into the product of four probabilities: $\alpha_t(i)$, A_{ij}, $b_j(o_{t+1})$, and $\beta_{t+1}(j)$, as shown in Figure 12.5. For convenience of reading, we list the HMM variables in Table 12.1. Now we have

$$\xi_t(i,j) = \frac{\alpha_t(i) A_{ij} b_j(o_{t+1}) \beta_{t+1}(j)}{\Pr(o_{1:T}|\lambda)}. \tag{12.49}$$

Table 12.1 Summary of the variables in HMM learning.

	Definition	Recursion/calculation
α	$\alpha_t(i) = \Pr(o_{1:t}, Q_t = S_i \mid \lambda)$	$\alpha_{t+1}(i) = \left(\sum_{j=1}^{N} \alpha_t(j) A_{ji}\right) b_i(o_{t+1})$
β	$\beta_t(i) = \Pr(o_{t+1:T} \mid Q_t = S_i, \lambda)$	$\beta_t(i) = \sum_{j=1}^{N} A_{ij} b_j(o_{t+1}) \beta_{t+1}(j)$
γ	$\gamma_t(i) = \Pr(Q_t = S_i \mid o_{1:T}, \lambda)$	$\gamma_t(i) = \frac{\alpha_t(i)\beta_t(i)}{\sum_{j=1}^{N} \alpha_t(j)\beta_t(j)}$
δ	$\delta_t(i) = \max_{Q_{1:t-1}} \Pr(Q_{1:t-1}, o_{1:t}, Q_t{=}S_i \mid \lambda)$	$\delta_{t+1}(i) = \max_{1 \le j \le N} \left(\delta_t(j) A_{ji} b_i(o_{t+1})\right)$
ξ	$\xi_t(i,j) = \Pr(Q_t{=}S_i, Q_{t+1}{=}S_j \mid o_{1:T}, \lambda)$	$\xi_t(i,j) = \frac{\alpha_t(i) A_{ij} b_j(o_{t+1}) \beta_{t+1}(j)}{\sum_{i=1}^{N} \sum_{j=1}^{N} \alpha_t(i) A_{ij} b_j(o_{t+1}) \beta_{t+1}(j)}$

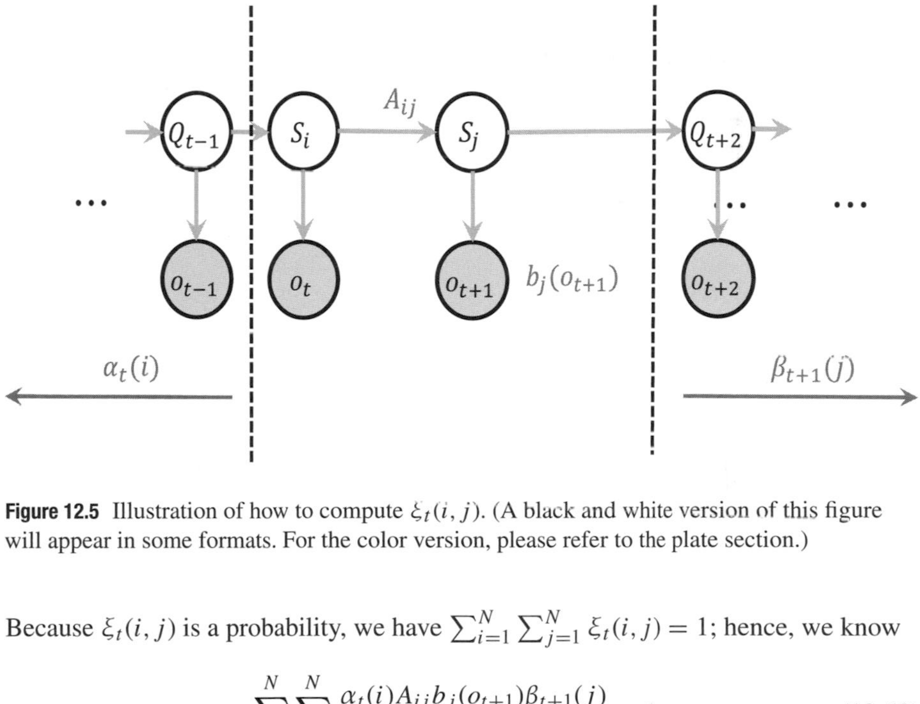

Figure 12.5 Illustration of how to compute $\xi_t(i,j)$. (A black and white version of this figure will appear in some formats. For the color version, please refer to the plate section.)

Because $\xi_t(i,j)$ is a probability, we have $\sum_{i=1}^{N} \sum_{j=1}^{N} \xi_t(i,j) = 1$; hence, we know

$$\sum_{i=1}^{N} \sum_{j=1}^{N} \frac{\alpha_t(i) A_{ij} b_j(o_{t+1}) \beta_{t+1}(j)}{\Pr(o_{1:T} \mid \lambda)} = 1, \tag{12.50}$$

or in an equivalent form,

$$\Pr(o_{1:T} \mid \lambda) = \sum_{i=1}^{N} \sum_{j=1}^{N} \alpha_t(i) A_{ij} b_j(o_{t+1}) \beta_{t+1}(j), \tag{12.51}$$

for any $1 \le t \le T-1$. This equation provides yet another way to solve the evaluation problem.

And, comparing the definitions of γ and ξ, we immediately get (by the law of total probability)

$$\gamma_t(i) = \sum_{j=1}^{N} \xi_t(i,j). \tag{12.52}$$

The parameters $\lambda = (\pi, A, B)$ can be updated using γ and ξ.

- Since $\gamma_1(i)$ is the expected proportion of $Q_1 = S_i$, we can update π_i using $\gamma_1(i)$.
- The expected probability of transition from S_i to S_j is $\xi_t(i,j)$ at time t. Hence, the expected number of transitions from S_i to S_j in the training sequence is $\sum_{t=1}^{T-1} \xi_t(i,j)$, while $\sum_{t=1}^{T-1} \gamma_t(i)$ is the expected number of times any state is S_i. Then A_{ij}, the probability of transiting from S_i to S_j, is the proportion of transitions $S_i \to S_j$ in all transitions starting from S_i, i.e.,

$$\frac{\sum_{t=1}^{T-1} \xi_t(i,j)}{\sum_{t=1}^{T-1} \gamma_t(i)}.$$

- To update B, we need to estimate two terms: the expected number of times in hidden state S_j ($\sum_{t=1}^{T} \gamma_t(j)$), and the number of times the hidden state is S_j *and* the observation is V_k at the same time ($\sum_{t=1}^{T} [\![o_t = k]\!] \gamma_t(j)$), in which $[\![\cdot]\!]$ is the indicator function. Then we can update $b_j(k)$ as the ratio between these two terms.

Summarizing the results till now, we arrive at the Baum–Welch algorithm, which is described in Algorithm 11.

12.6 Miscellaneous Notes and Additional Resources

Rabiner (1989) is an excellent tutorial for various aspects of HMM techniques and applications, while details of the application of HMM in speech recognition can be found in Rabiner & Juang (1993).

Details of recurrent neural networks can be found in Chapter 10 of Goodfellow et al. (2016), and Zhou et al. (2016) provides a succinct description and comparison of LSTM, GRU, and MGU.

We will introduce a little bit more on Kalman filtering in the next chapter. A tutorial on this topic can be found in Bishop & Welch (2001).

We have not elaborated on probabilistic graphical models in this book. Chapter 8 of Bishop (2006) and Jensen (1997) are good reading for beginners to this field, while Koller & Friedman (2009) has more advanced material.

In the exercise problems, we provide examples to understand conditional independence and the d-separation algorithm, which can also be found in the aforementioned books.

Message passing or belief propagation is an important algorithm for graphical models, and Kschischang et al. (2001) is a good resource for understanding this algorithm and its extensions.

Algorithm 11 The Baum–Welch algorithm

Initialize the parameters $\lambda^{(1)}$ (e.g., randomly).
$r \leftarrow 1$.
while the likelihood has not converged **do**
    Use the forward procedure to compute $\alpha_t(i)$ for all t $(1 \le t \le T)$ and all i $(1 \le i \le N)$ based on $\lambda^{(r)}$.
    Use the backward procedure to compute $\beta_t(i)$ for all t $(1 \le t \le T)$ and all i $(1 \le i \le N)$ based on $\lambda^{(r)}$.
    Compute $\gamma_t(i)$ for all t $(1 \le t \le T)$ and all i $(1 \le i \le N)$ according to the equation in Table 12.1.
    Compute $\xi_t(i,j)$ for all t $(1 \le t \le T-1)$ and all i, j $(1 \le i, j \le N)$ according to the equation in Table 12.1.
    Update the parameters to $\lambda^{(r+1)}$:

$$\pi_i^{(r+1)} = \gamma_1(i), \qquad 1 \le i \le N, \tag{12.53}$$

$$A_{ij}^{(r+1)} = \frac{\sum_{t=1}^{T-1} \xi_t(i,j)}{\sum_{t=1}^{T-1} \gamma_t(i)}, \qquad 1 \le i, j \le N, \tag{12.54}$$

$$b_j^{(r+1)}(k) = \frac{\sum_{t=1}^{T} [\![o_t = k]\!] \gamma_t(j)}{\sum_{t=1}^{T} \gamma_t(j)}, \qquad 1 \le j \le N,\ 1 \le k \le M. \tag{12.55}$$

    $r \leftarrow r + 1$.
end while

In this chapter, we have not proved that Baum–Welch will converge. In the exercise problem for Chapter 14, we will derive Baum–Welch as an application of the EM algorithm. Because EM is guaranteed to converge to a local minimum, we are assured that Baum–Welch will also converge.

Exercises

12.1 Suppose a DTMC models the evolution of a random variable X, which is discrete and has N possible values (states). Show that we need $N^2 - 1$ numbers to fully specify this DTMC.

12.2 Let A be the transition matrix of an HMM model. Prove that $A^k = \overbrace{A \ldots A}^{kA\text{'s}}$ is a right stochastic matrix for any positive integer k.

12.3 (Conditional independence) We say that A and B are conditionally independent given C, denoted as

$$A \perp B \mid C,$$

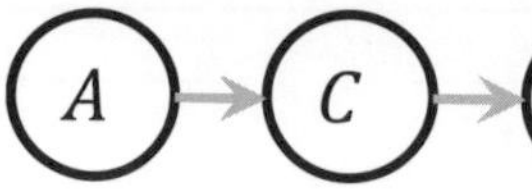
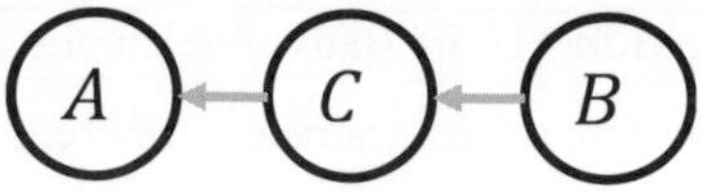

(a) Case 1.1 (b) Case 1.2

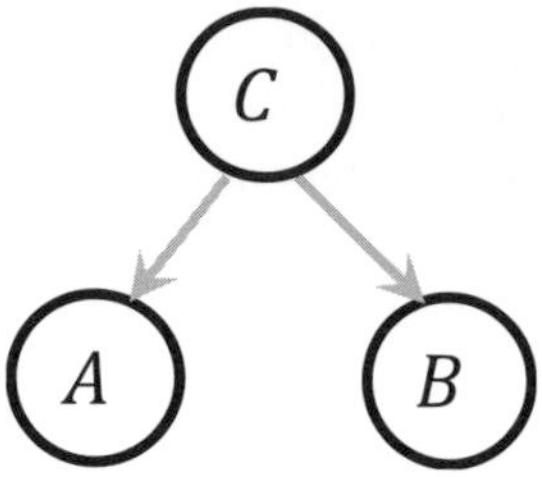

(c) Case 2

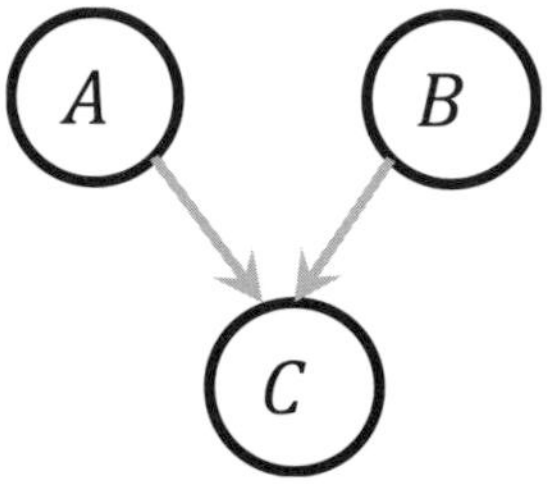
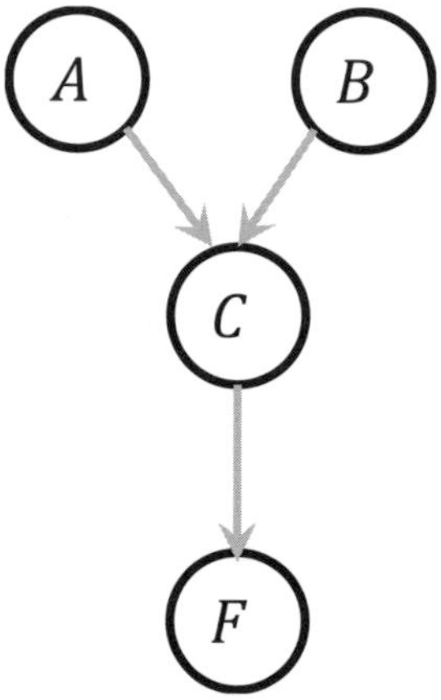

(d) Case 3.1 (e) Case 3.2

Figure 12.6 Various graphical model structures.

if $p(A,B|C) = p(A|C)p(B|C)$ always holds. The random variables A, B, and C can be discrete or continuous and can be either single variate or multivariate. In this exercise, we use various simple probabilistic graphical models in Figure 12.6 to illustrate the conditional dependence among sets of variables.

In a directed graphical model, the arrows indicate direct dependencies—one node depends on its parents (those who have edges pointing to it). For example, Figure 12.6a says C depends on A, B depends on C, but A depends on nothing—that is, the joint density can be factored as

$$p(A,B,C) = p(A)p(C|A)p(B|C).$$

(a) For the simple case 1.1 in Figure 12.6a, prove $A \perp B \mid C$.

(b) For the simple case 1.2 in Figure 12.6b, prove $A \perp B \mid C$.

(c) For the simple case 2 in Figure 12.6c, prove $A \perp B \mid C$.

(d) Case 3.1 in Figure 12.6d is a little more delicate. Show that when C is *not* observed, we have $p(A, B) = p(A)p(B)$—that is, A and B are independent. However, when C is observed, A and B are *not* conditionally independent. Try to find an intuitive example to explain this phenomenon.

This phenomenon is called *explaining away*. When two (or more) causes can both cause the same effect, these causes become dependent on each other after we observe that effect.

(e) Case 3.2, which is a variant of case 3.1, is shown in Figure 12.6e. Explain intuitively the following fact: even if C is not observed, A and B become dependent when any of C's descendants is observed.

12.4 (d-separation) We have been quite sloppy in this chapter when dealing with dependence or independence among variables in the hidden Markov model. In this problem, we will introduce d-separation, an algorithm that can precisely determine any conditional dependence or independence in HMM. In fact, d-separation works well in Bayesian networks, a more general class of probabilistic graphical models. HMM is an example of a Bayesian network.

Let A, B, and C be three sets of random variables, which are denoted as nodes in a directed probabilistic graphical model. A *trail* is an undirected path (i.e., ignoring the arrow directions and without any loop) in the graph. We say a trail is *d-separated* by Z if one or more of the following three situations happen:

(i) There is a directed chain and one of its middle nodes (i.e., excluding the starting and the ending nodes) is in Z. Cases 1.1 and 1.2 in Figure 12.6 are examples of such cases, but a directed chain can have more than three nodes.

(ii) There are nodes in the path that form a "common cause" (i.e., case 2 in Figure 12.6) and the middle node is in Z.

(iii) There are nodes in the path that form a "common effect" (i.e., cases 3.1 or 3.2 in Figure 12.6,), and the middle node is *not* in Z. Furthermore, *none of the descendants* of the middle node is in Z. Note that the descendant of the middle node may *not* be in the path.

Let u be a node in A and v be a node in B; let P be a trail that starts with u and ends at v. The d-separation rule states that $A \perp B \mid C$ if and only if all P is d-separated by Z for an arbitrary such trail P.

Use the d-separation rule to decide whether the following statements concerning Figure 12.7 are correct or not. Justify your answers.

(a) $B \perp C \mid A$.

(b) $C \perp D \mid F$.

12.5 Prove that the joint distribution of an HMM model is correctly calculated by Eq. (12.7). (Hint: Mathematical induction is useful.)

12.6 Prove the following equations. (Hint: Use d-separation to determine conditional independence.)

(a) $\alpha_{t+1}(i) = \left(\sum_{j=1}^{N} \alpha_t(j) A_{ji}\right) b_i(o_{t+1})$.

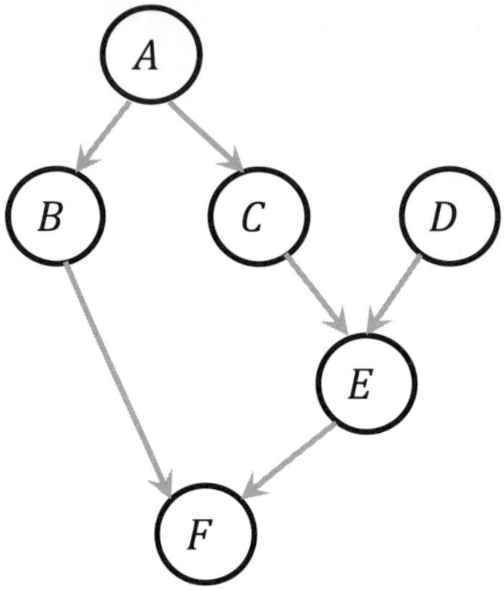

Figure 12.7 Example of d-separation.

(b) $\beta_t(i) = \sum_{j=1}^{N} A_{ij} b_j(o_{t+1}) \beta_{t+1}(j)$.

(c) $\Pr(o_{1:T}|\lambda) = \sum_{i=1}^{N} \pi_i b_i(o_1) \beta_1(i)$.

12.7 (n-step transition matrix) The transition matrix A can also be called a one-step transition matrix, because A_{ij} is the probability of transferring from one state S_i to another state S_j in one time step (though it is possible that $i = j$). The n-step transition matrix $A(n)$ is defined as

$$A_{ij}(n) \triangleq \Pr(X_{t+n} = S_j | X_t = S_i), \tag{12.56}$$

i.e., the probability of transferring from one state S_i to another state S_j in *exactly* n one-step transitions.

The *Chapman–Kolmogorov equations* state that

$$A_{ij}(m+n) = \sum_{k=1}^{N} A_{ik}(m) A_{kj}(n), \tag{12.57}$$

in which m and n are positive integers.

(a) Explain the meaning of the Chapman–Kolmogorov equations.

(b) Use the Chapman–Kolmogorov equations to find $A(n)$, whose (i, j)th entry is $A_{ij}(n)$.

(c) Show that $\mathbf{1} \in \mathbb{R}^N$ (a vector of all 1s) is an eigenvector of $A(n)$ for any positive integer n.

Part V

Advanced Topics

13 The Normal Distribution

The normal distribution is the most widely used probability distribution in statistical pattern recognition, computer vision, and machine learning. The nice properties of this distribution might be the main reason for its popularity.

In this chapter, we try to organize the *basic* facts about the normal distribution. There is no advanced theory in this chapter. However, in order to understand these facts, some linear algebra and mathematical analysis basics are needed, which are not covered sufficiently in undergraduate texts or in Chapter 2. We put this preliminary knowledge at the end of this chapter (Section 13.9).

13.1 Definition

We will start by defining the normal distribution.

13.1.1 Univariate Normal

The probability density function (p.d.f.) of a univariate normal distribution has the form

$$p(x) = \frac{1}{\sqrt{2\pi}\sigma} e^{-\frac{(x-\mu)^2}{2\sigma^2}}, \tag{13.1}$$

in which μ is the expected value, and σ^2 is the variance. We assume that $\sigma > 0$.

We have first to verify that Eq. (13.1) is a valid probability density function. It is obvious that $p(x) \geq 0$ always holds for $x \in \mathbb{R}$. From Eq. (13.98) in Section 13.9.1, we know that

$$\int_{-\infty}^{\infty} \exp\left(-\frac{x^2}{t}\right) \mathrm{d}x = \sqrt{t\pi}.$$

Applying this equation, we have

$$\int_{-\infty}^{\infty} p(x)\,\mathrm{d}x = \frac{1}{\sqrt{2\pi}\sigma} \int_{-\infty}^{\infty} \exp\left(-\frac{(x-\mu)^2}{2\sigma^2}\right) \mathrm{d}x \tag{13.2}$$

$$= \frac{1}{\sqrt{2\pi}\sigma} \int_{-\infty}^{\infty} \exp\left(-\frac{x^2}{2\sigma^2}\right) \mathrm{d}x \tag{13.3}$$

$$= \frac{1}{\sqrt{2\pi}\sigma} \sqrt{2\sigma^2\pi} = 1, \tag{13.4}$$

which verifies that $p(x)$ is a valid p.d.f.

The distribution with p.d.f. $\frac{1}{\sqrt{2\pi}} \exp\left(-\frac{x^2}{2}\right)$ is called the standard normal distribution (whose $\mu = 0$ and $\sigma^2 = 1$). In Section 13.9.1, we show that the mean and standard deviation of the standard normal distribution are 0 and 1, respectively. By making a change of variables, it is easy to show that

$$\mu = \int_{-\infty}^{\infty} x p(x) \, \mathrm{d}x$$

and

$$\sigma^2 = \int_{-\infty}^{\infty} (x-\mu)^2 p(x) \, \mathrm{d}x$$

for a general normal distribution.

13.1.2 Multivariate Normal

The probability density function of a multivariate normal distribution X has the form

$$p(\boldsymbol{x}) = \frac{1}{(2\pi)^{d/2}|\Sigma|^{1/2}} \exp\left(-\frac{1}{2}(\boldsymbol{x}-\boldsymbol{\mu})^T \Sigma^{-1} (\boldsymbol{x}-\boldsymbol{\mu})\right), \tag{13.5}$$

in which $\boldsymbol{x}$ is a d-dimensional vector, $\boldsymbol{\mu}$ is the d-dimensional mean, and Σ is the $d \times d$ covariance matrix. We assume that Σ is a symmetric positive definite matrix.

We have first to verify that Eq. (13.5) is a valid probability density function. It is obvious that $p(\boldsymbol{x}) \geq 0$ always holds for $\boldsymbol{x} \in \mathbb{R}^d$. Next we diagonalize Σ as $\Sigma = U^T \Lambda U$ in which U is an orthogonal matrix containing the eigenvectors of Σ, $\Lambda = \mathrm{diag}(\lambda_1, \lambda_2, \ldots, \lambda_d)$ is a diagonal matrix containing the eigenvalues of Σ in its diagonal entries, and their determinants satisfy

$$|\Lambda| = |\Sigma|.$$

Let us define a new random vector Y as

$$\boldsymbol{y} = \Lambda^{-1/2} U (\boldsymbol{x} - \boldsymbol{\mu}). \tag{13.6}$$

The mapping from $\boldsymbol{y}$ to $\boldsymbol{x}$ is one-to-one. The determinant of the Jacobian is

$$\left|\frac{\partial \boldsymbol{y}}{\partial \boldsymbol{x}}\right| = |\Lambda^{-1/2} U| = |\Sigma|^{-1/2}$$

because $|U| = 1$ and $|\Lambda| = |\Sigma|$. Now we are ready to calculate the integral:

$$\int p(\boldsymbol{x})\,\mathrm{d}\boldsymbol{x} = \int \frac{1}{(2\pi)^{d/2}|\Sigma|^{1/2}} \exp\left(-\frac{1}{2}(\boldsymbol{x}-\boldsymbol{\mu})^T\Sigma^{-1}(\boldsymbol{x}-\boldsymbol{\mu})\right)\mathrm{d}\boldsymbol{x} \tag{13.7}$$

$$= \int \frac{1}{(2\pi)^{d/2}|\Sigma|^{1/2}}|\Sigma|^{1/2} \exp\left(-\frac{1}{2}\boldsymbol{y}^T\boldsymbol{y}\right)\mathrm{d}\boldsymbol{y} \tag{13.8}$$

$$= \prod_{i=1}^{d}\left(\int \frac{1}{\sqrt{2\pi}} \exp\left(-\frac{y_i^2}{2}\right)\mathrm{d}y_i\right) \tag{13.9}$$

$$= \prod_{i=1}^{d} 1 \tag{13.10}$$

$$= 1, \tag{13.11}$$

in which y_i is the ith component of $\boldsymbol{y}$—i.e., $\boldsymbol{y} = (y_1, y_2, \ldots, y_d)^T$. This equation gives the validity of the multivariate normal density function.

Since $\boldsymbol{y}$ is a random vector, it has a density, which we denote as $p_Y(\boldsymbol{y})$. Using the inverse transform method, we get

$$p_Y(\boldsymbol{y}) = p_X\left(\boldsymbol{\mu} + U^T\Lambda^{1/2}\boldsymbol{y}\right)\left|U^T\Lambda^{1/2}\right| \tag{13.12}$$

$$= \frac{\left|U^T\Lambda^{1/2}\right|}{(2\pi)^{d/2}|\Sigma|^{1/2}} \exp\left(-\frac{1}{2}\left(U^T\Lambda^{1/2}\boldsymbol{y}\right)^T\Sigma^{-1}\left(U^T\Lambda^{1/2}\boldsymbol{y}\right)\right) \tag{13.13}$$

$$= \frac{1}{(2\pi)^{d/2}} \exp\left(-\frac{1}{2}\boldsymbol{y}^T\boldsymbol{y}\right). \tag{13.14}$$

The density defined by

$$p_Y(\boldsymbol{y}) = \frac{1}{(2\pi)^{d/2}} \exp\left(-\frac{1}{2}\boldsymbol{y}^T\boldsymbol{y}\right) \tag{13.15}$$

is called a spherical normal distribution.

Let $\boldsymbol{z}$ be a random vector formed by a subset of the components of $\boldsymbol{y}$. By marginalizing $\boldsymbol{y}$, it is clear that

$$p_Z(\boldsymbol{z}) = \frac{1}{(2\pi)^{d_z/2}} \exp\left(-\frac{1}{2}\boldsymbol{z}^T\boldsymbol{z}\right),$$

in which d_z is the dimensionality of $\boldsymbol{z}$. More specifically, we have

$$p_{Y_i}(y_i) = \frac{1}{\sqrt{2\pi}} \exp\left(-\frac{y_i^2}{2}\right).$$

Using this fact, it is straightforward to show that the mean vector and covariance matrix of a spherical normal distribution are $\boldsymbol{0}$ and I, respectively.

Using the inverse transform of Eq. (13.6), we can easily calculate the mean vector and covariance matrix of the density $p(\boldsymbol{x})$:

$$\begin{aligned}\mathbb{E}[\boldsymbol{x}] &= \mathbb{E}\left[\boldsymbol{\mu} + U^T \Lambda^{1/2} \boldsymbol{y}\right] && (13.16)\\ &= \boldsymbol{\mu} + \mathbb{E}\left[U^T \Lambda^{1/2} \boldsymbol{y}\right] && (13.17)\\ &= \boldsymbol{\mu}, && (13.18)\\ \mathbb{E}\left[(\boldsymbol{x}-\boldsymbol{\mu})(\boldsymbol{x}-\boldsymbol{\mu})^T\right] &= \mathbb{E}\left[(U^T \Lambda^{1/2} \boldsymbol{y})(U^T \Lambda^{1/2} \boldsymbol{y})^T\right] && (13.19)\\ &= U^T \Lambda^{1/2} \mathbb{E}\left[\boldsymbol{y}\boldsymbol{y}^T\right] \Lambda^{1/2} U && (13.20)\\ &= U^T \Lambda^{1/2} \Lambda^{1/2} U && (13.21)\\ &= \Sigma. && (13.22)\end{aligned}$$

13.2 Notation and Parameterization

When we have a density of the form in Eq. (13.5), it is often written as

$$X \sim N(\boldsymbol{\mu}, \Sigma), \tag{13.23}$$

or

$$N(\boldsymbol{x}; \boldsymbol{\mu}, \Sigma). \tag{13.24}$$

In most cases we will use the mean vector $\boldsymbol{\mu}$ and the covariance matrix Σ to express a normal density. This is called the *moment parameterization*. There is another parameterization of the normal density. In the *canonical parameterization*, a normal density is expressed as

$$p(\boldsymbol{x}) = \exp\left(\alpha + \boldsymbol{\eta}^T \boldsymbol{x} - \frac{1}{2}\boldsymbol{x}^T \Lambda \boldsymbol{x}\right), \tag{13.25}$$

in which

$$\alpha = -\frac{1}{2}\left(d \log(2\pi) - \log(|\Lambda|) + \boldsymbol{\eta}^T \Lambda^{-1} \boldsymbol{\eta}\right)$$

is a normalization constant that does not depend on $\boldsymbol{x}$. The parameters in these two representations are related to each other by the following equations:

$$\begin{aligned}\Lambda &= \Sigma^{-1}, && (13.26)\\ \boldsymbol{\eta} &= \Sigma^{-1}\boldsymbol{\mu}, && (13.27)\\ \Sigma &= \Lambda^{-1}, && (13.28)\\ \boldsymbol{\mu} &= \Lambda^{-1}\boldsymbol{\eta}. && (13.29)\end{aligned}$$

Notice that there is a conflict in our notation: Λ has different meanings in Eqs. (13.25) and (13.6). In Eq. (13.25), Λ is a parameter in the canonical parameterization of a normal density, which is not necessarily diagonal. In Eq. (13.6), Λ is a diagonal matrix formed by the eigenvalues of Σ.

It is straightforward to show that the moment parameterization and the canonical parameterization of the normal distribution are equivalent to each other. In some cases the canonical parameterization is more convenient to use than the moment parameterization; an example of this case will be shown later in this chapter.

13.3 Linear Operation and Summation

In this section, we will touch on some basic operations among several normal random variables.

13.3.1 The Univariate Case

Suppose $X_1 \sim N(\mu_1, \sigma_1^2)$ and $X_2 \sim N(\mu_2, \sigma_2^2)$ are two *independent* univariate normal variables. It is obvious that

$$aX_1 + b \sim N(a\mu_1 + b, a^2\sigma_1^2),$$

in which a and b are two scalars.

Now consider a random variable $Z = X_1 + X_2$. The density of Z can be calculated by a convolution, i.e.,

$$p_Z(z) = \int_{-\infty}^{\infty} p_{X_1}(x_1) p_{X_2}(z - x_1)\, \mathrm{d}x_1. \tag{13.30}$$

Define $x_1' = x_1 - \mu_1$; we get

$$p_Z(z) = \int p_{X_1}(x_1' + \mu_1) p_{X_2}(z - x_1' - \mu_1)\, \mathrm{d}x_1' \tag{13.31}$$

$$= \frac{1}{2\pi\sigma_1\sigma_2} \int \exp\left(-\frac{x^2}{2\sigma_1^2} - \frac{(z - x - \mu_1 - \mu_2)^2}{2\sigma_2^2} \right) \mathrm{d}x \tag{13.32}$$

$$= \frac{\exp\left(-\frac{(z-\mu_1-\mu_2)^2}{2(\sigma_1^2+\sigma_2^2)} \right)}{2\pi\sigma_1\sigma_2} \int \exp\left(-\frac{\left(x - \frac{(z-\mu_1-\mu_2)\sigma_1^2}{\sigma_1^2+\sigma_2^2}\right)^2}{2\sigma_1^2\sigma_2^2/(\sigma_1^2+\sigma_2^2)} \right) \mathrm{d}x \tag{13.33}$$

$$= \frac{1}{2\pi\sigma_1\sigma_2} \exp\left(-\frac{(z - \mu_1 - \mu_2)^2}{2(\sigma_1^2 + \sigma_2^2)} \right) \sqrt{\frac{2\sigma_1^2\sigma_2^2}{\sigma_1^2 + \sigma_2^2}\pi} \tag{13.34}$$

$$= \frac{1}{\sqrt{2\pi}\sqrt{\sigma_1^2 + \sigma_2^2}} \exp\left(-\frac{(z - \mu_1 - \mu_2)^2}{2(\sigma_1^2 + \sigma_2^2)} \right), \tag{13.35}$$

in which the transition from the third last to the second last line used the result of Eq. (13.98).

In short, the sum of two univariate normal random variables is again a normal random variable, with the mean value and variance summed respectively, i.e.,

$$Z \sim N(\mu_1 + \mu_2, \sigma_1^2 + \sigma_2^2).$$

The summation rule is easily generalized to n independent normal random variables. However, this rule cannot be used if x_1 and x_2 are dependent.

13.3.2 The Multivariate Case

Suppose $X \sim N(\boldsymbol{\mu}, \Sigma)$ is a d-dimensional normal random variable, A is a $q \times d$ matrix, and $\boldsymbol{b}$ is a q-dimensional vector; then $Z = AX + \boldsymbol{b}$ is a q-dimensional normal random variable:

$$Z \sim N(A\boldsymbol{\mu} + \boldsymbol{b}, A\Sigma A^T).$$

This fact is proved using the characteristic function (see Section 13.9.2). The characteristic function of Z is

$$\begin{aligned}
\varphi_Z(\boldsymbol{t}) &= \mathbb{E}_Z\left[\exp(i\boldsymbol{t}^T \boldsymbol{z})\right] && (13.36)\\
&= \mathbb{E}_X\left[\exp\left(i\boldsymbol{t}^T(A\boldsymbol{x} + \boldsymbol{b})\right)\right] && (13.37)\\
&= \exp\left(i\boldsymbol{t}^T\boldsymbol{b}\right)\mathbb{E}_X\left[\exp\left(i(A^T\boldsymbol{t})^T\boldsymbol{x}\right)\right] && (13.38)\\
&= \exp\left(i\boldsymbol{t}^T\boldsymbol{b}\right)\exp\left(i(A^T\boldsymbol{t})^T\boldsymbol{\mu} - \frac{1}{2}(A^T\boldsymbol{t})^T\Sigma(A^T\boldsymbol{t})\right) && (13.39)\\
&= \exp\left(i\boldsymbol{t}^T(A\boldsymbol{\mu} + \boldsymbol{b}) - \frac{1}{2}\boldsymbol{t}^T(A\Sigma A^T)\boldsymbol{t}\right), && (13.40)
\end{aligned}$$

in which the transition to the last line used Eq. (13.108) in Section 13.9.2.

Section 13.9.2 also states that if a characteristic function $\varphi(\boldsymbol{t})$ is of the form $\exp(i\boldsymbol{t}^T\boldsymbol{\mu} - \frac{1}{2}\boldsymbol{t}^T\Sigma\boldsymbol{t})$, then the underlying density is normal with mean $\boldsymbol{\mu}$ and covariance matrix Σ. Applying this fact to Eq. (13.40), we immediately get

$$Z \sim N(A\boldsymbol{\mu} + \boldsymbol{b}, A\Sigma A^T). \tag{13.41}$$

Suppose $X_1 \sim N(\boldsymbol{\mu}_1, \Sigma_1)$ and $X_2 \sim N(\boldsymbol{\mu}_2, \Sigma_2)$ are two independent d-dimensional normal random variables, and define a new random vector $Z = X_1 + X_2$. We can calculate the probability density function $p_Z(\boldsymbol{z})$ using the same method as we used in the univariate case. However, the calculation is complex, and we have to apply the matrix inversion lemma in Section 13.9.3.

The characteristic function simplifies the calculation. Using Eq. (13.111) in Section 13.9.2, we get

$$\begin{aligned}
\varphi_Z(\boldsymbol{t}) &= \varphi_X(\boldsymbol{t})\varphi_Y(\boldsymbol{t}) && (13.42)\\
&= \exp\left(i\boldsymbol{t}^T\boldsymbol{\mu}_1 - \frac{1}{2}\boldsymbol{t}^T\Sigma_1\boldsymbol{t}\right)\exp\left(i\boldsymbol{t}^T\boldsymbol{\mu}_2 - \frac{1}{2}\boldsymbol{t}^T\Sigma_2\boldsymbol{t}\right) && (13.43)\\
&= \exp\left(i\boldsymbol{t}^T(\boldsymbol{\mu}_1 + \boldsymbol{\mu}_2) - \frac{1}{2}\boldsymbol{t}^T(\Sigma_1 + \Sigma_2)\boldsymbol{t}\right), && (13.44)
\end{aligned}$$

which immediately gives us

$$Z \sim N(\boldsymbol{\mu}_1 + \boldsymbol{\mu}_2, \Sigma_1 + \Sigma_2).$$

The summation of two independent multivariate normal random variables is as easy to compute as in the univariate case: sum the mean vectors and covariance matrices. This rule remains the same for summing several multivariate normal random variables.

Now we use the tool of linear transformation, and revisit Eq. (13.6). For convenience we retype the equation here: $X \sim N(\boldsymbol{\mu}, \Sigma)$, and we get Y by

$$\boldsymbol{y} = \Lambda^{-1/2} U(\boldsymbol{x} - \boldsymbol{\mu}). \tag{13.45}$$

Using the properties of linear transformations on a normal density, Y is indeed normal (in Section 13.1.2 we painfully calculated $p_Y(\boldsymbol{y})$ using the inverse transform method), and has mean vector $\mathbf{0}$ and covariance matrix I.

The transformation of applying Eq. (13.6) is called the whitening transformation, because the transformed density has an identity covariance matrix and zero mean (cf. Chapter 5).

13.4 Geometry and the Mahalanobis Distance

Figure 13.1 shows a bivariate normal density function. Normal density has only one mode, which is the mean vector, and the shape of the density is determined by the covariance matrix.

Figure 13.2 shows the equal probability contour of a bivariate normal random variable. All points on a given equal probability contour must have the following term

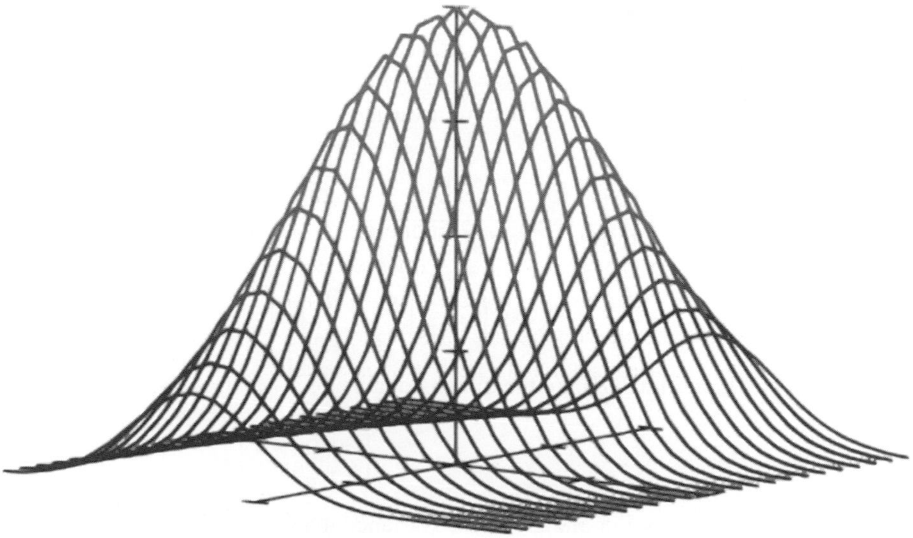

Figure 13.1 Bivariate normal p.d.f.

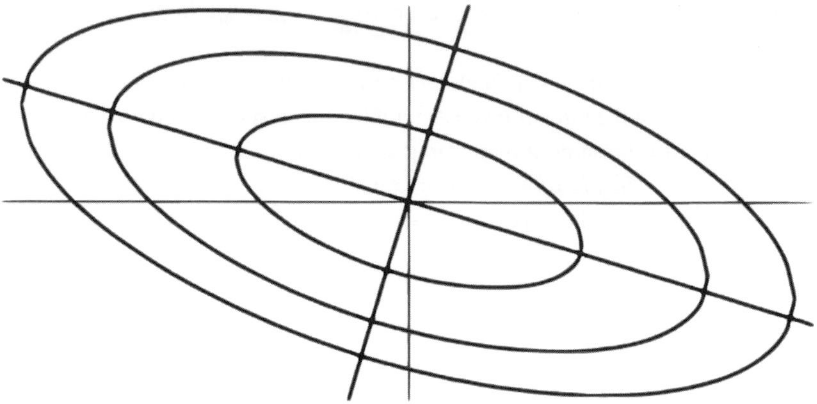

Figure 13.2 Equal probability contour of a bivariate normal distribution.

evaluated to a constant value:

$$r^2(\boldsymbol{x}, \boldsymbol{\mu}) = (\boldsymbol{x} - \boldsymbol{\mu})^T \Sigma^{-1} (\boldsymbol{x} - \boldsymbol{\mu}) = c. \tag{13.46}$$

The quantity $r^2(\boldsymbol{x}, \boldsymbol{\mu})$ is called the Mahalanobis distance from $\boldsymbol{x}$ to $\boldsymbol{\mu}$, given the covariance matrix Σ. Equation (13.46) defines a hyperellipsoid in d-dimensional space, which means that the equal probability contour is a hyperellipsoid in d-dimensional space. The principal component axes of this hyperellipsoid are given by the eigenvectors of Σ, and the lengths of these axes are proportional to the square roots of the eigenvalues associated with these eigenvectors (cf. Chapter 5).

13.5 Conditioning

Suppose X_1 and X_2 are two multivariate normal random variables, which have a joint p.d.f.

$$p\left(\begin{bmatrix} \boldsymbol{x}_1 \\ \boldsymbol{x}_2 \end{bmatrix}\right) = \frac{1}{(2\pi)^{(d_1+d_2)/2} |\Sigma|^{1/2}}$$
$$\cdot \exp\left(-\frac{1}{2} \begin{bmatrix} \boldsymbol{x}_1 - \boldsymbol{\mu}_1 \\ \boldsymbol{x}_2 - \boldsymbol{\mu}_2 \end{bmatrix}^T \begin{bmatrix} \Sigma_{11} & \Sigma_{12} \\ \Sigma_{21} & \Sigma_{22} \end{bmatrix}^{-1} \begin{bmatrix} \boldsymbol{x}_1 - \boldsymbol{\mu}_1 \\ \boldsymbol{x}_2 - \boldsymbol{\mu}_2 \end{bmatrix} \right),$$

in which d_1 and d_2 are the dimensionality of X_1 and of X_2, respectively, and

$$\Sigma = \begin{bmatrix} \Sigma_{11} & \Sigma_{12} \\ \Sigma_{21} & \Sigma_{22} \end{bmatrix}.$$

The matrices Σ_{12} and Σ_{21} are covariance matrices between $\boldsymbol{x}_1$ and $\boldsymbol{x}_2$, satisfying

$$\Sigma_{12} = (\Sigma_{21})^T.$$

The marginal distributions $X_1 \sim N(\boldsymbol{\mu}_1, \Sigma_{11})$ and $X_2 \sim N(\boldsymbol{\mu}_2, \Sigma_{22})$ are easy to get from the joint distribution. We are interested in computing the conditional probability $p(\boldsymbol{x}_1|\boldsymbol{x}_2)$.

We will need to compute the inverse of Σ, and this task is completed by using the Schur complement (see Section 13.9.3). For notational simplicity, we denote the Schur complement of Σ_{11} as S_{11}, defined as

$$S_{11} = \Sigma_{22} - \Sigma_{21}\Sigma_{11}^{-1}\Sigma_{12}.$$

Similarly, the Schur complement of Σ_{22} is

$$S_{22} = \Sigma_{11} - \Sigma_{12}\Sigma_{22}^{-1}\Sigma_{21}.$$

Applying Eq. (13.121) and noticing that $\Sigma_{12} = (\Sigma_{21})^T$, we get (writing $\boldsymbol{x}_1 - \boldsymbol{\mu}_1$ as $\boldsymbol{x}'_1$, and $\boldsymbol{x}_2 - \boldsymbol{\mu}_2$ as $\boldsymbol{x}'_2$ for notational simplicity)

$$\begin{bmatrix} \Sigma_{11} & \Sigma_{12} \\ \Sigma_{21} & \Sigma_{22} \end{bmatrix}^{-1} = \begin{bmatrix} S_{22}^{-1} & -S_{22}^{-1}\Sigma_{12}\Sigma_{22}^{-1} \\ -\Sigma_{22}^{-1}\Sigma_{12}^T S_{22}^{-1} & \Sigma_{22}^{-1} + \Sigma_{22}^{-1}\Sigma_{12}^T S_{22}^{-1}\Sigma_{12}\Sigma_{22}^{-1} \end{bmatrix} \tag{13.47}$$

and

$$\begin{aligned} &\begin{bmatrix} \boldsymbol{x}_1 - \boldsymbol{\mu}_1 \\ \boldsymbol{x}_2 - \boldsymbol{\mu}_2 \end{bmatrix}^T \begin{bmatrix} \Sigma_{11} & \Sigma_{12} \\ \Sigma_{21} & \Sigma_{22} \end{bmatrix}^{-1} \begin{bmatrix} \boldsymbol{x}_1 - \boldsymbol{\mu}_1 \\ \boldsymbol{x}_2 - \boldsymbol{\mu}_2 \end{bmatrix} \\ &= \boldsymbol{x}_1'^T S_{22}^{-1}\boldsymbol{x}'_1 + \boldsymbol{x}_2'^T(\Sigma_{22}^{-1} + \Sigma_{22}^{-1}\Sigma_{12}^T S_{22}^{-1}\Sigma_{12}\Sigma_{22}^{-1})\boldsymbol{x}'_2 \\ &\quad - \boldsymbol{x}_1'^T S_{22}^{-1}\Sigma_{12}\Sigma_{22}^{-1}\boldsymbol{x}'_2 - \boldsymbol{x}_2'^T\Sigma_{22}^{-1}\Sigma_{12}^T S_{22}^{-1}\boldsymbol{x}'_1 \\ &= (\boldsymbol{x}'_1 - \Sigma_{12}\Sigma_{22}^{-1}\boldsymbol{x}'_2)^T S_{22}^{-1}(\boldsymbol{x}'_1 - \Sigma_{12}\Sigma_{22}^{-1}\boldsymbol{x}'_2) + \boldsymbol{x}_2'^T\Sigma_{22}^{-1}\boldsymbol{x}'_2. \end{aligned} \tag{13.48}$$

Thus, we can split the joint distribution as

$$\begin{aligned} &p\left(\begin{bmatrix} \boldsymbol{x}_1 \\ \boldsymbol{x}_2 \end{bmatrix}\right) \\ &= \frac{1}{(2\pi)^{d_1}|S_{22}|^{1/2}} \exp\left(-\frac{(\boldsymbol{x}'_1 - \Sigma_{12}\Sigma_{22}^{-1}\boldsymbol{x}'_2)^T S_{22}^{-1}(\boldsymbol{x}'_1 - \Sigma_{12}\Sigma_{22}^{-1}\boldsymbol{x}'_2)}{2}\right) \\ &\quad \cdot \frac{1}{(2\pi)^{d_2}|\Sigma_{22}|^{1/2}} \exp\left(-\frac{1}{2}\boldsymbol{x}_2'^T\Sigma_{22}^{-1}\boldsymbol{x}'_2\right), \end{aligned} \tag{13.49}$$

in which we have used the fact that

$$|\Sigma| = |\Sigma_{22}|\,|S_{22}|,$$

a fact that is obvious from Eq. (13.117) in Section 13.9.3.

Since the second term on the right-hand side of Eq. (13.49) is the marginal $p(\boldsymbol{x}_2)$ and $p(\boldsymbol{x}_1,\boldsymbol{x}_2) = p(\boldsymbol{x}_1|\boldsymbol{x}_2)p(\boldsymbol{x}_2)$, we now get the conditional probability $p(\boldsymbol{x}_1|\boldsymbol{x}_2)$ as

$$p(\boldsymbol{x}_1|\boldsymbol{x}_2) = \frac{1}{(2\pi)^{d_1}|S_{22}|^{1/2}} \exp\left(-\frac{\left(\boldsymbol{x}_1' - \Sigma_{12}\Sigma_{22}^{-1}\boldsymbol{x}_2'\right)^T S_{22}^{-1}\left(\boldsymbol{x}_1' - \Sigma_{12}\Sigma_{22}^{-1}\boldsymbol{x}_2'\right)}{2}\right), \tag{13.50}$$

or

$$\boldsymbol{x}_1|\boldsymbol{x}_2 \sim N(\boldsymbol{\mu}_1 + \Sigma_{12}\Sigma_{22}^{-1}\boldsymbol{x}_2', S_{22}) \tag{13.51}$$

$$\sim N(\boldsymbol{\mu}_1 + \Sigma_{12}\Sigma_{22}^{-1}(\boldsymbol{x}_2 - \boldsymbol{\mu}_2), \Sigma_{11} - \Sigma_{12}\Sigma_{22}^{-1}\Sigma_{21}). \tag{13.52}$$

Note that $\boldsymbol{x}_1' - \Sigma_{12}\Sigma_{22}^{-1}\boldsymbol{x}_2' = \boldsymbol{x}_1 - \left(\boldsymbol{\mu}_1 + \Sigma_{12}\Sigma_{22}^{-1}\boldsymbol{x}_2'\right)$.

13.6 Product of Gaussians

Suppose $X_1 \sim p_1(\boldsymbol{x}) = N(\boldsymbol{x};\boldsymbol{\mu}_1,\Sigma_1)$ and $X_2 \sim p_2(\boldsymbol{x}) = N(\boldsymbol{x};\boldsymbol{\mu}_2,\Sigma_2)$ are two independent d-dimensional normal random variables. Sometimes we want to compute the density, which is proportional to the product of the two normal densities, i.e.,

$$p_X(\boldsymbol{x}) = \alpha p_1(\boldsymbol{x})p_2(\boldsymbol{x}),$$

in which α is a proper normalization constant to make $p_X(\boldsymbol{x})$ a valid density function.

In this task, the canonical parameterization (see Section 13.2) will be extremely helpful. Writing the two normal densities in the canonical form

$$p_1(\boldsymbol{x}) = \exp\left(\alpha_1 + \boldsymbol{\eta}_1^T\boldsymbol{x} - \frac{1}{2}\boldsymbol{x}^T\Lambda_1\boldsymbol{x}\right), \tag{13.53}$$

$$p_2(\boldsymbol{x}) = \exp\left(\alpha_2 + \boldsymbol{\eta}_2^T\boldsymbol{x} - \frac{1}{2}\boldsymbol{x}^T\Lambda_2\boldsymbol{x}\right), \tag{13.54}$$

the density $p_X(\boldsymbol{x})$ is then easy to compute as

$$\begin{aligned} p_X(\boldsymbol{x}) &= \alpha p_1(\boldsymbol{x})p_2(\boldsymbol{x}) \\ &= \exp\left(\alpha' + (\boldsymbol{\eta}_1 + \boldsymbol{\eta}_2)^T\boldsymbol{x} - \frac{1}{2}\boldsymbol{x}^T(\Lambda_1 + \Lambda_2)\boldsymbol{x}\right), \end{aligned} \tag{13.55}$$

in which α' summarizes all terms that are not dependent on $\boldsymbol{x}$. This equation states that in the canonical parameterization, in order to compute the product of two Gaussians we just sum the parameters.

This result is readily extendable to the product of n normal densities. Suppose we have n normal distributions $p_i(\boldsymbol{x})$, whose parameters in the canonical parameterization are $\boldsymbol{\eta}_i$ and Λ_i, respectively ($i = 1,2,\ldots,n$). Then $p_X(\boldsymbol{x}) = \alpha\prod_{i=1}^n p_i(\boldsymbol{x})$ is also a normal density, given by

$$p_X(\boldsymbol{x}) = \exp\left(\alpha' + \left(\sum_{i=1}^{n} \eta_i\right)^T \boldsymbol{x} - \frac{1}{2}\boldsymbol{x}^T \left(\sum_{i=1}^{n} \Lambda_i\right) \boldsymbol{x}\right). \tag{13.56}$$

Now let us go back to the moment parameterization. Suppose we have n normal distributions $p_i(\boldsymbol{x})$, in which $p_i(\boldsymbol{x}) = N(\boldsymbol{x}; \boldsymbol{\mu}_i, \Sigma_i)$, $i = 1, 2, \ldots, n$. Then $p_X(\boldsymbol{x}) = \alpha \prod_{i=1}^{n} p_i(\boldsymbol{x})$ is normal,

$$p(\boldsymbol{x}) = N(\boldsymbol{x}; \boldsymbol{\mu}, \Sigma), \tag{13.57}$$

where

$$\Sigma^{-1} = \Sigma_1^{-1} + \Sigma_2^{-1} + \cdots + \Sigma_n^{-1}, \tag{13.58}$$

$$\Sigma^{-1}\boldsymbol{\mu} = \Sigma_1^{-1}\boldsymbol{\mu}_1 + \Sigma_2^{-1}\boldsymbol{\mu}_2 + \cdots + \Sigma_n^{-1}\boldsymbol{\mu}_n. \tag{13.59}$$

13.7 Application I: Parameter Estimation

We have listed some properties of the normal distribution. Next, let us show how these properties are applied.

The first application is parameter estimation in probability and statistics.

13.7.1 Maximum Likelihood Estimation

Let us suppose that we have a d-dimensional multivariate normal random variable $X \sim N(\boldsymbol{\mu}, \Sigma)$, and n i.i.d. (independent and identically distributed) samples $\mathcal{D} = \{\boldsymbol{x}_1, \boldsymbol{x}_2, \ldots, \boldsymbol{x}_n\}$ sampled from this distribution. The task is to estimate the parameters $\boldsymbol{\mu}$ and Σ.

The log-likelihood function of observing the dataset $\mathcal{D}$ given parameters $\boldsymbol{\mu}$ and Σ is

$$\ell\ell(\boldsymbol{\mu}, \Sigma|\mathcal{D}) \tag{13.60}$$

$$= \log \prod_{i=1}^{n} p(\boldsymbol{x}_i) \tag{13.61}$$

$$= -\frac{nd}{2}\log(2\pi) + \frac{n}{2}\log|\Sigma^{-1}| - \frac{1}{2}\sum_{i=1}^{n}(\boldsymbol{x}_i - \boldsymbol{\mu})^T \Sigma^{-1}(\boldsymbol{x}_i - \boldsymbol{\mu}). \tag{13.62}$$

Taking the derivative of the log-likelihood with respect to $\boldsymbol{\mu}$ and Σ^{-1} gives (see Section 13.9.4)

$$\frac{\partial \ell\ell}{\partial \boldsymbol{\mu}} = \sum_{i=1}^{n} \Sigma^{-1}(\boldsymbol{x}_i - \boldsymbol{\mu}), \tag{13.63}$$

$$\frac{\partial \ell\ell}{\partial \Sigma^{-1}} = \frac{n}{2}\Sigma - \frac{1}{2}\sum_{i=1}^{n}(\boldsymbol{x}_i - \boldsymbol{\mu})(\boldsymbol{x}_i - \boldsymbol{\mu})^T, \tag{13.64}$$

in which Eq. (13.63) used Eq. (13.126) and the chain rule, and Eq. (13.64) used Eqs. (13.133) and (13.134), and the fact that $\Sigma = \Sigma^T$. The notation in Eq. (13.63) is a little confusing. There are two Σs on the right-hand side: the first represents a summation and the second represents the covariance matrix.

In order to find the maximum likelihood solution, we want to find the maximum of the likelihood function. Setting both Eqs. (13.63) and (13.64) to $\mathbf{0}$ gives us the solution:

$$\boldsymbol{\mu}_{\text{ML}} = \frac{1}{n}\sum_{i=1}^{n} \boldsymbol{x}_i, \tag{13.65}$$

$$\Sigma_{\text{ML}} = \frac{1}{n}\sum_{i=1}^{n} (\boldsymbol{x}_i - \boldsymbol{\mu}_{\text{ML}})(\boldsymbol{x}_i - \boldsymbol{\mu}_{\text{ML}})^T. \tag{13.66}$$

These two equations clearly state that the maximum likelihood estimation of the mean vector and the covariance matrix are just the sample mean and the sample covariance matrix, respectively.

13.7.2 Bayesian Parameter Estimation

In this Bayesian estimation example, we assume that the covariance matrix Σ is known. Let us suppose that we have a d-dimensional multivariate normal density $X \sim N(\boldsymbol{\mu}, \Sigma)$, and n i.i.d. samples $\mathcal{D} = \{\boldsymbol{x}_1, \boldsymbol{x}_2, \ldots, \boldsymbol{x}_n\}$ sampled from this distribution. We also need a prior on the parameter $\boldsymbol{\mu}$. Let us assume that the prior is $\boldsymbol{\mu} \sim N(\boldsymbol{\mu}_0, \Sigma_0)$. The task is then to estimate the parameters $\boldsymbol{\mu}$.

Note that we assume $\boldsymbol{\mu}_0$, Σ_0, and Σ are all known. The only parameter to be estimated is the mean vector $\boldsymbol{\mu}$.

In Bayesian estimation, instead of finding a point $\hat{\boldsymbol{\mu}}$ in the parameter space that gives maximum likelihood, we calculate $p(\boldsymbol{\mu}|\mathcal{D})$, the posterior density for the parameter. And we use the entire distribution of $\boldsymbol{\mu}$ as our estimation for this parameter.

Applying Bayes' rule, we get

$$p(\boldsymbol{\mu}|\mathcal{D}) = \alpha\, p(\mathcal{D}|\boldsymbol{\mu})\, p_0(\boldsymbol{\mu}) \tag{13.67}$$

$$= \alpha\, p_0(\boldsymbol{\mu}) \prod_{i=1}^{n} p(\boldsymbol{x}_i), \tag{13.68}$$

in which α is a normalization constant that does not depend on $\boldsymbol{\mu}$.

Applying the result in Section 13.6, we know that $p(\boldsymbol{\mu}|\mathcal{D})$ is also normal, and

$$p(\boldsymbol{\mu}|\mathcal{D}) = N(\boldsymbol{\mu}; \boldsymbol{\mu}_n, \Sigma_n), \tag{13.69}$$

where

$$\Sigma_n^{-1} = n\Sigma^{-1} + \Sigma_0^{-1}, \tag{13.70}$$

$$\Sigma_n^{-1}\boldsymbol{\mu}_n = n\Sigma^{-1}\boldsymbol{\mu} + \Sigma_0^{-1}\boldsymbol{\mu}_0. \tag{13.71}$$

Both μ_n and Σ_n can be calculated from known parameters and the dataset. Thus, we have determined the posterior distribution $p(\mu|\mathcal{D})$ for μ.

We choose the normal distribution to be the prior family. Usually, the prior distribution is chosen such that the posterior belongs to the same functional form as the prior. A prior and posterior chosen in this way are said to be *conjugate*. We have just observed that the normal distribution has the nice property that both the prior and the posterior are normal—i.e., the normal distribution is auto-conjugate.

After $p(\mu|\mathcal{D})$ is determined, a new sample is classified by calculating the probability

$$p(\boldsymbol{x}|\mathcal{D}) = \int_{\mu} p(\boldsymbol{x}|\mu)p(\mu|\mathcal{D})\,\mathrm{d}\mu. \tag{13.72}$$

Equations (13.72) and (13.31) have the same form. Thus, we can guess that $p(\boldsymbol{x}|\mathcal{D})$ is normal again, and

$$p(\boldsymbol{x}|\mathcal{D}) = N(\boldsymbol{x};\mu_n,\Sigma+\Sigma_n). \tag{13.73}$$

This guess is correct, and is easy to verify by repeating the steps from Eq. (13.31) to Eq. (13.35).

13.8 Application II: Kalman Filter

The second application is Kalman filtering.

13.8.1 The Model

The Kalman filter addresses the problem of estimating a state vector $\boldsymbol{x}$ in a discrete time process, given a linear dynamic model

$$\boldsymbol{x}_k = A\boldsymbol{x}_{k-1} + \boldsymbol{w}_{k-1} \tag{13.74}$$

and a linear measurement model

$$z_k = H\boldsymbol{x}_k + \boldsymbol{v}_k. \tag{13.75}$$

Note that in this example we use lowercase letters to denote random variables.

The process noise $\boldsymbol{w}_k$ and measurement noise $\boldsymbol{v}_k$ are assumed to be normal:

$$\boldsymbol{w} \sim N(\boldsymbol{0}, Q), \tag{13.76}$$

$$\boldsymbol{v} \sim N(\boldsymbol{0}, R). \tag{13.77}$$

These noises are assumed to be independent of all other random variables.

At time $k-1$, assuming that we know the distribution of $\boldsymbol{x}_{k-1}$, the task is to estimate the posterior probability of $\boldsymbol{x}_k$ at time k, given the current observation z_k and the previous state estimation $p(\boldsymbol{x}_{k-1})$.

From a broader perspective, the task can be formulated as estimating the posterior probability of $\boldsymbol{x}_k$ at time k, given all the previous state estimates and all the observations up to time step k. Under certain Markovian assumptions, it is not hard to prove that these two problem formulations are equivalent.

In the Kalman filter setup, we assume that the prior is normal—i.e., at time $t = 0$, $p(\boldsymbol{x}_0) = N(\boldsymbol{x}; \boldsymbol{\mu}_0, P_0)$. Instead of using Σ, here we use P to represent a covariance matrix, in order to match the notation in the Kalman filter literature.

13.8.2 The Estimation

Now we are ready to see that with the help of the properties of Gaussians that we have obtained so far, it is quite easy to derive the Kalman filter equations. The derivation in this section is neither precise nor rigorous, and mainly provides an intuitive way to interpret the Kalman filter.

The Kalman filter can be separated into two (related) steps. In the first step, based on the estimation $p(\boldsymbol{x}_{k-1})$ and the dynamic model (Eq. 13.74), we get an estimate $p(\boldsymbol{x}_k^-)$. Note that the minus sign means that the estimation is done before we take the measurement into account.

In the second step, based on $p(\boldsymbol{x}_k^-)$ and the measurement model (Eq. 13.75), we get the final estimation $p(\boldsymbol{x}_k)$. However, we want to emphasize that this estimation is in fact conditioned on the observation $\boldsymbol{z}_k$ and previous state $\boldsymbol{x}_{t-1}$, although we have omitted these dependencies in our notation.

First, let us estimate $p(\boldsymbol{x}_k^-)$. Assume that at time $k-1$, the estimation we have already obtained is a normal distribution

$$p(\boldsymbol{x}_{k-1}) \sim N(\boldsymbol{\mu}_{k-1}, P_{k-1}). \tag{13.78}$$

This assumption coincides well with the prior $p(\boldsymbol{x}_0)$. We will show that under this assumption, after the Kalman filter updates, the estimation $p(\boldsymbol{x}_k)$ will also become normal, and this makes the assumption a reasonable one.

Applying the linear operation equation (Eq. 13.41) on the dynamic model (Eq. 13.74), we immediately get the estimation for $\boldsymbol{x}_k^-$:

$$\boldsymbol{x}_k^- \sim N(\boldsymbol{\mu}_k^-, P_k^-), \tag{13.79}$$

$$\boldsymbol{\mu}_k^- = A\boldsymbol{\mu}_{k-1}, \tag{13.80}$$

$$P_k^- = AP_{k-1}A^T + Q. \tag{13.81}$$

The estimate $p(\boldsymbol{x}_k^-)$ conditioned on the observation $\boldsymbol{z}_k$ gives $p(\boldsymbol{x}_k)$, the estimation we want. Thus the conditioning property (Eq. 13.52) can be used.

Without observing $\boldsymbol{z}_k$ at time k, the best estimate for it is

$$H\boldsymbol{x}_k^- + \boldsymbol{v}_k,$$

which has a covariance

$$\text{Cov}(z_k) = HP_k^- H^T + R,$$

by applying Eq. (13.41) to Eq. (13.75). In order to use Eq. (13.52) we compute

$$\text{Cov}(z_k, \boldsymbol{x}_k^-) = \text{Cov}(H\boldsymbol{x}_k^- + \boldsymbol{v}_k, \boldsymbol{x}_k^-) \tag{13.82}$$

$$= \text{Cov}(H\boldsymbol{x}_k^-, \boldsymbol{x}_k^-) \tag{13.83}$$

$$= HP_k^-; \tag{13.84}$$

the joint covariance matrix of $(\boldsymbol{x}_k^-, z_k)$ is

$$\begin{bmatrix} P_k^- & P_k^- H^T \\ HP_k^- & HP_k^- H^T + R \end{bmatrix}. \tag{13.85}$$

Applying the conditioning property (Eq. 13.52), we get

$$p(\boldsymbol{x}_k) = p(\boldsymbol{x}_k^- | z_k) \tag{13.86}$$

$$\sim N(\boldsymbol{\mu}_k, P_k), \tag{13.87}$$

$$P_k = P_k^- - P_k^- H^T \left(HP_k^- H^T + R\right)^{-1} HP_k^-, \tag{13.88}$$

$$\boldsymbol{\mu}_k = \boldsymbol{\mu}_k^- + P_k^- H^T \left(HP_k^- H^T + R\right)^{-1} (z_k - H\boldsymbol{\mu}_k). \tag{13.89}$$

The two sets of equations (Eqs. 13.79 to 13.81 and Eqs. 13.86 to 13.89) are the Kalman filter updating rules.

The term $P_k^- H^T \left(HP_k^- H^T + R\right)^{-1}$ appears in both Eqs. (13.88) and (13.89). Defining

$$K_k = P_k^- H^T \left(HP_k^- H^T + R\right)^{-1}, \tag{13.90}$$

these equations are simplified as

$$P_k = (I - K_k H)P_k^-, \tag{13.91}$$

$$\boldsymbol{\mu}_k = \boldsymbol{\mu}_k^- + K_k(z_k - H\boldsymbol{\mu}_k^-). \tag{13.92}$$

The term K_k is called the Kalman gain matrix and the term $z_k - H\boldsymbol{\mu}_k^-$ is called the innovation.

13.9 Useful Math in This Chapter

Although Chapter 2 provides some useful mathematical results, for convenience we supplement this chapter with a few mathematical facts at the end.

13.9.1 Gaussian Integral

We will compute the integral of the univariate normal p.d.f. in this section. The trick in doing this integration is to consider two independent univariate Gaussians at one time:

$$\int_{-\infty}^{\infty} e^{-x^2}\,\mathrm{d}x = \sqrt{\left(\int_{-\infty}^{\infty} e^{-x^2}\,\mathrm{d}x\right)\left(\int_{-\infty}^{\infty} e^{-y^2}\,\mathrm{d}y\right)} \tag{13.93}$$

$$= \sqrt{\int_{-\infty}^{\infty}\int_{-\infty}^{\infty} e^{-(x^2+y^2)}\,\mathrm{d}x\,\mathrm{d}y} \tag{13.94}$$

$$= \sqrt{\int_{0}^{\infty}\int_{0}^{2\pi} re^{-r^2}\,\mathrm{d}r\,\mathrm{d}\theta} \tag{13.95}$$

$$= \sqrt{2\pi\left[-\frac{1}{2}e^{-r^2}\right]_0^{\infty}} \tag{13.96}$$

$$= \sqrt{\pi}, \tag{13.97}$$

in which a conversion to polar coordinates is performed in Eq. (13.95), and the extra r that appears inside the equation is the determinant of the Jacobian.

The above integral can be easily extended as

$$f(t) = \int_{-\infty}^{\infty} \exp\left(-\frac{x^2}{t}\right)\,\mathrm{d}x = \sqrt{t\pi}, \tag{13.98}$$

in which we assume $t > 0$. Then we have

$$\frac{\mathrm{d}f}{\mathrm{d}t} = \frac{\mathrm{d}}{\mathrm{d}t}\int_{-\infty}^{\infty} \exp\left(-\frac{x^2}{t}\right)\,\mathrm{d}x \tag{13.99}$$

$$= \int_{-\infty}^{\infty} \frac{x^2}{t^2}\exp\left(-\frac{x^2}{t}\right)\,\mathrm{d}x \tag{13.100}$$

and

$$\int_{-\infty}^{\infty} x^2 \exp\left(-\frac{x^2}{t}\right)\,\mathrm{d}x = \frac{t^2}{2}\sqrt{\frac{\pi}{t}}. \tag{13.101}$$

As a direct consequence, we have

$$\int_{-\infty}^{\infty} x^2 \frac{1}{\sqrt{2\pi}}\exp\left(-\frac{x^2}{2}\right)\,\mathrm{d}x = \frac{1}{\sqrt{2\pi}}\frac{4}{2}\sqrt{\frac{\pi}{2}} = 1, \tag{13.102}$$

and it is obvious that

$$\int_{-\infty}^{\infty} x \frac{1}{\sqrt{2\pi}}\exp\left(-\frac{x^2}{2}\right)\,\mathrm{d}x = 0, \tag{13.103}$$

since $x\exp\left(-\frac{x^2}{2}\right)$ is an odd function.

The last two equations prove that the mean and variance of a standard normal distribution are 0 and 1, respectively.

13.9.2 Characteristic Functions

The characteristic function of a random variable with p.d.f. $p(\boldsymbol{x})$ is defined as its Fourier transform

$$\varphi(\boldsymbol{t}) = \mathbb{E}\left[e^{i\boldsymbol{t}^T\boldsymbol{x}}\right], \tag{13.104}$$

in which $i = \sqrt{-1}$.

Let us compute the characteristic function of a normal random variable:

$$\varphi(\boldsymbol{t}) \tag{13.105}$$

$$= \mathbb{E}\left[\exp\left(i\boldsymbol{t}^T\boldsymbol{x}\right)\right] \tag{13.106}$$

$$= \int \frac{1}{(2\pi)^{d/2}|\Sigma|^{1/2}} \exp\left(-\frac{1}{2}(\boldsymbol{x}-\boldsymbol{\mu})^T\Sigma^{-1}(\boldsymbol{x}-\boldsymbol{\mu}) + i\boldsymbol{t}^T\boldsymbol{x}\right) \mathrm{d}\boldsymbol{x} \tag{13.107}$$

$$= \exp\left(i\boldsymbol{t}^T\boldsymbol{\mu} - \frac{1}{2}\boldsymbol{t}^T\Sigma\boldsymbol{t}\right). \tag{13.108}$$

Since the characteristic function is defined as a Fourier transform, the inverse Fourier transform of $\varphi(\boldsymbol{t})$ will be exactly $p(\boldsymbol{x})$—i.e., a random variable is completely determined by its characteristic function. In other words, when we see that a characteristic function $\varphi(\boldsymbol{t})$ is of the form

$$\exp\left(i\boldsymbol{t}^T\boldsymbol{\mu} - \frac{1}{2}\boldsymbol{t}^T\Sigma\boldsymbol{t}\right),$$

we know that the underlying density is normal with mean $\boldsymbol{\mu}$ and covariance matrix Σ.

Suppose X and Y are two *independent* random vectors with the same dimensionality, and we define a new random vector $Z = X + Y$. Then

$$p_Z(\boldsymbol{z}) = \iint_{\boldsymbol{z}=\boldsymbol{x}+\boldsymbol{y}} p_X(\boldsymbol{x})p_Y(\boldsymbol{y})\,\mathrm{d}\boldsymbol{x}\,\mathrm{d}\boldsymbol{y} \tag{13.109}$$

$$= \int p_X(\boldsymbol{x})p_Y(\boldsymbol{z}-\boldsymbol{x})\,\mathrm{d}\boldsymbol{x}, \tag{13.110}$$

which is a convolution. Since convolution in the function space is a product in the Fourier space, we have

$$\varphi_Z(\boldsymbol{t}) = \varphi_X(\boldsymbol{t})\varphi_Y(\boldsymbol{t}), \tag{13.111}$$

which means that the characteristic function of the sum of two independent random variables is just the product of the characteristic functions of the summands.

13.9.3 Schur Complement and the Matrix Inversion Lemma

The Schur complement is very useful in computing the inverse of a block matrix.

Suppose M is a block matrix expressed as

$$M = \begin{bmatrix} A & B \\ C & D \end{bmatrix}, \tag{13.112}$$

in which A and D are nonsingular square matrices. We want to compute M^{-1}.

Some algebraic manipulation gives

$$\begin{aligned}
&\begin{bmatrix} I & \mathbf{0} \\ -CA^{-1} & I \end{bmatrix} M \begin{bmatrix} I & -A^{-1}B \\ \mathbf{0} & I \end{bmatrix} && (13.113)\\
&= \begin{bmatrix} I & \mathbf{0} \\ -CA^{-1} & I \end{bmatrix} \begin{bmatrix} A & B \\ C & D \end{bmatrix} \begin{bmatrix} I & -A^{-1}B \\ \mathbf{0} & I \end{bmatrix} && (13.114)\\
&= \begin{bmatrix} A & B \\ \mathbf{0} & D - CA^{-1}B \end{bmatrix} \begin{bmatrix} I & -A^{-1}B \\ \mathbf{0} & I \end{bmatrix} && (13.115)\\
&= \begin{bmatrix} A & \mathbf{0} \\ \mathbf{0} & D - CA^{-1}B \end{bmatrix} = \begin{bmatrix} A & \mathbf{0} \\ \mathbf{0} & S_A \end{bmatrix}, && (13.116)
\end{aligned}$$

in which I and $\mathbf{0}$ are identity and zero matrices of appropriate size, respectively, and the term

$$D - CA^{-1}B$$

is called the *Schur complement of* A, denoted as S_A.

Taking the determinant of each side of the above equation gives

$$|M| = |A|\,|S_A|. \tag{13.117}$$

Equation $XMY = Z$ implies that $M^{-1} = YZ^{-1}X$ when both X and Y are invertible. Hence, we have

$$\begin{aligned}
M^{-1} &= \begin{bmatrix} I & -A^{-1}B \\ \mathbf{0} & I \end{bmatrix} \begin{bmatrix} A & \mathbf{0} \\ \mathbf{0} & S_A \end{bmatrix}^{-1} \begin{bmatrix} I & \mathbf{0} \\ -CA^{-1} & I \end{bmatrix} && (13.118)\\
&= \begin{bmatrix} A^{-1} & -A^{-1}BS_A^{-1} \\ \mathbf{0} & S_A^{-1} \end{bmatrix} \begin{bmatrix} I & \mathbf{0} \\ -CA^{-1} & I \end{bmatrix} && (13.119)\\
&= \begin{bmatrix} A^{-1} + A^{-1}BS_A^{-1}CA^{-1} & -A^{-1}BS_A^{-1} \\ -S_A^{-1}CA^{-1} & S_A^{-1} \end{bmatrix}. && (13.120)
\end{aligned}$$

Similarly, we can also compute M^{-1} by using the Schur complement of D, in the following way:

$$\begin{aligned}
M^{-1} &= \begin{bmatrix} S_D^{-1} & -S_D^{-1}BD^{-1} \\ -D^{-1}CS_D^{-1} & D^{-1} + D^{-1}CS_D^{-1}BD^{-1} \end{bmatrix}, && (13.121)\\
|M| &= |D|\,|S_D|. && (13.122)
\end{aligned}$$

Equations (13.120) and (13.121) are two different representations of the same matrix M^{-1}, which means that the corresponding blocks in these two equations must be equal, for example,

$$S_D^{-1} = A^{-1} + A^{-1} B S_A^{-1} C A^{-1}.$$

This result is known as the *matrix inversion lemma*:

$$S_D^{-1} = (A - BD^{-1}C)^{-1} = A^{-1} + A^{-1}B(D - CA^{-1}B)^{-1}CA^{-1}. \tag{13.123}$$

The following result, which comes from equating the two upper right blocks, is also useful:

$$A^{-1}B(D - CA^{-1}B)^{-1} = (A - BD^{-1}C)^{-1}BD^{-1}. \tag{13.124}$$

This formula and the matrix inversion lemma are useful in the derivation of the Kalman filter equations.

13.9.4 Vector and Matrix Derivatives

Suppose y is a scalar, A is a matrix, and $\boldsymbol{x}$ and $\boldsymbol{y}$ are vectors. The partial derivative of y with respect to A is defined as

$$\left(\frac{\partial y}{\partial A}\right)_{ij} = \frac{\partial y}{\partial a_{ij}}, \tag{13.125}$$

where a_{ij} is the (i, j)th component of the matrix A.

Based on this definition, it is easy to get the following rule:

$$\frac{\partial}{\partial \boldsymbol{x}}(\boldsymbol{x}^T \boldsymbol{y}) = \frac{\partial}{\partial \boldsymbol{x}}(\boldsymbol{y}^T \boldsymbol{x}) = \boldsymbol{y}. \tag{13.126}$$

For a square matrix A that is $n \times n$, the determinant of the matrix defined by removing from A the ith row and jth column is called a *minor* of A, and denoted as M_{ij}. The scalar $c_{ij} = (-1)^{i+j} M_{ij}$ is called a *cofactor* of A. The matrix A_{cof} with c_{ij} in its (i, j)th entry is called the *cofactor matrix* of A. Finally, the *adjoint* matrix of A is defined as the transpose of the cofactor matrix

$$A_{\text{adj}} = A_{\text{cof}}^T. \tag{13.127}$$

There are some well-known facts about the minors, determinant, and adjoint of a matrix:

$$|A| = \sum_j a_{ij} c_{ij}, \tag{13.128}$$

$$A^{-1} = \frac{1}{|A|} A_{\text{adj}}. \tag{13.129}$$

Since M_{ij} has the ith row of A removed, it does not depend on a_{ij} and neither does c_{ij}. Thus, we have

$$\frac{\partial}{\partial a_{ij}}|A| = c_{ij} \tag{13.130}$$

$$\text{or} \quad \frac{\partial}{\partial A}|A| = A_{\text{cof}}, \tag{13.131}$$

which in turn shows that

$$\frac{\partial}{\partial A}|A| = A_{\text{cof}} = A_{\text{adj}}^T = |A|(A^{-1})^T. \tag{13.132}$$

Using the chain rule, we immediately get that for a positive definite matrix A,

$$\frac{\partial}{\partial A}\log|A| = (A^{-1})^T. \tag{13.133}$$

Applying the definition, it is also easy to show that for a square matrix A,

$$\frac{\partial}{\partial A}(\boldsymbol{x}^T A\boldsymbol{x}) = \boldsymbol{x}\boldsymbol{x}^T, \tag{13.134}$$

since $\boldsymbol{x}^T A\boldsymbol{x} = \sum_{i=1}^n \sum_{j=1}^n a_{ij}x_i x_j$, where $\boldsymbol{x} = (x_1, x_2, \ldots, x_n)^T$.

Exercises

In the exercises for this chapter, we will discuss a few basic properties of the *exponential family*. The exponential family is probably the most important class of distributions, with the normal distribution being a representative of it.

We say that a p.d.f. or p.m.f. (for continuous or discrete random vectors) is in the exponential family with parameters $\boldsymbol{\theta}$ if it can be written as

$$p(\boldsymbol{x}|\boldsymbol{\theta}) = \frac{1}{Z(\boldsymbol{\theta})}h(\boldsymbol{x})\exp\left(\boldsymbol{\theta}^T\phi(\boldsymbol{x})\right). \tag{13.135}$$

Various items of notation involved in this definition are explained as follows:

- *Canonical parameters.* $\boldsymbol{\theta} \in \mathbb{R}^d$ are the canonical parameters or natural parameters.
- $\boldsymbol{x} \in \mathbb{R}^m$ are the random variables, which can be either continuous or discrete.
- *Sufficient statistics.* $\phi(\boldsymbol{x}) \in \mathbb{R}^d$ is a set of sufficient statistics for $\boldsymbol{x}$. Note that $m = d$ may not (and often does not) hold. Let X be a set of i.i.d. samples from $p(\boldsymbol{x}|\boldsymbol{\theta})$. Loosely speaking, the term "sufficient" means that the set $\phi(X)$ contains all the information (i.e., sufficient) to estimate the parameters $\boldsymbol{\theta}$. Obviously, $\phi(\boldsymbol{x}) = \boldsymbol{x}$ is a trivial set of sufficient statistics with respect to $\boldsymbol{x}$.
- $h(\boldsymbol{x})$ is a scaling function. Note that $h(\boldsymbol{x}) \geq 0$ is required to make $p(\boldsymbol{x}|\boldsymbol{\theta})$ a valid p.d.f. or p.m.f.

- *Partition function.* $Z(\boldsymbol{\theta})$ is called a partition function, whose role is to make $p(\boldsymbol{x}|\boldsymbol{\theta})$ integrate (or sum) to 1. Hence,

$$Z(\boldsymbol{\theta}) = \int h(\boldsymbol{x}) \exp\left(\boldsymbol{\theta}^T \phi(\boldsymbol{x})\right) \mathrm{d}\boldsymbol{x}$$

  in the continuous case. In the discrete case, we simply replace the integration with a summation.
- *Cumulant function.* We can define a *log partition function* $A(\boldsymbol{\theta})$ as

$$A(\boldsymbol{\theta}) = \log(Z(\boldsymbol{\theta})).$$

  With this new notation, Eq. (13.135) has an equivalent form:

$$p(\boldsymbol{x}|\boldsymbol{\theta}) = h(\boldsymbol{x}) \exp\left(\boldsymbol{\theta}^T \phi(\boldsymbol{x}) - A(\boldsymbol{\theta})\right). \tag{13.136}$$

  Note that $A(\boldsymbol{\theta})$ is also called a cumulant function, the meaning of which will be made clear soon.

Note that these functions or statistics are not unique. For example, we can multiply the parameters $\boldsymbol{\theta}$ by a constant $c > 0$, multiply the sufficient statistics ϕ by $1/c$, and change h and Z accordingly to obtain an equivalent $p(\boldsymbol{x}|\boldsymbol{\theta})$. Similarly, we can change the scale h and partition function Z simultaneously. It is often the case that we choose $h(\boldsymbol{x}) = 1$ for any $\boldsymbol{x}$.

13.1 Answer the following questions:

(a) Show that the canonical parameterization (Eq. 13.25) is equivalent to the more common moment parameterization in Eq. (13.5).

(b) Show that a normal distribution is in the exponential family.

(c) The Bernoulli distribution is a discrete distribution. A Bernoulli random variable X can be either 0 or 1, with $\Pr(X = 1) = q$ and $\Pr(X = 0) = 1 - q$, in which $0 \leq q \leq 1$. Show that the Bernoulli distribution is in the exponential family.

13.2 (Cumulant function) In statistics, the first cumulant of a random variable X is the expectation $\mathbb{E}[X]$, and the second cumulant is the variance (or covariance matrix) $\mathbb{E}[(X - \mathbb{E}X)^2]$. In the exponential family, the cumulant function $A(\boldsymbol{\theta})$ has close relationships to these cumulants of the sufficient statistics $\phi(\boldsymbol{x})$.

(a) Prove that

$$\frac{\partial A}{\partial \boldsymbol{\theta}} = \mathbb{E}[\phi(X)].$$

(Hint: You can safely exchange the order of the integration and differentiation operators in this case.)

(b) Prove that

$$\frac{\partial^2 A}{\partial \boldsymbol{\theta}\, \partial \boldsymbol{\theta}^T} = \operatorname{Var}\left(\phi(X)\right).$$

(c) Use the above theorems to find the expectation and variance of the Bernoulli distribution. Check the correctness of your calculations using the definition of mean and variance.

13.3 (Beta distributions) The beta distribution is a continuous distribution. The support of a beta distribution is $[0, 1]$—i.e., its p.d.f. is 0 for values that are negative or larger than 1. For simplicity, we use the range $(0, 1)$ as a beta distribution's support in this problem—i.e., excluding $x = 0$ and $x = 1$.

A beta distribution has two *shape parameters* $\alpha > 0$ and $\beta > 0$, which determine the shape of the distribution. And a beta random variable is often denoted as $X \sim \text{Beta}(\alpha, \beta)$ when the two shape parameters are α and β, respectively. Note that $\text{Beta}(\alpha, \beta)$ and $\text{Beta}(\beta, \alpha)$ are two different distributions when $\alpha \neq \beta$.

(a) The p.d.f. of a beta distribution is

$$p(x) = \frac{1}{\mathrm{B}(\alpha, \beta)} x^{\alpha-1}(1-x)^{\beta-1} \tag{13.137}$$

for $0 < x < 1$, in which

$$\mathrm{B}(\alpha, \beta) = \int_0^1 t^{\alpha-1}(1-t)^{\beta-1}\,\mathrm{d}t$$

is the *beta function*. The p.d.f. is 0 for other x values. Show that a beta distribution is in the exponential family. What is the partition function?

(b) The gamma function is defined as

$$\Gamma(x) = \int_0^\infty t^{x-1} e^{-t}\,\mathrm{d}t.$$

Read the information at `https://en.wikipedia.org/wiki/Gamma_function` and `https://en.wikipedia.org/wiki/Beta_function` to pick up a few important properties of the gamma and beta functions, especially the following ones (proofs are not required):

(i) $\Gamma(0.5) = \sqrt{\pi}$.

(ii) $\Gamma(-\frac{1}{2}) = -2\sqrt{\pi}$.

(iii) $\Gamma(n) = (n-1)!$ for any positive integer n, in which ! means the factorial function.

(iv) $\mathrm{B}(x, y) = \frac{\Gamma(x)\Gamma(y)}{\Gamma(x+y)}$.

(v) $\mathrm{B}(x+1, y) = \mathrm{B}(x, y) \cdot \frac{x}{x+y}$.

(vi) $\mathrm{B}(x, y+1) = \mathrm{B}(x, y) \cdot \frac{y}{x+y}$.

(c) Write your own code to draw curves for the p.d.f. of $\text{Beta}(0.5, 0.5)$, $\text{Beta}(1, 5)$, and $\text{Beta}(2, 2)$. Calculate the p.d.f. values for $x = 0.01n$ using Eq. (13.137) to draw the curves, where $1 \leq n \leq 99$ enumerates positive integers between 1 and 99.

13.4 (Conjugate prior) The exponential family is particularly useful in Bayesian analysis, because their conjugate priors exist. Given a distribution $p(\boldsymbol{x}|\boldsymbol{\theta})$ in the exponential family (hence the likelihood function is in the exponential family too), we can always find another distribution $p(\boldsymbol{\theta})$ such that the posterior distribution $p(\boldsymbol{\theta}|\boldsymbol{x})$ is in the same family as that of $p(\boldsymbol{\theta})$. We say that the prior is a *conjugate prior for the likelihood function* if the prior and the posterior have the same form. In this chapter, we have shown that the normal distribution is conjugate to itself.

In this problem, we will use the Bernoulli–beta pair as an example to further illustrate the conjugate priors for exponential family distributions. Similar procedures can be extended to handle other exponential family distributions and the exponential family in general.

(a) Let $\mathcal{D} = \{x_1, x_2, \ldots, x_n\}$ be i.i.d. samples from a Bernoulli distribution with $\Pr(X = 1) = q$. Show that the likelihood function is

$$p(\mathcal{D}|q) = (1-q)^n \exp\left(\ln\left(\frac{q}{1-q}\right)\sum_{i=1}^{n} x_i\right).$$

(b) Because $\theta^x \cdot \theta^y = \theta^{x+y}$, it is natural to set the prior $p(q)$ to

$$p(q|\nu_0, \tau_0) = c(1-q)^{\nu_0} \exp\left(\ln\left(\frac{q}{1-q}\right)\tau_0\right),$$

in which $c > 0$ is a normalization constant, and ν_0 and τ_0 are parameters for the prior distribution. Show that

$$p(q|\nu_0, \tau_0) \propto q^{\tau_0}(1-q)^{\nu_0-\tau_0},$$

and further show that it is a beta distribution. What are the parameters of this beta distribution? And what is the value of c in terms of ν_0 and τ_0?

(c) Show that the posterior $p(q|\mathcal{D})$ is a beta distribution. What are the parameters of this beta distribution?

(d) Intuitively explain what the prior does.

14 The Basic Idea behind Expectation-Maximization

Statistical learning models are very important in many areas inside computer science, including but not confined to machine learning, computer vision, pattern recognition, and data mining. It is also important in some deep learning models, such as the restricted Boltzmann machine (RBM).

Statistical learning models have parameters, and estimating such parameters from data is one of the key problems in the study of such models. Expectation-maximization (EM) is arguably the most widely used parameter estimation technique. Hence, it is worthwhile knowing some basics of EM.

However, although EM is must-have knowledge in studying statistical learning models, it is not easy for beginners. This chapter introduces the basic idea behind EM. We want to emphasize that the main purpose of this chapter is to introduce the *basic idea* (or to emphasize the *intuition*) behind EM, not to cover all the details of EM or to present completely rigorous mathematical derivations.

14.1 GMM: A Worked Example

Let us start from a simple worked example: the Gaussian mixture model (GMM).

14.1.1 Gaussian Mixture Model

In Figure 14.1 we show three curves corresponding to three different probability density functions (p.d.f.s). The blue curve is the p.d.f. of a normal distribution $N(10,16)$—i.e., a Gaussian distribution—with mean $\mu = 10$ and standard deviation $\sigma = 4$ (and $\sigma^2 = 16$). We denote this p.d.f. as

$$p_1(x) = N(x; 10, 16).$$

The red curve is a normal distribution $N(30,49)$ with $\mu = 30$ and $\sigma = 7$. Similarly, we denote it as

$$p_2(x) = N(x; 30, 49).$$

We are interested in the black curve, whose first half is similar to the blue one, while the second half is similar to the red one. This curve is also the p.d.f. of a distribution,

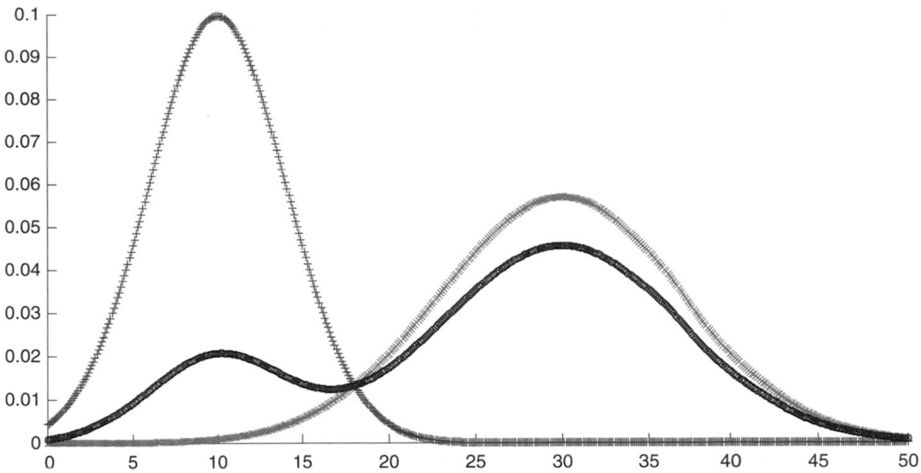

Figure 14.1 A simple GMM illustration. (A black and white version of this figure will appear in some formats. For the color version, please refer to the plate section.)

denoted as p_3. Since the black curve is similar to parts of the blue and red curves, it is reasonable to conjecture that p_3 is related to both p_1 and p_2.

Indeed, p_3 is a *weighted* combination of p_1 and p_2. In this example,

$$p_3(x) = 0.2p_1(x) + 0.8p_2(x). \tag{14.1}$$

Because $0.2 + 0.8 = 1$, it is easy to verify that $p_3(x) \geq 0$ always holds and $\int_{-\infty}^{\infty} p_3(x)\,\mathrm{d}x = 1$. Hence, p_3 is a valid p.d.f.

Thus p_3 is a *mixture* of two Gaussians (p_1 and p_2), hence a *Gaussian mixture model*. The definition of a GMM is in fact more general: it can have more than two components, and the Gaussians can be multivariate.

A GMM is a distribution whose p.d.f. has the form

$$p(\boldsymbol{x}) = \sum_{i=1}^{N} \alpha_i N(\boldsymbol{x}; \boldsymbol{\mu}_i, \Sigma_i) \tag{14.2}$$

$$= \sum_{i=1}^{N} \frac{\alpha_i}{(2\pi)^{d/2}|\Sigma_i|^{1/2}} \exp\left(-\frac{1}{2}(\boldsymbol{x} - \boldsymbol{\mu}_i)^T \Sigma_i^{-1} (\boldsymbol{x} - \boldsymbol{\mu}_i)\right), \tag{14.3}$$

in which $\boldsymbol{x}$ is a d-dimensional random vector.

In this GMM, there are N Gaussian components, with the ith Gaussian having mean vector $\boldsymbol{\mu}_i \in \mathbb{R}^d$ and covariance matrix $\Sigma_i \in \mathbb{R}^{d \times d}$. These Gaussian components are mixed together using a linear combination, where the weight for the ith component is α_i (called the *mixing coefficient*). The mixing coefficients must satisfy

$$\sum_{i=1}^{N} \alpha_i = 1, \tag{14.4}$$

$$\alpha_i \geq 0 \quad \forall i. \tag{14.5}$$

Figure 14.2 GMM as a graphical model.

It is easy to verify that under these conditions, $p(\boldsymbol{x})$ is a valid multivariate probability density function.

14.1.2 The Hidden Variable Interpretation

We can have a different interpretation of the Gaussian mixture model, using the hidden variable concept, as illustrated in Figure 14.2.

In Figure 14.2, the random variable X follows a Gaussian mixture model (cf. Eq. 14.3). Its parameters are

$$\boldsymbol{\theta} = \left\{\alpha_i, \boldsymbol{\mu}_i, \Sigma_i\right\}_{i=1}^{N} . \tag{14.6}$$

If we want to sample an instance from this GMM, we could directly sample from the p.d.f. in Eq. (14.3). However, there is another two-step way to perform the sampling.

Let us define a random variable Z, where Z is a multinomial discrete distribution, taking values from the set $\{1,2,\ldots,N\}$. The probability that Z takes the value $Z = i$ is α_i—i.e., $\Pr(Z = i) = \alpha_i$ for $1 \le i \le N$. Then the two-step sampling procedure is

Step 1. Sample from Z, and get a value i $(1 \le i \le N)$.
Step 2. Sample $\boldsymbol{x}$ from the ith Gaussian component $N(\boldsymbol{\mu}_i, \Sigma_i)$.

It is easy to verify that the sample $\boldsymbol{x}$ achieved from this two-step sampling procedure follows the underlying GMM distribution in Eq. (14.3).

In learning GMM parameters, we are given a sample set $\{\boldsymbol{x}_1, \boldsymbol{x}_2, \ldots, \boldsymbol{x}_M\}$, where the $\boldsymbol{x}_i$ are i.i.d. (independent and identically distributed) instances sampled from the p.d.f. in Eq. (14.3). From this set of samples, we want to estimate or learn the GMM parameters $\boldsymbol{\theta} = \left\{\alpha_i, \boldsymbol{\mu}_i, \Sigma_i\right\}_{i=1}^N$.

Because we are given the samples $\boldsymbol{x}_i$, the random variable X (cf. Figure 14.2) is called an *observed* (or observable) random variable. As shown in Figure 14.2, observed random variables are usually shown as filled circles.

The random variable Z, however, is not observable, and is called a *hidden variable* (or a latent variable). Hidden variables are shown as empty circles, as for the Z node in Figure 14.2.

14.1.3 What If We Can Observe the Hidden Variable?

In real applications, we do not know the value (or instantiation) of Z, because it is hidden (not observable). This fact makes estimating GMM parameters rather difficult, and techniques such as EM (the focus of this chapter) have to be employed.

However, for the sample set

$$\mathcal{X} = \{\boldsymbol{x}_1, \boldsymbol{x}_2, \ldots, \boldsymbol{x}_M\},$$

let us consider the scenario in which we can further suppose that some oracle has given us the value of Z:

$$\mathcal{Z} = \{z_1, z_2, \ldots, z_M\}.$$

In other words, we know that $\boldsymbol{x}_i$ is sampled from the z_ith Gaussian component.

In this case, it is easy to estimate the parameters $\boldsymbol{\theta}$. First, we can find all those samples that are generated from the ith component, and use $\mathcal{X}_i$ to denote this subset of samples. In precise mathematical language,

$$\mathcal{X}_i = \left\{\boldsymbol{x}_j \mid z_j = i,\ 1 \le j \le M\right\}. \tag{14.7}$$

The mixing coefficient estimation is a simple counting. We can count the number of examples that are generated from the ith Gaussian component as

$$m_i = |\mathcal{X}_i|,$$

where $|\cdot|$ is the size (number of elements) of a set. Then the maximum likelihood estimation for α_i is

$$\hat{\alpha}_i = \frac{m_i}{\sum_{j=1}^N m_j} = \frac{m_i}{M}. \tag{14.8}$$

Second, it is also easy to estimate the $\boldsymbol{\mu}_i$ and Σ_i parameters for any $1 \le i \le N$. The maximum likelihood estimation solutions are the same as those single Gaussian equations:

$$\hat{\boldsymbol{\mu}}_i = \frac{1}{m_i} \sum_{\boldsymbol{x} \in \mathcal{X}_i} \boldsymbol{x}, \tag{14.9}$$

$$\hat{\Sigma}_i = \frac{1}{|m_i|} \sum_{\boldsymbol{x} \in \mathcal{X}_i} (\boldsymbol{x} - \hat{\boldsymbol{\mu}}_i)(\boldsymbol{x} - \hat{\boldsymbol{\mu}}_i)^T. \tag{14.10}$$

In short, if we know the hidden variable's instantiations, the estimation is straightforward. Unfortunately, we are given only the observed sample set $\mathcal{X}$. The hidden variables $\mathcal{Z}$ are unknown to us. This fact complicates the entire parameter estimation process.

14.1.4 Can We Imitate an Oracle?

It is natural to ask ourselves, if we do not have an oracle to teach us, whether we can imitate the oracle's teaching. In other words, can we *guess* the value of z_j for $\boldsymbol{x}_j$?

As we will see, EM is an iterative process, in which we use a variable t to denote the iteration index. We will update the parameters $\boldsymbol{\theta}$ in every iteration, and use $\boldsymbol{\theta}^{(t)}$ to denote their values in the tth iteration. Then a natural choice for our guess is to use the posterior $p(z_j|\boldsymbol{x}_j, \boldsymbol{\theta}^{(t)})$ as a replacement for z_j. This term is the probability of z_j given the sample $\boldsymbol{x}_j$ and the current parameter values $\boldsymbol{\theta}^{(t)}$, which seems to be the best educated guess we can have given the information available.

In this guessing game, we have at least two issues in our way. First, an oracle is supposed to know everything, and will be able to tell us, with 100% confidence, that $\boldsymbol{x}_7$ comes from the third Gaussian component. If an oracle exists, we can simply say $z_7 = 3$ for this example $\boldsymbol{x}_7$. However, our guess will never be deterministic—it can at best be a probability distribution for the *random variable* z_j.

Hence, we will assume that for every observed sample $\boldsymbol{x}$, there is a corresponding hidden vector $\boldsymbol{z}$, whose values can be guessed but cannot be observed. We still use Z to denote the underlying random variable, and use

$$\mathcal{Z} = \{\boldsymbol{z}_1, \boldsymbol{z}_2, \ldots, \boldsymbol{z}_M\}$$

to denote the set of hidden vectors for the observable training examples

$$\mathcal{X} = \{\boldsymbol{x}_1, \boldsymbol{x}_2, \ldots, \boldsymbol{x}_M\}.$$

In the GMM example, a vector $\boldsymbol{z}_j$ will have N dimensions, corresponding to the N Gaussian components. One and only one of these dimensions will be 1, and all others will be 0.

Second, the guess we have about $\boldsymbol{z}_j$ is a distribution determined by the posterior $p(\boldsymbol{z}_j|\boldsymbol{x}_j, \boldsymbol{\theta}^{(t)})$. However, what we really want are values instead of a distribution. How are we going to use this guess? A common trick in statistical learning is to use its expectation. We will leave to later sections the details of how the expectation is computed and used.

14.2 An Informal Description of the EM Algorithm

Now we are ready to give an informal description of the EM algorithm.

- We first initialize the values of $\boldsymbol{\theta}$ in any reasonable way.
- Then we can estimate the best possible $\mathcal{Z}$ (or the expectation of its posterior distribution) using $\mathcal{X}$ and the current $\boldsymbol{\theta}$ estimation.
- With this $\mathcal{Z}$ estimation, we can find a better estimate of $\boldsymbol{\theta}$ using $\mathcal{X}$.
- A better $\boldsymbol{\theta}$ (combined with $\mathcal{X}$) will lead to a better guess for $\mathcal{Z}$.
- This process (estimating $\boldsymbol{\theta}$ and $\mathcal{Z}$ in alternating order) can proceed until the change in $\boldsymbol{\theta}$ is small (i.e., when the procedure converges).

In still more informal language, after proper initialization of the parameters, we can perform the following steps:

E-step. Find a better guess of the nonobservable hidden variables by using the data and current parameter values.

M-step. Find a better parameter estimation by using the current guess for the hidden variables and the data.

Repeat. Repeat the above two steps until convergence.

In the EM algorithm, the first step is usually called the expectation step, abbreviated as the E-step, and the second step is usually called the maximization step, abbreviated as the M-step. The EM algorithm repeats E- and M-steps in alternating order. When the algorithm converges, we get the desired parameter estimations.

14.3 The Expectation-Maximization Algorithm

Now we will show more details of the EM algorithm. Suppose we are dealing with two sets of random variables: the observed variables X and the hidden variables Z. The joint p.d.f. is $p(X,Z;\boldsymbol{\theta})$, where $\boldsymbol{\theta}$ are the parameters. We are given a set of instances of X to learn the parameters:

$$\mathcal{X} = \{\boldsymbol{x}_1, \boldsymbol{x}_2, \dots, \boldsymbol{x}_M\}.$$

The task is to estimate $\boldsymbol{\theta}$ from $\mathcal{X}$.

For every $\boldsymbol{x}_j$, there is a corresponding z_j, which we denote collectively as

$$\mathcal{Z} = \{z_1, z_2, \dots, z_M\}.$$

And we want to clarify that $\boldsymbol{\theta}$ now include the parameters that are associated with Z. In the GMM example, $\{z_i\}_{i=1}^M$ are estimates for Z, $\left\{\alpha_i, \boldsymbol{\mu}_i, \Sigma_i\right\}_{i=1}^N$ are parameters specifying X, and $\boldsymbol{\theta}$ include both sets of parameters.

14.3.1 Jointly Nonconcave Incomplete Log-Likelihood

If we use the maximum likelihood (ML) estimation technique, the ML estimate for $\boldsymbol{\theta}$ is

$$\hat{\boldsymbol{\theta}} = \arg\max_{\boldsymbol{\theta}} p(\mathcal{X}|\boldsymbol{\theta}). \tag{14.11}$$

Or equivalently, we can maximize the log-likelihood

$$\hat{\boldsymbol{\theta}} = \arg\max_{\boldsymbol{\theta}} \ln p(\mathcal{X}|\boldsymbol{\theta}) \tag{14.12}$$

because $\ln(\cdot)$ is a monotonically increasing function.

Then parameter estimation becomes an optimization problem. We will use the notation $\ell\ell(\boldsymbol{\theta})$ to denote the log-likelihood, that is,

$$\ell\ell(\boldsymbol{\theta}) = \ln p(\mathcal{X}|\boldsymbol{\theta}). \tag{14.13}$$

Recent developments in optimization theory tell us that we can generally consider a minimization problem "easy" if it is *convex*, but nonconvex problems are usually difficult to solve. Equivalently, a *concave* maximization problem is generally considered easy, while nonconcave maximization is often difficult, because the negation of a convex function is a concave one, and vice versa.

Unfortunately, the log-likelihood is nonconcave in most cases. Let us take the Gaussian mixture model as an example. The likelihood $p(\mathcal{X}|\boldsymbol{\theta})$ is

$$p(\mathcal{X}|\boldsymbol{\theta}) = \prod_{j=1}^{M} \left(\sum_{i=1}^{N} \frac{\alpha_i}{(2\pi)^{d/2}|\Sigma_i|^{1/2}} \exp\left(-\frac{1}{2}(\boldsymbol{x}_j - \boldsymbol{\mu}_i)^T \Sigma_i^{-1} (\boldsymbol{x}_j - \boldsymbol{\mu}_i) \right) \right). \tag{14.14}$$

The log-likelihood has the form

$$\sum_{j=1}^{M} \ln \left(\sum_{i=1}^{N} \frac{\alpha_i}{(2\pi)^{d/2}|\Sigma_i|^{1/2}} \exp\left(-\frac{1}{2}(\boldsymbol{x}_j - \boldsymbol{\mu}_i)^T \Sigma_i^{-1} (\boldsymbol{x}_j - \boldsymbol{\mu}_i) \right) \right). \tag{14.15}$$

This equation is nonconcave with respect to $\left\{\alpha_i, \boldsymbol{\mu}_i, \Sigma_i\right\}_{i=1}^{n}$, the joint optimization variables. In other words, this is a difficult maximization problem.

We have two sets of random variables X and Z. The log-likelihood in Eq. (14.15) is called the *incomplete data* log-likelihood because Z is not in that equation.

14.3.2 (Possibly) Concave Complete Data Log-Likelihood

The complete data log-likelihood is

$$\ln p(\mathcal{X}, \mathcal{Z}|\boldsymbol{\theta}), \tag{14.16}$$

in which the hidden variable Z is assumed to be known. Knowing the hidden variable can often simplify the optimization. For example, the complete data log-likelihood may become concave.

Let us use GMM as an example once more. In GMM, the z_j vectors (which form $\mathcal{Z}$) are N-dimensional vectors with $(N-1)$ 0s and only one dimension with value 1. Hence, the complete data likelihood is

$$p(\mathcal{X},\mathcal{Z}|\boldsymbol{\theta}) = \prod_{j=1}^{M}\prod_{i=1}^{N}\left[\frac{\alpha_i}{(2\pi)^{d/2}|\Sigma_i|^{1/2}}\exp\left(-\frac{1}{2}(\boldsymbol{x}_j-\boldsymbol{\mu}_i)^T\Sigma_i^{-1}(\boldsymbol{x}_j-\boldsymbol{\mu}_i)\right)\right]^{z_{ij}}. \tag{14.17}$$

This equation can be explained using the two-step sampling process. Let us assume that $\boldsymbol{x}_j$ is generated by the i'th Gaussian component. Then if $i \neq i'$ we know that $z_{ij} = 0$; otherwise $z_{ij} = z_{i'j} = 1$. In other words, the term inside the two products will equal 1 for the $N-1$ times when $z_{ij} = 0$, and the remaining single entry will be evaluated to

$$\alpha_{i'}N(\boldsymbol{x};\boldsymbol{\mu}_{i'},\Sigma_{i'}),$$

which exactly matches the two-step sampling procedure. In the two-step sampling, the first step has probability $\alpha_{i'}$, and the second step has density $N(\boldsymbol{x};\boldsymbol{\mu}_{i'},\Sigma_{i'})$. These two steps are independent of each other, hence the product rule applies to obtain the above density.

Then the complete data log-likelihood is

$$\sum_{j=1}^{M}\sum_{i=1}^{N} z_{ij}\left(\frac{1}{2}\left(\ln|\Sigma_i^{-1}| - (\boldsymbol{x}_j-\boldsymbol{\mu}_i)^T\Sigma_i^{-1}(\boldsymbol{x}_j-\boldsymbol{\mu}_i)\right) + \ln\alpha_i\right) + \text{const}, \tag{14.18}$$

in which 'const' refers to constant values that are not affected by the parameters $\boldsymbol{\theta}$.

Let us consider the scenario when the hidden variable z_{ij} is known, but $\alpha_i, \boldsymbol{\mu}_i$, and Σ_i are unknown. Here we suppose Σ_i is invertible for $1 \le i \le N$. Instead of considering the parameters $(\boldsymbol{\mu}_i,\Sigma_i)$, we consider $(\boldsymbol{\mu}_i,\Sigma_i^{-1})$. In fact, it is more natural to understand this choice as using a variant of the canonical parameterization of a normal distribution, which was explained in detail in Chapter 13.

Now we can look at the three remaining items in Eq. (14.18):

- It is well known that the log-determinant function

$$\ln|\Sigma_i^{-1}| = \ln\det\left(\Sigma_i^{-1}\right)$$

  is concave with respect to Σ_i^{-1}.
- It is also obvious that the quadratic term

$$(\boldsymbol{x}_j-\boldsymbol{\mu}_i)^T\Sigma_i^{-1}(\boldsymbol{x}_j-\boldsymbol{\mu}_i)$$

  is jointly convex with respect to variables $(\boldsymbol{\mu}_i,\Sigma_i^{-1})$, which directly implies that its negation is concave.
- It is easy to prove that the logarithm function $\ln\alpha_i$ is concave with respect to α_i.

Because the sum of concave functions is concave, Eq. (14.18) can be efficiently solved.

From this optimization perspective, we can understand the EM algorithm from a different point of view. Although the original maximum likelihood parameter estimation problem is difficult to solve (jointly nonconcave), the EM algorithm can usually (but not always) make concave subproblems, hence becoming efficiently solvable.

14.3.3 The General EM Derivation

Now we discuss EM in the general case. We have observable variables X and samples $\mathcal{X}$. We also have hidden variables Z and unobservable samples $\mathcal{Z}$. The overall system parameters are denoted by $\boldsymbol{\theta}$.

The parameter learning problem tries to find optimal parameters $\hat{\boldsymbol{\theta}}$ by maximizing the incomplete data log-likelihood

$$\hat{\boldsymbol{\theta}} = \arg\max_{\boldsymbol{\theta}} \ln p(\mathcal{X}|\boldsymbol{\theta}). \tag{14.19}$$

As a simplification, we assume that Z is discrete, and hence

$$p(\mathcal{X}|\boldsymbol{\theta}) = \sum_{\mathcal{Z}} p(\mathcal{X},\mathcal{Z}|\boldsymbol{\theta}). \tag{14.20}$$

However, this assumption is mainly for notational simplicity. If Z is continuous, we can replace the summation with an integral.

Although we have mentioned previously that we can use the posterior of Z—i.e., $p(\mathcal{Z}|\mathcal{X},\boldsymbol{\theta})$—as our guess, it is also interesting to observe what will happen to the complete data likelihood if we use an *arbitrary* distribution for Z (and hence understand why the posterior is special and why we should use it).

Let q be any valid probability distribution for Z. We can measure how different q is to the posterior using the classic Kullback–Leibler (KL) divergence measure:

$$\mathrm{KL}(q\|p) = -\sum_{\mathcal{Z}} q(\mathcal{Z}) \ln\left(\frac{p(\mathcal{Z}|\mathcal{X},\boldsymbol{\theta})}{q(\mathcal{Z})}\right). \tag{14.21}$$

Probability theory tells us that

$$p(\mathcal{X}|\boldsymbol{\theta}) = \frac{p(\mathcal{X},\mathcal{Z}|\boldsymbol{\theta})}{p(\mathcal{Z}|\mathcal{X},\boldsymbol{\theta})} \tag{14.22}$$

$$= \frac{p(\mathcal{X},\mathcal{Z}|\boldsymbol{\theta})}{q(\mathcal{Z})}\frac{q(\mathcal{Z})}{p(\mathcal{Z}|\mathcal{X},\boldsymbol{\theta})}. \tag{14.23}$$

Hence,

$$\ln p(\mathcal{X}|\boldsymbol{\theta}) = \left(\sum_{\mathcal{Z}} q(\mathcal{Z})\right) \ln p(\mathcal{X}|\boldsymbol{\theta}) \tag{14.24}$$

$$= \sum_{\mathcal{Z}} q(\mathcal{Z}) \ln p(\mathcal{X}|\boldsymbol{\theta}) \tag{14.25}$$

$$= \sum_{\mathcal{Z}} q(\mathcal{Z}) \ln \left(\frac{p(\mathcal{X}, \mathcal{Z}|\boldsymbol{\theta})}{q(\mathcal{Z})} \frac{q(\mathcal{Z})}{p(\mathcal{Z}|\mathcal{X}, \boldsymbol{\theta})} \right) \tag{14.26}$$

$$= \sum_{\mathcal{Z}} \left(q(\mathcal{Z}) \ln \frac{p(\mathcal{X}, \mathcal{Z}|\boldsymbol{\theta})}{q(\mathcal{Z})} - q(\mathcal{Z}) \ln \frac{p(\mathcal{Z}|\mathcal{X}, \boldsymbol{\theta})}{q(\mathcal{Z})} \right) \tag{14.27}$$

$$= \sum_{\mathcal{Z}} q(\mathcal{Z}) \ln \frac{p(\mathcal{X}, \mathcal{Z}|\boldsymbol{\theta})}{q(\mathcal{Z})} + \mathrm{KL}(q \| p) \tag{14.28}$$

$$= \mathcal{L}(q, \boldsymbol{\theta}) + \mathrm{KL}(q \| p). \tag{14.29}$$

We have decomposed the incomplete data log-likelihood into two terms. The first term is $\mathcal{L}(q, \boldsymbol{\theta})$, defined as

$$\mathcal{L}(q, \boldsymbol{\theta}) = \sum_{\mathcal{Z}} q(\mathcal{Z}) \ln \frac{p(\mathcal{X}, \mathcal{Z}|\boldsymbol{\theta})}{q(\mathcal{Z})}. \tag{14.30}$$

The second term is a KL-divergence between q and the posterior,

$$\mathrm{KL}(q \| p) = - \sum_{\mathcal{Z}} q(\mathcal{Z}) \ln \left(\frac{p(\mathcal{Z}|\mathcal{X}, \boldsymbol{\theta})}{q(\mathcal{Z})} \right), \tag{14.31}$$

which was copied from Eq. (14.21).

KL–divergence has some nice properties. For example,

$$D(q \| p) \geq 0 \tag{14.32}$$

always holds, and the equality is true if and only if $q = p$ (cf. Chapter 10). One direct consequence of this property is that

$$\mathcal{L}(q, \boldsymbol{\theta}) \leq \ln p(\mathcal{X}|\boldsymbol{\theta}) \tag{14.33}$$

always holds, and

$$\mathcal{L}(q, \boldsymbol{\theta}) = \ln p(\mathcal{X}|\boldsymbol{\theta}) \text{ if and only if } q(\mathcal{Z}) = p(\mathcal{Z}|\mathcal{X}, \boldsymbol{\theta}). \tag{14.34}$$

In other words, we have found a lower bound of $\ln p(\mathcal{X}|\boldsymbol{\theta})$. Hence, in order to maximize $\ln p(\mathcal{X}|\boldsymbol{\theta})$, we perform two steps:

- The first step is to make the lower bound $\mathcal{L}(q, \boldsymbol{\theta})$ equal $\ln p(\mathcal{X}|\boldsymbol{\theta})$. As aforementioned, we know the equality holds if and only if

  $$\hat{q}(\mathcal{Z}) = p(\mathcal{Z}|\mathcal{X}, \boldsymbol{\theta}).$$

  With this optimal $\hat{q}(\mathcal{Z})$ value, we have

  $$\ln p(\mathcal{X}|\boldsymbol{\theta}) = \mathcal{L}(\hat{q}, \boldsymbol{\theta}), \tag{14.35}$$

  and $\mathcal{L}$ now depends only on $\boldsymbol{\theta}$. This is the expectation step (E-step) in the EM algorithm.

- In the second step, we maximize $\mathcal{L}(\hat{q}, \boldsymbol{\theta})$ with respect to $\boldsymbol{\theta}$. Since $\ln p(\mathcal{X}|\boldsymbol{\theta}) = \mathcal{L}(\hat{q}, \boldsymbol{\theta})$, an increase of $\mathcal{L}(\hat{q}, \boldsymbol{\theta})$ also means an increase of the log-likelihood $\ln p(\mathcal{X}|\boldsymbol{\theta})$. And, because we are maximizing $\mathcal{L}(\hat{q}, \boldsymbol{\theta})$ in this step, *the log-likelihood will always increase* if we are not already at a local maximum of the log-likelihood. This is the maximization step (M-step) in the EM algorithm.

14.3.4 The E- and M-Steps

In the E-step, we already know that we should set

$$\hat{q}(\mathcal{Z}) = p(\mathcal{Z}|\mathcal{X}, \boldsymbol{\theta}), \tag{14.36}$$

which is straightforward (at least in its mathematical form).

Then how will we maximize $\mathcal{L}(\hat{q}, \boldsymbol{\theta})$? We can substitute $\hat{q}$ into the definition of $\mathcal{L}$, and then find the optimal $\boldsymbol{\theta}$ that maximizes $\mathcal{L}$ after plugging in $\hat{q}$. However, note that $\hat{q}$ involves $\boldsymbol{\theta}$ too. Hence, we need some more notation.

Suppose we are in the tth iteration. In the E-step, $\hat{q}$ is computed using the current parameters as

$$\hat{q}(\mathcal{Z}) = p(\mathcal{Z}|\mathcal{X}, \boldsymbol{\theta}^{(t)}). \tag{14.37}$$

Then $\mathcal{L}$ becomes

$$\mathcal{L}(\hat{q}, \boldsymbol{\theta}) = \sum_{\mathcal{Z}} \hat{q}(\mathcal{Z}) \ln \frac{p(\mathcal{X}, \mathcal{Z}|\boldsymbol{\theta})}{\hat{q}(\mathcal{Z})} \tag{14.38}$$

$$= \sum_{\mathcal{Z}} \hat{q}(\mathcal{Z}) \ln p(\mathcal{X}, \mathcal{Z}|\boldsymbol{\theta}) - \hat{q}(\mathcal{Z}) \ln \hat{q}(\mathcal{Z}) \tag{14.39}$$

$$= \sum_{\mathcal{Z}} p(\mathcal{Z}|\mathcal{X}, \boldsymbol{\theta}^{(t)}) \ln p(\mathcal{X}, \mathcal{Z}|\boldsymbol{\theta}) + \text{const}, \tag{14.40}$$

in which $\text{const} = -\hat{q}(\mathcal{Z}) \ln \hat{q}(\mathcal{Z})$ does not involve the variable $\boldsymbol{\theta}$, hence can be ignored.

The remaining term is in fact an expectation, which we denote by $\mathcal{Q}(\boldsymbol{\theta}, \boldsymbol{\theta}^{(t)})$:

$$\mathcal{Q}(\boldsymbol{\theta}, \boldsymbol{\theta}^{(t)}) = \sum_{\mathcal{Z}} p(\mathcal{Z}|\mathcal{X}, \boldsymbol{\theta}^{(t)}) \ln p(\mathcal{X}, \mathcal{Z}|\boldsymbol{\theta}) \tag{14.41}$$

$$= \mathbb{E}_{\mathcal{Z}|\mathcal{X}, \boldsymbol{\theta}^{(t)}} \left[\ln p(\mathcal{X}, \mathcal{Z}|\boldsymbol{\theta}) \right]. \tag{14.42}$$

That is, in the E-step, we compute the posterior of Z. In the M-step, we compute the expectation of the complete data log-likelihood $\ln p(\mathcal{X}, \mathcal{Z}|\boldsymbol{\theta})$ with respect to the posterior distribution $p(\mathcal{Z}|\mathcal{X}, \boldsymbol{\theta}^{(t)})$, and we maximize the expectation to get a better parameter estimate:

$$\boldsymbol{\theta}^{(t+1)} = \arg\max_{\boldsymbol{\theta}} \mathcal{Q}(\boldsymbol{\theta}, \boldsymbol{\theta}^{(t)}) \tag{14.43}$$

$$= \arg\max_{\boldsymbol{\theta}} \mathbb{E}_{\mathcal{Z}|\mathcal{X}, \boldsymbol{\theta}^{(t)}} \left[\ln p(\mathcal{X}, \mathcal{Z}|\boldsymbol{\theta}) \right]. \tag{14.44}$$

Thus, three computations are involved in EM: (1) posterior, (2) expectation, (3) maximization. We treat (1) as the E-step and (2)+(3) as the M-step. Some researchers prefer to treat (1)+(2) as the E-step and (3) as the M-step. However, no matter how the computations are attributed to different steps, the EM algorithm does not change.

14.3.5 The EM Algorithm

We are now ready to write down the EM algorithm.

Algorithm 12 The expectation-maximization algorithm

1: $t \leftarrow 0$.
2: Initialize the parameters to $\boldsymbol{\theta}^{(0)}$.
3: The **E**(expectation)-step: Find $p(\mathcal{Z}|\mathcal{X}, \boldsymbol{\theta}^{(t)})$.
4: The **M**(aximization)-step 1: Find the expectation

$$\mathcal{Q}(\boldsymbol{\theta}, \boldsymbol{\theta}^{(t)}) = \mathbb{E}_{\mathcal{Z}|\mathcal{X}, \boldsymbol{\theta}^{(t)}} \left[\ln p(\mathcal{X}, \mathcal{Z}|\boldsymbol{\theta}) \right]. \tag{14.45}$$

5: The **M**(aximization)-step 2: Find a new parameter estimate

$$\boldsymbol{\theta}^{(t+1)} = \arg\max_{\boldsymbol{\theta}} \mathcal{Q}(\boldsymbol{\theta}, \boldsymbol{\theta}^{(t)}). \tag{14.46}$$

6: $t \leftarrow t + 1$.
7: If the log-likelihood has not converged, go to the E-step again (line 3).

14.3.6 Will EM Converge?

The analysis of EM's convergence property is a complex topic. However, it is easy to show that the EM algorithm will help achieve higher likelihood and converge to a local maximum.

Let us consider two time steps $t - 1$ and t. From Eq. (14.35), we obtain

$$\mathcal{L}(\hat{q}^{(t)}, \boldsymbol{\theta}^{(t)}) = \ln p(\mathcal{X}|\boldsymbol{\theta}^{(t)}), \tag{14.47}$$

$$\mathcal{L}(\hat{q}^{(t-1)}, \boldsymbol{\theta}^{(t-1)}) = \ln p(\mathcal{X}|\boldsymbol{\theta}^{(t-1)}). \tag{14.48}$$

Note that we have added the time index to the superscript of $\hat{q}$ to emphasize that $\hat{q}$ also changes between iterations.

Now, because at the $(t - 1)$th iteration

$$\boldsymbol{\theta}^{(t)} = \arg\max_{\boldsymbol{\theta}} \mathcal{L}(\hat{q}^{(t-1)}, \boldsymbol{\theta}), \tag{14.49}$$

we have

$$\mathcal{L}(\hat{q}^{(t-1)}, \boldsymbol{\theta}^{(t)}) \geq \mathcal{L}(\hat{q}^{(t-1)}, \boldsymbol{\theta}^{(t-1)}). \tag{14.50}$$

Similarly, at the tth iteration, based on Eqs. (14.33) and (14.35), we have

$$\mathcal{L}(\hat{q}^{(t-1)}, \boldsymbol{\theta}^{(t)}) \leq \ln p(\mathcal{X}|\boldsymbol{\theta}^{(t)}) = \mathcal{L}(\hat{q}^{(t)}, \boldsymbol{\theta}^{(t)}). \tag{14.51}$$

Putting these equations together, we get

$$\begin{aligned}
\ln p(\mathcal{X}|\boldsymbol{\theta}^{(t)}) &= \mathcal{L}(\hat{q}^{(t)}, \boldsymbol{\theta}^{(t)}) && \text{(use Eq. 14.47)} && (14.52)\\
&\geq \mathcal{L}(\hat{q}^{(t-1)}, \boldsymbol{\theta}^{(t)}) && \text{(use Eq. 14.51)} && (14.53)\\
&\geq \mathcal{L}(\hat{q}^{(t-1)}, \boldsymbol{\theta}^{(t-1)}) && \text{(use Eq. 14.50)} && (14.54)\\
&= \ln p(\mathcal{X}|\boldsymbol{\theta}^{(t-1)}) && \text{(use Eq. 14.48).} && (14.55)
\end{aligned}$$

Hence, EM will converge to a local maximum of the likelihood. However, the analysis of its convergence rate is very complex and beyond the scope of this introductory book.

14.4 EM for GMM

Now we can apply the EM algorithm to GMM.

The first thing is to compute the posterior. Using Bayes' theorem we have

$$p(z_{ij}|\boldsymbol{x}_j, \boldsymbol{\theta}^{(t)}) = \frac{p(\boldsymbol{x}_j, z_{ij}|\boldsymbol{\theta}^{(t)})}{p(\boldsymbol{x}_j|\boldsymbol{\theta}^{(t)})}, \tag{14.56}$$

in which z_{ij} can be 0 or 1, and $z_{ij} = 1$ is true if and only if $\boldsymbol{x}_j$ is generated by the ith Gaussian component.

Next we will compute the $\mathcal{Q}$ function, which is the expectation of the complete data log-likelihood $\ln p(\mathcal{X}, \mathcal{Z}|\boldsymbol{\theta})$ with respect to the posterior distribution we just found. The GMM complete data log-likelihood has already been computed in Eq. (14.18). For easier reference, we copy this equation here:

$$\sum_{j=1}^{M}\sum_{i=1}^{N} z_{ij}\left(\frac{1}{2}\Big(\ln|\Sigma_i^{-1}| - (\boldsymbol{x}_j - \boldsymbol{\mu}_i)^T\Sigma_i^{-1}(\boldsymbol{x}_j - \boldsymbol{\mu}_i)\Big) + \ln\alpha_i\right) + \text{const.} \tag{14.57}$$

The expectation of Eq. (14.57) with respect to Z is

$$\sum_{j=1}^{M}\sum_{i=1}^{N} \gamma_{ij}\left(\frac{1}{2}\left(\ln|\Sigma_i^{-1}| - (\boldsymbol{x}_j - \boldsymbol{\mu}_i)^T\Sigma_i^{-1}(\boldsymbol{x}_j - \boldsymbol{\mu}_i)\right) + \ln\alpha_i\right), \tag{14.58}$$

where the constant term is ignored, and γ_{ij} is the expectation of $z_{ij}|\boldsymbol{x}_j, \boldsymbol{\theta}^{(t)}$. In other words, we need to compute the expectation of the conditional distribution defined by Eq. (14.56).

In Eq. (14.56), the denominator does not depend on Z, and $p(\boldsymbol{x}_j|\boldsymbol{\theta}^{(t)})$ is equal to $\sum_{i=1}^{N} \alpha_i^{(t)} N(\boldsymbol{x}_j; \boldsymbol{\mu}_i^{(t)}, \Sigma_i^{(t)})$. For the numerator, we can directly compute its expectation, as

$$\mathbb{E}\big[p(\boldsymbol{x}_j, z_{ij}|\boldsymbol{\theta}^{(t)})\big] = \mathbb{E}\big[p(z_{ij}|\boldsymbol{\theta}^{(t)})p(\boldsymbol{x}_j|z_{ij}, \boldsymbol{\theta}^{(t)})\big]. \tag{14.59}$$

Note that when $z_{ij} = 0$, we always have $p(\boldsymbol{x}_j|z_{ij}, \boldsymbol{\theta}^{(t)}) = 0$. Thus,

$$\mathbb{E}\big[p(z_{ij}|\boldsymbol{\theta}^{(t)})p(\boldsymbol{x}_j|z_{ij}, \boldsymbol{\theta}^{(t)})\big] = \Pr(z_{ij} = 1)p(\boldsymbol{x}_j|\boldsymbol{\mu}_i^{(t)}, \Sigma_i^{(t)}) \tag{14.60}$$

$$= \alpha_i^{(t)} N(\boldsymbol{x}_j; \boldsymbol{\mu}_i^{(t)}, \Sigma_i^{(t)}). \tag{14.61}$$

Hence, we have

$$\gamma_{ij} = \mathbb{E}\big[z_{ij}|\boldsymbol{x}_j, \boldsymbol{\theta}^{(t)}\big] \propto \alpha_i^{(t)} N(\boldsymbol{x}_j; \boldsymbol{\mu}_i^{(t)}, \Sigma_i^{(t)}), \tag{14.62}$$

or

$$\gamma_{ij} = \mathbb{E}\big[z_{ij}|\boldsymbol{x}_j, \boldsymbol{\theta}^{(t)}\big] = \frac{\alpha_i^{(t)} N(\boldsymbol{x}_j; \boldsymbol{\mu}_i^{(t)}, \Sigma_i^{(t)})}{\sum_{k=1}^N \alpha_k^{(t)} N(\boldsymbol{x}_j; \boldsymbol{\mu}_k^{(t)}, \Sigma_k^{(t)})} \tag{14.63}$$

for $1 \le i \le N, 1 \le j \le M$.

After γ_{ij} is computed, Eq. (14.58) is completely specified. We start the optimization from α_i. Because there is a constraint that $\sum_{i=1}^N \alpha_i = 1$, we use the Lagrange multiplier method. After removing irrelevant terms, we get

$$\sum_{j=1}^M \sum_{i=1}^N \gamma_{ij} \ln \alpha_i + \lambda \left(\sum_{i=1}^N \alpha_i - 1 \right). \tag{14.64}$$

Setting the derivative to 0 gives us that for any $1 \le i \le N$,

$$\frac{\sum_{j=1}^M \gamma_{ij}}{\alpha_i} + \lambda = 0, \tag{14.65}$$

or

$$\alpha_i = -\frac{\sum_{j=1}^M \gamma_{ij}}{\lambda}.$$

Because $\sum_{i=1}^N \alpha_i = 1$, we know that

$$\lambda = -\sum_{j=1}^M \sum_{i=1}^N \gamma_{ij}.$$

Hence,

$$\alpha_i = \frac{\sum_{j=1}^M \gamma_{ij}}{\sum_{j=1}^M \sum_{i=1}^N \gamma_{ij}}.$$

For notational simplicity, we define

$$m_i = \sum_{j=1}^M \gamma_{ij}. \tag{14.66}$$

From the definition of γ_{ij}, it is easy to prove

$$\sum_{i=1}^{N} m_i = \sum_{i=1}^{N}\sum_{j=1}^{M} \gamma_{ij} \tag{14.67}$$

$$= \sum_{j=1}^{M}\left(\sum_{i=1}^{N} \gamma_{ij}\right) \tag{14.68}$$

$$= \sum_{j=1}^{M} 1 \tag{14.69}$$

$$= M. \tag{14.70}$$

Then we get the updating rule for α_i:

$$\alpha_i^{(t+1)} = \frac{m_i}{M}. \tag{14.71}$$

Furthermore, using similar steps to deriving the single Gaussian equations, it is easy to show that for any $1 \le i \le N$,

$$\boldsymbol{\mu}_i^{(t+1)} = \frac{\sum_{j=1}^{M} \gamma_{ij}\boldsymbol{x}_j}{m_i}, \tag{14.72}$$

$$\Sigma_i^{(t+1)} = \frac{\sum_{j=1}^{M} \gamma_{ij}\left(\boldsymbol{x}_j - \boldsymbol{\mu}_i^{(t+1)}\right)\left(\boldsymbol{x}_j - \boldsymbol{\mu}_i^{(t+1)}\right)^T}{m_i}. \tag{14.73}$$

Putting these results together, we have the complete set of updating rules for GMM. If at iteration t, the parameters are estimated as $\alpha_i^{(t)}$, $\boldsymbol{\mu}_i^{(t)}$, and $\Sigma_i^{(t)}$ for $1 \le i \le N$, the EM algorithm updates these parameters (for $1 \le i \le N$, $1 \le j \le M$) as

$$\gamma_{ij} = \frac{\alpha_i N(\boldsymbol{x}_j; \boldsymbol{\mu}_i^{(t)}, \Sigma_i^{(t)})}{\sum_{k=1}^{N} \alpha_k^{(t)} N(\boldsymbol{x}_j; \boldsymbol{\mu}_k^{(t)}, \Sigma_k^{(t)})}, \tag{14.74}$$

$$m_i = \sum_{j=1}^{M} \gamma_{ij}, \tag{14.75}$$

$$\boldsymbol{\mu}_i^{(t+1)} = \frac{\sum_{j=1}^{M} \gamma_{ij}\boldsymbol{x}_j}{m_i}, \tag{14.76}$$

$$\Sigma_i^{(t+1)} = \frac{\sum_{j=1}^{M} \gamma_{ij}\left(\boldsymbol{x}_j - \boldsymbol{\mu}_i^{(t+1)}\right)\left(\boldsymbol{x}_j - \boldsymbol{\mu}_i^{(t+1)}\right)^T}{m_i}. \tag{14.77}$$

14.5 Miscellaneous Notes and Additional Resources

Good tutorials for the EM algorithm exist, e.g., Bilmes (1998) and Dellaert (2002).

Analyses of EM's convergence speed for GMM can be found in Xu & Jordan (1996).

In Exercise 14.2, we discuss detailed steps to show that the Baum–Welch algorithm for HMM parameter learning is a special case of EM.

More on RBM can be found in Hinton (2012).

Exercises

14.1 Derive the updating equations for Gaussian mixture models by yourself. You should not refer to Section 14.4 during your derivation. If you have just finished reading Section 14.4, wait at least two or three days before working on this problem.

14.2 In this problem, we will use the expectation-maximization method to learn parameters in a hidden Markov model (HMM). As will be shown in this problem, the Baum–Welch algorithm is indeed performing EM updates. To work out the solution for this problem, you will also need knowledge and facts learned in the HMM chapter (Chapter 12) and the information theory chapter (Chapter 10).

We will use the notation in the HMM chapter. For your convenience, the notation is repeated here:

- There are N discrete states, denoted as $S_1, S_2, \ldots, S_N$.
- There are M output discrete symbols, denoted as $V_1, V_2, \ldots, V_M$.
- Assume one sequence with T time steps, whose hidden state is Q_t and whose observed output is O_t at time t ($1 \le t \le T$). We use q_t and o_t to denote the indexes for state and output symbols at time t, respectively—i.e., $Q_t = S_{q_t}$ and $O_t = V_{o_t}$.
- The notation $1:t$ denotes all the ordered time steps between 1 and t. For example, $o_{1:T}$ is the sequence of all observed output symbols.
- An HMM has parameters $\lambda = (\pi, A, B)$, where $\pi \in \mathbb{R}^N$ specifies the initial state distribution, $A \in \mathbb{R}^{N\times N}$ is the state transition matrix, and $B \in \mathbb{R}^{N\times M}$ is the observation probability matrix. Note that $A_{ij} = \Pr(Q_t = S_j | Q_{t-1} = S_i)$ and $b_j(k) = \Pr(O_t = V_k | Q_t = S_j)$ are elements of A and B, respectively.
- In this problem, we use a variable r to denote the index of EM iterations, which starts from $r = 1$. Hence, $\lambda^{(1)}$ are the initial parameters.
- Various probabilities have been defined in the HMM chapter, denoted as $\alpha_t(i)$, $\beta_t(i)$, $\gamma_t(i)$, $\delta_t(i)$, and $\xi_t(i,j)$. In this problem, we assume that at the rth iteration, $\lambda^{(r)}$ are known, and these probabilities are computed using $\lambda^{(r)}$.

The purpose of this problem is to use the EM algorithm to find $\lambda^{(r+1)}$ using a training sequence $o_{1:T}$ and $\lambda^{(r)}$, by treating Q and O as the hidden and observed random variables, respectively.

(a) Suppose the hidden variables can be observed as $S_{q_1}, S_{q_2}, \ldots, S_{q_T}$. Show that the complete data log-likelihood is

$$\ln \pi_{q_1} + \sum_{t=1}^{T-1} \ln A_{q_t q_{t+1}} + \sum_{t=1}^{T} \ln b_{q_t}(o_t). \tag{14.78}$$

(b) The expectation of Eq. (14.78) with respect to the hidden variables Q_t (conditioned on $o_{1:T}$ and $\lambda^{(r)}$) forms an auxiliary function $\mathcal{Q}(\lambda, \lambda^r)$ (the E-step). Show that the expectation of the first term in Eq. (14.78) equals $\sum_{i=1}^{N} \gamma_1(i) \ln \pi_i$, i.e.,

$$\mathbb{E}_{Q_{1:T}}[\ln \pi_{Q_1}] = \sum_{i=1}^{N} \gamma_1(i) \ln \pi_i. \tag{14.79}$$

(c) Because the parameter π hinges on Eq. (14.79) only, the update rule for π can be found by maximizing this equation. Prove that we should set

$$\pi_i^{(r+1)} = \gamma_1(i)$$

in the M-step. Note that $\gamma_1(i)$ is computed using $\lambda^{(r)}$ as parameter values. (Hint: The right-hand side of Eq. (14.79) is related to the cross entropy.)

(d) The second part of the E-step calculates the expectation of the middle term in Eq. (14.78). Show that

$$\mathbb{E}_{Q_{1:T}}\left[\sum_{t=1}^{T-1} \ln A_{q_t q_{t+1}}\right] = \sum_{i=1}^{N} \sum_{j=1}^{N} \left(\sum_{t=1}^{T-1} \xi_t(i,j)\right) \ln A_{ij}. \tag{14.80}$$

(e) For the M-step relevant to A, prove that we should set

$$A_{ij}^{(r+1)} = \frac{\sum_{t=1}^{T-1} \xi_t(i,j)}{\sum_{t=1}^{T-1} \gamma_t(i)}. \tag{14.81}$$

(f) The final part of the E-step calculates the expectation of the last term in Eq. (14.78). Show that

$$\mathbb{E}_{Q_{1:T}}\left[\sum_{t=1}^{T} \ln b_{q_t}(o_t)\right] = \sum_{j=1}^{N} \sum_{k=1}^{M} \sum_{t=1}^{T} [\![o_t = k]\!] \gamma_t(j). \tag{14.82}$$

(g) For the M-step relevant to B, prove that we should set

$$b_j^{(r+1)}(k) = \frac{\sum_{t=1}^{T} [\![o_t = k]\!] \gamma_t(j)}{\sum_{t=1}^{T} \gamma_t(j)}, \tag{14.83}$$

in which $[\![\cdot]\!]$ is the indicator function.

(h) Are these results, obtained using EM, the same as those in the Baum–Welch method?

15 Convolutional Neural Networks

This chapter describes how a convolutional neural network (CNN) operates from a mathematical perspective. This chapter is self-contained, and the focus is to make it comprehensible for beginners in the CNN field.

The convolutional neural network (CNN) has shown excellent performance in many computer vision, machine learning, and pattern recognition problems. Many papers have been published on this topic, and quite a number of high-quality open source CNN software packages have been made available.

There are also well-written CNN tutorials and CNN software manuals. However, we believe that introductory CNN material specifically prepared for beginners is still needed. Research papers are usually very terse and lack detail. It might be difficult for beginners to read such papers. A tutorial targeting experienced researchers may not cover all the necessary details to understand how a CNN runs.

This chapter tries to present a document that

- is self-contained. It is expected that all required mathematical background knowledge is introduced in this chapter itself (or in other chapters in this book).
- has details of all the derivations. This chapter aims to explain all the necessary math in detail. We try not to ignore any important step in a derivation. Thus, it should be possible for a beginner to follow (although an expert may find this chapter a bit tautological).
- ignores implementation details. The purpose is for a reader to understand how a CNN runs at the mathematical level. We will ignore those implementation details. In CNN, making correct choices for various implementation details is one of the keys to its high accuracy (that is, "the devil is in the detail"). However, we have intentionally left this part out, in order for the reader to focus on the mathematics. After understanding the mathematical principles and details, it is more advantageous to learn these implementation and design details through hands-on experience by experimenting with CNN programming. The exercise problems in this chapter provide opportunities for this experience.

CNNs are useful in many applications, especially in image-related tasks. Applications of CNNs include image classification, image semantic segmentation, and object detection in images. We will focus on image classification (or categorization) in this chapter. In image categorization, every image has a major object that occupies a large portion of the image. An image is classified into one of the categories based on the identity of its main object—e.g., dog, airplane, bird.

15.1 Preliminaries

We start with a discussion of some background knowledge that is necessary in order to understand how a CNN runs. The reader familiar with these basics can ignore this section.

15.1.1 Tensor and Vectorization

Everybody is familiar with vectors and matrices. We use a symbol shown in boldface to represent a vector—e.g., $\boldsymbol{x} \in \mathbb{R}^D$ is a column vector with D elements. We use a capital letter to denote a matrix—e.g., $X \in \mathbb{R}^{H \times W}$ is a matrix with H rows and W columns. The vector $\boldsymbol{x}$ can also be viewed as a matrix with 1 column and D rows.

These concepts can be generalized to higher-order matrices—i.e., tensors. For example, $\boldsymbol{x} \in \mathbb{R}^{H \times W \times D}$ is an order 3 (or third-order) tensor. It contains HWD elements, and each of them can be indexed by an index triplet (i,j,d), with $0 \le i < H$, $0 \le j < W$, and $0 \le d < D$. Another way to view an order 3 tensor is to treat it as containing D channels of matrices. Every channel is a matrix with size $H \times W$. The first channel contains all the numbers in the tensor that are indexed by $(i,j,0)$. Note that in this chapter we assume the index starts from 0 rather than 1. When $D = 1$, an order 3 tensor reduces to a matrix.

We have interacted with tensors day-to-day. A scalar value is a zeroth-order (order 0) tensor, a vector is an order 1 tensor, and a matrix is a second-order tensor. A color image is in fact an order 3 tensor. An image with H rows and W columns is a tensor with size $H \times W \times 3$: if a color image is stored in the RGB format, it has three channels (for R, G, and B, respectively), and each channel is an $H \times W$ matrix (second-order tensor) that contains the R (or G, or B) values of each pixel.

It is beneficial to represent images (or other types of raw data) as a tensor. In early computer vision and pattern recognition, a color image (which is an order 3 tensor) was often converted to the grayscale version (which is a matrix) because we know how to handle matrices much better than tensors. The color information was lost during this conversion. But color is very important in various image- (or video-)based learning and recognition problems, and we do want to process color information in a principled way—e.g., using a CNN.

Tensors are essential in CNN. The input, intermediate representation, and parameters in a CNN are all tensors. Tensors with order higher than 3 are also widely used in CNNs. For example, we will soon see that the convolution kernels in a convolution layer of a CNN form an order 4 tensor.

Given a tensor, we can arrange all the numbers inside it into a long vector, following a prespecified order. For example, in MATLAB/GNU Octave, the `(:)` operator converts a matrix into a column vector in column-first order. An example is

$$A = \begin{bmatrix} 1 & 2 \\ 3 & 4 \end{bmatrix}, \quad A(:) = (1,3,2,4)^T = \begin{bmatrix} 1 \\ 3 \\ 2 \\ 4 \end{bmatrix}. \tag{15.1}$$

In mathematics, we use the notation "vec" to represent this vectorization operator. That is, $\mathrm{vec}(A) = (1,3,2,4)^T$ in the example in Eq. (15.1). In order to vectorize an order 3 tensor, we could vectorize its first channel (which is a matrix and we already know how to vectorize it), then the second channel, ..., till all channels are vectorized. The vectorization of the order 3 tensor is then the concatenation of the vectorization of all the channels in this order.

The vectorization of an order 3 tensor is a recursive process, which utilizes the vectorization of order 2 tensors. This recursive process can be applied to vectorize an order 4 (or even higher-order) tensor in the same manner.

15.1.2 Vector Calculus and the Chain Rule

The CNN learning process depends on vector calculus and the chain rule. Suppose z is a scalar (i.e., $z \in \mathbb{R}$) and $\boldsymbol{y} \in \mathbb{R}^H$ is a vector. If z is a function of $\boldsymbol{y}$, then the partial derivative of z with respect to $\boldsymbol{y}$ is a vector, defined as

$$\left[\frac{\partial z}{\partial \boldsymbol{y}}\right]_i = \frac{\partial z}{\partial y_i}. \tag{15.2}$$

In other words, $\frac{\partial z}{\partial \boldsymbol{y}}$ is a vector with the *same size* as $\boldsymbol{y}$, and its ith element is $\frac{\partial z}{\partial y_i}$. Also note that

$$\frac{\partial z}{\partial \boldsymbol{y}^T} = \left(\frac{\partial z}{\partial \boldsymbol{y}}\right)^T.$$

Furthermore, suppose $\boldsymbol{x} \in \mathbb{R}^W$ is another vector, and $\boldsymbol{y}$ is a function of $\boldsymbol{x}$. Then the partial derivative of $\boldsymbol{y}$ with respect to $\boldsymbol{x}$ is defined as

$$\left[\frac{\partial \boldsymbol{y}}{\partial \boldsymbol{x}^T}\right]_{ij} = \frac{\partial y_i}{\partial x_j}. \tag{15.3}$$

This partial derivative is an $H \times W$ matrix, whose entry at the intersection of the ith row and jth column is $\frac{\partial y_i}{\partial x_j}$.

It is easy to see that z is a function of $\boldsymbol{x}$ in a chain-like argument: a function maps $\boldsymbol{x}$ to $\boldsymbol{y}$, and another function maps $\boldsymbol{y}$ to z. The chain rule can be used to compute $\frac{\partial z}{\partial \boldsymbol{x}^T}$, as

$$\frac{\partial z}{\partial \boldsymbol{x}^T} = \frac{\partial z}{\partial \boldsymbol{y}^T} \frac{\partial \boldsymbol{y}}{\partial \boldsymbol{x}^T}. \tag{15.4}$$

A sanity check for Eq. (15.4) is to check the matrix/vector dimensions. Note that $\frac{\partial z}{\partial \boldsymbol{y}^T}$ is a row vector with H elements, or a $1 \times H$ matrix. (Be reminded that $\frac{\partial z}{\partial \boldsymbol{y}}$ is a column vector.) Since $\frac{\partial \boldsymbol{y}}{\partial \boldsymbol{x}^T}$ is an $H \times W$ matrix, the vector/matrix multiplication between them is valid, and the result should be a row vector with W elements, which matches the dimensionality of $\frac{\partial z}{\partial \boldsymbol{x}^T}$.

For specific rules to calculate partial derivatives of vectors and matrices, please refer to Chapter 2 and *The Matrix Cookbook* (Petersen & Pedersen 2012).

15.2 CNN Overview

In this section, we will see how a CNN trains and predicts at the abstract level, with the details left for later sections.

15.2.1 The Architecture

A CNN usually takes an order 3 tensor as its input—e.g., an image with H rows, W columns, and 3 channels (R, G, B color channels). Higher-order tensor inputs, however, can be handled by CNN in a similar fashion. The input then sequentially goes through a number of processes. One processing step is usually called a layer, which could be a convolution layer, a pooling layer, a normalization layer, a fully connected layer, a loss layer, etc.

We will introduce the details of these layers later in this chapter. We will give detailed introductions to three types of layers: convolution, pooling, and ReLU, which are the key parts of almost all CNN models. Proper normalization—e.g., batch normalization—is important in the optimization process for learning good parameters in a CNN. Although it is not introduced in this chapter, we will present some related resources in the exercise problems.

For now, let us give an abstract description of the CNN structure first:

$$\boldsymbol{x}^1 \longrightarrow \boxed{\boldsymbol{w}^1} \longrightarrow \boldsymbol{x}^2 \longrightarrow \cdots \longrightarrow \boldsymbol{x}^{L-1} \longrightarrow \boxed{\boldsymbol{w}^{L-1}} \longrightarrow \boldsymbol{x}^L \longrightarrow \boxed{\boldsymbol{w}^L} \longrightarrow z. \tag{15.5}$$

Equation (15.5) illustrates how a CNN runs layer by layer in a forward pass. The input is $\boldsymbol{x}^1$, usually an image (order 3 tensor). It goes through the processing in the first layer, which is the first box. We denote the parameters involved in the first layer's processing collectively as a tensor $\boldsymbol{w}^1$. The output of the first layer is $\boldsymbol{x}^2$, which also acts as the input to the second layer's processing. This processing proceeds till all layers in the CNN have been finished, and then outputs $\boldsymbol{x}^L$.

One additional layer, however, is added for backward error propagation, a method that learns good parameter values in the CNN. Let us suppose that the problem at hand is an image classification problem with C classes. A commonly used strategy is to output $\boldsymbol{x}^L$ as a C-dimensional vector, whose ith entry encodes the prediction (posterior probability of $\boldsymbol{x}^1$ coming from the ith class). To make $\boldsymbol{x}^L$ a probability mass function, we can set the processing in the $(L-1)$th layer as a softmax transformation of $\boldsymbol{x}^{L-1}$ (cf. Chapter 9). In other applications, the output $\boldsymbol{x}^L$ may have other forms and interpretations.

The final layer is a loss layer. Let us suppose $\boldsymbol{t}$ is the corresponding target (groundtruth) value for the input $\boldsymbol{x}^1$; then a cost or loss function can be used to measure the discrepancy between the CNN prediction $\boldsymbol{x}^L$ and the target $\boldsymbol{t}$. For example, a simple loss function could be

$$z = \frac{1}{2}\|\boldsymbol{t} - \boldsymbol{x}^L\|^2, \tag{15.6}$$

although more complex loss functions are usually used. This squared ℓ_2 loss can be used in a regression problem.

In a classification problem, the cross entropy (cf. Chapter 10) loss is often used. The groundtruth in a classification problem is a categorical variable t. We first convert the categorical variable t to a C-dimensional vector $\boldsymbol{t}$ (cf. Chapter 9). Now both $\boldsymbol{t}$ and $\boldsymbol{x}^L$ are probability mass functions, and the cross entropy loss measures the distance between them. Hence, we can minimize the cross entropy loss. Equation (15.5) explicitly models the loss function as a loss layer, whose processing is modeled as a box with parameters $\boldsymbol{w}^L$, although in many cases a loss layer does not involve any parameter—i.e., $\boldsymbol{w}^L = \emptyset$.

Note that there are other layers that do not have any parameter—that is, $\boldsymbol{w}^i$ may be empty for some $i < L$. The softmax layer is one such example. This layer can convert a vector into a probability mass function. The input to a softmax layer is a vector, whose values may be positive, zero, or negative. Suppose layer l is a softmax layer and its input is a vector $\boldsymbol{x}^l \in \mathbb{R}^d$. Then its output is a vector $\boldsymbol{x}^{l+1} \in \mathbb{R}^d$, which is computed as

$$x_i^{l+1} = \frac{\exp(x_i^l)}{\sum_{j=1}^d \exp(x_j^l)}, \tag{15.7}$$

that is, a softmax transformed version of the input. After the softmax layer's processing, values in $\boldsymbol{x}^{l+1}$ form a probability mass function, and can be used as input to the cross entropy loss.

15.2.2 The Forward Run

Suppose all the parameters of a CNN model $\boldsymbol{w}^1, \boldsymbol{w}^2, \ldots, \boldsymbol{w}^{L-1}$ have been learned; then we are ready to use this model for prediction. Prediction involves running the CNN model forward only—i.e., in the direction of the arrows in Eq. (15.5).

Let us take the image classification problem as an example. Starting from the input $\boldsymbol{x}^1$, we make it pass the processing of the first layer (the box with parameters $\boldsymbol{w}^1$), and get $\boldsymbol{x}^2$. In turn, $\boldsymbol{x}^2$ is passed into the second layer, etc. Finally, we achieve $\boldsymbol{x}^L \in \mathbb{R}^C$, which estimates the posterior probabilities of $\boldsymbol{x}^1$ belonging to the C categories. We can output the CNN prediction as

$$\arg\max_i x_i^L. \tag{15.8}$$

Note that the loss layer is not needed in prediction. It is useful only when we try to learn CNN parameters using a set of training examples. Now the problem is how we learn the model parameters.

15.2.3 Stochastic Gradient Descent (SGD)

As in many other learning systems, the parameters of a CNN model are optimized to minimize the loss z—i.e., we want the predictions of a CNN model to match the groundtruth labels on the training set.

Let us suppose one training example $\boldsymbol{x}^1$ is given for training such parameters. The training process involves running the CNN network in both directions. We first run the network in the forward direction to get $\boldsymbol{x}^L$ to achieve a prediction using the current CNN parameters. Instead of outputting this prediction, however, we need to compare it with the target $\boldsymbol{t}$ corresponding to $\boldsymbol{x}^1$—that is, continue running the forward pass till the last loss layer. Finally, we achieve a loss z.

The loss z is then a supervision signal, guiding how the parameters of the model should be modified (updated). And the stochastic gradient descent (SGD) way of modifying the parameters is

$$\boldsymbol{w}^i \longleftarrow \boldsymbol{w}^i - \eta \frac{\partial z}{\partial \boldsymbol{w}^i}. \tag{15.9}$$

A cautious note about the notation: In most CNN materials, a superscript indicates the "time" (e.g., training epochs). But in this chapter, we use the superscript to denote the layer index. Please do not get confused. We do not use an additional index variable to represent time. In Eq. (15.9), the $\longleftarrow$ sign implicitly indicates that the parameters $\boldsymbol{w}^i$ (of the i-layer) are updated from time t to $t+1$. If a time index t is used explicitly, this equation will look like

$$\left(\boldsymbol{w}^i\right)^{t+1} = \left(\boldsymbol{w}^i\right)^t - \eta \frac{\partial z}{\partial \left(\boldsymbol{w}^i\right)^t}. \tag{15.10}$$

In Eq. (15.9), the partial derivative $\frac{\partial z}{\partial \boldsymbol{w}^i}$ measures the rate of increase of z with respect to the changes in different dimensions of $\boldsymbol{w}^i$. This partial derivative vector is called the *gradient* in mathematical optimization. Hence, in a small local region around the current value of $\boldsymbol{w}^i$, to move $\boldsymbol{w}^i$ in the direction determined by the gradient will increase the objective value z. In order to minimize the loss function, we should update $\boldsymbol{w}^i$ along the opposite direction of the gradient. This updating rule is called gradient descent. Gradient descent is illustrated in Figure 15.1, in which the gradient is denoted by $\boldsymbol{g}$.

If we move too far in the negative gradient direction, however, the loss function may increase. Hence, in every update we change the parameters by only a small proportion of the negative gradient, controlled by η—with $\eta > 0$—which is called the learning rate and is usually set to a small number (e.g., $\eta = 0.001$) in deep neural network learning.

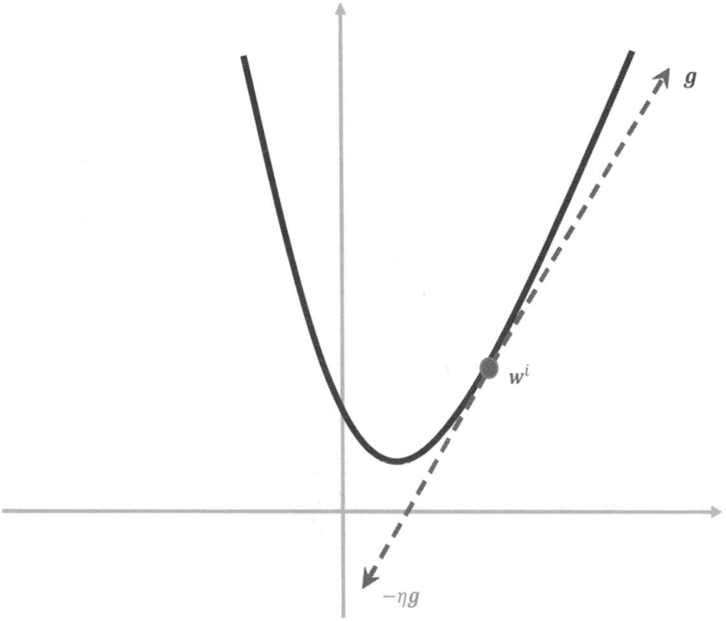

Figure 15.1 Illustration of the gradient descent method, in which η is the learning rate.

One update based on $\boldsymbol{x}^1$ will make the loss smaller for this particular training example if the learning rate is not too large. However, it is very possible that it will cause the loss of some other training examples to become larger. Hence, we need to update the parameters using all training examples. When all training examples have been used to update the parameters, we say that one *epoch* has been processed.

One epoch will in general reduce the average loss on the training set until the learning system overfits the training data. Hence, we can repeat the gradient descent updating for many epochs and terminate at some point to obtain the CNN parameters (e.g., we can terminate when the average loss on a validation set increases).

Gradient descent may seem simple in its math form (Eq. 15.9), but it is a very tricky operation in practice. For example, if we update the parameters using the gradient calculated from only one training example, we will observe an unstable loss function: the average loss of all training examples will bounce up and down at very high frequency. This is because the gradient is estimated using only one training example instead of the entire training set—the gradient computed using only one example can be very unstable.

Contrary to single-example-based parameter updating, we can compute the gradient using all training examples and then update the parameters. However, this *batch* processing strategy requires a lot of computations because the parameters are updated only once in an epoch, and hence it is impractical, especially when the number of training examples is large.

A compromise is to use a *mini-batch* of training examples, to compute the gradient using this mini-batch, and to update the parameters correspondingly. Updating the parameters using the gradient estimated from a (usually) small subset of training examples is called *stochastic* gradient descent. For example, we can set 32 or 64 examples as a mini-batch. Stochastic gradient descent (using the mini-batch strategy) is the mainstream method used to learn a CNN's parameters. We also want to note that when mini-batches are used, the input of the CNN becomes a fourth-order tensor—e.g., $H \times W \times 3 \times 32$ if the mini-batch size is 32.

A new problem now becomes apparent, and seems a very complex task: How do we compute the gradient?

15.2.4 Error Back Propagation

The last layer's partial derivatives are easy to compute. Because $\boldsymbol{x}^L$ is connected to z directly under the control of parameters $\boldsymbol{w}^L$, it is easy to compute $\frac{\partial z}{\partial \boldsymbol{w}^L}$. This step is needed only when $\boldsymbol{w}^L$ is not empty. In the same spirit, it is also easy to compute $\frac{\partial z}{\partial \boldsymbol{x}^L}$. For example, if the squared ℓ_2 loss is used, we have an empty $\frac{\partial z}{\partial \boldsymbol{w}^L}$, and

$$\frac{\partial z}{\partial \boldsymbol{x}^L} = \boldsymbol{x}^L - \boldsymbol{t}.$$

In fact, for every layer, we compute two sets of gradients: the partial derivatives of z with respect to the layer parameters $\boldsymbol{w}^i$, and that layer's input $\boldsymbol{x}^i$:

- The term $\frac{\partial z}{\partial \boldsymbol{w}^i}$, as seen in Eq. (15.9), can be used to update the current (ith) layer's parameters.
- The term $\frac{\partial z}{\partial \boldsymbol{x}^i}$ can be used to update parameters backward—e.g., to the $(i-1)$th layer. An intuitive explanation is that $\boldsymbol{x}^i$ is the output of the $(i-1)$th layer and $\frac{\partial z}{\partial \boldsymbol{x}^i}$ is how $\boldsymbol{x}^i$ should be changed to reduce the loss function. Hence, we could view $\frac{\partial z}{\partial \boldsymbol{x}^i}$ as the part of the "error" supervision information propagated from z backward to the current layer, in a layer-by-layer fashion. Thus, we can continue the back propagation process, and use $\frac{\partial z}{\partial \boldsymbol{x}^i}$ to propagate the errors backward to the $(i-1)$th layer.

This layer-by-layer backward updating procedure makes learning a CNN much easier. In fact, this strategy is also the standard practice for other types of neural networks beyond CNN; it is called error back propagation, or simply back propagation.

Let us take the ith layer as an example. When we are updating the ith layer, the back propagation process for the $(i+1)$th layer must have been finished. That is, we have already computed the terms $\frac{\partial z}{\partial \boldsymbol{w}^{i+1}}$ and $\frac{\partial z}{\partial \boldsymbol{x}^{i+1}}$. Both are stored in memory and ready for use.

Now our task is to compute $\frac{\partial z}{\partial \boldsymbol{w}^i}$ and $\frac{\partial z}{\partial \boldsymbol{x}^i}$. Using the chain rule, we have

$$\frac{\partial z}{\partial(\operatorname{vec}(\boldsymbol{w}^i)^T)} = \frac{\partial z}{\partial(\operatorname{vec}(\boldsymbol{x}^{i+1})^T)} \frac{\partial \operatorname{vec}(\boldsymbol{x}^{i+1})}{\partial(\operatorname{vec}(\boldsymbol{w}^i)^T)}, \tag{15.11}$$

$$\frac{\partial z}{\partial(\operatorname{vec}(\boldsymbol{x}^i)^T)} = \frac{\partial z}{\partial(\operatorname{vec}(\boldsymbol{x}^{i+1})^T)} \frac{\partial \operatorname{vec}(\boldsymbol{x}^{i+1})}{\partial(\operatorname{vec}(\boldsymbol{x}^i)^T)}. \tag{15.12}$$

Since $\frac{\partial z}{\partial \boldsymbol{x}^{i+1}}$ has already been computed and stored in memory, it requires just a matrix reshaping operation (vec) and an additional transpose operation to get $\frac{\partial z}{\partial(\operatorname{vec}(\boldsymbol{x}^{i+1})^T)}$, which is the first term on the right-hand side of both equations. So long as we can compute $\frac{\partial \operatorname{vec}(\boldsymbol{x}^{i+1})}{\partial(\operatorname{vec}(\boldsymbol{w}^i)^T)}$ and $\frac{\partial \operatorname{vec}(\boldsymbol{x}^{i+1})}{\partial(\operatorname{vec}(\boldsymbol{x}^i)^T)}$, we can easily get what we want (the left-hand side of both equations).

In fact, $\frac{\partial \operatorname{vec}(\boldsymbol{x}^{i+1})}{\partial(\operatorname{vec}(\boldsymbol{w}^i)^T)}$ and $\frac{\partial \operatorname{vec}(\boldsymbol{x}^{i+1})}{\partial(\operatorname{vec}(\boldsymbol{x}^i)^T)}$ are much easier to compute than directly computing $\frac{\partial z}{\partial(\operatorname{vec}(\boldsymbol{w}^i)^T)}$ and $\frac{\partial z}{\partial(\operatorname{vec}(\boldsymbol{x}^i)^T)}$, because $\boldsymbol{x}^i$ is directly related to $\boldsymbol{x}^{i+1}$, through a function with parameters $\boldsymbol{w}^i$. The details of these partial derivatives will be discussed in the following sections for different layers.

15.3 Layer Input, Output, and Notation

Now that the CNN architecture is clear, we will discuss in detail the different types of layers, starting from the ReLU layer, which is the simplest layer among those we discuss in this chapter. But before we start, we need to further refine our notation.

Suppose we are considering the lth layer, whose inputs form an order 3 tensor $\boldsymbol{x}^l$ with $\boldsymbol{x}^l \in \mathbb{R}^{H^l \times W^l \times D^l}$. Thus, we need a triplet index set (i^l, j^l, d^l) to locate any specific element in $\boldsymbol{x}^l$. The triplet (i^l, j^l, d^l) refers to one element in $\boldsymbol{x}^l$, which is in the d^lth channel, and at spatial location (i^l, j^l) (at the i^lth row and j^lth column). In actual CNN learning, the mini-batch strategy is usually used. In that case, $\boldsymbol{x}^l$ becomes an order 4 tensor in $\mathbb{R}^{H^l \times W^l \times D^l \times N}$ where N is the mini-batch size. For simplicity we assume that $N = 1$ in this chapter. The results in this chapter, however, are easy to adapt to mini-batch versions.

In order to simplify the notation that will appear later, we follow the zero-based indexing convention, which specifies that $0 \le i^l < H^l$, $0 \le j^l < W^l$, and $0 \le d^l < D^l$.

In the lth layer, a function will transform the input $\boldsymbol{x}^l$ to an output $\boldsymbol{y}$, which is also the input to the next layer. Thus, we notice that $\boldsymbol{y}$ and $\boldsymbol{x}^{l+1}$ in fact refer to the same object, and it is very helpful to keep this point in mind. We assume that the output has size $H^{l+1} \times W^{l+1} \times D^{l+1}$, and an element in the output is indexed by a triplet $(i^{l+1}, j^{l+1}, d^{l+1})$, $0 \le i^{l+1} < H^{l+1}$, $0 \le j^{l+1} < W^{l+1}$, $0 \le d^{l+1} < D^{l+1}$.

15.4 The ReLU Layer

A ReLU layer does not change the size of the input—that is, $\boldsymbol{x}^l$ and $\boldsymbol{y}$ share the same size. In fact, the rectified linear unit (hence the name ReLU) can be regarded as a truncation performed individually for every element in the input tensor:

$$y_{i,j,d} = \max\{0, x^l_{i,j,d}\}, \tag{15.13}$$

with $0 \le i < H^l = H^{l+1}$, $0 \le j < W^l = W^{l+1}$, and $0 \le d < D^l = D^{l+1}$.

There is no parameter inside a ReLU layer, hence no need for parameter learning in this layer.

Based on Eq. (15.13), it is obvious that

$$\frac{\mathrm{d}y_{i,j,d}}{\mathrm{d}x^l_{i,j,d}} = \left[\!\left[x^l_{i,j,d} > 0 \right]\!\right], \tag{15.14}$$

where $[\![\cdot]\!]$ is the indicator function, which is 1 if its argument is true and 0 otherwise.

Hence, we have

$$\left[\frac{\partial z}{\partial \boldsymbol{x}^l}\right]_{i,j,d} = \begin{cases} \left[\frac{\partial z}{\partial \boldsymbol{y}}\right]_{i,j,d} & \text{if } \boldsymbol{x}^l_{i,j,d} > 0, \\ 0 & \text{otherwise.} \end{cases} \tag{15.15}$$

Note that $\boldsymbol{y}$ is an alias for $\boldsymbol{x}^{l+1}$.

Strictly speaking, the function $\max(0, x)$ is not differentiable at $x = 0$, hence Eq. (15.14) is a little problematic in theory. In practice, it is not an issue and ReLU is safe to use.

The purpose of ReLU is to increase the nonlinearity of the CNN. Since the semantic information in an image (e.g., a person and a husky dog sitting next to each other on a bench in a garden) is obviously a highly nonlinear mapping of pixel values in the input, we want the mapping from CNN input to its output also to be highly nonlinear. The ReLU function, although simple, is a nonlinear function, as illustrated in Figure 15.2.

We may treat $x^l_{i,j,d}$ as one of the $H^l W^l D^l$ *features* extracted by CNN layers 1 to $l - 1$, which can be positive, zero, or negative. For example, $x^l_{i,j,d}$ may be positive if a region inside the input image has certain patterns (like a dog's head or a cat's head or some other patterns similar to that) and $x^l_{i,j,d}$ is negative or zero when that region does not exhibit these patterns. The ReLU layer will set all negative values to 0, which means that $y^l_{i,j,d}$ will be *activated* only for images possessing these patterns in that particular region.

Intuitively, this property is useful for recognizing complex patterns and objects. For example, it is only weak evidence to support "the input image contains a cat" if a feature is activated and that feature's pattern looks like a cat's head. However, if we find many activated features after the ReLU layer whose target patterns correspond to cat's head, torso, fur, legs, etc., we have higher confidence (at layer $l + 1$) to say that a cat probably exists in the input image.

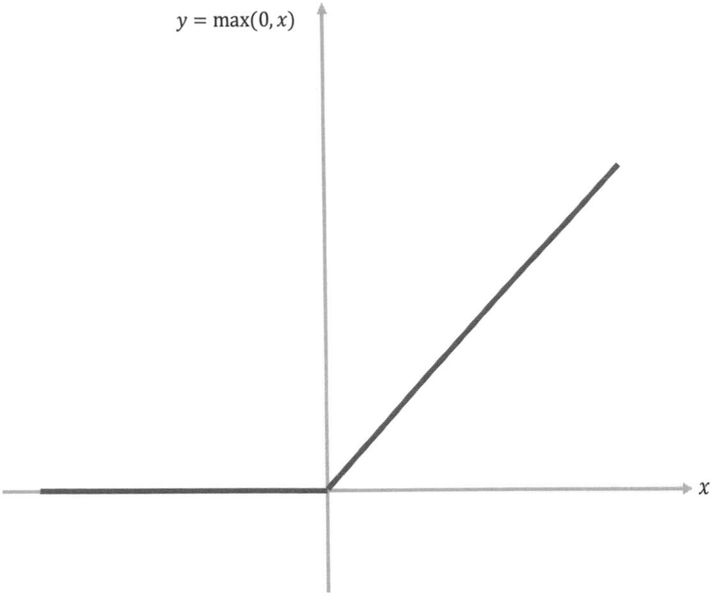

Figure 15.2 The ReLU function.

Other nonlinear transformations have been used in the neural network community to produce nonlinearity, for example the logistic sigmoid function

$$y = \sigma(x) = \frac{1}{1 + \exp(-x)}.$$

However, the logistic sigmoid function performs significantly worse than ReLU in CNN learning. Note that $0 < y < 1$ if a sigmoid function is used and

$$\frac{\mathrm{d}y}{\mathrm{d}x} = y(1-y),$$

so we have

$$0 < \frac{\mathrm{d}y}{\mathrm{d}x} \leq \frac{1}{4}.$$

Hence, in the error back propagation process, the gradient $\frac{\partial z}{\partial x} = \frac{\partial z}{\partial y}\frac{\mathrm{d}y}{\mathrm{d}x}$ will have much smaller magnitude than $\frac{\partial z}{\partial y}$ (at most $\frac{1}{4}$). In other words, a sigmoid layer will cause the magnitude of the gradient to significantly reduce, and after several sigmoid layers, the gradient will *vanish* (i.e., all its components will be close to 0). A vanishing gradient makes gradient-based learning (e.g., SGD) very difficult. Another major drawback of the sigmoid function is that it is saturated. When the magnitude of x is large—e.g., when $x > 6$ or $x < -6$—the corresponding gradient is almost 0.

On the other hand, the ReLU layer sets the gradient of some features in the lth layer to 0, but these features are not activated (i.e., we are not interested in them). For those activated features, the gradient is back propagated without any change, which is beneficial for SGD learning. The introduction of ReLU to replace the sigmoid function is an important change in CNN, which significantly reduces the difficulty in learning CNN parameters and improves its accuracy. There are also more complex variants of ReLU, for example, parametric ReLU and exponential linear unit, which we do not touch on in this chapter.

15.5 The Convolution Layer

Next, we turn to the convolution layer, which is the most involved one among those we discuss in this chapter. It is also the most important layer in a CNN, hence the name convolutional neural networks.

15.5.1 What Is a Convolution?

Let us start by convolving a matrix with one single convolution kernel. Suppose the input image is 3×4 and the convolution kernel size is 2×2, as illustrated in Figure 15.3.

If we overlay the convolution kernel on top of the input image, we can compute the product between the numbers at the same location in the kernel and the input, and we

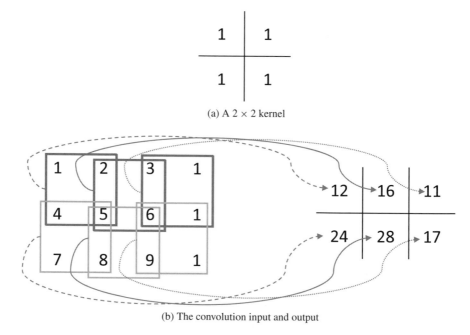

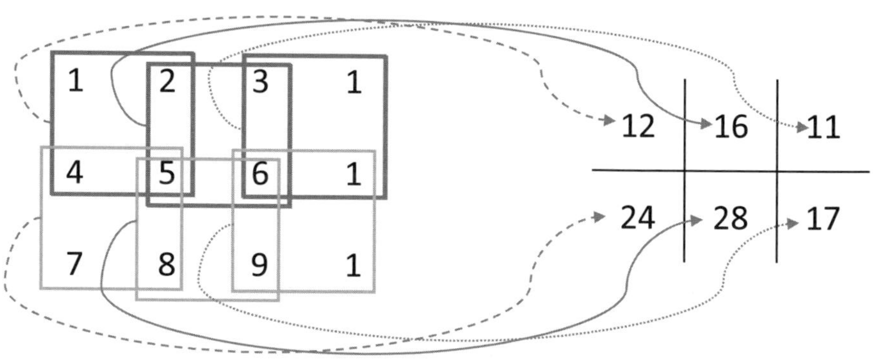

(a) A 2×2 kernel

(b) The convolution input and output

Figure 15.3 Illustration of the convolution operation. (A black and white version of this figure will appear in some formats. For the color version, please refer to the plate section.)

get a single number by summing these products together. For example, if we overlay the kernel with the top-left region in the input, the convolution result at that spatial location is

$$1 \times 1 + 1 \times 4 + 1 \times 2 + 1 \times 5 = 12.$$

We then move the kernel down by one pixel and get the next convolution result as

$$1 \times 4 + 1 \times 7 + 1 \times 5 + 1 \times 8 = 24.$$

We keep moving the kernel down till it reaches the bottom border of the input matrix (image). Then we return the kernel to the top, and move the kernel to its right by one element (pixel). We repeat the convolution for every possible pixel location until we have moved the kernel to the bottom-right corner of the input image, as shown in Figure 15.3.

For order 3 tensors, the convolution operation is defined similarly. Suppose the input in the lth layer is an order 3 tensor with size $H^l \times W^l \times D^l$. One convolution kernel is also an order 3 tensor with size $H \times W \times D^l$. When we overlay the kernel on top of the input tensor at the spatial location $(0,0,0)$, we compute the products of corresponding elements in all the D^l channels and sum the HWD^l products to get the convolution result at this spatial location. Then we move the kernel from top to bottom and from left to right to complete the convolution.

In a convolution layer, multiple convolution kernels are usually used. Assuming D kernels are used and each kernel is of spatial span $H \times W$, we denote all the kernels as $\boldsymbol{f}$, where $\boldsymbol{f}$ is an order 4 tensor in $\mathbb{R}^{H \times W \times D^l \times D}$. Similarly, we use index variables $0 \le i < H$, $0 \le j < W$, $0 \le d^l < D^l$, and $0 \le d < D$ to pinpoint a specific element in the kernels. Also note that the set of kernels $\boldsymbol{f}$ refers to the same object as the notation $\boldsymbol{w}^l$ in Eq. (15.5). We change the notation slightly to make the derivation a little simpler. It is also clear that even if the mini-batch strategy is used, the kernels remain unchanged.

As shown in Figure 15.3, the spatial extent of the output is smaller than that of the input so long as the convolution kernel is larger than 1×1. Sometimes we need the input and output images to have the same height and width, and a simple padding trick can be used. If the input is $H^l \times W^l \times D^l$ and the kernel size is $H \times W \times D^l \times D$, the convolution result has size

$$(H^l - H + 1) \times (W^l - W + 1) \times D.$$

For every channel of the input, if we *pad* (i.e., insert) $\lfloor \frac{H-1}{2} \rfloor$ rows above the first row and $\lfloor \frac{H}{2} \rfloor$ rows below the last row, and pad $\lfloor \frac{W-1}{2} \rfloor$ columns to the left of the first column and $\lfloor \frac{W}{2} \rfloor$ columns to the right of the last column of the input, the convolution output will be $H^l \times W^l \times D$ in size—i.e., having the same spatial extent as the input ($\lfloor \cdot \rfloor$ is the floor function). Elements of the padded rows and columns are usually set to 0, but other values are also possible.

Stride is another important concept in convolution. In Figure 15.3, we convolve the kernel with the input at every possible spatial location, which corresponds to the stride $s = 1$. However, if $s > 1$, every movement of the kernel skips $s - 1$ pixel locations (i.e., the convolution is performed once every s pixels both horizontally and vertically). When $s > 1$, a convolution's output will be much smaller than that of the input—H^{l+1} and W^{l+1} will be roughly $1/s$ of H^l and W^l, respectively.

In this section, we consider the simple case when the stride is 1 and no padding is used. Hence, we have $\boldsymbol{y}$ (or $\boldsymbol{x}^{l+1}$) in $\mathbb{R}^{H^{l+1} \times W^{l+1} \times D^{l+1}}$, with $H^{l+1} = H^l - H + 1$, $W^{l+1} = W^l - W + 1$, and $D^{l+1} = D$.

In precise mathematics, the convolution procedure can be expressed as an equation:

$$y_{i^{l+1},j^{l+1},d} = \sum_{i=0}^{H-1} \sum_{j=0}^{W-1} \sum_{d^l=0}^{D^l-1} f_{i,j,d^l,d} \times x^l_{i^{l+1}+i,\, j^{l+1}+j,\, d^l}. \tag{15.16}$$

Equation (15.16) is repeated for all $0 \le d < D = D^{l+1}$, and for any spatial location (i^{l+1}, j^{l+1}) satisfying

$$0 \le i^{l+1} < H^l - H + 1 = H^{l+1}, \tag{15.17}$$

$$0 \le j^{l+1} < W^l - W + 1 = W^{l+1}. \tag{15.18}$$

In this equation, $x^l_{i^{l+1}+i,\, j^{l+1}+j,\, d^l}$ refers to the element of $\boldsymbol{x}^l$ indexed by the triplet $(i^{l+1} + i, j^{l+1} + j, d^l)$.

A bias term b_d is usually added to $y_{i^{l+1},j^{l+1},d}$. We omit this term in this chapter for clearer presentation.

15.5.2 Why Convolve?

Figure 15.4a shows a color input image and its convolution results using two different kernels (Figures 15.4b and 15.4c). A 3×3 convolution matrix

$$K = \begin{bmatrix} 1 & 2 & 1 \\ 0 & 0 & 0 \\ -1 & -2 & -1 \end{bmatrix}$$

is used. The convolution kernel should be of size $3 \times 3 \times 3$, in which we set every channel to K. When there is a horizontal edge at location (x, y) (i.e., when the pixels at spatial location $(x + 1, y)$ and $(x - 1, y)$ differ by a large amount), we expect the convolution result to have high magnitude. As shown in Figure 15.4b, the convolution results indeed highlight the horizontal edges. When we set every channel of the convolution kernel to K^T (the transpose of K), the convolution result amplifies vertical edges, as shown in Figure 15.4c. The matrices (or filters) K and K^T are called Sobel operators.[1]

[1] The Sobel operator is named after Irwin Sobel, an American researcher in digital image processing.

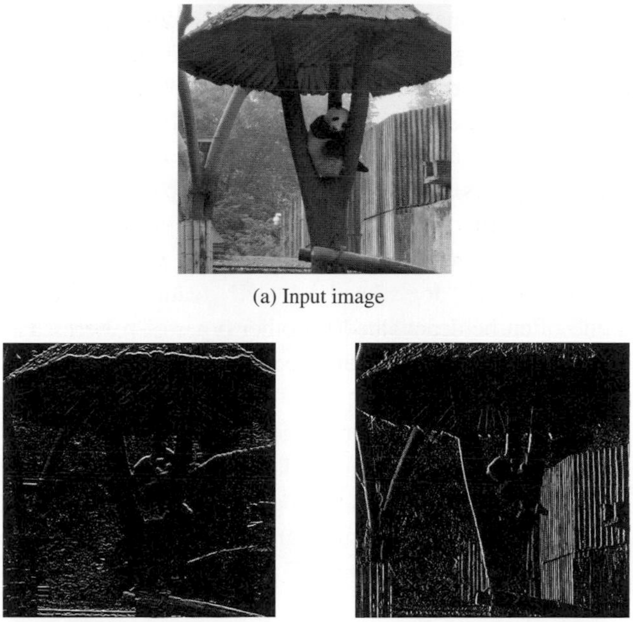

(a) Input image

(b) Horizontal edge

(c) Vertical edge

Figure 15.4 An image and the effect of different convolution kernels. (A black and white version of this figure will appear in some formats. For the color version, please refer to the plate section.)

If we add a bias term to the convolution operation, we can make the convolution result positive at horizontal (or vertical) edges in a certain direction (e.g., a horizontal edge with the pixels above it brighter than the pixels below it), and negative at other locations. If the next layer is a ReLU layer, its output in fact defines many "edge detection features," which activate only at horizontal or vertical edges in certain directions. If we replace the Sobel kernel by other kernels (e.g., those learned by SGD), we can learn features that activate for edges with different angles.

When we move further down in the deep network, subsequent layers can learn to activate only for specific (but more complex) patterns—e.g., groups of edges that form a particular shape. This is because any feature in layer $l + 1$ considers the combined effect of many features in layer l. These more complex patterns will be further assembled by deeper layers to activate for semantically meaningful object parts or even a particular type of object—e.g., dog, cat, tree, beach.

One more benefit of the convolution layer is that all spatial locations share the same convolution kernel, which greatly reduces the number of parameters needed for a convolution layer. For example, if multiple dogs appear in an input image, the same "dog-head-like pattern" feature might be activated at multiple locations, corresponding to heads of different dogs.

In a deep neural network setup, convolution also encourages parameter sharing. For example, suppose "dog-head-like pattern" and "cat-head-like pattern" are two features learned by a deep convolutional network. The CNN does not need to devote two sets of disjoint parameters (e.g., convolution kernels in multiple layers) to them. The CNN's bottom layers can learn "eye-like pattern" and "animal-fur-texture pattern," which are shared by both these more abstract features. In short, the combination of convolution kernels and deep and hierarchical structures is very effective in learning good representations (features) from images for visual recognition tasks.

We want to add a note here. Although we have used phrases such as "dog-head-like pattern," the representation or feature learned by a CNN may not correspond exactly to semantic concepts such as "dog's head." A CNN feature may activate frequently for dogs' heads and often be deactivated for other types of patterns. However, there are also possible false activations at other locations, and possible deactivations at dogs' heads.

In fact, a key concept in CNN (or more generally deep learning) is *distributed representation*. For example, suppose our task is to recognize N different types of objects, and a CNN extracts M features from any input image. It is most likely that any one of the M features is useful for recognizing all N object categories, and to recognize one object type requires the joint effort of all M features.

15.5.3 Convolution as Matrix Product

Equation (15.16) seems pretty complex. However, there is a way to expand $\boldsymbol{x}^l$ and simplify the convolution as a matrix product.

Let us consider a special case with $D^l = D = 1$, $H = W = 2$, and $H^l = 3$, $W^l = 4$. That is, we consider convolving a small single channel 3×4 matrix (or image) with one 2×2 filter. Using the example in Figure 15.3, we have

$$\begin{bmatrix} 1 & 2 & 3 & 1 \\ 4 & 5 & 6 & 1 \\ 7 & 8 & 9 & 1 \end{bmatrix} * \begin{bmatrix} 1 & 1 \\ 1 & 1 \end{bmatrix} = \begin{bmatrix} 12 & 16 & 11 \\ 24 & 28 & 17 \end{bmatrix}, \tag{15.19}$$

where the first matrix is denoted as A, and $*$ is the convolution operator.

Now let's run a MATLAB/GNU Octave command `B=im2col(A, [2 2]);` we arrive at a B matrix that is an expanded version of A:

$$B = \begin{bmatrix} 1 & 4 & 2 & 5 & 3 & 6 \\ 4 & 7 & 5 & 8 & 6 & 9 \\ 2 & 5 & 3 & 6 & 1 & 1 \\ 5 & 8 & 6 & 9 & 1 & 1 \end{bmatrix}.$$

It is obvious that the first column of B corresponds to the first 2×2 region in A, in a column-first order, corresponding to $(i^{l+1}, j^{l+1}) = (0,0)$. Similarly, the second to last columns of B correspond to regions in A with (i^{l+1}, j^{l+1}) being $(1,0)$, $(0,1)$, $(1,1)$, $(0,2)$ and $(1,2)$, respectively. That is, the MATLAB/GNU Octave `im2col` function explicitly expands the required elements for performing each individual convolution into a column in the matrix B. The transpose of B, B^T, is called the `im2row` expansion of A. Note that the parameter `[2 2]` specifies the convolution kernel size.

Now, if we vectorize the convolution kernel itself into a vector (in the same column-first order) $(1,1,1,1)^T$, we find that[2]

$$B^T \begin{bmatrix} 1 \\ 1 \\ 1 \\ 1 \end{bmatrix} = \begin{bmatrix} 12 \\ 24 \\ 16 \\ 28 \\ 11 \\ 17 \end{bmatrix}. \tag{15.20}$$

If we reshape this resulting vector in Eq. (15.20) properly, we get the exact convolution result matrix in Eq. (15.19).

That is, the convolution operator is a linear operator. We can multiply the expanded input matrix and the vectorized filter to get a result vector, and by reshaping this vector properly we get the correct convolution result.

We can generalize this idea to more complex situations and formalize them. If $D^l > 1$ (that is, the input $\boldsymbol{x}^l$ has more than one channel), the expansion operator could first expand the first channel of $\boldsymbol{x}^l$, then the second, ..., till all D^l channels are expanded. The expanded channels will be stacked together, that is, one row in the `im2row` expansion will have $H \times W \times D^l$ elements, rather than $H \times W$.

More formally, suppose $\boldsymbol{x}^l$ is a third-order tensor in $\mathbb{R}^{H^l \times W^l \times D^l}$, with one element in $\boldsymbol{x}^l$ being indexed by a triplet (i^l, j^l, d^l). We also consider a set of convolution kernels $\boldsymbol{f}$, whose spatial sizes are all $H \times W$. Then the expansion operator (`im2row`) converts $\boldsymbol{x}^l$ into a matrix $\phi(\boldsymbol{x}^l)$. We use two indexes (p,q) to index an element in this matrix. The expansion operator copies the element at (i^l, j^l, d^l) in $\boldsymbol{x}^l$ to the (p,q)th entry in $\phi(\boldsymbol{x}^l)$.

From the description of the expansion process, it is clear that given a fixed (p,q), we can calculate its corresponding (i^l, j^l, d^l) triplet, because obviously

$$p = i^{l+1} + (H^l - H + 1) \times j^{l+1}, \tag{15.21}$$

$$q = i + H \times j + H \times W \times d^l, \tag{15.22}$$

$$i^l = i^{l+1} + i, \tag{15.23}$$

$$j^l = j^{l+1} + j. \tag{15.24}$$

In Eq. (15.22), dividing q by HW and taking the integer part of the quotient, we can determine which channel (d^l) it belongs to. Similarly, we can get the offsets inside the convolution kernel as (i,j), in which $0 \le i < H$ and $0 \le j < W$. Thus q completely determines one specific location inside the convolution kernel by the triplet (i, j, d^l).

[2] The notation and presentation of this chapter is heavily affected by the MatConvNet software package's manual (`http://arxiv.org/abs/1412.4564`, which is MATLAB based). The transpose of an `im2col` expansion is equivalent to an `im2row` expansion, in which the numbers involved in one convolution form one row in the `im2row` expanded matrix. The derivation in this section uses `im2row`, complying with the implementation in MatConvNet. Caffe, a widely used CNN software package (`http://caffe.berkeleyvision.org/`, which is C++ based) uses `im2col`. These formulations are mathematically equivalent to each other.

Note that the convolution result is $\boldsymbol{x}^{l+1}$, whose spatial extent is $H^{l+1} = H^l - H + 1$ and $W^{l+1} = W^l - W + 1$. Thus, in Eq. (15.21) the remainder and quotient of dividing p by $H^{l+1} = H^l - H + 1$ will give us the offset in the convolved result (i^{l+1}, j^{l+1}), or the top-left spatial location of the region in $\boldsymbol{x}^l$ (which is to be convolved with the kernel).

Based on the definition of convolution, it is clear that we can use Eqs. (15.23) and (15.24) to find the offset in the input $\boldsymbol{x}^l$ as $i^l = i^{l+1} + i$ and $j^l = j^{l+1} + j$. That is, the mapping from (p,q) to (i^l, j^l, d^l) is one-to-one. However, we want to emphasize that the reverse mapping from (i^l, j^l, d^l) to (p,q) is one-to-many, a fact that is useful in deriving the back propagation rules in a convolution layer.

Now we use the standard vec operator to convert the set of convolution kernels $\boldsymbol{f}$ (order 4 tensor) into a matrix. Let us start from one kernel, which can be vectorized into a vector in $\mathbb{R}^{HWD^l}$. Thus, all convolution kernels can be reshaped into a matrix with HWD^l rows and D columns (remember that $D^{l+1} = D$.) Let us call this matrix F.

Finally, with all this notation, we have a beautiful equation to calculate convolution results (cf. Eq. (15.20), in which $\phi(\boldsymbol{x}^l)$ is B^T):

$$\operatorname{vec}(\boldsymbol{y}) = \operatorname{vec}(\boldsymbol{x}^{l+1}) = \operatorname{vec}\left(\phi(\boldsymbol{x}^l)F\right). \tag{15.25}$$

Note $\operatorname{vec}(\boldsymbol{y}) \in \mathbb{R}^{H^{l+1}W^{l+1}D}$, $\phi(\boldsymbol{x}^l) \in \mathbb{R}^{(H^{l+1}W^{l+1})\times(HWD^l)}$, and $F \in \mathbb{R}^{(HWD^l)\times D}$. The matrix multiplication $\phi(\boldsymbol{x}^l)F$ results in a matrix of size $(H^{l+1}W^{l+1}) \times D$. The vectorization of this resultant matrix generates a vector in $\mathbb{R}^{H^{l+1}W^{l+1}D}$, which matches the dimensionality of $\operatorname{vec}(\boldsymbol{y})$.

15.5.4 The Kronecker Product

A short detour to the Kronecker product is needed to compute the derivatives.

Given two matrices $A \in \mathbb{R}^{m\times n}$ and $B \in \mathbb{R}^{p\times q}$, the Kronecker product $A \otimes B$ is an $mp \times nq$ matrix, defined as a block matrix

$$A \otimes B = \left[\begin{array}{c|c|c} a_{11}B & \cdots & a_{1n}B \\ \hline \vdots & \ddots & \vdots \\ \hline a_{m1}B & \cdots & a_{mn}B \end{array}\right]. \tag{15.26}$$

The Kronecker product has the following properties that will be useful for us:

$$(A \otimes B)^T = A^T \otimes B^T, \tag{15.27}$$

$$\operatorname{vec}(AXB) = (B^T \otimes A)\operatorname{vec}(X), \tag{15.28}$$

for matrices A, X, and B with proper dimensions (e.g., when the matrix multiplication AXB is defined.) Note that Eq. (15.28) can be utilized from both directions.

With the help of $\otimes$, we can write

$$\operatorname{vec}(\boldsymbol{y}) = \operatorname{vec}\left(\phi(\boldsymbol{x}^l)FI\right) = \left(I \otimes \phi(\boldsymbol{x}^l)\right)\operatorname{vec}(F), \tag{15.29}$$

$$\operatorname{vec}(\boldsymbol{y}) = \operatorname{vec}\left(I\phi(\boldsymbol{x}^l)F\right) = (F^T \otimes I)\operatorname{vec}(\phi(\boldsymbol{x}^l)), \tag{15.30}$$

Table 15.1 Variables, their sizes, and meanings. Note that "alias" means that a variable has a different name or can be reshaped into another form.

Variable	Alias	Size & meaning
X	$\boldsymbol{x}^l$	$H^l W^l \times D^l$, the input tensor
F	$\boldsymbol{f}, \boldsymbol{w}^l$	$HWD^l \times D$, D kernels, each $H \times W$ and D^l channels
Y	$\boldsymbol{y}, \boldsymbol{x}^{l+1}$	$H^{l+1}W^{l+1} \times D^{l+1}$, the output, $D^{l+1} = D$
$\phi(\boldsymbol{x}^l)$		$H^{l+1}W^{l+1} \times HWD^l$, the `im2row` expansion of $\boldsymbol{x}^l$
M		$H^{l+1}W^{l+1}HWD^l \times H^l W^l D^l$, the indicator matrix for $\phi(\boldsymbol{x}^l)$
$\frac{\partial z}{\partial Y}$	$\frac{\partial z}{\partial\, \mathrm{vec}(\boldsymbol{y})}$	$H^{l+1}W^{l+1} \times D^{l+1}$, gradient for $\boldsymbol{y}$
$\frac{\partial z}{\partial F}$	$\frac{\partial z}{\partial\, \mathrm{vec}(\boldsymbol{f})}$	$HWD^l \times D$, gradient to update the convolution kernels
$\frac{\partial z}{\partial X}$	$\frac{\partial z}{\partial\, \mathrm{vec}(\boldsymbol{x}^l)}$	$H^l W^l \times D^l$, gradient for $\boldsymbol{x}^l$, useful for back propagation

where I is an identity matrix of proper size. In Eq. (15.29), the size of I is determined by the number of columns in F; hence $I \in \mathbb{R}^{D\times D}$ in Eq. (15.29). Similarly, in Eq. (15.30), $I \in \mathbb{R}^{(H^{l+1}W^{l+1})\times(H^{l+1}W^{l+1})}$.

The derivation for gradient computation rules in a convolution layer involves many variables and much notation. We summarize the variables used in this derivation in Table 15.1. Note that some of this notation will soon be introduced in later sections.

15.5.5 Backward Propagation: Updating the Parameters

As previously mentioned, we need to compute two derivatives: $\frac{\partial z}{\partial\, \mathrm{vec}(\boldsymbol{x}^l)}$ and $\frac{\partial z}{\partial\, \mathrm{vec}(F)}$, where the first term $\frac{\partial z}{\partial\, \mathrm{vec}(\boldsymbol{x}^l)}$ will be used for backward propagation to the previous $((l-1)$th) layer, and the second term will determine how the parameters of the current (lth) layer will be updated. A friendly reminder is to remember that $\boldsymbol{f}$, F, and $\boldsymbol{w}^i$ refer to the same thing (modulo reshaping of the vector or matrix or tensor). Similarly, we can reshape $\boldsymbol{y}$ into a matrix $Y \in \mathbb{R}^{(H^{l+1}W^{l+1})\times D}$; then $\boldsymbol{y}$, Y, and $\boldsymbol{x}^{l+1}$ refer to the same object (again modulo reshaping).

From the chain rule (Eq. 15.11), it is easy to compute $\frac{\partial z}{\partial\, \mathrm{vec}(F)}$ as

$$\frac{\partial z}{\partial (\mathrm{vec}(F))^T} = \frac{\partial z}{\partial (\mathrm{vec}(Y)^T)} \frac{\partial\, \mathrm{vec}(\boldsymbol{y})}{\partial (\mathrm{vec}(F)^T)}. \tag{15.31}$$

The first term on the right-hand side has already been computed in the $(l+1)$th layer as (equivalently) $\frac{\partial z}{\partial (\mathrm{vec}(\boldsymbol{x}^{l+1}))^T}$. The second term, based on Eq. (15.29), is pretty straightforward:

$$\frac{\partial\, \mathrm{vec}(\boldsymbol{y})}{\partial (\mathrm{vec}(F)^T)} = \frac{\partial \left((I \otimes \phi(\boldsymbol{x}^l))\, \mathrm{vec}(F) \right)}{\partial (\mathrm{vec}(F)^T)} = I \otimes \phi(\boldsymbol{x}^l). \tag{15.32}$$

Note that we have used the fact $\frac{\partial X \boldsymbol{a}^T}{\partial \boldsymbol{a}} = X$ or $\frac{\partial X \boldsymbol{a}}{\partial \boldsymbol{a}^T} = X$ so long as the matrix multiplications are well defined. This equation leads to

$$\frac{\partial z}{\partial (\operatorname{vec}(F))^T} = \frac{\partial z}{\partial (\operatorname{vec}(\boldsymbol{y})^T)} (I \otimes \phi(\boldsymbol{x}^l)). \tag{15.33}$$

Making a transpose, we get

$$\frac{\partial z}{\partial \operatorname{vec}(F)} = \left(I \otimes \phi(\boldsymbol{x}^l)\right)^T \frac{\partial z}{\partial \operatorname{vec}(\boldsymbol{y})} \tag{15.34}$$

$$= \left(I \otimes \phi(\boldsymbol{x}^l)^T\right) \operatorname{vec}\left(\frac{\partial z}{\partial Y}\right) \tag{15.35}$$

$$= \operatorname{vec}\left(\phi(\boldsymbol{x}^l)^T \frac{\partial z}{\partial Y} I\right) \tag{15.36}$$

$$= \operatorname{vec}\left(\phi(\boldsymbol{x}^l)^T \frac{\partial z}{\partial Y}\right). \tag{15.37}$$

Note that both Eq. (15.28) (from right-hand to left-hand side) and Eq. (15.27) are used in the above derivation.

Thus, we conclude that

$$\frac{\partial z}{\partial F} = \phi(\boldsymbol{x}^l)^T \frac{\partial z}{\partial Y}, \tag{15.38}$$

which is a simple rule to update the parameters in the lth layer: the gradient with respect to the convolution parameters is the product between $\phi(\boldsymbol{x}^l)^T$ (the `im2col` expansion) and $\frac{\partial z}{\partial Y}$ (the supervision signal transferred from the $(l+1)$th layer).

15.5.6 Even-Higher-Dimensional Indicator Matrices

The function $\phi(\cdot)$ has been very useful in our analysis. It is pretty high-dimensional—e.g., $\phi(\boldsymbol{x}^l)$ has $H^{l+1}W^{l+1}HWD^l$ elements. From the above, we know that an element in $\phi(\boldsymbol{x}^l)$ is indexed by a pair p and q.

A quick recap about $\phi(\boldsymbol{x}^l)$: (1) from q we can determine d^l, which channel of the convolution kernel is used and we can also determine i and j, the spatial offsets inside the kernel; (2) from p we can determine i^{l+1} and j^{l+1}, the spatial offsets inside the convolved result $\boldsymbol{x}^{l+1}$; (3) the spatial offsets in the input $\boldsymbol{x}^l$ can be determined as $i^l = i^{l+1} + i$ and $j^l = j^{l+1} + j$.

That is, the mapping $m\colon (p,q) \mapsto (i^l, j^l, d^l)$ is one-to-one, and thus is a valid function. The inverse mapping, however, is one-to-many (thus not a valid function). If we use m^{-1} to represent the inverse mapping, we know that $m^{-1}(i^l, j^l, d^l)$ is a set S, where each $(p,q) \in S$ satisfies $m(p,q) = (i^l, j^l, d^l)$.

Now we take a look at $\phi(\boldsymbol{x}^l)$ from a different perspective. In order to fully specify $\phi(\boldsymbol{x}^l)$, what information is required? It is obvious that the following three types of information are needed (and only those) for *every* element of $\phi(\boldsymbol{x}^l)$:

(A) Which region does it belong to—i.e., what is the value of p $(0 \le p < H^{l+1}W^{l+1})$?

(B) Which element is it inside the region (or equivalently inside the convolution kernel)—i.e., what is the value of q $(0 \le q < HWD^l)$?

The above two pieces of information determine a location (p,q) inside $\phi(\boldsymbol{x}^l)$. There is one item of missing information:

(C) What is the value in that position—i.e., $\left[\phi(\boldsymbol{x}^l)\right]_{pq}$?

Since every element in $\phi(\boldsymbol{x}^l)$ is a verbatim copy of one element from $\boldsymbol{x}^l$, we can turn (C) into a different but equivalent one:

(C.1) For $\left[\phi(\boldsymbol{x}^l)\right]_{pq}$, where is this value copied from? Or, what is its original location inside $\boldsymbol{x}^l$—i.e., an index u that satisfies $0 \le u < H^l W^l D^l$?

(C.2) The entire $\boldsymbol{x}^l$.

It is easy to see that collectively, (A, B, C.1) (for the entire range of p, q, and u) and (C.2) (i.e., $\boldsymbol{x}^l$) contain exactly the same amount of information as $\phi(\boldsymbol{x}^l)$.

Since $0 \le p < H^{l+1}W^{l+1}$, $0 \le q < HWD^l$, and $0 \le u < H^l W^l D^l$, we can use a matrix

$$M \in \mathbb{R}^{(H^{l+1}W^{l+1}HWD^l)\times(H^l W^l D^l)}$$

to encode the information in (A, B, C.1). One row index of this matrix corresponds to one location inside $\phi(\boldsymbol{x}^l)$ (i.e., a (p,q) pair). One row of M has $H^l W^l D^l$ elements, and each element can be indexed by (i^l, j^l, d^l). Thus, each element in this matrix is indexed by a 5-tuple: (p, q, i^l, j^l, d^l).

Then we can use the "indicator" method to encode the function $m(p,q) = (i^l, j^l, d^l)$ into M. That is, for any possible element in M, its row index x determines a (p,q) pair, and its column index y determines a (i^l, j^l, d^l) triplet, and M is defined as

$$M(x,y) = \begin{cases} 1 & \text{if } m(p,q) = (i^l, j^l, d^l), \\ 0 & \text{otherwise.} \end{cases} \tag{15.39}$$

The M matrix has the following properties:

- It is very high-dimensional.
- However, it is also very sparse: there is only one nonzero entry in the $H^l W^l D^l$ elements in one row, because m is a function.
- M, which uses information (A, B, C.1), encodes only the one-to-one correspondence between any element in $\phi(\boldsymbol{x}^l)$ and any element in $\boldsymbol{x}^l$; it does not encode any specific value in $\boldsymbol{x}^l$.
- Most importantly, putting together the one-to-one correspondence information in M and the value information in $\boldsymbol{x}^l$, obviously we have

$$\operatorname{vec}(\phi(\boldsymbol{x}^l)) = M \operatorname{vec}(\boldsymbol{x}^l). \tag{15.40}$$

15.5.7 Backward Propagation: Preparing the Supervision Signal for the Previous Layer

In the lth layer, we still need to compute $\frac{\partial z}{\partial \operatorname{vec}(\boldsymbol{x}^l)}$. For this purpose, we want to reshape $\boldsymbol{x}^l$ into a matrix $X \in \mathbb{R}^{(H^l W^l)\times D^l}$, and use these two equivalent forms (modulo reshaping) interchangeably.

The chain rule states that (cf. Eq. 15.12)

$$\frac{\partial z}{\partial(\operatorname{vec}(\boldsymbol{x}^l)^T)} = \frac{\partial z}{\partial(\operatorname{vec}(\boldsymbol{y})^T)} \frac{\partial \operatorname{vec}(\boldsymbol{y})}{\partial(\operatorname{vec}(\boldsymbol{x}^l)^T)}.$$

We will start by studying the second term on the right-hand side (utilizing Eqs. 15.30 and 15.40):

$$\frac{\partial \operatorname{vec}(\boldsymbol{y})}{\partial(\operatorname{vec}(\boldsymbol{x}^l)^T)} = \frac{\partial(F^T \otimes I)\operatorname{vec}(\phi(\boldsymbol{x}^l))}{\partial(\operatorname{vec}(\boldsymbol{x}^l)^T)} = (F^T \otimes I)M. \tag{15.41}$$

Thus,

$$\frac{\partial z}{\partial(\operatorname{vec}(\boldsymbol{x}^l)^T)} = \frac{\partial z}{\partial(\operatorname{vec}(\boldsymbol{y})^T)}(F^T \otimes I)M. \tag{15.42}$$

Since (using Eq. (15.28) from right to left)

$$\frac{\partial z}{\partial(\operatorname{vec}(\boldsymbol{y})^T)}(F^T \otimes I) = \left((F \otimes I)\frac{\partial z}{\partial \operatorname{vec}(\boldsymbol{y})}\right)^T \tag{15.43}$$

$$= \left((F \otimes I)\operatorname{vec}\left(\frac{\partial z}{\partial Y}\right)\right)^T \tag{15.44}$$

$$= \operatorname{vec}\left(I\frac{\partial z}{\partial Y}F^T\right)^T \tag{15.45}$$

$$= \operatorname{vec}\left(\frac{\partial z}{\partial Y}F^T\right)^T, \tag{15.46}$$

we have

$$\frac{\partial z}{\partial(\operatorname{vec}(\boldsymbol{x}^l)^T)} = \operatorname{vec}\left(\frac{\partial z}{\partial Y}F^T\right)^T M, \tag{15.47}$$

or equivalently,

$$\frac{\partial z}{\partial(\operatorname{vec}(\boldsymbol{x}^l))} = M^T \operatorname{vec}\left(\frac{\partial z}{\partial Y}F^T\right). \tag{15.48}$$

Let us have a closer look at the right-hand side. Here $\frac{\partial z}{\partial Y}F^T \in \mathbb{R}^{(H^{l+1}W^{l+1})\times(HWD^l)}$ and $\operatorname{vec}\left(\frac{\partial z}{\partial Y}F^T\right)$ is a vector in $\mathbb{R}^{H^{l+1}W^{l+1}HWD^l}$. On the other hand, M^T is an indicator matrix in $\mathbb{R}^{(H^l W^l D^l)\times(H^{l+1}W^{l+1}HWD^l)}$.

In order to pinpoint one element in $\operatorname{vec}(\boldsymbol{x}^l)$ or one row in M^T, we need an index triplet (i^l, j^l, d^l), with $0 \le i^l < H^l$, $0 \le j^l < W^l$, and $0 \le d^l < D^l$. Similarly, to locate a column in M^T or an element in $\frac{\partial z}{\partial Y}F^T$, we need an index pair (p,q), with $0 \le p < H^{l+1}W^{l+1}$ and $0 \le q < HWD^l$.

Thus, the (i^l, j^l, d^l)th entry of $\frac{\partial z}{\partial(\text{vec}(\boldsymbol{x}^l))}$ equals the multiplication of two vectors: the row in M^T (or the column in M) that is indexed by (i^l, j^l, d^l), and $\text{vec}\left(\frac{\partial z}{\partial Y} F^T\right)$.

Furthermore, since M^T is an indicator matrix, in the row vector indexed by (i^l, j^l, d^l), only those entries whose index (p,q) satisfies $m(p,q) = (i^l, j^l, d^l)$ have a value 1; all other entries are 0. Thus, the (i^l, j^l, d^l)th entry of $\frac{\partial z}{\partial(\text{vec}(\boldsymbol{x}^l))}$ equals the sum of these corresponding entries in $\text{vec}\left(\frac{\partial z}{\partial Y} F^T\right)$.

Transferring the above description into precise mathematical form, we get the following succinct equation:

$$\left[\frac{\partial z}{\partial X}\right]_{(i^l, j^l, d^l)} = \sum_{(p,q)\in m^{-1}(i^l, j^l, d^l)} \left[\frac{\partial z}{\partial Y} F^T\right]_{(p,q)}. \tag{15.49}$$

In other words, to compute $\frac{\partial z}{\partial X}$, we do not need to explicitly use the extremely high-dimensional matrix M. Instead, Eqs. (15.49) and (15.21)–(15.24) can be used to efficiently find $\frac{\partial z}{\partial X}$.

We use the simple convolution example in Figure 15.3 to illustrate the inverse mapping m^{-1}, which is shown in Figure 15.5.

In the right half of Figure 15.5, the 6×4 matrix is $\frac{\partial z}{\partial Y} F^T$. In order to compute the partial derivative of z with respect to one element in the input X, we need to find which elements in $\frac{\partial z}{\partial Y} F^T$ are involved and add them. In the left half of Figure 15.5, we show that the input element 5 (shown in larger font) is involved in four convolution operations, shown by the red, green, blue, and black boxes, respectively. These four convolution operations correspond to $p = 1,2,3,4$. For example, when $p = 2$ (the green box), 5 is the third element in the convolution; hence $q = 3$ when $p = 2$, and we put a green circle in the $(2,3)$th element of the $\frac{\partial z}{\partial Y} F^T$ matrix. After all four circles

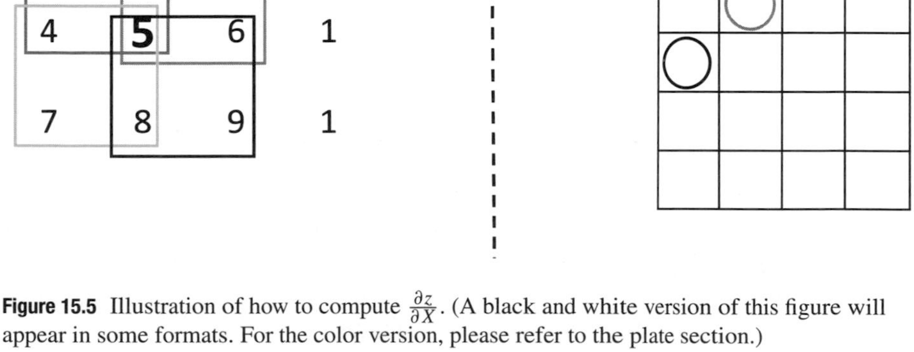

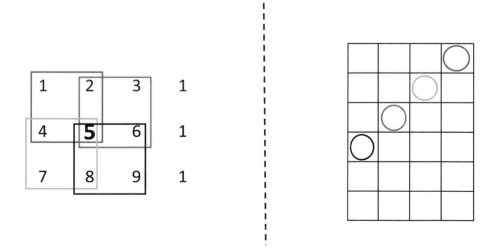

Figure 15.5 Illustration of how to compute $\frac{\partial z}{\partial X}$. (A black and white version of this figure will appear in some formats. For the color version, please refer to the plate section.)

have been put in the $\frac{\partial z}{\partial Y} F^T$ matrix, the partial derivative is the sum of elements in these four locations of $\frac{\partial z}{\partial Y} F^T$.

The set $m^{-1}(i^l, j^l, d^l)$ contains at most HW elements. Hence, Eq. (15.49) requires at most HW summations to compute one element of $\frac{\partial z}{\partial X}$.[3]

15.5.8 Fully Connected Layer as a Convolution Layer

As aforementioned, one benefit of the convolution layer is that convolution is a local operation. The spatial extent of a kernel is often small (e.g., 3×3). One element in $\boldsymbol{x}^{l+1}$ is usually computed using only a small number of elements in its input $\boldsymbol{x}^l$.

A fully connected layer refers to a layer where the computation of any element in the output $\boldsymbol{x}^{l+1}$ (or $\boldsymbol{y}$) requires all elements in the input $\boldsymbol{x}^l$. A fully connected layer is sometimes useful at the end of a deep CNN model. For example, if after many convolution, ReLU, and pooling (which will be discussed soon) layers, the output of the current layer contains distributed representations for the input image, we want to use all these features in the current layer to build features with stronger capabilities in the next one. A fully connected layer is useful for this purpose.

Suppose the input of a layer $\boldsymbol{x}^l$ has size $H^l \times W^l \times D^l$. If we use convolution kernels whose size is $H^l \times W^l \times D^l$, then D such kernels form an order 4 tensor with size $H^l \times W^l \times D^l \times D$. The output is $\boldsymbol{y} \in \mathbb{R}^D$. It is obvious that to compute any element in $\boldsymbol{y}$, we need to use all elements in the input $\boldsymbol{x}^l$. Hence, this layer is a fully connected layer, but can be implemented as a convolution layer. Hence, we do not need to derive learning rules for a fully connected layer separately.

15.6 The Pooling Layer

We will use the same notation inherited from the convolution layer to introduce pooling layers.

Let $\boldsymbol{x}^l \in \mathbb{R}^{H^l \times W^l \times D^l}$ be the input to the lth layer, which is now a pooling layer. The pooling operation requires no parameter (i.e., $\boldsymbol{w}^i$ is null, hence parameter learning is not needed for this layer). The spatial extent of the pooling ($H \times W$) is specified in the design of the CNN structure. Assume that H divides H^l, W divides W^l, and the stride equals the pooling spatial extent;[4] the output of pooling ($\boldsymbol{y}$ or equivalently $\boldsymbol{x}^{l+1}$) will be an order 3 tensor of size $H^{l+1} \times W^{l+1} \times D^{l+1}$, with

$$H^{l+1} = \frac{H^l}{H}, \quad W^{l+1} = \frac{W^l}{W}, \quad D^{l+1} = D^l. \tag{15.50}$$

[3] In Caffe, this computation is implemented by a function called `col2im`. In MatConvNet, this operation is operated in a `row2im` manner, although the name `row2im` is not explicitly used.

[4] That is, the strides in the vertical and horizontal directions are H and W, respectively. The most widely used pooling setup is $H = W = 2$ with a stride of 2.

A pooling layer operates on $\boldsymbol{x}^l$ channel by channel independently. Within each channel, the matrix with $H^l \times W^l$ elements is divided into $H^{l+1} \times W^{l+1}$ nonoverlapping subregions, each subregion being $H \times W$ in size. The pooling operator then maps a subregion into a single number.

Two types of pooling operators are widely used: max pooling and average pooling. In max pooling, the pooling operator maps a subregion to its maximum value, while the average pooling maps a subregion to its average value. In precise mathematics,

$$\text{max:} \quad y_{i^{l+1},j^{l+1},d} = \max_{0 \le i < H, 0 \le j < W} x^l_{i^{l+1} \times H + i,\, j^{l+1} \times W + j,\, d}, \tag{15.51}$$

$$\text{average:} \quad y_{i^{l+1},j^{l+1},d} = \frac{1}{HW} \sum_{0 \le i < H, 0 \le j < W} x^l_{i^{l+1} \times H + i,\, j^{l+1} \times W + j,\, d}, \tag{15.52}$$

where $0 \le i^{l+1} < H^{l+1}$, $0 \le j^{l+1} < W^{l+1}$, and $0 \le d < D^{l+1} = D^l$.

Pooling is a local operator, and its forward computation is pretty straightforward. Now we focus on the back propagation. Only max pooling is discussed, and we can resort to the indicator matrix again. Average pooling can be dealt with using a similar idea.

All we need to encode in this indicator matrix is where each element in $\boldsymbol{y}$ comes from in $\boldsymbol{x}^l$.

We need a triplet (i^l, j^l, d^l) to pinpoint one element in the input $\boldsymbol{x}^l$, and another triplet $(i^{l+1}, j^{l+1}, d^{l+1})$ to locate one element in $\boldsymbol{y}$. The pooling output $y_{i^{l+1},j^{l+1},d^{l+1}}$ comes from $x^l_{i^l,j^l,d^l}$, if and only if the following conditions are met:

- They are in the same channel.
- The (i^l, j^l)th spatial entry belongs to the (i^{l+1}, j^{l+1})th subregion.
- The (i^l, j^l)th spatial entry is the largest one in that subregion.

Translating these conditions into equations, we get

$$d^{l+1} = d^l, \tag{15.53}$$

$$\left\lfloor \frac{i^l}{H} \right\rfloor = i^{l+1}, \quad \left\lfloor \frac{j^l}{W} \right\rfloor = j^{l+1}, \tag{15.54}$$

$$x^l_{i^l,j^l,d^l} \ge y_{i+i^{l+1} \times H,\, j+j^{l+1} \times W,\, d^l} \quad \forall 0 \le i < H, 0 \le j < W, \tag{15.55}$$

where $\lfloor \cdot \rfloor$ is the floor function. If the stride is not H (W) in the vertical (horizontal) direction, Eq. (15.54) must be changed accordingly.

Given a $(i^{l+1}, j^{l+1}, d^{l+1})$ triplet, there is only one (i^l, j^l, d^l) triplet that satisfies all these conditions. Thus, we define an indicator matrix

$$S(\boldsymbol{x}^l) \in \mathbb{R}^{(H^{l+1}W^{l+1}D^{l+1}) \times (H^l W^l D^l)}. \tag{15.56}$$

One triplet of indexes $(i^{l+1}, j^{l+1}, d^{l+1})$ specifies a row in S, while (i^l, j^l, d^l) specifies a column. These two triplets together pinpoint one element in $S(\boldsymbol{x}^l)$. We set that element to 1 if Eqs. (15.53) to (15.55) are simultaneously satisfied, and 0 otherwise. One row of $S(\boldsymbol{x}^l)$ corresponds to one element in $\boldsymbol{y}$, and one column corresponds to one element in $\boldsymbol{x}^l$.

With the help of this indicator matrix, we have

$$\operatorname{vec}(\boldsymbol{y}) = S(\boldsymbol{x}^l)\operatorname{vec}(\boldsymbol{x}^l). \tag{15.57}$$

Then it is obvious that

$$\frac{\partial \operatorname{vec}(\boldsymbol{y})}{\partial (\operatorname{vec}(\boldsymbol{x}^l)^T)} = S(\boldsymbol{x}^l), \quad \frac{\partial z}{\partial (\operatorname{vec}(\boldsymbol{x}^l)^T)} = \frac{\partial z}{\partial (\operatorname{vec}(\boldsymbol{y})^T)} S(\boldsymbol{x}^l), \tag{15.58}$$

and consequently

$$\frac{\partial z}{\partial \operatorname{vec}(\boldsymbol{x}^l)} = S(\boldsymbol{x}^l)^T \frac{\partial z}{\partial \operatorname{vec}(\boldsymbol{y})}. \tag{15.59}$$

The matrix $S(\boldsymbol{x}^l)$ is very sparse. It has exactly one nonzero entry in every row. Thus, we do not need to use the entire matrix in the computation. Instead, we need to record the locations of just those nonzero entries—there are only $H^{l+1}W^{l+1}D^{l+1}$ such entries in $S(\boldsymbol{x}^l)$.

A simple example can explain the meaning of these equations. Let us consider a 2×2 max pooling with stride 2. For a given channel d^l, the first spatial subregion contains four elements in the input, with $(i,j) = (0,0)$, $(1,0)$, $(0,1)$, and $(1,1)$, and let us suppose the element at spatial location $(0,1)$ is the largest among them. In the forward pass, the value indexed by $(0,1,d^l)$ in the input (i.e., $x^l_{0,1,d^l}$) will be assigned to the element in the $(0,0,d^l)$th element in the output (i.e., $y_{0,0,d^l}$).

If the strides are H and W, respectively, one column in $S(\boldsymbol{x}^l)$ contains at most one nonzero element. In the above example, the columns of $S(\boldsymbol{x}^l)$ indexed by $(0,0,d^l)$, $(1,0,d^l)$, and $(1,1,d^l)$ are all zero vectors. The column corresponding to $(0,1,d^l)$ contains only one nonzero entry, whose row index is determined by $(0,0,d^l)$. Hence, in the back propagation, we have

$$\left[\frac{\partial z}{\partial \operatorname{vec}(\boldsymbol{x}^l)}\right]_{(0,1,d^l)} = \left[\frac{\partial z}{\partial \operatorname{vec}(\boldsymbol{y})}\right]_{(0,0,d^l)}$$

and

$$\left[\frac{\partial z}{\partial \operatorname{vec}(\boldsymbol{x}^l)}\right]_{(0,0,d^l)} = \left[\frac{\partial z}{\partial \operatorname{vec}(\boldsymbol{x}^l)}\right]_{(1,0,d^l)} = \left[\frac{\partial z}{\partial \operatorname{vec}(\boldsymbol{x}^l)}\right]_{(1,1,d^l)} = 0.$$

However, if the pooling strides are smaller than H and W in the vertical and horizontal directions, respectively, one element in the input tensor may be the largest element in several pooling subregions. Hence, there can be more than one nonzero entry in one column of $S(\boldsymbol{x}^l)$. Let us consider the example input in Figure 15.5. If a 2×2 max pooling is applied to it and the stride is 1 in both directions, the element 9 is the largest in two pooling regions: $\left[\begin{smallmatrix} 5 & 6 \\ 8 & 9 \end{smallmatrix}\right]$ and $\left[\begin{smallmatrix} 6 & 1 \\ 9 & 1 \end{smallmatrix}\right]$. Hence, in the column of $S(\boldsymbol{x}^l)$ corresponding to the element 9 (indexed by $(2,2,d^l)$ in the input tensor), there are two nonzero entries whose row indexes correspond to $(i^{l+1}, j^{l+1}, d^{l+1}) = (1, 1, d^l)$ and $(1, 2, d^l)$. Thus, in this example, we have

$$\left[\frac{\partial z}{\partial \operatorname{vec}(\boldsymbol{x}^l)}\right]_{(2,2,d^l)} = \left[\frac{\partial z}{\partial \operatorname{vec}(\boldsymbol{y})}\right]_{(1,1,d^l)} + \left[\frac{\partial z}{\partial \operatorname{vec}(\boldsymbol{y})}\right]_{(1,2,d^l)}.$$

15.7 A Case Study: The VGG16 Net

We have introduced the convolution, pooling, ReLU, and fully connected layers so far, and have briefly mentioned the softmax layer. With these layers, we can build many powerful deep CNN models.

15.7.1 VGG-Verydeep-16

The VGG-Verydeep-16 CNN model is a pretrained CNN model released by the Oxford VGG group.[5] We use it as an example to study the detailed structure of CNN networks. The VGG16 model architecture is listed in Table 15.2.

Table 15.2 The VGG-Verydeep-16 architecture and receptive field

	Type	Description	R. size		Type	Description	R. size
1	Conv	64;3x3;p=1,st=1	212	20	Conv	512;3x3;p=1,st=1	20
2	ReLU		210	21	ReLU		18
3	Conv	64;3x3;p=1,st=1	210	22	Conv	512;3x3;p=1,st=1	18
4	ReLU		208	23	ReLU		16
5	Pool	2x2;st=2	208	24	Pool	2x2;st=2	16
6	Conv	128;3x3;p=1,st=1	104	25	Conv	512;3x3;p=1,st=1	8
7	ReLU		102	26	ReLU		6
8	Conv	128;3x3;p=1,st=1	102	27	Conv	512;3x3;p=1,st=1	6
9	ReLU		100	28	ReLU		4
10	Pool	2x2;st=2	100	29	Conv	512;3x3;p=1,st=1	4
11	Conv	256;3x3;p=1,st=1	50	30	ReLU		2
12	ReLU		48	31	Pool		2
13	Conv	256;3x3;p=1,st=1	48	32	FC	(7x7x512)x4096	1
14	ReLU		46	33	ReLU		
15	Conv	256;3x3;p=1,st=1	46	34	Drop	0.5	
16	ReLU		44	35	FC	4096x4096	
17	Pool	2x2;st=2	44	36	ReLU		
18	Conv	512;3x3;p=1,st=1	22	37	Drop	0.5	
19	ReLU		20	38	FC	4096x1000	
				39	σ	(softmax layer)	

[5] www.robots.ox.ac.uk/~vgg/research/very_deep/

There are six types of layers in this model.

Convolution A convolution layer is abbreviated as "Conv." Its description includes four parts: number of channels, kernel spatial extent (kernel size), padding ("p"), and stride ("st") size.

ReLU No description is needed for a ReLU layer.

Pool A pooling layer is abbreviated as "Pool." Only max pooling is used in VGG16. The pooling kernel size is always 2×2 and the stride is always 2 in VGG16.

Fully connected A fully connected layer is abbreviated as "FC." Fully connected layers are implemented using convolution in VGG16. Their size is shown in the format $n_1 \times n_2$, where n_1 is the size of the input tensor and n_2 is the size of the output tensor. Although n_1 can be a triplet (such as $7 \times 7 \times 512$), n_2 is always an integer.

Dropout A dropout layer is abbreviated as "Drop." Dropout is a technique to improve the generalization of deep learning methods. It sets the weights connected to a certain percentage of nodes in the network to 0 (and VGG16 sets the percentage to 0.5 in the two dropout layers).

Softmax This is abbreviated as "σ."

We want to add a few notes about this example deep CNN architecture.

- A convolution layer is always followed by a ReLU layer in VGG16. The ReLU layers increase the nonlinearity of the CNN model.
- The convolution layers between two pooling layers have the same number of channels, kernel size, and stride. In fact, stacking two 3×3 convolution layers is equivalent to one 5×5 convolution layer, and stacking three 3×3 convolution kernels replaces a 7×7 convolution layer. Stacking a few (two or three) smaller convolution kernels, however, computes faster than a large convolution kernel. In addition, the number of parameters is also reduced—e.g., $2 \times 3 \times 3 = 18 < 25 = 5 \times 5$. The ReLU layers inserted in between small convolution layers are also helpful.
- The input to VGG16 is an image with size $224 \times 224 \times 3$. Because the padding is 1 in the convolution kernels (meaning 1 row or column is added outside the four edges of the input), convolution will not change the spatial extent. The pooling layers will reduce the input size by a factor of 2. Hence, the output after the last (fifth) pooling layer has spatial extent 7×7 (and 512 channels). We may interpret this tensor as $7 \times 7 \times 512 = 25\,088$ "features." The first fully connected layer converts these into 4096 features. The number of features remains at 4096 after the second fully connected layer.
- The VGG16 is trained for the ImageNet classification challenge, which is an object recognition problem with 1000 classes. The last fully connected layer (4096×1000) outputs a length 1000 vector for every input image, and the softmax layer converts this length 1000 vector into the estimated posterior probability for the 1000 classes.

15.7.2 Receptive Field

Another important concept in CNN is the receptive field size (abbreviated as "r. size" in Table 15.2). Let us look at one element in the input to the first fully connected layer (`32 | FC`). Because it is the output of a max pooling, we need values in a 2×2 spatial extent in the input to the max pool layer to compute this element (and we need elements in this spatial extent only). This 2×2 spatial extent is called the *receptive field* for this element. In Table 15.2 we listed the spatial extent for any element in the output of the last pooling layer. Note that because the receptive field is square, we use only one number (e.g., 48 for 48×48). The receptive field size listed for one layer is the spatial extent in the input to that layer.

A 3×3 convolution layer will increase the receptive field by 2, and a pooling layer will double the spatial extent. As shown in Table 15.2, receptive field size in the input to the first layer is 212×212. In other words, in order to compute any single element in the $7 \times 7 \times 512$ output of the last pooling layer, a 212×212 image patch is required (including the padded pixels in all convolution layers).

It is obvious that the receptive field size increases when the network becomes deeper, especially when a pooling layer is added to the deep net. Unlike traditional computer vision and image processing features that depend only on a small receptive field (e.g., 16×16), deep CNN computes its representation (or features) using large receptive fields. The larger receptive field characteristic is an important reason why CNN has achieved higher accuracy than classic methods in image recognition.

15.8 Hands-On CNN Experiences

We hope this introductory chapter on CNN is clear, self-contained, and easy to understand for our readers.

Once a reader is confident of understanding CNN at the mathematical level, in the next step it is very helpful to get some hands-on CNN experience. For example, one can validate what has been talked about in this chapter using the MatConvNet software package if you prefer the MATLAB environment.[6] For C++ lovers, Caffe is a widely used tool.[7] The Theano package is a Python package for deep learning.[8] Many more resources for deep learning (not only CNN) are available—e.g., Torch,[9] PyTorch,[10] MXNet,[11] Keras,[12] TensorFlow,[13] and more. The exercise problems in this chapter are offered as appropriate first-time CNN programming practice.

[6] www.vlfeat.org/matconvnet/
[7] http://caffe.berkeleyvision.org/
[8] http://deeplearning.net/software/theano/
[9] http://torch.ch/
[10] http://pytorch.org/
[11] https://mxnet.incubator.apache.org/
[12] https://keras.io/
[13] www.tensorflow.org/

15.9 Miscellaneous Notes and Additional Resources

In the exercise problems for this chapter, we provide links to resources for more important CNN techniques, including dropout, VGG-Verydeep and GoogLeNet network architectures, batch normalization, and residual connections. For more information about CNN and other deep learning models, please refer to Goodfellow et al. (2016).

For more on the Sobel operator, please refer to Gonzalez & Woods (2017).

Bengio et al. (2013) contains a good summary of the distributed representation property.

Convolutional neural networks have achieved top accuracy in many computer vision tasks, for example, object recognition (He et al. 2016), object detection (Girshick 2015), semantic segmentation (Shelhamer et al. 2017), and single image depth estimation (Liu et al. 2015).

Exercises

15.1 Dropout is a very useful technique in training neural networks, proposed by Srivastava et al. (2014).[14] *Carefully* read this paper and answer the following questions (please organize your answer to each question into one brief sentence):
(a) How does dropout operate during training?
(b) How does dropout operate during testing?
(c) What is the benefit of dropout?
(d) Why can dropout achieve this benefit?

15.2 The VGG16 CNN model (also called VGG-Verydeep-16) was publicized by Simonyan & Zisserman (2015)[15] and the GoogLeNet model was publicized by Szegedy et al. (2015).[16] These two papers were publicized around the same time and share some similar ideas. *Carefully* read both papers and answer the following questions (please organize your answer to each question into one brief sentence):
(a) Why do they use small convolution kernels (mainly 3×3) rather than larger ones?
(b) Why are both networks quite deep (i.e., with many layers, around 20)?
(c) What difficulties are caused by the large depth? How are they solved in these two networks?

15.3 Batch normalization (BN) is another very useful technique in training deep neural networks, which was proposed by Ioffe & Szegedy (2015).[17] *Carefully* read this paper and answer the following questions (please organize your answer to each question into one brief sentence):
(a) What is internal covariate shift?

[14] Available at `http://jmlr.org/papers/v15/srivastava14a.html`.
[15] Available at `https://arxiv.org/abs/1409.1556`, later published in ICLR 2015 as a conference track paper.
[16] Available at `https://arxiv.org/abs/1409.4842`, later published in CVPR 2015.
[17] Available at `http://jmlr.org/proceedings/papers/v37/ioffe15.pdf`

(b) How does BN deal with this?
(c) How does BN operate in a convolution layer?
(d) What is the benefit of using BN?

15.4 ResNet is a very deep neural network learning technique proposed by He et al. (2016).[18] *Carefully* read this paper and answer the following questions (please organize your answer to each question into one brief sentence):
(a) Although VGG16 and GoogLeNet have encountered difficulties in training networks of around 20–30 layers, what enables ResNet to train networks as deep as 1000 layers?
(b) VGG16 is a feed-forward network, where each layer has only one input and only one output. Conversely, GoogLeNet and ResNet are DAGs (directed acyclic graphs), where one layer can have multiple inputs and multiple outputs, so long as the data flow in the network structure does *not* form a cycle. What is the benefit of DAGs vs. feed forward?
(c) VGG16 has two fully connected layers (fc6 and fc7), while ResNet and GoogLeNet do not have fully connected layers (except the last layer for classification). What is used to replace FC layers in them? What is the benefit?

15.5 *AlexNet* refers to the deep convolutional neural network trained on the ILSVRC challenge data, which is groundbreaking work on deep CNN for computer vision tasks. The technical details of AlexNet are reported in Krizhevsky et al. (2012).[19] It proposed the ReLU activation function and creatively used GPUs to accelerate the computations. *Carefully* read this paper and answer the following questions (please organize your answer to each question into one brief sentence):
(a) Describe your understanding of how ReLU helps its success. And how do the GPUs help out?
(b) Using the average of predictions from several networks helps to reduce the error rates. Why?
(c) Where is the dropout technique applied? How does it help? And what is the cost of using dropout?
(d) How many parameters are there in AlexNet? Why is the dataset size (1.2 million images) important for the success of AlexNet?

15.6 We will try different CNN structures on the MNIST dataset. We denote the "baseline" network in the MNIST example in MatConvNet as BASE in this question.[20] In this question, a convolution layer is denoted as "$x \times y \times \text{nIn} \times \text{nOut}$," whose kernel size is $x \times y$, with nIn input and nOut output channels, with stride 1 and pad 0. The pooling layers are 2×2 max pooling with stride equal to 2. The BASE network has four blocks. The first consists of a $5 \times 5 \times 1 \times 20$ convolution and a max pooling, the second block is composed of a $5 \times 5 \times 20 \times 50$ convolution and a max pooling, the

[18] Available at `https://arxiv.org/pdf/1512.03385.pdf`.
[19] This paper is available at `http://papers.nips.cc/paper/4824-imagenet-classification-with-deep-convolutional-neural-networks`.
[20] MatConvNet version 1.0-beta20. Please refer to MatConvNet for all the details of BASE, such as parameter initialization and learning rate.

third block is a $4 \times 4 \times 50 \times 500$ convolution (FC) plus a ReLU layer, and the final block is the classification layer ($1 \times 1 \times 500 \times 10$ convolution).

(a) The MNIST dataset is available at `http://yann.lecun.com/exdb/mnist/`. Read the instructions on that page, and write a program to transform the data to formats that suit your favorite deep learning software.

(b) Learning deep learning models often involves random numbers. Before the training starts, set the random number generator's seed to 0. Then use the BASE network structure and the *first* 10 000 *training examples* to learn its parameters. What is the test set error rate (on the 10 000 test examples) after 20 training epochs?

(c) From now on, if not otherwise specified, we assume the first 10 000 training examples and 20 epochs are used. Now we define the BN network structure, which adds a batch normalization layer after every convolution layer in the first three blocks. What is its error rate? What can you say about BN vs. BASE?

(d) If you add a dropout layer after the classification layer in the fourth block, what is the new error rate of BASE and BN? Comment on the use of dropout.

(e) Now we define the SK network structure, which refers to small kernel size. SK is based on BN. The first block (5×5 convolution plus pooling) is now changed to two 3×3 convolutions, and BN + ReLU is applied after every convolution. For example, block 1 is now $3 \times 3 \times 1 \times 20$ convolution + BN + ReLU + $3 \times 3 \times 20 \times 20$ convolution + BN + ReLU + pool. What is SK's error rate? Comment on that (e.g., how and why the error rate changes).

(f) Now we define the SK-s network structure. The notation "s" refers to a multiplier that changes the number of channels in convolution layers. For example, SK is the same as SK-1, and SK-2 means that the number of channels in each convolution layer (except the one in block 4) is multiplied by 2. Train networks for SK-2, SK-1.5, SK-1, SK-0.5, and SK-0.2. Report their error rates and comment on them.

(g) Now we experiment with different training set sizes using the SK-0.2 network structure. Using the first 500, 1000, 2000, 5000, 10 000, 20 000, and 60 000 (all) training examples, what error rates do you achieve? Comment on your observations.

(h) Using the SK-0.2 network structure, study how different training sets affect its performance. Train 6 networks, and use the $(10\,000 \times (i-1)+1)$th to the $(i \times 10\,000)$th training examples in training the ith network. Are CNNs stable in terms of different training sets?

(i) Now we study how randomness affects CNN learning. Instead of setting the random number generator's seed to 0, use 1, 12, 123, 1234, 12 345, and 123 456 as the seeds to train 6 different SK-0.2 networks. What are their error rates? Comment on your observations.

(j) Finally, in SK-0.2, change all ReLU layers to sigmoid layers. Comment on the comparison of error rates between using ReLU and sigmoid activation functions.

Bibliography

Aharon, M., Elad, M., & Bruckstein, A. (2006), "K-SVD: An Algorithm for Designing Overcomplete Dictionaries for Sparse Representation", *IEEE Trans. Signal Processing* **54**(11), 4311–4322.

Akbani, R., Kwek, S., & Japkowicz, N. (2004), Applying Support Vector Machines to Imbalanced Datasets, *in* "Proc. European Conf. Machine Learning", Vol. 3201 of *Lecture Notes in Computer Science*, Springer, pp. 39–50.

Aloise, D., Deshpande, A., Hansen, P., & Popat, P. (2009), "NP-Hardness of Euclidean Sum-of-Squares Clustering", *Machine Learning* **75**(2), 245–248.

Arthur, D. & Vassilvitskii, S. (2007), k-means++: The Advantages of Careful Seeding, *in* "Proc. ACM-SIAM Symposium on Discrete Algorithms", pp. 1027–1035.

Beck, A. & Teboulle, M. (2009), "A Fast Iterative Shrinkage-Thresholding Algorithm for Linear Inverse Problems", *SIAM Journal on Imaging Sciences* **2**(1), 183–202.

Belhumeur, P. N., Hespanha, J. P., & Kriegman, D. J. (1997), "Eigenfaces vs. Fisherfaces: Recognition Using Class Specific Linear Projection", *IEEE Trans. Pattern Analysis and Machine Intelligence* **19**(7), 711–720.

Belkin, M. & Niyogi, P. (2002), Laplacian Eigenmaps and Spectral Techniques for Embedding and Clustering, *in* "Proc. Advances in Neural Information Processing Systems 14", pp. 585–591.

Bellman, R. E. & Dreyfus, S. E. (2015), *Applied Dynamic Programming*, Princeton Legacy Library, Princeton University Press.

Ben-Israel, A. & Greville, T. N. (2003), *Generalized Inverses: Theory and Applications*, CMS Books in Mathematics, 2nd edn, Springer.

Bengio, S., Pereira, F., Singer, Y., & Strelow, D. (2009), Group Sparse Coding, *in* "Proc. Advances in Neural Information Processing Systems 22", pp. 82–89.

Bengio, Y., Courville, A., & Vincent, P. (2013), "Representation Learning: A Review and New Perspectives", *IEEE Trans. Pattern Analysis and Machine Intelligence* **35**(8), 1798–1828.

Bengio, Y., Simard, P., & Frasconi, P. (1994), "Learning Long-Term Dependencies with Gradient Descent Is Difficult", *IEEE Trans. Neural Networks* **5**(2), 157–166.

Bertsekas, D. P. (2009), *Convex Optimization Theory*, Athena Scientific Optimization and Computation, Athena Scientific.

Bertsekas, D. P. (2016), *Nonlinear Programming*, Athena Scientific Optimization and Computation, 3rd edn, Athena Scientific.

Bertsimas, D. & Tsitsiklis, J. N. (1997), *Introduction to Linear Optimization*, Athena Scientific Optimization and Computation, Athena Scientific.

Bi, J., Bennett, K., Embrechts, M., Breneman, C., & Song, M. (2003), "Dimensionality Reduction via Sparse Support Vector Machines", *Journal of Machine Learning Research* **3**, 1229–1243.

Bilmes, J. A. (1998), A Gentle Tutorial of the EM Algorithm and its Application to Parameter Estimation for Gaussian Mixture and Hidden Markov Models, Technical Report TR-97-021, International Computer Science Institute and Computer Science Division, Department of Electrical Engineering and Computer Science, UC Berkeley.

Bingham, E. & Mannila, H. (2001), Random Projection in Dimensionality Reduction: Applications to Image and Text Data, *in* "Proc. ACM SIGKDD Int'l Conf. Knowledge Discovery and Data Mining", pp. 245–250.

Bishop, C. M. (1995a), *Neural Networks for Pattern Recognition*, Oxford University Press.

Bishop, C. M. (1995b), "Training with Noise Is Equivalent to Tikhonov Regularization", *Neural Computation* **7**(1), 108–116.

Bishop, C. M. (2006), *Pattern Recognition and Machine Learning*, Springer.

Bishop, G. & Welch, G. (2001), "An Introduction to the Kalman Filter, Course at SIGGRAPH 2001".

Borg, I. & Groenen, P. J. F. (2005), *Modern Multidimensional Scaling: Theory and Applications*, Springer Series in Statistics, 2nd edn, Springer.

Boughorbel, S., Tarel, J.-P., & Boujemaa, N. (2005), Generalized Histogram Intersection Kernel for Image Recognition, *in* "Proc. Int'l Conf. Image Processing", Vol. 3, pp. 161–164.

Boyd, S. & Vandenberghe, L. (2004), *Convex Optimization*, Cambridge University Press.

Bradley, A. P. (1997), "The Use of the Area under the ROC Curve in the Evaluation of Machine Learning Algorithms", *Pattern Recognition* **30**(7), 1145–1159.

Bradski, G. & Kaehler, A. (2008), *Learning OpenCV: Computer Vision with the OpenCV Library*, O'Reilly Media.

Breiman, L. (1996a), "Bagging Predictors", *Machine Learning* **24**(2), 123–140.

Breiman, L. (1996b), Bias, Variance and Arching Classifiers, Technical Report 460, Department of Statistics, University of California, Berkeley.

Breiman, L. (2001), "Random Forests", *Machine Learning* **45**(1), 5–32.

Breiman, L., Friedman, J. H., Olshen, R. A., & Stone, C. J. (1984), *Classification and Regression Trees*, Chapman and Hall/CRC.

Brockwell, P. J. & Davis, R. A. (2009), *Time Series: Theory and Methods*, Springer Series in Statistics, 2nd edn, Springer.

Brunelli, R. & Poggio, T. (1993), "Face Recognition: Features versus Templates", *IEEE Trans. Pattern Analysis and Machine Intelligence* **15**(10), 1042–1052.

Burges, C. J. (1998), "A Tutorial on Support Vector Machines for Pattern Recognition", *Data Mining and Knowledge Discovery* **2**(2), 121–167.

Candès, E. J., Romberg, J., & Tao, T. (2006), "Robust Uncertainty Principles: Exact Signal Reconstruction from Highly Incomplete Frequency Information", *IEEE Trans. Information Theory* **52**(2), 489–509.

Caruana, R., Lawrence, S., & Giles, L. (2001), Overfitting in Neural Nets: Backpropagation, Conjugate Gradient, and Early Stopping, *in* "Proc. Advances in Neural Information Processing Systems 13", pp. 381–387.

Chambers, J. M., Cleveland, W. S., Tukey, P. A., & Kleiner, B. (1983), *Graphical Methods for Data Analysis*, Duxbury Press.

Chang, C.-C. & Lin, C.-J. (2011), "LIBSVM: A Library for Support Vector Machines", *ACM Transactions on Intelligent Systems and Technology* **2**(3), 27:1–27:27.

Chawla, N. V., Bowyer, K. W., Hall, L. O., & Kegelmeyer, W. P. (2002), "SMOTE: Synthetic Minority Over-Sampling Technique", *Journal of Artificial Intelligence Research* **16**, 321–357.

Cho, K., van Merrienboer, B., Gulcehre, C., Bahdanau, D., Bougares, F., Schwenk, H., & Bengio, Y. (2014), Learning Phrase Representations using RNN Encoder-Decoder for Statistical Machine Translation, *in* "Proc. Conf. Empirical Methods in Natural Language Processing (EMNLP)", pp. 1724–1734.

Clevert, D.-A., Unterthiner, T., & Hochreiter, S. (2016), Fast and Accurate Deep Network Learning by Exponential Linear Units (ELUs), *in* "Proc. Int'l Conf. Learning Representations".

Comaniciu, D. & Meer, P. (2002), "Mean Shift: A Robust Approach toward Feature Space Analysis", *IEEE Trans. Pattern Analysis and Machine Intelligence* **24**(5), 603–619.

Cormen, T. H., Leiserson, C. E., Rivest, R. L., & Stein, C. (2009), *Introduction to Algorithms*, 3rd edn, MIT Press.

Cortes, C. & Mohri, M. (2004), AUC Optimization vs. Error Rate Minimization, *in* "Proc. Advances in Neural Information Processing Systems 16", pp. 313–320.

Cortes, C. & Vapnik, V. N. (1995), "Support-Vector Networks", *Machine Learning* **20**(3), 273–297.

Cover, T. M. & Thomas, J. A. (2006), *Elements of Information Theory*, 2nd edn, Wiley-Interscience.

Crammer, K. & Singer, Y. (2001), "On the Algorithmic Implementation of Multiclass Kernel-Based Vector Machines", *Journal of Machine Learning Research* **2**, 265–292.

Criminisi, A., Shotton, J., & Konukoglu, E. (2012), "Decision Forests: A Unified Framework for Classification, Regression, Density Estimation, Manifold Learning and Semi-Supervised Learning", *Foundations and Trends in Computer Graphics and Vision* **7**(2-3), 81–227.

Cristianini, N. & Shawe-Taylor, J. (2000), *An Introduction to Support Vector Machines and Other Kernel-based Learning Methods*, Cambridge University Press.

Crow, F. C. (1984), Summed-Area Tables for Texture Mapping, *in* "Annual Conf. Computer Graphics and Interactive Techniques (SIGGRAPH)", pp. 207–212.

DasGupta, A. (2011), *Probability for Statistics and Machine Learning: Fundamentals and Advanced Topics*, Springer Science & Business Media.

Datta, R., Joshi, D., Li, J., & Wang, J. Z. (2008), "Image Retrieval: Ideas, Influences, and Trends of the New Age", *ACM Computing Surveys (CSUR)* **40**(2), Article No. 5.

Davis, J. & Goadrich, M. (2006), The Relationship between Precision-Recall and ROC Curves, *in* "Proc. Int'l Conf. Machine Learning", pp. 233–240.

Davis, J. V., Kulis, B., Jain, P., Sra, S., & Dhillon, I. S. (2007), Information-Theoretic Metric Learning, *in* "Proc. Int'l Conf. Machine Learning", pp. 209–216.

DeGroot, M. H. & Schervish, M. J. (2011), *Probability and Statistics*, 4th edn, Pearson.

Dellaert, F. (2002), The Expectation Maximization Algorithm, Technical Report GIT-GVU-02-20, College of Computing, Georgia Institute of Technology.

Dempster, A. P., Laird, N. M., & Rubin, D. B. (1977), "Maximum Likelihood from Incomplete Data via the EM Algorithm", *Journal of the Royal Statistical Society. Series B (Methodological)* **39**(1), 1–38.

Demšar, J. (2006), "Statistical Comparisons of Classifiers over Multiple Data Sets", *Journal of Machine Learning Research* **7**, 1–30.

Devroye, L., Györfi, L., & Lugosi, G. (1996), *A Probabilistic Theory of Pattern Recognition*, Applications of Mathematics, Springer.

Dietterich, T. G. (1998), "Approximate Statistical Tests for Comparing Supervised Classification Learning Algorithms", *Neural Computation* **10**(7), 1895–1923.

Dietterich, T. G. (2000), "An Experimental Comparison of Three Methods for Constructing Ensembles of Decision Trees: Bagging, Boosting, and Randomization", *Machine Learning* **40**(2), 139–158.

Dinuzzo, F. & Schölkopf, B. (2012), The Representer Theorem for Hilbert Spaces: A Necessary and Sufficient Condition, *in* "Proc. Advances in Neural Information Processing Systems 25", pp. 189–196.

Djuric, N., Lan, L., Vucetic, S., & Wang, Z. (2013), "BudgetedSVM: A Toolbox for Scalable SVM Approximations", *Journal of Machine Learning Research* **14**, 3813–3817.

Domingos, P. (1999), MetaCost: A General Method for Making Classifiers Cost-Sensitive, *in* "Proc. ACM SIGKDD Int'l Conf. Knowledge Discovery and Data Mining", pp. 155–164.

Domingos, P. (2000), A Unified Bias-Variance Decomposition and Its Applications, *in* "Proc. Int'l Conf. Machine Learning", pp. 231–238.

Donoho, D. L. (1995), "De-noising by Soft-Thresholding", *IEEE Trans. Information Theory* **41**(3), 613–627.

Donoho, D. L. (2006), "Compressed Sensing", *IEEE Trans. Information Theory* **52**(4), 1289–1306.

Drucker, H., Burges, C. J., Kaufman, L., Smola, A., & Vapnik, V. (1997), Support Vector Regression Machines, *in* "Proc. Advances in Neural Information Processing Systems 9", pp. 155–161.

Drummond, C. & Holte, R. C. (2003), C4.5, Class Imbalance, and Cost Sensitivity: Why Under-Sampling Beats Over-Sampling, *in* "Proc. Int'l Conf. Machine Learning Workshop on Learning from Imbalanced Data Sets II".

Dubuisson, M.-P. & Jain, A. K. (1994), A Modified Hausdorff Distance for Object Matching, *in* "Proc. IAPR Int'l Conf. Pattern Recognition", Vol. 1.

Duda, R. O., Hart, P. E., & Stork, D. G. (2001), *Pattern Classification*, 2nd edn, Wiley.

Dudewicz, E. J. & Mishra, S. N. (1988), *Modern Mathematical Statistics*, Wiley.

Duin, R. P. (1976), "On the Choice of Smoothing Parameters for Parzen Estimators of Probability Density Functions", *IEEE Trans. Computers* **C-25**(11), 1175–1179.

Elkan, C. (2001), The Foundations of Cost-Sensitive Learning, *in* "Proc. Int'l Joint Conf. Artificial Intelligence", Vol. 2, pp. 973–978.

Fan, R.-E., Chang, K.-W., Hsieh, C.-J., Wang, X.-R., & Lin, C.-J. (2008), "LIBLINEAR: A Library for Large Linear Classification", *Journal of Machine Learning Research* **9**, 1871–1874.

Fan, W., Stolfo, S. J., Zhang, J., & Chan, P. K. (1999), AdaCost: Misclassification Cost-Sensitive Boosting, *in* "Proc. Int'l Conf. Machine Learning", pp. 97–105.

Fawcett, T. (2006), "An Introduction to ROC Analysis", *Pattern Recognition Letters* **27**(8), 861–874.

Fayyad, U. M. & Irani, K. B. (1992), "On the Handling of Continuous-Valued Attributes in Decision Tree Generation", *Machine Learning* **8**(1), 87–102.

Forsyth, D. A. & Ponce, J. (2011), *Computer Vision: A Modern Approach*, 2nd edn, Pearson.

Fox, C. & Roberts, S. (2011), "A Tutorial on Variational Bayesian Inference", *Artificial Intelligence Review* **38**(2), 85–95.

Fox, E., Sudderth, E. B., Jordan, M. I., & Willsky, A. S. (2011), "Bayesian Nonparametric Inference of Switching Linear Dynamical Systems", *IEEE Trans. Signal Processing* **59**(4).

Frey, B. J. & Dueck, D. (2007), "Clustering by Passing Messages between Data Points", *Science* **315**(5814), 972–976.

Friedman, J., Hastie, T., & Tibshirani, R. (2000), "Additive Logistic Regression: A Statistical View of Boosting", *Annals of Statistics* **28**(2), 337–407.

Fukumizu, K., Bach, F. R., & Jordan, M. I. (2004), "Dimensionality Reduction for Supervised Learning with Reproducing Kernel Hilbert Spaces", *Journal of Machine Learning Research* **5**, 73–99.

Fukunaga, K. (1990), *Introduction to Statistical Pattern Recognition*, Academic Press, San Diego.

Gao, B.-B., Xing, C., Xie, C.-W., Wu, J., & Geng, X. (2017), "Deep Label Distribution Learning with Label Ambiguity", *IEEE Trans. Image Processing* **26**(6), 2825–2838.

Gao, S., Tsang, I. W.-H., & Chia, L.-T. (2013), "Laplacian Sparse Coding, Hypergraph Laplacian Sparse Coding, and Applications", *IEEE Trans. Pattern Analysis and Machine Intelligence* **35**(1), 92–104.

Gao, W. & Zhou, Z.-H. (2013), "On the Doubt about Margin Explanation of Boosting", *Artificial Intelligence* **203**, 1–18.

Geman, S., Bienenstock, E., & Doursat, R. (1992), "Neural Networks and the Bias/Variance Dilemma", *Neural Computation* **4**(1), 1–58.

Genuer, R., Poggi, J.-M., & Tuleau-Malot, C. (2010), "Variable Selection Using Random Forests", *Pattern Recognition Letters* **31**(14), 2225–2236.

Georghiades, A. S., Belhumeur, P. N., & Kriegman, D. J. (2001), "From Few to Many: Illumination Cone Models for Face Recognition under Variable Lighting and Pose", *IEEE Trans. Pattern Analysis and Machine Intelligence* **23**(6), 643–660.

Girshick, R. (2015), Fast R-CNN, *in* "Proc. IEEE Int'l Conf. Computer Vision", pp. 1440–1448.

Girshick, R., Donahue, J., Darrell, T., & Malik, J. (2014), Rich Feature Hierarchies for Accurate Object Detection and Semantic Segmentation, *in* "Proc. IEEE Int'l Conf. Computer Vision and Pattern Recognition", pp. 580–587.

Glorot, X., Bordes, A., & Bengio, Y. (2011), Deep Sparse Rectifier Neural Networks, *in* "Proc. Int'l Conf. Artificial Intelligence and Statistics", pp. 315–323.

Golub, G. H. & van Loan, C. F. (1996), *Matrix Computations*, Johns Hopkins Studies in the Mathematical Sciences, Johns Hopkins University Press.

Gonzalez, R. C. & Woods, R. E. (2017), *Digital Image Processing*, 4th edn, Pearson.

Goodfellow, I., Bengio, Y., & Courville, A. (2016), *Deep Learning*, MIT Press.

Goodfellow, I., Pouget-Abadie, J., Mirza, M., Xu, B., Warde-Farley, D., Ozair, S., Courville, A., & Bengio, Y. (2014), Generative Adversarial Nets, *in* "Proc. Advances in Neural Information Processing Systems 27", pp. 2672–2680.

Graham, R. L., Knuth, D. E., & Patashnik, O. (1994), *Concrete Mathematics: A Foundation for Computer Science*, 2nd edn, Addison-Wesley Professional.

Guyon, I. & Elisseeff, A. (2003), "An Introduction to Variable and Feature Selection", *Journal of Machine Learning Research* **3**, 1157–1182.

Ham, J., Lee, D. D., Mika, S., & Schölkopf, B. (2004), A Kernel View of the Dimensionality Reduction of Manifolds , *in* "Proc. Int'l Conf. Machine Learning".

Han, J., Kamber, M., & Pei, J. (2011), *Data Mining: Concepts and Techniques*, Morgan Kaufmann Series in Data Management Systems, 3rd edn, Morgan Kaufmann.

Hartigan, J. A. & Wong, M. A. (1979), "Algorithm AS 136: A K-Means Clustering Algorithm", *Journal of the Royal Statistical Society. Series C (Applied Statistics)* **28**(11), 100–108.

Hastie, T., Tibshirani, R., & Friedman, J. (2009), *The Elements of Statistical Learning: Data Mining, Inference, and Prediction*, Springer Series in Statistics, 2nd edn, Springer Science & Business Media.

Haykin, S. (2008), *Neural Networks and Learning Machines*, 3rd edn, Pearson.

He, H., Bai, Y., Garcia, E. A., & Li, S. (2008), ADASYN: Adaptive Synthetic Sampling Approach for Imbalanced Learning, *in* "Proc. Int'l Joint Conf. on Neural Networks (IEEE World Congress on Computational Intelligence)".

He, H. & Garcia, E. A. (2009), "Learning from Imbalanced Data", *IEEE Trans. Knowledge and Data Engineering* **21**(9), 1263–1284.

He, K., Zhang, X., Ren, S., & Sun, J. (2015), Delving Deep into Rectifiers: Surpassing Human-Level Performance on ImageNet Classification, *in* "Proc. IEEE Int'l Conf. Computer Vision and Pattern Recognition", pp. 1026–1034.

He, K., Zhang, X., Ren, S., & Sun, J. (2016), Deep Residual Learning for Image Recognition, *in* "Proc. IEEE Int'l Conf. Computer Vision and Pattern Recognition", pp. 770–778.

He, X. & Niyogi, P. (2004), Locality Preserving Projections, *in* "Proc. Advances in Neural Information Processing Systems 16", pp. 153–160.

Hinton, G. E. (2012), A Practical Guide to Training Restricted Boltzmann Machines, *in* "Neural Networks: Tricks of the Trade", Vol. 7700 of *Lecture Notes in Computer Science*, Springer, pp. 599–619.

Hochreiter, S. & Schmidhuber, J. (1997), "Long Short-Term Memory", *Neural Computation* **9**(8), 1735–1780.

Hodge, V. & Austin, J. (2004), "A Survey of Outlier Detection Methodologies", *Artificial Intelligence Review* **22**(2), 85–126.

Hoerl, A. E. & Kennard, R. W. (1970), "Ridge Regression: Biased Estimation for Nonorthogonal Problems", *Technometrics* **12**(1), 55–67.

Hsieh, C.-J., Chang, K.-W., Lin, C.-J., Keerthi, S. S., & Sundararajan, S. (2008), A Dual Coordinate Descent Method for Large-Scale Linear SVM, *in* "Proc. Int'l Conf. Machine Learning", pp. 408–415.

Hsu, C.-W. & Lin, C.-J. (2002), "A Comparison of Methods for Multiclass Support Vector Machines", *IEEE Trans. Neural Networks* **13**(2), 415–425.

Huang, J., Zhang, T., & Metaxas, D. (2011), "Learning with Structured Sparsity", *Journal of Machine Learning Research* **12**, 3371–3412.

Huang, K., Yang, H., King, I., & Lyu, M. R. (2006), "Imbalanced Learning with a Biased Minimax Probability Machine", *IEEE Trans. Systems, Man, and Cybernetics, Part B (Cybernetics)* **36**(4), 913–923.

Huffman, D. A. (1952), "A Method for the Construction of Minimum-Redundancy Codes", *Proceedings of the IRE* **40**(9), 1098–1101.

Huttenlocher, D. P., Klanderman, G. A., & Rucklidge, W. J. (1993), "Comparing Images Using the Hausdorff Distance", *IEEE Trans. Pattern Analysis and Machine Intelligence* **15**(9), 850–863.

Ioffe, S. & Szegedy, C. (2015), Batch Normalization: Accelerating Deep Network Training by Reducing Internal Covariate Shift, *in* "Proc. Int'l Conf. Machine Learning", pp. 448–456.

Jain, A. K., Duin, R. P., & Mao, J. (2000), "Statistical Pattern Recognition: A Review", *IEEE Trans. Pattern Analysis and Machine Intelligence* **22**(1), 4–37.

Jain, A. K. & Vailaya, A. (1996), "Image Retrieval Using Color and Shape", *Pattern Recognition* **29**(8), 1233–1244.

Jegou, H., Douze, M., & Schmid, C. (2011), "Product Quantization for Nearest Neighbor Search", *IEEE Trans. Pattern Analysis and Machine Intelligence* **33**(1), 117–128.

Jensen, F. V. (1997), *Introduction to Bayesian Networks*, Springer.

Joachims, T. (1999), Transductive Inference for Text Classification Using Support Vector Machines, *in* "Proc. Int'l Conf. Machine Learning", pp. 200–209.

Kearns, M. J. & Vazirani, U. V. (1994), *An Introduction to Computational Learning Theory*, MIT Press.

Keerthi, S. S. & Lin, C.-J. (2003), "Asymptotic Behaviors of Support Vector Machines with Gaussian Kernel", *Neural Computation* **15**(7), 1667–1689.

Keogh, E. J. & Pazzani, M. J. (2000), Scaling Up Dynamic Time Warping for Datamining Applications, *in* "Proc. ACM SIGKDD Int'l Conf. Knowledge Discovery and Data Mining", pp. 285–289.

Kohavi, R. (1995), A Study of Cross-Validation and Bootstrap for Accuracy Estimation and Model Selection, *in* "Proc. Int'l Joint Conf. Artificial Intelligence", Vol. 2, pp. 1137–1143.

Kohavi, R. & Wolpert, D. (1996), Bias plus Variance Decomposition for Zero-One Loss Functions, *in* "Proc. Int'l Conf. Machine Learning", pp. 275–283.

Kohonen, T. (1982), "Self-Organized Formation of Topologically Correct Feature Maps", *Biological Cybernetics* **43**(1), 59–69.

Koller, D. & Friedman, N. (2009), *Probabilistic Graphical Models: Principles and Techniques*, Adaptive Computation and Machine Learning, MIT Press.

Kong, X., Ng, M. K., & Zhou, Z.-H. (2013), "Transductive Multilabel Learning via Label Set Propagation", *IEEE Trans. Knowledge and Data Engineering* **25**(3), 704–719.

Korte, B. & Vygen, J. (2006), *Combinatorial Optimization: Theory and Algorithms*, Algorithms and Combinatorics, Springer.

Krizhevsky, A., Sutskever, I., & Hinton, G. E. (2012), ImageNet Classification with Deep Convolutional Neural Networks, *in* "Proc. Advances in Neural Information Processing Systems 25", pp. 1097–1105.

Kschischang, F. R., Frey, B. J., & Loeliger, H.-A. (2001), "Factor Graphs and the Sum-Product Algorithm", *IEEE Trans. Information Theory* **47**(2), 498–519.

Lanckriet, G. R., Ghaoui, L. E., Bhattacharyya, C., & Jordan, M. I. (2002), "A Robust Minimax Approach to Classification", *Journal of Machine Learning Research* **33**, 555–582.

Lange, K. (2013), *Optimization*, Springer Texts in Statistics, 2nd edn, Springer Science & Business Media.

Lasserre, J. A., Bishop, C. M., & Minka, T. P. (2006), Principled Hybrids of Generative and Discriminative Models, *in* "Proc. IEEE Int'l Conf. Computer Vision and Pattern Recognition".

Lawrence, N. D. (2012), "A Unifying Probabilistic Perspective for Spectral Dimensionality Reduction: Insights and New Models", *Journal of Machine Learning Research* **13**, 160–9–1638.

LeCun, Y., Bengio, Y., & Hinton, G. (2015), "Deep Learning", *Nature* **521**, 436–444.

LeCun, Y., Bottou, L., Bengio, Y., & Haffner, P. (1998), "Gradient-Based Learning Applied to Document Recognition", *Proceedings of the IEEE* **86**(11), 2278–2324.

Lee, J. (2004), *A First Course in Combinatorial Optimization*, Cambridge Texts in Applied Mathematics, Cambridge University Press.

Li, M. & Yuan, B. (2005), "2D-LDA: A Statistical Linear Discriminant Analysis for Image Matrix", *Pattern Recognition Letters* **26**(5), 527–532.

Li, Y.-F., Kwok, J. T., & Zhou, Z.-H. (2009), Semi-Supervised Learning Using Label Mean, *in* "Proc. Int'l Conf. Machine Learning", pp. 633–640.

Lin, G., Liu, F., Shen, C., Wu, J., & Shen, H. T. (2017), "Structured Learning of Binary Codes with Column Generation for Optimizing Ranking Measures", *Int'l Journal of Computer Vision* **123**(2), 287–308.

Lin, H.-T., Lin, C.-J., & Weng, R. C. (2007), "A Note on Platt's Probabilistic Outputs for Support Vector Machines", *Machine Learning* **68**(3), 267–276.

Liu, F., Shen, C., & Lin, G. (2015), Deep Convolutional Neural Fields for Depth Estimation from a Single Image, *in* "Proc. IEEE Int'l Conf. Computer Vision and Pattern Recognition", pp. 5162–5170.

Liu, G., Wu, J., & Zhou, S. (2011), Probit Classifiers with a Generalized Gaussian Scale Mixture Prior, *in* "Proc. Int'l Joint Conf. Artificial Intelligence", pp. 1372–1377.

Liu, G., Wu, J., & Zhou, S. (2013), "Probabilistic Classifiers with a Generalized Gaussian Scale Mixture Prior", *Pattern Recognition* **46**, 332–345.

Liu, H. & Yu, L. (2005), "Toward Integrating Feature Selection Algorithms for Classification and Clustering", *IEEE Trans. Knowledge and Data Engineering* **17**(4), 491–502.

Liu, X.-Y., Wu, J., & Zhou, Z.-H. (2009), "Exploratory Undersampling for Class-Imbalance Learning", *IEEE Trans. Systems, Man, and Cybernetics, Part B (Cybernetics)* **39**(2), 539–550.

Lloyd, S. (1982), "Least Squares Quantization in PCM", *IEEE Trans. Information Theory* **28**(2), 129–137.

Loader, C. R. (1999), "Bandwidth Selection: Classical or Plug-In?", *Annals of Statistics* **27**(2), 415–438.

Long, J., Shelhamer, E., & Darrell, T. (2015), Fully Convolutional Networks for Semantic Segmentation, *in* "Proc. IEEE Int'l Conf. Computer Vision and Pattern Recognition", pp. 3431–3440.

Luo, J.-H., Wu, J., & Lin, W. (2017), ThiNet: A Filter Level Pruning Method for Deep Neural Network Compression, *in* "Proc. IEEE Int'l Conf. Computer Vision", pp. 5058–5066.

Maccone, C. (2009), A Simple Introduction to the KLT (Karhunen—Loève Transform), *in* "Deep Space Flight and Communications: Exploiting the Sun as a Gravitational Lens", Springer Praxis Books, Springer, pp. 151–179.

MacKay, D. J. (2003), *Information Theory, Inference and Learning Algorithms*, Cambridge University Press.

Mairal, J., Bach, F., Ponce, J., & Sapiro, G. (2009), Online Dictionary Learning for Sparse Coding, *in* "Proc. Int'l Conf. Machine Learning", pp. 689–696.

Maji, S. & Berg, A. C. (2009), Max-Margin Additive Classifiers for Detection, *in* "Proc. IEEE Int'l Conf. Computer Vision", pp. 40–47.

Maji, S., Berg, A. C., & Malik, J. (2008), Classification Using Intersection Kernel Support Vector Machines Is Efficient, *in* "Proc. IEEE Int'l Conf. Computer Vision and Pattern Recognition", pp. 1–8.

Manning, C. & Schütze, H. (1999), *Foundations of Statistical Natural Language Processing*, MIT Press.

Masud, M. M., Gao, J., Khan, L., Han, J., & Thuraisingham, B. M. (2011), "Classification and Novel Class Detection in Concept-Drifting Data Streams under Time Constraints", *IEEE Trans. Knowledge and Data Engineering* **23**(6), 859–874.

Mika, S., Ratsch, G., Weston, J., Scholkopf, B., & Mullers, K.-R. (1999), Fisher Discriminant Analysis with Kernels, *in* "Proc. IEEE Signal Processing Society Workshop on Neural Networks for Signal Processing IX".

Mingers, J. (1989), "An Empirical Comparison of Pruning Methods for Decision Tree Induction", *Machine Learning* **4**(2), 227–243.

Mitchell, T. M. (1997), *Machine Learning*, McGraw-Hill Education.

Moghaddam, B. & Pentland, A. (1997), "Probabilistic Visual Learning for Object Representation", *IEEE Trans. Pattern Analysis and Machine Intelligence* **19**(7), 696–710.

Montgomery, D. C., Peck, E. A., & Vining, G. G. (2007), *Introduction to Linear Regression Analysis*, 4th edn, Wiley-Interscience.

Muja, M. & Lowe, D. G. (2014), "Scalable Nearest Neighbor Algorithms for High Dimensional Data", *IEEE Trans. Pattern Analysis and Machine Intelligence* **36**(11), 2227–2240.

Murphy, K. P. (2012), *Machine Learning: A Probabilistic Perspective*, Adaptive Computation and Machine Learning, MIT Press.

Murphy, K. P., Weiss, Y., & Jordan, M. I. (1999), Loopy Belief Propagation for Approximate Inference: An Empirical Study, *in* "Proc. Conf. Uncertainty in Artificial Intelligence", pp. 467–475.

Navarro, G. (2001), "A Guided Tour to Approximate String Matching", *ACM Computing Surveys (CSUR)* **33**(1), 31–88.

Ng, A. Y. & Jordan, M. I. (2002), On Discriminative vs. Generative Classifiers: A Comparison of Logistic Regression and Naive Bayes, *in* "Proc. Advances in Neural Information Processing Systems 14", pp. 841–848.

Nocedal, J. & Wright, S. J. (2006), *Numerical Optimization*, Springer Series in Operations Research and Financial Engineering, 2nd edn, Springer.

Osuna, E., Freund, R., & Girosi, F. (1997), Training Support Vector Machines: An Application to Face Detection, *in* "Proc. IEEE Int'l Conf. Computer Vision and Pattern Recognition", pp. 130–136.

Papadimitriou, C. H. & Steiglitz, K. (1998), *Combinatorial Optimization: Algorithms and Complexity*, Dover Publications.

Pearl, J. (1982), Reverend Bayes on Inference Engines: A Distributed Hierarchical Approach, *in* "Proc. National Conf. Artificial Intelligence (AAAI)", pp. 133–136.

Pearl, J. (1988), *Probabilistic Reasoning in Intelligent Systems: Networks of Plausible Inference*, Morgan Kaufmann Series in Representation and Reasoning, Morgan Kaufmann.

Pearl, J. (2009), *Causality: Models, Reasoning, and Inference*, 2nd edn, Cambridge University Press.

Peng, H., Long, F., & Ding, C. (2005), "Feature Selection Based on Mutual Information Criteria of Max-Dependency, Max-Relevance, and Min-Redundancy", *IEEE Trans. Pattern Analysis and Machine Intelligence* **27**(8), 1226–1238.

Perronnin, F., Sánchez, J., & Liu, Y. (2010), Large-Scale Image Categorization with Explicit Data Embedding, *in* "Proc. IEEE Int'l Conf. Computer Vision and Pattern Recognition", pp. 2297–2304.

Petersen, K. B. & Pedersen, M. S. (2012), "The Matrix Cookbook", `http://www2.imm.dtu.dk/pubdb/views/publication_details.php?id=3274`.

Platt, J. (1998), Sequential Minimal Optimization: A Fast Algorithm for Training Support Vector Machines, Technical Report MSR-TR-98-14, Microsoft Research.

Platt, J. (2000), Probabilistic Outputs for Support Vector Machines and Comparison to Regularized Likelihood Methods, *in* "Advances in Large Margin Classifiers", MIT Press.

Platt, J. C., Cristianini, N., & Shawe-Taylor, J. (2000), Large Margin DAGs for Multiclass Classification, *in* "Proc. Advances in Neural Information Processing Systems 12", pp. 547–553.

Prechelt, L. (1998), "Automatic Early Stopping Using Cross Validation: Quantifying the Criteria", *Neural Networks* **11**(4), 761–767.

Press, W. H., Flannery, B. P., Teukolsky, S. A., & Vetterling, W. T. (1992), *Numerical Recipes in C: The Art of Scientific Computing*, 2nd edn, Cambridge University Press.

Provost, F. J., Fawcett, T., & Kohavi, R. (1998), The Case against Accuracy Estimation for Comparing Induction Algorithms, *in* "Proc. Int'l Conf. Machine Learning", pp. 445–453.

Pudil, P., Novovičová, J., & Kittler, J. (1994), "Floating Search Methods in Feature Selection", *Pattern Recognition Letters* **15**(11), 1119–1125.

Puntanen, S. & Styan, G. P. H. (1989), "The Equality of the Ordinary Least Squares Estimator and the Best Linear Unbiased Estimator", *The American Statistician* **43**(3), 153–161.

Quinlan, J. R. (1992), *C4.5: Programs for Machine Learning*, Morgan Kaufmann Series in Machine Learning, Morgan Kaufmann.

Rabiner, L. & Juang, B.-H. (1993), *Fundamentals of Speech Recognition*, Prentice Hall.

Rabiner, L. R. (1989), "A Tutorial on Hidden Markov Models and Selected Applications in Speech Recognition", *Proceedings of the IEEE* **77**(2), 257–286.

Rahimi, A. & Recht, B. (2007), Random Features for Large-Scale Kernel Machines, *in* "Proc. Advances in Neural Information Processing Systems 20", Vancouver, Canada, pp. 1177–1184.

Ripley, B. D. (1996), *Pattern Recognition and Neural Networks*, Cambridge University Press.

Rosen, K. H. (2011), *Discrete Mathematics and Its Applications*, 7th edn, McGraw-Hill Education.

Ross, S. M. (2003), *Introduction to Probability Models*, 8th edn, Academic Press.

Roweis, S. T. & Saul, L. K. (2000), "Nonlinear Dimensionality Reduction by Locally Linear Embedding", *Science* **290**(5500), 2323–2326.

Rui, Y., Huang, T. S., Ortega, M., & Mehrotra, S. (1998), "Relevance Feedback: A Power Tool for Interactive Content-Based Image Retrieval", *IEEE Trans. Circuits and Systems for Video Technology* **8**(8), 644–655.

Rumelhart, D. E., Hinton, G. E., & Williams, R. J. (1986), "Learning Representations by Back-Propagating Errors", *Nature* **323**, 533–536.

Safavian, S. R. & Landgrebe, D. A. (1991), "A Survey of Decision Tree Classifier Methodology", *IEEE Trans. Systems, Man, and Cybernetics* **21**(3), 660–674.

Samaria, F. & Harter, A. (1994), Parameterisation of a Stochastic Model for Human Face Identification, *in* "Proc. IEEE Workshop on Applications of Computer Vision".

Sánchez, J., Perronnin, F., Mensink, T., & Verbeek, J. (2013), "Image Classification with the Fisher Vector: Theory and Practice", *Int'l Journal of Computer Vision* **105**(3), 222–245.

Schapire, R. E., Freund, Y., Bartlett, P., & Lee, W. S. (1998), "Boosting the Margin: A New Explanation for the Effectiveness of Voting Methods", *Annals of Statistics* **26**(5), 1651–1686.

Schmidhuber, J. (2015), "Deep Learning in Neural Networks: An Overview", *Neural Networks* **61**, 85–117.

Scholkopf, B. (2001), The Kernel Trick for Distances, *in* "Proc. Advances in Neural Information Processing Systems 13", pp. 301–307.

Scholkopf, B., Herbrich, R., & Smola, A. J. (2001), A Generalized Representer Theorem, *in* "Proc. Int'l Conf. Computational Learning Theory", Vol. 2111 of *Lecture Notes in Computer Science*, Springer, pp. 416–426.

Scholkopf, B. & Smola, A. J. (2002), *Learning with Kernels: Support Vector Machines, Regularization, Optimization, and Beyond*, MIT Press.

Scholkopf, B., Smola, A., & Müller, K.-R. (1998), "Nonlinear Component Analysis as a Kernel Eigenvalue Problem", *Neural Computation* **10**(5), 1299–1319.

Schroff, F., Kalenichenko, D., & Philbin, J. (2015), FaceNet: A Unified Embedding for Face Recognition and Clustering, *in* "Proc. IEEE Int'l Conf. Computer Vision and Pattern Recognition", pp. 815–823.

Schwarz, H. R. & Waldvogel, J. (1989), *Numerical Analysis: A Comprehensive Introduction*, Wiley.

Scott, D. W. (2015), *Multivariate Density Estimation: Theory, Practice, and Visualization*, Wiley Series in Probability and Statistics, 2nd edn, Wiley.

Shalev-Shwartz, S., Singer, Y., & Srebro, N. (2007), Pegasos: Primal Estimated sub-GrAdient SOlver for SVM, *in* "Proc. Int'l Conf. Machine Learning", pp. 807–817.

Shelhamer, E., Long, J., & Darrell, T. (2017), "Fully Convolutional Networks for Semantic Segmentation", *IEEE Trans. Pattern Analysis and Machine Intelligence* **39**(4), 640–651.

Silverman, B. W. (1986), *Density Estimation for Statistics and Data Analysis*, Chapman and Hall.

Sim, D.-G., Kwon, O.-K., & Park, R.-H. (1999), "Object Matching Algorithms Using Robust Hausdorff Distance Measures", *IEEE Trans. Image Processing* **8**(3), 425–429.

Simonyan, K. & Zisserman, A. (2014), Two-Stream Convolutional Networks for Action Recognition in Videos, *in* "Proc. Advances in Neural Information Processing Systems 27", pp. 568–576.

Simonyan, K. & Zisserman, A. (2015), Very Deep Convolutional Networks for Large-Scale Image Recognition, *in* "Proc. Int'l Conf. Learning Representations".

Smeulders, A. W., Worring, M., Santini, S., Gupta, A., & Jain, R. C. (2000), "Content-Based Image Retrieval at the End of the Early Years", *IEEE Trans. Pattern Analysis and Machine Intelligence* **22**(12), 1349–1380.

Smola, A. J. & Scholkopf, B. (2004), "A Tutorial on Support Vector Regression", *Statistics and Computing* **14**(3), 199–222.

Srivastava, N., Hinton, G., Krizhevsky, A., Sutskever, I., & Salakhutdinov, R. (2014), "Dropout: A Simple Way to Prevent Neural Networks from Overfitting", *Journal of Machine Learning Research* **15**, 1929–1958.

Strang, G. (2018), *Linear Algebra and Its Applications*, 5th edn, Cengage Learning.

Sun, Y., Chen, Y., Wang, X., & Tang, X. (2014), Deep Learning Face Representation by Joint Identification-Verification, *in* "Proc. Advances in Neural Information Processing Systems 27", pp. 1988–1996.

Suykens, J. A. & Vandewalle, J. (1999), "Least Squares Support Vector Machine Classifiers", *Neural Processing Letters* **9**(3), 293–300.

Szegedy, C., Liu, W., Jia, Y., Sermanet, P., Reed, S., Anguelov, D., Erhan, D., Vanhoucke, V., & Rabinovich, A. (2015), Going Deeper with Convolutions, *in* "Proc. IEEE Int'l Conf. Computer Vision and Pattern Recognition", pp. 1–9.

Szeliski, R. (2010), *Computer Vision: Algorithms and Applications*, Springer.

Tan, M., Tsang, I. W., & Wang, L. (2014), "Towards Ultrahigh Dimensional Feature Selection for Big Data", *Journal of Machine Learning Research* **15**, 1371–1429.

Tenenbaum, J. B., de Silva, V., & Langford, J. C. (2000), "A Global Geometric Framework for Nonlinear Dimensionality Reduction", *Science* **290**(5500), 2319–2323.

Tibshirani, R. (1996), "Regression Shrinkage and Selection via the Lasso", *Journal of the Royal Statistical Society. Series B (Methodological)* **58**(1), 267–288.

Tipping, M. E. & Bishop, C. M. (1999), "Probabilistic Principal Component Analysis", *Journal of the Royal Statistical Society. Series B (Statistical Methodology)* **61**(3), 611–622.

Tsang, I. W., Kwok, J. T., & Cheung, P.-M. (2005), "Core Vector Machines: Fast SVM Training on Very Large Data Sets", *Journal of Machine Learning Research* **6**, 363–392.

Turk, M. & Pentland, A. (1991), "Eigenfaces for Recognition", *Journal of Cognitive Neuroscience* **3**(1), 71–86.

Ueda, N. & Nakano, R. (1998), "Deterministic Annealing EM Algorithm", *Neural Networks* **11**(2), 271–282.

van der Maaten, L. & Hinton, G. (2008), "Visualizing High-Dimensional Data Using t-SNE", *Journal of Machine Learning Research* **9**, 2579–2605.

Vapnik, V. N. (1999), *The Nature of Statistical Learning Theory*, Springer.

Vazirani, V. V. (2001), *Approximation Algorithms*, Springer.

Vedaldi, A. & Zisserman, A. (2012a), "Efficient Additive Kernels via Explicit Feature Maps", *IEEE Trans. Pattern Analysis and Machine Intelligence* **34**, 480–492.

Vedaldi, A. & Zisserman, A. (2012b), Sparse Kernel Approximations for Efficient Classification and Detection, *in* "Proc. IEEE Int'l Conf. Computer Vision and Pattern Recognition", pp. 2320–2327.

Vidal, R., Ma, Y., & Sastry, S. S. (2016), *Generalized Principal Component Analysis*, Interdisciplinary Applied Mathematics, Springer.

Viola, P. A. & Jones, M. J. (2004), "Robust Real-Time Face Detection", *Int'l Journal of Computer Vision* **57**(2), 137–154.

Viola, P. A., Jones, M. J., & Snow, D. (2003), Detecting Pedestrians Using Patterns of Motion and Appearance, *in* "Proc. IEEE Int'l Conf. Computer Vision", pp. 734–741.

Wainwright, M. J. & Jordan, M. I. (2008), "Graphical Models, Exponential Families, and Variational Inference", *Foundations and Trends in Machine Learning* **1**(1-2), 1–305.

Wan, J., Wang, D., Hoi, S. C. H., Wu, P., Zhu, J., Zhang, Y., & Li, J. (2014), Deep Learning for Content-Based Image Retrieval: A Comprehensive Study, *in* "ACM International Conference on Multimedia", pp. 157–166.

Wasserman, L. (2003), *All of Statistics: A Concise Course in Statistical Inference*, Springer Texts in Statistics, Springer Science & Business Media.

Wasserman, L. (2007), *All of Nonparametric Statistics*, Springer Texts in Statistics, Springer Science & Business Media.

Webb, A. R. (1999), *Statistical Pattern Recognition*, Oxford University Press, New York.

Wei, X.-S., Luo, J.-H., Wu, J., & Zhou, Z.-H. (2017a), "Selective Convolutional Descriptor Aggregation for Fine-Grained Image Retrieval", *IEEE Trans. Image Processing* **26**(6), 2868–2881.

Wei, X.-S., Wu, J., & Zhou, Z.-H. (2017b), "Scalable Algorithms for Multi-Instance Learning", *IEEE Trans. Neural Networks and Learning Systems* **28**(4), 975–987.

Wei, X.-S., Zhang, C.-L., Li, Y., Xie, C.-W., Wu, J., Shen, C., & Zhou, Z.-H. (2017c), Deep Descriptor Transforming for Image Co-localization, *in* "Proc. Int'l Joint Conf. Artificial Intelligence", pp. 3048–3054.

Weinberger, K. Q. & Saul, L. K. (2009), "Distance Metric Learning for Large Margin Nearest Neighbor Classification", *Journal of Machine Learning Research* **10**, 207–244.

Weston, J. & Watkins, C. (1998), Multi-class Support Vector Machines, Technical Report CSD-TR-98-04, Royal Holloway, University of London.

Widmer, G. & Kubat, M. (1996), "Learning in the Presence of Concept Drift and Hidden Contexts", *Machine Learning* **23**(1), 69–101.

Williams, C. K. & Seeger, M. (2000), Using the Nyström Method to Speed Up Kernel Machines, *in* "Proc. Advances in Neural Information Processing Systems 13", pp. 682–688.

Witten, I. H., Frank, E., Hall, M. A., & Pal, C. J. (2016), *Data Mining: Practical Machine Learning Tools and Techniques*, Morgan Kaufmann Series in Data Management Systems, 4th edn, Morgan Kaufmann.

Wolpert, D. H. (1992), "Stacked Generalization", *Neural Networks* **5**(2), 241–260.

Wolpert, D. H. (1996), "The Lack of A Priori Distinctions between Learning Algorithms", *Neural Computation* **8**(7), 1341–1390.

Wright, J., Ganesh, A., Rao, S., Peng, Y., & Ma, Y. (2009a), Robust Principal Component Analysis: Exact Recovery of Corrupted Low-Rank Matrices via Convex Optimization, *in* "Proc. Advances in Neural Information Processing Systems 22", pp. 2080–2088.

Wright, J., Yang, A. Y., Ganesh, A., Sastry, S. S., & Ma, Y. (2009b), "Robust Face Recognition via Sparse Representation", *IEEE Trans. Pattern Analysis and Machine Intelligence* **31**(2), 210–227.

Wu, J. (2011), Balance Support Vector Machines Locally Using the Structural Similarity Kernel, *in* "Proc. Pacific-Asia Conf. Advances in Knowledge Discovery and Data Mining", Vol. 6634 of *Lecture Notes in Computer Science*, Springer, pp. 112–123.

Wu, J. (2012a), "Efficient HIK SVM Learning for Image Classification", *IEEE Trans. Image Processing* **21**, 4442–4453.

Wu, J. (2012b), Power Mean SVM for Large Scale Visual Classification, *in* "Proc. IEEE Int'l Conf. Computer Vision and Pattern Recognition", pp. 2344–2351.

Wu, J., Brubaker, S. C., Mullin, M. D., & Rehg, J. M. (2008), "Fast Asymmetric Learning for Cascade Face Detection", *IEEE Trans. Pattern Analysis and Machine Intelligence* **30**(3), 369–382.

Wu, J., Liu, N., Geyer, C., & Rehg, J. M. (2013), "C^4: A Real-Time Object Detection Framework", *IEEE Trans. Image Processing* **22**(10), 4096–4107.

Wu, J., Mullin, M. D., & Rehg, J. M. (2004), Learning a Rare Event Detection Cascade by Direct Feature Selection, *in* "Proc. Advances in Neural Information Processing Systems 16", pp. 1523–1530.

Wu, J., Mullin, M. D., & Rehg, J. M. (2005), Linear Asymmetric Classifier for Cascade Detectors, *in* "Proc. Int'l Conf. Machine Learning", pp. 993–1000.

Wu, J. & Rehg, J. M. (2009), Beyond the Euclidean Distance: Creating Effective Visual Codebooks Using the Histogram Intersection Kernel, *in* "Proc. IEEE Int'l Conf. Computer Vision", pp. 630–637.

Wu, J., Tan, W.-C., & Rehg, J. M. (2011), "Efficient and Effective Visual Codebook Generation Using Additive Kernels", *Journal of Machine Learning Research* **12**, 3097–3118.

Wu, J. & Yang, H. (2015), "Linear Regression Based Efficient SVM Learning for Large Scale Classification", *IEEE Trans. Neural Networks and Learning Systems* **26**(10), 2357–2369.

Wu, J. & Zhou, Z.-H. (2002), "Face Recognition with One Training Image per Person", *Pattern Recognition Letters* **23**(14), 1711–1719.

Xie, J. & Qiu, Z. (2007), "The Effect of Imbalanced Data Sets on LDA: A Theoretical and Empirical Analysis", *Pattern Recognition* **40**(2), 557–562.

Xing, E. P., Ng, A. Y., Jordan, M. I., & Russell, S. (2003), Distance Metric Learning, with Application to Clustering with Side-Information, *in* "Proc. Advances in Neural Information Processing Systems 15", pp. 521–528.

Xu, L. & Jordan, M. I. (1996), "On Convergence Properties of the EM Algorithm for Gaussian Mixtures", *Neural Computation* **8**(1), 129–151.

Xu, R. & Wunsch II, D. (2005), "Survey of Clustering Algorithms", *IEEE Trans. Neural Networks* **16**(3), 645–678.

Yan, S., Xu, D., Zhang, B., Zhang, H.-J., Yang, Q., & Lin, S. (2007), "Graph Embedding and Extensions: A General Framework for Dimensionality Reduction", *IEEE Trans. Pattern Analysis and Machine Intelligence* **29**(1), 40–51.

Yang, J., Zhang, D., Frangi, A. F., & Yang, J.-Y. (2004), "Two-Dimensional PCA: A New Approach to Appearance-Based Face Representation and Recognition", *IEEE Trans. Pattern Analysis and Machine Intelligence* **26**(1), 131–137.

Yuan, G.-X., Ho, C.-H., & Lin, C.-J. (2012), "Recent Advances of Large-Scale Linear Classification", *Proceedings of the IEEE* **100**, 2584–2603.

Zeiler, M. D. & Fergus, R. (2014), Visualizing and Understanding Convolutional Networks, *in* "Proc. European Conf. Computer Vision", Vol. 8689 of *Lecture Notes in Computer Science*, Springer, pp. 818–833.

Zhang, X. (2013), *Matrix Analysis and Applications (in Chinese)*, 2nd edn, Tsinghua University Press.

Zhang, Y., Wu, J., & Cai, J. (2014), Compact Representation for Image Classification: To Choose or to Compress?, *in* "Proc. IEEE Int'l Conf. Computer Vision and Pattern Recognition", pp. 907–914.

Zhang, Y., Wu, J., & Cai, J. (2016), "Compact Representation of High-Dimensional Feature Vectors for Large-Scale Image Recognition and Retrieval", *IEEE Trans. Image Processing* **25**(5), 2407–2419.

Zhao, W.-Y., Chellappa, R., Phillips, P. P. J., & Rosenfeld, A. (2003), "Face Recognition: A Literature Survey", *ACM Computing Surveys (CSUR)* **35**(4), 399–458.

Zhou, G.-B., Wu, J., Zhang, C.-L., & Zhou, Z.-H. (2016), "Minimal Gated Unit for Recurrent Neural Networks", *Int'l Journal of Automation and Computing* **13**(3), 226–234.

Zhou, Z.-H. (2012), *Ensemble Methods: Foundations and Algorithms*, Chapman & Hall/CRC Machine Learning & Pattern Recognition, Chapman and Hall/CRC.

Zhou, Z.-H. (2016), *Machine Learning (in Chinese)*, Tsinghua University Press.

Zhou, Z.-H. & Liu, X.-Y. (2006), "Training Cost-Sensitive Neural Networks with Methods Addressing the Class Imbalance Problem", *IEEE Trans. Knowledge and Data Engineering* **18**(1), 63–77.

Zhou, Z.-H., Wu, J., & Tang, W. (2002), "Ensembling Neural Networks: Many Could Be Better Than All", *Artificial Intelligence* **137**(1-2), 239–263.

Zou, H. & Hastie, T. (2005), "Regularization and Variable Selection via the Elastic Net", *Journal of the Royal Statistical Society. Series B (Statistical Methodology)* **67**(2), 301–320.

Index